When I was growing up in a more "fundame̶n̶t̶a̶l̶i̶s̶t̶ ̶s̶e̶t̶t̶i̶n̶g̶, I was often frustrated because I felt that the conservative church had found the truth in Scripture but seemed to be unwilling to address the tough—often controversial—questions facing life and society. Conversely, the liberal church seemed to be willing to address the difficult questions but the answers seemed to be inadequate and without authority. But, we must bring God's revelation to bear upon the big concerns of our culture—and I'm convinced, only then will we find help. This book both addresses the big issue of division in society with courage and it does so from the perspective of God's Word. It is desperately needed.

> Greg Waybright
> President, Trinity International University
> and Trinity Evangelical Divinity School

What should be a distinguishing characteristic that will allow the evangelical church to have a powerful impact on the fractured world of the twenty-first century? This collection of essays passionately argues that Christians must reach across all the barriers created by society and embody a constructive unity in Chirst. Read this book, and *dare to be stretched!*

> M. Daniel Carroll R.
> Professor of Old Testament, Denver Seminary

Editor Dr. Perry provides the evangelical community with extremely helpful resources in this timely volume, *Building Unity in the Church of the New Millennium.* The selected subjects are the center of debate, discussion and mission within most Christian institutions.

> Dr. Manuel Ortiz
> Professor of Ministry and Urban Mission,
> Westminster Theological Seminary

Unity, reconciliation, and transethnic understanding are among those issues that are obviously highest on the worldwide Christian church's agenda today. *Building Unity in the Church of the New Millennium* redirects Christians toward laying concrete foundations of unity and reconciliation that Christ, the Cornerstone of the church, intended for His kingdom.

> Johng O. Lee, Ph.D.
> Professor, Moody Bible Institute

BUILDING
UNITY
IN THE CHURCH
OF THE
NEW
MILLENNIUM

DWIGHT PERRY
General Editor

MOODY PRESS
CHICAGO

Quotations from *Divided by Faith: Evangelical Religion and the Problem of Race in America* are by Michael O. Emerson and Christian Smith. Copyright © Oxford Univ. Press, 2000. Used by permission.

All Scripture quotations, unless otherwise indicated, are taken from the *Holy Bible, New International Version*®. NIV®. Copyright © 1973, 1978, 1984 by International Bible Society. Used by permission of Zondervan Publishing House. All rights reserved.

Scripture quotations marked KJV are taken from the King James Version.

Scripture quotations marked NASB are taken from the *New American Standard Bible*®, © Copyright The Lockman Foundation 1960, 1962, 1963, 1968, 1971, 1972, 1973, 1975, 1977, 1995. Used by permission.

Scripture quotations marked TLB are taken from *The Living Bible* copyright © 1971. Used by permission of Tyndale House Publishers, Inc., Wheaton, Illinois 60189. All rights reserved.

Scripture quotations marked THE MESSAGE are from *The Message,* copyright © by Eugene H. Peterson 1993, 1994, 1995. Used by permission of NavPress Publishing Group.

Library of Congress Cataloging-in-Publicaton Data

Building unity in the church of the new millennium / Dwight Perry, general editor.
    p. cm.
  Includes bibliographical references.
  ISBN 0-8024-1589-X
   1. Evangelicalism--United States. 2. Church and minorities--United States. I. Perry, Dwight.

BR1642.U5 B85 2002
261.8'34--dc21

2001054645

1 3 5 7 9 10 8 6 4 2

To my Uncle Barry Batson:
Uncle Barry, thanks for being the father
I never was privileged to grow up with.
You are proof that even under great racial and class oppression,
God was still about the business of raising up
some godly African-American men,
such as you, who even in the midst of the "ghetto"
loved their families and took time out
for the orphans of the world like me.

CONTENTS

Part Two
Unity Between Classes in the Church

Part Three
Unity Between Genders in the Church

ABOUT THE CONTRIBUTORS

Henry Lee Allen is Associate Professor of Sociology at Wheaton College. He received a Bachelor of Arts degree in Biblical Studies from Wheaton College and a masters degree and Ph.D. from the University of Chicago. He has published numerous articles about sociology, ethnicity, and American higher education. A number of these publications examine the role of Christian faith in resolving key issues of concern to churches and the African-American community. Dr. Allen has held faculty positions at Bethel College (Minn.), Calvin College, the graduate school of education at the University of Rochester, and the Rochester Institute of Technology. He has served on the board of directors or advisory board of a number of organizations and Chicago churches and has served as a consultant in higher education. Most recently, Professor Allen has become the principal investigator for a major survey research project conducted for the American Bible Society. He is married to the former Juliet Cooper of Liberia, West Africa. They live in Wheaton, Illinois, with their eight children.

Vincent Bacote is an Assistant Professor of Theology at Wheaton College. He received his Bachelor of Science degree from the Citadel, earned his Masters of Divinity from Trinity Evangelical Divinity School, and is currently finishing his Ph.D. in Theological and Religious Studies at Drew University in Madison, New Jersey. Professor Bacote is also a licensed Baptist minister and has published articles in *The Journal for Christian Theological Research, Re:generation Quarterly,* and *Christianity Today.* He has contributed to the books *The Best Christian Writing 2000* and *The Gospel in Black and White.* He lives in Naperville, Illinois, with his wife, Shelley, and daughter, Laurel.

Ellen Lowrie Black (Ed.D., Temple University; M.Ed., East Texas State University; B.S., Eastern Mennonite University) is an educational consultant who works primarily in the areas of organizational development within a higher education setting. She has been Vice President of Equip in Norcross, Georgia; Vice President of Planning, Research, and Assessment and Dean of Education for Liberty University; and an accreditation committee member of the Commission on Colleges, Southern Association of Colleges and Schools. She has served as a Professor of Education at Liberty University and on visiting graduate faculty of Columbia International University and Grace Theological Seminary. She is a keynote and workshop speaker at numerous educational conferences annually, as well as speaking internationally. She has written on Christian education in various journals. Ellen has been married to Robert Black for twenty-two years, and they live in Lawrenceville, Georgia. They have a daughter and two sons.

Robert M. Boyd, Director of Church and Pastoral Vitality for the Minnesota Baptist Conference, earned his B.A. at Gordon College and his M.Div. from Gordon-Conwell Theological Seminary. He and his wife, Janet, have three married children and nine grandchildren. He worked for eleven years in Argentina, held pastorates in Minnesota, and served as director of Hispanic Ministries and of the Hispanic Bible School in Chicago. He worked for ten years as director of Baptist General Counference Multicultural Ministries. Since 1992 he has lived in St. Paul, Minnesota, where his major responsibilities include the care of pastors, aiding churches in revitalization, and special care of the ethnic and cultural churches and outreach in the state.

Evelyn Christenson is an author, speaker, and teacher. She has been a prayer seminar and conference speaker for more than twenty-five years, including international speaking for seventeen years. Her first book, *What Happens When Women Pray,* has sold more than three million copies. She has written several other books on prayer and received numerous awards. Mrs. Christenson is founder and chairman of the board of Christian Women United, formerly known as the AD2000 North America Women's Track, a networking movement committed to reaching the spiritually lost for Jesus Christ. She is also founder and president of United Prayer Ministry, which has included twenty years of broadcasting into China, India, and the Caribbean through Trans World Radio. Her involvement for more than twenty years as a member of the National Prayer Committee has, in part, focused on sponsoring and participating in the National Day of Prayer in Washington, D.C., and the annual televised prayer program. She and her husband, Harold, live in St. Paul, Minnesota. They have three married children and eight grandchildren.

David K. Clark is the dean of the Center for Biblical and Theological Foundations and Professor of Theology at Bethel Theological Seminary. He consults on leadership and theology with churches; speaks at colleges, churches, and conferences; and dialogues with all sorts of people about why it makes sense to follow Jesus Christ. He is writing his eighth book and has published forty articles in both professional and popular periodicals. David lives with his family in New Brighton, Minnesota. His wife, Sandy, is a grant writer in the development office at Bethel College and Seminary. The Clarks have two sons, Tyler and Ryan. David was born and reared in Tokyo, Japan, of missionary parents. He attended Houghton College in New York, Trinity Evangelical Divinity School for seminary, and Northwestern University for his Ph.D. He taught for ten years at Toccoa Falls College in Georgia.

Rod Cooper is the Hansen Professor of Leadership and Discipleship at Gordon-Conwell Theological Seminary. In 1998, prior to his appointment at Gordon-Conwell, Dr. Rodney Cooper was appointed Associate Professor of Leadership and Director of the M.A. in Leadership program at Denver Seminary. Dr. Cooper earned his Ph.D. and M.A. degrees in Clinical/Counseling Psychology at George Fox University/Western Seminary, his Th.M. degree in Pastoral Ministries from Dallas Theological Seminary and his B.A. degree in Psychology from Ohio State University. He has been National Director of Educational Ministries for Promise Keepers. Along with these teaching and speaking positions, Dr. Cooper was also a chaplain for the Houston Oilers and the Houston Astros franchises. He is a licensed psychologist in Colorado and served on one of the licensing examining panels for psychologists. Dr. Cooper has written numerous books, articles, and published sermons. He is the author of *We Stand Together* and *Double Bind: Escaping the Contradictory Demands of Manhood*. Dr. Cooper and his wife, Nancy, live in the Boston area.

Rosalie de Rosset is a professor of literature, English, and biblical message preparation at Moody Bible Institute in Chicago, Illinois. She has been speaking to various groups, including churches, seminars, and conferences, for twenty years. She has also spoken at conferences in Russia, Hawaii, and New Zealand. Prior to becoming a professor, she was a script writer for WMBI AM and FM in Chicago. Over the years, she has also appeared on Moody Broadcasting Network programs as a guest and co-host and has had articles and book reviews published in various Christian publications. Dr. de Rosset has an M.A. in English, a Masters of Divinity from Trinity Evangelical Divinity School, and a Ph.D. in English from the University of Illinois at Chicago. The daughter of career missionaries, Rosalie was born and raised in Peru, South America. She lives in Chicago.

Brad Grammer founded and led Face-to-Face Ministries, an outreach of Breakthrough Urban Ministries in Chicago, for five years. His ministry included evangelistic outreach in the gay bars on the Northside and to men struggling with homosexuality and/or AIDS incarcerated at the Cook County Jail in Chicago. In 1998 Brad moved to Indianapolis to become director of Hope & New Life Ministries, an Exodus International referral ministry, with the same focus of reaching out to those seeking freedom from homosexual desires. Brad received his undergraduate degree in Human Development from the University of Nebraska-Lincoln and a Certificate of Biblical Studies from Moody Bible Institute. He wrote a chapter on ministry to homosexuals in *A Heart for the City*, a Moody Press book edited by John Fuder. He and his wife, Laura, live in Indianapolis and have two sons.

Craig S. Keener (Ph.D. in New Testament from Duke University) is Professor of New Testament at Eastern Seminary and an associate minister at Enon Tabernacle Baptist Church in Philadelphia. He has written eleven books and numerous articles; the books include . . . *And Marries Another: Divorce and Remarriage in the Teaching of the New Testament; Paul, Women & Wives: Marriage and Women's Ministry in the Letters of Paul;* two books coauthored with Glenn Usry (*Black Man's Religion: Can Christianity be Afrocentric?* and *Defending Black Faith: Answers to Tough Questions about African-American Christianity*); and the highest-ranking biblical studies works in the *Christianity Today* book awards in their respective years: The *IVP Bible Background Commentary: New Testament,* 1993; *A Commentary on the Gospel of Matthew,* 1999.

Glen A. Kehrein was the founder of Circle Urban Ministries and has been the Executive Director for more than twenty-five years. Glen is a graduate of Moody Bible Institute and Wheaton College and was also one of the first Americans to receive the Doctor of Peacemaking degree granted by Westminster College in 1997. Glen has co-authored *Breaking Down Walls* with Raleigh Washington, on racial reconciliation, and he continues to travel and speak extensively on that subject. He and his wife, Lonni, have raised their son and two daughters in the Austin community on the Westside of Chicago.

Shirley Wright Masongezi has been working with the Baptist General Conference eleven years in Cameroon and Ivory Coast, West Africa, where she is focusing on work among Muslim women, discipleship, and church planting. Shirley recently married Wilondja Masongezi, father of four daughters and two sons. At Eureka College she had a double major in Mathematics and Physical Education, and she received a Masters of Science in Educational Administration from Northern Illinois University. She has been a mathematician and taught math in middle school, high school, and college; served with Campus Crusade for Christ for eight years in Nigeria, West Africa, and the Legacy Ministry in Atlanta.

Bill McCartney is Founder and President of Promise Keepers. For eight years he was head football coach for the University of Colorado, leading his team in 1990 to win the Associated Press National Championship. He graduated with a B.A. in Education from the University of Missouri, where he played as linebacker for the school's football team. He has written or contributed to numerous books, including *Sold Out* and *The Seven Promises of a Promise Keeper.* He is married to Lyndi.

Larry Mercer (B.A., East Carolina University; Th.M. and D.Min., Dallas Theological Seminary) is Senior Vice President of Media and Church Ministries at Moody Bible Institute in Chicago. He speaks at churches, conferences, and universities in the United States and abroad. He has been a counselor in a junior high school; Executive Director of Buckner Children & Family Services of North Texas, a multi-service Christian social service agency; and Associate Pastor of Christian Education at Oak Cliff Bible Fellowship in Dallas. He is the featured speaker on the weekly radio program "Look Into the Word." He and his wife, Annie, are the parents of four children.

Michelle Obleton is the director of the women's ministry WINGS (Women IN Godly Services) at Waukegan Church in Waukegan, Illinois, and served as the Coordinator of Women's Ministries at Oak Cliff Bible Fellowship for three years. She wrote a chapter about minister's wives in the book *Woman to Woman.* She has compiled several Bible study guides and has led marriage workshops with her husband. She and her husband, Fred, have a son, Shelby, and a daughter, Andrea.

Cynthia Perry serves as a Professor of Education at Benedictine University in Lisle, Illinois. She has served as an adjunct professor in the Educational Psychology department at Governors State University. She is an educational consultant and women's ministry leader, and she serves on the National Prayer Commission of the Baptist General Conference. She has spoken at churches, women's ministry conferences, marriage conferences with her husband, Dwight, and educational forums during twenty years of full-time ministry. She earned an Ed.D. in Curriculum and Instruction from Loyola University. Her dissertation was on the teacher's perception of Attention Deficit Hyperactive (ADHD) children in the reading content area.

Dwight Perry is Professor of Pastoral Studies at Moody Bible Institute. He has been a pastor and has worked with the Baptist General

Conference, first as National Coordinator of Black Ministries and then as Associate Director of Home Missions. He earned a B.A. in History Education (with an African-American concentration) from the University of Illinois, an M.Ed. in Educational Psychology from the University of Illinois, a D.Min. from Covington Theological Seminary, and a Ph.D. from Trinity Evangelical Divinity School, where he now teaches in the M.A. urban ministries program as an adjunct professor. He was the first African American in the history of Trinity Evangelical Divinity School to earn a Ph.D. in any discipline. His first book, *Breaking Down Barriers,* focused on a historical analysis of the black church.

Sandy Rios is President of Concerned Women for America in Washington, D.C., one of the most powerful lobbying organizations in the nation's capitol. For eight years, Sandy was the host and executive producer of the "Sandy Rios Show" for the Salem network on WYLL, AM 1160 in Chicago, Illinois, where she was known for her courage in tackling any issue, from tough political questions to compassionate challenges to unsaved callers. A former recording artist with Diadem records, Sandy's best known songs include "I'm Going Home," which was number four on the Christian Contemporary Music charts, and "My Shepherd Became a Lamb." Sandy is a graduate of Oklahoma Baptist University and the proud mother of two adult children, Sasha Richelle and Jeremy.

Clarence Shuler (M.Div., Southwestern Baptist Theological Seminary; B.A., Covenant College) has thirty years of cross-cultural ministry experience. He developed and managed Focus on the Family's Black Families Ministries Department. He presently serves as co-pastor of Northview Church in Colorado Springs and is founder and President of Building Lasting Relationships, Inc., which facilitates marriage and biblical diversity seminars that he and his wife, Brenda, do internationally. He teaches at Denver Institute for Urban Studies. He is the author of *Winning the Race to Unity* and *Your Wife Can Be Your Best Friend.* Clarence and Brenda live with their three daughters in Colorado Springs, and they are speakers for Dennis Rainey's FamilyLife Marriage Conferences.

A. Charles Ware (B.R.E., Baptist Bible College of Pennsylvania; M.Div., Capital Bible Seminary; D.D., Baptist Bible Seminary) is President of Crossroads Bible College (formerly Baptist Bible College of Indianapolis), a biblically conservative evangelical institution dedicated to training Christian leaders to reach a multi-ethnic urban world for Christ. He is also the senior pastor of Crossroads Bible Church, that meets at the college. The college is predominantly African American with a healthy mix of whites and other ethnics; it is becoming nationally recognized as a leader in modeling multicultural ministry and biblical racial reconciliation. Dr. Ware co-founded and served seven years as pastor of Scranton Revival Baptist Church while directing a summer camp for inner city youth. He was senior pastor for thirteen years of the Bethel Bible Church in Camp Springs, Maryland, and organized and administered the Bethel Bible Christian School. He co-founded and led the Voice of Biblical Reconciliation. Dr. Ware speaks regularly in the United States and abroad. He co-edited and contributed to *Reuniting the Family of God,* is the author of *Prejudice and the People of God,* and has written articles for the *Christian Advocate, AWANA Cross-Training,* and the *Indianapolis Star* and *World* magazines. He and his wife, Sharon, are parents of Kristin, Timothy, Jonathan, Matthew, Karen, and Justin.

Raleigh B. Washington (D.Div., Trinity International University; M.Div., Trinity Evangelical Divinity School; B.A., Florida A & M University) is Executive Vice President of Global Ministries with Promise Keepers. He was previously Vice President for Reconciliation and a member of the board of directors. Dr. Washington is the founder and Pastor Emeritus of Rock of Our Salvation Evangelical Free Church in Chicago, an urban church reaching across racial barriers in the inner city, and he is a member of the board of directors for Circle Urban Ministries in Chicago. He developed Trinity's Urban Ministries master's program, which he directed for six years. He is the co-author, with Glen Kehrein, of *Breaking Down Walls: A Model of Reconciliation in an Age of Racial Strife.* He attained the rank of Lieutenant Colonel in the U.S. Army, earning the Bronze Star for meritorious service in Vietnam. He is a featured speaker for numerous organizations. He and his wife, Paulette, live in Denver.

FOREWORD

by JOHN PERKINS

E vangelicalism has often been accused of being insensitive to people with social problems—strong on doctrine, weak in good works. In this book twenty-one Bible-believing Christians respond to the issue of class, race, and gender discrimination. They recognize that the church has often failed in these areas, and they point the way toward time-tested solutions. The authors are not armchair theorists, but instead they are battle-scarred veterans, many with years of firsthand experience. They relate the Bible to the real life of the poor, abused women, etc. The hard questions are thoughtfully addressed.

From as far back as the early 1960s, I have longed for a book that could serve as a handbook for the church as it works toward the intricate process of building unity in the church. Finally, such a book has been written in the name of *Building Unity in the Church of the New Millennium*. I envision this book serving as a guide for evangelical Christians who desire to increase unity in the church. This could be a book that evangelical Christians use to see some of the complexity that we have created within the church, the body of Christ, and to understand the impact of racism and other forms of discrimination upon people who are created in the image of God. Instead of Christians enhancing and reflecting this image, the light of God that He has placed in humanity to shine brightly, we have managed to dim this light.

I pray that *Building Unity in the Church of the New Millennium* will be just the resource that will cultivate a profound desire among Christians to proclaim the gospel, which is the power of God unto salvation. This power of God was evident in the conversion experience of the apostle Paul, in that his life before conversion was characterized by bigotry toward Christians, whereas his life after his conversion was characterized by a genuine passion and compassion for proclaiming the gospel to *all* people regardless of race, gender, and religion.

Therefore, it is with deep gratitude to God that I commend the men and women God has ordained and inspired to share their insights and experiences, which has resulted in the work of *Building Unity in the Church of the New Millennium*. I further commend Dwight for doing such a marvelous job of connecting the thoughts of all these writers, as well as editing this invaluable and timely handbook. I can almost say as Simeon said when he saw the child Jesus, "Now may this old man depart in peace." I know my son, Spencer, is shouting with joy in heaven to know that these brothers and sisters have put together a handbook for this millennium and is comforted in knowing that his three biracial children will have an opportunity to experience the fruits of the unity-building efforts of the church. Consequently, they will rejoice in being a part of the people of God.

I welcome and recommend *Building Unity in the Church of the New Millennium,* and it is my hope and prayer that it will be received by *everyone,* not only within the evangelical community, but also within the entire Christian community throughout the world.

Dr. John M. Perkins
President, John M. Perkins Foundation

FOREWORD

It happened about 1900, in response to a modernizing America that emphasized evolution, rationality, and science. Christians, especially white Christians, split over how to deal with the modernizing world.

Some Christians decided that their theology must "modernize" as well, and they made the decision to downplay a personal relationship with Christ in favor of stressing issues of justice and inclusiveness. In their eyes, to say that Christ is the only way to salvation was exclusive, maybe even naive. The true faith, according to those who followed what some called "the social gospel," focused on making society fair and just for all, and in doing so showed God's power and love in tangible ways. Followers of the social gospel helped workers unionize, were concerned with racial oppression and poverty, campaigned for shorter work days, and were concerned with ecumenism, a big word that simply means unity and cooperation across religious boundaries without regard to doctrinal differences.

Other Christians decided that the way to deal with the modernizing world was to reject most of it. They focused on what they viewed as the fundamentals of Christianity—that Jesus died for each person's sins, that He was raised on the third day, that He ascended to heaven, that salvation comes only through a personal relationship with Jesus Christ, and that those who do not accept Christ as their Savior will suffer eternally in hell. The focus on these issues, to the exclusion of issues of social justice, was in clear reaction to social gospel folks, who were downplaying or rejecting these very tenets of the Christian faith.

Those Christians who focused on the specific beliefs of salvation and conservative living came to be called Fundamentalists. Fundamentalists also developed a theology called premillennialism—the belief that the world will get worse and worse until Christ comes back. Given this understanding, they viewed our purpose on earth to be individually saved and to help save others. Anything else—such as making on earth more fair and just—was time wasted, because it was not possible in this kingdom ruled by the devil.

And such was the beginning of the Unfortunate Century. The Bible and the Faith were violently and unnaturally ripped in half, each group grasping a core component of God's message, and each group rejecting a core component of God's message. This was a clear break from the Christianity of the previous century, which emphasized personal salvation *and* making the world a better place for all of God's children.

Many of us born in the Unfortunate Century were given a half faith. We were taught to follow one part of Christianity and distrust the other part. Either we were to focus on salvation and evangelism, or we were to focus on unity and justice. As part of this, we learned to read the Bible selectively, downplaying God's words that speak to the ignored half of the faith.

It is time to bury the Unfortunate Century. We must return to being a true people of the Book, whole and complete followers of God. May our children not have to be forced to make a choice between evangelism and justice. But to bury the Unfortunate Century and enter God's new millennium, we shall have to return to a deep exploration of the very heart of our Creator. We must work to understand and live out His fullness.

Building Unity in the Church of the New Millennium is a dynamic, powerful shift in this direction. This book contains exactly the type of thought and discussion we need to move past the Unfortunate Century and return to God. It brings together the whole faith, applying it to issues that matter. I thank God for Dwight Perry, who has labored for decades to bring the fullness of God's message. He has assembled in this volume an amazing array of God's leaders to speak to us about vital aspects of our faith, teaching us how to reunite that which has been separated. This book is compelling, each chapter unfolding important truths. I read this volume with excitement, as I kept learning more with each page.

With its contents and the excellent discussion questions at the end of each chapter, this book is ideal for individuals hoping to learn more about God's plans for unity. It is also ideal for small groups, from Sunday school classes to discipleship classes, from in-home groups to college courses. In fact, this volume will be most valuable when Christians come together to discuss the meaning and implications of its chapters.

May God use the words of this book, your heart, and your mind in working to fulfill His Design.

Michael Emerson, Ph.D.
Professor, Rice University
Author of *Divided by Faith*

ACKNOWLEDGMENTS

One of the things we learn growing up in the inner city is that it truly "takes a village to raise a child." I can still remember Mrs. Powell and many of the other good folks of the neighborhood who looked out for me and my brother, including those who did not live in the neighborhood, like my uncle Barry, who was the father I never experienced. I also want to thank, from the bottom of my heart, my godly mother, Mrs. Bernice Perry, who literally prayed me into the kingdom.

In writing this book there are many whom I must acknowledge. First and foremost are my twenty co-authors. It is mind-boggling to think that twenty-one people can work together to accomplish anything, let alone a book of this magnitude, but I found each of them not only engaging with the subject but a real joy to work with.

My General Editor, Cheryl Dunlop, is a godsend. She not only is extremely competent in her craft, but has a passion for a subject like this and was outstanding in her input, not only about such issues as writing style and grammar, but content as well.

I also want to thank Greg Thornton, Vice President of publishing for Moody Press. Greg did not have to publish a book like this, yet he has been behind this project from day one.

Last but certainly not least, I want to thank the Love of my life, Cynthia. She has walked with me throughout the last twenty-two-plus years, first as a friend, and then as a partner in life and ministry. Cynthia, I owe you my life.

INTRODUCTION

Growing up in the inner city of Chicago in the 1950s and volatile '60s, I never imagined that I would someday have the privilege of serving on the faculty of one of the premier evangelical Bible colleges in the entire world, the Moody Bible Institute. Part of the reason that this was not even a part of my frame of reference was the fact that, as an African American in America, I lived in a country that was truly, as Andrew Hacker says in his book *Two Nations,* "a country that is divided, two nations both hostile and unequal." As far as I can recall I saw only one Caucasian in person up to junior high, and I was extremely limited in my interaction with what we would come to call the "world" outside the ghetto I was being raised in. Especially with the "evangelical world," which during this time was for the most part fleeing the cities of our country for the suburbs.

This was a world that from my perspective has not only marginalized people because of their race, but also has failed to grapple satisfactorily and biblically with its relationship and response to women (especially those who have gifts in the area of leadership), those of a different class background, and those who for any reason do not fit into the unofficial American dream of being under forty, a middle- to upper-class Caucasian male with no physical disabilities or challenges.

The main problem I have with this mind-set is that, if we are going to believe Michael Emerson in his now famous book *Divided by Faith,* the evangelical church is one of the main perpetrators of these divisions. Some could ask, "Dwight, why are you writing a book like this? What do you hope to accomplish?" A better question in my judgment is "Why is there still a need for such a book?"

Unfortunately if we are to believe the statement made by Dr. King more than thirty-five years ago, that eleven o'clock Sunday morning is the most segregated hour in the country—and not just segregated racially, but in terms of interaction among classes and genders and with those who have physical disabilities—then not only is there still a need for such a book, but we might even be running out of time in this relativistic, postmodern era to see the church become a major player in bringing biblical solutions to this all-encompassing dilemma.

This book will address discrimination, and biblical answers to it, specifically within the evangelical church. It is different from other books that have dealt with this topic (including my own book *Breaking Down Barriers*) in that it does not deal solely with the area of racial discrimination within the church, but also looks at other areas, including gender, age, physical disability, and class. I have solicited the help of twenty other scholars and practitioners in these areas. The book is thus divided into four sections. One or two of the topics might particularly resonate with you. Maybe we deal with an area you really care about or one you know you need to study more. But undoubtedly, as you look through what has been written in other areas and wonder whether that area has affected your own church, you will be challenged to think even more carefully about some of the implications this book conveys. (For additional reading on any particular subject, see the bibliography at the end of the book.)

It is my hope, and that of others who have worked with me on this project, that it can be a resource to both church and parachurch ministries, as well as to individual believers who are seeking answers in some of these critical areas. My main focus in selecting those who will help me tell the story of this book was that they needed to be people who loved Jesus and His Word above all else. I wanted the book to be evangelical yet frank in its treatment of this very painful and at times controversial subject. It is my prayer, as one who has had the privilege of serving Christ more than a quarter century, that this book will truly help us as the body of Christ to fulfill Christ's wonderful words found in John 17: that the world will know that Jesus is the Savior by the experience of true unity we have with one another in the body of Christ, regardless of race, class, gender, age, or any other physical characteristic.

PART ONE

UNITY BETWEEN RACES IN THE CHURCH

CHAPTER ONE

DEVELOPING A BIBLICAL THEOLOGY OF RACIAL RECONCILIATION:

How Do Institutions Perpetuate Racism?

DWIGHT PERRY

Michael Emerson in his book *Divided by Faith* gives the most profound definition of societal racism that I have ever heard. He says that a racist society is "a society wherein race matters profoundly for differences in life experiences, life opportunities, and social relationships. A racialized society can also be said to be 'a society that allocates differential economic, political, social, and even psychological rewards to groups along racial lines; lines that are socially constructed.'"[1]

As one who has lived in two worlds going on five decades and has ministered for more than twenty-seven years in both the white and black culture, all I can say is a hardy Amen! However, the critical question that this chapter will address is not whether we live, as Emerson says, in a racialized society, but why do we see very little difference within evangelical, conservative churches? Those churches and institutions that supposedly possess the truth, as I said in my book *Breaking Down Barriers*, have the "right theology but the wrong sociology."

Andrew Hacker gives further definition to this all-consuming problem when he says,

> Black Americans are Americans, yet they still subsist as aliens in the only land they know. Other groups may remain outside the mainstream—some religious sects, for example—but they do so voluntarily. In contrast, blacks must endure a segregation that is far from freely chosen. So America may be seen as two separate nations. Of course, there are places where the races mingle. Yet in most significant respects, the separation is pervasive and penetrating. As a social and human division, it surpasses all others—even gender—in intensity and subordination.[2]

Joseph Barndt puts it like this,

> Racism is clearly more than simple prejudice or bigotry. Everyone is prejudiced, but not everyone is racist. To be prejudiced means to have opinions without the facts and to hold on to those opinions, even after contrary facts are known. To be racially prejudiced means to have distorted opinions about people of other races. Racism goes beyond prejudice. It is backed up by power. Racism is the power to enforce one's prejudices. More simply stated, racism is prejudice plus power.[3]

We as believers have done very little to address the issue of race and more specifically the issue of institutional racism. If we have entered into this conversation, we have tended to respond to this issue on more of a personal rather than a theological and structural level, not truly understanding the deeply theological and structural implications of an integrated perspective on racial reconciliation.

Racism on a Systemic Level

John Piper, renowned pastor and theologian who serves as pastor of the Bethlehem Baptist Church in inner-city Minneapolis, spoke at the February 2001 Moody Bible Institute's Founder's Week Bible Conference. Dr. Piper gave the best theological treatment from Revelation

5 as to why this is ultimately "a blood issue" and not just something that is politically correct. John, a friend of mine, allowed me the privilege of having breakfast with him and his wife and six-year-old adopted daughter (who is black) the day after his address. I commended him for what was the greatest theological treatment of this issue that I had heard. Then I said that he still needed to add one more piece to his outworking of the issue that is critical for every person in America: the importance of understanding that true reconciliation cannot take place unless there is a strong structural component along with a strong theological and personal compoent.

The issue of racial reconciliation cannot be addressed simply on a personal level as it has been positioned, but must include the great structural implications of dealing with racism on a systemic level.

In thinking about the interaction with Dr. Piper that morning, I developed what I call an integrated philosophy of racial reconciliation.

PERRY'S DEFINITION OF AN INTEGRATED
PHILOSOPHY OF RACIAL RECONCILIATION
Racial Reconciliation =
(1) A strong biblical/theological foundation plus
(2) personal repentance and interaction with someone else of a different race, with
(3) a continued emphasis and call to structural and systemic change.

The call to changing the way we do things must be confronted head on by those who are a part of the problem, white middle-class conservative believers. For as long as blacks and other minorities are the only ones confronting the issue, it will remain marginalized. Only when Caucasian spiritual leaders begin to exercise leadership in this area more than persons of color who live in the cycle of racism will this issue be seen as something that is legitimate. When it is not solely addressed by people of color but is aggressively addressed by those in the Caucasian evangelical setting, the issue of racism will be seen as more than just a black issue that bitter, unforgiving blacks can't seem to recover from, but as a legitimate issue that is hurting the church.

All three of these components must be addressed in an in-depth and comprehensive manner by each of us as believers. Any response to institutional racism that is missing any one of the three critical components of my definition of racial reconciliation leaves those involved in the process only partially in tune with the issues that institutional racism in this country has been able to perpetuate, especially within conservative evangelical structures. For if one accepts the underlying premise of Michael Emerson's work *Divided by Faith,* one of the major stumbling blocks to the races (especially blacks and whites) being able to come together is religion, and specifically evangelical Christianity:

> Emboldened by the sacred, religion can be a powerful source for change. And indeed, as part of what we examine in Chapter Two, religion has been a source for change in American race relations, from abolition to the Civil Rights movement. Thus, religion can provide the moral force for people to determine that something about their world so excessively violates their moral standards that they must act to correct it. It can also provide the moral force necessary for sustained, focused, collective action to achieve the desired goal.
>
> Nevertheless, we argue that religion, as structured in America, is unable to make a great impact on the racialized society. In fact, far from knocking down racial barriers, religion generally serves to maintain these historical divides, and helps to develop new ones.[4]

Levels of Institutional Racism

Let's explore the implications of each of the three major components of an integrated perspective on how to solve the problem of institutional racism. Before we delve into this subject we need to define very clearly what we mean when we talk about institutional racism.

Institutional racism is an intentional or unintentional system of excluding persons based solely on race, color, or ethnic background from a shared participation within the organization, usually through covert, subtle means. Please notice that institutional racism does not have to be intentional; it can be systemic and be just as devastating. As a matter of fact, especially since the onslaught of the civil rights movement, the more overt forms of racism, which still do exist, are not the majority expressions of institutional racism as they were even fifty years ago in many parts of this country.

Joseph Barndt in his book *Dismantling Racism* defines institutional racism on three levels. It will help us to look briefly at all three.

Level One: Racism in Personnel

One individual's racist and prejudicial behavior can skew the entire system. For example, the Rodney King riots in Los Angeles were precipitated by the actions of a few racist policemen who violated the civil rights of Mr. King. These few racist policemen set up the impression that the entire police department was thus racist, a statement that is far from the truth. Similarly a salesperson who is racist can make an entire department store chain look racist, when in essence it is institutional racism being perpetrated through one person or a small group of individuals. Out of the three levels, this level is the easiest to identify and begin to seek resolution. Many of the programs of an organization can be geared toward addressing institutional racism as reflected in this level. It is even possible to dismiss people from employment if they persist in these types of behaviors.

Level Two: Racism in Policy and Practice

Working on the area of institutional racism on solely a personal level is not going to be sufficient. It is the central thesis of this chapter that institutional racism cannot truly be addressed unless we move past personal reconciliation and begin to look at some of the structural implications of racist behavior and attitudes. Level two is the beginning of this structural process, because it attacks the issue of institutional racism from the point of view of an institution's policy and practice. It is on the policy level that even many conservative evangelicals have attacked institutions. For it is on the policy and practice levels that the institution's decision and organizational ethos is guided and shaped.

The workers in an organization may also be carrying out racist policies and practices without even realizing it. An excellent example of this is found in Joseph Barndt's book *Dismantling Racism*: "A city police department may have a stated policy of equal protection for all neighborhoods, but its practice may be very different."[5] Of course, many such instances have made the news each year for the last several years—and many more go unreported. Sometimes companies hire enough minorities to stay ahead of the law, but most of the minorities are in entry-level or low-skill jobs.

Level Three: Racism in Structures and Foundations

This is the most important and is the hardest to eradicate. Change is most difficult on this level because the racism that is found within the organization is rooted in the very foundation and structures of the organization. "Structural racism exists when the designated boundaries of the institution's services exclude people of color or do not serve them equally. It also exists when a product or service is of inferior quality when provided to people of color." Another example mentioned by Barndt is "when staff or leadership of a multicultural community or institution is predominately white and does not represent proportionately its membership."[6]

Institutions can also function according to white people's values in such a way that minority employees or constituents are left at a distinct disadvantage. For example, middle-class white America appears at time to value "being on time" more than relationships, white Christians speak out on lateness as a *sin* (bad stewardship of time, disrespect of others, poor priorities, etc.). White pastors performing weddings for minority couples have been known to get started "on time" and consider it the fault of the wedding guests that most don't make it until the ceremony is over. Companies may give time off for employees to attend relative funerals, but they are unlikely to think it necessary to include such "distant" relatives as uncles, aunts, and cousins—who might be very close relatives to African-American or Hispanic employees.

Most conservative white people dislike affirmative action, thinking it unfairly gives jobs to large numbers of unqualified minorities rather than to them, yet they don't blink an eye at the fact that many companies hire almost exclusively based on who the applicant knows in the company—a distinct disadvantage for minority applicants trying to get into mostly white companies or rise to management positions in them.

An institution's foundations are the underlying core values, stated purposes, and historical traditions that the institution is built upon.

This is a very complex issue. The reason that so many Caucasians cannot understand why it is even an issue is that the foundational base of many of the institutions in this country is rooted in and corrupted by racism. Slavery and the economic and social foundation that so encompassed the land laid the foundation of a white, Anglo worldview that looked at life through the lens of race.

In an April 1994 issue of *Time* magazine, the lead story was about the supposed glass ceiling that many African-American executives face on a continual basis. It is perceived totally differently by blacks and whites. Blacks see the issue of institutional racism as systemic and at the very core of our existence in this culture, whereas many whites see it as something that took place in history and does not have any real bearing on our world today.

The Biblical Foundation of Racial Reconciliation

As evangelicals we "love the Bible." One of the unfortunate realities in this whole treatment of institutional racism by many conservative evangelicals is that in the zeal to try to grapple with this complex issue, we have jumped over what the Bible says about the issue of racism. (At least that's true for a very few of us; most Christians couldn't care less about this issue if the truth be known!) We have by our actions given the impression that our response to this issue is primarily rooted in our desire to be right with our fellow man, and not necessarily as an application of being in a right relationship with our God. From Genesis to Revelation we see a God who not only values diversity but who demands that His people, the bride of Christ, be a multiracial, -ethnic, -language people. In John Piper's profound Founder's Week message, he said, "Part of the problem is that many evangelical believers do not think this issue is a big issue when in reality it is an all-consuming issue because it is critical to the heart of God."

Revelation 7:9 says, "After this I looked and there before me was a great multitude that no one could count, from every nation, tribe, people and language, standing before the throne and in front of the Lamb. They were wearing white robes and were holding palm branches in their hands."

Galatians 3:28 says, "There is neither Jew nor Greek, slave nor free, male nor female, for you are all one in Christ Jesus."

One of the most profound passages in the area of laying a biblical and theological foundation for a proper response to institutional racism is found in James 2:1–13. The author James, the half brother of Jesus, is writing to a group of Jewish believers who, due to persecution for their faith, had been dispersed abroad from Jerusalem. Their lives were filled with intense pressure and pain, which is why James in his little letter to these saints is seeking to exhort them to live out their faith even in the midst of tough times. Some have called this letter "the Proverbs of the New Testament" because of its pithy, practical instructions.

James 2:1–13 is the third in this series of short exhortations, with the focus of this passage being James's exhortation to saints not to be like those individuals in the world who exclude others based on their social status. Rather, they were to be people who truly demonstrate the law of love by breaking down the walls of partiality seeking to rise up among these New Testament believers. He uses three keys in the text to exhort these saints: number one, the importance of not falling into the faulty thinking of the sin of partiality (vv. 1–4); number two, understanding the significant role that the poor will play in God's kingdom and should play right now in our churches (vv. 5–6); and number three, realizing that the issue of power (vv. 6–13) is at the root of all partiality, and only as we apply the law of love can we hope to overcome its tentacles.

We have just touched on a few of the relevant Scriptures in this area. There are at least 1,200 passages in both the Old and New Testament that look at the issues of the poor, the downtrodden, the oppressed, and those who are discriminated against.

Personal Responsibility to Those of Other Races

The second critical component to the development of an integrated response to institutional racism is one's personal response. I thank God that especially over the last ten years or so, and in direct response to the Promise Keepers movement, we have seen a real emphasis among conservative evangelicals in this area. Men especially, but women and children as well, have had to come to grips with their own racist attitudes and behaviors. Such speakers and authors as Glen Kehrein, Raleigh Washington, Bill McCartney, Spencer Perkins, John

Perkins, Chris Rice, and many others have helped people see the reality of racism in their own individual experience.

In the best-selling book *Breaking Down Walls* by Raleigh Washington and Glen Kehrein we find these words:

> *This book is about a solution.* The reality of racial strife in our society is obvious. If the recent Los Angeles riots taught us anything, it is that we have been traveling in circles. Riots, fermenting in the hotbed of racial inequity and poverty, lie dormant only to rise again; each time more vile and destructive. Each time a new generation will write increasingly articulate works about the causes and little about the remedy.
>
> This book talks about a remedy. A remedy coming from the timeless book of irrefutable truth—the Bible. Neither Congress nor the president can apply a remedy to cure our country's ills. However, you, individually, can apply the principles described in this book, regardless of your place in life. Our remedy is distinctly Christian, calling upon those of faith in Christ to be "salt and light" and to "break down walls of hostility." This remedy is at the very foundation of the Christian faith. It is *the remedy of reconciliation;* specifically, the power of the cross of Christ to bring racial reconciliation. The authenticity of the gospel is demonstrated when the dividing walls of racial hostility are broken down.[7]

In *More Than Equals,* Spencer Perkins mirrors these words by saying,

> As a Black Christian I thought our freedom struggle in the sixties would lead to reconciliation. I was wrong. Race seems to be the one nut that even Christianity is having a hard time cracking. Chris [his white co-author] and I believe that the first step in the reconciliation process is admitting that the race problem exists and that our inability to deal with race has weakened the credibility of our gospel.[8]

Institutional racism at its core is a reflection of individual bias and self-deception. Organizations are no more than the people who are involved in them, and organizations reflect those people's values.

Dr. Rod Cooper in his profound work *We Stand Together* says it like this:

Describing the United States as a melting pot—an overused expression—is suggestive of a country where people of every class, creed, and color with different customs have melded together to create a new culture. However, the United States is not now, and never was, some kind of homogenized culture where people from around the globe with their many differences somehow softened into a new kind of supra-culture. Since its beginning, one and only one racial-ethnic group has dominated and become the standard for others to emulate—namely, Western Europeans.[9]

Ironically, this is one area where the culture is doing better than the church. Black musicians have become mainstream, appealing even to white suburban teenagers (as noted by major news magazines). Most white people are beginning to be aware of the huge number of inventions African-Americans have given America, and Spanish is used on advertising billboards in many parts of the country. Consumer products are likely to carry a picture of a black family, or a Chinese person, or people of several races, and white people will still buy them. But in the church, the fear of color—or fear of hypothetical other people's fear of color—still keeps most sermons, promotional materials, and publications safely white, unless they're specifically intended to appeal to people of color.

Individual repentance has always been at the core of corporate repentance. Hundreds of years ago Solomon had just completed the fulfillment of his father's dream of the temple being built. As part of the dedication of the temple he prayed that the temple might be the place where God would adjudicate wrongs between individuals, where He would forgive the nation when it was defeated in battle because of sin, and where He would hear their prayers of repentance when drought and other disasters befell them as a result of divine judgment (2 Chronicles 6:22–31). For seven days the festivities went on with the people of the Lord gathered. Finally on the eighth day, which followed the seven-day Feast of Tabernacles (Leviticus 23:36), the people assembled once more just before returning home. Then, Scripture tells us,

When Solomon had finished the temple of the Lord and the royal palace, and had succeeded in carrying out all he had in mind to do in the temple of the Lord and in his own palace, the Lord appeared to him at night and

said: "I have heard your prayer and have chosen this place for myself as a temple for sacrifices. When I shut up the heavens so that there is no rain, or command locusts to devour the land or send a plague among my people, if my people, who are called by my name, will humble themselves and pray and seek my face and turn from their wicked ways, then will I hear from heaven and will forgive their sin and will heal their land."
(2 Chronicles 7:11–14)

There can be no revival until there is repentance. This may be one of the reasons that the national prayer initiatives put forth by many Caucasian evangelicals are simply, in this author's opinion, a waste of time, as we cry out to a God who refuses to hear us because of our unwillingness to truly repent of the sin of racism both individually and also within our evangelical structures.

Eugene Peterson in THE MESSAGE paraphrases the prophet Isaiah in a way that even though not inspired is indeed profound:

Shout! A full-throated shout! Hold nothing back—a trumpet-blast shout! Tell my people what's wrong with their lives, face my family Jacob with their sins! They're busy, busy, busy at worship, and love studying all about me. To all appearances they're a nation of right-living people—law-abiding, God-honoring. They ask me, "What's the right thing to do?" and love having me on their side. But they also complain, "Why do we fast and you don't look our way? Why do we humble ourselves and you don't even notice?"

Well, here's why:

The bottom line on your "fast days" is profit. You drive your employees much too hard. You fast, but at the same time you bicker and fight. You fast, but you swing a mean fist. The kind of fasting you do won't get your prayers off the ground. Do you think this is the kind of fast day I'm after: a day to show off humility? To put on a pious long face and parade around solemnly in black? Do you call that fasting, a fast day that I, God, would like?

This is the kind of fast day I'm after: to break the chains of injustice, get rid of exploitation in the workplace, free the oppressed, cancel debts. What I'm interested in seeing you do is: sharing your food with the hungry, inviting the homeless poor into your homes, putting clothes on the shivering ill-clad, being available to your own families. Do this and the lights will turn on, and your lives will turn around at once. Your righ-

*teousness will pave your way. The God of glory will secure your passage.
Then when you pray, God will answer. You'll call out for help and I'll say,
"here I am." (Isaiah 58:1–12)*

Confronting Structural and Systemic Racism

Individual repentance on a personal level is thus basic if we are
going to address the problem of institutional racism. Even though it
is critical, if stopped here, as most evangelicals have done (if they have
done anything at all about racial reconciliation), it continues to fall
short of what is truly necessary to deal with the insidious and satanic evil of institutional racism. There is one more part to my equation of essential factors in addressing the evil of institutional racism:
that of confronting the structural inequalities that we see throughout
our society and even more specifically within the church, that continue to exclude people, based on race, from accessing all that God
has entrusted to these organizations.

Many people have asked the question for what purpose was the
nation of Israel selected to be God's chosen people. Was it because
God wanted to have a people for Himself? Was it because He was
enamored in some special way with the Jewish people? No, quite simply so that they as His chosen people could be used by God to share
the richness of faith in Jehovah with all the nations and could be a
living illustration of His mercy and grace. Unfortunately they largely
failed to do that and looked at their special relationship with God as
a privilege that was exclusively for them because they were better than
the rest of the world, instead of the servant of the world.

In similar manner we who are part of the American evangelical
conservative church have mistaken God's blessing as a license to spend
more and more on ourselves and to exclude those who look different
from us and who are in a different social class than we are. We maintain in our own personal lives the very same institutional attitudes and
practices that the broader culture has continued to hold on to in this
country to protect our own economic and social interest.

An involvement in structural change goes right to the heart of the
gospel. Jesus says in Luke 4:18, quoting from the prophet Isaiah, "The
Spirit of the Lord is on me, because he has anointed me to preach good
news to the poor. He has sent me to proclaim freedom for the pris-

oners and recovery of sight for the blind, to release the oppressed, to proclaim the year of the Lord's favor."

Now I know many white conservative evangelical commentators have chosen to exegetically defuse the social and structural implications of this passage in favor of the prophetic emphasis on Jesus as the Messiah. I wholeheartedly agree that this is the clear focus of the text exegetically; however, one cannot help but see that, in fulfilling His ministry as the Messiah, Jesus had a very specific agenda that included the confrontation of unjust structures and the liberation of those who were being oppressed. As was the custom of that day, Jesus introduced Himself to those in the synagogue by telling the ministry that His Father had called Him to do. His call was to preach the good news (gospel—Greek *Euaggelizo*, which means "to evangelize, to proclaim"). That good news will literally set people free not only spiritually but also emotionally and physically.

This theme of deliverance of the poor and the oppressed is not something that Jesus initiated in the Gospels, but it is seen throughout the Old Testament. The word *just* or *justice* in the Old Testament has two primary meanings: The first, *Mispat*, occurs more than four hundred times and is usually found where the NIV speaks of "doing what is just or justice" and has to do primarily with the execution of judicial decision, the execution of judgment, and even a statement of code. The second, *Sadaq*, has in common the idea that "moral and ethical norms exist and that actions in harmony with the norms are just, while actions not in harmony with the norm are unjust or constitute injustice."[10]

One needs only to do a perusal of both the Major and Minor Prophets to see the theme of justice and righteousness amplified over and over again with the prophet being God's voice in a dark and unjust world on behalf of those who were being oppressed. Even as we move to the New Testament Epistles we see the continued emphasis on the fact that, because we have a God who is just, He will exact justice on those who disobey Him.

Implications of Perry's Formula for True Reconciliation

Let's consider some implications of people taking this formula for reconciliation seriously.

No. 1: Institutional racism cannot be tolerated, because it is not a politically correct issue; it is a blood issue. In other words it is not a side issue, but an integral issue of the gospel and the implications of the gospel.

No. 2: Caucasian evangelicals can no longer focus on personal reconciliation as the catchall to the problem of institutional racism but must confront structural and systemic racism within their spheres of influence. It is expected for a person of color to speak out against these issues; however, it does not have the same impact on the majority culture as when a Caucasian speaks out against these issues.

No. 3: A clear theological motif must undergird any of our efforts in the area of a Christian response to institutional racism. Theology cannot be set aside as an area that does not have a direct connection to this very important area.

No. 4: Persons of color must learn how to be more confrontative within white evangelical structures and not just simply leave quietly, fearing the ramifications of such action. Truth must be proclaimed in a spirit of love, but it must be proclaimed. We cannot fall prey to the tendency Raleigh Washington and Glen Kehrein have described so well in their book *Breaking Down Walls* as the "BBW Syndrome"—Black people talk to Black people about White people. (Neither can white people fall prey to the "WWB Syndrome" of White people talking to White people about Black people.)

No. 5: The issue of the fear of sharing financial and other types of resources that go along with the area of white privilege must be addressed. There can be no true reconciliation without redistribution and sharing of resources.

No. 6: Training, mission, denominational, and other types of parachurch ministries need to understand what true contextualization means within a North American context. There are many ways of doing things, not simply one right way, even though there is only one correct principle that undergirds the methodology.

Conclusion

Jesus said during His last few hours here on earth a most profound statement: The world will know that He is the Christ by our unity (John 17:21). From that day to this day, the Enemy of our souls has done everything he can to stifle the unity that you and I already possess in Christ (Ephesians 4:3). One of the major ploys he uses in this country is the devastating lie of racial division. He has been able to gain a foothold not only in many of our individual lives, but also in the structures that continue to reinforce the reality that we are truly two nations divided and unequal, even in the church. Only as we as evangelicals develop an integrated philosophy of racial reconciliation that looks at this issue of institutional racism from the three-fold perspective of the personal, theological, and structural can we show the world the unified church Christ desires.

What is at stake if we do not begin to do the hard work of reconciliation? A generation of people whose view of God is skewed because they cannot see the manifestation of the power of God among His people living a redeemed and reconciled experience.

DISCUSSION STARTER QUESTIONS

1. Define institutional racism. How is it different from prejudice? Why is it important to be able to distinguish between the two?
2. Have you ever experienced institutional racism? If you have, tell another person in your group how and what impact it had on you. If not, tell whether you have been exposed to this concept through the experience of another and what your reaction was to the person. Tell any examples of it being effectively resolved. State in detail the process that took place.
3. React to Perry's contention that racial reconciliation is a "blood issue"—in other words, that it is an issue that is central to our understanding and application of the gospel and cannot be pushed aside as a tertiary social issue but is deeply theological.

CHAPTER TWO

FADE TO WHITE:

How White Is Evangelical Theology?

VINCENT BACOTE

The term "evangelical" is associated with many things, from certain streams of tradition more or less rooted in the Protestant Reformation to particular forms of piety to a broad set of cultural norms and values. Beyond such associations, to be "evangelical" means to be "biblical" in the sense that God's self-disclosure in the sixty-six books of the Bible is considered authoritative. The Bible is understood to be God's Word and thus to convey the truth about whatever it addresses in the text. When theology is constructed in the evangelical framework, then, the objective is to articulate the truth about God, Jesus Christ, the church, etc. in a way that accurately reflects what the Bible says about the topic at hand. J. I. Packer articulates this "classical" approach to systematic theology as follows:

> The aim of this theology . . . is to function as a science: that is . . .
> to give the world a body of analyzed, tested, correlated knowl-
> edge concerning God in relation to his creatures in general and

to mankind in particular. The method whereby it pursues its aim requires the student to be conscientiously Bible-based, Christ-centered, and church-oriented, with a sustained life-changing and world-changing interest. These perspectives of concern hang together, and Bible-based thinking requires one to embrace them all, as all major systematic theologians from Origen on have in fact done.[1]

From an evangelical perspective, the Bible-based thinking referred to above is central to the task of systematic theology, regardless of methodological nuances. With the Bible at the center, evangelicals intend to articulate theology in a way that would yield coherent, biblically faithful results, indeed results that are, ideally, free from the myopic influences of culture, class, or political influence. To most Bible-believing Christians, irrespective of a self-conscious identity as evangelical, this would probably be construed as the ideal way to undertake the theological enterprise.

Like most endeavors, the theological task has potential pitfalls. Packer articulates a significant danger: All theology suffers contextual handicaps. He notes that there are two kinds of errors in theological systems: those resulting from defective methodology and those resulting from the failure to meet the demands of a right method.[2] It is in regard to the latter that Packer notes the greatest of theological handicaps:

> It needs to be stated that the systematic theologian's biggest problem is always *himself*—that is, the unmortified arrogance and continuing darkness of his own intellect, which leads him unwittingly, in perfect sincerity and often with painstaking labor, to offer God's people theological constructions that are unbiblical, man-centered, culturally determined, unpractical, undevotional, undoxological, Spirit-quenching and self-aggrandizing —theological constructions that in effect put God in a box of one's own manufacture, claiming in effect to master him by knowing exhaustively what he will and will not do. Theologians who allowed themselves to speak as if they had God in their pocket would indeed be presenting a mirage of unreality! But the true systematic theologian will be carefully, prayerfully watching himself all the time so as to avoid doing any such thing.[3]

Packer tells us that idolatry is always a danger for the theologian. It is too easy to make an apparently biblical theology that is in reality constructed in the image of the theologian or the theologian's community. Does evangelical theology exhibit an attention to Packer's concerns, and, if so, has it done so in such a way as to counteract the legacy of discrimination and racism in the church? This raises the central question of this essay: How "white" is evangelical theology? Is it just theology that exhibits a high level of biblical fidelity, or are there sociocultural influences that significantly shape it? Though Packer is an evangelical theologian aware of this concern, it is not clear that this concern has permeated the theology of evangelicalism's professional theologians and the larger evangelical populace.

Evangelicals' Racial Division

Divided by Faith, by Michael O. Emerson and Christian Smith, reveals the entrenchment of racial division in evangelicalism. Tracing evangelicals' approaches to race and religion in America from 1700, they note that the evangelical focus on evangelism and discipleship led them

to avoid issues that hinder these activities. Thus, they are generally not countercultural. With some significant exceptions, they avoid "rocking the boat," and live within the confines of the larger culture. At times they have been able to call for and realize social change, but most typically their influence has been limited to alterations at the margins. So, despite having the subcultural tools to call for radical changes in race relations, they most consistently call for changes in persons that leave the dominant social structures, institutions, and culture intact. This avoidance of boat-rocking unwittingly leads to granting power to larger economic and social forces. It also means that evangelicals' views to a considerable extent conform to the socioeconomic conditions of their time. Evangelicals usually fail to challenge the system not just out of concern for evangelism, but also because they support the American system and enjoy its fruits. They share the Protestant work ethic, support laissez-faire economics, and sometimes fail to evaluate whether the social system is consistent with their Christianity.[4]

This observation reveals that evangelicalism, although committed to biblical fidelity, is also significantly shaped and influenced by the American context. As Emerson and Smith demonstrate, white evangelicals not only acquiesced but sometimes contributed to the development of America as a racialized society, a society in which whites were understood to be normative (whether this was explicitly stated or not).[5] In terms of self-concept, this implies that evangelicals have arrived at their self-perception as a result of culture as much as exegesis, if not more. Theologically, this pervasive influence of American cultural values (as they developed throughout the birth and growth of the nation) has left its mark in ways that may not always be readily visible, though they are revealed as evangelicals attempt to fully articulate and practice the Christian life.

The Individualism of the American Church

In what way has the American culture affected evangelical thinking on race, particularly in ways that reveal an explicit or subtle influence on the evangelical approach to theology? Emerson and Smith, drawing on sociologist Ann Swidler, examine the religio-cultural "tool kit" of white evangelicals. The tool kit metaphor refers to ideas, habits, skills, and styles used by individuals and groups to organize experience and evaluate reality.[6] According to Emerson and Smith, a form of individualism is one of the primary tools of white evangelicals. The influence of individualism is not only pivotal to the religious world of white evangelicals, but also extends to their interpretation of the race problem in America. More specifically, white evangelicals use a form of individualism that emphasizes personal accountability, interpersonal relationships, and antistructuralism.[7]

Evangelicals talk a lot about being part of the "body" of Christ—a term with corporate ramifications. But does evangelical practice follow this terminology? If not, why not, since the whole imagery of the New Testament presupposes the church is a corporate entity? Besides biblical guidance, two influences come together in any discussion of the church: its own history and the culture in which it is set.[8] American evangelicals lean heavily on the history of the Reformation and on the more recent history of revivalism. In addition, the church is heavily affected by American culture, with influences ranging from marketing tools to a psychological understanding of the human being.

The Protestant Reformation had as its explicit purpose to return the church to a more biblical foundation. An unintended side effect was splintering the church into multiple denominations. In telling believers that only Scripture is the Christian's ultimate authority, that God's revelation is given today only through the Word, and that the church is in error when it contradicts Scripture, and in emphasizing the priesthood of the individual believer (all biblically true), the seeds were sown for individuals to stand ultimately above the church, judging it and not considering themselves accountable to it, but rather the other way around. In other words, rather than Scripture being one's final authority, one's *private interpretation* of Scripture is. This of course is radically different both from Scripture and from the intentions of the Reformers. But it has led to multiple denominations splitting from one another on various points of theology, to parachurch organizations that stand beyond the authority of any church, and to believers who jump from church to church on a whim. To evangelicals, "ministry" has also been seen as the most important career choice a believer can make, with options ranging from missionary service to the pastorate or work with a parachurch organization; interaction with the culture for other than explicitly evangelistic influence has thus been limited and in fact often discouraged.

The story of revivalism is also based on a scriptural truth: Through the Cross Christ offers to sinners the chance to have an individual relationship with Him, not just with the church and its traditions. It is true that salvation comes through repentance and a relationship with Christ, not through following church traditions. But once again, the unintended consequence was further individualism in church members. If the most important thing in life was one's private relationship with Jesus, initiated by "asking Jesus into my heart," then the church one attended could be self-chosen or even optional. (Today some families, dissatisfied with any church, are choosing to have "home churches" made up only of their immediate families.) And of course at its worst, there is no place in Protestantism to call cultic branches to accountability under Scripture or any corporate authority.

If the church is not an authority, then it is only a place to worship and fellowship with like-minded individuals, and not an agent of accountability that speaks for God. The church music of the last couple of centuries has likewise become more and more individually driven ("I love you, Lord"). With the fundamentalist call, early in the twentieth century, for believers to be radically "separate" from the world, many (white) believers became ever more isolated from anyone other than their own immediate nuclear families and their own churches, which contained people much like them. If the church isn't an authority, the extended family's role is largely absent, and the culture's role is seen as negative (threatening to one's holiness and distracting to one's calling), then individualism can be almost total—just me, my family, and Jesus.

Of course, evangelicalism and fundamentalism have been strong in the calls to personal holiness of members, which is a good thing. They have also emphasized believers' responsibility to read and memorize Scripture. Hundreds of American colleges and seminaries, hospitals and homes for needy children, and eventually various activist organizations, including those that fight against aborting the next generation, have their roots in American conservative evangelicalism. Various branches of the church have also been very active in sending missionaries; many countries in the world have been evangelized because of American churches. But the effects of the evangelical church on the larger American culture, and on people from other subcultures, have probably been minimized in recent decades because of the tendency to look inward.

In addition to the influence of churches' focus on the priesthood of the believer, and in fact probably largely because of it, American society would itself eventually be known around the world for its individualism. From the fact that even educated Americans are usually only proficient in one language, English, to the icon of the "self-made" rugged Western cowboy, from the rise of the Freudian "self-help" culture to advertising that makes the individual consumer king, from the cultural oddity of Americans commuting to work with one person per car (as opposed to mass public transportation of many countries) to the overthrow of tradition in favor of the "new," with each generation creating its own culture, American society is a breed apart. And the church self-consciously copies culture, if it tends to do so a decade later. "Church marketing" (figuring out what appeals to individuals and offering it), up-to-the-minute music and technology, psychological profiling of members, and the burying of any concepts (including sin) that might not be popular to the masses—in many ways the American church looks very American. And that means, ironically, that in many ways the more the white American church comes together, the more it stays apart from its neighbors. Since the average white church has few, if any, black members, and since issues outside the church are outside its private sense of calling and often even seen as conflicting with it, the problems of the poor and of minorities have unfortunately often been invisible.

When evaluating the problem of race in America, the overwhelming evangelical tendency is to interpret it on an individual level, as a matter of interpersonal conflict, and there is a notable absence of discussion of social structural factors in racism.[9]

Individualism and Evangelical Theology

How does this individualism and its effect on an approach to race affect evangelical theology? First, it serves as an example of the effect of sociocultural context on the theological task. Although it may be true that some evangelical theologians are aware of the impact of history and culture, the Bible-centered approach to theology given at the beginning of this essay would tend to lead most white American evangelicals (and others) to undertake the theological task in a manner identical or similar to that found in Wayne Grudem's *Systematic Theology: An Introduction to Biblical Doctrine*. Grudem's text defines systematic theology as "any study that answers the question, 'What does the whole Bible teach us today?' about any given topic,"[10] and describes the task of theology as "collecting and understanding all the relevant passages in the Bible on various topics and then summarizing their teachings clearly so that we know what to believe about each topic."[11] This definition of theology and its method is explicit in its fidelity to the Bible, but as Alister McGrath observes, "Biblical passages are treated as timeless and culture-free statements that can be assembled to yield a timeless and culture-free theology that stands over and above the shifting sands of our postmodern culture."[12] When theology is approached in this way, the results of the one's study are assumed to strictly reflect the Bible alone and not one's culture.

Individualism and Our Sense of Sin

The impact of individualism that is central to the white evangelical tool kit reveals itself in the articulation of a doctrine such as sin. This can be seen not only in discussions of the race problem, but even in theology textbooks. A well-known text such as Millard Erickson's *Christian Theology* contains a section on social sin,[13] but texts such as Grudem's (and its predecessors such as A. H. Strong and Louis Berkhof) limit the discussion to a relationship between individuals and God. Grudem defines sin as "any failure to conform to the moral law of God in act, attitude, or nature."[14]

The Scriptures discuss the relationship between individual and corporate sin, but in evangelicalism this failure in conformity is generally conveyed only as a problem of sinful individuals. Although this is clearly central to an evangelical doctrine of sin, the absence of any reference to social, corporate, or structural sin is remarkable in a text that is intended to be exhaustively biblical.

Can sin really be seen corporately? Let's touch briefly on some biblical examples. Prophets and leaders often confessed for the sins of the people; whether or not they were personally responsible for the sins committed, they accepted their role in the corporate responsibility. For example, Nehemiah prayed, "I confess the sins we Israelites, including myself and my father's house, have committed against you. We have acted very wickedly toward you. We have not obeyed the commands, decrees and laws you gave your servant Moses" (1:6–7; see also Daniel 9:1–19). Joel 2:12–18 calls for a corporate sacred assembly. In 2 Chronicles 7:14 God says, "If my people, who are called by my name, will humble themselves and pray and seek my face and turn from their wicked ways, then will I hear from heaven and will forgive their sin and will heal their land." Corporate sin had led to corporate punishment, and corporate repentance was expected. In fact, Joshua 7 tells the story of the sin of one man, Achan, being considered a corporate sin—to the extent that the Israelites lost their next battle. Not only were fellow ("innocent") Israelites killed in battle, but Achan's whole family was stoned at God's command. In the New Testament, Ephesians 5:27 suggests the corollary of corporate purity.

The silence concerning nonindividualistic forms of sin makes sense when one attempts to understand the absence in light of the tool kit metaphor. The presence or absence of certain tools helps us to see how it is possible that certain theological aspects are included and others are left out. The pervasive individualism that diverts the gaze of most white evangelicals from structural factors as significant to the race problem[15] helps to explain a narrowly personalistic doctrine of sin.

Although sin is only one point of doctrine, it is a facet of doctrine that has far-reaching consequences. If sin is strictly an individual matter, then it affects the way that one understands the essence of the gospel and how one understands the scope of salvation. Another way to think of this is to consider the possibility that if the lenses of evangelical perception are ground by American individualism, and if the majority of United States evangelicals experience life as a series of choices and interpersonal relationships, and if these evangelicals pursue and enjoy the American way of life, then an individualistic understanding of sin and salvation may be all that is perceived as necessary for understanding the gospel. A structural perspective of the sin problem may seem foreign and even perplexing. The influence of culture that results in an individualistic perspective on sin and salvation reveals a theology that reflects its contextual origins, even if this happens unconsciously.

If, on the other hand, one extends the doctrine of sin to include social/structural sin, then one may have a broader concept of the sinful dilemma and the richness of salvation. For those who view sin as both an individual and a structural matter, not only is there a need for personal transformation, but also for social renewal at the structural level. From this perspective, for example, the Exodus means not only a symbol of deliverance from spiritual slavery, but also a physical and temporal deliverance from evil structures to a better life (in some sense) in the present. Further, a broader conception of the sin problem leads us to not only ask how are individuals saved, but how are families, neighborhoods, nations, and even the entire creation saved in the end? We are also prompted to ask questions about the nature of the church if we consider a broader view of sin. We must not only ask what kind of community is the church, but what are the responsibilities and benefits of church membership if we embrace a corporate identity (as opposed to the church as a voluntary association)? The expansion of a doctrine of sin beyond individualistic concerns can lead to theological reflection in areas that tend to be neglected in many evangelical circles.

The influence of individualism demonstrates that evangelical theology, though biblical, is far from "culture-free." It reveals that evangelical theology may not have fully heeded Packer's warning concerning theology that reflects one's own image. In this sense it might be said that evangelical theology tends to reflect the concerns of its predominantly white constituency. Although it must be said that such texts do not explicitly articulate a "white agenda," they do reflect the interests of the white community by virtue of the absence of valid biblical emphases that are explicit to minority communities yet not seen as important by the white evangelical majority.[16] This is significant because evangelical theology seeks to be fully biblical and to present itself as above culture and contextual influence. This, as we have seen, is not the case. This can lead to the conclusion that evangelical theology may be unconsciously reflective of cultural influences such as individualism while intending to be "merely biblical." Willie James Jennings argues that this reflects a docetic[17] tendency, particularly in terms of race:

> Our docetism in matters of race surfaces in our articulation of a social redemption that is beyond the actual realities and operations of our humanity. Our docetic tendency is not merely our inability to deal with human "differences." Our docetism in matters of race comes to light in our desire to see racial harmony and peace without the actual transformation identity rooted in the real conversion of our forms of social existence and community. We docetists say, "I don't see anyone as black or white, just my sister or brother in Christ. There is no such thing as race; we are all one in Christ." Or we say, "We just need to learn how to forgive, respect and live together and go on to the future." . . . These kinds of statements commonly found in the mouths of Christians exhibit the worst kind of theological deception. Here we claim a commitment to a changed perspective without the requirement of any significant display of that commitment.[18]

Of course, people who say, "I don't see a person as black or white, just as a person" generally don't *mean* to deny the significance of another's culture or history. But because culture is very significant to most African Americans, that sounds demeaning—and whatever the motives of the person speaking, it's obviously best to avoid saying something that sounds demeaning to the people he's talking to. Part of the issue is that "white" isn't consciously much of a culture to most white people, so the person saying this may be thinking, *Why should I care what color your skin is, any more than I care whether a particular friend has blue or brown eyes?* Of course it's true that skin color doesn't determine someone's value—but skin color does often say something about the person's heritage, which is an important part of who the person is. Ignoring it is ignoring something that matters to him.

Docetism describes the attempt to arrive at a culture-free theology. In the attempt to be biblical and free from culture, humanity is denied. It is true that humanity is a central concern when many evangelicals talk about "applying" their theology, but might it be better to recognize the human clothing on our theology even as we pursue the task?

Becoming Aware of Our Own Individualism

Having seen that culture is embedded in our theological reflection, it is important that the larger evangelical populace becomes aware of this reality. Evangelical theology must become consciously aware of its contextual nature. This is a difficult but necessary task if Packer's warning is to be taken seriously, and one that highlights the corporate and ecclesiological nature of the theological enterprise. Theology is a communal task that requires the multiple voices, or multiple and differing members of the body, to faithfully and fully articulate the Christian faith. If several members are in conversation with one another, then it is possible for those with differing perspectives to make one another aware of blind spots and to help one another recognize facets of the faith that may be missed if the task is pursued alone.

If theology is seen as the work of the church, then it is possible to suggest a way forward by attending to theology as a truly global, catholic[19] task. An interesting metaphor for this approach is found in Kevin J. Vanhoozer's essay "The Voice and the Actor: A Dramatic Proposal about the Ministry and Minstrelsy of Theology." Vanhoozer uses the metaphor of the theater to describe the theological task. In response to God's speech and acts in Jesus Christ, theologians respond in speech and performance and attempt to faithfully perform the gospel story.

He articulates it as follows:

What does the church have to say and do—to communicate through its action—that no other institution can say and do?

What is the main idea of the play we call the Christian life? Theology yields doctrines—dramatic directions—learned from the canon and formulated to answer for our time just such questions. . . . Like the medieval minstrel, theologians should think of themselves as part of a performing troupe. The etymology of *minstrel* (Provençal, Latin) is related to our term for minister. Yet the term *minstrel* specifies the way in which we minister the Word— through voice and action. The minstrelsy of the word is its performance.[20]

If we engage the concerns of this essay with the metaphor of the theater, it can lead to the suggestion that the play put on by evangelical theology is a good play, but one whose performance is limited by the speaking and acting of the minstrels.[21] This limitation leads to a performance that is not quite complete. The way to completion is through bringing other minstrels onto the stage, minstrels with speaking parts who deepen the performance of the story by contributing their unique voices and actions. If the cast is enlarged by the addition of these minstrels, then evangelical theology will not fade into whiteness but instead reflect a kaleidoscopic richness. Theology as a catholic and ecclesiological enterprise can only enrich our understanding of the faith.

DISCUSSION STARTER QUESTIONS

1. Why does the writer say evangelical theology is largely driven by white culture? Do you agree or disagree, and why? What are some other ways you have seen that it is influenced by whiteness or American thinking?
2. What are two or three ways a Christian can consciously step outside his cultural influences in understanding Scripture? How can you personally, and your church or ministry, do so?
3. How does your church reflect your own culture? How might that limit attendance by people of other subcultures?

CHAPTER THREE

THE "RIGHT" WAY TO PRAISE GOD:

Is Our Style
Biblical,
or Is It
Simply Cultural?

CLARENCE SHULER

Y ou've probably heard of (or even seen) the "worship wars" that pit lovers of one musical style against those who like to use another in the worship service. Yet that is only a small segment of the "culture wars/style wars" in the church, and in this chapter we'll take a look at a larger issue. As we attempt to distinguish what is biblical from what is simply cultural, we will limit our discussion to several church practices. We'll look at a few examples so there is no confusion as to what is being evaluated. Then we'll attempt to define culture and, finally, see if we can determine why some churches are so culturally different from others in their church and/or worship practices. The purpose of this chapter is simply to cause us to think more closely about why we do some of the things we do in our churches and whether these practices are biblical or simply cultural. Once we have seen that, it will be easier for us to recognize when culture gets in the way of our worship or our fellowship with people who are different from us.

What Are Some Cultural Differences in Worship Styles?

What are some examples of cultural differences practiced in American churches today? Churches vary on how they take the offering, whether they use common cups or individual ones for communion, when and how they greet visitors during the service, whether or not members clap during singing, whether people kneel at some point during the service, whether people sing from memory or song sheets or the hymnal or the overhead, and even *who* leads music. And that's just looking at issues that are culturally neutral with few or no theological issues involved.

In many churches, particularly African-American ones, the raising of hands is an accepted and often an expected expression of worship and praise. Is such an expression of worship just a cultural norm, or is it biblical? In 1 Timothy 2:8, Paul writes to Timothy saying, "I want men everywhere to lift up holy hands in prayer, without anger or disputing." So are those who practice lifting their hands to God in worship demonstrating too much emotion, or could their response to worship result from *their* interpretation of Scripture? Could their actions be viewed as a natural response to God that is biblically acceptable? Are those who choose not to raise their hands sinning or being less spiritual? Certainly many of us who have found ourselves in the minority in either of these camps of worship have felt out of place or even questioned our own spirituality or commitment to God.

A closer examination of the aforementioned verse reveals that it is Paul's *desire,* not a command, that men everywhere lift their hands to God. Therefore, no sin is committed regardless of what you do with your hands.

Another aspect of this emotional expression of worship is that it is loud. Yet in Revelation 1:10, John says, "On the Lord's Day [which is usually identified as Sunday in the New Testament] I was in the Spirit, and I heard behind me a *loud* voice like a trumpet" (italics added). In verse 15 of this same chapter, Christ's voice is described as being "like the sound of rushing waters." Rushing waters are loud. Throughout the remainder of the book of Revelation, at worship and other times, the phrase "in a loud voice" is used. So if the people in Revelation are not hard of hearing, then even though it is not a biblical command to be loud, it could be a biblical example or, at the very least, it is not unbiblical to be loud in activities that relate to the Lord of lords and King of kings.

Most men who like sports, regardless of culture, have no difficulty clapping, shouting, yelling, etc. when supporting their favorite team. African Americans and other minorities often struggle in understanding how some of these same men criticize this emotional expression when African Americans and other minorities worship God. Adding insult to injury is the all-too-common complaint by many of European descent that such an emotional and passionate worshipful expression is unnecessary, distracting to their worship, and unfortunately even a result having less intelligence, instead of people attempting to follow what they consider a biblical example.

Due to the historical oppression of African Americans in this country, we see God as our Deliverer. Therefore, nothing is too great to do for our Lord and Savior. Some worship words actually have physical implications. The Hebrew word *shahah* literally means "one being bowing down." *Hallel* can be translated as "to look foolish before God." I believe these words imply doing things one would not normally do, because such a person understands that worship is not about him, but that worship is giving reverence and homage to God. Therefore, the mediums of raising your hands, bowing down, etc. may seem to make a person look foolish, but they may be motivated by that person's love of God.

The flipside of this situation is that some African Americans feel that whites aren't really spiritually in tune. Some resulting comments about worship services in Caucasian churches have been "God's frozen chosen" and "church of the deep freeze." All cultures and/or races must be careful in viewing the various worship styles of those who are different from them. It is not our place to judge worship, but *to worship*.

It seems that we sometimes forget that worship is about giving to God and for God. We are to honor *Him*.

This gap between different cultures may be closing. Promise Keeper events have crossed denominational lines, promoting racial reconciliation—accepting people of different cultures. This movement has helped the overflow of accepting the different cultural worship styles as well.

A few years ago, I was able to pair my mentor, the Rev. Don Sharp, the pastor of Faith Tabernacle Baptist Church of Chicago, with the

Rev. Jim Campbell of a Baptist church in Tahlequah, Oklahoma. The influence of Faith Tabernacle, a black church, tremendously affected Jim's church, a predominantly white church. This traditional white Southern Baptist church went to two services. One was traditional for the older members. This traditional service was primarily composed of one culture. In the second service, if you closed your eyes, it would be difficult to tell where you were. This service, which has an African-American flavor, is packed with African Americans, Asians, Caucasians, and Hispanics. God does have a sense of humor. In Oklahoma, a Southern Baptist church that has a five-point Calvinist theology has a multicultural congregation with an African-American flavor in worship.

What Are Some Historic Black Worship Patterns?

One of the prominent practices in most African-American churches is seen in the dress for Sunday church services. Historically, from slavery, African Americans have always worn their best clothes for Sunday to honor the God who helped them endure their plight in life. These clothes were often called "Sunday-go-to-meeting" clothes.

In the black church, worship is participatory. In the black church, most preachers expect the congregation to respond verbally to their preaching during the sermon. In fact, a seasoned black preacher usually can tell by the congregation's comments whether he or she is doing well. If the congregation is yelling, "Preach," "Say it," "Don't stop," etc., the preacher knows he is usually doing well and can go deeper into his text. If the congregation is saying, "Lord help him," "Make it plain," etc., the preacher knows he is in trouble, because he isn't connecting with the congregation. If the congregation is saying, "Take your time," it could mean he is talking too fast and slow down, or it could mean that "what you are saying is good, preach as long as you want" (knowing which requires being in tune with the congregation). Even the phrase "Make it plain" could mean "you are making it practical, so we are understanding you—keep going."

Exodus 19:8 ("We will do everything the Lord has said") is a biblical example of "talking back" to the preacher. In fact, some black preachers find it difficult to preach in white churches—it is hard to evaluate if they are communicating because there is not the usual response. They find themselves silently asking questions while preaching: "Am I connecting here and should I go deeper?" or "Do I need to sit down as soon as possible because I'm bombing?" Many white preachers, on the other hand, say they love preaching in black churches. Verbal encouragement for preachers is like saying "sic 'em" or "go get it" to a bulldog, regardless of what one's culture is.

Preaching is another example of difference. In most white evangelical churches the pastors preach technically precise sermons, just the way they were taught in seminary. Homiletics as taught in predominantly white Christian undergraduate schools and seminaries encourages a cognitive approach to the text and a sermon that does not exceed thirty minutes. This style can be traced back to Europe before the Mayflower. The emphasis is on making sure a biblical text has been explained to the congregation so they know what it means and how it should affect their lives. In black preaching, the number of points isn't as critical as preaching *reality theology*, a phrase coined by Dr. Bishop Dantley of Cincinnati. This is preaching where the people live daily. This is to encourage a persecuted people by giving them biblical hope so they can survive the week. The sermon may last for an hour in an African-American church.

In a traditional black Baptist church, it is common at Sunday morning service to have a time of testimony, anytime before the pastor preaches or even after the sermon. Someone from the congregation tells what God has recently done for him or her. There may be one or several testimonies. It depends on how the Spirit is *leading*. It is also appropriate and expected at Wednesday night prayer service at church. These testimonies may have nothing to do with what has been or will be preached. Sometimes the pastor is so moved that he or she changes the sermon. The Holy Spirit can change the direction of the service. This is a spontaneous occurrence.

White churches also have testimonies. The time periods allotted for them tend to be shorter, as in most white churches the service must be completed by noon. Yet the Bible doesn't give a time schedules for worship. So can we say one group is more spiritual than the other?

In many black churches, everybody can be somebody of importance. This traditionally has been one of the drawing forces of the black church. This is probably seen most clearly in the role of the usher in the black church. From the days of slavery, black ushers have been in church to make the worship experience enjoyable for all.

They not only welcome you at the door and give you a bulletin, but they personally lead you to a seat. Their responsibilities don't end there. They direct the congregation during the offering. In some black churches, for the offering, everyone has to walk down to the front and put their tithes in the offering plate. Some of the motivation for this practice comes from Malachi 3:10—"Bring the whole tithe into the storehouse." To be honest, the peer pressure is greater when everyone has to walk down and give money instead of simply passing the plate down the pew.

In many traditional black Baptist churches, the ushers are all in uniform dress; some churches even require white gloves for men and women. Ushers don't allow the chewing of gum, especially by children, who will often leave the gum somewhere on the pew for an unsuspecting guest. They will also discipline unruly, loud children and/or assist a mother with taking a crying baby out of the sanctuary. These ushers are the ones who determine when late arrivals can enter the worship services.

Many black churches still have an annual Ushers' Day. Some churches have a Men's Ushers' Day and a Women's Ushers' Day. This day originated as a time when the men and women competed in fundraising in order to supplement the pastor's salary. Usually, the pastor was bi-vocational. As full-time pastors became more common, Ushers' Day remained, and the money now may go for building additions or repairs. Therefore, the usher's role is one of importance and high visibility.

Black churches also celebrate the Pastor's Anniversary. This is a special day when the pastor and family are honored for years of service. Similar to Ushers' Day, its original purpose was to help the pastor to pay all of his bills. Today, it is a huge perk. Many black pastors of large churches no longer need the money, but it is not uncommon for them to receive much more than $10,000 on this day. Their white counterparts don't seem to have their anniversaries celebrated to this extent.

Another aspect still practiced in most black churches is the invitation for salvation and church membership. The phrase often used for this invitation is "the doors of the church are now open." When I was a boy and heard this term, I had no idea what it meant. A little research traced this phrase back to slavery. It was an invitation for a person to leave the sinful life of the world and to join a better life in the church. This idea of invitation is based on Jesus' many invitations for people to join Him that we find in the Gospels.

Many white churches and some black churches no longer give an invitation because they believe the music might manipulate people into doing something that they don't want to do. Churches also don't want to embarrass or offend anyone. This thinking wants everyone to come to church but assumes that eventually they will become Christians without ever being directly challenged on the issue.

Black churches tend to model verses such as Matthew 10:33—"But whoever disowns me before men, I will disown him before my Father in heaven" by being sure they "own" their relationship to God. And Luke 9:26 promotes a similar thought, "If anyone is ashamed of me and my words, the Son of Man will be ashamed of him when he comes in his glory and in the glory of the Father and of the holy angels." There is the idea of being proud to stand up for a God who has stood up and delivered you.

In any discussion of church traditions, we certainly can't omit the music. Without question, the most readily identifiable cross-cultural expression of worship has been African-American music.

I visited a prestigious traditional church in Oklahoma and was puzzled that when hymns are sung, if people are sitting, on the third verse everyone stands up and sits when the fourth verse of that song is begun. I had never seen this before. Many of the adults didn't know why they did it. As I spoke with one of the "mothers" of the church (an older lady in the church who is greatly respected because of her walk with Christ and her age), she told me that this tradition had been passed down from slavery. The slaves sat on roughly made benches. In order to keep circulation in their bottoms and stay awake, they developed the tradition of standing up on the third verse of every hymn.

The black spiritual as an art form was given international recognition through the concerts of the Fisk Jubilee Singers, who took their music to the capitals of Europe to raise funds for the struggling college a hundred years ago.[1] C. Eric Lincoln says of the importance of music to black people historically:

> In the darkness of bondage, it [music] was his light; in the morn of his freedom, it was his darkness; but as the day advances, and he is being gradually lifted up into a higher life, it is becoming not only his proud heritage, but a support and powerful inspiration.

Undisturbed and unafraid, he could always unburden his heart in these simple songs pregnant with faith, hope and love. The man, though a slave, produced the song, and the song, in turn, produced a better man.[2]

Too little has changed for the African American since his arrival in America. He is still working for equality, especially from white Christians in America. Therefore, the songs of African Americans continue to play the same role in their lives. This is why when African Americans sing, their songs are more than notes on paper. They are singing life: pain from the past and present and hope for the future. This is possibly why people of other cultural groups are moved when they hear African Americans sing: The emotions of pain, faith, and hope come through.

The Cost of Cultural Insensitivity

Two friends of mine, Andy and Arlene from Trinidad told their experience with white missionaries. As I tell their tale, maybe it will help you better understand music and the passions minorities have for it.

Andy and Arlene were teenagers and new Christians, and like many of their Christian peers they loved music, both before and after their salvation. They encountered a group of white missionaries from Illinois who came to Trinidad to minister. Andy and Arlene initially appreciated the arrival of this group.

In Trinidad, the steel drum had become the instrument of choice. It was a grassroots creation born out of innate impetus to express oneself musically and the economic inaccessibility of wind, string, or percussion instruments from the European culture. Coupled with this local innovation was a balladic form of poetry—precursor to rap—that in essence served the islanders as a griot would an African. Other familiar objects also became musical instruments: a metal afro comb or spoon applied to a soda or beer bottle, any piece of metal applied to tire rims, an afro comb applied to an ordinary kitchen grater, etc.

To Andy and Arlene and their peers, these musical instruments and the islander form of poetic ballads were the vehicles of choice for new believers exploding with inner joy. They made music with every part of their heart, soul, mind, and body—loudly, frankly, and energetically.

The islanders based their style of music and worship on David's celebration of the victories God gave him, resulting in David's dancing and his not being afraid to look foolish to others as he worshiped his God. The missionaries were intellectually familiar with David's epic victory dances and musical extravaganzas, but God's harvesters from Illinois had yet to personally experience this type of expression. Uneasy, they responded with fear to this highly rhythmic exuberance and multiplicity of vigorously played loud instruments—completely failing to hear the words of joy and hope. Their biblical interpretation made them protective. They felt deeply called to guard God's Word that had been entrusted to them. Unable to assess, value, or really see what was before them, they responded by labeling this form of expression as sin and carnality. Missed was an opportunity to inform and transform the content of an emerging art form by strengthening its biblical foundation.

They failed to use the creativity of the Holy Spirit in the context of their biblical knowledge to objectively evaluate what was before their eyes. They failed in responding to use what was in their hands for the furtherance of the gospel (cf. Moses and the rod, the little boy with the five loaves and two fishes, Nehemiah and the wall, etc.).

Handicapped by their own cultural biases, the missionaries failed to remember that the musicians and poets of early Christianity merely used the media of their day to express their love for our Lord. Their passion and exuberance were exhibited in the great music of the hymnal that has withstood the passage of time. Played with the abandon for which its score calls, Handel's *Messiah* is a perfect example of wonderful music and beautiful heartfelt poetry. A legacy to be appreciated, remembered, and built upon became instead a cultural ramrod for a foreign culture gloved in the truth of the gospel.

Andy and Arlene felt that these missionaries were used by God, but limited because they were unable to do as 2 Peter 3:1 suggests, "to stimulate you to wholesome thinking." The missionaries tried to make everyone worship just like them—white Americans. The result of such efforts is that to this day, though Andy and Arlene are grown with Christian teenagers of their own, they, especially Arlene, have little use for white American Christians. It is sad because Arlene has much to offer, but she refuses to share God's blessings with those who are not like her—ironic, isn't it? She is no different from children of alcoholics. The very thing they despise and vow to never become, they become.

Andy and Arlene have one question: "How can you love, share, look out for your brother when you have learned to devalue that which God has *given* you?"

Andy and Arlene have unnecessary pain they carry because of being wounded by Christians. These well-intentioned missionaries evaluated another culture's music as sinful and, thus, defined difference as sin.

In black music, it is common for certain choruses to be repeated numerous times. This annoys some of the majority culture. The majority culture's style of worship tends to be more quiet because its spiritual heritage is from Europe. Again, Revelation 4:8 states, "Day and night they never stop saying: 'Holy, holy, holy is the Lord God Almighty, who was, and is, and is to come.'" Thus, it is not uncommon for minorities to have significant praise time as a part of the worship service. Today this is true of a large percentage of white churches as well.

Similar to Andy and Arlene's experience, it is not uncommon to hear some white evangelicals who have attended an African-American service in America or some missionaries who have been with Africans to negatively describe these worshipers as being emotional. This is probably an accurate observation, but is this emotion just a cultural characteristic of some people of color, or is there biblical justification? Unfortunately, this emotion is usually evaluated by many conservative white Christians as not in any way intellectual and bordering on sinful, possibly even falling into Satan's deception.

Clapping is a response to worship and a form of praise. This expression of worship is extremely common in African-American churches and those of other minorities, and is becoming much more common in white churches. Isaiah 55:12 and Psalms 47:1 and 98:8 all mention praise from humans or nature. Most of them are not biblical commands, but could be used as biblical examples for celebrating/praising God.

A Definition of Culture

Webster's New Collegiate Dictionary defines culture as "the integrated pattern of human behavior that includes thought, speech, action, and artifacts and depends upon man's capacity for learning and transmitting knowledge to succeeding generations; the customary beliefs, social forms, and material traits of a racial, religious or social group."

Thomas Sowell, in his book, *Race and Culture: A World View,*

defines culture as a particular people, which usually has its own particular set of skills for dealing with the economics and social necessities of life—and its own particular set of values as to what are the higher and lower purposes of life. These sets of skills and values typically follow them wherever they go. Despite prevailing "social science" approaches which depict people as creatures of their surrounding environment, or as victims of social institutions immediately impinging on them, both emigrants and conquerors have carried their own patterns of skills and behavior —their cultures—to the farthest regions of the planet, in the most radically different societies, and these patterns have often persisted for generations or even centuries.[3]

If Webster and Sowell are correct in their definitions, then culture is not just what we do, but who we are.

Our challenge as Christians, if forced to choose, is putting God first, before our culture. Or maybe it means being willing to sacrifice some aspects of our culture for the sake of developing lasting cross-cultural relationships that result in worshiping together in the same church.

Why Are Black Churches and White Churches So Different?

Two of my white friends told me that the friendliest churches they have ever attended were black churches. They asked me why. My response was, "Most minorities are relationship-oriented." I also told them that being a minority puts an entirely different perspective on being welcomed or rejected; consequently, minorities tend to be more accepting of people, regardless of their culture.

Here's an example, as told to me by Dr. Vernard Gant, Director of Urban School Services for the Association of Christian Schools International. He said that he was in a cross-cultural church during a time of greeting visitors. A white attendee expressed his dissatisfaction by saying, "This should be a solemn time of concentrating on the Lord—I don't come to church to fellowship. I come to worship God. I can't concentrate on God with all these people standing up." Rather than seeing this as part of the communal aspect of worshiping God, he saw it as a distraction. It seems he was not understanding that 1 John 4:20–21 demands that we love our brother. In fact, these verses strongly state that if we don't love our brother, whom we have seen, we really don't love God, whom we have not seen.

As mentioned earlier, minorities in general tend to be more relationship-oriented than the majority culture, which means people are more important than programs. Another aspect is that minorities have to deal with issues of persecution or the perception of persecution and justice. Therefore, in a black church a pastor must attempt to heal the wounds from the previous week as well as inspire hope for the upcoming week. The pastor must encourage the flock when justice seems a long time coming.

The black church historically has been, and, for many, continues to be a refuge for blacks from the cruelties of the world. It is a place where everyone can be someone. The black church is a place where the dignity of an oppressed people can be restored for a few hours.

Why Does the White Church Do Things Differently?

This different perspective for church in the white community is different simply because it is a church of the majority culture. One of the dynamics of a majority culture is its security of its heritage. Thus, the pastor may never feel a need to preach on justice, persecution, or suffering. The white pastor may need to warn against apathy, etc. The white church seems to be more of a program, institutional, and documented organization.

Black churches are more likely to have multiple generations of families in the same church; in white churches, pastors preach largely to individual nuclear families and to singles who have no relatives in the church. That means that white churches deal less with family and community influences, and that they may be more subject to the influences of pop culture than of tradition.

White churches speak less to the culture (except political-influence issues, such as abortion) and more to individual Christians.

Many white churches have a strong call to personal holiness, individual study of the Word and Scripture memorization, and support of missions. Although the church is often slow to take up "social" issues such as slavery, civil rights, abortion, and care of the disenfranchised such as prisoners, white leaders have worked within the church as they begin to develop a heart for a needy people group or important cause, or they have established parachurch organizations whose power has been felt on such issues.

The songs in the African-American church and the white church are different. There will be more songs about suffering in the black church, whereas in the white church, there will be more songs about victory. These are the dynamics of majority and minority being played out in churches. Therefore, the local church plays a different role in various cultures.

What is the gospel to the socially comfortable? Many in the majority culture are socially comfortable and have never known poverty, discrimination, or injustice. Therefore, it is easy for their theology to become ethereal. Though many have shown true compassion and help to others, some want to relieve their conscience by doing short-term projects in deprived areas across the country or overseas and then return to a comfortable life. Others want to seal their place in heaven. There is often the tendency to look inward instead of outward. The proliferation of self-help books means something is missing on the inside. Members are not compelled to look outside, but to look inside, which is what many whites want in their churches.

Black people who have been socially deprived attempt to find churches that try to meet their temporal needs, which means they sometimes focus more on the cultural experience of a church than on its doctrine. White churches deal more with people's relationship with God than with their relationship with other people. Some white churches may have little social relevance and thus less of a concept of social justice, which is true of many of those in the religious right.

Why Do We Do the Things We Do?

Walt Henrichsen, author and former Navigator says, "Remember, the local church is a cultural, not a biblical, phenomenon. The believer is free to do whatever the Bible does not prohibit. Thus, unless you break a command, any cultural implementation is fine."

As I questioned Walt more, especially about worship in Hebrews 10:25, he responded in the following way. "As you know, this is the only command to congregate in the New Testament. It doesn't mention how often or on what days. In the Old Testament, the people gathered three times a year. The Sabbath was a day of rest, not gathering. The synagogue came into existence during the Babylonian Captivity with no mention of it until you come to the Gospels. Hebrews 10:25 must be understood in light of Romans 14:5–6." Several New Testament verses suggest that after Christ's resurrection believers began the habit or tradition of gathering on the first day of the week, Sunday. But there is no command on which day or how many times to meet on that day. All of the previously mentioned habits or traditions are examples of cultural implementation. I'm not suggesting that we stop worshiping on Sunday but Walt makes an interesting point in that our culture affects how we view Scripture.

One of my Christian neighbors, Jen Samuels, says, "We tend to get into a habit of doing things. Then we begin to believe these things we are doing are right, which we then, consciously or subconsciously feel that others are probably wrong; then since what we are doing what is right, it must be biblical. Once we believe it is biblical, then we would rather fight than switch or accept that some of our church practices may be cultural with no biblical support." I think she makes a good point.

The problem is that the different cultures, which do it differently, tend to think their way is right and biblical. Therefore, if a person doesn't worship their way, that person isn't quite as spiritual.

We tend to create myths about other cultures and the way their church practices. A deep part of the mythmaking comes from *the way we view religion*. Peter Glasner illustrates the various models created by the science of sociology to define the secularization process of human religions. The models are ideologized by science into social myths. And the myths, he says, are included in our perception of truth without being analyzed. So, for example, there is preoccupation in much Western sociology with the institutionalized aspects of "religiosity." The assumption here is that a usable definition of Christianity must focus on function and be concerned with membership, ritual, and attendance. These become crucial elements of a definition of religion, so any move away from this institutional participation involves religious decline and secularism, yet mere church attendance is counted as proper religious action.

If we are to break with this way of evaluating, we will have to see religion in a more sweeping, more holistic way. Can we do it by saying that human life, in its entirety, is religion, humanity's integral response action to God? Because it is totalitarian in its scope in that God's demands are all-embracing (Deuteronomy 10:12–13; 2 Corinthians 10:5), its progress or decline cannot be measured merely by church buildings or a lack of them; its measuring stick becomes its commitment to the words of the Preacher: "Fear God and keep his commandments, for this is the whole duty of man" (Ecclesiastes 12:13).[4]

What Is a Biblical Approach to Cultural Differences?

In Acts, the Jewish believers were having a difficult time embracing Gentiles as fellow believers. Acts 11 reveals the Jewish believers' criticism of Peter for witnessing of Christ to Gentiles. They reluctantly accepted the fact that Gentiles were believers when they said in Acts 11:18, "So then, God has granted *even* the Gentiles repentance unto life" (italics added). Gentiles were formerly called dogs by Jewish believers. Dogs in New Testament times weren't pets; they ran in packs and attacked people and other animals.

The problem of accepting Gentiles as fellow believers simply got worse. In Acts 15, at the Council at Jerusalem there was a division among the Jewish believers accepting Gentile believers as legitimate Christians. Some Jews, those who belonged to the party of the Pharisees, were attempting to exclude Gentiles from enjoying all the benefits of Christian fellowship and equality with all believers. Those Pharisees are similar to many of today's Christians who view a political party as America's only hope for salvation. Thus, there is little emphasis on the gospel. These Christians have become legalists. There is little room for mercy or grace in their practical theology. They promote a cloning mentality—"You need to be just like me and I will accept you." Intellectually, as Christians, on our core values we would agree, but they focus on the disagreements.

These Pharisees were demanding that the Gentiles "must be circumcised and required to obey the law of Moses" (Acts 15:5). They insisted that the Gentiles practice the customs of Moses. Yet many of these practices were no longer necessary because of Christ's death, burial, and resurrection. This included the eating of certain foods (Acts 10:9–16).

Paul and Barnabas strongly disagreed with these Pharisees. After much prayer and debate, the council stated its decision in Acts 15:28–29: "It seemed good to the Holy Spirit and to us not to burden you with anything beyond the following requirements: You are to abstain from food sacrificed to idols, from blood, from the meat of strangled animals and from sexual immorality. You will do well to avoid these things." There was no need to burden these new Gentile, culturally different believers with what were now simply Jewish customs, which were no longer necessary for New Testament believers. What occurred at the Council at Jerusalem? The Jewish believers modeled what Christianity is all about: self-sacrifice. Isn't this what Christ did for us? The Jewish believers sacrificed what was important to them in order not to be a stumbling block for these new Gentile believers (Romans 14:5–10, 13–22).

Another example is seen in Galatians 2:11–21. Paul confronted Peter because, when the Jewish believers were not around, Peter ate with the Gentile believers, but, when the Jewish believers were present, then Peter would not eat with the Gentiles. It was against Jewish tradition for Jews to eat with Gentiles or even enter their homes (Acts 11:2–3). Peter was attempting to be politically correct at the expense of being biblically correct. It is important that we Christians take a stand against hypocrisy at all times, regardless of the cost.

Dr. Karen Wilson-Starks, president/CEO of Transleadership, Inc., has suggested some practical considerations in our efforts to determine if something is biblical or simply cultural. Dr. Starks recommends that we ask ourselves several questions: Who is God? What is the character of God? What would God do in this situation? and How does God deal with His people? She encourages us in our biblical interpretation not to take isolated texts of Scripture on which to build a tradition. She says, "God created all of us. Therefore, He created a diverse world and wants this diverse world to get along. But this doesn't mean we will do everything the same."

If Christians are going to learn to accept the cultural church practices that are different from our own, then we must learn about each other. First Corinthians 12:21–26 (reinforcing the importance of all the parts of the body to the whole body) provides some principles that may help Christians with cultural differences get along. These verses may be where people of faith err the most, because it seems that we do so little together. There is a tendency to think of ourselves as superior and others inferior, to be divisive, and not to realize that when one part of the body hurts we all hurt. We seem unable to rejoice in the Lord when one part of the body is honored. But if we are not honored specifically, we are honored in general when one believer is honored, because we are all part of the same body. Of course, this demands we learn how to serve each other in a way that the other culture or race appreciates.

This Scripture makes it obvious that we all have some work to do. Dag Hammarskjold said that he learned a radical lesson from the Gospels. "All men are equals as God's children and should be met and treated by us as [by] our master." Theologically, few Christians will disagree with this statement, but our actions in the evangelical community clearly demonstrate we don't believe it.

If the body of Christ is serious in practicing the parallel applications of truth in 1 Corinthians 12, a good starting place is learning about other cultures, which will make it easier to understand and accept differences.

Today, Christians must closely examine ourselves, why we do what we do in light of biblical principles and not our cultural preferences. Remember, as Walt Henrichsen has said, the local church is a cultural phenomenon, not a biblical phenomenon. If this is true, then we can worship God in many ways as long as these styles don't violate biblical principles. And equally importantly, we must not force our cultural preference of worship on anyone. And we should be willing to evaluate our cultural practices if they seem to be keeping people from other cultures from being comfortable in our churches.

The rapidly changing demographics of the United States will test the maturity of local churches in America as long-time church practices will be evaluated and challenged. Because it is hard to change what has been ingrained and hard to change the way we have been trained, this could be an incredibly painful blessing in disguise as the cross-cultural influences may help purify our worship.

DISCUSSION STARTER QUESTIONS

1. What do you think are some of the primary differences
   between minority churches and white churches? Have
   you ever attended a church where you were a minority?
   What did you find different, and what was the same?
2. What are some ways the church can evaluate which of its
   practices are biblical absolutes and which are cultural
   options? How does a church know when it's time to modify
   some of its cultural traditions?
3. What Scriptures would you use with someone who believes
   that it's better for separate cultures just to have their own
   churches and not even try to interact with other believers of
   different races? What do you think are two or three blessings
   of different cultures worshiping together?

CHAPTER FOUR

ONE WHITE MAN'S PERSONAL JOURNEY

*What Does It
Take to Understand
People Who Are
Different from Us?*

ROBERT M. BOYD

For the first forty years of life I looked at every new challenge with the fear that I would never make it. I approached each grade in school saying, "Well, I got through first grade, but I'll never make it through second." I didn't fit the standard U.S. stereotypes for males—independent, strong, self-sufficient, athletic, mechanical, adventurous risk takers. Instead I was an overweight "mama's boy" who was fearful, a klutz, and a dreamer—intimidated by everyone and scared to death of anyone in authority.

A counselor in college told me that one day when I was about five years old someone who was an authority figure shouted at me and told me to "shut up," and I did so for the next fifteen years. I became a stutterer, and it was so profoundly entrenched even in private conversation that I could only make myself understood with great difficulty. I spent five years during elementary school going to special classes for speech therapy, but the problem continued to such an extent that I could not read out loud in class even at the end of high school. I know what it's like to be handicapped, to be laughed at and ridiculed and picked on, and to feel helpless and inferior constantly.

Unknown to me at the time, God was already preparing me for my future. I needed to know what it felt like to be an outsider. I needed to know I had no strength of my own, so I would be willing to lean on Him. Perhaps I even needed to have a hard time making friends so I would learn to value relationships. But when I was a child, I knew nothing of God's desire to place me as an adult in cross-cultural relationships around the nation and the world. I knew only that I was an outsider in my own neighborhood.

My Spiritual Foundation

From the time I was born my mother (Esther Boyd) took me regularly to an evangelical church near where we lived in Philadelphia. She was a strong believer, very involved with the church, and influential in my spiritual development. Often after evangelistic meetings at church the invitation was given to raise one's hand and come forward to talk with the pastor to receive Christ as Savior. I never could do that since I was not able to talk. So several times I asked my mother to pray with me beside my bed to receive Christ into my heart. We did that again and again because I lacked assurance since I couldn't do it the way I saw everyone else doing it.

My mother's sister, Florence Tilley, was a missionary in Africa. Every four or five years when she came back to the U.S. she lived with us. I know that she prayed for me regularly. Through her I was exposed to lots of missionaries, who often stayed in our home, and many pictures of her beloved Africans. My aunt's deep love for the African people was so sincere and so evident that it undoubtedly left its unconscious mark on me.

My mother and my aunt took me to many "deeper life" meetings, and so I was exposed to this at a young age and developed a passion for the pursuit of holiness, which has continued all of my life. I continued to struggle with my assurance of salvation into my high school years, until one day a teacher in a Bible class talked about the marks of a Christian. He said first of all that a Christian finds that the Bible is not like a history book: When a Christian reads the Bible it speaks to his inner being. The second mark of a Christian is that Christ is the top priority in his life, and the third is that when he is with other Christians he feels an immediate kinship with them. To each of these my spirit said a resounding yes. Suddenly the long-desired assurance flooded over me. It was a great cause for rejoicing, and within a short time after that I felt a desire to serve God in full-time ministry.

I decided to pursue missionary service partly because of the great need overseas, but also because I was sure I could never make it in ministry in the United States. I was still stuttering, unable to speak in public, and still "not going to make it through second grade." But I graduated from high school and was accepted at college, to the surprise of many.

Preparation for Ministry

Gordon College in Boston was a wonderful experience for me. Solid evangelical teaching, strong Christian friends, and a healthy atmosphere contributed to rapid growth in faith and maturity. I dated and courted a great classmate all through college, and we were married the same week we graduated. Janet too was committed to missionary service, and she taught school while I went to Gordon seminary. God used her belief in me, the chance to sing in the college choir, and a year as the preacher in a city mission church to conquer my stuttering problem. For the last two and one-half years of seminary I pastored a tiny church in a nearby city. I fell in love with the pastorate.

On graduation from seminary we applied to the World Mission Board of the Baptist General Conference and were appointed to serve in Argentina. After our support was raised, we went to San Jose, Costa Rica, for a year of language study. Here began our orientation to a culture that was different from our own.

Learning a New Language

It is really a great advantage for cross-cultural missionaries to be obligated to learn the language of the people among whom they will be working. People speak the way they speak because they are the way they are. When we learn their language and how they use it, we learn about them—about their culture that is also different from our own. I learned their language not because I wanted to do so, but because it was a necessity—an obligation.

Actually, language study was like a "necessary evil," as it was a long, hard, frustrating, humbling job. After graduate school to be reduced to the level of "Dick and Jane" and "see Spot catch the big red ball" is quite humiliating. But we learned two important lessons here: First, one ought always to approach learning about another culture with great humility as a beginner, and, second, it is good to put ourselves in a position where we are obligated to do that which is good for us, that which we ought to do. It is important to step away from our own ways of thinking and acting and embrace and love those of another culture. Language learning helps us do that.

Cultural Immersion

Our arrival in Argentina touched some of our deepest emotions. This was the land and the people we intended to serve among for the rest of our lives. Our strong commitment to minister here inspired within us the resolute decision to immerse ourselves and our family in the culture of this people. This was a laudable commitment, but between the ideal and the actuality there was a long, hard road to travel. Their culture and their way of living every day had so many differences from our own that the culture shock was a difficult thing to bear on many of the days of ordinary living. As I look back on the cultural adjustment process I would describe it like this:

- During the first epoch of immersion (nine months to a year), you look around at those in the new culture and you think, *This is sure a dumb way to do things.*
- During the second epoch of living in another culture, you watch how they live and you think, *This is a dumb way to do things, but they seem to like it.*
- During the third period of your immersion, you look at how the people of the new culture act and you think, *This is a dumb way to do things, but they do seem to like it, and actually it seems to work for them.*
- During your fourth epoch living in a new culture, you watch how they do things and suddenly you are struck with a startling

realization. You think, *You know what? Some of their ways of doing things are better than the way we do them at home!*

Once you go through this process, you are never the same again. You never again think that *my way of doing, thinking, relating, and living are the best or the only way to live.* And once you open up to a second culture, it is easier to open to a third and a fourth, just as once you learn a second language, it is easier to learn a third. The reason for this is, of course, not that the third culture or language is easy. It actually has little to do with the nature of the third and fourth. The major difficulty in accepting another culture or learning a second language is getting out of your own. It's recognizing and admitting that "my way of thinking, my way of talking, my way of relating, and my way of living are not the only way there is to live, and they are not necessarily the best either."

Some of the Things I Learned About the Hispanic Culture

These are some of the things I have learned about the Hispanic culture that I have written up more extensively for use in seminars about Hispanic culture.

Patterns of Response Commonly (But Not Exclusively) Found in Hispanic Cultures
- **The Hispanic Response to Emotional Feelings.** How a person *feels* about something important and about his own relation to it is more crucial for Hispanics than are cold, impersonal rules in a given situation.
- **The Hispanic Response to Process in Communication.** When involved in even a casual encounter with another person, the feeling that the conversation itself should be pleasant is more important to Hispanics than the details involved in the exchange.
- **The Hispanic Response to Positional Distance.** In order to feel at ease in discussing important or sensitive things with another person, distance or objects that separate these persons are seen as barriers to intimacy.
- **The Hispanic Response to Time Duration.** Each day is looked upon as a period for living. It is not considered as a precise

mathematical sum of twenty-four-hour-long periods. The *quality* of the day's experience is more important than the *quantity* of the day's accomplishments. Spontaneity is powerful and appealing. Organization should not be so evident that it stifles spontaneous participation.

- **The Hispanic Response to Regimentation**. Participation in an important event in a meaningful and spontaneous way is more crucial than being there when it begins or being there during every moment in which the event is taking place. Time is not regimented because the event is more important than the time. Hispanics place tremendous value on the present. What is happening now is of greater importance than anything in the past or the future.

- **The Hispanic Response to Building Trust**. Trust in another person comes only after time has shown many small successful opportunities to observe that one is trustworthy. One earns the right to be trusted personally with every individual. Trust is not transferred from another person, nor is it given by virtue of a position or a title.

- **The Hispanic Response to Friendship**. A true friendship that one person has established with another person is a sacred trust. It has been built through a series of personal encounters over a period of time and has included many important and meaningful events. Friendship is one of the priorities of life.

Learning to Recognize My Cultural Biases

Being born and raised in the United States of America at that time (at least if you were a white man), one was without doubt imbued with a sense of the greatness of our country. Its wealth, power, and influence in the world were well known. Our language and culture affect the whole world. For many, America is the land of hope—the huge land of unlimited opportunity, the land of the future. In so many ways it has dominated the markets of the world and for a time, at least in the 1950s and '60s, we had the idea that we produced the best of almost everything (except perhaps bananas). So I must admit that in spite of my personal feelings of inferiority and intimidation among my own peers, unconsciously at least I had in the back of my mind that on going to the third world countries of Latin America to share the glorious gospel of the grace and love and forgiveness found in Jesus Christ, I would also be taking with me my superior culture. I would be able to share that strength with the disadvantaged people with whom I was going to live.

As I look back on the decade of missionary service that I was privileged to spend in Latin America, I see that I was able to be a very imperfect channel through which God's Holy Spirit was able nonetheless to do His eternal work. But as far as what I myself was able to give to the Argentines, I see only that I received from them so much more than what I gave.

I am clearly indebted to the Latino culture. The people have left an immense impact on my life. They are so very gracious, sensitive, warm, and affectionate. They hug and kiss and love people deeply. They know how to celebrate, and they do it often. For about the first three years when they hugged me I had goose bumps run up my spine, but then I ran out of goose bumps and joined them. When standing freely, white people stand about twenty inches apart to feel comfortable. Latinos stand about eight inches away—so they can hold on. I have come to think that so many good, warm, valuable human things are expressed through a simple appropriate touch that it is a great loss to deprive ourselves of proper touching in our relationships with those we know and care about. We know what a "good" touch is, and it says so eloquently but simply "You are important," "I'm glad you're here," "I care about you," and "I like to be with you."

It was quite ironic to us to remember that some of our relatives had said to us when we took our children to Argentina in 1959, "Aren't you concerned about taking your children to South America?" I say it was ironic because when we left Argentina in 1970, after the tumultuous '60s in the States, the Argentines said to us, "Aren't you concerned for the safety of your children in the U.S.A.?" Without a doubt the second concern was far greater than the first.

A New Phase of Ministry

The windy frozen frontier of Minnesota became our next home. This beautiful upper Midwestern "land of 10,000 lakes" was home to many hardy offspring of Scandinavian and German heritage and not much other ethnic or cultural diversity. Afraid to be a pastor yet unsure of what I could do for a living, I accepted the call of a church in the northern suburbs of Minneapolis to be the associate to their pastor while I began to deal seriously with accepting who I was and what I was going to do.

I took courses in pastoral psychology in three different Twin Cities seminaries, which helped me to deal with all of those issues of inferiority, terror, and intimidation that had plagued me since childhood. I wanted to be somebody I wasn't. I wanted to give to God who I hoped to be, but I realized that was a cop-out. Yet I didn't value who I was, so who I was seemed so paltry in comparison to what I hoped to be that it seemed like an offense to offer that to God. The gifts that God had given me were a "funny bone" that wouldn't quit and a love for people that rivaled a stereotypical grandmother's. I didn't think that would play very well on Broadway or look very good on a résumé. But the people of the church I served accepted and loved me, and my senior pastor, Frank Voth, began the healing touch that turned my life around.

Pastor Voth was a very wise and exceptionally capable pastor, and he affirmed and praised me both privately and publicly. Because of that I began to heal. By 1972, after working with him for two years, I had grown so much that I accepted the call to be the pastor of the Grace Baptist Church in Minneapolis. In two years I turned forty, and the people of this church accepted me as I was and loved and trusted me. I felt like I wanted to stay there forever. In a matter of a few weeks, in January of 1974, as this reality dawned on me I felt like I was liberated. A freedom to be myself took hold of me so, though it hadn't seemed to me like much to give the few gifts I had to God, I did so at last. Life began at forty for me.

Soon it became evident to me and to my congregation that when I was able to love and understand people and empathize with them, I was being authentic. God blessed our ministry together profoundly in the years that followed. Somewhere I read that if you find someone who is truly empathetic, if you scratch very deeply, you will almost inevitably find suffering. It seemed like I qualified on that score.

The years I served as pastor of Grace Baptist Church were so exciting, inspiring, challenging, and delightful that I never thought about leaving. But in 1977 the Hispanic Bible School in Chicago was just four years old, and Batist General Conference's Home Missions Department was looking for someone to become the first full-time director of the school and of Hispanic church ministries. Friends and former missionary colleagues in Chicago urged me to accept the position. I resisted successfully until I gave in to their invitation to "just come to observe." The Latino youth recaptured my heart, and I had to go. It seemed like all of my past experiences came together to prepare me for this opportunity. For the next six years I was once again immersed in the Hispanic culture—this time based not in northwest Argentina, but in Chicago, the heartland of the United States. But I realized that the best way for the Hispanic Bible School to flourish was to have a Hispanic person to lead it. In 1983 I was able to turn it over to a Hispanic director.

A New Area of Cross-Cultural Ministry

After the successful transfer of responsibility, my boss, Clifford Anderson, the director of home missions, came to me and said, "Rob, there are a lot of other cultures out there in our country besides Hispanics —I'd like you to work at developing our ministry with them as well." I'm sorry to confess that my first thought was *I've spent twenty years relating and adapting to the Hispanic culture, including ten years of total immersion in the interior of a South American country—I don't have twenty more years to try to understand another one.* But since this was a request from my boss, I had to at least find a way to begin to comply.

I decided I'd begin by reading what I could about the next two major areas of cultural ministry in our fellowship of churches— African American and Native American. I was at least wise enough to determine to read what Native American and African-American authors wrote about their own journeys instead of only reading what some Anglo-American "cultural expert" said about them.

As I began to read, my eyes, my head, and my heart were opened in two ways. The most obvious way was that I began my pilgrimage toward understanding the African American and the Native American experience in America. I say I *began to move toward* understanding, because the more I learn and experience and am intimately involved in these cultures, the more I realize that as a white man I can never fully understand what it's like to be black or Indian in America.

It's interesting that, in choosing these next two largest cultural ministries in our conference to study, I unknowingly studied the two U.S. minority cultures that have many similarities at least in their relation to the dominant white culture here. These are the two "resident minorities" in contrast to the many "immigrant" ones. Our society is pretty aware of the Indians being in America before the white man came, but not nearly as aware of the fact that at the time of the American Revolution a full one-quarter of the four million population was black and that very little immigration of blacks occurred after the Civil War. This means that it could be said that African Americans are "more American" or "have more rights here" than most white Americans. Other similarities that Indians and blacks have are related to the way they have been treated by the white majority—that is, discriminated against, physically abused, murdered, and segregated by being isolated in ghettos in cities or on distant reservations.

The second way that my eyes, head, and heart were opened is that I began to realize how blind and ignorant I had been about these my fellow Americans and, therefore, how blind and ignorant much of the rest of the white population might be as well. Worse than the rest though, I began to realize that because of my involvement with Hispanics, I had been kind of mentally "spraining my arm patting myself on the back" at how broad-minded I was for being bilingual and bicultural, when actually I had blinders on that obscured any other cultures around me.

My reading began with Richard Wright's *Native Son*. This book affected me so profoundly that for days afterward I wanted to weep. I remember coming out of a grocery store the next day and, on seeing a black lady approach the door, I had the urge to run over and open it for her. That was an extreme reaction and would have been an unnecessary thing to do for someone who was quite capable of coming in on her own. But I remember well how I felt inside—wishing somehow, some way to try to make up for the terrible injustices we had heaped on the shoulders of those who were black in America.

So, I went on reading anything I could find by Richard Wright, and then by James Baldwin, W. E. B. DuBois's *The Souls of Black Folk*, Vincent Harding's *There Is a River,* Albert Raboteau's *Slave Religion,* and J. Deotis Roberts' *Roots of a Black Future: Family and Church*. These works among others touched my heart and informed my mind.

A Personal Encounter

My job took me to various parts of the country to speak on behalf of home missions, which still included being the liaison between the administration of the Hispanic Bible School in Chicago and the home missions department in the national office that owned and operated it. So in 1980 I was asked to go to the Elim Baptist Church in the outskirts of Detroit, Michigan, to be the speaker for their missions conference. By that time my title was Director of Cultural Ministries for the Baptist General Conference.

One of our first African-American churches was also in Detroit, and a couple of the young associate pastors there heard that I was coming to the Elim church. They asked that pastor to arrange a time when they could meet with me while I was there.

I'll never forget that meeting. They came to hear me speak, and we met in the pastor's office after the service was over. They were bright, articulate, knowledgeable young ministers—both graduates of William Tyndale Bible College in Detroit. We talked for about half an hour about all kinds of things—just asking and answering questions and getting to know each other. After years more experience I've learned that African Americans are much more adept at sizing up white men than we are at getting to know them. They have had to develop that ability in order to survive and get ahead in American society—Caucasian people have not had to do that. So, after the half hour was up, one of the pastors, Charles Oliver, stopped and looked me right in the eye for a minute and smiled at me. I'll never forget what he said to me. He said, "When we heard that your title was Director of Cultural Ministries for the Baptist General Conference, we thought maybe that might include us, so we wanted to come to meet you. After talking with you now, I think that we can ask you the question we came here to ask you tonight."

I said, "Thank you—I'm so glad you are willing to ask me."

Then he said, "We have been members for a long time at the BGC African-American church here in Detroit, and we have learned a lot there over the years and have served as associates to the pastor there. Now we have graduated from Tyndale Bible College, and we want you to know that we like what we have come to know about the BGC. The question we came to ask you tonight is this—is there room for us to serve in the BGC?"

That question has rung in my ears and on my heart ever since that day. I answered them according to the desire of my heart. I said, "Yes, my dear brothers, of course there is room for you to serve with us."

How could I help but love these dear young brothers—ready, eager, and passionate about serving God. But the truth was, at that time there was not nearly as much room as there could be or should be for them to serve. That was a God-ordained encounter because that question has driven me from that day on. I have told about that encounter many times in church after church in our conference. I have challenged congregations every way I could imagine. Even in totally white churches in totally white communities I have said, "If fifty black families moved into your neighborhood next month—the way you must answer that question is—'Would you hire Charles Oliver to be an associate pastor at your church in order to reach them for Christ?'"

Thankfully, over the last fifteen years since that date there is a lot more room to serve in the BGC for others who are like those young men that day in Detroit. Our Conference has done intentional African-American church planting and has celebrated our old established churches in changing neighborhoods that have become filled and flourishing under capable African-American leadership. And Charles Oliver has honored me by becoming a very dear friend. It just so happens that we are both "blessed" with the same personality characteristics. Charles's dear wife, Marilyn, calls me "the vanilla Charles Oliver" because she sees how much alike we are. We have had the joy of visiting in each other's homes, serving together in His church, and working together often at conference gatherings. I had the honor to have a part in leading the very church where we first met, Elim Baptist in Detroit, to call him to be their pastor in 1982, and he has served there faithfully and well now for almost twenty years. Charles became the first African-American trustee of our Bethel College and Seminary and the first African American to be moderator of the Conference Annual Meeting. Yes, God has been good, but his question still keeps ringing in my ears and heart. It will never stop. "Is there room for us to serve in the BGC?" Yes, there is, and there must be more and more.

"Immersed" in Black Culture

What has gone on inside of me during these years? I have read more than twenty books by African Americans and have cherished friendships with many other BGC African-American pastors. I did some graduate seminary work in the area of cultural ministries in the

U.S.—specializing in Hispanic and African-American studies. Part of that study was at a seminary on the Southside of Chicago.

One course was for graduate students on the history of the black church in America. The text was by a black author, the professor was black, the south Chicago area was "black turf," the students—more than twenty of them—were all black except for me and two others.

I remember feeling exhilarated that I was able in this setting to be in what seemed to me to be total immersion in black culture. I listened and felt and watched and learned so much. I felt like an unnoticed speck or a fly on the wall. None of the three of us whites ever spoke—we were all in the "taking in" mode.

On the last day of class the professor led the students in a verbal evaluation of the class, which I considered to be a customary procedure. Several students spoke about various aspects of the study materials and how the class went. Then one student shocked me when he said, "The class was very helpful and the materials were profound, but I felt we could have been more free and open with each other if the white students weren't here."

I was floored. I was shocked not just because his statement was so straightforward, but because I had been sure that my presence was so incredibly tiny as to be all but unnoticed, but in his mind that little bit was way too much. This was a lesson that has profound implications and I have never forgotten it. When I have asked my trusted black brothers about it subsequently, they say, "Yes, I understand what he meant."

I try to let it help me on my pilgrimage of learning to understand what it is like to be black in America. I think about it when I'm driving too fast and I see a police car, and I only have to hope he didn't have his radar on and make me pay a fine, but I don't have to worry about what he may do to me when he sees my face like my black brothers do. I think about it when I take my kids to register in school, or at the pool, or when I register to vote, or I go into a bank, or I jog around the block—I don't face any of those things like my black brothers and sisters do.

And I have learned to consider also the many advantages that have been mine that I take for granted and never thought about—my corporate advantages. The years when I was growing up as a child in a white neighborhood, in white schools, with parents who could get good well-paying jobs so they could send me to college. Though unknown to me, I profited greatly by the years of institutional and overt racism that my forefathers had perpetrated on the African Americans. Having never even visited the Southern states, I had no idea of the depths of segregation that existed there. But I was also blind to the more subtle discrimination that existed right around me for many years, because no black children were ever depicted on the television screen using the newest toothpaste or shown as adults driving the new model cars.

Learning About Slavery and Stereotypes

The infliction of slavery on the black race has been called "America's national sin." Black slavery has been compared to internment in Nazi concentration camps. But even the official end of slavery did not solve the problem for blacks in America. They were free, but free to die of starvation and illness and all the efforts to help them face countermeasures. Laws to protect blacks were inadequate and unenforced. Whites used any and all methods to destroy racial reconstruction, and their efforts largely succeeded for many years.

Not until Dr. Martin Luther King Jr. was catapulted to prominence in the civil rights struggle of black Americans by his leadership of the successful Montgomery, Alabama, boycott of public transportation in 1956 did real major change begin in the struggle against discrimination and race prejudice. Dr. King expressed so clearly and perfectly the central message of Christian doctrine that he could not be dismissed as a fool, a quack, or a cultist. His credentials in faith and learning were impressive, coming from some of white America's most respected institutions. He is a hero of the highest order not only to people in America but across the whole world.

Dr. Martin Luther King Jr. may be the best known African-American hero of the twentieth century, but he is by no means the only one. George Washington Carver is another one of many outstanding African Americans in as wide a variety of areas of knowledge and experience as exist in America. A visit to the Harriet Tubman Museum in Macon, Georgia, is an eye-opening experience that every American of every race ought to experience. There one will find room after room full of murals depicting countless famous African Americans, beautiful works of art of all kinds, and rooms full of everyday articles that were invented by African Americans. You leave that museum with your mouth open and any remaining stereotypes you had in your head exploded and dissolved.

More Lessons I Needed to Learn

Stereotypes and Blind Spots

I was surprised and chagrined to find stereotypes and blind spots in myself, and I am frustrated and angry to see how pervasive they are in the lives of white Americans. I find myself impatient with my white brothers and sisters when they seem like Archie Bunker and I can't make them change. I forget how long a pilgrimage I have had and the tremendous advantages along the way, that having a speech handicap and being immersed for ten years in a foreign culture, have been for me. The Gospel of John, chapter 9, has been my "life passage" of Scripture. It begins with the stereotypes held by the Lord's first disciples. They had blinders on and put people in boxes. In their minds there were only two possibilities as to why the man was born blind, but Jesus said neither one was correct. Instead Jesus said that this happened to him "so that the work of God might be displayed in his life." The blind man's parents wouldn't answer questions because of fear for themselves, and the man himself didn't really understand everything, but he knew his experience was real. As he said, "One thing I do know, I was blind but now I see!" Stereotyping and blind spots—there are plenty of each in this Bible passage.

For thirty years I had anger in my heart that God allowed me to be handicapped and suffer so much teasing and harassment and inferiority and so many helpless feelings because of it. People put me in their mental box of a "useless introverted stutterer who will never be able to make it anywhere." But in a tiny city way back in the interior of a poor province in a South American country I met a man named Victor who had a Bible study in his home and for months had pleaded by letter with me to come and help them start a church there. When I finally went to meet him I found that he stuttered. He had never had anyone in that far off place who knew how to help him. I had studied all I could about it and spent days with him over the next couple years telling him all I had learned. There is a church in that place today because of my dear brother Victor. For the first time in my life I lifted my heart to God and thanked Him that stuttering had happened to me "so that the work of God might be displayed" in my life and in Victor's.

Some Advantages I Had in Learning

Without a doubt there were three major "advantages" that God gave to me to move me along in my pilgrimage toward understanding other cultures in America and coming to deeply love so many people of other races. All three of these "advantages" were imposed on me; they were not of my own making or initiative: the stuttering handicap, the total immersion in Hispanic culture, and my boss's directive to expand my focus to include other cultural groups.

Some of the lessons I have learned along the way have been a great help in my journey. Studying what people say about their own cultural group instead of what others say about them is crucial. Learning about what people of another group have accomplished and celebrating their successes gives us a sense of gratitude and of indebtedness to them for how our own lives have been enriched by them. Third, if we get the chance to get close enough to many individuals of another group and let ourselves fall in love with these individuals, we will find that we begin to generalize about the whole culture or the racial group through our love for the individuals instead of generalizing about individuals through cold stereotypes we may have formed about the culture as a whole. We can criticize, rationalize, or theorize about some impersonal cultural group, but if we start with individuals whom we know and appreciate, trust, respect, and love, we give them the benefit of the doubt in areas that we don't know about or understand. In all human interactions, if we are going to have healthy, growing, helpful relationships, we must consistently be giving one another the benefit of the doubt.

Two Guidelines

Finally, I want to mention two ideas that I have learned somewhere sometime along the years of this pilgrimage that have directed my mind and heart like lighthouses on a rocky coast. I don't remember where I got them, but I know they have provided much-needed guidance to me and to many others with whom I've been able to share them. The first is this: In the twenty-first century, wherever in the world you find a dominant class of people in a society, you find that since they have the agenda in their hands they are future-oriented. I hear this expressed often by leaders in the dominant class in America—"The last century is gone," "We are in a whole new millennium," "You have to look ahead," "What is your three-year, five-year, ten-year plan?" "Don't get trapped in the past—let it go." We get the feeling that anyone who has half a brain will be future-oriented, period. So those who have the agenda in their hands can easily be future-oriented, but what of those who are in the oppressed class in society? The oppressed class has history! Once we get hold of this reality, we begin to see how these two different groups can view the same incident that happened in 1985 so differently.

This was the fortieth anniversary year of the end of World War II. The staunchest and strongest ally that America had in Europe in 1985 was Germany. Forty long years had passed since the war—we had long been in a "new world scene" after Europe's reconstruction and prosperity, and a friendship had developed between the U.S. and Germany that was profound and crucial to the future of the Western powers. As an act of friendship, U.S. President Ronald Reagan, visiting Germany in 1985 at a small city named Bittberg, placed a wreath of flowers on the graves of German soldiers who died forty years before. To the dominant future-oriented communities, it was a non-event— flowers on forty-year-old graves of soldiers of a valued friend—just a simple courteous gesture. But the Jewish people in America were absolutely scandalized. How could our president do such a horrendous thing? Yes, an oppressed people have *history!*

So how do the dominant and the oppressed people in the U.S. look at slavery, at Selma and Birmingham and Montgomery, Alabama? How do they look at Forsythe County, Georgia, at the Little Rock school integration, at Rodney King in Los Angeles, at the O. J. Simpson verdict, and at the disenfranchised voters in Florida and other places in the November 2000 election? The dominant class has the agenda in their hands and so are "future-oriented." The oppressed classes have *history!*

The second idea is this: In order to truly allow a minority group to be empowered, the majority must give them two parallel things. Like railroad tracks, there must be both of these tracks simultaneously in order for the train of "empowerment" to run. If only one or the other is given, it may appear to be enough, but the result will be isolation and not empowerment. The two tracks are access to power and opportunity for self-determination. More commonly used terms for the same things are "being part of the mainstream," and "bringing their own agenda."

If a minority group is invited to have some of their members on the organization's governing board but without an inclusion and a celebration of the minority's agenda, there is no empowerment. If the minority group is allowed to work on and celebrate their own agenda but apart from the mainstream, they are isolated off in some corner and are not empowered. Of course, it can be threatening to the majority agenda to bring a minority representation onto the power board and have them bring their agenda there. That is why the majority tries to avoid real empowerment. This realization has determined for me many a course of action over the years, and the result has been that both I and the groups I have been able to influence have been greatly enriched and some magnificent groups of people have been empowered. Alas, however, we have only begun—there is yet a long pilgrimage ahead. My great joy is that on this journey I now have brothers and sisters of other racial groups who actually love and trust me, and with deep gratitude in my heart we are traveling together.

Formidable Obstacles

During the years that I was patting myself on the back as broadminded for being bilingual and immersed in the Hispanic culture, I thought that the language barrier was the greatest obstacle for minorities to get over in order to be empowered in our society. But learning a language, though difficult, is a rather mechanical obstacle to be conquered. Many "immigrant minority" groups scale their obstacles to integration quite rapidly and well. I have come to believe that the obstacles that our two "resident minority" groups have to overcome are more formidable.

Another incident that is deeply imbedded in my consciousness is again something that occurred with my dear friend, Charles Oliver. By this time in our relationship we had stayed in each other's homes, knew each other's families, and had ministered to each other and alongside each other in many ways for some years. Our relationship long since had gotten to the place where he could tease me about things, like when he told me, "Black people don't eat that white cottage cheese," and I believed him (though that was his excuse to me for not eating it when he really just didn't like it). And he constant-ly reminded me of the funny nickname that he had heard my moth-er call me but that nobody else knew. Another time when I gently tried to close the trunk of his new car and it didn't close, he came over and pushed it down hard and closed it, then looked at me and said, "Black Power."

It happened during one of the number of times we roomed to-gether at one of our denomination's weeklong seminars. It was near the end of another week that we had walked and talked with each oth-er all day every day and shared the same room in the dormitory at night. I was driving him to a local mall to pick up his suitcase that was being repaired. I have no recollection of what we were talking about in the car—we talked about anything and everything. As we got out, crossed the street, and walked toward the mall together, he turned to me and said, "Rob, I think you are really for real."

I could guess what he meant, but I needed to hear him say it. So I asked, "What do you mean?"

He said, "I think you really care about me—I think you really love me."

I was astonished and said, "Charles, we've been friends for a long time—we are brothers in the Lord and we've had lots of experiences together. That's been true for years—how come you are saying that now?"

His response has been another one of those messages that are imbedded in my heart. He said, "You have no idea how long it takes here for a black man to really trust a white man." He was right—I didn't know, but I am beginning to move along the path "toward un-derstanding" what the minority experience in America is like.

DISCUSSION STARTER QUESTIONS

1. What minority groups are you most familiar with? What studying have you done to become better acquainted with this or other groups? What additional studying can you do in the next six months?
2. Does the story at the conclusion of this essay, showing how long it might take a black man to trust a white man, surprise

you? Why or why not? What are ways that you can be intentional about earning the trust of people in other ethnic groups? Can you think of any lessons you have learned or experiences in your own difficulties that can be of help to you or others?

3. If you are in a position of power or authority in any setting, what are ways you can share some of that authority with people in other ethnic groups or come alongside them and get to know them better?

CHAPTER FIVE

GETTING TO KNOW EACH OTHER:

Are We Willing to Break Down the White Power Structure Within Evangelicalism?

BILL McCARTNEY

In the mid-1980s, I had been the football coach at the University of Colorado for a few years when a black Denver attorney named Teddy Woods died at the age of forty. In his college days, Teddy had excelled as a student-athlete at CU. Although he didn't play for me, I had met him and knew his prowess and influence in the Denver area.

I arrived early for the funeral and found a seat in the front of the church. By the time the service began, the auditorium was full. Now, bear in mind that I didn't know the other people and had only met Teddy in passing. I was there to pay my respects because he had played football for CU, and I was the current coach.

However, what happened to me that day changed my life. When I sat down and started listening to the music I was deeply affected. The mournful singing of the mostly black congregation expressed a level of pain I hadn't seen or felt before. As I looked from side to side across the crowd, I realized their grief over the loss of Teddy Woods was bringing to the surface an even deeper hurt. This wasn't just a funeral; it was also a gathering of wounded, long-suffering believers.

In response, I began to weep uncontrollably. I tried to cover my tears, fearing someone would see me and recognize that I barely knew Teddy Woods. I thought they might accuse me of grandstanding to gain acceptance and approval in the inner city as a recruiting ploy. Yet I couldn't hold back the tears. The grieving and groaning exceeded anything I had ever experienced.

I have never been the same since then. I had come in touch for the first time with the pain, struggle, despair, and anguish of black people. Stunned by that experience, I felt a great desire to understand what I had observed. I also wanted to pursue what I had felt in my spirit. Although Boulder, the city where I live, is 98 percent white, I worked with black families during recruiting season every year. As I worked with these families, I had a sense that God was calling me to a deeper understanding of their lives that would greatly influence me both personally and in my role as a leader of Promise Keepers.

So I began to question black people I had known for years. It amazed me that despite wide differences in their ages and places where they had grown up, they all identified directly with the pain I had felt in the church that day. They told stories about dramatic experiences and everyday examples of the injustices they face as Americans.[1]

The Veil Between Us

As I have been privileged to lead Promise Keepers, I have rubbed shoulders with many great men of the faith. They are each men of genuine hearts and vibrant faith. They are an inspiration to millions of people every day throughout our country. In spite of this, I have observed a fact that confronts us all. It is a "veil." Even as Paul speaks of a veil that covers the hearts of unbelievers, I believe a veil covers the hearts of believers today with regard to the subtle forms of racism and racial insensitivity that exist in ministries today. Now don't get me wrong. This is not a matter of condemnation, ridicule, or arrogant criticism. Rather, it is on my heart that we come together as the body of Christ to reflect the *fullness* of His body in all that we do. As long as the veil exists, we will not see what we need to see about becoming sensitive to the experiences and pain of our black brothers and sisters.

You may be asking, "So, what breaks down this veil?" That is exactly what I hope to address in this chapter. I would like to look at some basic principles that might give us an answer to this question. I *will* give you a hint, though. It's all about intimacy. Just as God tore the veil of the temple in two so that He might have intimacy with us in a new way through Jesus Christ, so too we must tear the veil that divides us even at the most basic level of where we work and where we worship.

A Desire for Intimacy

I find a powerful analogy regarding prayer that we can draw upon as we explore the topic of intimacy and its relationship to overcoming the barriers that exist in ministries and churches today. When we consider prayer, we need to ask ourselves about our motivation. Why do I pray? Is it out of duty? Is it out of love for the God who saved me? Each of us has to answer this question to determine the motivation that drives us in our times with almighty God. If it is merely out of duty, then it will quickly become dry and lifeless. It will become an empty ritual that means little but fulfills some requirement we have come to believe marks a Christian.

On the other hand, if our time in prayer grows out of a heart that is overflowing with love for Jesus Christ and what He did for us at the Cross and through His resurrection, then our time in prayer will be rich, fulfilling, and spiritually fresh and powerful. Motivation matters. Heart matters. The reality is that once we have experienced the intimacy that flows out of a heart of love and passion for God, we will never want to return to the dry, lifeless ritual we once practiced.

The same is true when it comes to overcoming barriers that divide us in our ministries and churches. Without a passion for intimacy and understanding, we will never have the determination and perseverance necessary to understand one another. We will not have the guts to move into another person's world to understand his pain without getting defensive.

I could have easily sat in Teddy Woods's funeral and decided that what I was feeling was unreasonable since I had no part in the pain that was expressed in that music. After all, I was just there to represent CU. I believe that it was nothing short of the Holy Spirit breaking through my heart to help me to see the pain of my brothers and sisters in order to ignite in me a passion for understanding brothers who are different from me.

That is what it takes for us as well. I believe that God uses a willing heart, and He does the rest in revealing to us what we need to know and understand in order to develop the intimacy necessary to break down these barriers. Intimacy becomes the launch pad from which we move with intentionality toward changing the world around us, whether that is in a ministry, a church, or even a family. That is why this principle is the first to be mentioned. It provides us with the vision necessary to sustain the course of making the changes within our organizations so that in some small way (and even great ways) they reflect the body of Christ. Scripture tells us, "Where there is no vision, the people perish" (Proverbs 29:18 KJV). The same is true with regard to making *real* changes in how we conduct ourselves in our ministries, churches, and seminaries. Without the vision for intimacy that we can have in the body of Christ, which is almighty God's desire, we will make little progress in having all areas of ministry and life reflecting unity and diversity.

That has been the guiding principle and passion for me as I have been honored to be a part of Promise Keepers through its first decade. That experience at Teddy Woods's funeral gave me the desire and passion to understand at a level that has guided my actions ever after. It hasn't required an edict from above. Intimacy has drawn me as it does in prayer. As Promise Keepers has moved to take on the giant of racism in our country and in the church, we have taken tremendous hits both from within the church and from outside of it. In spite of all this, the desire for intimacy and understanding has guided me as I have been part of the leadership team at PK.

The Need of Empathy for Others

Once we have been drawn by our desire for intimacy with our brothers and sisters different from us, empathy begins to develop. We need to tap into other people's pain and their joys. We need to understand their world from *their* perspective and not just our own. That is the only way that true empathy will develop. By doing it this way, we can move a little farther down the road of making things different.

How do leaders develop empathy? It is no different than what Christ modeled for us after the seventy disciples returned from their first journey to the lost sheep of Israel. He listened and rejoiced in their experiences. As leaders, there is an added burden for us to listen with new ears, to listen with an ear for experiences different from our own, and to use the knowledge that we get from that to develop the empathy we need to "turn the world upside down." This kind of empathy develops sensitivity in us that we would not otherwise have.

When we lack the commitment to understand others' pain, we run the risk of diminishing the respect we should give them. The reality is that when we refuse to understand others' pain and empathize with them, we are stealing their dignity. In essence, we are saying, "Only *my* perspective on your experience counts." That may not be what we say, but our actions betray us.

If I may call upon a football example, it's a little like you are on "injured reserve." You are thoroughly prepared for the game, but you're injured. The reality is that you can't be in the game like your teammates. All you can do is watch from the sidelines. Unfortunately, from the sidelines you can get a distorted sense of the game. You really can't get a sense of the flow of the game, the opposing players, or what will work and what won't. You are not in the game, so you cannot really get a "feel" for what is going on. You can't eyeball the opposing players, you can't get a sense of what your teammates are thinking, and you certainly can't begin to know how to adapt in your own position to make the plays that need to be made. The bottom line is that you simply can't be part of the solution for your team. Essentially, the person in the game is the one who clearly understands what is going on out on the field. Coaches know that—that's why they not only stand on the sidelines, but also have guys up in the box to gain a different perspective on the game that can't be seen from the sidelines.

What's important to understand here is that unless you are in the game with your brothers and sisters, you can't adequately understand what they are experiencing. You may be able to watch from the sidelines and have an intellectual understanding. But that doesn't cut it when it comes to understanding our ethnically different brothers and sisters. What they respect the most is when we are willing to "get dirty" with them. That means that when we understand, we will understand from a perspective that we can share with them.

Thankfully, our actions can also strengthen our message of understanding and empathy. Take the men of Gilead, for example. These were guys who were in the game with their brothers. They *did* understand what their brothers were going through.

Moses' ministry was coming to an end, so he set out to deliver his final sermon. In it, he describes the nation of Israel's conquests. Prior to delivering the actual content of this sermon, Moses gives the hill country of Gilead to the Reubenites, the Gadites, and the half-tribe of Manasseh. The bequeathing of this inheritance didn't come without a price, though. Moses tells them:

> I commanded you at that time: "The LORD your God has given you this land to take possession of it. But all your able-bodied men, armed for battle, must cross over ahead of your brother Israelites. However, your wives, your children and your livestock (I know you have much livestock) may stay in the towns I have given you, until the LORD gives rest to your brothers as he has to you, and they too have taken over the land that the LORD your God is giving them, across the Jordan. After that, each of you may go back to the possession I have given you." (Deuteronomy 3:18–20)

That was the command given these three tribes. They had stiffer duty than the rest of the fighting men of Israel. They had to lead the way! Of course, they *could* have bailed out, and said, "Forget it, Moses! We're here, and we aren't going any further. We're home. Let the rest of them fend for themselves!"

But they didn't bail out. Later, in Joshua 13, when the tribes are apportioned the land inheritance that is theirs, the men of Gilead finally receive what they have been promised. That means that they fulfilled their mission. They had fought until their brothers found their rest just as they had to the east of the Jordan River. In other words, these valiant men of Gilead had fought with (and in front of) their brothers for something they had already received. Their actions spoke loudly to their brothers about their commitment to see to it that their brothers received what they already had waiting for them back in the hill country of Gilead.

That is our mission as well when it comes to our brothers and sisters who are ethnically different from us. If we are members of the predominant ethnic group, we must commit ourselves to fight to understand the world from our brothers' and sisters' perspective, and also commit ourselves like the men of Gilead to go ahead of them so that they may find the rest with which we have already been blessed.

This perspective has implications for the corporate culture as well. This principle is certainly something I have seen at PK as we have sought to be intentional in developing an ethnically diverse management team. In my opinion, it is incumbent upon on us white men and women to make a way for our brothers and sisters of other ethnicities. We are blessed with an incredible opportunity of opening a door for them to excel as we have been given the opportunity to excel. We have seen that lived out in the halls of PK as we have made the effort to increase the diversity of our staff.

That doesn't mean that we won't take our shots. I believe that every time we seek to do the right thing, we can plan to take our hits for it. That has certainly happened at PK, just like any other ministry or organization. There has been grumbling about our choices for our leadership team. In order to stand my ground with these decisions, I have been driven by my conviction that this is the heart of God Himself for us to turn the tables and serve our brothers and sisters in this way. I realize that it takes time to change a corporate culture. We must be intentional, patient, and determined to see our decisions through in this area. The power behind it is that it speaks volumes to our brothers and sisters of the darker hue that we are ready to "walk our talk" when it comes to ethnic diversity.

The Value of Experience

There is no substitute for experience to refine our understanding and sharpen our efforts to make real change. The first Boulder PK conference helped me to identify the disturbing reality of racism in the body of Christ. Toward the end of the program, as I casually gazed out on the crowd, my eye caught something that sent a chill down my spine. The crowd was almost entirely white. I knew the Holy Spirit was prompting me. As we were about to close in prayer, I walked back up on stage with a simple word of caution, one that would drastically alter my own life. If each man in the arena brought twelve friends the following summer, we said, we'd have fifty thousand men. "Men," I said, "next year at Folsom Stadium we expect a sellout. But I believe that if we fail to gather a fair representation of *all* of God's people, God will not join us." I didn't mean by this statement that God doesn't manifest Himself when this aspect of diversity isn't fulfilled. But I wanted to communicate with every fiber in my being that we simply wouldn't experience the fullness of God's presence without the full representation of the *diverse* body of Christ as is pictured in Revelation 5.

The crowd left on a wave of exhilaration that would only be multiplied in the years to come. But my last remarks on the racial issue had clearly hit a raw nerve, igniting a minor firestorm of hate mail and caustic letters, chastising me, saying, "How dare you imply that in a stadium filled with men glorifying Jesus Christ, God won't be there." Others stated angrily, "God did not state in Scriptures, 'Go ye therefore and eradicate racism.' He said, 'Go preach the gospel to all nations.'"

Many quoted the Scripture where Jesus says, "For where two or three come together in my name, there am I with them" (Matthew 18:20) to debunk my exhortation. And I understood their point. But what it really gave me was a first glimpse of the seething *giant* of racism lurking within the fabric of the Christian church.

I never backed off my original statement. As I have since learned, Matthew 18:20 probes deeper into the heart of the character of His church than most want to believe. For I believe that in order for God to bless His people with a true fullness of power and blessing, He requires more than mere proximity, numbers, and verbal assent. God's commands always convict; they expose our true condition. God knows it's easy enough for His people to *say* they agree when they gather in Christ's name. But His gaze is all-discerning. It knows whether or not His children are truly joined in wholehearted purity and oneness of spirit; if we are bonded at heart, in undisturbed harmony, in seamless unity; if we are truly humbled, broken, and contrite.

God knows when we are authentically "together," or when we're simply paying lip service. He knows when we are truly of one accord by how easily we defer to one another with servants' hearts and count others as better than ourselves. I venture a guess that when *those* conditions are in their proper place, we have full right to expect God to come and dwell among us in all His unfathomable abundance and to bless the prayers of His chastened saints.

I therefore make no apologies for concluding that in ministries, churches, and other institutions of the church, God's heart is for the full complement of His people represented in all the incalculably rich, heavenly splendor of racial and cultural diversity. Where could it be more clear than in Colossians 3:11: "Here there is no Greek or Jew, circumcised or uncircumcised, barbarian, Scythian, slave or free, but Christ is all, and is in all."

Let me give one last example of what experience can accomplish for us as we seek to change our organizations and ministries to reflect the fullness of the body of Christ. With the help of Christian broadcaster James Dobson, I began scheduling speaking engagements at churches across the country, delivering a controversial message on racial reconciliation. I'd show up to churches filled with men eager to hear about the marvelous move of God called Promise Keepers— and I'd begin to talk. I spoke of my experience as a football coach, recognizing in my players' faces a conditioned resignation toward cultural injustice; I tried to explain how a subtle spirit of white superiority has unwittingly alienated and wounded our brothers and sisters within the church, and how the eleven o'clock hour on Sunday morning is the country's most segregated hour of the week.

"My heart is broken for why I am standing here today," I cried out. "The church is standing on the shore while the tide is taking our brothers and sisters of color out to sea. We must get in touch with reality. We have oppressed men and women of color. We will not have revival until we have reconciliation."

But always when I finished there was no response—nothing. No applause. No nods. Everyone instead looked sober. In city after city (more than sixty), in church after church, it was the same story—wild enthusiasm while I was being introduced, followed by a morgue-like chill as I stepped away from the microphone. It was as if God had commissioned me to single-handedly burst everyone's bubble. I repeatedly returned to my prayer room shaken and dejected. "Am I hearing You, Lord?" I asked. "Is this really the message You want me to share?" And every time He would impress on me, "Just be faithful. Just be obedient."

As my speaking tour came to a close, I had an engagement at a church in Portland, Oregon. My message ended to the usual wall of silence. Yet before I could leave the podium, a black speaker at the back of the platform stood up. I paused as he began to walk toward me. As he got closer, I could see tears in his eyes. He approached the podium and stood there for what seemed like minutes, trying to gather himself. After a long delay, in a broken voice, he finally said,

"I never thought . . . that in my lifetime . . . I'd ever hear a white man say . . . what this man has said." He paused to compose himself. The church was stone silent. His face was still contorted in a pain I would never know. In spite of this, there glimmered in his heart a sliver of hope. He continued in a tone that was determined but weary of the dashed hopes in the past, "Maybe there is hope."

Maybe there is hope. Those were the words I'd waited to hear. They validated me, confirming that what I'd been saying was truly from God's heart. Over the years, I have held meetings with ethnic pastors in U.S. cities. Everywhere I go, pastors of color are profoundly encouraged, eagerly waiting to see good intentions put into action, while some among the white clergy remain veiled. It's such a simple message: We are all one in Christ and should treat one another as such. Even within Promise Keepers there has been pressure to de-emphasize or soften the racial message. But we hold firm. We press on, taking our cue from ethnic brothers and sisters who, for the first time, are expressing hope of seeing these racial veils fall once and for all.[2]

Experience sharpens us; experience hardens our resolve; experience confirms that indeed we are acting consistent with God's heart. That is certainly what experience has done for me and the way I lead the ministry of Promise Keepers. Without intimacy, I cannot shape my actions to be sensitive to my brothers and sisters of color. Without empathy, I cannot see the world through their eyes and tap into their pain. Without experience, I cannot sharpen and focus what I do and think as I continue my journey of faith.

I believe in my heart that the exponential growth of the early years of Promise Keepers was because of our obedience to God's desire for diversity and unity in His body. It was a hard message to carry, but one that was absolutely in tune with God's desire for His body.

I have been convicted beyond measure by Ezekiel 16:49: "Now this was the sin of your sister Sodom: She and her daughters were arrogant, overfed and unconcerned; they did not help the poor and needy."

As I meditated on this Scripture, I was struck by something. I had always thought that the only reason that Sodom was destroyed was because of its rampant sexual immorality. Yet here in this passage she was being indicted because she was "arrogant, overfed and unconcerned." The upshot of this condition was her response to the poor and the needy. Then the light went on in my head, and my heart was pierced. *That's me!* I can be held accountable for the same things as Sodom. I, too, am arrogant, overfed, and unconcerned. This has left a conviction in my heart that I need to do everything I can to pierce the veil of my heart that blinds me to the condition, pain, and perspective of my brothers and sisters of color. Armed with that conviction and sensitivity, we can all make a difference in our ministries, churches, and seminaries.

So what are the keys to overcoming the white-power barriers in our evangelical organizations? First, it takes a commitment to intimacy to truly know our brothers and sisters of color. Because of this knowledge and understanding, we will necessarily take certain actions, including intentionally seeking ways to open the door for them in our organizations.

The second key is empathy. It requires empathy from us to see the world through the eyes of our ethnically different brothers and sisters. Again, this sensitivity forces action from us. If nothing else, this action is seen in our efforts to communicate our support and willingness to understand the world through their eyes.

Finally, it takes experience to sharpen and focus our resolve to act in a way that will change our world forever. My desire is that when others look from the outside, they will say we are indeed disciples of Christ because "we love one another" *and* because they see *all* of us represented.

DISCUSSION STARTER QUESTIONS

1. What do you think has allowed Promise Keepers to be as effective as it has been in getting out the message of racial reconciliation? What specific points can your ministry copy from them? What do you need to do differently?
2. Do you agree or disagree that all of God's people must be present for God's power to fully dwell in a ministry? Support your answer with Scripture.
3. What three things can you pray for your own church or ministry as you think seriously about moving forward in unity with brothers and sisters of other races?

CHAPTER SIX

THE ALTERNATIVE TO ETHNIC-FOCUSED CHURCH PLANTING:

How Can We Build Diversity As We Build Churches?

RALEIGH B. WASHINGTON

And they sang a new song, saying, "Worthy are You to take the book and to break its seals; for You were slain, and purchased for God with Your blood men from every tribe and tongue and people and nation." (Revelation 5:9 NASB)

Diversity is an undeniable desire in the very heart of almighty God. John tells us in chapter 5 of Revelation that Jesus was slain to purchase for God with His very blood people from every tribe and tongue and people and nation. The Cross did not simply represent the redemption of believers in a general or generic sense. Rather, God's Word makes it unmistakable that the Cross was designed to redeem a kingdom of people for God that would be incomplete if this kingdom did not include an appropriate, representative group of people consistent with His creation. This group of people would be a thoroughly diverse representation of mankind.

The axiom for church growth and development of homogeneity

that has been used for many years, while it predicts success, is not consistent with Scripture, and I believe it has grave consequences for the global body of Christ. We must be careful with human knowledge and understanding of church development that produces the desired effect, but sidesteps the issue of consistency with Scripture. Clearly, as Peter Wagner suggests, homogeneity does produce rapid growth and stability within church structures. At the same time, though, we must ask the question: Is this at the heart of God for the physical manifestation of His body and bride?

Homogeneity: Problems and Pitfalls

Many theoreticians of church growth over the last decade have made the observation that churches grow in proportion to the sameness of their members. The simple adage "birds of a feather flock together" applies. As a matter of fact, the conclusion is that churches grow when people feel the most comfortable with the people in the church. Quite naturally, then, the more the church reflects them— values, ethnicity, socioeconomic status, age, etc.—the more likely they are to attend.

In spite of this, homogeneity has its own set of problems and pitfalls. One of the most compelling of these problems is the simple fact that we do not exist in a homogeneous world. An incredible diversity is part of our everyday experience. From the lowest forms of life to God's crowning glory of man himself, we see diversity. Therefore, when homogeneity is sought, it is done so on the basis of something other than growth alone. Perhaps this principle of homogeneity is profound more because it simply allows (or should I say gives permission to) people to be comfortable.

I don't think anyone would argue that we all like comfort and ease. As a matter of fact, many of the choices we make during our lives, from the people with whom we associate (including our spouses) to the career toward which we gravitate, are powerfully influenced by comfort. This is not to say that comfort is wrong. It is important, though, that we not deny its power in shaping our decisions even when it comes to the church we choose. The power (and the problem) of homogeneity lies in the fact that it creates an artificially "safe" environment in the church. We unwittingly provide a sanctuary for the people in the pews in which they never confront the reality they see as they leave the front door of the church. Even more so, we could well be co-conspirators to a subtle form of racism. To be sure, it is not purposeful, intentional racism, but a passive acquiescence for the "great divide" to exist between the races on Sunday.

A second problem that must be considered when denominations or parachurch organizations apply this principle in their efforts to plant ministries and churches is the contribution it makes to the already firmly entrenched racial separation that exists in the church on any given Sunday morning. I realize that there is often no conscious effort to create local church bodies that are uniform and homogeneous. Yet it appears that in our effort to reach people for Christ, we have missed the very heart of God for diversity. The effort needed to reach into various ethnic communities, whether they be Hispanic, African American, Caucasian, or Asian, seems to outweigh the importance of those intentional decisions that have to be made in order to plant churches that reflect the glory of diversity. Of course, that is not to say that these efforts are in vain because they create communities of believers that are the same ethnically. On the other hand, though, are we to sacrifice our efforts to address this "great divide" that exists in the church simply because it is *easier* to avoid it?

No matter what our effort to win the world for Christ, the heart of God must guide us as we reach out in His name rather than with pragmatic concerns. The efforts that are driven by homogeneity are indeed productive and successful. Perhaps that is part of the problem. They are so successful that we begin to believe that we have the ability in ourselves to grow a church. The wonder and beauty of pursuing diversity in our communities is that there is a miracle in it that reflects the heart of the Almighty. There is no human way that such communities could grow or even exist without God's hand on them because they reflect His desire articulated in Revelation 5—people from every tongue, nation, tribe, and people.

A last problem I would like to highlight is related to our definitions of "success." We must all grapple with how we define success as we pursue church-planting efforts. On the surface, the definition of success rests in the increase of churches and the number of souls won to Christ. That measure can, indeed, be used with powerful validity. After all, why are we planting churches? Yet the key issue is *how* are we planting churches, not simply *that* we are planting churches. It is far easier to plant a church with the intentionality of reflecting the diversity of God's people than it is to change it midstream. To call upon the horticultural metaphor, it is far easier to plant with the intention of growing a particular kind of plant than it is to attempt to prune that same plant into shape after it has been left to grow its own way.

People, like plants, tend to follow their nature even in churches. It is because of this tendency that the homogeneity principle of church growth is so powerful. Therefore, when the plant begins to grow and blossom into its full nature, it is difficult to attempt to coax it into some other kind of plant or even to make it look like one. God seems to be far more effective in grafting into an original plant and making it blossom than humans are. In various settings, including churches, the effort it takes is beyond humans and their ability to transform into something more diverse than they were originally. One of the reasons that churches are not more diverse in this country is that diversity is a supernatural work. It cannot be done on a human level but takes divine intervention. But we have a God who *is* supernatural, and our churches can be too.

It is truly the calling of the church to "go and make disciples of all nations." It is also true that the vision of Revelation 5 is the calling of the church. That vision is to be a true representation of the fullness of the body of Christ with "all nations" being represented—every tribe, tongue, people, and nation. Perhaps our measure of success should rest not only on the people being won to Christ but the diversity of the group they are being won into.

An Alternative to Ethnic-Focused Church Planting

One might object to the assertion that churches should reflect the diversity of the body of Christ reflected in Revelation 5. It seems unfair to expect a church to have diversity when it isn't even in an environment that has diversity. For example, the question can be posed: Can churches that are in ethnically homogeneous communities be expected to have a diverse body of believers? The answer to this question is both yes and no.

The "no" part of our answer reflects the fact that we should be circumspect about condemning a church when its immediate surroundings do not offer a viable opportunity to reach out to people of different ethnicities. Such a church could have a true heart of diversity, but have no chance to express such a desire. An example of this would be a church that is in a county in which there is no (or very little) ethnic diversity.

On the other hand, it will fall far short of meeting the desire of God's heart if there are no intentional efforts made by a church body to include diverse people in the context of worshiping God and serving man. Every church can include initiatives that would provide this diversity. Such initiatives would include mission efforts within the urban centers and Native American reservations, short-term mission initiatives to nations around the world, international exchange programs, and local church-sponsored mission teams. The opportunity to become diverse is virtually unlimited where there is intentionality on the part of the pastor and his pastoral team, whether they are paid or volunteer. Other specific suggestions will be provided later in this chapter, including a living, breathing example that continues today in Minnesota.

Commitment

Diverse and truly reconciled church bodies are built upon the foundation of committed relationships. Time alone doesn't heal. It never has, and it never will. Racial alienation in this country goes back for centuries and affects everyone. Effort is needed to bridge the pain of past experiences. We who are Christians need a *deep commitment* to cross the chasm and build significant relationships across racial lines.

Committed personal relationships are the foundation of racial understanding and acceptance. They are the essential catalyst for setting the miracle of unity into motion. To begin the process of reconciliation, each of us must get involved personally in a friendship. Many folks would welcome friendships with people of other races if those relationships happened easily and were automatically filled with joy, peace, and success. But the fact is that cross-cultural relationships require effort; they often break down over misunderstandings, disappointments, and defensive attacks. Misunderstandings are hard enough to settle with people who are like us. But in this country, every disappointment between blacks and whites reminds people of darker hue of centuries of bad history. It's normal to want to avoid pain, so most people, both black and white, walk away from interracial relationships, saying, "I don't need this hassle."

True diversity in our churches won't happen among Christians unless we commit ourselves to developing relationships across racial lines. Of course, this flies in the face of the homogeneity principle of church growth. We can't stop with a commitment to diversity; it must be put into action. Genuine reconciliation happens only between people who make a commitment to relationships and who consider the relationships so important that they won't let them go, even when the going gets tough. Where can we find this kind of courage to make such a commitment?

Jesus once described the quality of lasting commitment using the image of a farmer plowing a field. Jesus had called people to follow Him. Sometimes they responded in the first flush of enthusiasm with "I'll follow You wherever You go, Master!" But when He challenged them to put their enthusiasm into action, He heard a lot of excuses: "After my elderly parents die, then I'll follow You"; "I've got a lot of family responsibilities. Let me wrap up the family business; then I'll follow You."

To this second excuse Jesus responded simply, "No one who puts his hand to the plow and looks back is fit for service in the kingdom of God" (Luke 9:62). Jesus was saying, "If you want to follow Me, you can't stand on the sidelines. It's going to take effort and hard work to plow up this field. Be sure you count the cost, because once you grab the plow, you have to keep going. Anyone who looks back when the going gets tough isn't worthy of the kingdom of God." Jesus was very clear that the way of the Cross isn't easy; it takes commitment.

This is the kind of commitment needed for all serious relationships: husband/wife, business partners, deacons in the church, and cross-cultural church plants. It's like plowing virgin sod—four feet deep and never opened up; conflicts are inevitable. But when you keep your hand on the plow, the end result is a deeply enriched relationship. This is the first step you must take to accomplish true diversity in a church body: Be committed to any relationship you begin to develop.

Intentionality

Intentionality is the purposeful, positive, and planned activity that facilitates reconciliation and true diversity in the church body. Diversity and racial reconciliation don't happen spontaneously. Blacks and whites can work side by side, live side by side, even go to church together, and still not be in a meaningful relationship with each other. The reality as we begin the twenty-first century is that most blacks and whites are still separated and alienated from each other, and eleven o'clock Sunday morning is still the most segregated hour of the week.

We may agree that God has given Christians the ministry of reconciliation. We may recognize that developing relationships across racial lines is the key to true reconciliation. But all too often our beliefs and good intentions lie dormant and unheeded. That is where intentionality comes in. Intentionality gives priority to purposeful, positive, and planned activity that facilitates reconciliation and a true appreciation for the wonderful diversity God has ordained.

Intentionality is the locomotive that drives racial reconciliation and our desire to plant churches that are truly multi- and cross-cultural. We must want to know the other race, to contribute to the other person's spiritual, social, and emotional growth, and to allow him to contribute to ours. Our attitude must be *I will be intentional in pursuing a relationship with this person*. That is as true in our efforts in planting churches. We must be equally intentional to reach across racial differences and facilitate local church bodies that pursue reconciliation on the most basic level of their operations and functioning.

Paul wrote, "Your attitude should be the same as that of Christ Jesus" (Philippians 2:5). What attitude? That of humility. Christ, who was "in very nature God" and equal with God, nonetheless humbled Himself, took on the nature of a servant, and was obedient even to the point of death. Not just any death, but death on the cross! *That* took intentionality. He intended to be involved with sinful, inconvenient people. So He entered their lives by coming to earth.

In many ways, that model lays the framework for our modern-day efforts to plant churches in a variety of communities that are diversity-focused. We must pursue the same kind of intentionality that Christ did by entering into others' world and inviting them into ours.

Sensitivity

Separation from people who are different develops and even encourages distrust. Human beings have a tendency not to trust across ethnic, social, national, and denominational lines. We don't trust people or situations we don't know or understand. We've heard from others everything we know about these different people. The lack of authentic, meaningful relationships means we talk mainly with others like us, who reinforce our negative preconceptions and limited understanding.

We tend to interpret the actions of others based on our own life experiences. Without knowledge of the other person's life, we may jump to incorrect or unfair conclusions. Prejudice can develop and be encouraged by this lack of truth. If we base our opinions of others only on the statements of those who are like us, we're liable to get a biased viewpoint.

From a church-planting perspective, therefore, we inadvertently perpetuate the ongoing misunderstandings between people within God's church when we choose to pursue an ethnic-focused church planting process. Only through purposeful, planned, and positive activities that are intended to heighten sensitivity (which must be done cross-culturally and cross-ethnically) will we truly avoid this. Accordingly, the outcome will be a church that deepens in its understanding of people different from the prevailing, dominant ethnic group and that deepens in its understanding of God's heart for diversity in His church.

Sincerity

Casual relationships with Christians across racial lines are a good beginning. But members of the body of Christ must move beyond casual relationships to loving, caring, trusting friendships that last.

The principle of sincerity says we must talk to each other and honestly disclose our thoughts. This takes us back to previous principles, because such efforts will not happen without intentionality or outside committed relationships. Talking about those things that divide us, especially racial issues, can be very threatening. We fear even using the "r" words (*racism* or *racist*). We may believe that discussing them would be asking for trouble or conflict. Such fear entraps us in our isolation. Paul told us, "God did not give us a spirit of timidity, but a spirit of power, of love and of self-discipline" (2 Timothy 1:7). In practice, the revealing of ourselves brings understanding, which leads to resolution of differences.

Developing this kind of environment in a church takes time and a lot of energy. Expressing ourselves in sincerity requires us to be humble and risk vulnerability. It also requires an act of faith and trust in God and the principles He has given us for relating to each other (e.g., honesty, truthfulness, sincerity). You may ask yourself, "If I say this, will God take care of me?" Inevitably someone will say, "I revealed myself like that once, and they really hurt me. I won't do that again." Such a response to rejection is understandable, but it closes the door on reconciliation in the name of self-protection. When we conform to the likeness of Christ, we can expect to suffer for His sake at times. If you experience rejection or hurt because you took the risk of vulnerability, God can take those experiences and use them to help you grow into maturity:

> Consider it pure joy, my brothers, whenever you face trials of many kinds, because you know that the testing of your faith develops perseverance. Perseverance must finish its work so that you may be mature and complete, not lacking anything. (James 1:2–4)

As we enter into a relationship of sincerity, God deepens our dependence on Him and equips us to be ambassadors of reconciliation.

Sacrifice

The final principle I would like to highlight is that of sacrifice. This principle is particularly powerful in terms of church planting. Sacrifice here is defined as the willingness to give up anything to see God's will in reconciliation and diversity happen.

To one degree or another, all previous principles for an alternative to ethnic-focused church planting might make some practical sense to the world. Sacrifice does not. Human pride and selfishness refuse to give up position, status, security, or personal rights for the sake of someone else. Applying the principle of sacrifice will require that you allow Christ and His Spirit to work in and through you. For the one who has Christ inside, sacrifice is possible—even if it requires your life someday.

As applied to church planting this is especially relevant. The very act of planting a diverse church in an area that is culturally and ethnically diverse, one that is designed to build itself on the principles outlined above, is the embodiment of sacrifice. Without sacrifice, meaningful change in our patterns of relating is doomed. The tighter we hold on to our own desires, the more we separate ourselves from others. That is the real danger in homogeneity of churches. We are setting up a process that supports, and even gives permission for, this continuance of separateness. Therefore, the true sacrifice that is necessary to see true diversity in the body of Christ is never really achieved. Sacrifice is really giving in to God—yielding everything we have to His use. It will require that we trust God to care for us as we pioneer ways to truly facilitate reconciliation through our efforts in planting churches.

The Journey Toward Diversity: Two Church Models

One church plant of which I have intimate knowledge is that of Rock of Our Salvation Evangelical Free Church on the West Side of Chicago, Illinois. Rock Church was raised up with the intentional strategy of planting a church that would be a culturally diverse church. By the end of its fifteenth year of ministry, the composition of the congregation has moved from being 30 percent diverse to being 35 percent diverse. Over those fifteen years we had an increase of 5 percent in our congregation in which people other than African American came to be involved in the life of our congregation. Because of our intentionality, the diversity not only held during this fifteen-year period, but increased.

At that time, the neighborhood in which Rock Church was planted was 95 percent African American, yet the church was more than 30 percent Caucasian. This means that Anglo people caught the vision of racial reconciliation and diversity and moved into the neighborhood to be part of the bigger vision of Rock Church.

In addition to those who actually moved into our neighborhood, Rock Church has had very close relationships with a number of churches, most of which are Evangelical Free churches. However, its closest and most intimate relationship was, and continues to be, with Wayzata Evangelical Free Church in Wayzata, Minnesota.

Our relationship with the Wayzata church came into being as a result of one man's passionate desire to embrace the vision for reconciliation. I had been invited to speak at a regional conference for the Evangelical Free Church, and Maury Kapsner was in attendance. Maury was a leader in missions at his church in Wayzata. After listening to my message, Maury caught the vision for the partnering of churches that were culturally and ethnical diverse. He took this same passion and vision back to his church and challenged them to get involved. As a result, Maury and his wife, Linda, invited me to speak to their church about this same message of reconciliation. There was an outpouring of support and, beyond that, a willingness to put action to their enthusiasm.

This church is a wonderful example of a church that thinks beyond its boundaries, both physical and spiritual. In its journey toward diversity, this predominantly white church could have stopped at its borders and concluded that it really couldn't do anything since the community in which it was planted was no more diverse than the church itself. With the help of some passionate people like Maury and Linda Kapsner who had a heart for diversity and reconciliation, this church reached beyond its physical boundaries and enfolded Rock Church with love and tangible support.

As a matter of fact, within the last week of the time in which I am writing this chapter, Linda Kapsner, Judy Craig, and Gretchen Buckmiller are giving leadership to the Wayzata ladies as they host a retreat in Minnesota for the women of Rock Church. The theme of this retreat is a reconciliation theme—"TRUST: True Religion is Urban and Suburban Together." My wife, Paulette, and my sister-in-law, Lisa Washington (wife of Abraham Lincoln Washington, pastor of Rock Church) are the keynote speakers for this retreat.

How does such a thing happen? It happens in response to a heart that is convinced and convicted that we must have intentional and positive activities in order to facilitate diversity in our churches. Linda Kapsner and the Wayzata ladies raised the money and paid for the airfare of the women of Rock Church to attend the weekend retreat so that they could pray, study, and live out the truth of committed relationships. Incidentally, this weekend is not the first time this has happened. It has been an annual event for the past seven or eight years.

The bottom line is that, while Wayzata may not have a significant percentage of diverse families in its church, you'd better believe the church is diverse in its thinking and ministry directly related to what is happening among these ladies.

The pastor of Wayzata, Dr. George Kenworthy, has also caught the vision. In addition to his relationship with me, and now with my brother, Abraham, he has established a committed relationship with an African-American pastor in the Twin Cities of Minnesota. What is key to notice is the God-inspired "snowball effect" that has been created by these ladies who have a heart for intentional, committed relationships across racial lines.

Wayzata is a study in overcoming the obstacles and barriers that exist in raising up a church with a heart and a vision for reconciliation in spite of its surroundings.

Conclusion

Ethnic-focused church planting, in spite of its allure and apparent success, deviates from the miracle that happens when people pursue the heart of God through diversity. Revelation 5 makes it clear that God's heart is for the fullness of His body to display the richness of diversity He has created in it.

We can do no less in our efforts to plant churches with a vision for a diverse local body of believers than to reflect what is in God's heart for His saints. That means we are bargaining for the difficulty and tension that come with working out committed relationships, sacrificing for each other, cultivating sincerity and sensitivity, and moving intentionally into each other's worlds. Yet that is where the miracle lies in His church blossoming and welcoming even more lost souls into its ranks. It is worth the effort to see such a miracle. No doubt being ethnically focused is easier, but it may well rob us of the opportunity of seeing God's hand knit the hearts of diverse people together through the blood of His Son.

DISCUSSION STARTER QUESTIONS

1. What has your own church done toward encouraging diversity within its own walls or in outreaches such as missions, church plants, and relationships with other churches?
2. What more is your church able to do with its current resources, location, etc.? What could it plan to do within the next few years?
3. How important is it to you that your church be diverse in various ways (ethnic, class, age, etc.)? What would you personally be willing to sacrifice to see it happen?

CHAPTER SEVEN

UNDERSTANDING INTERRACIAL FAMILIES:

Can the Church
Welcome
Mixed-Race
Couples?

A. CHARLES WARE

U nity with diversity is a growing challenge for both the American society and the church. Christian ministries are beginning to desire modeling ethnic diversity in a nation that has greater diversity than any other nation in the world.

The church has a responsibility to stand on moral principles while seeking to reach a diverse world for Christ. What does this mean when it comes to social relationships, especially interracial marriage? Should the church seek to preserve and maintain the "God ordained" racial distinctions by prohibiting intermarriage? Or should the church become the one true family of God embracing one another across racial lines, including intermarriage? Scriptural answers to these questions and the resultant responsibility of the people of God are needed as we minister within a diverse society.

Interracial marriage has been a long-term concern for the American society. In an attempt to protect the purity of the white gene pool, interracial marriages were long considered socially, morally, and legally wrong. It was as recently as 1967 that the U.S. Supreme Court struck down laws in sixteen states that made mixed-race marriage a crime.

The social transition is illustrated by the June 10, 1991, cover story of *JET* magazine: "Black/White Love Affair Sparks 'Jungle Fever.'" "Jungle Fever" is described as "a movie that tackles the ultimate taboo, Black men dating White women."[1] This movie, which depicted an adulterous interracial affair, was considered socially challenging not because of adultery but rather because of the interracial love theme.

As the social, moral, and legal walls fall, the number of interracial marriages continues to increase. In the article "Interracial Marriages Becoming Commoner," based upon U.S. Census Bureau's 2000 data, Tony Pugh states:

> Mixed marriages, once rare in the United Sates, are surging. . . .
>
> Nearly 34 years after the U.S. Supreme Court struck down the last laws prohibiting mixed-marriages, the once forbidden unions now total 1.5 million. That's a tenfold increase since 1960. Adding Hispanics who marry outside their ethnic group brings the total of mixed marriages to 3 million based on an analysis of recent survey data.
>
> Today only 5% of all U.S. marriages are mixed. But the steady growth of mixed marriages is powerful evidence that racial and ethnic barriers are softening as the nation's population becomes more diverse.[2]

The church realizes that not all social change is good, and the legalization of an act does not make it morally right. So the church needs biblically clear direction concerning mixed-race marriages. Do such unions break the moral law of God, just as a homosexual or lesbian couple do? Or have the spouses made an unwise, although not immoral decision that will lead to a lifetime of trouble if not the ultimate failure of the marriage? Have they created a union that will curse their children with a lifetime of rejection? Have they severely limited their usefulness in ministry by consummating a marriage that the church will not accept? Whether in private counseling or public teaching, the church must communicate the mind of God on these issues.

Scriptural Arguments Used Against Interracial Marriages

Historically, many evangelical/fundamentalist believers have considered interracial marriage to be either sin or socially unwise. The belief that interracial marriage was a violation of Scripture motivated some Christians to discourage such unions. Discouragement took the form of everything from public proclamations of "Scriptures"[3] to private counseling, from segregated institutions[4] to special policies or rules forbidding interracial dating. Mixed marriages, generally, were not and in some cases still are not welcomed in the church.

The church is to be the pillar and ground of truth in a community. However, often the church has proclaimed error in the community due to misinterpretation of certain Scriptures. In *Prejudice and the People of God*, I stated that "misinterpretation leads to misapplication which leads to misdirection."[5] A biblical change of direction requires a proper interpretation of the text, followed by a proper application. An examination of several Scriptures used to assert that mixed marriages are wrong will demonstrate how misinterpretation and poor application of Scripture mislead the church.

Genesis 9–10: The Hamitic Curse

The so-called "Hamitic curse" and the resultant inferiority (servitude) of the black race has been used to prohibit interracial relationships. The pronouncement that Canaan was to be a "servant of servants" unto his brothers has been used to support color-based, that is black, slavery and marital segregation.

An urban missionary sought an explanation as to why he was asked to instruct his black youth not to date any white campers. He reasoned that a blanket "no dating" policy would be more acceptable than singling out his youth. The camp director responded that he simply believed that God never intended for the descendants of the three sons of Noah to intermarry.

Accurate interpretation of a text requires an examination of a text within its context. First, Genesis 9 never addresses the subject of marriage but rather the unity of humanity. After the flood the world was populated from Noah and his three sons, Shem, Ham, and Japheth (Genesis 9:18–19). Second, the curse was pronounced upon Canaan (Ham's son) and his descendents, not Ham (Genesis 9:25–27). The

Scriptures attest to the sin of the Canaanites and their consequent judgment when Joshua led Israel into the Promised Land (Genesis 15:16; 18:32; Leviticus 18; Joshua 9:15–19, 22–27).[6]

In conclusion, this text does not address the question of marriage. It does clearly teach that all of mankind is united at the family tree trunk of Noah and his three sons.

Genesis 11: Separation of Languages

Some contend that, when God confused the people's languages in Genesis 11, He separated the races. The modern movement toward one world is identified with the unity described in Genesis 11. Anything that promotes the one-world system, such as intermarriage, is considered contrary to God's will.

The text clearly teaches that God's concern was the self-reliance of the people and their plan of building a city unto heaven (idolatry), contrary to the will of God (cf. Genesis 11:3–6). Again, marriage is not an issue in the text.

God stepped into human history and stopped a human project by confusing the languages of the people and scattering them. This divine division robbed the people of the strength of a unified effort. Thus an ungodly plan was halted by divine intervention. God still, at times, intervenes to stop ungodly people from accomplishing unbiblical goals, but this has no application to Christians forming unions in obedience to and for the purpose of glorifying God.

Rather than segregating believers, the New Testament argues strongly for unity (cf. Ephesians 2:14–21; 3:6–13; 4:1–6). Interracial marriages may provide a visible symbol of oneness in Christ. After all, marriage is one of the symbols of the church (Ephesians 5:22–32).

Furthermore, if the Genesis 11 text is applied to intermarriage it would teach that no two language groups (e.g., Italian, French, German, Zulu, or Swahili), even of the same race, could marry.

Scriptures Forbidding Israel's Intermarriage with Other Nations

Scriptures forbidding the nation of Israel from marrying those of other nations are purported to support the assumption that God is against Christian interracial marriages (Deuteronomy 7:3; 20:16–18; 1 Kings 11:1, 8; Ezra 10:2, 11, 14, 17–18, 44; Nehemiah 13:23, 26).

It is asserted that purity of the races was God's primary motivation for prohibiting Israel's intermarriage with other nations. Therefore Christians should honor God's desire for racial purity by discouraging intermarriage.

Purity of faith, not race, was God's actual concern. The issue was to keep Israel from being drawn into idolatry (Deuteronomy 7:4–6; 1 Kings 11:2–10). God provided guidelines for Israel to marry those from another nation (Deuteronomy 21:10–14). There were interracial marriages within Israel and in the line of Christ (cf. Matthew 1:5). Purity of faith in marriage is consistent with the New Testament prohibition of intimate relationships between believers and unbelievers (cf. 2 Corinthians 6:14–18).

Marriage with "Strange Women" Forbidden

Some strange hermeneutics have concluded that biblical texts forbidding marriage to "strange women" (KJV wording) clearly demonstrate God's displeasure with interracial marriages (Proverbs 2:16; 5:3, 20; 6:24; 7:5; 20:16; 23:27; 27:13; Malachi 2:11). Yet examinations of these texts reveal that they are addressing immoral relationships such as adultery or prostitution and idolatry (Proverbs 2:16–17; 6:24; 23:27; Malachi 2:11–15), and such is reflected in most newer versions. Sexual immorality is sin regardless of the race(s) involved.

Christian unions are a family affair. Brothers and sisters in Christ are entering into a covenant relationship for the purpose of glorifying God together. Does the church dare cast a shadow of immorality over such holy unions?

Numbers 36: Marriage Within the Tribe

It has been asserted that "Numbers 36:6 indicates that people with a closer background have better marriages." The obvious application is that, since individuals from the same race have closer backgrounds, intermarriage is wrong.

Godly counsel requires an accurate interpretation and application of the Scriptures. The Numbers passage is addressing a special situation involving the inheritance of family property (36:1–9; cf. 27:1–11). There was no male through whom the family inheritance could be kept within the family. Zelophehad's daughters upon marriage would transfer the family inheritance to the family represented by their husbands. Therefore to keep the family property at least within the tribe, since it could not be kept within the family, the daughters were to marry within the tribe.

The Numbers passage addressed a unique historical marriage issue. This was a legal issue applied only to Israel. In fact, research has demonstrated that marriages between close relatives have a greater risk of birth defects.

Acts 17: Bounds of Habitation

Acts 17:26–29 has been referenced as support of God's intent to segregate races (cf. Deuteronomy 32:8). It is argued that since God has established the bounds, the national boundaries, man should not destroy these boundaries through intermarriage.

The passage is actually arguing for the unity of humanity. Please note that the passage speaks of a common ancestry or creation, for God has "made of one blood all nations of men" (Acts 17:24–27 KJV; "of one man," NIV). The unity theme continues by addressing the universal guilt, or sin, of humanity (vv. 29–31; cf. Romans 5:12, 19). The ultimate point of the passage is the universal invitation for all humanity to seek salvation (Acts 17:23, 26–27, 30–31).

Clearly these texts are not addressing marriage but rather the common origin, universal sin, and only hope of salvation for humanity. There are clear and compelling arguments both from Scripture and science that all of humanity is from one blood.[7]

If the text were to be applied to intermarriage, the prohibition would not be inter-color but inter-national. Thus Italian and Swedes, German and Dutch, Japanese and Koreans would be prohibited from marriage.

1 Corinthians 8: Voluntarily Limiting One's Freedom

Some contend that although one may have the biblical freedom to intermarry, that freedom does not make such unions the best (1 Corinthians 6:12; Galatians 5:13; Romans 13:10; 1 Corinthians 9:5–6, 19; 8:13; 10:32). It is believed that exercising one's right to intermarry will hinder one's Christian growth or testimony.

Some conclude that mature Christians will always forgo intermarriage for the success of their ministry. A number of foreign missionaries have told me their conviction that marriage between a missionary and a national would adversely affect the ministry. A black pastoral student from a predominately white Bible college was counseled that if he was to marry a white woman, his ministry would suffer. Following the counsel given, he ended an interracial dating relationship.

Marriage is a choice that should be exercised with great wisdom. The question is, Should believers allow two individuals the freedom to consider the wisdom of their union without judgment from the church? Christian liberty issues, which include interracial marriage, give Christians the freedom to make individual choices without being judged by other Christians (Romans 14:1–10). The Scriptures clearly teach that believers are free to marry in the Lord (1 Corinthians 7:39; 2 Corinthians 6:14–18). Of course, for any union social and spiritual implications of marriage should be weighed before marriage. What is wise in the eyes of one may be unwise in the eyes of another, but some of the unlikeliest looking marriages end up being some of the strongest ones. Time is the only true test of the wisdom of certain choices.

Somewhat confusing is the biblical argument that intermarriage is a stumbling block for weaker Christians (1 Corinthians 8:9–13). I am not sure what proponents of this view are saying. There seem to be at least two possibilities. First is that weaker Christians would be encouraged by the examples of interracial couples to enter such marriages to their own detriment. The second is that a segregated society would cause weaker Christians to reject a religion that supported such unions.

Some mission agencies have believed it to be a wise policy to forbid any marriage between a national and a missionary. Such policies are usually defended on the basis of a genuine concern for the nationals and the cause of Christ. In many countries there are definitely cultural issues to be considered before considering such relationships. Yet we must be careful that our American commitment to segregation does not pervert our thinking on these matters.

The truth of the matter is that the public proclamation of love and inclusion for all who come to Christ and the private segregation, including prohibition of interracial relationships, has caused many to stumble. A missionary told me that when a national man married a missionary woman and came back to America, the national was confused when a supporting church refused to allow the couple in the building. He could not understand how a church could give money to send someone to his country to preach the gospel but refuse to receive him as a brother. This man's disillusionment caused him to stop attending church altogether. I have heard of numerous accounts where the faith of Christians has been severely tested by rules and policies that encouraged or enforced "racial purity" for the good of the "Christian testimony."

The real stumbling blocks, in the biblical sense, are those who have been denied full access into the family by the church seeking to regulate their relationships in an unscriptural manner. Some have concluded that the church is no better than the world and stopped attending church as a result. Others begin attending churches that are doctrinally unsound but that accept interracial relationships.

In conclusion, the Bible does not prohibit intermarriage. Previous misinterpretation of certain biblical texts and the resultant misapplication resulted in the misdirection of the church.

Social Arguments Used Against Interracial Marriage

It seems that the most popular religious opposition to interracial marriage, even to this present time, is that such unions may not be sin but are socially unwise.[8]

Marriage is a serious commitment and should be entered only after serious contemplation. Individuals should honestly consider the challenges that their personalities, cultures, and society may bring to their union. These warnings need to be weighed both by individuals considering such unions and the church as a whole. Of course, that's true of any marriage, and it doesn't automatically rule out cross-cultural marriages.

Warning: Love Is Blinding

The understanding that God does not disapprove of interracial marriages for racial reasons has blinded some to obvious character problems with their relationships. Being married interracially myself, individuals sometimes seek my advice when considering such a union.

A young couple came seeking my approval of their interracial relationship. Discovering that the young man was possessive and abusive, I confronted the couple that they were not ready for marriage. The problem was not color but character.

Family Rejection

The divorce statistics attest to the challenges married couples are facing today. Many believe that marriage is difficult enough without the added stress of possible rejection of family, friends, and community. In *Mixed Messages: Responding to Interracial Marriages,* Fred Prinzing gives an honest account of his journey from shock to acceptance of his family's blending through the interracial marriages of two of his children.

Prinzing recalled, "Mark dropped his bombshell. . . . 'I'm dating a girl over here,' he told each family member separately. 'Let's just say that Granddad wouldn't approve.' None of us needed any further explanation. Mark was dating a black woman!"[9]

Some Christian families struggle, at least at the emotional level, with welcoming interracial unions in their family or circle of friends. The family unit is very important. Sometimes an interracial couple will be rejected by one or both spouses' families. Creating a new family at the cost of total loss of prior family relationships should be done only after careful and prayerful contemplation. It can be argued that parents are biblically wrong when they reject a relationship simply because it is interracial. Yet the couple can help the transition by demonstrating patience and understanding. Seeking to get to know the partner's parents, listening to their concerns, and prayerfully attempting to address any legitimate concerns demonstrates maturity.

Couples who are in this situation should continue to show love and honor to parents. That would include remembering birthdays, anniversaries, and other important family traditions. Wise ones will learn to express gratitude for the positive benefits seen in the spouse that are the result of the home in which he or she was raised. Exposing parents to sound literature and successful intermarriages may be part of a divine process in bringing mental and emotional change.

A couple must never forget the power of God in reconciling relationships. Husband and wife should both passionately seek daily personal spiritual growth. Likewise there should be regular prayer for God to knit the families together by His love.

The above ideas do not guarantee that a family will accept intermarriage. Yet couples who follow this advice make themselves available to God as instruments of healing. The Prinzings are living illustrations of the fact that God may use intermarriage to enlarge the hearts of extended family.

Social Rejection

Certainly people who contemplate interracial relationships need to be mature enough to handle varied negative reactions from others. They will get the disapproving stares in the mall or church. Statements from the pulpit intended to be positive about one race may be offensive to one spouse. Whenever hate groups are in an area, there is always the possibility that an interracial marriage may become a target of their outrage. A couple must have a commitment to each other and a resolve to face such challenges in a Christlike spirit to avoid the undoing of their relationship by outside influences.

Relationships are unhealthy when real issues are not addressed. Fragile is the union where problems such as pride, selfishness, or even adultery cannot be addressed because the smoke screen of racial incompatibility clouds the real issues. Couples considering marriage need a commitment and practice of resolving differences by addressing specific issues rather than hiding behind racial generalities.

Successful marriages require two people who are committed to each other regardless of the external challenges that test them. They know how to find healthy resolutions to the inevitable interpersonal conflicts as well.

Cultural Differences

Another social argument discouraging interracial marriages is that the cultural differences are too great to overcome. Individuals' aesthetic preferences, entertainment, food, dress, and financial, intellectual, and spiritual tastes and values greatly affect emotional closeness. The question is whether racial difference alone creates a cultural divide too wide to bridge.

The stain of racial segregation sometimes colors our personalities in ways we don't realize. It is possible for two individuals to bring society's war, i.e., politics, heroes, history, and superiority/inferiority, into the relationship. Relationships may degenerate because individuals are more identified with an outside group, those of their own race, than with each other.

Cultural compatibility within marriage is an advantage. However, one should acknowledge that similar backgrounds are not always color- or race-coded. A black raised in the inner city of Harlem and a black raised on an Iowa farm have different backgrounds. A black and a white raised in the same middle-class suburban town may have similar cultural backgrounds.

Children Without a Race

Yet another social argument against interracial marriages is that the children will be without a race and brought into a stressful environment. A segregated society may scar a child in many ways. The questions about interracial parentage and possible rejection by peers may leave one with a deep sense of loneliness. Extended family on one or both sides may reject or unknowingly create an atmosphere that says loudly to the child, "You do not belong in our family."

Questions of heritage may leave a child from a blended family confused as to who he is historically. Should the child embrace one parent's heritage, usually the minority's? Such a choice could pit him against the other parent in the "my race is better than yours" game. This may become a greater problem if the child is raised in a single culture community that exalts its superiority above all others. The historic racism of America can evoke strong emotions within a child from a blended family as he seeks to identify with one group while denouncing the other.

Racial categories defy sound reasoning. If your great-grandmother was Native American, one grandfather Italian, and your father African-American, who are you? It is interesting how over the years an attempt to protect the purity of the "white gene pool" has forced individuals to identify with an individual racial group contrary to science and logic. Ever since slave masters impregnated slaves the practice has been to identify the offspring with the slaves, or blacks. Have you ever wondered why blacks span the color scale from ebony black to a slightly tanned look? Or why the hair ranges from a coarse and kinky texture to long and straight? A truly "pure race" would be hard to find in America.

Parents have sought to help children from blended families over-

come these challenges in several ways. First some parents emphasize one's Christian identity above any ethnic identity. Second, human history is emphasized, beginning with a common ancestor,
Adam. Third, learning the historic struggle of racism and those with
the courage to oppose it helps children to realize that their struggle
is not new. Fourth, exposure to historic heroes of blended ancestry
both from past and present history gives children role models. Fifth,
parents can discuss the ethnic background of both parents and teach
the child that he shares both. Sixth, many parents seek to raise their
children in a cross-cultural community, school, and/or church. Sev-
enth, parents can fervently pray that God would help the child to
value God's approval above all and that he would understand God's
love and plan for his life. Ultimately each child must decide how he
will respond to his environment. All or a combination of these strategies should prove helpful for children of blended families trying to
understand where they fit.

Blended Families Don't Fit

A potential couple's desire to protect their children from the abuses
of a segregated society and church may cause some to avoid interracial marriage. It's not just the children who are faced with some
emotional challenges. How should a white mother respond when her
child is considered to be solely African American because of the father's color? Or what about the assumption that you must be baby-
sitting these children whose color verifies that you could not be their
parent? If such an assumption can create a challenge for parents who
adopt cross-culturally, what must a natural parent feel? It is understandable how someone seeking to address the child's parent might
overlook a parent whose color is considerably different from the
child's. But how does such action make the parent feel? Adults should
be better prepared to handle such things, and such issues certainly
should be considered before entering a marriage.

Blended families may face some unique challenges, but they are
not insurmountable. Other couples believing their marriage to be
sanctioned by God chose to trust their children's future to Him. Science attests to the fact that all of humanity is of one blood. The assumed "great differences" between races are actually very small.
Webster's dictionary defines *race* as

1. any of the different varieties of mankind, mainly the Caucasoid, Mongoloid, and Negroid groups, distinguished by kind of hair, color of skin, etc. 2. Any geographical, national, or tribal ethnic grouping 3. Any group of people having the same ancestry or the same habits, ideas, etc.

In *One Blood,* Ken Ham discusses this point.[10] Many blended families, including interracial marriages and cross-racial adoptions seek to expose their children to a broader view of life than a superior monocultural perspective.

History and ethnic history should be taught children from a wholistic view. Accurate history will attest to the fact that while many, yes the majority, of whites supported slavery and segregation, there were whites who opposed such practices. White abolitionists and participants in the Underground Railroad must be acknowledged. Taking the broader view of history helps one to make truth and error, justice and injustice rather than race the issues around which to unite and divide.

Some blended families will look to the church for a place to call home. The question is whether the church can create an alternative culture. Can this "chosen people [and] . . . holy nation" (1 Peter 2:9) create an environment where Christians, even from blended families, sense an identity not known in secular society?

The Possibility of a Limited Ministry

Finally, some discourage interracial marriage on the basis that such marriages will limit a couple's ministry for the Lord. The reasoning is that society, and in many cases the church, will not accept leadership from such couples.

Leadership from an intermarried couple is a concern for some ministries. After my interracial marriage I was denied admission to a fundamental seminary. My denial was based upon the seminary leadership's assumption that, due to my marriage, I would not be able to pastor a church in their fellowship. Therefore, it would be fruitless to educate me.

Only God really knows the scope of your ministry. Just because men, even religious men, reject your ministry does not mean you are wrong. Consider the ministry of Jesus Christ and His rejection by the leaders of His day! Yet Christians desiring to effectively serve God should consider the impact of marriage on their ministry.

Part of an interracial married couple's ministry may be to lead the church toward the biblical model of oneness. Change usually comes at a cost. Many Christians look back on their own rejection and exclusion of fellow Christians on the basis of race with great embarrassment. The struggle still exists, but many ministries honestly desire cross-cultural, even interracial, leadership to provide a visible symbol of their commitment to the unity of the body of Christ.

Since our marriage I have served two churches as senior pastor and a Bible college as president. Presently I am an elder at a local church that is sending me to pastor a local cross-cultural church while continuing as president of the college. I have a very demanding public speaking schedule, including churches, schools, colleges, seminaries, and national conferences. I serve on a number of boards, have written numerous articles including a monthly column for the *Indianapolis Star,* and had a book published. We have six children; two are adopted, fulfilling a passion of my wife's. Although there is always room to do more, my wife and I have had a very active and full schedule in serving the Savior.

Directives for the Church

The church as the "pillar and ground of truth" needs to gives clear direction to the people of God concerning interracial marriage. The pulpit is commanded to proclaim the mind of God to the people of God (1 Peter 4:10–11). If such unions are sin, they need to be prohibited and repented as a prerequisite for a proper relationship with God and the church. If these unions are personal decisions, the church needs to create an environment where racially blended families are welcome.

The Big Picture

Premarital counsel is good for any couple considering marriage. Biblical counsel must be founded upon the clear teaching of the Word of God and godly wisdom. The following are some scriptural principles concerning interracial relationships. First, the Bible teaches that all of mankind originates from one couple, Adam and Eve. The human family survived and multiplied after the worldwide flood through Noah and his three sons. God divided the human family through confusion of languages.

God chose, during the old covenant, to entrust His Word and the Messiah's lineage to the nation of Israel. Israel was neither morally nor racially pure. Note the family tree inclusion of Rahab and Ruth (Matthew 1:5). If God did not require a racially pure lineage for Christ, does it not seem rather arrogant for the church to demand such of Christians?

The church age represents a time period when the people of God are transitioned from ethnic separation, i.e., Israel and other nations, to unity. The church is composed of born-again believers from all nations and ethnic groups. We are one in Christ (1 Corinthians 12:12–13; Galatians 3:28; Ephesians 2:11–22; Acts 17:26–31). The Word of God is committed to the church as a whole (Acts 10:15, 28, 43; 13:1; Galatians 2:11–14; 1 Corinthians 10:32). The Scriptures forbid marriage between believers and unbelievers (1 Corinthians 7:39), but the New Testament Scriptures on marriage do not prohibit interracial marriage. Ethnic diversity is not addressed in these texts. The church should devote more energy to seeking to maintain unity in the one body of Christ.

So called mixed marriages occurred in the Scriptures. Some biblical illustrations of intermarriages include Joseph and Asenath (Genesis 41:45), Moses and the Cushite (Numbers 12:1), Rahab and her Jewish husband (Matthew 1:5), Ruth and Kilion (Ruth 1:2–5), and Ruth and Boaz (Ruth 4:13). Timothy, the recipient of two New Testament books, was the child of an interracial marriage (Acts 16:1).

Marriage: A Covenant Agreement

Marriage is a lifetime commitment and should not be entered without serious preparation. Christians considering marriage should desire the will of God above everything (Romans 12:1–2).

Christian living, including marriage, requires the grace of God. Individuals considering marriage should be mature in the faith, because mature Christians are better prepared to handle the inevitable difficulties of life. The church should encourage the saints to seek personal maturity. A good scale to measure spiritual growth is found in 2 Peter 1:5–9.

A mature couple welcomes godly counsel (Proverbs 1:5). The

church should provide counsel from families who have developed godly wisdom over years of marriage. During counsel a couple must seek to communicate about every issue that will affect their lives and ministry (Ephesians 4:15–16). This includes finances, family planning, childrearing, church involvement, and cultural differences.

Couples should seek God's guidance through every phase of counseling with a commitment to do His will (Ephesians 4:17–32). Counsel should be approached with the understanding that during counsel something may be discovered that would warrant delaying or even calling a wedding off.

Conclusion

The church must correctly communicate the truth that the Bible does not forbid interracial marriage. Premarital counseling that addresses both biblical and social issues should be encouraged and provided. The church should seek to be a haven for all God's people. As my pastor says, we want the church on earth to reflect what the church in heaven looks like (Revelation 7:9).

DISCUSSION STARTER QUESTIONS

1. When you started reading this article, would you have said your view of interracial marriage was: (1) It's probably wrong; (2) It's probably acceptable but socially unwise or bad for ministry; (3) As long as the couple has godly counsel, it's as legitimate as any other marriage? After reading this article, how would you summarize the objections and their answers?

2. Look up some of the Scripture passages discussed in this chapter as examples for or against interracial marriage. Do they address this issue? If so, how do they answer it?

3. What would you say, based on Scripture used in this article or other passages you're aware of, is God's view on interracial marriage? What is your church/ministry's stated or unstated view? What are the ramifications of this issue on the church and on the culture?

PART TWO

UNITY BETWEEN CLASSES IN THE CHURCH

CHAPTER EIGHT

DISMANTLING CLASS BARRIERS:

Can the Church Avoid Wealth-Based Prejudice?

LARRY MERCER

Are you in the upper, middle, or lower class of your community?

I know you are probably thinking, *That's a personal question.* Well, it is a personal question. But the way you interpret and respond to the question of class may say more about the condition of your heart than about your income level or the size of your bank account. Do you make value judgments about yourself or other people based on class? Do you choose whom you worship with based on their class?

Why is it important to answer that question? *Every believer has a powerful opportunity to illustrate to those who watch his life that obedience to Christ transcends culture and class preferences.*

Social class is amoral. It is neither good nor bad. It could be the result of one of a number of circumstances: being born into a wealthy or poor family, experiencing personal hardship, or hard work. So you should not assign value to people based on their social class.

Is it wrong to be more comfortable worshiping with people in the same economic class as you? No. In the same way that class is amoral, the income level of those we worship with is amoral.

The Scripture does not prescribe for us the income level of the people with whom we choose to worship. So it would be inappropriate to suggest that people who worship with people in the same social class as they are always do so in violation of Scripture.

We should ask ourselves two key questions: (1) *How do I feel about and treat others who are not in the same class as I am?* (2) *Do I allow social class to influence where and with whom I worship?*

Class Limitations Hurt the Church's Testimony

Unfortunately, for some believers their class is not only a reference to their economic status, it is the mark of how they evaluate their personal significance. It forms the basis for how they evaluate *all* their professional and spiritual relationships.

Why do I make such a strong statement? Take a drive with me to two different churches, the "Prosperity Community Church" and the "Church of the Financially Challenged." Let's see what we learn from these two very different churches about the people who make up their memberships.

"Prosperity Community Church" is located in a very nice neighborhood and has exuberant worship services. If you want to hang out with people who are successful financially, it is the place to be. One glance at the cars in the parking lot outside this church or the quality of the suits and dresses of those entering the sanctuary gives a very clear signal. It appears that those who worship inside this church are doing OK financially, and many appear to be wealthy, in terms of their bank accounts.

On the other hand, at "Church of the Financially Challenged," although it has just as strong a commitment to Christ and an equally exuberant worship service, the attendees look very, very different. *The worshipers at this church appear to have a much more desperate need for God's help to make it through each day.* Their cars could easily find their place on the local used car lot, and their suits and dresses look like they came from the discount rack at the local thrift store. Instead of financial "success," their life focus is simply surviving the next day's call from the bill collectors.

So by now maybe you are beginning to make a value judgment. If your background or present circumstances afford you a parking spot on the lot of a church like the "Prosperity Community Church," you may be tempted to turn up your nose at the persons you encounter who don't "dress for success," "drive for success," or have an "address for success." If you are from the "other side of the tracks" and attend the "Church of the Financially Challenged," you may have limited material resources, and those who have great wealth may represent the bad side of materialism to you, which means you are judging a person based socially on social class. When we engage in the judgment of a person's value based on economic status, we participate in a destructive process that limits the full expression of all the implications of the gospel.

There you have it—the barrier of classism exists in the church.

Classism in the church is a very real challenge to the authentic message of the gospel. Unfortunately, the church is sometimes confused about the importance of class. This is evidenced by a tendency of some to equate spiritual maturity with financial success and of others who make the automatic assumption that if a person has great wealth he has compromised his commitment to Christ.

So which person is, inherently, more spiritual? Is the person with less, in terms of earthly possessions, more spiritual? Or does the person with more, by material standards, have a closer walk with God? The answer is simple: Neither. The Scripture teaches and illustrates a very powerful spiritual principle: *Christ transcends class and culture.*

Therefore, the expression of our commitment to Christ must transcend class and culture. Our spirituality is not defined by social class or cultural background. Spirituality is reflected through our faith and obedience *in* our class and culture. "Prosperity Community Church" and "Church of the Financially Challenged" are fictitious in this story, but the tension is a very common experience for believers every week in churches throughout the community.

When Class Divides, Christ's Name Is Compromised

It is a familiar scene. Different names and faces, but very similar circumstances exist for the participants of the average worship service on a Sunday morning. It is a commonly accepted sociological conviction that people from similar economic, educational, and ethnic backgrounds are more comfortable worshiping together than with people who are different. That may be "comfortable," but the question we need to ask ourselves is, *Does that reflect the model from Scripture?*

In some instances a case could be made that it is not only natural for people of similar economic levels to worship and serve together; it is the most effective way to meet the spiritual needs of people. One example normally offered is that a person who has been homeless and doesn't have the type of clothing traditionally worn at a Sunday morning worship service wouldn't be comfortable in a typical worship setting. At least that example focuses on the comfort level not of the wealthy worshipers but of the person who finds himself in a challenging economic situation. There should be only one reason that a ministry experience is exclusively focused on people of one economic or social class—it promotes the best possible worship experience for all.

Even in those instances the ultimate goal should be to create a community of believers that represents all economic and social classes, because that is what the body of Christ looks like. The intentional exclusion of people from a different background simply on the basis of their economic level compromises the testimony of Christ. You say, "Would anyone intentionally exclude someone from worship because of their social class?" I wish the answer was no. But we have not reached heaven yet, and the negative impact of classism sometimes takes our hearts places that don't honor God.

Unfortunately, that happens all too often. Let me give two different examples from a number of personal observations of acceptance or rejection based on external characteristics in the church during more than twenty years of ministry. My wife and I walked into a church filled with people who looked very different from us in terms of ethnic and class background. The cold stares and pulpit comments made it clear to us we were not welcome in this church service. We stayed through the entire service, but at the benediction we walked down the large pathway the usher showed us and hurried out. Later in the week I had a chance to talk with one of the members of that church. He was embarrassed about the way his church had received my family and the guests we had taken along with us to his church. His words were a window into the heart of many people in his home church: "Our church doesn't feel comfortable accepting people who are different from us in terms of culture and class." I appreciated his candor and apology. He said what many people feel every Sunday they enter the sanctuary of their church. I wish that were the only personal example of classism in the church I have personally experienced.

But is this only a problem across ethnic lines? No, it's not. Let me tell you about New Jerusalem Community Church (name changed). This church was in a community where most of the people were from the same ethnic background I am. I walked into New Jerusalem Community Church and immediately admired the stained glass windows and velvet-covered pews and enjoyed the beauty of the environment. My initial impressions were that it was probably a wonderful place to worship. Then I talked to the deacon conducting the tour, who let me know that the church made sure the people in the neighborhood who were not able to appreciate and take care of the beautiful furniture were discouraged from attending. All of a sudden the beautiful environment lost its attraction. The church had placed its décor over the privilege of discipleship of people from the same ethnicity, but a different class.

But what about the argument some people make that it is natural to worship primarily with people like you? Yes, it is true that it is natural for people to worship and serve with people who are from the same economic level—but isn't the church supposed to be *su-pernatural*? In many situations, while it is more convenient and comfortable for people who are in the same economic class to worship and serve God together, it is a poor reflection on the power of God to bring people together based largely on class and economic status. When Jesus walked on this earth, He interacted with people of all economic levels and cultural backgrounds.

When the church includes only people who are on the same economic level, we are missing an opportunity to demonstrate that the gospel of Jesus Christ unifies classes.

The distinction that believers sometimes make, to determine value and significance based on culture and class is outside of the will of God. Some homogenous groups are simply the result of community demographics; others are the result of conscious congregational choice. That leads to the observation that some homogenous worship groups are often inconsistent with the models presented in the New Testament.

People of All Classes Are Equal at the Cross

From the earliest days of the church, up to the return of Jesus Christ, a close examination of the Scripture shows God's heart for people of all races, cultures, and economic levels: "You are all sons of God through faith in Christ Jesus, for all of you who were baptized into Christ have clothed yourselves with Christ. There is neither Jew nor Greek, slave nor free, male nor female, for you are all one in Christ Jesus" (Galatians 3:26–28). Although people of different classes may dress differently, talk differently, and live in different places, they are equal in worth and value in the eyes of God, at the cross of Jesus Christ.

During a recent flight to Spokane, Washington, I saw a lot of beautiful terrain. From my window seat I could see the outline of valleys, hills, mountains, and rivers. It was interesting to me that the higher the plane went the more level all the landforms appeared. At some points mountains and rivers seemed to be the same height. Their levels faded into an image of unity. I take great comfort in knowing that, as God looks down from heaven, He does not see distinctions in our value to Him based on the "net worth" of those who follow Him. Class distinctions are blurred from heaven's vantage point.

In the same way, the more we see people around us from a heavenly viewpoint, the smaller our focus will be on the material wealth and the social status of the person. We should ask ourselves the question, *What difference should this make in the way we relate to each other as believers?* Our personal relationship with Jesus Christ should create a powerful platform for relationships with other people, no matter where they fall on the social ladder. So what difference should that make in our social gatherings?

The Gospel Should Build a Bridge Between the Classes

Jesus illustrated the importance of holding inclusive gatherings in His teachings in the Gospels: "When you give a luncheon or dinner, do not invite your friends, your brothers or relatives, or your rich neighbors; if you do, they may invite you back and so you will be repaid. But when you give a banquet, invite the poor, the crippled, the lame, the blind, and you will be blessed. Although they cannot repay you, you will be repaid at the resurrection of the righteous"

(Luke 14:12–14). Here Jesus provides a clear message. Reach out to people who are different from you and don't exclusively support and fellowship with those who can reciprocate. If the church follows the model Jesus presented in Luke 14, it will create gatherings that represent people from all social and economic levels.

The bridges between economic classes don't always have to include actual weekly fellowship and service in the same location. The bridges between classes could be focused on occasional shared opportunities for spiritual growth. There are a number of instances in the New Testament when those who had resources were given the opportunity to demonstrate a spirit of sacrifice and service to less fortunate believers. Acts 5–6 offers a concrete picture of the powerful community of believers in the New Testament church. It is clear that all who placed their personal faith in Jesus Christ had the opportunity to share their strengths and advantages with those who had limited resources.

Motives Are Foundational

The New Testament communicates a powerful principle that levels the economic "playing field" in the eyes of God:

> My brothers, as believers in our glorious Lord Jesus Christ, don't show favoritism. Suppose a man comes into your meeting wearing a gold ring and fine clothes, and a poor man in shabby clothes also comes in. If you show special attention to the man wearing fine clothes and say, "Here's a good seat for you," but say to the poor man, "You stand there" or "Sit on the floor by my feet," have you not discriminated among yourselves and become judges with evil thoughts? (James 2:1–4)

This passage makes it clear that we should resist any tendency to give people preferential treatment based on their economic or social class. In the eyes of God, the person dressed in fine clothes has no greater significance than the person who cannot afford to get his clothing dry-cleaned every week. In fact, the text suggests that if we make distinctions between people of differing economic levels, without regard to their spiritual status, our motives are in question.

Church should be the place where people are given dignity and respect because they are created in the image of God, period. Educational level, economic status, and cultural background are all important personal characteristics that can dramatically impact a person's life experience, but they should not exclusively determine "rank" in the family of God. Leaders have an excellent opportunity to serve people in the church from all types of backgrounds. That is why if the leadership group has spiritually mature representation from all economic levels it can be more effective in efforts to be sensitive and responsive to the needs of all people in the church.

Churches Can Transcend Class and Culture

So what can churches do to move beyond the easy classifications of the bank book? Let me review a few important scirptural themes and then make some practical suggestions.

- God made all men in His image, and rich and poor have a common bond (Genesis 1:27; Proverbs 22:2).
- God has a special concern for the poor and disadvantaged and properly gained wealth (Exodus 22; Psalm 146; Proverbs 10:4).
- God grants some the power to make wealth (Deuteronomy 8:18).
- Scripture warns about the perils of wealth and poverty from irresponsibility (Proverbs 24:30–34; Matthew 19:16–24).
- Personal wealth can be a great ministry tool (Acts 5; 1 Timothy 6:17–19).
- Persons both of poverty and of wealth hold high positions before God (James 1:9–10).

1. Teach a scriptural perspective of poverty and wealth.

There is a great deal of ignorance among believers about the significance of wealth in a person's spiritual life. Some people believe that the presence of wealth is always an evidence of God's blessing. Wealth may simply be the result of being born into a family with resources or being fortunate enough to have the right stocks at the right time. It will be helpful for believers to understand that wealth is amoral. It is neither good (moral) nor bad (immoral). The morality of our lives is not defined by our wealth; it is demonstrated as we make daily decisions in our walk with God.

2. *Cultivate respect for people based on their devotion to God rather than their financial portfolio.*

Unfortunately, there is a perception in our society that a person's economic status determines the level of respect he or she should receive. Jesus made a conscious decision to forgo accumulation of material wealth so He could focus on His mission for being on the earth. His life and influence are examples of the fact that impact doesn't necessarily follow wealth. He made an eternal impact, although He would have been considered very poor even by the standards of His day.

3. *Create opportunities for believers to experience mutual growth opportunities across economic levels.*

Believers who are poor in material goods have a lot to teach those who are materially wealthy. One of the reasons Jesus said that "it is easier for a camel to go through the eye of a needle than for a rich man to enter the kingdom of God" is that when you have access to resources, there is a subtle temptation to trust riches rather than God. Poverty or lack of guaranteed resources conversely can force a more consistent focus on the source of support and resources. People who know they have nowhere to turn have a wonderful incentive to pray and ask God for help.

4. *Encourage people who have been blessed with more resources and material possessions than they need to share some of their excess with people less fortunate than they are.*

Communicating and designing ministries that encourage believers to share their excess with other believers provides an excellent way to present a biblical perspective concerning class and culture. Obviously, savings and investments are important outlets for placing the resources God gives us. But helping people cultivate a practice of sensitivity to meeting the needs of others is a special blessing we can enable them to experience.

5. *Allow people on all economic levels to fill positions of leadership in the church.*

Leadership positions in many local churches are held, regrettably almost exclusively, by people who have achieved the appearance of "financial success." If that financial success is simply an extension of their spiritual maturity and dedication to Christ and their local church, it is a well-deserved appointment to a position of leadership. It is safe to assume that in most ministry situations the people appointed to leadership positions deserve those positions of leadership because of their character, not simply their "financial success," but perhaps churches need to be more intentional here.

The point of this discussion is not to challenge the credibility of people currently in positions of leadership, but to highlight the fact that committed and mature people who don't have a lot of material resources have a great deal to offer local church ministries by serving in leadership positions. A person with limited financial resources has a perspective on challenge and difficulty that can help the church demonstrate compassion and sensitivity in an authentic way. Search for people in your congregation from all economic levels who have demonstrated a love for God and a commitment to the ministry of the church.

6. *Through teaching and personal counsel, address unspiritual expressions of classism when you are exposed to it.*

When you see other believers display unhealthy attitudes toward financial resources, use your relationship with them as a platform to teach and encourage them. Help them understand their opportunity to bring glory to God through the way they handle their money and other material possessions.

7. *Develop personal relationships with people on all economic levels so you can experience the benefits of learning from each other.*

Don't limit your network of friends to people who live in the same type of neighborhood or drive the same type of car you do. God can teach you some very important spiritual principles from mature believers who have more and those who have less than you do.

You can learn a deeper level of dependence and trust from believers who have learned to watch God literally "provide their daily bread." A relationship with someone who has to depend on God on that level could demonstrate God's goodness in a fresh new way. Don't look down on another person because he or she has limited resources, or you could miss some very special spiritual lessons.

On the other hand, a believer who has learned to share from his abundance instead of hoarding resources could be a great model. Perhaps an even greater peril than poverty is misuse of God's provision. Watch those who have learned to hold on to their wealth loosely. You will learn that it is possible to have access to everything in the world and still be "poor in spirit."

This poem by an unknown author illustrates in a powerful way the fact that the way we treat people who are different from us is a window into the condition of our hearts.

The Cold Within

Six humans trapped by happenstance
In dark and bitter cold.
Each one possessed a stick of wood,
Or so the story's told.

Their dying fire in need of logs,
The first woman held hers back.
For on the faces around the fire,
She noticed one was black.

The next man looking cross the way,
Saw one not of his church,
And couldn't bring himself to give
The fire his stick of birch.

The rich man just sat back and thought
Of the wealth he had in store,
And how to keep what he had earned
From the lazy, shiftless poor.

The black man's face bespoke revenge
As the fire passed from his sight,

For all he saw in his stick of wood
Was a chance to spite the white.

The last man of this forlorn group
Did naught except for gain
Giving only to those who gave
Was how he played the game.

The logs held tight in death's still hands
Was proof of human sin.
They didn't die from the cold without,
They died from—The Cold Within.
                              Author Unknown

DISCUSSION STARTER QUESTIONS

1. How wide a range of income and education levels is represented in your church? Is the profile of your church membership a function of community demographics or congregational choice?
2. Are the people who are in leadership positions in your church or ministry a good representation of your membership or clientele? If not, how can you intentionally include a fuller representation?
3. Why is financial success such an important indicator of personal significance to Americans? To what extent has the evangelical church bought into this facet of "the American dream"? What aspects of this are good, and how can the church transcend what isn't good in that measure?

CHAPTER NINE

PEOPLE JUST LIKE ME:

Does the Bible Give Us Freedom to Build Deliberately Homogeneous Churches?

ROD COOPER

There is a story about an American Indian and an Anglo brother walking together on a downtown street. Cars were going by, honking their horns, a plane flew overhead, and street vendors loudly hyped the need to buy their goods. In the midst of all these distractions, the American Indian stopped and said, "Did you hear that?"

"Hear what?" asked the white man.

"That cricket," said the American Indian.

"Come on," said the Anglo. "You have got to be kidding—in the midst of all of these distractions and noise, you tell me you hear a cricket?"

The two men happened to be standing by a park. Casually the American Indian went over to a bush and pulled back the branches. Sure enough, there was a cricket singing his song.

The white man said in disbelief, "You must have the best hearing of any person alive!"

The American Indian replied, "No, my hearing is no better than yours. Let me show you what I mean." He reached into his pocket and pulled out a handful of coins and tossed them up into the air. When the coins began to clank against the concrete sidewalk, people stopped all up and down the city block to see where the coins were landing. The American Indian then said, "You see, my hearing is no better than theirs, but the difference is in what we are listening for."

Homogeneity Versus Heterogeneity

It would seem that the same is true concerning the issue of the nature of the church and church growth. There are various perspectives, but when all is said and done, there really are two key perspectives.

One perspective is called the HUP principle, which stands for "Homogenous Unit Principle." The word *homogenous* literally means "of the same or similar kind of nature." Advocates of this position seem to believe that the world is a vast mosaic with each piece sorting itself to be with others like it to form a homogenous unit defined by its language, ethnic, economic, or other unique characteristics. This principle states, "People like to become Christians without crossing racial, linguistic, or class barriers."[1] Even though advocates of this perspective would argue it has biblical merits, this writer is hard pressed to find such a basis. It would seem that regarding ethnically homogenous churches, this philosophy is based more on a sociological principle than a biblical one. The driving ideas behind this type of philosophy are couched in the need for effective evangelism and the maintaining of the group's "cultural" identity. Although this seems quite noble, even biblical, it perpetuates a "separate but equal" mentality within the church, which can subtly maintain racist and separatist attitudes toward the socioeconomically deprived in the name of bringing people to Christ.

There is no argument that evangelism is one of the key purposes of the church. Yet the very nature and impact of the church upon society is evidenced in the church's ability to do something society cannot do, namely, have unity in the midst of diversity. Jesus emphasized this unity in John 17 and John 13:34–35.

The New Testament gives no evidence that the church focused on a homogenous mentality of establishing churches according to people groups. Instead, the principle was that of heterogeneity. The word *heterogeneous* means "consisting of dissimilar or diverse ingredients or constituents; mixed" according to Webster's Dictionary. The apostle Paul, in all of his missionary journeys, did not plant one homogeneous church. These churches were made up of poor, rich, young, old, and ethnically diverse people.

It would seem that the homogeneous principle stems more from a pragmatic and sociological approach, whereas the heterogeneous principle centers more upon a biblical and theological basis.

Numerous passages are relevant to the issue of the church being a diverse entity. Two key passages most directly address this issue. One critical passage is Acts 15, centering in on the issue of inclusiveness, and the other is Ephesians 2:14–18, which clearly addresses the nature of the church and the work of Christ in our lives as believers. Let's look at both.

Guess Who's Coming to Church? (Acts 15:1–35)

Acts 15 contains a paradigm shift concerning those who had been in the church and those who were entering. The church up until Acts 15 was predominantly Jewish. Most people who had come to know Jesus Christ had come from a Jewish background. There were a few exceptions, but even they had some connection to Judaism. For instance, the Samaritans were at least half Jewish and understood the rites and rituals of Judaism. In Acts chapter 10 we have the first Gentile convert, Cornelius, who found favor with the Jews because he was willing to accept and even convert to Jewish ways.

In chapter 13, Paul and Barnabas were going on their first missionary journey, and as they traveled throughout Asia Minor their strategy at first was to go to the lost house of Israel. So they went to the synagogues and found themselves being rejected and hostilely treated by their Jewish brethren. Paul declared in Acts 13:46–49 that he was no longer going to use that strategy, but from now on he was going to the Gentiles as well, preaching this radical message of grace.

Sure enough, like a dry spiritual sponge, the Gentiles soaked up the gospel message. At the end of chapter 14, Paul and Barnabas came back to Antioch and began to rehearse the great spiritual awakening that was now taking place among the Gentiles.

Now that Gentiles were coming into the church, some Jewish believers came down from the mother church in Jerusalem and began to contend with Paul and Barnabas about their Gentile converts. They confronted Paul and Barnabas, telling them that the Gentiles could only be saved if they trusted Jesus and also came through the rituals of Moses and Judaism. In chapter 15 verse 2 the writer, Luke, uses the words "sharp dispute and debate," which means they were divided. We have here the possibility of a church split. And like most church fights, this one is cloaked in theological garb.

According to many in the discussion, somehow those Gentiles had to become Jews if they were to be a part of the church. Like most church fights, there was an underlying issue. Possibly the Jews realized that if the gospel spread within the Roman world to the Gentiles, the church might become predominantly Gentile, because there were more of them. The Jews had not always fared well under Gentile rule, and the church at Jerusalem could end up being controlled by Gentiles. There could, then, be some cause for concern about flooding the church with those Gentiles if there were not some controls in force. You see, Paul was "giving away the farm," and they wanted to keep it.

This is a classic power struggle. It is like a new pastor going into a small community church. A group of older, seasoned people has been there for a while, has been in leadership, has built the church to where it is now, and has given time and effort to it. But, all of a sudden, the church begins to grow and new people start coming in. The older leadership becomes threatened because the power base is beginning to shift. They may no longer have the influence they once had in the decision making, and they may lose their place.

It sounds familiar, doesn't it? What is it going to take for the body of Christ to come together? Well, it might mean having to change my opinions where they are questionable theologically or give up some of my stereotypes or give up some control.

Statistics tell us that we have more Jews in this country than in Israel, more blacks than in any other country outside of Nigeria, Africa, more Irishmen than in Ireland, and we are the third largest Spanish-speaking country in the world. According to the latest census figures, one out of four people is a minority.

The neighborhood is changing. It seems that in every issue we face we want to know what the Bible says, but when it comes to church growth and inclusiveness, we all of a sudden become more concerned about sociology than theology. For instance, if a man in the church was committing adultery we would approach him, tell him what the Bible says, and ask him to repent. If he didn't, we would tell him to leave the church until he was ready to repent. This would happen on a number of issues, but when it comes to culture, we all of a sudden jump social.

The Jerusalem Council (Acts 15)

How did the early church settle this dispute concerning those who wanted the Gentiles to trust Christ *and* Judaism? The church had a trial. In this trial, Luke gives us three witnesses or presentations. It is interesting whom he chooses to include in this debate. The first presenter was Peter. He said they needed to go to the Gentiles, which must have shocked the Judaizers. This is the same apostle who was rebuked by Paul when he was in Galatia for trying to separate himself from the Gentiles due to the pressure from the Jews there. This is the same man who had to have a vision to prepare him to go to Cornelius's house to present the gospel. You remember in Acts 10 when Peter was staying with Simon the tanner. Peter got hungry and had a vision of a sheet filled with unclean animals. The first time the sheet appears and a voice says, "Arise, Peter, slay and eat," Peter says, "No way, I don't like chittlins, Lord." The sheet goes up. The second time the sheet appears and the voice says, "Arise, Peter, slay and eat," Peter says, "Never has a ham sandwich passed these lips, Lord." The third time the sheet appears—ever notice how it seems to take Peter three times to get anything? But finally he gets it. God says, "Do not call anything impure that God has made clean."

Peter informs us that we *must not put God in a box.* Peter is telling us that God does the choosing. When God sets a people apart, they are a special people, because God says they belong to Him. God is saying, "Do not put Me in a box—I am bigger than your denomination—I am bigger than your race—I am God and I will decide who gets into the kingdom, not you. My job is the choosing—your job is to get along with those I've chosen."

In fact, Paul and Barnabas in Acts 15:12 back Peter up. They have been on the front lines, and they have seen God working in Gentiles' lives over and over again. The Jerusalem council concluded that Gentiles could be a part of the church without having to become Jews first. The only issues they were to address had to do with a moral issue (immorality) and a liberty issue (eating meat with blood), which could hurt the possibility of future fellowship between Gentiles and Jews. Notice, they were not being asked to stop being Gentiles or completely give up their culture. This passage clearly shows that the church intentionally broke down barriers so that there could be a shift from a strictly homogeneous body to a heterogeneous body.

What We Can Learn from the Sheet

God wanted to show Peter and us that you never know whom He is going to use in your life to change you. God used a vision of a sheet filled with unclean beasts to show Peter this message.

God had to figuratively let a sheet down out of heaven for me so I could change my mind. I had a problem with a certain group—to be blunt, they were Southern white males. I had lived in two Southern cities and did not have the best experiences. Some Southern white guys on my dorm floor in Bible college made fun of black preaching. I was one of just three blacks on the campus. But God has a great sense of humor. You see—I was also in a Bible study with six other men, all white brothers, including one who happened to be a Southern white male. His name was John. Because of some of my negative experiences with the other guys on the floor, I began to miss the Bible study and distance myself from my white brothers, John in particular. I even got the nickname the "Bear" because of my bad attitude.

But one day as I was walking down the hall an arm reached out and pulled me into the room. And there in front of me was John. I was placed on a chair and surrounded by the other members of the Bible study. John looked at me and in that Southern drawl said, "I do not know what is happening to you, Rod—you have shut us out. In fact, if you were to graduate from here today, you couldn't minister to a rock, let alone people. What is the problem? Because you are not leaving here until we get this straightened out."

I looked at him and the others and said, "Who are you to tell me to change?" Then I looked at John and said, "You white people are the problem."

He put his hands on my shoulders and said, "No, Rod, I am not the problem; the white guys bothering you are, and what gives me the right to tell you to change is because I love you—and I am your brother." I broke down in tears and we all began to cry. John and I hugged. On that day, I did not leave a bitter man but I left a better man because of a Christian man who happened to be a Southern white male. God has a way of shaking up our categories and reminding us not to box Him in, because you never know whom He might use in our lives to make a change.

What We Have in Common in Christ

But there is something else we must focus on if we are to have unity in the midst of diversity: We must *recognize that underneath the skin we are the same* (Acts 15:8–9). First of all, *we have the same need.* Notice what Peter points out in these verses. He says, "God, who knows the heart . . . made no distinction between us and them, for he purified their hearts." Peter is pointing out that we can have all the programs, strategies, and ideas for diversity in the church we want, but in reality diversity in the church starts with the heart. Notice that is what God concentrated on—the heart. If there is not a change on the inside, then what we do on the outside has very little consequence.

For diversity and unity in the church to take place, we must have heart surgery. Just recently my brother-in-law, Charlie, had to have bypass surgery for his heart. Four arteries were blocked. They had tried angioplasty, kind of a power-rodding method for cleaning out the arteries, but that did not seem to work. So they performed a quadruple bypass. I learned that during the surgery they also had to give my brother-in-law a blood transfusion. I asked them why. They said that his blood carried impurities and lacked the oxygen content for him to be healthy and for his body to operate effectively. So they needed to give him new blood, clean blood that would be full of oxygen, be free of the impurities of the old blood that clogged up the system, and have the nutrients necessary to keep his system operating smoothly.

When we trusted in Jesus Christ we not only got a new heart, but we got a blood transfusion. Jesus' blood cleansed us from the old impurities of hate and prejudice. We now have all the nutrients from the blood of Jesus to "love one another" as He commanded.

Notice the most important nutrient that we got when we trusted Christ: *We have the same Spirit.* We have the same Spirit who cries out

"Abba Father," the same Spirit who convicts of sin, and the same Spirit who empowers us to do His work—together.

Let me tell you two stories. I was in Ontario, California, doing a men's retreat for a Baptist church. The men were white and from a middle to upper-middle class background. Their idea of camping out was spending the night in an Embassy Suites hotel. But when we had worship, I saw all the trappings of success go. I saw men who began to cry out to God asking for Him to heal their marriages and their relationships with their children and to cleanse them of sin. I saw the Spirit of God moving in their lives and they left different— changed.

The next week I went to speak at a men's retreat in Barbados (somebody has to do it). It was very different. This was a charismatic church, and there was no praise band—we just sang. There were about sixty black men from all different socioeconomic groups. We stayed at a retreat center where it was hot and humid, and the mosquitoes had a feast every night. But I will never forget Sunday morning. We were praying and these men began to cry out before God. They began to ask God for healing concerning their families, their marriages and their children. Men were prostrate on the floor, and others were bowed down on their knees. I saw the Spirit of God moving in their lives and they left changed. One group white, one group black; one in the U.S., the other in Barbados; one group rich, the other group not so rich—but one thing in common: They had the same Spirit whom they had from the same Father. I have noticed that when God moves and His Spirit is at work, classism, racism, and denominationalism are not primary issues but become secondary issues because *we are one in the Spirit and we are one in the Lord.*

Third, *we are saved by the same grace,* as Peter points out in Acts 15:11. Peter is pointing out that we have the same faith in the gospel of Jesus Christ.

The final argument made for diversity and unity in the church is that *we have the same future.* Look at what James, Jesus' half-brother, points out in verses 13–18. As he quotes the prophet Amos, he says God had foreordained there would be diversity in His church. The prophet Amos essentially asserts that God is going to have representatives of *all* people in His church.

Breaking Down the Walls (Ephesians 2:14–18)

This second classic passage clearly articulates that Jesus Christ's death not only brought redemption but established peace between God and man as well as between Jew and Gentile. Dr. Bruce Fong has done a masterful work on the implications of these key verses in his book *Racial Equality in the Church*. Dr. Fong states,

> Basic to the mission of the church is the proclamation of the one-ness that is accomplished by the Gospel. Peace between all men was achieved by the death of Christ and is to be a part of the re-ality of the church in the world. Mutual acceptance does not ar-gue that such cultural or ethnic distinctions are nullified. Rather, it calls for recognition *that such differences are not the priority de-termination of fellowship between Christians* (italics added).[2]

Jesus Christ's death broke down the dividing wall between Jew and Gentile, thus establishing peace and creating "one new man out of the two" (Ephesians 2:15). This "new man" is supernaturally em-powered due to the saving work of Christ and transcends cultural dif-ferences. Christian believers, both Jew and Gentile, have more in common through Christ's love than the differences that kept them apart before conversion. It is our love for one another that opens up for us the opportunity to demonstrate the power of the gospel through our fellowship in community with one another and mutu-ally celebrating the cultural differences brought to the body of Christ.

It is this writer's view that the "dividing wall" (v. 14) does not refer to an actual physical barrier but to the enmity and animosity that existed between Jew and Gentile. What separated Jews and Gen-tiles in history was far more than a physical wall but their hatred and animosity toward one another. They distrusted one another after numerous wars and slavery and subjugation of one over the other at various times in history.

Paul emphasizes that there is now peace between Jew and Gen-tile because of the work of Christ. For those who become part of the community of believers, the hostile attitudes are left behind because of their relationship to Christ and His work on the cross. Now the laws that separated the Jew from the Gentile and the Gentiles' overt disregard for the Jews' laws were broken down through the finished work of Christ. No longer are they to be separated, but they now have become a "new man" together as a result of their newfound faith in Jesus Christ. Even though they retain their ethnic distinction, they become much more and share something in common that is greater than their ethnicity—their salvation in Christ.

If the church is to be a visible representation of the power of God and of heaven and if, according to Revelation 7:9–12, *all* of the saints from *all* cultures and backgrounds are *together* proclaiming the one reason they are together, namely salvation, then it stands to reason reconciliation would be most visibly demonstrated through various cultures and people worshiping together here on earth. The church functions best in community and not some separate-but-equal mentality that brings us together only on special occasions.

Implications for the Church

It seems, based at least on the two passages discussed above, that true salvation breaks down walls and establishes unity between us. The gospel of Christ puts an end to the barriers that separate us. As Dr. Fong states,

> All Christians are one together in Christ and their organization into the Church should depict that essence. There is no theological basis for separating members of Christ's church because of ethnicity or race. . . . The *imago dei* [image of God] calls for mutual respect for each other's humanity with those ethnic features. Such differences call for acceptance not separation.[3]

Salvation and sanctification, which leads to maturity as evidenced in the fruit of the Spirit, would seem to be the keys in building the church and establishing unity within the body of Christ.

The implications for the church seem clear. The mandate of the church is to make disciples regardless of socioeconomic status or ethnic background. According to Matthew 28:18–20 the gospel is to be presented to all *ethne* or "all nations." Evangelism is not exclusively to one group, but to all groups regardless of economic categories, ethnic roots, cultural distinctives, or socioeconomic status. Each group helps make up the vast mosaic of the body of Christ. How else will the world know that "you are my disciples, if you love one another"

(John 13:35) except in the context of community or *koinonia*. A Christocentric philosophy of church growth is based upon our love for one another through mutual acceptance, which will draw people to Christ. A Christocentric philosophy asserts that when we become Christians we have much more in common than differences. Our love for one another is the glue that holds us together—in Christ.

The making of disciples then leads to the second major implication for the church, which is a proper view of sanctification. Sanctification is part of disciple making and is a process whereby the teaching of the Word of God and the power of the Holy Spirit in applying that Word make it possible to love other kinds of Christians and celebrate their cultural contributions to the body of Christ. Also, it is through sanctification that those parts of culture that fit with Christianity can be redeemed and those that do not are put to the side. The lordship of Christ transforms us and allows us to make the necessary changes.

Another key implication is based upon what drives the ministries of the church. If the church is problem-centered or need-oriented, then the focus will be upon the people and therefore anthropological, or man-centered. If the theological center is upon "making disciples," then, like the apostles in Acts 6, leaders will address the needs of the people but not compromise their calling to preach and teach the Word of God. New Testament principles will drive the ministries of the church, and the programs designed to deal with these problems will be theologically based.

Another implication for the church is to embrace a term used by Dr. Bruce Fong: "mutual acceptance." According to Fong, "mutual acceptance is based upon a mutual relationship among all Christians because of a commonness in Christ." Fong says, "The more mixed the congregation is, especially in class and color, the greater its opportunity to demonstrate the power of Christ. A truly interracial, inter-social Christian fellowship, whose members evidently care for one another and bear one another's burdens, is in itself an eloquent witness to the reconciling power of Jesus Christ."[4]

A final implication for the church is that by pursuing one particular ethnic or socioeconomic group there is a subtle message that those not "like us" are not welcome here. As a result of such an emphasis, racism and classism can subtly be propagated in the name of evangelism. Christ has broken down "all walls" and therefore, as people who have the same Savior and same Spirit and are made in the same *imago dei,* worship with one another is possible. It is critical for the church to realize that our unity in the midst of diversity, held together by the love of Christ, shows the power of the gospel in a world of division and racism.

Churches that are not multiethnic can do several things. They can have pulpit exchanges with churches of different ethnic backgrounds. They can have a time of joint worship on a regular basis with those same churches. The sermons of the pastor can strongly reinforce mutual acceptance and speak out against racism and classism.

Finally, churches can hire people of different ethnicities to be on their staff. Colorado Community Church in Colorado is a prime example. This church is predominately white but has two African-American pastors on its staff. One is the pastor of evangelism and regularly preaches from the pulpit. This sharing of leadership with a person of another ethnic background sends a clear message to people that we can indeed minister to one another. This church also has planted a multiethnic church and regularly fellowships together with this new church plant and counts the church plant as one of its campuses— not just another church.

Is it possible to have various ethnicities and classes in a church? As the story of the American Indian and the Anglo brother points out, it all depends on what you are listening for.

DISCUSSION STARTER QUESTIONS

1. What is it about being around people "different from us" that causes so much discomfort? What causes you to feel uncomfortable? What would make you feel comfortable? When you think of the term "separate but equal," what images come to your mind? Is this valid for the church? Why or why not?

2. What kept the early church from splitting into a Gentile church and a Jewish church, according to Acts 15? Did the leadership of the Jerusalem church focus more on culture or on the Word of God in making its decision to include Gentiles in Acts 15?

3. If a sheet were let down in your life to deal with your prejudices, what would it contain? What steps would you take to
   change? What role does sanctification (growing in Christ)
   have in bringing different classes and ethnic groups together
   in Christ?

CHAPTER TEN

THE QUEST FOR BIBLICAL COMMUNITY:

Is It Possible

to Unite

Oral and

Written Cultures?

HENRY LEE ALLEN

Years ago, a popular movie titled *The Gods Must Be Crazy* depicted the story of an African tribesman encountering a soft drink bottle that had fallen on his head from the sky. Apparently, an unseen passenger in a small airplane that flew above this tribesman had foolishly thrown the bottle out of the plane, causing it to fall precipitously upon the head of the unsuspecting African tribal native. What was most interesting about the ensuing plot that developed within this movie, however, was the clash of cultural perspectives it represented.

His nomadic culture had no scientific explanation of the physics that demystify the force of gravity. He had never read about airplanes or manufacturing. Lacking the technologies that could make a machine that flies like a bird riding invisible currents of air, our African protagonist was puzzled about how a strange glass artifact could emerge from the sky and connect with his head! Thus, within his pastoral culture, the default explanation was that the bottle was a sign from the gods who were trying to communicate with him. Picture then this tribesman trying to account for this episode; imagine his predicament in trying to explain this event to an oral culture that had no concepts such as airplane, gravity, and soda bottles.

Culture can exhibit many complexities, but such complications often produce humorous situations. (Many of the best comedians take advantage of this in their comic routines.) The hero of the movie cited above was quite perplexed by a series of events that could have been easily discerned even by most children in a literate, technological society.[1] The rest of the movie depicted how the culture of South African industrial society was a stark, rather vivid contrast to that experienced by our preliterate pastoral citizen. In short, culture shapes our sense of reality; it assigns meanings to the symbolic things we encounter or observe. Culture tells us how to interpret the people, places, events, and phenomena that we experience daily in time and space. Humans cannot exist without some form of culture. Our minds are designed to create and absorb its contents. To make an analogy familiar to those of us who inhabit the computer age, culture is to people what software is to a computer.

Anyone who has watched this humorous movie, *The Gods Must Be Crazy,* can easily perceive that the task of mixing oral and written cultures has many facets. To mix these divergent cultures presupposes a common point of reference, such as language, tradition or history, trade, or proximity. In short, some sort of sociological metric must be found that is agreeable to both cultures. Without such a metric, communication is impossible at worst, somewhat stifled at best.

More than two thousand years ago, Christ Jesus died on the cross and was resurrected to redeem lost humanity. As He conversed with His disciples just before His ascension into heaven, He told them to make disciples of all ethnic or cultural groups. Being God in the flesh, Christ knew fully that His cadre of Jewish disciples would have to encounter various cultural groups to fulfill the Great Commission. Undoubtedly, as members of a literate culture, they would meet persons from oral cultures. The task was to penetrate the full range of cultures with the gospel of Christ, as demonstrated by the power, grace, love, mercy, and faith exuding from the Holy Spirit. Across the centuries since, missionaries and translators have risked their lives to translate the Bible into the languages and cultural idioms of diverse peoples. In the wake of these efforts, martyrs have spilled their blood. My comments below are to be discerned within the confines of this worldview.

My task in this article is to unpack or analyze the social elements and processes necessary before one can mix oral and written cultures into one shared community. Since obviously the reader of this book is part of a literate culture, for us that means figuring out how best to interact with those who belong to an oral culture, so we will spend more time in this chapter addressing the strengths of oral cultures than looking at the strengths of literate societies.

I begin my remarks by discussing problematic aspects of culture in order to identify typical patterns. Next, I address the practicalities of any effective social exchange between cultures, relying on social scientific insights. Third, I comment on selective biblical imperatives or injunctions regarding culture. Finally, I relate this background schema to mixing oral and written cultures, whether in communities in the U.S. or overseas.

The Underpinnings of Culture

We often get frustrated, angry, and judgmental in social interactions as well as interpersonal communications when we fail to understand another person's or group's cultural distinctiveness. We often blame others and vice versa whenever we are unaware of the hidden meanings assigned to symbols, rituals, and artifacts we take for granted. *Ethnocentrism,* the tendency to think that the ideas and practices of our cultural group are inherently superior to those of anybody outside our cultural or ethnic group, is one major impetus for social conflict. This scourge of ethnocentrism can blind any person from a literate culture from seeing the good, unique, and adaptable aspects of people who are socialized within an oral culture. However, instead of seeing one culture as superior to another, it is far better to discover the social forces (and divine ingenuity) that shape any cultural group's uniqueness.

Sociologist Gerhard Lenski and others have written about how various societies and cultures around the world resemble certain patterns, from the nomadic villages or tribes of hunter-gatherers to horticultural societies, feudal societies, industrial-urban societies, and postindustrial (information-age) societies.[2] Regardless of their outward physical traits, peoples who live in these cultures share similar lifestyles. Their cultures are symbolic and behavioral adaptations to the historical, environmental, and social complications they have experienced to date. Of course the church brings a new dimension, crossing cultural distinctions and in effect bringing its own culture.

Low- and High-Context Cultures

During the 1960s and 1970s, Edward T. Hall published several crucial books on the hidden dimensions of culture.[3] Basically, he distinguished poignantly between what he called *low-context* and *high-context* cultural systems, while carefully explicating their unconscious impact on social interactions. (In a high-context situation, much of the communication is nonverbal or understood because of the common context.) I paraphrase his main tenets below:

Low-Context Cultures	**High-Context Cultures**
1. individualistic	1. communal
2. time is monochronic (linear)	2. time is polychronic (cyclical)
3. bureaucratic ties (social positions)	3. kinship ties
4. spatial distance	4. spatial proximity
5. private display of emotions	5. open/public display of emotions

Low-context cultures, according to Hall, display the tendency to be more individualistic, bureaucratic, formal, fragmented, and distant in social relations. In contrast, high-context cultures emphasize kinship ties, communalism, local ties, close spatial interaction, and a polychronic approach to time. (Notice that the biblical pattern combines aspects of both, encouraging community and kinship ties yet presenting time as moving forward in a linear fashion.) Low-context cultures appear to be more formalized; hence they are likely to favor literacy. High-context cultures appear to be more tribal, less inclined toward codification (use of symbols such as written language), and more inclined toward emergent, visible expression. These divergent cultural tendencies can easily create the conditions for misunderstanding and conflict if they are misunderstood, mishandled, or ignored.

Hall, as interviewed, went on to demonstrate that cultural differences matter much more than most of us would admit. For him, the Peoples Republic of China represented a high-context culture; meanwhile, the United States exhibited, in contrast, a low-context cultural orientation in its public policies. Urging Americans to look beyond their cultural biases in business and foreign policies, Hall seeks to minimize misunderstandings that could lead to tragic conflicts between societies. In the spring of 2001, Hall's ideas have proved to be prophetic, since, at this writing, the United States and China are embroiled in an international dispute over a captured spy plane. The Chinese demand an apology for an incident that resulted in the death of one of its pilots, while the U.S. tries to respond with suitable diplomatic language to protect its military interests. According to Hall, cultural differences are the underpinnings of several other international disputes, including the Arab-Israeli conflict.

Oral and Written Cultures

Many of Hall's observations have implications for the mixing of oral and written cultures. For instance, he classifies African Americans as having a high-context cultural style, whereas whites typically exhibit a low-context cultural orientation. Hall noted that African Americans were more visual in expression, used gestures more effectively, and were more likely to sustain eye contact with strangers than whites were. It may well be the case that oral cultural styles are more compatible with high-context groups. Hence, problems often attributed to the differences between oral and written cultures might be rather reflections of the divergences between high-context versus low-context cultures.

The above generalizations are not meant to rigidly classify cultural groups or persons within them, for countertendencies surely occur in very similar cultures.[4] Human beings from every cultural pattern have the ability to adapt to new surroundings, as proven by successive waves of immigrants to the United States across the centuries. Of course, those from societies that are extremely different from one another will have insurmountable obstacles to overcome to enter simpler or more complicated societies, as the feral child named Mowgli did in Rudyard Kipling's fascinating popular novel *Jungle Book.*

Social Exchanges Between Cultures

Every inquisitive social scientist has to be fascinated by the beauty and diversity of human cultures. Joel Charon, a sociologist, informs us that all cultures are reinforced or maintained by social ties, social statuses, and social institutions.[5] Thus, oral cultures are likely to have different patterns of social relationships, statuses, and institutional forms than literate cultures. When people or groups have been socialized in these distinctive social contexts, they often imbibe the incipient ethnocentrism contained in their social spheres. If they meet a person from the opposite camp, a typical response can be fear, flight, or anxiety—precipitated by a selective focus on cultural differences at the expense of obvious commonalities. For example, a person from Culture A will likely prefer his food, music, clothing, and other paraphernalia to that of his or her exotic counterpart from Culture B. Unless our citizen from Culture A is bored or dissatisfied with the accoutrements of his culture, ethnocentrism, xenophobia (fear of what is strange or foreign), and suspicion will probably prevail as he interacts with the citizen from Culture B. In many ways they are like proverbial aliens meeting together, aliens who have different modes of thinking about reality and other life forms.

Joseph Feagin, a renowned scholar in the study of ethnic groups, has developed six baseline principles that can be applied in understanding different cultures:[6]

1. Learn how groups enter a particular area; study the origins of their migration.
2. Discern how cultural groups adapt to their physical and social environments.
3. Identify stereotypes and how they are used to help or hurt those who differ.
4. Recognize how groups resolve conflict: Are tactics constructive or destructive? Are tactics proactive or reactive?
5. Examine how groups are treated as they enter positions within social institutions.
6. Note how groups are and are not integrated among other groups in society.

Feagin's principles are relevant to cultural groups in diverse settings, such as communities, schools, business organizations, civic groups, and churches. They also pertain to mixing oral and written cultures.

One must probe the conditions leading to the reason particular oral and written cultures have come into contact with each other. Was it voluntary or involuntary, chosen or coerced? Voluntary patterns on both sides may encourage cooperation; dominance or paternalism on behalf of any one side can undermine social exchanges or interaction patterns between groups. Power—in both its formal and informal dimensions—must be identified, understood, shared, and reciprocated, as Clarence Shuler implies in his book on racial reconciliation among evangelicals.[7]

To mix written and oral cultures, one must understand how each has adapted to conditions, restraints, and opportunities. It is necessary to *respect* the other culture and to see how the ways it operates are based in its history and its values.

To interact with those of a very different culture, one must combat the toxic effects of stereotypes, prejudice, and discrimination, for these—along with ethnocentrism and xenophobia—are the breeding grounds of fear, hate, bitterness, and violence.[8] Many modern atrocities among cultural groups in Europe, Africa, Asia, Australia, and Latin America attest to this fact. Efforts to dehumanize different cultures are rampant, emanating from the viruses of racism and colonialism. Whereas the Bible, instead of focusing on race, refers to family ancestry or lineage, the cultural notion of race is rooted in the idea of separate origins for humans who differ in color, observable physical traits, perhaps even language. In our era, it is easy to be confused about cultural differences and resort to racial stereotypes in explaining them to ourselves.[9]

If all humans have descended from the same parents' blood, as the apostle Paul reminds us in Acts 17:26, no racial or cultural group can ever be inherently superior or inferior to another—they came from the same genetic source. Thus, notions of cultural, social, and racial hierarchies are human creations, not divine in substance or conceptualization. Racism and cultural ethnocentrism dehumanize persons and groups because they are different or unique, undermining the sacred image of God contained within every human, whether saint or sinner. The book of James, in chapter 3, reminds us that we cannot claim moral virtue or wisdom if we use our tongues to praise God, on the one hand, and curse those made in His image with that same tongue, on the other hand.

To mix written and oral cultures, one must resolve covert as well as overt conflicts in constructive ways. Note a biblical example of this in how Abraham resolved a serious dispute between his clan and that of his nephew Lot. Here, the spiritual elder—Abraham—took the initiative to resolve the dispute and yielded the first choice of a constructive resolution to Lot. As a result of his wisdom and faith, God blessed Abraham abundantly. Whichever cultural group considers itself superior or mature must do likewise, if oral and written cultures are to evolve spiritually into one faith community. Social scientists target three key conditions to resolving conflicts among cultural groups;[10] given my extensive professional experiences, I now add a fourth condition to the set:

1. Encourage interaction among those from each group with similar talents and interests in an effort to build an intergroup consensus.
2. Reduce the social tendency to see persons or groups as categories rather than unique individuals who share a similar observable trait.
3. Organize people into interdependent groups and assign them interdependent tasks.
4. Select leaders who reflect these principles within and across diverse groups.

Obviously, the practical steps and ramifications associated with these matters must be considered carefully as well as systematically by the actual parties involved. In his excellent book *A World of Difference*, the late Thom Hopler wrote about encountering such a world.[11] As a missionary to Africa and an urban missionary to the United States, he recognized the importance of establishing reciprocal networks of communication between different cultural groups. His book provides a relevant background rationale for implementing the above conditions between cultures.

A fifth principle for mixing oral and written cultures is to monitor, mentor, sponsor, and minister to their peoples at all levels within social institutions. Social institutions include family, school, church, businesses, civic groups, media, governments, healthcare, and law enforcement. Talented individuals must be nurtured in all kinds of services. For example, those skilled at writing can record the oral histories and stories of their colleagues or counterparts from an oral culture. Note that Alex Haley's book *Roots*, which stunned the world in its movie version, was the consequence of listening to and writing oral stories. Conversely, oral speakers can help those from written cultures with memorization and speaking. Frequently, great leaders in church and society are those who can motivate and mobilize crowds by their use of words. Both skill sets are needed in a global era. Both could be shared in a community seeking interdependence between cultural groups. Some areas of work endeavor are based in speaking or oral communication—for example, talk shows and other media—and other endeavors are anchored in written communication.

Mixing oral and written cultures does not transpire by accident; it cannot occur in a social vacuum. Wise servants will notice when unjustified discrimination and segregation, whether based on a misunderstanding of differences or politics, impede the progress of any group. Where there is a will, there is a way to accommodate written and oral tastes. For example, the most innovative or cosmopolitan social institutions often alternate between diverse cultural styles in food, music, recreational options, financing, recruitment, and other venues. The best leaders search for talent, innovation, creativity, and productivity wherever they can be found in unexpected settings; institutions are enriched by diversity.

To sum up, one must develop an appropriate social technology for handling cultural differences. It seems strange that ordinary people who are not at all reluctant to adapt to successive waves of technological diversity—witness the proliferation of radios, cellular telephones, televisions, computers, and automobiles across cultures—are stymied over mixing oral and written cultures. Within universities and libraries across the world lie unused secrets for mixing all types of cultures.

Biblical Imperatives for Mixing Oral and Written Cultures

In the Old Testament, God promised to send a Savior to redeem humans from sin after our first parents, Adam and Eve, fell into sin— spurred on by satanic deception. Adam and Eve are the source of all cultures. Across the generations thereafter, God looked for persons of faith in every culture, from Abel, Enoch, Methuselah, and Noah, down to Abraham. He sought to establish a covenant with any person or group that would place faith in Him alone. Abraham responded to this divine call. Building on Abraham's faith, God selected his family to bring the light of His revelation to all nations or cultures. Later, God designed the nation of Israel to serve as His conduit to attract the nations of the world to His glorious kingdom. God's plan has always been to redeem human beings from all cultures, for everyone in all cultures would die eternally in sin apart from accepting His Son, Christ Jesus, as each person's own substitute sacrifice for sin.

Christ is the apex of all cultures—oral or written in form or content. At His birth, recorded in Luke chapter 2, angels declared that the good news of His birth was for all cultures! Divine beings announced from Bethlehem that God had shown favor to all mankind in sending Christ. Christ revealed the love, mercy, grace, character, and provision of the heavenly Father as He walked on this planet. As He contemplated death, Christ said that if He were lifted up on the cross, He would draw all men and women to Him.

As Christ's gospel spread from Jewish culture to diversified Gentile cultures, the apostle Peter articulates this universal truth in Acts 10:34–35. He observes that "God does not show favoritism but accepts men from every nation [ethnic group or culture] who fear him and do what is right." This verse stands as the declaration of acceptance for all cultures in Christ as long as their diverse beliefs, customs, and practices are consistent with biblical mandates.

Probably more than anyone else in his era, the apostle Paul understood the relationship between cultural ramifications and biblical imperatives. In 1 Corinthians 9, he writes about how he adapted to different cultural types in order to communicate the gospel to as many people as possible. In the book of Acts, Luke records how Paul entered the intellectual mecca of his time, Athens, engaging their culture, quoting from their poets, and acknowledging their philosophic traditions in an effort to spread the gospel to intellectuals. In Romans 3, Paul discusses the universal plight of all cultures in order to present Christ as the salvation from God's wrath and atoning sacrifice for all sin. We could deduce much wisdom from Paul's insights about culture, especially in his remarks to the cosmopolitan imperial city of Rome.

First, in his epistle to the Romans, chapter 12, Paul urges believers in all ages not to be conformed to the cultural patterns of this world system. Rather, we are to be transformed in our thinking as the Holy Spirit reveals the wisdom of biblical revelation to us in our culture. Instead of allowing our inner selves to be automatons to culture's subtle dictates or popular inertia, we must allow the Holy Spirit to shape and infiltrate our lives and our responses to culture. Throughout the ages, the church's credibility has been undermined drastically whenever it has prostituted its unique, divine power by surrendering to the temptations and compromises of culture.

In Romans 12, Paul also teaches the principle of interdependence as he discusses spiritual gifts. Though they are different, each gift makes an important contribution to the welfare of the body of Christ. Elsewhere in the chapter, Paul urges believers to use all spiritual gifts, to love their enemies, and to overcome evil (including conflicts and misunderstandings) with good. In Romans 13–15, Paul urges obedience to institutional leaders, as long as they do good, as well as submission to offended saints. Would that those who desire to mix oral and written cultures would remember these pivotal insights! Both written and oral cultures have value before almighty God; one is not superior to the other. Their cultural differences are related to purpose and function. At the close of the New Testament, in the book of Revelation, the apostle John documents that Christ has redeemed men and women from every culture—oral or written!

Of course, God's *Word* has also been given to all cultures and languages. From the time of the apostles, missionaries have not only brought people to Christ, but they have taught them to understand Scripture, which often includes translating the Bible into their language and/or teaching them to read. That is, however, off the subject of this essay; the ramifications of when it is appropriate to teach literacy and how to do so in a culturally sensitive way are better left for theologians to address.

On Mixing Oral and Written Cultures

Thus far, we have perused different patterns of culture in order to show that cultures do matter to us. They give us meaning and identity as humans who enter this world in families or communities shaped by the atmosphere of culture as by the air that engulfs us.

We have likewise considered relevant social scientific insights about ethnic cultures, deducing principles to guide our social exchanges and interactions. Third, we have summarized key aspects of biblical truth as these pertain to culture. Our final task, then, is to probe the quest for community between oral and written cultures.

Let me start by saying that there can never be real community without truth. Many efforts at mixing written and oral cultures fail because of a horrid past of colonial domination or incipient paternalism. No culture wishes to surrender its beauty under the threat of extinction or dominance. On the other hand, no culture is perfect! We can all learn important things from cultural exchanges without succumbing to the toxic effects of moral relativism. Cultural relativism invites us to sample diversity and discern the best. Cultural relativism is not equal to moral relativism. Moral relativism denies the sanctity of biblical revelation. Paul was a cultural relativist, but not a moral relativist! Those seeking to mix oral and written cultures need to realize that there is much to gain from accentuating the positive in their social exchanges, while agreeing to disagree in love concerning the negatives or areas of unavoidable conflict. We also, as Christians, need to see ourselves as representing *the church,* which stands above all cultures, more than we represent our individual cultures.

The key is not to maximize opportunities for conflict, but rather, as hostage negotiators know so well, one must seek to enlarge commonalities and mutual benefits. According to psychologist Daniel Goleman, one must cultivate emotional intelligence by recognizing how emotions are refracted within culture.[12] In far too many cases, the ability to detect, understand, handle, harmonize, negotiate, and unify emotions across diverse cultural groups requires greater sociological competencies than can be gathered from mere grasp of cognitive facts or limited encounters. Our failure to accept cultural differences proactively and strategically can damage the emotional empathy that is the foundation of trust. And trust is the crucible of intercultural morality.

Gareth Morgan helps us to see that our cultural images affect how we work with others.[13] Some images produce or reinforce dominance, whereas others can encourage cooperation. Moreover, Jean Lipman-Blumen directs us toward connective leadership in managing our cultural differences.[14] Connective leadership listens to and serves the needs of diverse constituents. Of course, this should remind us of how the apostles chose Greek leaders as deacons in Acts 6 when the needs of Hellenistic (Greek) widows were not being met sufficiently in the early church. Such an incident ought to show all believers that cultural problems or conflicts are really disguised opportunities for growth, since the church blossomed after this incident was wisely resolved.

These ideas about truth, trust, and leadership are essential to mixing oral and written cultures. I have only scratched the surface of knowledge, yet I close with a few seasoned tips or guidelines:

Guidelines for Mixing Oral and Written Cultures

1. Carefully research the situation for mixing written and oral cultures. Discern the wisdom of biblical and scholarly exemplars.
2. Place in authority leaders who have demonstrated empathy and compassion for both camps. Let them lead in listening and serving the weak. Rotate leaders and agendas systematically among cultural groups.
3. Plan proactively to seek mutual benefits (goodness) as much as possible.
4. Cultivate troubleshooters or problem-solvers. Integrate spiritual gifts.
5. See problems and conflicts as opportunities for greatness, to expand beyond our ethnocentric horizons.

We must attend to these matters if we are ever to successfully integrate or mix oral and written cultures into a genuine community. Being vulnerable is often the prelude to humility. But establishing authentic communities requires something more: Mixing cultures of any vintage also requires *vision*, an overarching idea, even models, to channel collective aspirations. Most people are far more inspired by example than exhortation. I urge the readers of this chapter to study those churches and social institutions that have become diverse. What challenges did they face? What struggles did they endure? How did they overcome?

I close this article on mixing cultures with two models of a diverse vision, one in the secular realm, the other in the church realm. Connoisseurs of popular culture and science fiction already know that the mythological ideals behind *Star Trek* exemplify a vision of a diverse, unified humanity off exploring extraterrestrial civilizations. Many scientists and others have been inspired by this utopian vision. It pictures a world where diversity is assumed, as infinite diversity in infinite combinations is the normative framework. I believe *Star Trek* is contagious because it imitates the harmony of cultures that will exist in heaven as Christ's kingdom is inaugurated someday in the future. Lest anyone doubt the power of this secular vision to inspire this planet's most brilliant scientists, I urge you to consult Michio Kaku's dynamic book, *Visions: How Science Will Revolutionize the 21st Century*.

The second model is Times Square Church, a church that I have visited on several occasions while in New York City, an assembly of saints pastored by the legendary David Wilkerson, whose early ministry is depicted in the book and movie *The Cross and the Switchblade*. This church is amazing to behold, the most diverse church I have ever seen. The congregation is made up of saints from all walks of life, representing an estimated 120 different nationalities from around the world. After seeing churches like this, one knows the beauty and glory of cultural diversity as God intended it. Those who have visualized or experienced cultural diversity at its best, according to its potential, can never again be satisfied with the laziness and naive determinism of homogeneity.

These visions cited above leave little doubt that mixing oral and written cultures is possible should community members and leaders choose to pursue this goal diligently and wisely. Efforts fail for lack of knowledge, wisdom, truth, love, and faith. Yet the gain outweighs the pain, for only thus unified is the glory of God manifested fully—all other renditions are partial, dim, or incomplete reflections. Unity need not imply uniformity; genuine, divine love can absorb cultural differences across the individual, group, community, organization, and systemic levels. Where there is no vision, people do perish.

DISCUSSION STARTER QUESTIONS

1. In what direct or indirect ways do you or your ministry interact with people in oral cultures? What have been some of your interactions—good and bad?
2. How can the strengths of oral or high-context cultures help the body of Christ?
3. Why does paternalism hurt the cause of Christ and the church? How did the apostles avoid it?

CHAPTER ELEVEN

THE PROMISE AND PERIL OF SEMINARY EDUCATION:

Is Evangelical Theological Education Bound by Class and Culture?

DAVID K. CLARK

S chools come in many shapes and sizes. A karate school teaches people to break chunks of wood with their bare hands. A medical school teaches students to stitch up the hands of those who didn't do so well at karate school. Those who start schools shape them to do a specific job, and they also follow the values, procedures, and expectations that their cultures have instilled in them. Every school, like every social institution, exists in a complicated relationship to its cultural surrounding. This reality leads to several questions. First, what are evangelical seminaries[1] like? How did the various European cultures influence theological schools, and how does this affect people of other cultures who work at or study at such schools? Second, what is the future of seminaries? How can theological schools best serve a world church—people from every tribe and nation?

The Impact of Cultures on Schools

Culture clearly affects every school. No school is culturally "pure." Consider an example. The original seal of Harvard featured the word *Veritas* ("truth") surrounded by *Por Christo et Ecclesia* ("for Christ and the church"). More than a century ago, Harvard deleted the latter phrase, leaving only *Veritas* on its seal. What does this subtle change mean? Some might say that Harvard ceased to be a *Christian* university—committed to Christian values—and became a *neutral* university—committed to an unbiased pursuit of *veritas*. But no, a secular university isn't a neutral university. In deciding not to be Christian, Harvard chose to become a university of a different, but still very particular sort. "There is no such thing as a university pure and simple."[2] Every school follows certain ideals, specific values, and particular practices. Every school reflects the priorities and goals of certain groups of people and not others. No school—no social institution of any sort—escapes the ethos, ideals, and practices of particular cultures.

In one sense, then, the reply to our question, "Is evangelical theological education bound by class and culture?" is obvious. Suppose the word *bound* has a softer sense, meaning *influencing and affecting*. Are theological schools *shaped by the values and practices of certain cultures and classes of people?* Clearly, *yes*. Seminaries mirror the customs, priorities, and habits of those who founded them, those who lead, work at, and support them. Certainly, those who enter schools from cultures other than the majority culture will encounter many cultural differences.

In another sense, however, the answer isn't quite so clear. Assume the word *bound* has a harder connotation, meaning that European cultural traditions *handcuff and hamper seminaries* so much that they can't connect to or helpfully serve members of non-European cultures. Are theological schools *in cultural captivity, in bondage to a European ethos, so they can't address the needs of the worldwide church?* Frankly, I believe, *no*—or at least, potentially no. Even if some seminaries are so bound by cultural traditions that they can't serve the whole church, others will develop leaders for multiple cultural situations.

The harder sense of the word *bound* correlates to a theory about the incompatibility of cultures that is probably false. Some scholars argue that cultures differ *radically*. The word *radically* doesn't mean that cultures are just *different*. That's obvious. Adding this qualifying word means that the differences among cultures are *extreme*. The values, rational principles, language patterns, customs, and world-views of unique cultures are *completely distinct*. They share almost no common ground. Some claim that this radical gap between cultures means that cross-cultural communication isn't possible, that cross-cultural ethics has no moral force, and that cross-cultural truth doesn't exist.

Benjamin Whorf defends this idea using a famous example. He explains that the Hopi Native American language is built on a distinctive worldview. This worldview is so alien to Anglo[3] modes of thought, says Whorf, that English speakers can't understand it. Hopi and English just can't be "calibrated." They don't exist on the same scale. There's no translation system. The two languages and cultures represent two utterly irreconcilable conceptual frameworks. Remember the early days when the operating systems of Mac and IBM couldn't communicate with each other? If Whorf were right, a dominantly white seminary, bound by European cultural values and norms, could never teach students and serve churches from non-European cultures without tearing them away from their culture.

Whorf, however, overstates his point. In illustrating his case, Whorf explains Hopi metaphysics to non-Hopi peoples *in English*. He successfully uses English words and Anglo thought patterns to help English speakers understand how the Hopi language is different from English. If cultures were as radically different as Whorf claims, there'd be no way Whorf could make this case.[4] I'm frankly very doubtful about claims to a radical *disconnection* between cultures. I lived for eighteen years as a minority person in Asia. I've experienced the uniqueness of cultures. Cross-cultural experiences are full of surprises. Cultures are distinct and different. But they are not *absolutely* so. It's unwise either to understate or to overstate these differences. So schools that arise in one cultural setting can learn to serve students from other cultures.

Eurocentric Higher Education

A balanced picture of the effects of European culture on seminaries will include several insights. First, it's sometimes argued that seminaries are *Eurocentric*. There's truth in this remark, but it's also misleading. It's misleading because there's just no such thing as European culture; there are many European cultures. Upon learning that I lived in Japan, many people say to me, "Oh, do you speak Chinese?" (This happened again only two weeks ago!) The fact is, of course, that China and Japan are worlds apart, and only from a great distance do they look at all the same. After teaching in several places in Europe, I realize that this continent, too, is a kaleidoscope of cultures. Europe is hardly one big, unified culture.

Second, what's right about the claim that seminaries are Eurocentric is this: Non-Anglo-Americans pursue higher education in a culturally alien ethos. Excepting traditionally non-Anglo universities, like Howard University, educational institutions do operate in Anglo ways. This affects all the features of culture. At simple levels, it influences dress and cuisine; at more important levels, relational and communication patterns, aesthetic and musical preferences, and attitudes toward time and personal space; and at fundamental levels, questions of curriculum and educational resources plus issues of identity and belonging. It is undeniable that non-Anglo students feel these kinds of differences—as does any person who lives in a culture not her own. It's white people who enjoy the luxury of feeling culturally at home when they go to seminary. This means Anglos generally experience a greater sense of power and inclusion in these schools than non-Anglos do.

Third, higher education has not just a European past, but a Christian heritage. Before the New Testament was finished, Christians started preparing church leaders. Paul studied in Jerusalem with Peter and James (Galatians 1:18–19). Paul also instructed Timothy to emphasize leadership preparation (2 Timothy 2:2). Out of the medieval systems for developing Christian leaders, Christians formed the first university. The University of Paris emerged from the cathedral schools connected with the Cathedral of Notre Dame. The Reformers— Luther, Melanchthon, Zwingli, Bucer, and Calvin—all studied in the universities and defended university education for their clergy. In the United States, Christians established schools for clergy education. The first, Harvard College, formed in 1636—sixteen years after the arrival of the Pilgrims. The education followed the English system: A single master tutored nine students in the Puritan theology of the early colonists. A 1643 brochure justified Harvard's existence: "To advance Learning and perpetuate it to Posterity; dreading to leave an illiterate Ministry to the Churches." The beginnings of higher education reflect not only European biases, but Christian values and purposes.

Fourth, secular European philosophy altered Western culture's views on the purposes of higher education. Renaissance and Enlightenment thinking affected Western higher education so that it now focuses more on secularized knowledge. Modern values—secularity, unrestrained freedom, and the independent self—powerfully influenced Western universities. Enlightenment thinkers came to see tradition— especially *religious* tradition—as a hindrance to intellectual progress. Of course, church politics and theological agendas shouldn't control academic study politically. And a scientist studying the migration of sperm whales doesn't gather her data primarily from the book of Jonah. But secularized Western culture exaggerates this valid point. A divinity school official at the University of Chicago said, "Religious special claims cannot be allowed in the University, even—or perhaps especially—in its Divinity School." In this official's view, commitment to biblical authority sabotages academic work. Good scholarship cannot submit to the authority of Christian revelation.[5] Ironically, therefore, although universities grew out of the church, many scholars today believe that religious ideas must *never* "interfere" with scholarship. This trend justifies the words of scholar Stephen Carter: "We should stop the steady drumbeat, especially in our popular culture, for the proposition that the religiously devout are less rational than more 'normal' folks."[6]

The Purposes of Seminary Education

The secularization of American culture affects how people view the purposes of seminary education. The common view is that graduate educational systems discover new knowledge and educate students in the methods of finding that knowledge. This knowledge is objective, analytic, and theoretic. So the purposes of education are seen as purely intellectual. (Undergraduates more often think that education leads to well-paying jobs.) In contrast, before the twentieth century, many held that all education should focus, not just on intellectual content and vocationally useful techniques, but also on developing character. Education builds persons. This view goes back to

Plato, who founded the first academy. Augustine advised, "Attract [students] by your way of life if you want them to receive . . . teaching from you."[7] Until a century or so ago, those who taught in public universities shared this perspective, generally agreeing that a central purpose of education is teaching virtue.

This view isn't held today. That hit me when I began teaching at a college that advertised the motto: "Where Character Is Developed with Intellect." Despite my Christ-centered college and seminary education, I reacted against the idea. *This stifles academic quality,* I thought. I fell victim to the attitude Carter identifies: I feared that "the religiously devout are less rational than more 'normal' folks" and felt that seeking to form character in students only makes that problem worse. My view was that excellent education is entirely intellectual and conceptual. To be honest, my teachers never defended this view. But somehow, somewhere, I picked it up, like the boy growing up in Green Bay and learning to be a Packer fan. Gradually, over some years, I saw the error of my youthful ways. I noticed the best teachers influencing their students most by their authentic relationships. Of course, mediocre teaching strategies are no virtue. But the inspiration produced through profound modeling, rooted in genuine, trustful relationships with students, is as essential to helping students learn and grow as are deep knowledge and sharp teaching strategy.

The secularized ethos in which I was socialized can infect any school. Although the roots of Western universities are profoundly Christian, the plants are now secular. Seminary deans, professors, and students, educated in the cultural ethos of this secularized Western university world, can feel pressure to keep up with universities, intellectually speaking, by adopting their assumptions. It's easy to believe that developing persons of character is anti-intellectual. It's easy to emphasize objective knowledge, to idolize reason, and to pretend that institutions are culturally neutral. There's good in Western education, but when it's not self-critical and is placed in a secular milieu, it can poison ministry education.

The Biblical Scholar Model

Seminaries breathe the fumes of secularized Western education. Often they implicitly follow what I call the Biblical Scholar Model. This model begins with:

1. A view on how people are spiritually transformed—which forces us to think about:
2. A theory of how to accomplish effective ministry—which pushes us back to consider:
3. A model of effective theological education.

Here's how the Biblical Scholar Model answers these questions:

1. *How are people changed spiritually?* By understanding God's truth intellectually. The proper strategy for growing as a Christian is to expand biblical literacy.
2. *What form should effective ministry take?* Accurate interpretation and explanation of the Bible. Christian leaders must offer clear proclamation of God's truth.
3. *What should theological education emphasize?* Formal academic study of the Bible. The top priority for pastors is conceptual skill in biblical interpretation.

After expressing this model boldly, I must qualify it. Of course, no one says overtly that spiritual vitality and church ministry aren't important. As evangelical professors, we see ourselves serving the church sacrificially, and we agree that spiritual growth and church work are important. We tend to act, however, as though these goals are best accomplished through the values and procedures—through the cultural ethos—of the Western academy. We assume that spiritual life and church growth happen best if pastors are very nearly like professors—like us! We act as though the best pastors must choose academic study and accurate explanation of the Bible as their overriding priority.

This model of seminary education is flawed. First, pastoral failures in evangelical ministry are typically not due to theological error, but to moral failure or leadership ineffectiveness. Second, spiritual growth does not follow automatically from conceptual knowledge. Psychological issues can block the application of biblical truth to a person's life. Some very intelligent people are dangerous leaders.[8] Third, pastors who did average work in academic theology often lead churches extraordinarily well. The spiritual gifts of effective leaders are different from those of star students. Fourth, in one study, in 42 percent of high quality, growing churches, the pastors are seminary educated. In contrast, for 85 percent of low quality, declining churches, the same is true.[9] These results call into question the Biblical Scholar Model.

The Spiritual Leader Development Model

What are effective churches doing? High quality, growing churches follow what I call the Spiritual Leader Development Model:

1. *How are people changed spiritually?* By integrating God's truth into character and life. Christian growth is partially conceptual, but more fundamentally personal. The soul grows organically like a body, gaining strength through repeated practice in relationship with a coach.
2. *What form should effective ministry take?* How do we pass on teaching of the Bible's message and its application to life? Effective Christian leaders connect with believers and unbelievers personally, both showing and telling, but mostly showing—living—the truth.
3. *What should theological education emphasize?* Formal biblical and theological study integrated with spiritual formation and leadership development.

The church needs seminaries to pursue the Spiritual Leader Development Model. I'm not saying the church doesn't need biblical scholars. No! The church *does need* theological scholars. The cause of Jesus Christ would suffer if thoughtful Christians never responded to academic callings. I don't devalue distinctively Christian scholarship in the least. But leaders of local church and ministry agencies shouldn't see their calling, first and foremost, as biblical scholars. They're not primarily scholars who produce new knowledge, but leaders who spawn transformed followers and transforming organizations. Scripture and theology must deeply inform their thought and practice. Yet they are, most essentially, change agents, people developers, team builders, worship leaders, gospel spokespersons, and enterprise builders for Christ.

Culture and the Future of Seminaries

The church everywhere needs enterprise builders. There is one gospel for all people. The principles of effective leadership are constant across cultures.[10] But transforming leaders who build communities of faith always do so *in particular cultural contexts.* There's no one style of communication that suits every context. So effective ministers bring together high levels of competence, *both* in theology and leadership *and* in interpreting cultures and societies. The deeply educated and effective Christian leader of the future will understand that the capacities to describe accurately, evaluate biblically, and respond powerfully to a whole host of cultural beliefs, attitudes, and practices are crucial.

If leaders of churches and ministry agencies are to fulfill their divine callings in the whole world—if they are to serve in culturally sensitive ways—they must become missiologists. If they are, first and foremost, change agents, people developers, team builders, gospel spokespersons, and enterprise builders for Christ, then they have to develop high levels of what I call CQ—cultural quotient. Similar to IQ (intelligence quotient) and EQ (emotional quotient),[11] CQ refers to high levels of cultural understanding and flexibility. Christians must see this as essential in *every* ministry context, including white America. If seminaries want to make a quantum leap to a higher level of effectiveness for the church, they will integrate the issues of cross-cultural skill into the core of the educational experience. The seminarian who cannot engage the Other—the person who is different, from another ethnicity, culture, class, or gender—cannot minister at a level of competence expected of a seminary graduate.

Can seminaries promote CQ? On the one hand, achieving this mission-critical educational outcome will mean adjusting seminary curricula. A curriculum maps out a student's educational journey. It has two parts. First, *Which courses must students take?* Second, *What happens inside the courses students must take?* Evangelical schools now generally follow the traditional, four-part curriculum: Bible, theology, history, and pastoral ministry. Regarding the *structure of the curriculum*—the courses students take—it's possible to teach these subjects and completely miss some essential aspects of preparation for ministry leadership. Regarding the *content of the curriculum*—what's inside those courses—the curriculum encourages students to compartmentalize rather than to integrate. A school that would free itself to serve peoples *from* many cultures and *for* many cultures should press its students to become leaders with global and highly integrated habits of thought and ministry.

On the other hand, certain Western education values and practices do enhance spiritual leader development. For example, living in Asia and teaching in Eastern Europe, I learned that in some cultures, teachers reward students for memorizing the teacher's thoughts. In the West, memorizing the teacher's opinions without processing and evaluating them is considered mediocrity. One of my international students struggled mightily at this point. Reciting his professors' thoughts had earned him high marks in his culture. On my exam, he repeated almost exactly something I said in class. Unfortunately, the memorized answer didn't relate to the question I asked. Since he faithfully repeated my words, this man couldn't understand why I gave him no credit for that answer. I spent considerable time helping him grasp the value of independent thinking. I convinced him, after long discussion, that I would do him a disservice if I allowed him simply to memorize my thoughts. That would never prepare him to respond fully to *his* cultural context. I challenged him to think for himself (a transcultural educational value that arose in the West). He needed to avoid the great cross-cultural "sin" of applying my American thoughts directly, without sensitivity, to his Asian cultural context.

This means that effective seminary education won't perpetuate *whiteness* or *middle-classness*. It won't try to turn black or Hispanic students into white people, or international students into North Americans. It won't neglect to challenge white students culturally by pretending that whites alone are culturally neutral. It won't enculturate students into an Enlightenment secularism that ignores cultural differences and pretends that total neutrality is possible. And it won't dictate a multicultural ideal as defined by secular thought.

Ideally, people at seminaries, regardless of their cultural background, will learn to acknowledge and own, with non-anxious clarity, their cultural identity. They will all see themselves spiritually united in ultimate allegiance to Christ. And they will sense an invitation into learning experiences designed to produce responsible theological reflection, mature spirituality, and global, cross-cultural leadership capacity. The purpose is to draw all students into a challenging, educational process that doesn't ask them to be something other than what they are *culturally,* and yet demands that they see the world *theologically* in new and truly global ways. It is to graduate spiritually centered, culturally intelligent leaders who respect the insights of Christians from Honduras as much as those of believers from Hyde Park. It is to form leaders who are not de-cultured, but who are comfortably, culturally aware of Self and Other, and, in the midst of that, ultimately committed to Christ.

Positive Trends in Today's Seminaries

Four trends in seminaries will help this process, and they deserve further encouragement. First, evangelical Bible study consciously values different cultural viewpoints. Evangelicals usually focus on a single meaning of a Bible text, though every passage certainly has multiple applications. Since God, by inspiration, is an author of the Bible, this single meaning of Scripture is what God wants it to say and do.[12] But although seeking a single, original meaning is right, whites easily equate that meaning with the interpretation common in white communities. The Bible's meaning and purposes are too rich for that. When people from two cultures read the Bible, they see different aspects of the Scripture's message. This doesn't say that the Bible *means different things.* It implies that the questions any reader asks of a text direct his attention to *part of* what the Bible is teaching.

Consider gender. Men and women open different windows onto biblical texts; our different windows help us see different dimensions of biblical teaching. Both can produce insights on the text. But neither my viewpoint nor my sister's has authority over the text. Our perspectives judge each other's, *and the Bible critiques both our perspectives equally.* So an American view of biblical teaching isn't automatically the standard, just because it's American, by which all biblical exegesis is evaluated. White Christians "have a lot to learn from interpreters of a wide variety of cultures if we are willing to read expositions we might otherwise ignore and raise questions we might otherwise never explore."[13]

Second, Bible study demands cross-cultural interpretive skill. Biblical scholars seek to read the Scripture in its truly ancient historical and cultural context. They correctly reject the practice of using Scripture as a source of quotations to support theological opinions. Students must be cross-cultural—they must cross into ancient cultures—in order to read the Bible well. Culture changes from place to place, from New York to New Delhi. It can also change from time to time, from twenty-first century to first century. So Bible study requires a person to become contextual. To understand the Bible in a historically responsible way demands high CQ. Biblical studies mandates sensitivity to other peoples—the Bible's original audience—requiring that students learn how to enter those cultural mind-sets and interpret them sympathetically.

Third, theological schools, responding to failures among clergy, are addressing spiritual formation more directly. This is critical to cross-cultural leadership preparation. Parker Palmer says, "People rise to leadership . . . in our society by operating very competently and effectively in the external world, sometimes at the cost of internal awareness."[14] Leaders sometimes lead out of an inward corruption without knowing it. Sometimes an inner shadow involves fear of the Other—the person of a different class, gender, culture, or group. Leaders must name and overcome this fear through inward character formation. People don't follow ideas or institutions; people follow people. By force of character, leaders inspire others to follow. Mother Teresa's deep commitments created her irresistible moral authority. "Great leadership comes from people who have made that downward journey through violence and terror, who have touched the deep place where we are in community with each other, and who can help take other people to that place."[15] Secure leaders, deeply nourished in the grace of Christ, can relate to and lead the other.

Fourth, evangelicals increasingly emphasize contextual theology and ministry. The goal of ministry is spreading God's transforming grace. A farmer can't cause his crops to grow, but he can create an environment where the miracle of life unfolds. Similarly, a transformational leader doesn't *cause* spiritual transformation, but she can *kindle* change by shaping an optimal environment that invites the human soul to open to the Spirit. While the values of the academy produce a valuable kind of knowledge—we certainly benefit from natural science—conceptual knowledge doesn't by itself bring spiritual transformation. Life change happens when people experience the gospel in the context of relationships they trust and in terms that make cultural sense to them. So analytic techniques aren't enough when inviting people to open their hearts to God. Ministry communication must touch deep, culturally meaningful levels of a person's heart. Effective leaders in the Kingdom will use deep-level modes of cultural expression.

Lamin Sannch of the World Religions Center at Harvard offers this example: The Xhosa people of South Africa have always followed uTikxo (God) who lives in Usezulwini (heaven). The Xhosa have long sung a hymn to uTikxo, and early missionaries adapted that hymn. Today that hymn ends with explicitly Christian lyrics, but its history, musical features, and cultural identity hark back to the prehistoric past of the Xhosa people. These Christians use culturally appropriate forms of worship to connect with God while escaping captivity to Western forms.[16]

Effective communication and transformational leadership must be situational and contextual. This idea may have surfaced in the West, but it's a transcultural principle. While ministering persons must develop a rich sense of historic Christian theology, they must also expend energy to find effective patterns of ministry practice and communication. If seminaries fulfill their purpose, they will see themselves developing high-capacity missiologists who cross cultural barriers of all sorts to connect appropriately with diverse people, sharing the biblical message in a form that makes sense to particular audiences culturally and that transforms hearts and communities.

All students will do cross-cultural analysis and study to be faithful to the biblical text. White students move out of their white cultural orbit, and nonwhite students do the same, as both are invited into the ancient cultures in which the Bible was written. Then all students will learn to think about how contemporary cultures work. This cultural analysis includes understanding how relationships, organizations, and communication operate within particular cultures. Students then learn to communicate the eternal truths and powerful purposes of Scripture to those contexts. All ministry, then, involves three cultures: the source culture of God's revelation, the culture that socialized the minister, and the culture of those among whom God calls that minister to serve Christ. All students, Anglo or not, will gain the benefits of graduate theological education only if they get balance on all three legs of this milking stool. Effective theological schools of the future will intentionally organize themselves for this outcome.

Life Together in a Learning Community

Both Anglo and non-Anglo students will benefit from a seminary that gains clarity on these three cultural points. For non-Anglo students to access these values without losing connection with their own culture, certain other structural issues need addressing. Most basically, a critical mass of students is crucial. If a substantial number of persons of color comes together in a school that's predominantly Anglo, they will more likely flourish.

At the same time, some students, both non-Anglo and Anglo, wrongly expect a seminary to function as their primary spiritual community. A seminary isn't a *primary, worshiping* community. Hopefully, students will experience a genuine sense of community at a theological school; ideally, they will feel invited into authentic relationships—they should *feel* they belong. Yet a school is always a *secondary, learning* community. It's critical for every student to remain connected to a worshiping community—a local church—where he feels he truly belongs and that reflects his cultural identity. It's spiritually risky to expect a seminary to replace one's church.

Faculty are key to students' experience. Students of color understandably want to attend schools where at least some of their professors share their experience as non-Anglo peoples. Of course, professors find they are attracted to schools where many of their students come from their own ethnic communities. Simply the physical presence of non-Anglo faculty communicates with powerful symbolism to non-Anglo students that they are valued and included—that they belong.

The orientation of Anglo faculty matters. It counts for something that Anglo faculty willingly learn and teach about different cultures, that they *benefit* from students whose experiences are different rather than *penalize* them for their uniqueness. Teaching includes selecting content and materials. A class on the doctrine of God could set Trinitarian thought in contrast, not just to the atheism of the Western academy, but also to the ancestor worship of traditional Japan. Illustrations of how to apply general theory to specific contexts could draw on various cultures—not just academic or suburban, but urban, rural, and international. A decade ago several colleagues assembled a bibliography of more than one hundred critical works in global theology.[17] Globalized education affects even such issues as library book purchasing policies.

Important studies show that faculty spirituality makes a difference. The spirituality a faculty member displays through honest and caring relationships to students (and students do evaluate this) directly affects the educational experience.[18] For holistic personal formation, nothing replaces the contact of person to person in genuine relationship. Seminary teachers should have capacity for transformational relationships with others. Those who lead theological schools must create the ethos where a formational learning environment is normal and valued. When faculty connect comfortably with students of varied cultural backgrounds, seminaries can *both* support their non-Anglo students *and* profoundly enrich the CQ of all students.

These issues require realistic expectations on all sides. A goal of theological education is to develop high level, CQ-savvy leaders. A school can't reach this goal if students are *de-cultured*—for example, if non-Anglo students are *re-cultured* as Anglicized persons who merely happen to have darker skin. Nor can it achieve this purpose if students are allowed to remain *monocultural*—for instance, if either Anglo or non-Anglo students simply remain in their culture and are cross-culturally naive. The purpose of graduate education is not just to feel affirmed in one's own culture. The goal is to develop leaders who are both *culturally centered* and *cross-culturally skilled.* By *culturally centered,* I mean they know who they are culturally, and are, in Christ, at peace in that awareness. By *cross-culturally skilled,* I mean they can relate comfortably to those who are culturally different. These are very challenging goals, spiritually and educationally. They can't happen with mere indoctrination. They require painful growth for all students. This inevitably involves some critical feedback and reality- based assessment. But wise teachers don't spoonfeed graduate students. They ask students of all cultures to think independently and grow spiritually—to develop as persons who can serve God in any context.

Conclusion

The European backgrounds of those who founded, lead, work at, support, and attend evangelical seminaries obviously shape those schools. So does the ethos of the Western academic world, inherited from the European Enlightenment, with its stress on objectivity, analysis, and theoretic explanation in research. Western education has followed Harvard in dropping any thought of serving "Christ and the church." By contrast, job one for seminaries is spiritual leader development, and this is especially necessary for the global church. So evangelical schools that would develop theologically informed, formationally oriented, culturally savvy spiritual leaders cannot merely imitate the Western educational establishment. At the same time, developing high-CQ leaders who are self-aware and self-critical is a mission that can *both* draw on certain Western educational traditions *and* learn valuable lessons from non-Western cultures.

God's creation is both delightfully diverse in its cultural expressions and deeply marred by sinful division and strife. So when God calls theological schools to develop CQ-savvy spiritual leaders, He calls them to a humanly impossible task. Only fools underestimate its difficulty. Yet profound changes in perspective and commitment are beginning to crop up, like the spring's first crocus, in some seminaries. The church needs these schools to raise up and educate more and more biblical, transformational, godly, high-CQ leaders from all cultural backgrounds. This vision *must* become reality, for the kingdom's sake, to the glory and praise of God.

DISCUSSION STARTER QUESTIONS

1. What are some practical ways for seminaries to encourage and affirm non-Anglo students and include other cultures' perspectives?
2. How do the challenges in this chapter translate to your own church or ministry?
3. What legs of the three-legged stool (biblical culture, your own culture, the culture or cultures in which you minister) are most developed in your ministry? If you minister in a setting where everyone is from your own cultural background, how can you develop greater cultural knowledge and sensitivity?

CHAPTER TWELVE

PURSUING FAITH-BASED OPPORTUNITIES:

How Can We Challenge Evangelical Prejudice Against the Poor?

GLEN KEHREIN

E veryone should get a chance to attend a White House briefing purely to feel the power of persuasion contained in that
office and facility. My opportunity came less than two months into
the George W. Bush administration and shortly after the new president's Faith-Based Initiative poverty program had been rolled out.

As a life-long "social entrepreneur" (current lingo of this initiative), I had been engrossed by a Republican president talking about
the poor. This was something new. The urban ministry organization
that I had founded on the Westside of Chicago had worked hard to
maintain a strong faith-based focus even though it often cost us funding. Government monies had never held a lot of attraction to us because of the accompanying purse strings. But what has happened,
ever so slowly but ever so surely, is the secularization of society. The
influence of religion in public life has increasingly become anathema.

For nearly thirty years we have been working with the poor from
a faith- and church-based foundation. Our ministry began in the era

when fundamentalists condemned such efforts as being the "social gospel"—the slippery slope toward liberalism. That was counterbalanced by the ever-increasing secularization of society. To secular humanists, we were immoral proselytizers—using human need to cram religion down the throats of the poor. How can anything be more immoral? "In God We Trust" has become an antiquated term as the secularization of America has been largely accomplished, often with governmental efforts leading the way.

Shifting Social Sands

By the latter half of the twentieth century, a modern interpretation of the doctrine of the separation of church and state had done a 180-degree flip from the framers' original intent. Historical abuses by the state church of England led early Americans to cherish freedom of religion. In the New World the church would be free from state control. The framers of the constitution guaranteed the right through the "Establishment Clause": Article I. *Congress shall make no law respecting an establishment of religion..."*

Just a cursory reading of history will confirm the intent of constitutional writers. But history has a way of evolving. Hollywood, long an unabashed agent for liberalization of morality, blatantly tips its hand at rewriting history in a movie called "The Contender" (2000). In classic Hollywood style, an evil cabal of right-wing politicians attempts to scuttle the appointment of what would be the first woman to become vice president. During the congressional hearing, where the nominee (played by Joan Allen) was attacked mercilessly, the candidate reviewed her liberal beliefs, including this classic reconstruction of history:

> Mr. Chairman, I stand for the separation of church and state, and the reason I stand for that is the reason, I believe, our forefathers did. It is not there to protect religion from the grasp of government, but to protect our government from the grasp of religious fanaticism.

The shifting sands of social and political philosophy have blown left and right, liberal and conservative. Social welfare and civil rights policies have similarly aligned to create the classic camps. Meanwhile the evangelical church has been largely silent about the decaying cities and the needs of America's poor. In essence, the church abdicated its biblical calling to the government to solve the problems of poverty.

The Old Paradigm

When the New Deal of the 1930s and later the Great Society of the 1950s emerged as the basic governmental strategy to address the poverty problem, the classic left/right social welfare philosophy emerged. When charted, the basic tenets of that philosophy look something like this after fifty years of development:

OLD SOCIAL WELFARE PARADIGM

Liberal =		Conservative =
Increase Welfare Spending & Programs Critique: "bleeding heart; for tax & spend; big government"	P H	Reduce Welfare Spending & Programs Critique: "mean-spirited, coldhearted; for the greedy not the needy"
Healthy Society = Just Society "if not justice for all, not justice at all"	I L	Healthy Society = Healthy Economy "trickle-down will help all"
Poor are Victims of Unjust Society "don't blame the victim"	O	"Problem Poor" Won't Help Themselves "boot strappism"
Government Compassion "guaranteed entitlement"	S O	Voluntary Charity "those concerned create a safety net"
More Government Intervention Social Engineering/ Corporate Responsibility	P H	Little to No Government Intervention Free Market/ Rugged Individualism
Civil Rights Got minorities on the field, but it is not yet level	Y	Civil Rights leveled the playing field
Ted Kennedy & Jesse Jackson New Deal/War on Poverty *Left*		Ronald Reagan & Newt Gingrich Reagan Revolution/Contract with America *Right*

Philosophy, of course, seldom is created in a vacuum. Rather, it is the foundation upon which practices are enacted. This philosophical right/left paradigm has been a tug of war, pulling the balance of power between liberal Democrats and conservative Republicans for the last seventy years. The poverty issues became the domain of the Democratic party, while the priority of a healthy economy became primary to the Republicans.

Much had been made of the bloated government welfare state dragging our society to ruins but, quite unexpectedly, that all changed in the 1990s when the country experienced an unprecedented economic boom. Seemingly overnight, the annual budget deficits evaporated, leaving a new phenomenon—a surplus. And all this was happening, most remarkably, on a Democratic watch.

For the poor it seemed the best of all possible worlds—a healthy economy while a liberal administration (Clinton's) was in power. But something was wrong. Neither philosophy, it seemed, was changing the plight of the permanent underclass. All social indicators—including out of wedlock births, educational disparity, drug use—continued to be high. Incarceration statistics were particularly alarming. The scandalous figure of one million Americans locked up by the mid 1980s had ballooned to an unfathomable two million by the year 2000.[1] Old paradigms were failing. Neither government spending nor a healthy economy was bringing about fundamental change for those scraping by at the lower rung of the societal ladder.

Hardliners from the left (LBJ et al.) and right (Reagan et al.) seem to have had their day. With answers fading from the extremes, an interesting centrist position began to emerge in the 1990s that became known as "compassionate conservatism." Borrowing values across the traditional boundaries, the new approach pulls toward the middle but with an interesting twist. Proponents of this philosophy submit that faith-based groups seem to be among the most effective poverty fighters, yet our ever-secularizing society has relegated faith to the fringes and, as such, anathema to governmental interventions.

Compassionate conservatives welcomed the faith-based "community healers" back into the poverty-fighting fold:

The answers to the problems America faces can be found in our own modern-day Josephs. Many of these community healers have come out of our prisons. They have experienced what it is to live in drug-infested, crime-ridden neighborhoods. Many have themselves fallen but have been able to recover through their faith in God. Their authority is attested to, not by their position and prestige in society, but by the thousands of lives they have been able to reach and change.[2]

Compassionate conservatism has become the magnetic force that is drawing together an unusual alignment of strange bedfellows under a broad tent. Conservative evangelicals like Gary Bauer, former head of the conservative Family Research Council, finds himself aligned with social activist Jim Wallis of the left-leaning *Sojourners* magazine. Charles Colson and Tony Campolo, both once aligned with controversial presidents of opposite camps (Nixon and Clinton, respectively), agree on this point: Hope for the inner cities will come through people of faith.

The Faith Dilemma

A problem exists. Like the political community, the faith community has fragmented into a left/right paradigm as well. From the early to mid twentieth century, white Protestant Christianity divided into two primary camps over the Modernist/Fundamentalist Movements. (It is very important to note that Hispanic and African-American church groups were not part of this schism.) When charted, the basic tenets of this philosophy/theology look something like this today:

Liberal =	Conservative =
Loving People is Righteous	Loving God is Righteous
Critique: "bleeding heart; no absolutes; unchristian in beliefs"	Critique: "ignorant; Bible thumpers; unchristian in actions"
God's Kingdom = Just/present Kingdom ". . . the least of these"	God's Kingdom = Righteous/future Kingdom ". . . seek after righteousness"
Gospel: Social & Corporate Purpose ". . . on earth as it is in heaven"	Gospel: Spiritual & Individualist Purpose "whosoever believeth in me"

Corporate Social Activism	Personal Piety
"separate the sheep from the goats"	". . . you must be born again"
More Social Intervention	More Spiritual Intervention
(Social Justice)	(Evangelism)
WWJD? Feed the Hungry	WWJD? Save the Lost
Bible/Jesus	Bible/Jesus
Motivational Book & Example	The Authority & Savior
Social Restoration	Spiritual Renewal
Walter Rauschenbusch	Billy Sunday

In effect, the gospel split into a vertical (personal piety and evangelism), conservative camp on one side and a horizontal (justice, social action), liberal camp on the other.[3]

When the raucous 1960s rolled around, accepted mores and values of general society were thrown up for grabs in a cultural revolution ignited by opposition to the undeclared war in Vietnam. Social welfare policy was also undergoing a revolution and a war of its own, the War on Poverty. The shakeout effect created an alliance of the political left with the theological left and the political right with the theological right.

As conservative theologians warned about the liberalizing effect upon the meaning of the gospel, they also warned about the slippery slope of involvement in all things social. Poverty and welfare issues became the property of the liberal politicians and the liberal theologians.

Fueling this conservative shift away from concern for the poor was a demographic shift. The middle class was fleeing the city for the lure of a suburban lifestyle. While blacks migrated north in the greatest population shift in American's history, whites built suburbs surrounding every major northern city. In the city the presence of the poor was inescapable, but the suburbs changed the need to deal with them. Evangelical Christians and their churches vacated the city during the second half of the twentieth century like never before. Middle-class and underclass suburbs created class-based churches. Although Christ's words predicting the perpetual existence of the poor remain true, the poor, in another sense, were no longer "with us."

Now the solid alignment of left-liberal-mainline-urban-democratic church position diametrically opposed the alignment of the right-conservative-evangelical-exurban church position. Those in the white Protestant Christian community took a position on the right or the left dependent upon their political/theological alignment.

But That's Just History, Isn't It?

Lost in this theological/political/geographic debate were the actual people who were struggling for civil rights and a piece of the American pie. Many were minorities shut out by bigotry and prejudice. The Jim Crow laws in the South were worse—but only by degree—than the inherent ethnic-based machine politics of the Northern cities that steered the new migrants into the ever-expanding public housing projects and surrounding ghettos.[4]

The political and theological left/right alignment was primarily an issue of the Anglo majority. It had been two hundred years before these debates that the church had segregated its major denominations (i.e., Baptists and Methodists). Even the relatively young mixed Pentecostal movement that had been initiated by the efforts of a black preacher, William Seymour, soon split racially. The traditional African-American churches neither entered the debate nor saw the relevance of dividing the gospel along vertical and horizontal lines. In fact, the church had been the single most stabilizing institution in the black community, being the center of both social and spiritual life. Like all institutions centuries old, the black church is not perfect, but it never lost the cause of justice and the poor. In fact, it was that cause that drew the black community into alignment with the left.

Taylor Branch's epic, Pulitzer-winning history of the civil rights era describes how the black community was not yet politically aligned. Many older blacks remembered Republicans as the party of Lincoln and the Dixie Democrats as the dismantlers of reconstruction and the fathers of segregation. In fact, the presidential election of 1960 was a toss-up in the African-American community. It was the eventual civil rights commitment of the Kennedy brothers and then President Johnson that sealed the political loyalty to the Democratic party.[5]

Further, many liberal denominations and churches embraced the justice sought by Dr. Martin L. King and other civil rights leaders.

When whites came to march alongside blacks in places like Birmingham and Selma, they were coming from liberal mainline churches, even producing martyrs from the ranks of their clerics.[6] Evangelicals solidly aligned with the status quo. Worse, many even parroted the communistic accusations slung toward King and other leaders by the egomaniacal and tyrannical leader of the FBI, J. Edgar Hoover.*

The impact of opposition by evangelical leaders to social-justice causes such as the civil rights movement cannot be overstated. Today it remains a reconciliation obstacle. History has a way of mellowing past racial figures as it turns them into heroes. Leaders of evangelical denominations and institutions that once opposed civil rights causes now celebrate this history and praise the most visible leader, Dr. M. L. King. Some even honor the cause with Black History events and holidays. However, many white evangelicals of today cannot understand the alignment of the black community with the Democratic party and liberal politicians. We have short memories.

This different worldview lies at the heart of the segregated church. In a new and powerfully revealing book, *Divided by Faith,* Christian sociologists Michael Emerson and Christian Smith interviewed two thousand white evangelicals by telephone and two hundred face-to-face for their study on race relations and the evangelical mind-set. The findings are important and illuminate the differences across racial lines:

> [For evangelicals] bigotry, anger, ignorance, lack of respect, and so forth are not just wrong in and of themselves, but they make for poor, unhealthy interactions between people. This, in their

---

* The idea that Dr. King and his organization, The Southern Christian Leadership Conference, was Communist-influenced or -infiltrated made an indelible historical impression upon the white majority. The historical record proves quite another thing. King's inner circle was extremely cognizant of the Communist party's desire to exploit the oppression of blacks, but knew them to be dangerous to the civil rights cause (i.e., the resulting mainstream backlash). Hoover illegally and constantly wiretapped King for years. He was elated to release the tapes that proved King's sexual indiscretions, but never produced one piece of evidence of communistic involvement. If it were fact, Hoover would have had proof. In fact, by the height of the civil rights movement, communistic oppression of citizenry (Russia) was abhorred by Dr. King, who went on record to condemn it. He was not about to exchange one system of oppression (segregation) for another (Communism). For detailed documentation of King and Communism read Taylor Branch's epic history classic, *America in the King Years,* volume 1 *Parting the Waters* and volume 2 *Pillar of Fire.* (The third is a work in process.)

minds, is one essence of the race problem. Christians are called to be in right relationship, individually, with God and with their fellow humans. Not to be is sin. This is much like evangelicals of the past who, even in the face of Jim Crow segregation, did not see such segregation as the key problem. Recall that during the Jim Crow era, "Most evangelicals, even in the North, did not think it their duty to oppose segregation; it was enough to treat blacks they knew personally with courtesy and fairness." The racialized system itself is not directly challenged. What is challenged is the treatment of individuals within the system.[7]

The individualism of the evangelical mind is a filter much different from the corporate ethos of the African-American experience, and for that matter of any people group with a history of oppression and struggle. Sports can serve as a great illustration. Although racism often limited genuine competition, some sports opened earlier than others. Boxing was among the first sports to open racially when the heavyweight contender Joe Lewis fought for more than himself. To hear the story told in the black community is intriguing enough to make one jealous to have missed the experience. Hundreds of thousands, perhaps millions of black people gathered around their radios. Many were not fight fans, but they were Joe Lewis fans. A roped-off canvas ring where only one man would emerge victorious was a genuinely level playing field in a very slanted world. The black community was eager to prove white supremacy wrong. Better yet, in an era where whites could routinely abuse black people with impunity, the idea of a black man freely punching a white man must have held ironic sweetness. When Joe Lewis lifted the championship belt, he lifted the hopes of every black person in America.

This is an experience white people might appreciate intellectually but seldom, if ever, experience. What Joe did for boxing, Jesse Owens did for track, Jackie Robinson did for baseball, and now Tiger Woods is doing for golf.

Jewish people, many of whom are far removed from personal acts of oppression, understand the corporate reality of being Jewish. The rally cry "Never again!" will long outlive the survivors who experienced the Holocaust's horrors. Undoubtedly this understanding of the need for corporate justice is why Jewish leaders marched for the civil rights of African Americans when evangelicals did not.

Corporate memory is more than musings from the dusty past; it shapes who we are. It is easy for me to dismiss ignorant and base neo-Nazis who want to march in a nearby suburb as fringe publicity hounds. Ignore them and it all will dry up and blow away, I might believe. Easily said by me, but not so easy if your name is Goldstein and your parents or grandparents died at Auschwitz. There is a corporate memory and a corporate responsibility to keep that sin from being visited upon future generations.

Evangelicals, Prejudice, the Bible, and the Poor

What we have seen in this chapter is that evangelicals have been historically removed from the poor by political affiliation, theological interpretation, historical indifference, and mind-set. It is not unusual that the distance created by these differences results in a kind of poor-prejudice—the kind of prejudice that grows from ignorance and lack of personal contact with the poor.

This becomes aggravated by evangelical cultural assumptions. Emerson and Smith documented that white Americans, and evangelicals even more than the norm, believe that the United States offers equal opportunity to all and inequality is a result of the lack of individual initiative and drive.

> Contemporary evangelicals' explanations for racial inequality, then, are essentially unchanged from a century ago (with the exception of the demise of the "inherently inferior" account). Now, as then, the racial gap is not explained by unequal opportunity or discrimination or shortcomings of the society as a whole, but rather by the shortcomings of blacks.[8]

Evangelicals' strong bent toward individualism drives the conclusions, conclusions that all too often are simplistic and drawn from personal limited experience. "I knew this guy once and he just didn't want to work" or "My family didn't have anything when I was growing up, but I worked hard and I made it." Because they are aggregationists (seeing society solely as the sum of individuals), evangelicals project the aggregate of many individual problems to account for societal problems. That historic corporate injustice (i.e., racist practices) might have predisposed large numbers of people toward poverty is unacceptable to many evangelicals. There is not a correlation between structural inequity and poverty (such as unequal access to quality education or segregated living that might lead to further social problems).

In short, the conclusion is that the poor are poor by their own making. The media's focus on the sensational stories of crime or abuse verifies this prejudice, and any anecdotal personal experience confirms it.

A number of years ago my wife and I traveled to the Republic of Congo (then known as Zaire). There I heard stories and saw many personal examples of the missionaries' sacrifice. Whether folklore or fact, the story of the resolve of the first missionaries was impressive. Missionaries, we were told, did not use barrels to ship their personal effects over from the United States; rather, they used coffins. Why? Coffins were deemed more practical and more likely to be needed than were barrels for a return trip. The drive, determination, and sacrifice of these white missionaries to reach the "dark continent" stands in stark contrast to the urban exodus of their stateside counterparts.

I thought of the community that we lived in on Chicago's Westside that had lost twenty-seven Bible-preaching churches when the neighborhood changed from white to black. But what Bible were these churches preaching? What accounts for this hypocrisy? On one side thousands of people believing the Bible and God's love for the lost enough to risk everything to traverse thousands of miles, while others of the same ilk flee their own homes. Might their new neighbors have been candidates for the same salvation message? Would the perceived sacrifice of remaining in the community have been greater than relocating to a foreign land with unknown languages and unforeseen peril?

After wrestling with this for many years, the only conclusion I can come to is that of a deep-seated prejudice. It is so ingrained that we easily overlook the implications of Paul's challenge to us.

Therefore, I urge you, brothers, in view of God's mercy, to offer your bodies as living sacrifices, holy and pleasing to God—this is your spiritual act of worship. Do not conform any longer to the pattern of this world, but be transformed by the renewing of your mind. Then you will be able to test and approve what God's will is—his good, pleasing and perfect will. (Romans 12:1–3)

Biblical injunctions to love and serve the poor abound. But Sunday morning sermons on the topic do not. I had already sat through thousands of sermons and completed Bible school when I heard that Jesus was anointed to "preach good news to the poor" (Luke 4:18).

Evangelicals have conformed to the prejudices of our political alignment. Poverty concerns, whether well intentioned or well initiated, do not "fit" the evangelical construct. They are "Democratic" and "liberal" agendas rather than biblical concerns. Politics, not biblical imperatives, define the mission practice of evangelicals when it comes to the establishment of ministries to the poor.

Without doubt, exceptions to these conclusions abound. Our ministry is just one of hundreds of such ministries to the poor around the country. It is a simple reading of God's Word that motivates our mission to the poor. But for the most part we are anomalies in the evangelical world.

Will We Miss New Opportunities?

Social development does tend toward pendulum swings, and gravity seems to be pulling against the historic right-left ideological extremes. The government of the United States is now admitting it cannot solve the dilemma of poverty without help from faith-based groups and "community healers." Now, it seems, the secular government—or at least this administration (G. W. Bush)—is ready to overcome prejudice against faith-based "poverty-fighting partnerships." Sitting within spitting distance at the White House briefing, I looked into the eyes and listened to the tone of voice of every senior official—from the president on down. I had diligently studied this philosophical shift, and it seemed to be holding up to personal observation from my naturally skeptical mind. An unusual opportunity seemed to be unfolding, old barriers falling, and a sensible approach to dealing with entrenched poverty in this country emerging: the church in action! It struck me that this is what evangelicals have been asking for.

For many years evangelicals and fundamentalists such as James Dobson and Jerry Falwell have been decrying society's constant movement away from its moral base. They have lamented, organized, and petitioned for more Christian influence in governing and setting of a moral compass. When Dr. Falwell retired from the Moral Majority, it signaled a bit of white-flag waving. Although these and many other evangelical leaders have certainly not quit or compromised their message, a sense of fatigue is nevertheless evident.

But might we be looking in all the wrong places? Might we be missing the opportunity God is opening?

The Old Testament cities of Sodom and Gomorrah have gone down as history's great moral lesson of depravity. Even pagans who never crack Holy Writ know about the evils of these cities consumed and eventually destroyed by lust. We know about Sodom and Gomorrah, right? But might there be more to be learned than we have thought?

The prophet Ezekiel goes to the root of the matter in these verses:

Now this was the sin of your sister Sodom: She and her daughters were arrogant, overfed and unconcerned; they did not help the poor and needy. They were haughty and did detestable things before me. Therefore I did away with them as you have seen. (Ezekiel 16:49–50)

Even the average person who lacks a medical degree knows that a cure involves treating the source of the disease, not merely its symptoms. In these verses, the prophet tells us the source of Sodom's moral disease was self-consumption. In its arrogance and selfishness Sodom served only itself, as demonstrated by neglect of the poor. Homosexuality and other moral "fruit" sins can be traced to the "root" sin of self-love: "arrogant, overfed and unconcerned; they did not help the poor and needy." This self-love, predictably, led to its most visible permutation, homosexuality.

Many evangelicals have turned from political activism of the Moral Majority to the Prayer and Revival movement. The National Day of Prayer led by Shirley Dobson and Bill Bright's promotion of fasting are calling us back to the basics of spiritual renewal. The rally cry comes straight from the Bible: "If my people, who are called by my name, will humble themselves and pray and seek my face and turn from their wicked ways, then will I hear from heaven and will forgive their sin and will heal their land" (2 Chronicles 7:14).

Attending such prayer gatherings has been stimulating and challenging, but they have also left me with a sense of incompleteness—a sense of eating only half of the loaf. That is because we focus upon the overt moral behavior (i.e., sexual perversion)—the "fruit sin," without speaking toward or praying about the motivating sin—the "root sin" of self-centered living.

Much of America's moral decay can be traced to its materialistic philosophy of conspicuous consumption. We live in a laissez-faire society: If it feels good, do it; if you want it, get it; if it will make you happy, have at it. Could God's prophet of today say, "Now this is the sin of your sister America: She and her daughters are arrogant, overfed and unconcerned; they did not help the poor and needy"?

When Jesus told His followers that they were to be the "salt and light" of the world, the meaning was clear. In the godless, hedonistic Roman-dominated culture where Jewish laws bred self-righteous hypocrisy, Jesus taught that a disciple is one who preserves society from rot and enlightens the pathway of righteousness. That is why, when the rich young ruler asked Jesus what he must do to inherit eternal life, Christ replied, "Sell your possessions and give to the poor, and you will have treasure in heaven. Then come, follow me" (Matthew 19:21).

Riches stood in the way of total commitment; sacrifice was required.

As the winds of politics would have it, a professing believer, George W. Bush, sits in the Oval Office as I write this. Unlike any modern Republican president, he talks about compassion for the poor and turns to the church for solutions. But will the evangelical church respond? In effect the president is calling the church to practice what the Bible preaches: compassion for the poor. But is the church too arrogant, overfed, and unconcerned? Has the evangelical community become so distant from the poor by class and geography that we will fail to seize this moment of opportunity to live out the gospel? Will our riches prevent us too?

What Do We Do?

We cannot redo history, only learn from it and change our future actions. Often, when I lecture on the gulf of separation described in this chapter, someone asks, "What do you want Christians to do, move from the suburbs back into the city?" Although God does lay that calling upon the hearts of some, I am not so naive as to suggest such a panacea. But here are a few starting points.

Preach the Word, Brother, the Whole Word

I grew up in the evangelical church and graduated from Moody Bible Institute and Wheaton College, but in these formative years never once did I hear a sermon about the poor. (I once sat down to calculate the total number of sermons on other subjects to be near four thousand). As the evangelical church has moved up the social status ladder, we have forgotten the poor. It is easy to do. The early church fathers even feared Paul would do that:

> *James, Peter and John, those reputed to be pillars, gave me and Barnabas the right hand of fellowship when they recognized the grace given to me. They agreed that we should go to the Gentiles, and they to the Jews. All they asked was that we should continue to remember the poor, the very thing I was eager to do. (Galatians 2:9–10)*

Such neglect begins with our individual biblical ignorance, so let's start there. Do a word study on "the poor" and related topics (i.e., alms giving)—computer programs make this so easy to do—and some interesting things will come to light, such as:

- The sheer volume jumps out first—literally hundreds of verses that might have escaped your notice before.
- The emphatic expression of God's compassion for the poor and oppressed balanced by injunctions that the poor act responsibly.
- New revelation of truth (i.e., did you know that the word for alms and righteousness are interchangeable?)

Then we should ask—and I do mean literally ask—our leaders, Why don't we hear more exhortation to be "conformed to the image of Christ" that reflects the biblical injunction of serving the poor? We should ask ourselves, Are my personal priorities conformed to the image of Christ? At our prayer meetings and conferences we should ask, Are our priorities conformed to the image of Christ? In our missions budgets we should ask, Are our priorities conformed to the image of Christ?

Live the Word

Earlier I wrote about evangelical isolation. Many of us could not name ten poor people. We have no context of interaction or relationship. Yet most Americans live within a short drive from a medium to large city where urban needs abound.

Volunteer opportunities and mission trips can be the bridge over this gap. Could God be calling you to be an ambassador of reconciliation and develop a relationship with an inner-city ministry or church? Circle Urban Ministries has been that bridge to many, with life-changing impact that reverberates both directions. Transformation testimonies to the power of Christian love are powerful when we seek to "be more like the Master."

Getting involved with a ministry to the poor is an "out-of-the-comfort-zone" experience. But it is the kind of thing we read about in the Bible. Ordinary people, walking in faith that is beyond one's personal ability, need dependence upon God. He will "show up and show out," as we say in the 'hood.

As you and your church reach out, remember these things:

Don't Expect Simple Fixes to Complex Problems

The problems of stagnant poverty in this country are complex and perplexing. Although I've spent my life in this calling, there is much I still have to learn. In our hyper-speed society, we tire of problems that can't be quickly solved. Jesus didn't call us to "fix" the problems of the poor, but to minister to the poor (Luke 4:18). When that ministry is holistic—that is, physical and spiritual—changed lives emerge; and enough changed lives reform communities. But such reformation takes time, personal involvement, and faithfulness.

Don't Expect Long-Distance Fixes or External Control

God's love is incarnational and Jesus, our model. No television evangelist or city crusade will transform the inner-city poor community. That job is given to those who will do as Jesus did, incarnate that love into personal action. The greater the "touch points," the greater the love. This was the power of Mother Teresa, who never stopped bathing the leper or tending his or her wounds. She, and the other Sisters of Charity, represented Jesus to the poor of Calcutta.

Cross-cultural sensitivity requires that we withhold judgment. A new subculture such as an inner-city minority community is a foreign land and takes time to understand. Even Jesus did not begin ministry before He was mature. When I jump to judge about things that I do not understand, I create serious damage. Come first to learn and grow. Start there, and God will show you where you can contribute. If you come first to contribute, you may never learn and grow, and never contribute much either.

We Don't Need Rugged Individuals

John Wayne is best left out in the Western plains. The urban poor need communities of believers (the local church) invested for the long haul. Individuals may come and go, but the body of Christ goes on. In every community, God has raised up people who are called by His name to serve and reach that neighborhood. Often the struggling urban church lacks even the most basic resources. Yet a few short miles away are affluent churches. We need partnerships built upon equality and trust that will join resources to serve the poor in the spirit of the New Testament church that Paul spoke of:

> Our desire is not that others might be relieved while you are hard pressed, but that there might be equality. At the present time your plenty will supply what they need, so that in turn their plenty will supply what you need. Then there will be equality. (2 Corinthians 8:13–14)

DISCUSSION STARTER QUESTIONS

1. Are you more familiar with political or theological discussions about helping the poor? Which have influenced you more?
2. Why do you think Christ made our attitudes toward the poor an indicator of our love for Him (Matthew 25:40)?
3. What opportunities of ministry to the poor has the church left for the government? Where can your own church or ministry reclaim some of the responsibility?

PART THREE

UNITY BETWEEN GENDERS IN THE CHURCH

CHAPTER THIRTEEN

SEEING THE INVISIBLE PREJUDICE:

*How Should
the Church
Respond to
Women in Leadership?*

ROSALIE DE ROSSET

*What would I have you do with woman? I would have you enforce her
responsibility to God for whatever He puts in her way to do. Sisters,
what would I have you do? I would have you study, of all things,
the higher Christian life. I would have you get away from
the things which are small and transitory.*[1]

Years ago I read an article in *Harper's* magazine that I have never forgotten. In fact, I found it so powerful that I incorporated it into some of the classes I teach. I have heard or read very little that has done as much to help me understand the plight of African-American men in this country. In a clever approach, the African-American narrator, editor, and journalist Brent Staples describes the way he must present himself in public places at night to prevent two problems: the arousal of fear in women he encounters on city streets and the dangers that misplaced fear may lead to.

Suffering insomnia as a student at the University of Chicago in the seventies, Staples sometimes walked the streets to get sleepy. While doing so, he noticed that he terrified many of the women he met; they crossed the street or fled from him. What he eventually realized was that, by being black, he had altered public space. In his words, he discovered that "a vast, unnerving gulf lay between night-time pedestrians—particularly women—and [him]."[2] Furthermore, he also knew that he, like other black men, had only to make a false move, and he would be approached by a policeman.

Staples admits that women are not hallucinating when they see themselves as particularly vulnerable to street violence, and he even states that young black males are "drastically over-represented among the perpetrators of that violence." However, he says poignantly, "these truths are no solace against the kind of alienation that comes of being ever the suspect."[3]

Over the years, he explains, he had to learn to subdue the rage he felt at being taken for a criminal so often because it would have driven him crazy. Instead, he built into his manner maneuvers that would calm those around him. He stayed far away from others he might make nervous on subway trains. He wore business clothes instead of jeans; he stayed calm and congenial if pulled over by the police. Finally, if he had to be out late at night, he whistled melodies from Beethoven and Vivaldi or other classical composers. He concludes his article with the following ironic words: "Virtually everybody seems to sense that a mugger wouldn't be warbling bright, sunny selections from Vivaldi's *Four Seasons*. It is my equivalent of the cowbell that hikers wear when they know they are in bear country."[4]

The Invisible Prejudice

Women in general, but Christian women in particular, also often unconsciously grow up understanding that there are games they must play, maneuvers they must employ, and ways they must look and be in order to be acceptable in their circles, be that in mainstream society or in the church. Although laws may change, attitudes don't necessarily follow.

Women understand that, if they want to succeed in many occupations or attain certain positions, they must work harder than men to prove themselves. They also realize that they must mute their voices, measure their words, remain calm and unflappable in the face of condescension and harassment, and hold back appropriate anger when treated unfairly. If they are intelligent, capable, and called, they must, like Brent Staples, keep men around them relaxed (a euphemism for unthreatened). Finally, they must, of course, look good and be as "feminine" as possible while trying to accomplish their goals.

Even in the professional secular world that pays lip service to equality, many stories are told by female film directors, corporate leaders, and other women in leadership of the unflattering names they have been called for being what any male leader is commended for: assertive, firm, proficient, intelligent, articulate, and determined, all qualities apparently often considered unfeminine. Yet as Dorothy Sayers reminds us, "A woman is just as much an ordinary human being as a man, with the same individual preferences, and with just as much right to the tastes and preferences of an individual. What is repugnant to every human being is to be reckoned as a member of a class and not as an individual person."[5]

Women fight regularly what Shirley Chisholm, the first black woman elected to Congress, called the "invisible prejudice." In fact, in an article entitled "I'd Rather Be Black Than Female," Chisholm once argued that being black seems at times less of a handicap than being a woman. One of the primary reasons she gives for this startling contention is that so few people realize how much prejudice actually exists against women, while America has been deliberately sensitized to prejudice against blacks for years. Racism is no longer an "invisible prejudice." She writes, "That there is prejudice against women is an idea that still strikes nearly all men—and, I am afraid, most women —as bizarre." In addition, she adds, "Women in America are much more brainwashed and content with their roles as second-class citizens than blacks ever were."[6] Women, then, often suffer at the hands of men and of other women, both groups affected by the above noted invisible prejudice, having been conditioned to live with a subtle or even overt disrespect and neglect they do not recognize.

Although things have changed since Chisholm wrote her article in the early seventies, and American women have achieved more status in the work and political worlds and are more protected from discrimination by legislation, the problem is far from solved. Furthermore, the conservative church, perhaps intimidated by the worst of the feminist movement's ideology (in the beginning feminism merely meant the belief that women are fully human, and that is still the basic dictionary definition), is running sadly behind, not giving the matter of women's significance in the church enough attention. Ironically, it is the church above all other institutions that should model the habit of giving worth and dignity to every individual, believing as Scripture teaches that each person is a valued creation of God.

The dilemmas that haunt women within society in general and within the evangelical community in particular simply aren't taken as seriously as those surrounding the victims of racial prejudice. It is almost unthinkable today to use certain ethnic slurs in institutions or public places. If the offensive words are spoken, serious consequences of some kind usually follow. For the most part, we are constantly reminded not to make differences between people based on their color or race. However, in public, within the church and inside the Christian institution, I have seen and heard women belittled, qualified, sidelined, condescended to, questioned inappropriately, sexually harassed, and otherwise put in a box in the most casual ways. Such behavior is rarely corrected by leaders who are in a position to make a difference, by those seeing or overhearing the offense, or by the women themselves.

Prejudice in the Christian Community

The sense of shock almost always present in the face of racial discrimination is curiously absent when it comes to gender prejudice. It is still fairly common to hear jokes at the expense of women from the pulpit (and I have heard women who speak out against these jokes referred to as humorless), whereas a joke at the expense of a racial minority would raise a public outcry in most settings. It is important to note here that, while both men and women may tell jokes at each other's expense in the company of their own sex, it is very different to tell those jokes publicly in a setting that is as authoritative as the pulpit.

Years ago, I took a homiletics course in seminary, a requirement for the degree I was working on. All of the members of that largely male class had to preach four sermons. We usually preached our messages in smaller groups and then critiqued one another. On the occasion of one of my sermons, two of the members of my cell group noted that I had used all female illustrations and that they found that to be a problem. Conditioned as I was (and as many women are) to feel that a man's critique must be right or, at the very least, his opinion more authoritative than mine, I immediately felt a sense of shame. I had not planned to use all female stories—I had simply used the illustrations that seemed most appropriate to my message, a couple of them the accounts of great missionary stateswomen such as Helen Roseveare. I began to apologize, never thinking that women have sat through endless illustrations that include men and their interests, in many cases sports. The teacher interrupted me kindly then turned to the young men in question and rebuked them soundly for their double standard, saying, "Your critique is inappropriate. And, think to yourself, when was the last time you used a female illustration in one of your sermons?" His handling of that situation is one of the few times in my experience I have seen such a defense.

Women as Second-class Christians

This incident points to another universal and historic problem: Women and their interests are considered secondary to men's interests.

By way of example, when one looks at the canon of literature before the twentieth century, almost no female names appear. In the eighteenth century, one finds the name of Jane Austen; in the nineteenth century, one sees Charlotte and Emily Bronte (both of them writing at the time under male pseudonyms) and George Eliot, whose real name was Mary Ann Evans but who knew she would not be acknowledged without disguising her gender.

The fact is that men made the decisions about what to include in the canon and couldn't seem to include women's books unless they thought they were men's. Women's gifts were not taken seriously. Obviously, although men and women share more in common in interests than is sometimes acknowledged, they also come to the narratives of their lives with distinctive patterns of living and dealing with the world that produce different points of view. The female point of view may not be easily accessible to men; they conceive it to be either odd or unimportant since the norms of culture are largely based on masculine experience and adapted to male roles and behavior.

To further illustrate what I am saying in a couple of down-to-earth ways, one hears men telling their wives or girlfriends that they don't want to see a certain movie because it's a "chick flick." Although some of the movies in question may be falsely sentimental, many of the ones

I have heard referred to in that way are films about relationship with poignant, dramatic overtones, certainly a higher standard for movie viewing than the action films, largely plot-driven and containing violence, gimmicks, and chase scenes that women patiently go to see with the men in their lives. On a personal note, I assign the novel *Jane Eyre* to many of my literature classes. It is a novel of deep principle, tremendous character development, and spiritual relevance. As a point of interest, I ask the men in my classes how many of them would read this book with a female name as title on their own. They almost all admit that they would not. When I ask them why, they reply that it sounds like it would be about "women's stuff." I do not get a similar response from my female students when I ask them about books like *Robinson Crusoe, David Copperfield,* and *Oliver Twist.* We are all, men and women, conditioned to see the male perspective as more significant and immune from criticism.

Even many children's books place male characters in the more important roles. Cheryl Dunlop, one of my friends who has worked extensively with children's curriculum and reading materials, pointed out that most of the make-believe characters in classic children's fiction are male: Peter Rabbit, Pinnochio, Tom and Jerry, Frog and Toad, etc. Cheryl also noted that, except in fairy tales (which often have female lead characters), females usually exist only as mothers, love interests, and occasional fairy godmothers. Male characters represent all children; female characters only speak to girls. She says she never particularly noticed this until some Sunday-school curriculum she used actually advised the teacher to use boys in modern-day parables told to illustrate a point. The teacher was told casually that girls would listen to stories about boys, but boys wouldn't listen to stories about girls. How much of this, she wondered, as do I, became a self-fulfilling prophecy: Girls *had to* listen to stories about boys, because that's about all they heard; while teachers rarely told stories about girls (and didn't expect boys to pay attention if they did tell a "girl" story).

The Basic Humanity of Women

In the foreword to a recent book, *Women as Risk-Takers for God*, well-known author and speaker Evelyn Christenson goes so far as to say, "The greatest need on Planet Earth, especially among Christians, may not be racial—but gender—reconciliation."[7] It is possible to suggest that such reconciliation has to begin with repentance in the body of Christ for the way in which the church has trivialized women. This has happened by seeing women's interests and needs as unimportant or secondary, by confining them to narrowly appointed tasks, and by failing to educate them about their responsibility to develop their individual gifts as a part of their obedience to Christ. Women are also trivialized when they are kept voiceless and afraid through neglect and condescension, unbiblical attitudes supported by a misuse of the biblical text. Change will involve a deliberate and concerted plan by the church and the Christian community to view women first as human beings, instead of simply in terms of their gender. Such vision will inevitably involve taking women seriously as valuable assets in the whole ministry of the church. Until this happens, women in leadership will continue to pay a high price; they will be, in Brent Staples's words, "suspect" when not invisible.

Seeing women or any other minority group as human is not as natural as it sounds. Writing in the 1920s, the great British scholar Dorothy Sayers understood the problem well and addressed it cogently in her little book called *Are Women Human?* She notes that men have asked frustratedly since the beginning of time, "What on earth do women want?" She answers their question by saying, "I do not know that women, as women, want anything in particular, but as human beings they want, my good men, exactly what you want yourselves: interesting occupation, reasonable freedom for their pleasures, and sufficient emotional outlet."[8] In other words, each man and woman, each *human* being wants to live a full life and have the opportunity to express him- or herself mentally, emotionally, and spiritually. Why has this concept been so difficult to understand since it makes so much sense?

In like manner, each Christian person should have the opportunity to express his or her God-given gifts and callings as fully as possible. This is a biblical injunction addressed to men and women alike. A woman is no less responsible to God than is a man for the use of her gifts. Each woman who knows Christ will stand at His judgment seat, alone, without another mediator (husband, pastor, male mentor) to answer for her life. Biblically, both men and women have only one mediator: Christ Jesus. Women must be encouraged to aspire to something beyond an identity lost in a man. In saying this, I am not at all denigrating the institution of marriage; marriage, however, can never rule out each individual's calling before God. If it does, it becomes a form of idolatry.

The crucial point being made here is that we are all members of the human race, and only then part of another subgroup or classification. As basic as this at first appears, this concept does not seem to be acknowledged and therefore practiced often enough. A former student, Beth Howard, wrote the following response to the problem Dorothy Sayers presents. Howard comments:

> We seem to assume default features about the term *human*. Our concept of human, unless otherwise specified, includes ideas such as white and male. In the States we often have the audacity to attach American and in evangelicalism we assume married of adults. A person who accomplishes something note-worthy but does not fit the categories white, male, American, married is always labeled for clarification.[9]

Howard goes on to illustrate her point saying:

> People would think it absurd to call a great evangelist a great white evangelist. How then is it acceptable to label Luis Palau as the Hispanic Billy Graham? Does race affect the ability to make a cogent presentation of the Gospel? Why is Tony Evans referred to as a great black pastor and preacher? A woman is seldom a hardworking Bible translator—she is a hardworking, single woman Bible translator. Do sex, race and marital status really contribute to a person's ability to teach or translate?[10]

In a similar vein, women are often labeled "pastors' or missionaries' wives" instead of individuals called by God to service on their own and not simply as an appendage to another person. I wonder if those who resort to these classifications have pondered for any length of time the exhaustion that comes to many of those who endure the labels, whose interests and gifts and callings are continually prefaced with an ethnic, gender, age, or marital-status qualifier? When I made the decision to go to seminary, I was asked innumerable times whether I was going to study women's issues or to prepare for women's ministry. I'm sure the same thing happens to members of different ethnic groups. In contrast, I doubt that white males are often if ever asked if they are going to seminary to study men's issues or prepare for male ministry. In fact, I was simply going to study church history, theology, biblical languages, and all the other disciplines that went into the Masters of Divinity degree. I was going, first of all, because I felt God's leading to do this and, secondly, because as a Christian *human* being I was interested in the Bible and in theology. Such false classification leads to trivialization—the classified point of view is smaller than the human point of view.

The church then needs to view everyone in the congregation, including women, first as human Christians and disciples instead of in terms of a subcategory (i.e., female, black, Hispanic, etc.). Secondly, the church must *encourage,* not just *allow,* women who have leadership gifts to lead, an encouragement that cannot remain an abstraction. Obviously, the direction that leadership will take will vary according to the theological position a church holds on the role of women in the church.

A Church's Position on Women

Furthermore, every church has an obligation before God to work through its position on the role of women carefully, refusing to allow background influences, psychological disposition, or unreflective acceptance of what has always been to dictate such a crucial issue, crucial because what is at stake here is the responsible use of a large percentage of the body of Christ. The church cannot be flippant about the exclusion of so many children of God. Conservative churches that decide to exclude women often do so with a force that suggests that they believe this limitation of women is as basic a theological issue as the Virgin Birth, the Deity of Christ, and other cardinal doctrines of evangelical faith. Is it not more important to discover what women *can* do than what they *can't* do since all Christians have some calling from God? Only a few texts address the matter in the New Testament, all of them open to various interpretations by evangelicals. It seems possible to note that, given that this is the case, the church should be working harder to find a way to include women; instead, it seems much more comfortable with confining and excluding them from significant service, a behavior that God will not leave unjudged.

A great deal of literature within the evangelical camp now exists addressing the scriptural texts and issues in question. A responsible church will make it a priority to study the subject, reading the best material on both positions, traditional and nontraditional, both of which can be defended from Scripture. Once a thorough and open study has been conducted and a decision has been reached, it is imperative that women be included without reservation in the work of God. They must be viable members of the church. Except for the most fundamentalist churches that sinfully choose to keep women completely silent, there is room in every evangelical body for women to exercise leadership, to make decisions, and to serve the whole body effectively without crossing traditional lines. But too many times, churches neglect to think about how to use women more fully. Or when women are granted positions of leadership or creative outlet, those end up being in name only, leaving the women frustrated and confused, often leading to passivity, inertia, and/or depression.

The Responsibility of Leaders to Use Members' Gifts

Insight and thoughtfulness in changing things is necessary on the part of those already in leadership. They must purpose, as they would with men, to notice the specific abilities of the women in their congregation so that those who have been unused to such liberty may begin to feel that they have a safe place to develop their gifts. As Lorry Lutz points out, men must help women work through the hurts of the past and allow them some anger over injustices that have occurred without labeling them as "radical feminists, aggressive or just plain unspiritual."[11] That in itself would be revolutionary in churches where women have been silenced and confined to the predictable capacities of food preparation, delivery of floral arrangements and food to the sick and infirm, and nursery care. There is nothing wrong with any of these duties. However, they need to be *chosen* by men or women and not presented as the only options available to individuals, usually women, who believe they have other things to give and who are insightful decision makers, teachers, and administrators.

In fact, a dual problem exists here: first, the conservative church's tendency to confine individuals to roles that have been understood to be the lot of their gender, not allowing that person to determine before God what he or she is called to do; and second, the church's placing more value on one kind of service over another. The fact of the matter is that most of what women do in churches where they have not been allowed to explore their gifts goes unremarked or condescendingly acknowledged as "the good the ladies do." Service to children, whether basic care or teaching, is seldom seen to be as crucial as it is. What the church does with children may make a difference for the rest of their lives because it is in those years that their imagination is either captured or lost for Christ. Yet too little attention is given to teaching the teachers of children, to training them to creatively interact with and develop curriculum, to prompting them to study as much if not more to teach a child as they would an adult. As an aside, and what an unrecognized need this is in an age of so many single-parent homes, men who want to teach children can be made to feel that this is an inferior position for them; teaching men or adults appears to be regarded by other men as having more dignity as permanent, long-term work in the church. Gender again becomes a basis for discrimination against men, women, and children.

Individuals, then, must be directed to explore their gifts, to decide on their realm of service, to seek confirmation of those gifts, and then to be commended and valued for whatever that service may prove to be. Ideally, all God-given gifts and perspectives should be appreciated. It is staggering to think about the joy and unity that would exist in a congregation where *people* work together, serving in responsibilities to which they are called and where they are respected.

Jesus' Response to Women

In an issue of *The Institute Tie*, an early Moody Bible Institute publication, Ellen Foster speaks to this need articulately. She begins the opinion piece by addressing a "complaint" to those who are public leaders in the church. Her complaint is that they are "inclined as a rule to emphasize that which is petty and small in woman's life and duties and not . . . as much that which is broad, wide and inspiring." Male leadership overemphasizes, she continues, the femininity of women rather than their humanity. They ought instead "to try more to lift woman to a comprehensive thought in Jesus Christ." Instead of continually exhorting women to be true to their homes, they need to be led to fellowship with Christ. Other matters of lifestyle and practice will follow.[12]

Foster also exhorts women to "study of all things the higher Christian life," to "get away from things which are small and transitory," to talk of the things of God as well as of the color of their children's eyes and of recipes. It is "soul-nurture" women need to be encouraged to be engaged in.[13] This is exactly what Christ seems to have encouraged so powerfully throughout His ministry on earth. As Lutz puts it, "From the beginning of time woman has suffered abuse, has been used, overworked and undervalued by almost all societies. She has been considered weak, lacking in intelligence, sexually seductive, emotionally unstable. Jesus honored women, taught them, healed them, treated them with equality, assigned them to proclaim his message. . . ."[14]

Many examples could be cited to demonstrate Jesus' regard for women, but particularly interesting are the passages that include Mary, the sister of Martha and Lazarus. Although the narrative is familiar to most Christians, it still bears repeating because of the force of the message. First, in Luke 10:38–42, Christ clearly commends as superior Mary's act of listening and giving attention to His presence, even though it is at the expense of household duty. He quickly sees that Martha is distracted and anxious and disturbed by what she considers Mary's neglect of the work appropriate to her. Mary was not doing the traditionally "feminine" job; she was, in Sayers's words, "behaving just like any other disciple, male or female."[15] Christ analyzes the situation quickly and says clearly to Martha, "Martha, Martha, you are worried and upset about many things, but only one thing is needed. Mary has chosen *what is better,* and it will not be taken away from her" (vv. 41–42, italics added). Clearly, Christ encourages women to do what is better, which is to study at His feet, making sure their priorities are straight.

In Mark 14:1–9, Christ again not only commends a woman's gift to Him, but He also refuses to tolerate criticism of her. In this account, Mary, the sister of Martha and Lazarus, comes into a gathering of Jesus and His disciples and anoints Jesus' head with very expensive perfume. One could speculate that her action was controversial on several fronts. She came into a gathering of men, Jesus and His disciples; she made what could be considered a scene by anointing Him; and she anointed Christ with a very expensive perfume, an act considered wasteful by at least one if not more of the disciples. (Was that really the issue?) Was Mary trying to cause trouble or get attention?

Or was she so taken with Jesus (as can be seen in other accounts) that she had to be near Him and give Him this gift she had planned so carefully? Some of the disciples (notably Judas Iscariot, as can be seen in the Matthew account) attack her verbally with harsh words.

In what is a wonderfully comforting passage to any woman who has been put down or ignored, Christ immediately and powerfully comes to Mary's defense and in no uncertain terms He rebukes her attackers, calling attention to their self-righteousness. Then, He commends her gift as "beautiful" and makes her part of the approaching events of the Passion. He finishes by telling those before Him that her story will be told "throughout the world . . . in memory of her." Mary let her heart burn within her as she sat in the presence of Jesus learning from Him, the description the disciples give of their experience with Jesus in Luke 24:32. What could make life seem fuller and more compelling to those observing the effect?

Finally, it must be pointed out that any church that limits women's work must give a great deal of attention to two things. First, it must affirm specifically and sincerely the work the women are given to do, giving them full rein in their appointed tasks. Second, it must instruct its members, particularly the men, about the dangers that exist when there is an imbalance of power, some of those dangers being pride, superiority, and a propensity to ignore a different and crucial perspective. The more the limitations a church places on women, the more those in power must pray for humility, examine their hearts and behaviors regularly, and insist on a high degree of respect for the women in the congregation, never limiting their opportunity to study the Bible, to learn theology, and to be a genuine part of the congregation's spiritual life.

The model for that behavior is, of course, no other than Jesus Christ. As Dorothy Sayers points out, it's no wonder that women were "first at the Cradle and last at the Cross. They had never known a man like this Man—there had [and has] never been such another."[16] Here was a man who took them seriously as human beings created by His Father God, loved and defended them, talked to and taught them, included and commended them. He used them in His illustrations, and they appear with Him in the accounts of His ministry and at His death and resurrection.

Change begins with recognition of failure leading to specific repentance, an act that always demands courage and humility. The following words of a "Prayer from Kenya" articulate well what must be the cry of every maturing believer.

> From the cowardice that dare not face new truth
> From the laziness that is contented with half truth
> From the arrogance that thinks it knows all truth,
> Good Lord, deliver me.[17]

DISCUSSION STARTER QUESTIONS

1. In what ways have churches or ministries in your experience diminished women or treated them as less than human? Has anyone spoken out against such instances?
2. How did Jesus elevate the status of women in His circle? In what ways were His responses seen as problematic by His disciples or the religious leaders? Does your church respond more like Jesus or the religious leaders in its treatment of women?
3. What are three ways your church or ministry can use women more effectively? What are two ways it can affirm them better in the roles they already hold?

CHAPTER FOURTEEN

A PLEA FOR GODLY PARTNERSHIP:

How Does the Church Condone Abuse and Silencing of Women?

ELLEN LOWRIE BLACK

A s the new millennium unfolds, the role of Christian women in culture, the church, and Christian organizations remains undetermined and precarious. While advertisers remind us, "You've come a long way, baby," issues of belonging, identity, and ministry have yet to be adequately addressed in the church. The mere mention of some of these issues leads to a backlash and accusations that Christian women, particularly in leadership roles, are sinning and stepping outside the will of God for their lives. Rather than being labeled a "feminist," a kiss of death in many evangelical circles, many women choose to avoid the conversation altogether. It is time, however, to honestly and biblically come to terms with the fact that too many women are abused, harassed, and demeaned. Many possess unused gifts, and often Christian men are responsible for intentionally holding back their sisters who have been equipped for ministry.

The future of evangelical organizations and the Christian family is contingent on the extent to which balance and mutual respect is obtained. Women have played a major role in the spread of Christianity worldwide. Strategically, the need to capture the vision and passion and energy that Christian women have is of paramount importance as the gospel continues to spread.

It seems obvious that Christians should examine Scripture closely to identify appropriate roles for men and women. Both testaments include many female characters in addition to verses that clearly address the nature of Christian womanhood. God is not silent on these issues.

Old Testament Accounts of Male-Female Relationships

In looking at the Genesis account, one finds Adam living an exciting, adventurous life. God created man with a mind, a body, and a soul. But it is apparent that Adam was not complete without Eve. This incompleteness was more than sexual; Adam's cognitive and emotional domains were not complete. Eve was created with a body, yes, but also a mind and soul.

The physical and sexual side of women, and of men, is powerful and strategic. Women bear children and historically are the nurturers of the world. This function of womanhood is God-given. It is not, however, the only part of womanhood. When woman's biological functions are acknowledged and the rest of her personhood disregarded or marginalized, a woman is left feeling disrespected and incomplete.

God did not create a bombshell or bimbo to partner with Adam. He created a woman with physical, mental, and spiritual domains, and the two complemented each other. Adam was more of a man with Eve in his life.

The most frequently used Scripture on Mother's Day is Proverbs 31, which talks about the virtuous woman. This woman is deified at one level, but would be relegated to obscurity in many organizations. How many young women are taught to model their lives after this woman? In order to do so, a business degree would be helpful, as would membership in the local gym. The Proverbs 31 woman was involved in commerce. Her children and home were well cared for, although she outsourced the cleaning to maids. She took time to take care of her physical needs, as Scripture tells us she strengthened her arms.

This is not June Cleaver or Susie Homemaker. The model given in Scripture is a complex one. The virtues exalted in this text are comprehensive as they encompass a woman's entire being: mind, body, and soul.

Women as well as men are commanded of God to witness and evangelize. The fact that women are commanded to do so puts those who stop this due to gender bias at odds with God. It is a fact that women can be prohibited from obeying God by men who claim to follow the same God.

Throughout history, women have been used of God to teach and evangelize. It is obvious that, to reach the next generation, women and children must be touched as well as men. One could argue that Christian women have a distinct advantage when it comes to evangelizing other women as well as children. Certainly the phenomenal growth of the Muslim faith will need vast numbers of Christian women to counteract. (Muslim women are beaten or worse if observed talking to men outside their families.)

In addition to evangelism, Scripture tells us that sons and daughters will prophesy (Joel 2:28). How many churches address the fact that God says daughters will prophesy? It sounds heretical in most circles, and yet we could ask ourselves, "What messages from God do we miss when the righteous women in our midst are not given the freedom to prophesy?"

New Testament Accounts of Male-Female Relationships

In the New Testament, we see Jesus interacting with many women. This was culturally radical and reflects Jesus' model of a new way of thinking about women. Most places Jesus traveled, it appears He took women along. Female companionship was sought after, and Jesus took time to talk openly with women. In a time when women were marginalized, Christ came to earth and demonstrated a new social order, one of equality and value.

Women were free to express their love and honor toward Christ. Emotions were not berated. Tenderness was nurtured, as illustrated by the pouring out of oils and the washing of feet with hair. This was very personal and rather sensuous. Perhaps Jesus was showing us that genuine friendship and even the senses are not wrong or inappropriate. As Hebrews teaches us, Jesus is the creator of the universe and He is the one who designed male and female bodies.

Women were close to minister to Jesus and stayed with Him in His darkest moments. The women had to be afraid as Jesus was captured and led to the cross. But they chose to stay with Jesus rather than run and hide in an effort to save themselves. The disciples were lousy models of what to do in frightening situations. Because women tend to be more emotionally attached to individuals and organizations, their strength in times of crises should not be overlooked.

Throughout His ministry, Jesus established significant roles for women. He turned the woman at the well into an evangelist. After the resurrection, women were given the game plan to tell the apostles. Living in a culture where women were disposable and not valued, Jesus walked and talked and lived a life socially contrary to the norms of the day.

The Biblical Model of Male-Female Interaction

Jesus' respect of women and the significant roles He gave them should be the model for Christian organizations. Organizations that follow this model benefit from the balance, wisdom, and knowledge women add. The executive director of a Christian accrediting body recently reported his disappointment in the loss of a talented Christian woman to secular higher education:

I thought many of our member institutions would jump at the chance to hire her. She has a Ph.D. from Regent, is well liked and highly professional. After waiting for an opening to serve in a Christian university, she was quickly hired at a large state institution, making much more money and with greater opportunities to progress.

This story illustrates the brain drain that is occurring as Christian women face rejection. We as Christians like to teach that God is the giver of gifts, the enabler, and the equipper. We do not corporately embrace, however, the fact that the sisters in our midst have been given various gifts, essential to Christian organizations fulfilling their potential. Meanwhile Christian women continue to go into the secular marketplace to use their God-given talents. (Certainly, many Christian women are called to this marketplace, and it is not about this group that we speak.)

There is particular concern for young Christian women entering the work force today. Churches that value women's ability beyond baking and changing diapers intentionally find places of ministry where Christian women can serve according to their gifting. This generation is much less likely to tolerate discriminatory behavior, and they vote with their feet quickly out the door.

Some estimate that women make up close to two-thirds of most congregations. A biblical model that exempts two-thirds of the Christian workers is ludicrous. There is so much to be accomplished, and workers are being held back or not enlisted. Loren Cunningham, in his profound discussion on this topic, states:

> Jesus said we should open our eyes, look at the fields, and see that the harvest is plenty but the workers are few. Why would anyone look at the huge harvest we face and the tiny workforce trying to gather in and seek to eliminate any workers whom God would call?
>
> We don't need fewer workers. We need more! But the enemy is trying to cut back on the number of workers for the harvest in every way he can. I believe he is behind the confusion in the church about women and their active participation in ministry. And sadly, some people are unknowingly part of this strategy as they allow tradition and the misunderstanding of certain scriptures to prevent or blunt the ministry of women.[1]

It is a sobering thought to consider that Christian men are being used by forces of evil to inhibit the work of God's kingdom.

Sexual Harassment and Abuse in Christian Settings

Rarely is the subject of harassment openly discussed in evangelical settings. It has been taboo for way too long. Perhaps that is because godly, righteous men cannot fathom that some of their brothers are vulgar and obscene. The quietness, however, serves as a catalyst to further empower abusers of women.

It is also true that our pulpits are sometimes used as platforms for pastors to joke about women or their wives. Humor that degrades is not innocent and sends the message that women are second-class citizens and not to be taken as seriously. Imagine being a visitor and not born again who is attending a service in which the pastor trashes women and then opens God's Word to teach and attract people to Christ. It is incongruous to expect women to want to follow the Christ of someone who is rude or insensitive.

The fact is that women in the world face harassment. This is very disturbing and should never be tolerated. However, sexual harassment in the pagan world does not have the same psychological effect on Christian women. When a Christian man, who is in fact a brother, inflicts physical or verbal harassment, the pain is greatly enhanced. Is it not incestuous for brothers to assault sisters? Is not family pain much more difficult to resolve than other pain?

Listen to the voices of Christian women.

- "I was pushed against the wall. My breasts and backside were groped. And yet I failed to scream. Who would believe me? Women ask for it, don't they?"

- "One Sunday night, the pastor went on a rampage against women working outside the home. As the sermon went on, he became more incensed and ended up referring to us working women as harlots. This was outrageous in light of the fact that this church has a Christian school and over 75 percent of the faculty are working moms. The church office is staffed by working mothers."

- "I came home from work and stood in the shower for an hour. I felt so dirty. Here was my boss, a Christian leader, asking for oral sex in his office. This happened many times before I moved away. The sad thing is, I left a job that I loved."

- "As the president of a Christian women's organization, I am asked often for our mailing list. Recently, I was in the offices of another Christian organization that was trying to get my list for their own purposes. We do not release it in order to protect the privacy of our women who are some of the wealthiest Christian women in the world. When I offered to speak to a group of women at this organization's annual event, I was told that would not be possible. They were not that brave! Think about it. They wanted my names and I was not allowed to speak to their group."

All of these testimonies are real and reflect a very small sampling of what women can experience in Christian organizations. These are our spiritual families. Families and homes are to be safe places where people are protected. How is it that in many organizations the perpetrators are protected to save face and avoid embarrassment? How often are women blamed for unsolicited advances? When a woman speaks up, are not lawsuits quietly settled?

Discrimination and harassment of women is sin. It is also woven into the fabric of our culture and Christian community. The challenge before us is to acknowledge the truth and discontinue our tacit approval of men who behave this way.

In order to reshape our thinking and behavior, men and women must actively combat and address harassers. Women must be willing to speak up, although there is great fear to do so. Christian men must speak on behalf of Christian women. Men must stop other men rather than subtly empowering them. They need to get in the face of men who mistreat women, holding them accountable for their behavior.

A Vision for the Future

The Christian family is facing up to failures worldwide in order to bring about healing. Reconciliation and forgiveness release spiritual power as bondage disappears. The first step to healing is to acknowledge reality. The next step is to discontinue damaging practices. The needs of the world are so great, and they demand a concerted effort of all of God's children. Change is never easy. It is always possible.

Loren Cunningham and David J. Hamilton tell of their dream:

> I see every little girl growing up knowing she is valued, knowing she is made in the image of God, and knowing that she can fulfill all the potential He has put in her. I see a body of Christ recognizing leaders whom the Holy Spirit indicates, the ones whom He has gifted, anointed, and empowered without regard to race, color, or gender. This generation will be the one that simply asks, "Who is it that God wants?" There will be total equality of opportunity, total equality of value, and a quickness to listen to and follow the ones the Holy Spirit sets apart.
>
> This new generation will not be bound by traditions hinder-

ing women from obeying God's call the way my generation has. Instead, they will take a fresh look at the Word of God, knowing that the Holy Spirit will never do anything that contradicts His Word. As this emerging generation studies the Bible free of cultural blinders, they will see that the Lord has always used both men and women to proclaim the Good News and to prophesy the Word of God to their generation.[2]

The time is now for Christian men and women to labor side by side, leveraging their entire God-given gifts for the kingdom of God.

DISCUSSION STARTER QUESTIONS

1. Do you think it's true, as the writer suggests, that Christian organizations tend to limit women to roles that are more or less defined by their sexuality?
2. How do churches and Christian organizations become "safe places" for men who abuse women? What safeguards does your ministry have in place to protect women? What additional ones might it need?
3. What would you say if you were to write your own dream for the future ministry of today's Christian girls?

CHAPTER FIFTEEN

MOVING PAST "WOMEN CAN'T PREACH":

What Are Some
Biblical Ways
to Include
Women in Ministry?

MICHELLE OBLETON

The room was quiet. No one dared talk. The door squeaked, and in walked the new potential pastor for Solomon Baptist Church,[1] wearing a stylish two-piece suit and carrying a briefcase. Pausing for a brief moment to exchange smiles and shake a few hands, the potential pastor walked to the front of the room and sat down. Strength and character were evident. The reputation of this individual had been impeccable. Here was one who stood for truth and not only boldly preached the Word of God but also lived it.

One of the elders of the church thanked everyone for coming out and formally introduced Pastor A. W. Billings to the congregation. After warm applause Billings stood and spoke to the congregation. The message was one of personal introduction and a God-given vision for Solomon Baptist. It was warm and inspiring. Many people still felt pain from the previous pastor who had been asked to leave only months ago. When the previous pastor left, half of the congregation left as well. The strained relationships with former members and the confusion the church went through were things they did not want to experience again. Could this new pastor bring healing and restoration to a hurting church?

On the following evening the membership got together to vote for or against Billings. Was this individual God-sent to Solomon? The church truly needed a strong leader committed to the things of God. Billings was a godly leader with a supporting family and a strong love for God. But Billings was voted down; 70 percent of the congregation voted against and only 30 percent voted for. Why would such a qualified person be turned down from such a needy congregation? A. W. Billings was a woman!

Andrea Billings did not give up her desire to serve God. She went on to develop a nationally known radio and TV ministry called Just for Him. Today she is a sought-after speaker throughout the country. Through her giftedness as a communicator she is now reaching thousands of people daily. Part of the ministry of Just for Him is to encourage women not to look at what they can't do, but to celebrate the many God-given opportunities they can achieve.

Andrea Billings's journey into successful ministry came as she allowed the Lord to use difficulties and misunderstandings to take her to new heights "just for Him."

Discerning the Role of Women

Whenever the role of women in the church is referred to today, there is much misunderstanding. Whether or not women can be pastors is usually the first question. Some women want to serve God and think there is little opportunity to do so unless they are pastors. As we embark upon the twenty-first century, we are seeing more female pastors than ever before. As a Christian African-American woman I regularly meet women attending seminary with plans to graduate and become a pastor in a local church.

The discussions of a woman's *role* and the term *submission* have caused much reaction from women today. Women have been told to submit in so many unhealthy situations that they have developed a totally negative reaction to the church, men, and ultimately the Word of God. Sad to say, much of the suffering and frustration of women regarding this topic has been done in the church or by leaders of the church in their own homes. Many times it has been described as the battle of the sexes.

In speaking to women regarding the role of women in the church, I have found a lack of understanding concerning what Scripture teaches. Submission and the God-given order between male and female is always one of the most intense sessions, with more discussion and questions than any other I can speak on. Following these times women will come to me and tell horror stories of how they have been made to submit to situations that were not of God with the Scripture thrown at them. Honest questions are answered with a reflexive, "Wives, submit to your husbands as to the Lord" (Ephesians 5:22). Or, on the other hand, women who are in abusive situations or know that their children are being abused will come to me with such expressions as "I am trying so hard to submit!"

In this chapter I wish to discuss the tension that has existed between men and women as far back in the beginning as the Garden of Eden, existed in the New Testament Scriptures, and still exists in the church. I would also like to offer solutions to the church by way of leadership and spiritual engagements for women that bring harmony and growth to the body of Christ. First we need to look at some background, then we will get to the places where women can have a larger role in participation in church life than they generally have today.

Tensions in the Garden

Most of the perplexities women face today point to Satan and his destructive schemes. It began way back in the beginning of time with Adam and Eve. In Genesis 3, Satan appeared before Eve and convinced her she would be like God if she ate of the fruit from the tree God had forbidden her and Adam to eat of: "When the woman saw that the fruit of the tree was good for food and pleasing to the eyes, and also desirable for gaining wisdom, she took some and ate it. She also gave some to her husband, who was with her, and he ate it" (Genesis 3:6). Eve really thought that she would be like God by eating the fruit.

The serpent deceived her and she ate. Immediately after her own fall into sin she offered the forbidden fruit to her husband. He willingly ate and also fell into sin. In this scene, a reversal of roles has occurred. Eve is now the leader over Adam. The ultimate responsibility before God rested with Adam, who knowingly allowed himself to be led astray by his wife.

That God considered Adam ultimately responsible, rather than Eve, is clear not only from Romans 5:12, which states that "sin entered the world through one man," but also by the fact that the all-knowing God first asked not Eve but Adam to explain his actions. Further, in Genesis 3:17, God told Adam that the curse would come on the earth "because you listened to your wife [rather than to Me] and ate from the tree about which I commanded you, 'You must not eat of it.'" The term "listen to" means "obeyed" in this case, as it often does in the Hebrew Old Testament.

Adam should have spoken up for Eve to the devil, since they both were there together, according to the passage. Instead he allowed his wife to be misled, resulting in such painful consequences that they can still be felt today. God intended for the man to lead. He gave him the responsibility of naming all creation and of preparing the way for his wife to come, and Adam was given the job of cultivating the garden and keeping it up each day. Eve was created after all creation was in order. God also gave the command not to eat the fruit of one tree, the Tree of the Knowledge of Good and Evil, to Adam, not Eve.

Because Adam did not step up in his God-given leadership regarding the trees, and because Eve stepped up when she was not supposed to, God dealt with them in these very areas. Eve, wanting to be like God, to be in control, was made to desire control and not have it. Adam, who didn't take control, perhaps didn't want the responsibility, was placed in control. Thus the tension began that still exists among mankind today. God also gave the man the frustration of hard work: "by the sweat of your brow" (Genesis 3:19). To the woman God gave great pain in childbirth (v. 16).

Tensions with New Testament Passages

The apostle Paul wrote several passages in Scripture about women. The main Scriptures are 1 Corinthians 11:2–16; Ephesians 5:22–33; and 1 Timothy 2:9–15. Sometimes the wording is rather strong, and women often wonder what exactly Paul meant by writing these strong words in Scripture. In order to understand these passages more clearly we need to understand three important points:

1. The historical setting in the church that evoked Paul's instructions from the passage.
2. The fact that Paul did not give a complete discussion on the role of women in the worship assembly.
3. That Paul was answering a question concerning the conduct of women in the worship assembly as it was known in the first century, not answering questions that are raised today in our society.

We won't take time to look at the second and third points, but rather will assume them as we look at the historical setting in which Paul wrote.

The Historical Setting

False teachers had arisen in the churches Paul was addressing. Quite possibly they came from within the church and may have included recognized elders. Paul was eager to refute them and to defend against further attacks through the teaching of correct doctrine.

There were problems relating to prayer. Believers were not being faithful in prayer, though they had been told to pray for all people, especially those in positions of governmental authority, that the church might have a peaceful life (1 Timothy 2:2). Such prayer has intrinsic excellence and is acceptable before God, who desires all people to be saved and has made salvation available through Christ's saving work on the cross.

First Timothy 2:8 seems to indicate that a quarrelsome spirit was taking over in the hearts of the men. Paul wanted special care given to overcoming this problem. Paul wanted men with cleansed consciences. He instructed the men in each of the home churches in Ephesus to pray with a cleansed conscience, free from the stain of interpersonal conflicts. Though it was not uncommon for believers to pray with raised hands, Paul's focus now was not on the physical act but on the heart attitude.

Women dressing inappropriately was another issue needing correction in the worship assemblies. Paul exhorted the women to adorn themselves both with modest apparel and with a modest attitude (vv. 9–10). By contrast they should not clothe themselves with ostentatious attire, but as women who profess godliness they should adorn themselves with good deeds.

The Role of Women in the Church

Since the beginning of the church at Pentecost, the congregation consisted of men and women. Together, both male and female joined in with fellowship, worship, prayer, teaching, and the Lord's Supper. In 1 Timothy 2:11–15 Paul wrote instructions on the role of women in the worship assembly. Paul desired the women to learn with an attitude of quiet submissiveness rather than to be involved improperly in teaching and leading the men in the assembly.

Paul's point is that the role reversal that caused such devastation at the beginning must not be repeated in the church. The woman must not be the one who leads the man. So when the teaching or preaching of the Word of God in the assembly goes forth, a qualified male leader or elder (able to teach sound doctrine) should fill the role.

Paul directed the women in the worship assembly to learn. This verb *learn* is used seven times in the Pastoral Epistles; in this verse it carries the connotation of *learning through instruction* (cf. John 7:15; 1 Corinthians 14:31; 2 Timothy 3:7, 14). The manner in which women were to learn is twofold. First they should learn "in quietness." The translation "quietness" is best here, since it would have been normal for women to speak in the worship assembly (1 Corinthians 11:5; 14:26). In addition to quietness, women were to learn in all (entire) submissiveness.

The question then arises to what or to whom a woman is to be submissive. Paul meant that a woman is to be submissive to the church elders. Since false teachers were leading believers astray, submission to church elders may have been part of Paul's solution to that problem. In essence women were to submit themselves to those elders who taught sound doctrine. Women were to receive instruction with an attitude of quiet receptivity and submissiveness. The emphasis here seems to be not so much on literal silence as on an inner attitude in which the spirit is at rest in submitting to the teaching and the teacher.

Paul's reasoning for instructing women in the worship assembly to learn in a quiet and submissive manner rather than to hold a position of teaching and exercising authority over a man is based on 1 Timothy 2:13–14, where Paul refers to the Genesis account of the creation and fall of mankind. In the New Testament the word *teaching* refers almost exclusively to public instruction. A teacher is one who systematically teaches or expounds the Word of God and who gives instruction in the Old Testament and apostolic teaching. The spiritual gift of teaching enables individuals to grasp revelation that already has been given and to communicate this truth effectively to others.

In 1 Timothy 2:15 Paul gives a blessing to women who adhere to the Bible regarding submission. There is one place where a woman can be strong, dominating, and powerful, and that is in regards to childbearing, mothering, and the nurturing of her children. But in order to be effective in these matters, a woman needs an attitude of faith, unconditional love, and self-control. Even a woman who has no children can nurture others.

Elder/Pastor versus Preaching

Part of the reason there has been so much tension between men and women in the church is due to the role of the "office of the elder." God has given the office of elder (pastor) to men (1 Timothy 2:12; Titus 1:6–9).

In both the Old and New Testaments, the term *elder* indicates one of advanced age or maturity who had a office of leadership among the people of God. The elders' task of oversight and discipline can be described in terms of keeping watch and shepherding on behalf of the Great Shepherd, Jesus Christ. In Paul's farewell to the Ephesian elders he said: "Keep watch over yourselves and all the flock of which the Holy Spirit has made you overseers. Be shepherds of the church of God, which he bought with his own blood" (Acts 20:28). The pastoral character of this task of oversight is also indicated when Peter writes:

> *To the elders among you, I appeal as a fellow elder. . . . Be shepherds of God's flock that is under your care, serving as overseers—not because you must, but because you are willing, as God wants you to be; not greedy for money, but eager to serve; not lording it over those entrusted to you, but being examples to the flock. And when the Chief Shepherd appears, you will receive the crown of glory that will never fade away. (1 Peter 5:1–4)*

The elder must be a blameless and God-fearing man who shows the fruit of the Spirit in his walk. He must also be able to teach others the way of the Lord and confute heretics (1 Timothy 3:2; 2 Timothy 3:14–17; Titus 1:9), but not be quarrelsome (1 Timothy 3:3) or enter into senseless controversies (1 Timothy 1:4; 6:4–5). A good knowledge of the Word of God is essential.

Use of the Word Preach

The word *preach* according to Webster means "to speak publicly on spiritual matters." Preaching and teaching are both used in a leadership capacity and are gifts given to the body of believers by the Holy Spirit.

According to the book *Network* by Bugbee, Cousins, and Hybels, the definition for preaching is the same as prophecy.[2] Its literal meaning is to speak before. Preaching is the divine enablement to reveal truth and proclaim it in a timely and relevant manner for understanding, correction, repentance, or edification. In 1 Timothy 2:12 Paul uses the term *teach*. The gift of teaching is the divine enablement to understand, clearly explain, and apply the Word of God, causing greater Christlikeness in the lives of listeners.

With definitions like these, it would be wrong to say women can't preach or teach in any setting. God has used women throughout the Bible from the Old Testament to the New Testament speaking forth His truths (Judges 4; John 20:18; Acts 18:26).

Authority over Men

However, the Bible is clear about women exercising authority over the man in teaching and preaching. These strong verses regarding the role of a woman are clear and are supported throughout the Word of God. Paul is not the initiator of these biblical passages concerning the role of women; God is. As long as a woman is teaching or preaching in a setting that is made up of women, children, and sometimes men (while the woman is under the authority of the pastor), she is free to use her God-given gifts to the glory of God. But when a woman becomes the central authority over men in the church, meaning she becomes the shepherd over the flock, she is out of order according to the Word of God.

Shepherding and Teaching Women and Girls

As a female leader, I have the spiritual gifts of shepherding and teaching. I feel used of God each and every week I stand to teach and preach. My ministry is to women and girls, and I feel the freedom to do this from such passages as Titus 2:3–5.

> *Older women likewise are to be reverent in their behavior, not malicious gossips, nor enslaved to much wine, teaching what is good, that they may encourage the young women to love their husbands, to love their children, to be sensible, pure, workers at home, kind, being subject to their own husbands, that the word of God will not be dishonored.* (NASB)

It is a biblical duty for a woman to teach other women. Many women refer to this as Titus 2:4 ministry.

Sometimes I have preached on Sunday for our church congregation on such occasions as Mother's Day and various appreciation Sundays. It was made clear to the congregation that I was speaking under the authority of the elder (pastor). Because of the special occasion, having a message from a female perspective made it fresh and well received.

Dr. Cynthia Perry, in her chapter "Looking at Women in Ministry," says,

> Some people . . . believe that Paul hated women and felt they were inferior to men. They interpret his writings as severely limiting the role of women in the church; in fact, setting boundaries for women that make men look superior. This was not true of the apostle Paul. At the same time Paul [wrote the Epistles, he] had women on his ministry team and spoke highly of them. It was Paul who wrote, "There is neither Jew nor Greek, slave nor free, male nor female, for you are all one in Christ Jesus" (Galatians 3:28).[3]

Women in the early church were given positions of leadership and responsibility. Paul mentioned several women who collaborated with him in the gospel ministry, including Euodias and Syntyche, Mary, Tryphena, and Tryphosa. Priscilla and her husband Aquila were such assets that Paul brought them with him to Ephesus. There he left them to establish the work while he went to discharge a vow in Jerusalem.

During his absence, Priscilla and Aquila instructed Apollos so that with great power he proclaimed Jesus as the Messiah. When Paul determined to go to Rome, it appears that he again sent Priscilla and her husband to do the advance work. Of the six times that this couple is mentioned, the wife's name comes first four times, seemingly indicating that she was more active in Christian service. When Paul sent the letter to the Romans, it was apparently delivered by Phoebe, an officer of the church appointed by Paul.

Tension in the Church

Some churches spend so much time determining what a woman can't and won't do that it seems to rob the church of its harmony and unity for all believers.

It is true in some of the small-town churches in my community that women are not allowed to speak from the podium (or raised platform). On floor level is a lectern women can speak from.

Keeping Women "in Their Place"

One day I was invited to speak at a church for a Women's Day program. Women's Day programs are designed to honor women, they are generally held twice a year in black churches, and the participants in the program are women. I went a little early in case there would be an opportunity to pray before the program began. When I arrived there was no mention of a prayer time, so I sat down up close so I could make my way to the front easily. My husband was coming a little later with the children.

Before the service began I noticed the male leaders of the church came out and lined up on the platform. I wanted to introduce myself, but none of them came to introduce themselves to me, so I remained seated. Finally the service began and I noticed that all the women who took part in the service stayed on the floor speaking from the lectern and did not go up onto the platform. I decided to follow suit when I made my way to the front.

When I turned to the congregation I saw my husband and children sitting in the audience and found them a needed encouragement. My husband was the senior pastor of a growing church in the community, so I took time to speak about him as well as my children by

way of introduction. As I was speaking, I was interrupted by the senior pastor of the church, who stood up and made a special welcome to my husband. He had my husband stand up, and he invited
him up to the platform where all the other ministers of the church
were. My husband mentioned that he had the children and he would
not mind staying with them. (Our four-year-old son and three-year-
old daughter were in much need of adult supervision.) The pastor
asked one of the women of the church to go and watch the children,
and he insisted on my husband coming to the front. As my husband
walked past me, I couldn't help thinking about how much effort they
placed to bring my husband up front, yet I hadn't even been introduced to them as the speaker for the evening.

I felt of little importance in this male-oriented church. After the
program was over, I ran into the young lady who had invited me to
come and speak. She thanked me for coming, and we made small conversation. I finally mentioned to her that I was somewhat at a loss
in not knowing what to do at her church, and wondered whether I
should have spoken from the pulpit. One look at her face told it all.
She finally said, "Michelle, I am so glad you did not go up to the
pulpit. They would have come up there personally and had you come
to the floor to speak." She went on to say women are not allowed to
speak from the top, only from the bottom.

Some pastors and church leaders see women in lower and less
respected roles. Even with all the present-day equal rights for women
in the culture at large, in the church women are too often not treated
as people made in God's image, with gifts and abilities given by the
Holy Spirit to do the work of the ministry. The church suffers spiritually when women are not allowed to use their gifts to the glory of
God. Both men and women have a part to play biblically in order to
bring order and harmony to the church of Jesus Christ.

The Church and Sexual Abuse

In the book *Restoring Broken Vessels* by Victoria Johnson, April's
story is told:

A deacon at my church told me he could satisfy my sexual needs
if I had any as a single parent. I was so disgusted with this comment. When I confronted him about it, he told me he was just

teasing. But I think he would have taken me up on it if I had responded favorably. It has been a struggle to keep myself sexually pure after becoming a Christian as a widow. It almost makes you want to give up the struggle of a high standard when you have to deal with these things. But I've decided I need to do what God wants me to do no matter if all the deacons and pastors in the world don't want to go God's way.[4]

April's story is no different from hundreds of other stories told by women who see men in leadership in the church with double standards—men used by the devil to destroy the people of God, especially women. In the same book Victoria Johnson says pastors and church leaders need to become more aggressive in dealing with abusive or sexually addictive behaviors by leaders of the church. They need to hold these men accountable for their behavior toward their families, and they should exercise church discipline if they violate biblical principles.

Women struggle with submission when asked to submit to a male leader who is living in sin. Many of the same women have been victims of sexual abuse and wrong treatment by men. The church of God should be a place of healing and restoration, but in reality too many times it becomes a reminder of the pain that has haunted their lives for so long. I even heard of a case where a pastor had a wife and a girlfriend in the same church, and naturally the women in the church had a problem respecting male leadership. The church should be composed of God-fearing leadership able to address immorality and speak out on sexual sins such as adultery, pornography, and other sex offenses that are destroying the spiritual fiber of our nation. Sexual sins have become one of the silent issues of the church. Ask yourself, when was the last time you heard a message preached on sexual abuse, pornography, or adultery? If someone were to come to your church needing help and counseling regarding sexual abuse, would he or she be able to receive it?

Women's Ministries and the Church Today

So much emphasis is placed on what women can't do today and so little on what they can. Churches need to consider whether or not they are providing sufficient opportunities for women to receive ministry and not just to provide ministry to others. Women shoulder most of the responsibility for the health and vitality of the Christian faith in this country, and they need ministries that meet a personal spiritual need within their lives. Women can do so much more than watching children, cooking, and serving the general population of the church with dishes of food. Although these services rendered to the body are not to be looked down on, they are just a few of the many needs and opportunities women should be doing.

The Place of Women in the Church

Without women, Christianity would have nearly 60 percent fewer adherents. In other words, 60 percent of attendees on Sunday are women. In George Barna's recent report, half of the nation's women have beliefs that classify them as born again (46 percent), compared to just about one-third of men (36 percent). In other words, there are between 11 million and 13 million more born again women than there are born again men in the U.S.[5]

Christianity is still the "faith of choice" among Americans, but particularly among women. When asked to identify their religious affiliation, nine out of ten women nationwide (90 percent) said that they consider themselves to be Christian (compared to 83 percent of men).

Although women account for half of the U.S. adult population, they represent a majority of religiously active individuals in twelve out of the thirteen religious activities examined.[6] Women's participation levels outdistance that of men in the following areas:

1. 100 percent more likely (twice as likely) to be involved in a discipleship process at a church.
2. 57 percent more likely to participate in adult Sunday school; 22 percent of women said that they have attended an adult Sunday school class in the past week (14 percent of men have attended such classes).
3. 56 percent more likely to hold a leadership position such as a Sunday school superintendent, choir member, leader in women's ministry, deaconess, Christian education director, or church staff position. About one out of seven women (14 percent) in the country said that they have served in a lead-

ership capacity at a church, not including the role of pastor (9 percent of men have held such positions).

4. 54 percent more likely to participate in small groups. One out of every five women (20 percent) go to a small group that meets regularly for Bible study, prayer, or Christian fellowship (compared to 13 percent of men).

5. 46 percent more likely to disciple others; one out of five women —19 percent—are currently serving as the spiritual mentor to someone else (compared to 13 percent of men).

6. 39 percent more likely to have a devotional time or quiet time; 61 percent of women said that, during the last seven days, they have intentionally spent time alone reading the Bible, reviewing devotional material, or praying (44 percent of men had done this).

7. 33 percent more likely to volunteer for a church. One quarter of women (24 percent) said that during the last week they have volunteered some of their time to help a church (18 percent of men had done so).

8. 29 percent more likely to witness to others; more than one quarter of women—27 percent—have shared their faith with someone else during the past twelve months, in the hope that the person would accept Christ as Savior (21 percent among men).

9. 23 percent more likely to donate to a church; while a majority of women have donated to a church in the past thirty days (59 percent), slightly less than half of men (48 percent) have given money to a church.

10. 16 percent more likely to pray; 89 percent of women have prayed to God in the past seven days (as did 77 percent of men).

An Effective Ministry for Women

At my church we have established a ministry for women that is really working. It gives major opportunities for women to be ministered to as well as minister to others. As an important wing of the church, our ministry is called WINGS, which stands for Women IN Godly Services. It is a ministry for women by women. It started with the main event Bible study, but has grown with many other components that enhance the main event. Our ministry reaches women of all ages, beginning at eight years old. From ages eight to twelve, young girls are called Winglets. From ages thirteen to eighteen, young girls are called WingSpan. In addition to WingSpan, we have Wingsters, who are teenage mothers. From ages eighteen and up, we have our general class WINGS of women from all walks of life. WINGS is a weekly ministry geared for women, with major components that help engage women in spiritual growth and involvement:

1. Woman-to-Woman Bible Study. A Bible study taught by women for women is very important. It helps women get right down to the basic issues they are facing and allows for a deeper interaction among women. Such a ministry can become a needed Ladies' Night Out. The Bible study is the main event for the evening.
2. Counseling Ministry. This can be offered before the main event. Female lay counselors can take advantage of training for counseling women. A counseling ministry for women can be very effective in a church because it takes much of the pressure off the male leadership. With the sexualized society we are in today, women counseling women as much as possible is a very wise step. Who best to give counsel to a woman going through tough times than another woman.
3. Child Care. Because so many women, especially single mothers, have child-care issues, offering child care is a good solution. A low-cost child care that would defray the cost of supplies and snacks should be offered. Many older and younger women enjoy caring for children.
4. Physical Awareness. This is a great way to help women make friends with other women as they engage in various physical activities. Some of these activities can be weight-loss classes, exercise classes, and various physical topics like care for diabetes, care for aging parents, etc.
5. Worship Teams. Women enjoy praising the Lord through songs. This would be a great way to engage women who love to sing in using their talents and gifts for God. Each week before the main event they could lead the women in singing.
6. Praise Teams. Just like the need for women to express themselves in song, it is so inspiring to see praise in dance. A

specially developed praise team performing regularly would be a really needed ministry among women.

7. Drama Teams. Drama has a way of taking a theme or a main idea and bringing it even closer to the hearts of the audience. Women who enjoy acting can get involved in this ministry.

8. Hospitality. Any gracious hostesses out there? Hospitality requires a coordinator who makes sure that each night there will be light snacks for those attending the Ladies' Night Out.

9. Bookstore. Making resources available to women is helpful in their spiritual growth. The bookstore can be as small as a table or as large as a full-scale book room. Some women enjoy setting up tables, assisting women in purchases, and handling cash.

10. Teachers. Those who possess the gift or who enjoy encouraging women make good teachers. These teachers are trained and able to rightly divide the Word of God.

11. Greeters. This is a high position in our women's ministry because most women already know if they are coming back to WINGS fifteen minutes after they have arrived, which means they have not heard the Word of God yet. They know if they will return by the spirit of the women in the room. When greeters are warm and friendly, women relax and feel they can enjoy themselves.

12. Registrars. This group of women helps with nametags, directs women needing child care, and keeps up with the records of those attending each week.

There are many more avenues of ministry for women. Helping battered women, the homeless, and those who are in prison are a few more. The church can also select godly mature women to serve as deaconesses on the deacon board. Godly women can bring spiritual insight and freshness to any male leadership team. I am glad to share in the ministry with my husband. I am not a deaconess, but many times my husband seeks my advice concerning matters in the church. This makes me feel needed and appreciated. It has also increased my prayers and involvement within the church.

Conclusion

The pattern of male headship was established in Creation, and Paul wanted to see this principle affirmed in the church. The principle of male headship was violated through the reversal of authority roles in the Fall with devastating consequences, and Paul wanted believers to avoid such a role reversal and its consequences in the church.

Both men and women have a biblical part to play today in order to bring order and harmony to the church of Jesus Christ.

Elders (pastors) need to lead with clear consciences, realizing they are God's representatives to the church. If the church is to stem the tide of biblical illiteracy and waning commitment to the Christian faith, men will have to re-establish themselves as partners and leaders of the spiritual functions of families. Family unity is the key for spiritual growth and maturation in our decentralized, relationally isolated culture. The apparent lack of spiritual leadership exhibited by thousands of Christian men has significantly hampered the spiritual growth of tens of thousands of well-meaning but spiritually inert families.

Women should learn with an attitude of quiet submissiveness, rather than be involved improperly in teaching and leading men in the worship assembly. More specifically Paul directed women to learn in the worship assembly with a quiet and submissive attitude rather than to teach or have authority over a man in that context. But beyond that stipulation, the New Testament seems clear that women are to use their gifts, teaching other women, teaching children, and encouraging the body of Christ. Scripture tells of women who served God enthusiastically in a multitude of roles, and it seems that the bigger question is not, What are women *not* to do? but How can women best be equipped to serve God in our churches?

DISCUSSION STARTER QUESTIONS

1. Name at least two tensions described in the chapter. How do you view these tensions in your own life, your church, and other relationships? Describe the present ministry

opportunities women have to use their gifts and abilities in your local church. Is there room for improvement?

2. The pattern of male headship was established in creation (in the garden) in Genesis 1–3. Do you feel some of the strong passages written in the Word of God help us to see God's original plan for man and women in relationship to the church? Explain.

3. Women have been considered the backbone of the church throughout history. How do you see the strength women bring to the body of Christ through their personal commitment to God and the church? Do you believe women are able to preach using their giftedness today? Do you see any limitations placed on women in light of 1 Timothy 2:11–12? Explain.

PART FOUR

UNITY
ACROSS
OTHER
BARRIERS
IN THE
CHURCH

CHAPTER SIXTEEN

RETIRED AND SET ASIDE:

Is There a Place for Elderly Saints in the Body of Christ?

an edited interview with EVELYN CHRISTENSON

The Bible has a lot to say about respecting and learning from our elders, whether they be parents or other older relatives, godly church leaders, or just older people who are in our lives. But in America, much of the time old people are seen as useless, even a nuisance, mindless, and more or less outdated. Unfortunately, too often the church gets its cues for relationship to elders from American culture, not Scripture. On January 26, 2001, I (Dwight Perry) spoke with Evelyn Christenson, well known internationally for her speaking and writing, particularly her best-selling book *What Happens When Women Pray.* I wanted to get her perspective on the relationship between older and younger people in the church, as well as what our older saints have to offer us.

What is your view of how our culture views those who are elderly?

Many churches put a lot of time and energy into ministry to their elderly saints, sponsoring tours, planning fun times, and providing pastoral care. However this most often seems to be *to* and *for* the seniors, and unknowingly can miss the most important needs of their senior citizens—to be needed.

Senior church members are the happiest when they are like Jesus —who came not to be ministered unto, but to minister.

Perhaps there is a general underlying, usually unspoken, attitude of perceiving older people as not as intelligent because they don't keep up with all the newest technology and methods. So they're looked at as not as intelligent, and their contributions to the current culture frequently are ignored or downplayed.

Most younger people think most good things going on started with themselves, and were not built one generation on top of another. As Paul reminded young Timothy, the faith that was in him was first in his grandmother, Lois, and in his mother, Eunice (2 Timothy 1:5).

I think every generation of adolescents thinks that they have discovered or invented sex, and they can't figure out how all the parents ever had their children! I think they believe that many older people are financially a drain, have to be taken care of, and are leeches, as it were. But I think there is a resentment on the other side too. I remember when I got my first Social Security card, every paycheck I've gotten since I was in my early teens, they've taken out a big chunk, and so there are two sides to that misunderstanding.

Although most Christians take good and sometimes outstanding care of their elderly, many do seem to resent oldsters, who are a drain on their finances and their time. The added responsibility of taking care of parents is difficult because usually both partners are working and there is an incredible increase in family activities demanding the time and energy of the parents. Children are running to a different sports activity, club meeting, or lesson most every day plus school activities and homework. For the woman who works all day and comes home to the running of a home, the demands of her children, and needs of her husband, the caring for an elderly parent can understandably be a serious problem. But while some of them resent or withdraw—there are so many who are just beautiful in their love toward their parents and their attitude in this sacrificial lifestyle. We must not categorize everybody as either/or.

I think it's important to realize that this youth culture, this attitude towards elders, is in America, and it's not around the world. It's very exciting to see and to travel around the world, which I've done; I've taught in every continent, and we elderly people are perceived differently around the world. And I can say "we" because, I might as well interject here, next week I turn seventy-nine. I have been surprised in some places at the sudden respect, sometimes even bowing, when my age has been disclosed.

Now, however, there is a swinging of the pendulum. Many young people today are feeling cheated they were not taught moral values and the basic values of life by their materialistic, "if it feels good, do it" parents. There is a swing. One of our men, Rich Richardson, just got back from Urbana, and he said there was a definite swing of the young people wanting to go deeper into the silence before God, and morals, and learning the basics of walking with Jesus.

I hear a lot from the young people, down into their teens and twenties, and they feel that there's been a gap here, where their parents have really abandoned them and almost abdicated their responsibility in modeling and teaching biblical values. Some believe their parents, in seeking the good life, have almost abdicated their role toward them. Now, as those young people face the world, they realize they're not equipped because they weren't taught. So I'm finding that they're observing that the freedom and humanism of the 1960s and '70s did not work. So these young people are looking to the elders in the church for the solid moral and spiritual footing they missed.

How does the church in general reflect or counteract these attitudes towards the aged?

Well, first of all, the church is a composite of types of members; there's everything imaginable, and so they do all different kinds of things. I have a very comfortable situation in the church where I am, but that isn't true of everybody. In general, younger church members automatically are absorbing the *attitudes* of the world's culture toward the aging. But the church leadership may or may not be aware of a problem, or they may not be responding to it. I think the church has absorbed this worldly culture, this youth culture that's looking at the aged. It isn't biblical, and it isn't Christian, but the church has absorbed it. However, usually I have seen Christians more sensitive to the needs of their elderly, many of them hiring a pastor for seniors, or staff to care for them, so the church is trying.

Those churches that are not as sensitive to their seniors, what have you seen as some of the reasons why they're not as sensitive to their seniors?

I think there is a lot of pride. As every generation rightfully and by necessity takes over more and more jobs, they frequently develop an attitude of "I can do it myself, God." I think every generation goes through it. God through Paul warned against bringing on a church leader who was a new convert (inexperienced), or he may become conceited and fall into the devil's traps (1 Timothy 3:6). I remember when we were yound. I looked at some of these older ones and I thought, *Boy, we have all these wonderful ideas, and where are they being used?* They didn't see all that we're doing, nor did we see what they were.

I think there's the tendency for young people to think they have all the answers because "we're the productive ones, we're the strong ones, we're the leaders now, we're the deacons, we're the trustees," or whoever they are.

An even more important reason churches are not sensitive to their seniors is they really do not know how many elderly members may be hurting. When the elderly are ignored, as younger leaders seem to be conveying to them that they now are the strong and the wise ones, the former leaders may see the new ones as not only reinventing the wheels that already were there for years, but as being oblivious to answers the seniors themselves had to learn the hard way from God.

Most elderly people are hurting in some way. It is much more than the humorous quip that "old age is just one Band-Aid after the other." I believe the church truly is trying to be sensitive to seniors' needs, but am not sure they have touched many of the real problems yet.

In looking for a ministerial candidate, what role, if any, does age play?

This you hit on the head, Dwight. There is no question in my mind that almost all churches are looking for a thirty-five- to fifty-year-old, and this is even younger than the business culture in putting people out to pasture.

Taking a new church after fifty-five usually includes a step down the ladder, and a step down financially. Pastors almost always are given smaller churches with less sociological growth potential after they are fifty, and certainly after they are fifty-five. Many large successful works are pastored by those even older than sixty-five, but usually that pastor started earlier in years and built it. He doesn't get called to it, but he's allowed to stay.

Have you or anyone you know been discriminated against due to their age within the church?

Yes. I have to say yes, it goes on all the time. However there may be good reasons, such as a more qualified younger person, or one more able to keep up physically, or a need for new ideas and methods. But it certainly also can be just plain discrimination. There is a youth culture in America, and we're conforming our whole youth ministry to it — especially music. The entertainment world, all of it is youth-oriented. And the advertising world. Everything. Of course, now the secular world is beginning to recognize the value of appealing to the elderly as a growing financial market.

There is a difference in knowledge and wisdom. Knowledge personally applied becomes wisdom. I've seen unusually qualified teachers eager to share not just their head knowledge but their life-earned wisdom replaced by a much less qualified person—not necessarily at the request of those being taught but those selecting the teachers.

However, I am probably the wrong person to ask if I've been discriminated against in the church due to my age. With a full-time ministry still going at age seventy-nine and more open doors than I could possibly go through, I have not sensed that yet. I feel very accepted in my own church as groups of all ages ask me to pray with them, or for them, or to squeeze in a time in my busy schedule to speak to them. The first half of my adult ministry was while a pastor's wife within the church, and the other half has been outside the local church in all states and all continents—but always prayed for and with my radio broadcasts on other continents partially supported financially by my church.

In my church today, I see many of my old friends still skipping around doing one job after the other—and others having found their rocking chairs as early as forty-five. Perhaps the secret is, whether young or old, to be willing to be content with whatever job God gives us to do in the church—glamorous or humble, in the place of authority or behind the scenes.

There's just no question that the younger people get the bigger Sunday school classes, and this and that. That's OK. I went through those years. I am *so* content with where I am that I'm probably the wrong person to ask.

What are some specific action steps that the church needs to take in relating to the elderly in our churches?

This is where you said "sic 'em" to me, Dwight, because I just see so many of them. *First, there needs to be a comfortable relationship with elder members as equal members of the body of Christ,* including recognizing that their church is most likely there because of the sacrificing leadership and hard work of those elders. As I go to funeral after funeral lately, of people my age, it's just awesome to hear the accomplishments of some of tham and our foreign missionaries— what they actually did, how they built that church. But somehow all generations tend to date any movement at when *they* entered the scene. They fail to see what has gone on before, what they inherited without knowing they had inherited it. And so I think there needs to be a recognition of that.

Second, there needs to be an appreciation that the elders brought the scriptural teaching, preaching, and Bible studies to the current generation, grounding them in the basics of their current faith. As the younger Christian generation is trying to balance the worldly youth emphasis culture with the Bible, many are turning to the senior citizens for solid truth from the Bible. A growing number of them are not satisfied with just what they may have heard in Sunday school or youth group about what somebody thought and published as curriculum.

Recently I have been both surprised and thrilled at the number of young people who have begged me to be their spiritual mother or grandmother.

I remember in our church at Rockford Temple, for years and years and years we had the most students coming to Bethel of any church in the BGC [Baptist General Conference]. It was very exciting. We were very conscious of this test that the freshmen could take to get them out of taking the freshman Bible class. If they knew enough about the Bible then they didn't have to take it. Our students would come up and they would get really good marks, and so we were very proud of that in those days you know. It was something for which we really would strive. But there came a day at Bethel when they said, "It doesn't make any sense to give that test. There aren't enough freshmen who know enough about the Bible to even bother giving the test." That is because of the generation that studied everybody's books in Sunday school. They frequently weren't studying the Word of God; they were studying people's books. And this is still going on today. Good or bad books. That's what gets to you every once in a while.

Third, realize that traditions produce a sense of security in upcoming generations. But it is easy to take them for granted, not cherish them, or let them die. There is music from our elders that is full of deep theological truths from the Bible. This is good and we are poorer when we no longer sing any of them.

Our extended family always ends our Thanksgiving and ushers in the Christmas holidays by singing the "Hallelujah Chorus." We have a mixture of a few who can't read a note—all the way to one who has played piano with the Minnesota Orchestra. But what an awesome tradition that has been. When we finished the family funeral for my husband's mother, the matriarch of our extended family on that side, all generations of us gathered around the piano near her casket. We then lifted our hearts to heaven, where she already was, singing with a new fervor, "And He shall reign forever, and ever, and ever . . . !"

At a birthday party for one of the elders of our family, his daughter had brought the music for the hymns he and his wife especially loved to sing. As we sang around the piano, our son-in-law, who is just a great Christian, suddenly said, "Oh, I never realized what we gave up when we lost the theology in this old music. It isn't just taking a little phrase and singing it twenty-five times. There is an awesome scriptural theology in these songs."

It is so important to keep traditions going. The Muslims keep theirs going, the Jews keep theirs going, the Buddhists—they all do, except us. A friend went back to a traditional liturgical church because she was sick and tired of somebody reinventing the worship every Sunday morning. She didn't know what they were singing. And she was working like mad trying to keep up. We aren't worshiping when we're singing a song for the very first time; we've never heard it and we're trying to learn it. The music isn't even there for those who read music. Although frequently I have been thrilled while deeply worshiping God in those times, we don't usually get to real worship until we get deeper than learning new songs. But I love to worship with the younger generations!

Also, I think it's important that with mutual respect we communicate with each other. I mean we talk to each other, I don't look down at you, and you don't look down at me; we're members of the body of Christ with mutual respect. Taking steps to improve these relationships where needed in churches will greatly solve some of the age gaps keeping us from being one in Jesus as He prayed for us to be in His high priestly prayer in John 17.

However, I believe the Christian culture today is in danger of losing something precious and vitally important that was taken for granted by the elders—*communicating vertically with the sovereign God in heaven.* The most important kind of communicating is not interacting with other humans, but taking time to listen in silence to God in His Word and interacting with Him in prayer. Today I ask people, "Are we in danger of losing the most important thing, communicating with God—because we run around with earplugs in our ears, cell phones in our hands, or playing with our computers—listening to other people almost exclusively?"

One way this constant horizontal communicating shortchanges us is that everything we get is secondhand. We are missing out on the awesome new things Jeremiah 33:3 says the God of the universe absolutely will show us if we call on Him. Those "great and mighty things we know not!" How foolish to ignore all the fabulous things He wants to tell us as we settle for everything secondhand. (See Romans 11:3–36.)

Another danger of only listening to other people is the untruths and evil that come our way incessantly. What percentage of the input to those who are constantly glued to their computers is pornography, violence, hatred, lies—all of which God unabashedly calls *sin?* A very fine Christian young man friend of ours is in deep trouble at his college because he was caught carrying on a sexually explicit computer friendship with a girl who turned out to be a minor whom the authorities were using to trap students.

When our niece Elizabeth Morrison enrolled as a freshman in college, she said, "Aunt Evelyn, I'm worried about something. We all have computers in our rooms—which are connected to the finest libraries in the country. And I've learned how to get an A on my papers. All I do is download all this wonderful information, arrange it in outline form, add a few transition sentences, and I have my A. *All without any of it going through my brain, but just from machine to machine.* I don't like that!" And she stopped doing that immediately—and went on to be chosen Bethel College's "Student of the Decade" last year.

Since just communicating has all but replaced the silence of listening to God, in prayer and in His Word, I think this lifestyle should be taught again, I wrote about it in a book, in my *Lord Change Me* book in 1977. I have seven methods of how the Lord wants to change us, but perhaps the most important one is listening, staying in the Word until He speaks, praying and obeying what God says.

Another thing. *Use the elders, the older people of the church.* One of the greatest needs of the elderly is not cupcakes and a cute doily, or to be entertained, but to be used. Don't stop doing the nice little things for your elderly friends, but remember most of them want something real to fill the void in their lives of inactivity and not being involved any longer in what used to be life itself to them. They need to be needed. Here are a few ways the elderly really can help—not just do busy work:

Prayer. The greatest untapped prayer potential in the church today is their senior citizens. I know that experientially. On my board for my United Prayer Ministries I have senior citizens, and I have young ones too. But the older ones have time. And some of them are in pain at night. One retired school principal was in so much pain she couldn't sleep nights. So, instead of counting sheep, she talked to the Shepherd. And she always came to board meetings with a little pile of those she specifically had prayed into Jesus' kingdom that month while a missionary reached them personally!

When the elderly no longer are physically strong enough to teach us, preach, and do manual labor, they have the spiritual maturity and the time to wrestle in prayer. And they do. Some of course have restricted mental abilities, but even they often pray.

Prayer for Evangelistic Bible Studies. We had the little neighborhood Bible studies going out under the Christian Women's Clubs from our church in Rockford. There were 350 of them. A woman only had to go to one and with all the materialwritten out, she just had to invite five to six people to her home and they had the chance to accept Jesus. We were a pilot church for this project, but we had a secret.

We assigned a golden ager to each group. She contacted the hostess and the teacher every week. They told her all the problems and needs and the names of the people, and she prayed for the salvation of each of them. There was never less than one person saved in every one of those Bible studies. Yes the teacher was eager to share what she had just found in Jesus, but it was the prayer support of a golden ager who would take the six weeks of the course and give her all to praying fervently for it. I've done that with neighborhood vacation Bible school and using many of the older people. It works!

Telephone Prayer Chains. We had our telephone prayer chains going *all* the time in Rockford. We prayed for every facet of our church. And a lot of them who could really spend time in prayer were the golden agers. I find that with my own ministry board too.

Then we sent our prayer requests to a lady in a nursing home who was in a wheelchair. She had a little typewriter. We'd give her the prayer requests. Simple ones. Then she'd type them out and putter around in her little wheelchair and hand them out to bedridden Christians. Then we would send through the answers. She would go around with the answers, so they could see the worth of themselves in prayer. They need to be needed. This is one of the best ways we can use the eldest church members. It's awesome.

The church must honestly depend on God through prayer and must teach and practice it and preach it from the pulpit if they're going to act like they need the elderly people to pray. If the church is going to use them as pray-ers, the pastor has to admit that he needs prayer, and the whole church has to honestly depend on prayer, which is not true in most churches. Now some of the greatest churches do, but they don't all.

Bible Studies by and for the Elderly. We also can use the elderly in Bible studies and nursing homes or retirement homes. They can have simple little Bible studies, and maybe just stay in one chapter, or The Lord's Prayer, or the Twenty-third Psalm or something. These people in nursing homes and retirement homes can't always absorb a lot, but they certainly can get the basics, and they're looking for answers. They really are.

Another thing we can use elders for is *counselors.* I have a board member who is in her eighties who is still a Billy Graham phone counselor. She leads several people to the Lord every time she is online, and then she brings them to church. She nurtures them, she sees about their physical problems, and all this. She follows them up. It's absolutely incredible. Her name is Mary Lou. Golden agers' accumulated experience and wisdom are desperately needed. When Mary Lou talks, she has answers just like this: "Oh, well, now when that happened to me, this is how the Lord helped me." You know, spiritual maturity and experience are important.

Most elderly Christians have learned how to let God make finer gold out of their hottest fires. The faith of their younger years has turned into absolute knowing who God is and how He works. In 2 Corinthians 1:3–4 we read, "Praise be to the God and Father of our Lord Jesus Christ, the Father of compassion and the God of all comfort, who comforts us in all our troubles, so that we can comfort those in any trouble with the comfort we ourselves have received from God." Nobody can learn that overnight.

Then there is awesome *faith* of so many older Christians. The faith of their younger years, often with an unidentified bit of hoping in it, has turned into an absolute knowing who God is and how He works. In these uncertain times, our young people need to see their elders living out their unshakable faith in God.

When I was just twenty-three years of age and my life was extremely difficult from World War II and three lost babies, God clearly said to me, "It's Romans 8:28." I knew it by heart and kept reciting it over and over, "And we know that God works all things together for good to those who love Him, and are called according to His purpose."[1] But lying in that hospital bed as a young wife, it was just pure faith and trust in what God said. But now I can say absolutely, "I know!" After experiencing from age twenty-three to seventy-nine what God really has done that for me, my faith has turned to knowing.

Mentoring is another word you can use. The church needs to encourage the younger members to learn from the wisdom and experience of the elders. This can be formally, with a study, as they develop one-on-one relationships, or as always is going on—the younger are learning by example, good or bad. The church should teach the elders their responsibility for the example of their faith and their lifestyle.

Sharing Jesus. Nursing homes and retirement homes are fertile harvest fields for those sweetly living and lovingly sharing Jesus. That's important. You can't be an old grump and say, "I want you to be what I am," but if you are really a loving and caring older person, and there are those in nursing homes, people want what they have. Someone asked me, "What's your answer? Tell me what's your answer. Why aren't you afraid of dying?" My answer became hers too—Jesus!

For years our daughter Jan was a critical care doctor in her hospital, often the last person to see a patient before death. When I was writing down the verses in my international *Study Guide for Evangelism Praying* curriculum for women around the world to use to lead people to Jesus, Jan said, "Mother, be sure that you use 1 John 5:13, 'by this you can know that you have eternal life . . .' Those are the words I use, Mother—after I have shared Jesus with them, of course." Then Jan said, "Mother, there are exceptions of rebellious dying people dying flying angily in the face of God, but I have found most of them are fearful. Painkillers? Yes. But give them the dignity of not being afraid of dying and absolutely knowing where they're going."

Then we should stress the *joy* that elderly members should have in seeing the fruits of their labors taking root in the next generation. Now there are a lot of times that the elders are living in the "if onlys" and "oh, dear, if I wouldn't have"—living in the guilt of the past. But a lot of them are living in the joy of seeing the next generation serve Jesus. As my mother watched us mature, I watch my generation coming now under me. I was just down in Rockford, Illinois, for their wonderful Christmas festivity. Two young women came up to me, and they said they were Marion Ferrell's daughters. My heart almost exploded with joy. Marion Ferrell was the first person who was saved in my neighborhood Bible study.

I had become restless always teaching those who were already Christians, fishing in the aquarium as it were. So I started a new neighborhood evangelism Bible study. I let them read Scripture and then would let them discuss whatever they wanted to discuss about it. Amazingly, only two out of all the people who came through that Bible study in three years did *not* accept Jesus, only two. A few of them we found out, really did know Him, but weren't sure.

I got worried at first because nobody was accepting Jesus. That was during the time that we were doing *What Happens When Women Pray* experimentation in that church in Rockford. Tuesday morning was our prayer day, and we had filled this large room with pray-ers who had been praying for them. Then I told them that I was taking Marion to lunch to make sure she knew Christ; I wanted to lead her to the Lord that noon. They were praying and each prayed through the lunch hour. Well, I thought *I* was taking Marion, but she arrived in her big, white Cadillac convertible, the top down, and took me to her husband's country club, which he basically owned I guess. In spite of all of it, Marion accepted Christ that day, and that was my first convert in my Bible study. Those girls, her daughters, said, "Our mother taught us about Jesus and then led us to Jesus as our Savior, and then she taught us to pray. And we want you to know that because of your struggling so hard back there in that Bible study our mother then passed on to us what you taught her."

Elders are not giving themselves credit. They're saying, "Look what *God* did with my feeble little attempt." They didn't have anything written in those days about evangelism Bible study. This faithful attempt, that's all God wanted. That's what the elderly people want to look back at: when they succeeded or fell on their faces. Many stumbled and their testimony was so weak and feeble, and yet they look back and see a new generation did come through, they did accept Jesus and they are serving the Lord, and so that's a very, very important thing.

Deuteronomy 4:9 commands us "to give heed to yourself and keep your soul diligently, lest you forget the things which your eyes have seen . . . but make them known to your sons and your grandsons."

These past victories can be a real source of joy to those who no longer can be out on the front lines for Jesus. Not because they need recognition for themselves nearly as much as to tell others of how powerfully God worked—when they perhaps were weak, inexperienced, or feeling their way into an unknown future service for Jesus.

These past victories of seniors also can be a great learning tool in the church today—taking what worked in the past while those in this generation step into their own unknown future full of things God hasn't shown any other generation yet!

I have a board member, Fran Howard, who's working in the prisons nationally and overseas. She told me she has personally observed through the years that drug addicts beget drug addicts, child abusers beget child abusers, prostitutes beget prostitutes, and right down the line, but also Christians should beget Christians. What we are, that's what we beget. In our homes, in our neighborhoods, in our nursing homes, wherever we are. Of course that Steve Green song, "Find Us Faithful," reminds us of the importance of what we leave behind. We are all the product of those who have gone before us.

But it behooves the church to make sure that what's going on is what we want to leave behind. I think we're falling down there too. According to Psalm 145:4, "One generation shall praise thy works to another, and shall declare thy mighty acts" (KJV). The responsibility is awesome—but also is the incredible privilege given us by God.

What does the Bible say about how we should respond to our elders?

Judy Mbugua from Kenya is the president of PACWA (Pan Africa Christian Women's Association for all of Africa) and the international president of our AD 2000 International Women's Track under whom I worked as the director for North America. Judy to me was a perfect example of how to treat those older than yourself since I was already sixty-nine years old when I accepted that ten-year assignment.

Judy always encouraged me through thick and thin. But the greatest came when, after I had written the curriculum for our women all around the world teaching how to put evangelism into whatever they were doing for God, we met at an international board meeting. Judy put her arms around me and tears streamed down her cheeks as she said, "Evelyn, I want you to know, I have now put evangelism into all of PACWA!"

When my cardiologist advised against my going overseas, I missed the meeting of all of us directors held in Guatemala, but Judy sent me this verse from her heart to mine:

> *"Even to your old age, I shall be the same,*
> *And even to your graying years I shall bear you!*
> *I have done it, and I shall carry you;*
> *And I shall bear you, and I shall deliver you."*
> Isaiah 46:4

A young, powerful worldwide leader encouraging a golden ager! But not for me alone. This is the Lord speaking—encouraging all His children in their old age.

One of the most amazing things Jesus did on the cross was remember His mother. While He was in the throes of His physical and spiritual agony, while He took on Himself the sins of the whole world, Jesus stopped to give His mother into the hands of His disciple John and to tell John "Behold your mother." And from that hour John took her into his own house. *Are we really achieving our goal of being Christ-like if we fail in what was so important to Jesus—even while dying?*

Leviticus 19:32 says, "You shall rise up before the grayheaded, and honor the aged, and you shall revere your God; I am the Lord." The Ten Commandments from God firmly state the same: "Honor your father and your mother, that your days may be prolonged in the land which the Lord your God gives you" (Exodus 20:12).

Proverbs 16:31 states, "A gray head is a crown of glory, if it is found in the way of righteousness."

As the strength of youth fades, one of the most exasperating things for seniors is to have vision and even urgency about doing something for God, and then their strength fails before the vision. But Isaiah 40:29–31 encourages us by saying, "Though youths grow weary and tired, and vigorous young men stumble badly, yet those who wait for the Lord will gain new strength . . . like the eagles."

All through my senior years (and years before) I completely trusted the power of Christ as Paul did in his thorn in the flesh experience in 2 Corinthians 12:9–10, "My grace is sufficient for you, for power is perfected in weakness . . . for when I am weak, then I am strong." Through numerous major surgeries and a parasite attacking my heart leaving only about one-third of it living, beating muscle—God always has given me all the strength I have needed to travel and speak for Jesus. Never once has He let me down!

The promise that has encouraged me the most in times of wondering if I still can be of any use to God is Psalm 92:14–15, "They [the righteous] will still yield fruit in old age. They shall be full of sap and very green, to declare that the Lord is upright; He is my rock . . ."

What does God say about changing our obedience to His call when we age?

I don't think age makes any difference to God. A call is an ongoing thing—until He calls us to something else. I've written a lot about it in my new book, *What God Does When Women Pray*. There is no mandatory retirement age in the Bible; it is strictly man-made. See, at any age there's the passage in Luke 11 when Jesus said, "Oh no, it's not the one who gave birth and nursed Me, but it's anyone who hears the Word of God and obeys it who is blessed." So do I have the right suddenly when I turn sixty-five not to obey the Word of God and His call on my life anymore?

My call to the prayer ministry came in the fall of 1967 when I had received an invitation to take the women of my own church and, in six months' time, find out exactly what God does when women pray. No theories, just solid interviewing the people for whom we had prayed. Not having a clue how to do such an experiment, I stalled until God powerfully called me with the words from Revelation 3:8, "Behold I have put before you an open door." My obeying immediately opened the door to a now thirty-four-year international ministry and millions of copies of books on prayer.

Through the years whenever I asked God if I had gotten old enough to throw in at least part of the towel, He would powerfully recall to my mind Jesus' words to the church in Sardis in Revelation 3:2, "Wake up and strengthen the things that were about to die; for I have not found your deeds completed in the sight of My God."

The year I turned sixty-five, at our United Prayer Ministry's annual "Lord, Change Me" retreat, we were all silently getting instructions from the Lord out of Revelation chapter three. I wept before my board and God, repenting that I had even thought of perhaps retiring a little bit, for in prayer Jesus had said to me: "Where did you get the idea it is *your* door? It is Mine!" His Scripture to me had been, "He . . . who opens and no one will shut, and who shuts and no one opens, says this: . . . Behold I have set before you an open door."

No person (including myself) could shut the door—but if He shuts it, no human can open it. That is all I need directly from Jesus to keep going until He says stop. Time is in His hands.

However, still serving Him does not mean staying in the same thing forever. I am in the process of turning over the administrative side of my AD2000/Christian Women United commitment for the decade of the '90s—because it is finished. I will stay in a steering position until God changes that because I still feel a growing urgency to reach the lost for Jesus. I have stacks of penciled notes of things I want desperately to get written also. But to this point I have not been released from my most recent calling. I still want to meet Jesus "with my boots on."

Describe an experience that you perceive as positive in the way people have respected you for your age.

I have been on national committees such as the National Prayer Committee since 1973 and Mission America's various committees for the past ten years, always praying deeply about things I felt needed changing but rarely being assertive—because I have frequently been the token woman on many of them. However, I have been surprised at an unusual asking for my opinion recently—an old grandmother in her upper seventies.

One of the first times it happened we were having a Mission America "Light Your Street" meeting. Chris Cooper was there with his computer and then-new program where we all took turns talking and seeing the computer screen type out our words. We were all excitedly gushing over all the new communicating techniques including "spiritual mapping" of any area in the United States and our being able to sign up for all the data about every house in that area so we could reach them for Jesus. Suddenly the marketing agent for the world's largest international evangelism organization said, "Evelyn, you can't leave this committee." I asked him why not. And his reply was "Because you have such a loud voice."

Embarrassed, I tried to defend myself a little. "That is because I have been projecting it in my speaking for so long."

"Oh no," he replied, "It is because we know *how* to say it (with all this modern technology), but you know *what* to say."

Perhaps mine is not the normal senior citizen story, but I am not worthy of all the wonderful awards and respect I am given. True, the church may have many things to change to make a place for the elderly saints in the body of Christ, not retiring us and setting us aside. But here are few positive answers I've taught and seen work throughout my adult life:

Solution to All Discrimination Issues in the Church
(not just the elderly)

1. Both the ones hurt and the ones doing the hurting must realize that even these attitudes are called "sin" in God's Word. (See James 4:17.)

2. Admit that Satan gets an advantage (toehold in us) when we are grieved and do not follow the formula of 2 Corinthians 2:5–11, which includes forgiving.
3. Each side needs to pray "Lord, change *me*" not "change my adversary." Holding grudges, having a constant un-Christlike chip on our shoulder, not controlling our tongue, etc. are all biblical sins that need to be confessed and stopped.
4. There must be sincere prayers of repentance on both sides. First John 1:8–9 is written only to Christians. Then doing deeds "meet for repentance" is actually fellowshiping, working, playing, and praying together.
5. Jesus prayed for us in His prayer in John 17 that we would have unity, and He made it very clear that the world will not be interested in our evangelizing them if we can't get along with each other. Why should they want Christanity when they are having more fun at the corner bar?
6. Jesus commanded us to pray for those who persecute us—not retaliate.
7. Where there is a lack of love—so obvious in the Bible's requirement of Jesus' followers—we PRAY asking God to give it to us. This works amazingly well.

God's Ultimate Secret for Handling All Discrimination

However, the overall secret that will unequivocally handle all discrimination in our churches is what Jesus taught us to pray in His Lord's Prayer: "Our Father which art in heaven . . .Thy will be done on earth—as it is in heaven" (Matthew 6:10).

When we see every member of the body of Christ regardless of race, color, sex, age, social status, or financial success as a vital part of His purpose planned from eternity past, we will not only gladly accept but will want and encourage God's will in and for each member.

Second Timothy 1:9 explains it clearly: "[God] who has saved us, and called us with a holy calling, not according to our works but according to His own purpose and grace which was granted us in Christ Jesus from all eternity . . ."

When each person in the church sincerely wants God's will and not their own for every member of the body of Christ, including for himself or herself—then all criticism, defensiveness, trying to control others, and discrimination will fade away. And we will think we are in heaven already!

DISCUSSION STARTER QUESTIONS

1. What does the Bible say about our relationship to aged believers? Have your own attitudes/actions matched your beliefs?
2. Does your church/ministry put older Christians on the shelf or use them effectively? Do older men have the opportunities to teach younger men and older women, younger women?
3. If you were to develop a philosophy for effective, biblical responses to the older people in your ministry (or your community), what would you emphasize? What is the hardest point for you personally in Mrs. Christenson's list above? Why? Is there anything in your thinking, or your actions, that you must change to conform to the truths from God's Word you have just read?

CHAPTER SEVENTEEN

THE THEOLOGY OF THE WHEELCHAIR:

How Can We Minister Christ's Wholeness to Those with Disabilities?

SANDY RIOS

Sasha and the Theology of Wheelchairs

The patent leather shoe went flying through the air as Sasha bore down, a deep furrow in her brow, willing her stronger right leg to kick the footrest of her wheel chair, cracking the plastic and sending the shoe hurtling through the church hallway. Exasperated at the number of times we had chased the shoe, but at the same time grateful she could accomplish such a feat, we looked down on her determined countenance as she let out a giggle. We lifted her from the chair and carried her into the sanctuary, little-girl shoe in hand, as was our Sunday custom.

We took our usual seats, and, as the organ played the prelude, her big brown eyes were held in rapt attention. There was a brief pause as the organist released the final chord. Sasha held her breath for a moment, eyes still with wonder, then let out a high-pitched melody, loud and sweet, that only the angels could recognize. I clasped my

282 BUILDING UNITY IN THE CHURCH OF THE NEW MILLENNIUM

hand over her mouth, barely managing to muffle her song, but enjoying her enthusiasm and comforted with the knowledge that my church family knew her well and greeted her outbursts with humor and abundant patience. The organist next moved to a hymn that we all sang loudly—all of us but Sasha, who lapsed back into her silent, wide-eyed wonder, listening intently, waiting . . . waiting . . . until the hymn reached its conclusion and silence fell over the sanctuary once again. "Aaaaaaaaaaaaaaaah!" her sweet voice resounded in fortissimo as she launched into verse two of her Sunday morning solo. I was forced to walk out, hand gently over her mouth as she sang—walking laughing, half embarrassed, half delighted in her love of music and the expression of it in her own special way.

This was a typical Sunday morning at our home church of many years. Once, in the middle of the pastor's very serious sermon, Sasha waited for one of those dramatic pauses to insert a loud—always loud, but ever sweet—nonverbal response. The pastor looked our way, smiled, and thanked her tenderly by name for her input. The congregation laughed, and we felt the warmth that only family can feel in the safety and love of their own kind, the people of God. How blessed we were to have a church family like that!

The Sunday Marathon

With two babies, Sasha six but still in diapers, unable to feed herself, walk, talk, or manage any of the basic skills, and my strapping rolled roast of a baby boy, Jeremy, full of his own demands, Sundays were a challenge at best. By the time I had gotten Sasha up, fed her, bathed her, and dressed her, an hour and a half had transpired. For Jeremy it was nursing him in the early months, diapering, dressing him, and then using whatever time remained to ready myself. Then there was the loading into the car: carrying Sasha, carrying her chair and her bags, carrying Jeremy, his stroller or seat and his bags, and somehow carrying Bibles, purse, and whatever else the day called for. Once at church, there was the unloading ritual: each stroller out, each child in with each bag, wheeling them into church and then carrying them up or down stairs because the building was tri-level. That took us through Sunday school, at the end of which time we had to lift Sasha out of her wheelchair and carry her into the sanctuary to a pew. By the time I arrived at the main service, I was exhausted.

I am embarrassed to admit that it was the rare Sunday I didn't fall asleep in church from sheer exhaustion. Call it pride, but it was important to me that nobody was impositioned by my circumstances, that my responsibilities, however difficult, didn't define me or burden those around me. I would get to Sunday school, look around at the other young couples, and in a flash of self-pity wonder if they had any idea what I had just been through in order to be there, sitting beside them. Of course they didn't, and I wasn't going to waste their time explaining what I understood to be my unique circumstance to manage in the best way I could.

Nobody could shoulder my responsibility but me. But sometimes I failed. Not only was Sasha's disability severe, but she was often sick with fevers, infection, and allergies, and she had chronic seizures. There were as many Sundays when her outbursts were the animal groanings of a grand mal seizure while her limbs jerked violently and her face contorted as there were sweet solos. This could happen at any time and did. During songs, messages, Scripture readings—quiet moments and loud ones. It was impossible to predict, impossible to stop, impossible to carry her out, and it did not end with the passing of the attack. The seizure would end with loud choking, coughing, groans, and sometimes with another coming on its heels. And still our church family bore it with us . . . kindly . . . lovingly . . . patiently. How blessed we were!

Sometimes it was just seizures, sometimes it was infections, but illness was chronic. The greatest stress of her care was never being able, no matter how hard we tried or how much we did or how much we wanted to, to make things all right for her. After spending thirty to forty-five minutes feeding her, she might projectile vomit all her food, including her life-sustaining seizure medications. When seizures came, she would sleep for hours, moving into days, in which it was impossible to get liquids or food down. Worrying . . . worrying . . . waiting for the fever to lift or the seizures to stop, desperate to get some sustenance and medication into her fragile body. In a given week of school, she rarely attended all five days. In a given week, between her chronic needs and Jeremy's regular, normal baby needs, I rarely slept all night. The strain and stress, in spite of my efforts to shield my friends from the burden, often spilled over into Sundays.

Sometimes it was all I could do to hold back the tears as they insisted on making their way down my cheeks. Week after week I wept silently, feeling like an old woman before I ever was one and wondering if I could survive another day. Our Sunday school teacher's wife was the kindest, most empathetic woman I knew. She seemed always able to hear my sorrow without losing interest or patience. Week after week she saw me cry, and sometimes it seemed as if it were only her kind words and willingness to let me unburden myself that kept my sanity and ability to keep going.

It was without doubt my faith in the Lord Jesus and the strength I found in His Word, through His Spirit, and among His people that sustained me for the twenty years I kept Sasha Richelle. And because my brothers and sisters in Christ lived that drama with me, I hesitate to utter any complaint toward them or their response to me and my precious little one. Only for the purpose of instruction would I venture a criticism, for above all, I am grateful not only to God for His sustaining power, but to my various church families who often were His hands and feet.

So it is in that spirit I commit to paper the areas in which they could have expressed God's love more and represented His heart more faithfully, for there are thousands of Sashas out there in varying forms whose mothers don't have the kind of deep, abiding faith in and long history with God that I was blessed with, who might have fallen by the wayside or thought that the negligence of God's people was the negligence of God Himself. Many of those desperately need the Living Hope that only the Living God can give, and they have never experienced it because church people never knew what they did wrong, never understood the heart of God in these matters—and people like me never took time to present the need and help correct the course for parents struggling now, even as I write, and those coming in the future.

If I had never been Sasha's mother, I confess to you right here and now, I don't think I would have ever had the affinity to deal with people with disabilities. I am by nature a very impatient person, restless, not given to confinement or repetitious duty. I drive fast, talk faster, and simply can't stand to be held down for too long anywhere. So God in His infinite wisdom has allowed this thing in my life for a purpose and, to use a phrase from my good friend Joni Tada, I have been "held still." So knowing God's mind in dealing with the disabled has not come naturally to me. I was an unwilling pupil who found herself in a graduate-level course. But I had a wonderful partner, my precious mother, and together we prayed and wept and pleaded with

God, and studied His Word until at last we were at peace. The sorrow has never left. I don't think it ever will. But peace? Absolutely —beyond understanding. I could write a book on what God has done in my life and taught me in the process, but today and for now, I will confine my reflection to what He has shown me about the way the body of Christ should be serving the disabled.

Lopsided and Unblessed: A Diagnosis

Upon the death of newspaper publishing mogul Katherine Graham, the media were in awe of the number of celebrities and "important people" she had associated with and who were present at her funeral: Former Secretary of State Madeleine Albright, former Secretary of Defense Robert McNamara, renowned news anchor Walter Cronkite, billionaire "wunderkind" Bill Gates, Academy Award winning actor Tom Hanks. It was a virtual "Who's Who" of power and influence. Why in the world didn't Jesus surround Himself with people like that? He created these mortals and could have had a relationship with any of them. Why not an evening with Caesar or the senators of Rome? An Egyptian queen or a king or two? It could have been so glamorous, and much more convincing, His claim to Godhood, don't you think? How disappointing that the God of the universe should send His Son to earth to spend His three valuable years of ministry not with the worthy, but the unworthy—poor people, blind people, lame people, lepers, prostitutes, and beggars. What was God thinking?

When John the Baptist inquired if Jesus was the One they were waiting for, Jesus answered, "Go back and report to John what you hear and see: The blind receive sight, the lame walk . . ." (Matthew 11:4–5). The very presence of the disenfranchised and their resultant healing was the definitive sign the Messiah was present.

How many wheelchairs line the aisles of your church? How many blind people sit in the pews, and how many deaf are in the hearing-impaired section? If God is present, then why aren't they? Could it be that the people of God have failed to provide a place or to manifest His presence in such a way that the disenfranchised flock can receive comfort and God's healing as they did in the time of Jesus? Does their absence mean they don't exist, or does it illustrate our failure to exemplify the Great Physician's heart?

I recall an old gentleman who had been a faithful member of our church. For years he attended, served, and gave, but when a stroke came, managing the stairs became an impossible task. The only way he could get into the sanctuary was for several husky men to lift him up the stairs in his wheelchair. I remember seeing him cry over being unable to access the service without great difficulty. At the same time, Sasha was growing and our own efforts to get her into the sanctuary were becoming more difficult by the year. The church discussed the possibility of putting in an elevator, but it was very expensive, and in their logic there were, you see, only a few people who needed it. It would be such a terrible waste of resources. They contented themselves with providing tapes for the "shut-ins" and man power for the wheelchairs.

This was a wise use of God's money, they told themselves. Who were we to demand such an expense on our behalf, and who was this little old saint of a man to do the same? And so we continued to manage the situation, searching for help each time we arrived at church and each time we needed to move up or down the stairs. As Sasha grew bigger, I had just enough strength to lift and carry her to the left-hand side, fifth pew of the sanctuary, without any stops or pauses. It always puzzled me when well-meaning members of the flock would choose those moments for a chat as my arms began to shake and my knees trembled. I would have to push past them and declare breathlessly in the most spiritual Sunday morning way, "I can't stop right now!"

God didn't, however, fail to observe this struggle. One couple knew His mind, and at the end of the service, the husband, a former football player, would rush to my side, sweep Sasha up in his arms, load her into her wheelchair, carry her downstairs with the assistance of others, and see me, Sasha, and Jeremy, chairs and paraphernalia included, completely into the car. What a godsend. The kind of help I was embarrassed to ask for week after week, but the kind that brought tears as it was freely given. We were so blessed. And yet . . . something bothered me. What was God's mind in this? Would He have agreed that an elevator was a waste of His money? Would the elderly gentleman's situation alone have been enough to justify the expense? Would ours? Doesn't God expect us to be good stewards of our resources . . . and yet . . . ?

Jesus' Response to Waste and Brokenness

"Then Mary took about a pint of pure nard, an expensive perfume; she poured it on Jesus' feet and wiped his feet with her hair" (John 12:3). Judas Iscariot objected to this extravagant, seemingly wasteful action: "Why wasn't this perfume sold and the money given to the poor? It was worth a year's wages." "Leave her alone," Jesus replied. "It was intended that she should save this perfume for the day of my burial" (vv. 5, 7). I do realize that Jesus' burial was the most profound occasion the world would ever experience, but still it seems to me that in Jesus' mind there were occasions worth "wasting" money on.

In Luke chapter 5:18–26 comes the old familiar story of the paralyzed guy whose friends went to great extremes to get him to see Jesus. They dismantled a roof (how destructive and wasteful) and, in very dramatic and determined fashioned, lowered the man into the house. It was just one man, you see, and I'm sure the homeowner wasn't crazy about their disregard for his property. Those friends were probably responsible men with busy lives, but somehow, instinctively, they knew this one man was worth it and that bringing him to Jesus was the right thing to do, no matter the cost. What they in fact did was engineer a first-century handicap-accessible sanctuary.

Perhaps you're assuming they knew Jesus had the power to heal and that's what drove them to such extremes. He was their friend, he was unable to walk, and this was a once-in-a-lifetime opportunity to change that. But what was the first thing Jesus said to the man? It wasn't "Stand up and walk," it was "Friend, your sins are forgiven." The scribes and Pharisees became furious at what they heard as His blasphemy. Jesus read their thoughts and said, "'Which is easier: to say, "Your sins are forgiven," or to say, "Get up and walk"? But that you may know that the Son of Man has authority on earth to forgive sins. . . .' He said to the paralyzed man, 'I tell you, get up, take your mat and go home'" (Luke 5:23–24).

And the man got up, rolled up his sleeping mat, and walked home. It was an amazing miracle, but according to Jesus, just as miraculous that his sins be forgiven as that his body be healed. Do you think his friends were expecting that? Probably not, but Jesus taught all of us, including them, a valuable lesson about miracles. Today, for whatever reason, the Great Physician doesn't seem to be performing many dramatic healings to the physical body, but to the spirit, the miracles are just as incredible! Why can't we see that healing still awaits the disabled as well as the able-bodied and that we must go to heroic, dramatic efforts to bring them into His presence in the same way the friends of the paralytic did in the first century . . . even if it means installing an expensive elevator. I believe this is God's mind on the matter.

Our Own Priorities

Part of the problem is one of perspective. Sanctuaries are air-conditioned; pews are padded. Women's restrooms are decorated, and canopies are built over entrances to protect from the rain. None of these are necessities, but they provide comfort for able-bodied adults, teens, children—contributing members, financially and otherwise. Technically, these things are just as much a waste as ramps, elevators, and accessible bathrooms. Perhaps more so, because their absence won't make it impossible for people to attend church.

"Each of you should look not only to your own interests, but also to the interests of others" (Philippians 2:4). It isn't enough that the comfort of the strong and healthy and verbal is obtained; we must consider the silent and defenseless as well, as we care for the whole body of Christ. The truth of the matter is we really do think able-bodied people are more important. They contribute more but cost less . . . give input . . . keep things going. But remember the parable in Luke 14 in which Jesus instructed His listeners that when they gave a dinner party they were not to call their friends or rich neighbors who were able to reciprocate the invitation, but to invite the poor, the maimed, the lame, and the blind—and He told them, "You will be repaid at the resurrection of the righteous" (v. 14). The principle here? To give when you'll get nothing in return.

I don't really think churches intentionally decide the disabled are unworthy of special consideration, I just think they don't understand that God has asked us to provide not just for those who can give back but especially for those who have nothing to give and no voice even to express thanks. I believe this is God's mind on the matter.

When God looks upon mankind, just what do you think He sees? Does He see the lawyer's perfectly groomed hair and three-piece suit as he enters the courtroom, or does He see his thoughts, filled with strategy, deceit, and vanity? Does He see the beautiful face and fig-

ure of a young movie star, or does He see the heart filled with seduction and adultery? Does He see our fit bodies, or our selfish motives? Our wrinkle-free faces, or our disregard for a helpless stranger?
Our beautiful homes, or our monthly giving?

Sasha's Quiet Influence

"Man looks on the outward appearance, but God looks on the
heart" (1 Samuel 16:7). David and Jonathan's love for each other is
legendary. When Jonathan died, David demonstrated his love by inviting Jonathan's son, Mephibosheth, who was crippled in both feet, to
live with him and eat at his table. Mephibosheth responded by asking, "What is your servant, that you should notice a dead dog like
me?" (2 Samuel 9:8), reflecting of course the attitude of the culture
at the time toward a crippled man. David's response was countercultural. He insisted that Mephibosheth be brought into the palace
and treated like his own son. "So Mephibosheth ate at David's table
like one of the king's sons" (v. 11). The truth of the matter is that
we, you and I, are the truly disabled eating at the King's table as
though we were sons. Where would we be if God had regard only
for the physically or spiritually perfect?

At the same time, some have a foolish notion that if they make
the sacrifices necessary to tend to the disabled, they will get nothing in return. When my children were small, many times when Sasha
was in the kitchen with me and Jeremy was in the family room playing with his friends, he would call out, "Mom, can Sasha come in here
with us?" I would dutifully wheel her into the family room while
the boys made way and greeted her warmly. Now, Sasha can't say a
word, lift a toy, or contribute anything to little boy activities, so it
always made me chuckle when they did this. Chuckle, but also realize that in her silence, she was a presence that the boys, and our
family and our friends for some unknown, intangible reason, enjoyed
and longed for.

Ask any of our friends, Sasha's teachers, her baby-sitters, or our
church family if Sasha had an impact on their lives. There was
something in her fragile, helpless little body that drew something
deep from all of us. Was it a glimpse of innocent and true perfec-
tion? A mind devoid of ulterior motive or self-awareness? Was it
the struggle for life and sometimes for breath she waged valiantly

and repeatedly? Or was it the profound lesson of just what in this world really matters?

Dietrich Bonhoeffer said, "Not only do the weak need the strong, but the strong need the weak." When Sasha was eight years old, on a day when she was sick and having seizures, I sat down to write a song for her. I was determined it wouldn't be a sugary song about pie-in-the-sky faith, for my heart was breaking and I honestly didn't know if I could bear the pain for another day.

I gave you life one summer day.
Such joy had never come my way,
But quickly sorrow came to stay beside us.
My grief was great, my soul was stirred
With questions, doubts, and empty words,
Of platitudes and promises long treasured.

Would God sustain us through the years
Of heartache, disappointment, tears?
And show to us his strength through fears and failures?

My fragile child, so weak, so frail.
I bend to softly touch your pale
But silken cheeks to make you feel my loving.
I know that in that fragile form
Beats heart, thinks mind, lives soul in warm
And gentle ways the truth to me is showing

How God sustains us through the years
Of heartache, disappointment, tears.
And shows to us his strength through fears and failure.

"I may not walk or run or play
Or touch your hand to softly say,
'I love you, Mommy!' But someday, when we're in Heaven.
I'll fly so free so full that we will spend our time eternally
Embracing, loving, joyfully remembering

"How God sustained us through the years
Of heartache, disappointment, tears
And showed to us his strength through fears and failures!"[1]

I first performed that song in Chicago at a pro-life function attended by politicians who, at the end of the song, leapt to their feet in a standing ovation. What was it about Sasha's story that moved them so? The song became an album, and everywhere I sang it, it got the same response. Mothers and fathers and grandparents of disabled children from all over resonated with the words, but the response wasn't limited to those who had lived with the handicapped. God's people everywhere seemed to be deeply moved. Perhaps it is what Christopher De Vinck refers to in his book by that same name, as the "Power of the Powerless."[2] I found that, as I traveled around the United States and overseas, people enjoyed my singing, yes, but when the story of my daughter was told, the message wielded a megaton impact.

On a concert tour in Japan, I fervently prayed that God would somehow give me words to reach believing and nonbelieving audiences. How could I speak to them in a culturally relevant way about the message of the gospel of Jesus? I knew that having a disabled child was to them a shameful thing, and so I hesitated to tell my story. But one night I felt compelled, and as I spoke, it occurred to me the grace of God was best illustrated to them by its comparison to their legacy of shame. Japanese people feel shame over things they do or say, over family histories, many times over things they cannot control and have no hope of reversing. It is a heavy burden, often leading to suicide. I asked them to imagine a God who loved them so much that He provided a way to remove their shame—as far as the east is from the west. I could not believe the response. Many received Christ. As a by-product, people from all over the island heard about Sasha and broke custom by bringing their disabled children and family members to the concerts.

One night they gathered around and begged me to meet with them afterward to talk about the special needs of families and children with disabilities. A pediatric neurologist was among them, eager to know how to better serve his patients and their families. God moved in a mighty way, and the very thing I feared would be the wrong thing to tell became the key that unlocked their hearts. But you see, God was not surprised by that. He uses "the foolish things of the world to shame the wise," and His strength "is made perfect in weakness." So we cheat and rob ourselves by not bothering with the weak. We are lopsided and unblessed because our perspective is upside down and our world much too small.

So You Want to Get Rid of Your Disability?

So how can the body of Christ embrace the disabled and their families and really exemplify the heart of the Great Physician?

Go to Extraordinary Measures to Accommodate Them

"If you build it, he will come!" declares a voice (James Earl Jones) to an Iowa farmer, played by Kevin Costner, in the movie *Field of Dreams*. They were referring to a baseball stadium in the middle of nowhere, but the same thing applies to churches. You may have only a few people with disabilities in your congregation now, but "if you build 'it,' they will come!" Disabled people and their families are everywhere, silently surrounding you. I guarantee that elevator will never be wasted.

Get Your Theology Straight So You Can Truly Minister to Them

I'm not sure where I was the first time someone said to me, "God only gives a child like Sasha to someone like you because you're special." It didn't take me long to catch on to the fact that my "comforter" was at the same time thanking God he was not so "special." A few years ago a father in Indiana threw his newborn Down's Syndrome baby headfirst onto the delivery room floor and killed him. In other cultures, drowning seems to be the preferred method of eradicating broken babies, while the more sophisticated Christ Hospital in Oak Lawn, a Chicago suburb, in cooperation with mothers and dads, induces early labor and allows less than perfect babies to die in the soiled linen closet of the hospital. It must be that no one ever told these parents how special they are.

I realize people don't know what to say and frankly, if this were instruction to parents of the disabled, I would counsel them to absorb foolish comments and extend grace as often as possible in order to put people at ease who are just trying to bring comfort. However, I am not speaking to them, and so for the rest of you, I say, please stop! When this platitude was relayed to me, it was *never* a comfort. I was barely keeping my head above water emotionally, and the only thing holding me together was my faith in God's strength and ability to sustain, *not my own*.

The Bible is clear that God "sends rain on the righteous and the unrighteous." How we respond is our choice. We can run, or we can stand and face the crisis. People respond in both ways every day. Because of God's work in my life and my rich history with Him, I chose to stand fast. I was nothing special, just a young mom who experienced a trial of faith. Any "specialness" came much later as God perfected my character through my faith in Him in a way that wouldn't have been possible through ordinary circumstances.

Sasha was only a few months old when a call came from a friend who'd heard of our sorrow, suggesting I must have unconfessed sin in my life. She counseled me to think back and try to discover what it might be. She then moved to my husband with the same admonition. It struck me as funny and even pathetic because I understood then as I understand now that, by the standards of God's holiness, I had enough sin in my life to deserve much worse, and so did my husband. If God gave us what we deserved, we would all be blind quadriplegics, or worse . . . just plain dead and lost. Scripture is clear that Christ did "not come to call the righteous, but sinners" and that "there is no one who does good, not even one" (Luke 5:32; Psalm 14:3). "While we were still sinners, Christ died for us" (Romans 5:8). We were spared damnation because of His sacrifice. The price has been paid. God doesn't mete out judgment through the maiming of our children. When the disciples asked, "Who sinned?" Jesus told them, in effect, "No one, but the purpose in this is that God may be glorified" (see John 9:2–3).

When Sasha was very tiny, I asked the elders of our church to lay on hands, pray for healing, and anoint her with oil. I believed with all my heart that, if God could create mankind, He could certainly heal my child. Instead she got worse. The seizures increased, as did my despair. A few months later a group of Foursquare Gospel businessmen, upon my request, surrounded us and prayed fervently, passionately, that God would heal Sasha. Nothing changed.

On her first birthday, while visiting my parents in our small hometown, Sasha awoke with a fever and frequent seizures. As the day wore on, they became more intense, and finally around dinnertime, all hell broke loose as her body contorted violently and her face began to turn blue. I grabbed her from my father's arms to administer CPR as my sister ran for her car keys. As she flipped on the bedroom light switch to retrieve them, the ceiling light bulb blew out, forcing her to grope in the dark. Frantic, she ran back to the kitchen as we piled into the car, my father, my mother, my sister, little Sasha, and me, and made our way to the tiny local hospital.

The hospital admitted her to emergency, and she immediately began another grand mal seizure and another. In between she cried a cry I shall never forget as my tender dad paced the floor trying desperately to comfort her. And me? Her mother? At that moment something in me snapped to the point that it seemed I was simply an observer to the scene. I just wanted to get out of the room. I felt nothing. Nothing.

When things had calmed down and emergency room staff were tending her, they assigned us a room. Before her arrival, my parents, my sister, and I all gathered in that room. The gloom hung heavily . . . the silence was deafening. But I knew in that moment I had to pray. I felt nothing, but I had to pray. And I knew instinctively I was the only one who could do it. I bowed my head mechanically, with only the will and not the power, with the knowledge that for the last year I had prayed every prayer imaginable, cried every tear cryable, said all I could say that was speakable in every way I could possibly say it. With emotionless delivery and a heart devoid of religious notions, I simply said, "I don't understand, Lord. But I trust You."

Gradually I found myself in a new place. It seemed at first glance to be a lack of faith, but as I grew in knowledge and understanding, I began to see for the first time in my life what great faith is truly all about. I began to discover that great faith is not believing that, against all odds and reason, God will perform a miracle. *Great faith is still trusting Him when He doesn't.* How could I have missed those critical verses that state it so clearly? Job's declaration of faith was not "I'm believing God for a miracle! I know He wants me to be rich and healthy again, so I'm just sitting here, in spite of my boils, lost children, and lost fortune, waiting for the blessings!" No! In the midst of his pain and loss, with no hope of regaining anything, he declared, "Though he slay me, yet will I hope in him" (Job 13:15).

Shadrach, Meshach, and Abednego refused to serve the Babylonian gods. Their punishment? To be burned alive in a hot furnace. I used to think they marched into that furnace with confidence knowing full well that God would deliver them in triumph, but I was wrong. In Daniel, they declare, "Our God is able to deliver us from this furnace, but if he doesn't, we still won't serve your gods" (see

Daniel 3:17–18). They knew He could save them. They did have that kind of faith, that He could, but they showed greater faith by marching into the furnace with no assurance that He would, willing to be burned alive rather than deny their faith in Him.

And finally, in the famous faith chapter, Hebrews 11, the litany of the great women and men of faith and their mighty deeds ends with a simple aside, that many of them never "received what had been promised." To serve faithfully, to give all without miraculous signs, without miraculous delivery, and in the face of the most hopeless circumstances, to be willing to endure all of it in the absence of any tangible relief—*that* is great faith. The prayer I prayed in that hospital room changed my life. Don't be deceived by those who name it and claim it, those who would indicate to the disabled and their families that God would heal if only they had enough faith. These people know nothing about real faith.

After I had gone through the process of asking God to heal Sasha many times during her first few years of life, I came to a place of peace, understanding that His answer was no. When people have come to me in later years, insisting I go here or there to a faith healer or let them pray over Sasha for her healing, they sometimes don't understand my resistance. They think I lack faith, but if I do, I share that "lack of faith" with the apostle Paul, who after asking three times for a "thorn" to be removed from his flesh, accepted God's sovereignty and declared that his strength was "made perfect in weakness" (2 Corinthians 12:9).

Offer Practical Help—and Don't Wait to Be Asked

During those same difficult years of having two babies, I conducted a college choir that toured every spring for ten days. My parents came and stayed with the children, but they lived three hundred miles away and the days leading up to the tour were a challenge in which to find time to prepare. One year I had it all worked out, though, down to the minute and last list. I hadn't anticipated Sasha getting sick. I should have. Two days before I was to leave, the seizures began, which meant no school for her, which meant I wasn't able to leave the house. My husband was working full-time and in law school at nights, unable to help. I first called people I knew well to ask for a few hours of their time. Everyone was busy. I called people I knew less, and they were also unavailable. Then I began to panic. How could I run these errands and get everything packed and ready?

I needed just two hours, but oh, how I needed them. I hated being in that position. It's one thing to ask for help when you can do without it if it can't be given, quite another to feel desperate and needy as you pose the question.

I swallowed hard and called the church office—the same home church I described earlier that knew us well—and asked if the secretary knew of somebody, *anybody,* who might be able to come to my house just for two hours so I could leave and do these errands? She offered the name of a deaconess, whom I promptly called. Holding my breath, I tried not to sound as desperate as I was. She paused for a minute and then replied that, no, she wouldn't be able to come that morning, she had a deaconess meeting at church. I hung up, humiliated, angry, and burst into tears. A deaconess, specially chosen to meet the needs of church members, couldn't give me two hours of her time because she had a deaconess meeting? It would have been funny had I not been so overwhelmed.

Parents and family members of the disabled often need help. Don't wait for them to ask; just understand the need is there. Why not assign someone to ask their special needs? It might be weekly relief or monthly relief. It might be help in a special circumstance, but it might just be the need for a night out. The divorce rate among parents of disabled children is astronomical. Part of the problem is that the needs swallow up their time and they are not able to relate to each other as husband and wife, as lovers. They'll never ask you to help them with this. Don't wait for them to, because if you wait until they ask, it might be too late.

Staff your Sunday schools with workers willing to aid children and adults with special needs. Any willing person can learn how. Provide a way for the parents to go to Sunday school just like everyone else. The caregivers can take turns, if it seems too hard for one person. For your efforts, you may have just saved a marriage and by doing so done more to help the disabled child than any therapy, by giving the parents a break. They'll never ask you to help them with this. Don't wait for them to.

Learn to See Beyond the Disability

And Mephibosheth was "crippled in both feet," it says in 2 Samuel 9:3; and Mephibosheth "was crippled in both feet," it repeats in verse 13. Did the writer think we had forgotten in so short a time? No, he was like most of us—he simply never saw past Mephibosheth's obvious deformity. We are told that Mephibosheth had a son, and we can read that Mephibosheth was verbal and intelligent. I'm sure every morning when he woke up, his first and only thought was not that he was crippled in both feet. I bet he thought about his wife, his son, the weather, the political climate of the day.

Disabled people are far more than their obvious physical malady. Was Helen Keller merely deaf and dumb and blind? No! She was a woman of great intellect and character whose contribution to the world has been great. Was Franklin Delano Roosevelt just a crippled guy in a wheelchair? Hardly. In fact, few Americans knew of his disability during the time he served as president of the United States. Physically broken people are always far more than their disability. Start looking at the person, not the form. You'll be amazed what you'll learn when you get past your own discomfort and hangups. Find out what they can contribute, and put them to work!

Tell Them About Jesus

After you've done all this, and they have experienced the love of the Great Physician in tangible ways, tell them about Him. It's not enough to meet their physical needs; it's time to make the gospel clear so that they and their whole family can be restored in the most significant way. "Whatever you did for one of the least of these brothers of mine, you did for me" (Matthew 25:40). This, after all, is God's mind in the matter.

DISCUSSION STARTER QUESTIONS

1. How can your church represent Jesus to the disabled in your community? What physical barriers might stand in the way? What other barriers might?

2. What are some ways you personally might be able to come alongside those in your church or community who have physical limitations?

3. Do you agree or disagree with Sandy's conclusions about faith meaning trusting God in the hard times? Why?

CHAPTER EIGHTEEN

THOSE WE'D RATHER FORGET:

Are Homosexuals and People with AIDS Beyond the Hope of the Gospel?

BRAD GRAMMER

G od Hates Fags!" "Fags Can't Repent!" A beautiful day in southern California was completely disrupted by these repulsive signs. The individuals bearing the signs yelled condemning statements hoping to banish homosexuals to hell unless they repent. Yet one of the signs said that homosexuals *can't* repent. Was there any logic or truth in their assertions, or were they committed to a personal agenda *using* God as their authority?

Only feet away, a large group of men and women joined hands, forming a circle that faced those observing them. A large arch of balloons displaying the colors of a rainbow was placed near the entrance of the convention hall. Shirts worn by the demonstrators begged the church not to prevent "gay" Christians from serving in the church.

The convention hall in Long Beach, California, was the location for the annual General Assembly of the Presbyterian Church (USA) in the year 2000. As I stood looking at these two groups diametrically opposed in their positions, I couldn't keep the grief and anger from welling up within my heart. Are these the only two positions the church in America has to offer regarding the issue of homosexuality? Where are the Christians who are compassionate yet fervently committed to the truth of the Scriptures? The only two representations at this demonstration were either hateful and derogatory, or gentle and deceived.

Marion Soards, author of *Scripture and Homosexuality,* sums up my observations,

> For us the divine combination of judgment and grace, of condemnation and forgiveness, of wrath and reconciliation are hard to fathom, and so we tend to eliminate one or the other dimension of the paradox of God's relationship to humankind. We focus on judgment and wrath and contemplate damnation, or we savor reconciliation and grace and celebrate divine acceptance of sinful humanity. The tendency is to view God as a cosmic ogre, bound and determined to administer well-deserved punishment; or we envision God as an eternal Mr. Rogers, eager to welcome us all to the neighborhood of the kingdom. Wrath and reconciliation become theological oil and water, so that we opt for the ointment of righteous recompense or the refreshment of divine deliverance. Jesus, however, lived with the dynamic tension of God's wrath and grace; in fact, he embodied the paradox.[1]

My desire is to strike a balance between the wrath of God and His wonderful grace. Only when we are able to live in this balance will we, as Christians, be able to effectively handle the problem of homosexuality in a biblical manner.

The Theological Perspectives on Homosexuality

In recent years, there has been growing support for the perspective that homosexuality is acceptable in God's eyes. A "pro-gay" position has been transcribed by some theologians. Although these theologians still remain in the minority, they have acquired a following among Christians who agree that the Scriptures are not clear on the topic of homosexuality. In fact, they believe that the Bible does not condemn homosexual behavior per se but only *selfish, unloving* homosexual behavior.

Space would not allow for explanation of the two theological perspectives of homosexuality. Two good sources on this discussion include *Strong Delusions* by Joe Dallas and *Straight & Narrow?* by Thomas E. Schmidt. Both are excellent sources that address both sides. The perspective I take is that homosexuality is a sin. This conclusion comes from the following biblical passages that directly address homosexuality: Genesis 19; Leviticus 18:22; 20:13; Judges 19; Romans 1:18–32; 1 Corinthians 6:9–11; and 1 Timothy 1:10. Other biblical passages that speak of God's plan for sexuality include Genesis 2:24; Matthew 19:1–12; 1 Corinthians 6:9–7:11.

I have heard many tragic stories and seen many broken lives. What has been consistent in the testimonies of those with whom I've ministered is the experience that the church has not been of help to the homosexual struggler seeking freedom and support. In fact, many of the experiences of strugglers could be classified as discrimination. For those with AIDS, the stories are similar. Fear of contracting this disease has prevailed in the church as much as the culture. My belief is that Christians have not only been afraid of getting AIDS but of also somehow *contracting* the sin that may, or may not, have been associated with this deadly disease. In many instances, the real problem is not AIDS itself but the fear or rejection of the history of someone with this disease. Someone who has contracted AIDS through blood transfusions, or even drug use, doesn't face the same kind of discrimination as someone from a homosexual background.

Through the years, I have discipled men who have come from various denominations and racial backgrounds. What is interesting is that, despite their differences, there is commonality in their experience among Christians. Rather than being a place of healing and restoration, the church has become an institution of fear and rejection. Can we say this behavior is pleasing to our Father in heaven?

From my understanding of the Bible, the main reason Jesus came was to save us from our most difficult problem, which could not be handled by any other method—sin. This is good news for the one with homosexual desires. If we take the approach that homosexual behavior is a sin, then there is hope, because Christ died on the cross to take care of that sin problem. Second Peter 1:3 says, "For as you know him better, he will give you, through his great power, everything you need for living a truly good life: he even shares his own glory and his own goodness with us!" (TLB).

What encouragement to know that Christ's presence in my life gives me all I need to overcome any sin problem!

In relation to homosexuality, we know that there is hope for overcoming this struggle, even to the point of complete change. Paul speaks directly to the Corinthian church and says,

> Don't you know that those doing such things have no share in the Kingdom of God? Don't fool yourselves. Those who live immoral lives, who are idol worshipers, adulterers or homosexuals—will have no share in his Kingdom. Neither will thieves or greedy people, drunkards, slanderers, or robbers. There was a time when some of you were just like that but now your sins are washed away, and you are set apart for God, and he has accepted you because of what the Lord Jesus Christ and the Spirit of our God have done for you. (1 Corinthians 6:9–11 TLB, emphasis added)

There were homosexuals in the early church who found freedom from their sin.

My Own Story

I know of this freedom through the power of my own testimony. My earliest recollection of having strong desires for men goes back to the age of six. Throughout my adolescence and young adult life, I battled with homosexuality in silence. Incessant taunting from male peers in school solidified in my thinking that I was gay and that there would be no way of changing. Hopelessness and despair ruled my feelings for years.

During this entire time, I attended church and believed that Jesus was the answer for my life. However, overcoming this problem remained a mystery. I would have liked to tell my struggles to someone at church, but my sense was that church was not a safe place for such discussions. Rarely were problems discussed in church. Sexual struggles were never mentioned, and my conclusion was that this problem is beyond the scope of Christians and perhaps of God.

To make a long story short, I discovered that God is truly the answer to my sexual struggles. I won't be able to explain all of the intricacies of why homosexuality develops in an individual. Fortunately, many Christian books available today give these insights. My understanding of my emotional needs as well as my sinful ways of relating paved the way for freedom from my homosexual desires. As I repented of my sinful behavior and had my needs met in healthy ways, I experienced changes in my sexual desires.

Today, I can say that I am completely free from homosexual attractions. My wife and two boys are a testimony to God's transforming power. Not everyone can make this claim for his or her own journey, but God has worked in this way in my life. This is encouraging for many whom I counsel who are now struggling with this issue. What's not so encouraging is when I tell them that this process took approximately *ten years*. Homosexuality is a complex puzzle and requires attention to all of the pieces before everything fits together. I do believe that some harms in life may never be completely healed. Thus, some individuals may never be completely free from homosexual desires. However, if we are honest, all humanity carries the struggle between the Spirit and the flesh. Being free from homosexuality has not freed me from all sin. I still battle my flesh daily, only over more challenging sins like pride and selfishness. These sins may not seem significant when battling with broken sexuality, but the pain from these sins is no less. My life will always be a process of repentance, and I'm grateful that God's mercy and grace is sufficient throughout my life.

The Church's Response

What would you do if someone came up to you and confessed his or her struggle with homosexuality? How would you comfort someone who just discovered he has contracted AIDS? Would your thoughts immediately turn to judgment, or would you have the compassion of the Father?

Joe Dallas, in his book *Desires in Conflict,* speaks of how the church has traditionally responded to the problem of homosexuality. Typically, the church has responded in one of three ways: ignoring the problem, suppressing the problem, or rejecting the person.[2]

"This Problem Doesn't Exist in Our Church!"

Most churches do not have resources or a plan as to how to help those who are struggling sexually. Some are in denial about the fact that many individuals are struggling with various sexual issues. Recent statistics have revealed that as much as 10 percent of a church body is struggling with some kind of sexual addiction.[3] Another statistic states that at least 20 percent of pastors struggle with pornography of some kind.[4]

In my home church during my adolescence, an unexpected incident left the church stunned. A middle-aged man had been the treasurer for the church for thirty years. He was known by everyone and was married with one child. Numerous times, this kind man drove my mother and me home from various church activities. When I was a teenager, the church leadership discovered that this man had embezzled a significant amount of money from the church during the past thirty years and that he had a homosexual lover. After being exposed, the man left his wife. No one would have suspected that this sweet family could be divided and devastated by his sin.

What was amazing was that almost as soon as this problem surfaced, life went on as usual in the church. There didn't seem to be a lesson that developed from this tragedy, and this man and his family were quickly forgotten. The man's wife eventually left the church, most likely because there was little support for her. Who was there to help her understand what had happened? Who was going to help this man in the repentance process? There *was* no repentance process. There was no support. The church showed no response that revealed that it realized its need to address the issue of sexuality, not to mention homosexuality. If one man struggled for thirty years with no one knowing, could there be someone else? Did other leaders struggle also and just want to brush it under the rug so they didn't have to face their own sexual issues? No one will know. This church's response seemed to be "If our church has problems, we can just ignore them and they will go away."

"Just Don't Do It!"

Some church leaders have had good intentions in helping a struggler. All too often, though, their ignorance leads them to dole out simple solutions for a complex problem: "Just read your Bible and pray more often." "You just need to try dating girls more. Once you get comfortable with girls, you'll find your attractions will catch up." "Are you tithing?" "You need to be delivered from the demon of homosexuality!" Many strugglers who have sought help in the church have been met with these actual statements and little substance to carry them through the difficult journey. After the initial confession, people with AIDS are often quickly forgotten and rarely supported.

Most, if not all, who have faced the challenge of the journey out of homosexuality will tell you that the process is very difficult. Much pain comes along with facing reality in one's life. As I mentioned earlier, I had not only to face the emotional needs I harbored deep within, but also to wrestle with all of the sinful ways of relating that needed to be removed from my life. Repentance is not a painless process! One needs prayer support and words of encouragement, along with patience and warmth. All too often, the American church has a microwave attitude toward spirituality: "Ask God into your life and He will make everything work out . . . tomorrow!"

What if everything doesn't work out the way you imagine? How does one persevere through the difficulty of the process when expecting that things will smooth out in less than five years? Is there more to working on my life than just "trusting Jesus"?

Dan Allender writes,

> Don't assume that resolving your turbulent emotions is the key to meeting God. It is actually within the inner mayhem of life that a stage is built for the intrusive story of His light and hope. The absence of tumult, more than its presence, is an enemy of the soul. God meets you in your weakness, not in your strength. He comforts those who mourn, not those who live above desperation. He reveals Himself more often in darkness than in the happy moments of life.[5]

I believe that we are often more interested in using God to make our lives better than knowing Him and following Him through whatever life brings. This is why I believe we expect simple solutions to complex problems in this world. We have been influenced by our American culture that says that it's our *right* to have a comfortable life. Too often Christians have taken on this same perspective and use God to somehow reach their goal of comfort and problem-free living.

The true disciple of Christ understands that in this world we will have tribulation (John 16:33). The true disciple knows that suffering is a normal part of the Christian life (Romans 5:3; 1 Thessalonians 1:6; 2 Timothy 1:8–9; Hebrews 10:32–34; 1 Peter 2:19 and

4:12–13). Once this is realized, a follower of Christ doesn't make the main focus of life to try to overcome suffering, but continues to pursue Him regardless of the pain involved. Now I'm not saying I like suffering anymore than anyone else does. In fact, you can still see me running from it at times. However, I do know my goal is not to reach a plateau of problem-free living. My goal is to follow God regardless of the cost. This perspective enabled me to persevere through the homosexual struggle, even though I didn't have all the answers in the beginning. The answers came with time and patience and diligence.

Last year, I was asked to speak at a conference on sexual brokenness for the African-American church. One young man who struggled with homosexuality told me the confusion that permeates his church experience. He hears stern admonition from the pulpit not to live in sexual promiscuity. Yet, when he is not dating women, or even sleeping around, then the buzzword is that he must be "gay." How would you feel if you had this baffling dilemma thrust upon you in the midst of your own confusion? Would you feel hopeful and want to tell others your struggle?

"I Think the Church down the Street Could Help You"

Rather than helping someone seeking assistance in overcoming homosexual desires, many times the church has rejected that person. To put it more clearly, statements like the one actually expressed above are a clear example of discrimination in the church. I have heard many stories of homosexual men who, at one time, attended church faithfully but stopped because they were asked to leave upon confessing their struggle. Just last week, one of the men I counsel told of the pain he experienced at hearing his uncle boast about kicking a man out of his church because he struggled with homosexuality. In the uncle's exact words, "We don't accept those kind here." My question is, What kind do you accept? Perfect people. Well, who do you know who is perfect? And who did Jesus die for? (See Luke 5:32.)

Many cities around the country have gay pride parades during gay pride week. During one of these parades, I decided to attend and observe the activities. I placed myself along a strip of the street that was next to a church. A few individuals came out of the church to watch the parade, or so I thought. The next thing I knew, as the parade passed by us, these Christians began swinging the Bible around, calling participants sinners and screaming at them to repent.

In another event, there was a prayer gathering on the steps of the state capitol in Indianapolis. Approximately 100 to 150 people turned out for the gathering. What a passer-by may not have known was that these individuals were "gay Christians." However, several individuals held large signs in the back of this prayer gathering that said homosexuals were going to burn in hell. One of the demonstrators even barked out, "You oughta be hung!" After hearing this remark, I decided to interact with the individuals. As I approached them, the group seemed to assume that I was one of "them." I sensed this because of the lack of hands extended for greeting and the hateful glares. As I introduced myself, I explained that I was in ministry to help individuals coming out of the homosexual struggle. Of course, part of my position is that homosexuality is a sin. After hearing this, a "warmth" came to the individuals before me. They were *then* willing to shake my hand.

At other times in my interactions with demonstrators, I've asked for explanation of the admonition in Scripture not to judge those outside the church. First Corinthians 5:12–13 says it bluntly: "What business is it of mine to judge those outside the church? Are you not to judge those inside? God will judge those outside." This passage seems to be very clear about leaving the responsibility to God to judge nonbelievers. We are only given the responsibility of judging the church. In two of the demonstrations I've mentioned in this chapter, the group attacked claimed to be Christian. Even then, though, there are biblical guidelines as to how to go about such a confrontation. Galatians 6:1 says that "if a Christian is overcome by some sin, you who are godly should gently and humbly help that person back onto the right path, remembering that next time it might be one of you who is in the wrong" (TLB). The implication is that we are not to think so highly of ourselves that we believe we are above any sin another is trapped in. In addition, we are to restore the person "gently and humbly." "You oughta be hung" doesn't seem to fit in the category of gentleness and humility.

Reasons for Our Negative Responses

Why would a certain part of the body of Christ be so hateful in their responses to confronting sin or in some cases attacking unbelievers?

At its core, I believe the problem develops from a hatred of God and a hatred of others. Why would I make such a strong statement? If we look at the Scriptures, Jesus doesn't really give any room for something to exist between love and hate. We either love or we hate. First John 4:20 tells us, "If anyone says, 'I love God,' yet hates his brother, he is a liar. For anyone who does not love his brother, whom he has seen, cannot love God, whom he has not seen." We either love Him or hate Him. In like manner, we either love others or hate them. My contention is that we hate others whenever we do not respond in biblical love.

This begs to ask, "What does biblical love look like?" First Corinthians 13 gives a beautiful definition. Obviously, Jesus' example is a loving example. We know that He ate with "sinners" and was judged by the religious leaders because He did so. There were times also when Jesus confronted sin. When He saved the woman about to be stoned for adultery, He did tell her, "Go, and sin no more" (John 8:11 KJV). But I don't recall Jesus ever saying, "You oughta be hung!"

Going back to Galatians 6:1, let's remember that we are to restore in gentleness and be careful that we don't fall into the same temptation. The corollary seems to be that if we do not respond in gentleness, then we are communicating somehow that we will not fall into temptation because we are above the sin. Anytime we believe we are above any sin, we put ourselves in a position of false holiness. Once again, "all have sinned and fall short of the glory of God." No one is exempt from needing Jesus, our Savior, to save us from our wicked state. Jeremiah 17:9 states, "The heart is deceitful above all things and beyond cure. Who can understand it?" To my understanding, this passage does not restrict the wickedness of the heart to "nonbelievers." God includes all mankind in this verse.

So perhaps some motivation for hateful responses is due to an unwillingness to look at one's own sinful condition. Would not a sober realization of one's own sin cause a person to respond with patience and compassion to another sinner? My wife and I have two different ways of living in relation to housekeeping. My attitude in housekeeping is that there is a place for everything and everything in its place. My wife's attitude is more "relaxed." When we were first married, I naturally approached the topic of housekeeping from the position that my perspective is correct: One should always have a home looking like the cover of *Good Housekeeping*. This attitude caused numerous fights early in our marriage. My thought was that if I yelled loud enough, this would show I was really upset and produce the desired result. My formula (this may come as a surprise) didn't work.

The fights have been reduced in our marriage because I have taken on the attitude that perhaps housekeeping isn't as serious as I would like to think and that different isn't necessarily bad. I had to be willing to humble myself. In my tirades to show that my wife was in sin by not taking care of the house "well enough," I was falling into sin by attacking her.

Another aspect of my anger at the housekeeping issue was that I wanted control in my house. The more I felt chaotic on the inside, the more I needed to have the outside under control to help me feel at ease. The truth is that I needed to find out what was causing the discomfort within and treat it accordingly. I needed to seek God for comfort. I believe this is partly what motivates a hateful response as well. There is disturbance within a person's heart, for various reasons, and one way to address this disturbance is to try to gain order from the world.

Often, we turn to an unrighteous anger. Dan Allender states the following in relation to unrighteous anger:

> The anger expressed in most interactions has little to do with the redemptive purpose of destroying the ugliness in order to enhance what is good. The person filled with unrighteous anger suppresses the freedom of others, filling an emptiness that demands satisfaction and refuses to cry out in humble, vulnerable need. Unrighteous anger condemns any who stand opposed to its pursuit of control.[6]

Allender also says that, even though our anger is directed toward others, it's ultimately directed toward God and that we are infuriated with Him for inequality. He seems unwilling to dispense justice to those who are unjust and evil. In the words of Allender, "we want vengeance."[7]

In relation to the disease of AIDS, some Christians have said that this disease is God's judgment on the homosexual. Rather than argue whether this is true or not, I believe a more important question is, What do we as believers gain from shouting this message? Will this draw homosexuals to God by condemning them? Let's make it clear that AIDS *is* a consequence of sin. Although some individuals have obtained the AIDS virus through blood transfusions and are therefore innocent of contracting this disease directly through sinful behavior, the sins of others have affected them.

When we face illness honestly, though, all diseases/viruses/illnesses are a result of sin. In the words of Kay Arthur, "First, if man had not sinned, there would be no sickness. So in that sense all sickness is due to sin."[8] The Scriptures are clear, also, that "all have sinned and fall short of the glory of God" (Romans 3:23), and the "wages of sin is death" (Romans 6:23). So in that sense, we are *all* guilty of bringing sickness into the world. Homosexuals, therefore, are not the only ones under judgment through illness. All humanity fits in that category. We all suffer the consequences, physically, for our sins. The following passages in Scripture give some examples linking physical illness with sin: 1 Chronicles 21:10–14; Psalm 38:1–3; John 5:5–8, 14; 1 Corinthians 11:27–32; 1 Timothy 5:22–25; and James 5:14–16.

Positive Examples of Ministry to Homosexuals

Before you think that there is no Christian love in America, let me give a couple of positive examples. One church in Grand Rapids, Michigan, has developed a good reputation among the homosexual community because of the church's love for, and ministry to, those with AIDS. This church is seen as a place where homosexuals are welcomed, yet homosexual behavior is not condoned.

Another church in Rockford, Illinois, faced the challenge of a prominent member being involved with homosexual behavior. He confessed his sin and sought repentance and restoration in his marriage. The church leadership stood by him and loved him in the process as he sought to put the broken pieces of his past and present together.

When my wife and I attended a cell church located in the Uptown neighborhood of Chicago, we had the opportunity to minister to a man living with AIDS. At the time Uptown had the highest percentage of people diagnosed with AIDS in Chicago. A ministry to those with AIDS in the suburbs of Chicago, Love & Action, had contacted me about a man who needed assistance with daily tasks. Those in my cell church took on the duties of cleaning this man's house, taking him to the grocery store, and just sitting to talk with him. Bob was hard to love. He was bitter over his past life and he needed Jesus. Fortunately, there were Christians willing to make sacrifices to model the love of Christ.

Were it not for the wonderful examples like this that exist today, I would be more despairing over the condition of the church in America. Fortunately, God has touched the hearts of some believers and they have responded by obeying Jesus' commandment to love our neighbors. Are you one of those believers who is so full of love for your Savior that it compels you to reach out and touch the life of someone who has faced rejection and ridicule? I am not challenging you to reach out to a "community" but to *one person*.

What Can the Church Do?

The question begs to be asked, "What can the church do?" Some large churches may have the laborers and facilities needed to start a support group ministry of some kind. Many churches, however, lack the resources to start a group ministry.

My recommendation is that we recommit to a plan Christ started two thousand years ago. This plan can be summed up in one word: relationship. Relationship may not seem like a significant plan, but Christ has modeled the effectiveness of this strategy.

When Christ began His ministry, He chose twelve men in whom to invest Himself. These twelve disciples followed and learned from Jesus for three years. The result was that the entire world was turned upside down because of Christ's willingness to give Himself for them. Jesus had no building, no budget, and no volunteers when He started. He began by loving people.

I think a common assumption in the church today is that we *know* how to love. However, the evidence seems to indicate that we as Christians don't love much better than the world. George Barna gives some statistics from his surveys that are a reflection of how well we love. Two results showed that there is little difference in percentages between Christians and non-Christians in the areas of divorce and the amount of time donated to a non-profit organization.[9] One result revealed that non-Christians actually give more money to the homeless than Christians do (perhaps because Christians mostly give to Christian ministries, and few of these deal with the homeless).[10]

Another reflection of our lack of love is the fact that gay activists see Christians as hateful and homophobic.

From my understanding and experience, when others see love coming from a person, there is a tendency to want to draw closer, not pull away in wrath. Let me tell an example from my life.

For six years, I did evangelistic outreach to the gay bars on the North Side of Chicago. God provided me with the opportunity to share the gospel with around two hundred gay men. Most already knew the gospel message. One of the friendships that developed as a result of this outreach was with a man who lived as a homosexual for quite a number of years. Disillusionment had filled his heart as he experienced being regularly used and rejected in the gay community. Gene decided to become a Franciscan and live a celibate life.

Over the course of one year, we met for coffee every week and talked about spiritual matters. Eventually, my wife and I invited him over for a few dinners. One evening Gene came over when my wife wasn't feeling well. Rather than fix dinner, we decided to order pizza. As we were waiting for the delivery, some friends of ours dropped by with a container of homemade chicken soup because they had heard that Laura wasn't feeling well. After our friends left, Gene commented that these were the kind of people he wanted to be around. He was so moved by this simple expression of love, something unfamiliar in his life, that he was drawn to pursue relationship with these friends.

As I think about what Gene experienced, I ask myself this question: Was it the love of Christ that drew me to Him, or was it programs and activities to promote Christian living? My belief is that churches are more drawn to programs than relationship because relationships are too difficult. The love Jesus requires of us involves pain, something most of us wish to avoid.

The best method for reaching the homosexual struggler and/or AIDS victim is a loving relationship. The sexually broken need men and women who will model healthy masculinity and femininity. They need support to overcome their fears and insecurities about relating to members of their own sex. My desire is to see mentor relationships develop in every church. Can you imagine how the world could be changed if every Christian man and woman felt compelled to mentor even one person in his/her lifetime? Jesus spent time with twelve men and the gospel spread throughout the world. The Scriptures say that we could do greater things than what Jesus performed on earth (John 14:12). Perhaps this strategy of mentoring could be one possible answer.

The journey for me began with one godly man loving me well and modeling true masculinity. I never went to counseling or a support group ministry, but God used individuals to affect me significantly. Not that counseling or ministries are wrong to pursue. However, any professional will tell you that counseling and support groups alone are not enough. Everyone needs love and support. Everyone needs to see the love of God manifested in tangible ways through ordinary people like you and me.

Ask the Lord to give you one person to mentor. Allow God to use that relationship to guide you where *He* wants you to go. Involve a couple of other individuals in your church in this mentoring process. As you grow in this endeavor, God may eventually lead you to start up a support group ministry through your church or to join up with another church to do the work of ministry to the sexually broken.

Seek the Scriptures to see what God has to say about how to love. Ask God to teach you what it really means to love. This is a difficult prayer because most of us are blind to our own lack of love for others and God will reveal our weaknesses. Prayer in this manner, though, pleases the Lord and aligns with His sovereign will for all of us (Matthew 22:37–40). Ask Him to strengthen you for the journey deeper into the love of Christ. Will you join Christ on this journey toward godly love for those we'd rather forget?

DISCUSSION STARTER QUESTIONS

1. What category of "sexually broken" people do you most resonate with? What would be their particular needs in ministry and relationship?
2. Why are relationships more important than programs, particularly in reaching the sexually broken? Is your church a safe place for these relationships to happen?
3. What are practical ways that a church can communicate "sinners are welcome here" without condoning sin?

CHAPTER NINETEEN

KIDS IN CONSTANT MOTION:

How Can the Church Work More Effectively with Children with ADD/ADHD?

CYNTHIA PERRY

When I was a young mother of four small children, I was often discouraged about going to church. My second child was extremely active and very hard to keep quiet in church. I dreaded being there, because it was in the church that I received the most criticism, even though I was the pastor's wife. I regularly received such comments as "Why can't you control your son?" or "All you need to do is discipline him more" or "The Bible says that he who spares the rod spoils the child."

Week after week I heard similar types of comments. As my son grew older, my inability to control him increased. I couldn't put him in Sunday school because he disturbed the class, the nursery wouldn't keep him, and he was constantly put out of children's church. The majority of fights and arguments that involved children were my son and someone else. The children began picking on him because they knew that he was an easy prey.

This frustration that I experienced in the church began to spill over into our home. Constant fights and bickering took place between this son and the other three children. I could barely keep up with his demands to go here and do this. What made things worse were the demands of my husband's ministry, which always kept us in the public eye under constant scrutiny and criticism. As the pastor's wife, I not only felt like a failure as a mother, but also a failure as one of the leaders in the church. This reached a boiling point in about our ninth year of marriage. I felt so alone and misunderstood, not only by the people in my family, but especially by those in the church. It was at this point that God laid on my heart to go back to school to seek some answers about what was happening to my son. I didn't know where to turn. I couldn't turn to my family or church, so I felt that if I could begin to understand what he was going through, that could provide some solution. This began a ten-year journey that eventually led to my earning a doctorate from Loyola University of Chicago in the area of Curriculum and Instruction. The focus of my dissertation was the very disorder that I had come to discover was the major cause of my son's problems: Attention Deficit Hyperactivity Disorder.

Today a growing number of children suffer from Attention Deficit Hyperactivity Disorder (ADHD). It is estimated that about 20 million people in the United States either have attention deficit disorder or some form of it. Many people learn to cope with their disability, depending on the severity of the disorder. However, children who cannot defend themselves and who are dependent on others for support and guidance suffer the most abuse from the disorder. One reason for this abuse is that many people do not understand ADHD.

In my experience and my interaction with Sunday school teachers in many different settings, I've seen that ADHD children in the church have become a major concern to the body of Christ, especially for Sunday school teachers. In most churches, Sunday school teachers are not regular educators who might have encountered ADHD students in the classroom and have some strategies for working with them. They are generally parents, business people, retired adults, and young adults who are interested in teaching children.

Reid et al. in their article, "An Analysis of Teachers—Perceptions of Attention Deficit-Hyperactivity Disorders," said they believed that little information is available detailing how to prepare general-education teachers to work effectively with ADHD students.[1] Yet Sunday school teachers are expected to teach ADHD children without having knowledge of the disorder, how to establish the proper learning environment, or developing proper teaching strategies and classroom management.

In this chapter we are going to define ADHD, symptoms associated with it, and classroom management and teaching strategies for the Sunday school teachers' classroom.

What Is ADD/ADHD?

Attention Deficit Hyperactivity Disorder (ADHD) is ADD with hyperactivity and impulsivity as primary characteristics. Since ADD and ADHD are closely related, I will use the term ADHD to include both disorders.

The National Institute of Mental Health explains,

ADD, once called hyperkinesis or minimal brain dysfunction, is one of the most common mental disorders among children. It affects 3 to 5 percent of all children, perhaps as many as 2 million American children. Two to three times more boys than girls are affected.[2]

ADHD is a chronic neurobiological condition characterized by developmentally inappropriate attention skills, which include impulsivity, distractibility, and hyperactivity or excess energy.[3] ADHD is currently seen as a medical/psychiatric condition and is listed in the DSM-III-R (American Psychiatric Association, 1987).

According to Taylor and Larson, ADHD is a lifelong neurodevelopmental disorder that affects the brain and results in a variety of inappropriate and maladaptive behaviors.[4] ADHD is not a disease but a processing deficit that results in children having difficulty with inhibitory control. That is, children with ADHD lack self-control, something they cannot help. In children with ADHD, the parts of the brain that control attention and stop inappropriate behavior are underdeveloped.[5]

The Cause of ADHD

More helpful for families than figuring out the cause of the disorder is finding out what will help their child. No one knows what causes ADD, although health officials believe there is likely to be a genetic base for it. Some of "the literature shows that attention disorders tend to run in families, so there are likely to be genetic influences. Children who have ADHD usually have at least one close relative who also has ADHD."[6] Taylor and Larson stated that many doctors believe that there is a hereditary link to ADHD.

> In 1990, the *New England Journal of Medicine* published the results of a landmark study in which researchers at the National Institute for Mental Health used advanced brain imaging techniques to compare brain metabolism between adults with ADD and adults without ADD. The study documented that adults with ADD utilized glucose, the brain's main energy source, at a lesser rate than did adults without ADD. This reduced brain metabolism rate was most evident in the portion of the brain that is important for attention, handwriting, motor control, and inhibition of responses. These brain metabolism studies, combined with other data including family history studies and drug responses studies, have convinced researchers that ADD is a neurobiological disorder and not caused by a chaotic home environment.[7]

Symptoms of ADHD

The hyperactivity, difficulty focusing, and impulsivity of ADHD begins its manifestation in early childhood and is displayed across a variety of settings (school, home, and play).[8]

Hyperactivity is sometimes noticed even in the womb, and the disorder becomes obvious by the age of three. Parents often describe these children as "driven," "continuously on the go," or "nonstop." In the classroom, these children fidget and squirm, jump in and out of their seats, disturb their classmates, speak when they aren't supposed to, have problems waiting for their turn, and take risks without thinking about the consequences, to name a few characteristics. Outside, they tend to be overaggressive, play extremely hard, and have difficulty settling down once playtime is over.[9]

> Children with ADD often make life difficult for themselves and everyone around them. They can easily produce chaos in a classroom or turn a family home into a battleground. Sometimes they

seem to be provoking conflict just for the love of excitement. Exasperated parents and teachers may regard them as lazy, irresponsible, and arrogant; other children often find them obnoxious and avoid them. They rarely perform up to the expectations generated by the abilities they erratically display, and they almost inevitably develop a poor opinion of themselves in reaction to constant criticism and failure.[10]

According to the National Institute for Mental Health, the Individuals with Disabilities Act (IDEA) was recently modified, and "For the first time, IDEA specifically lists ADHD as a qualifying condition for special education services."[11]

ADHD affects adults as well. Although it begins in childhood, researchers in the last twenty years have shown that it is also a disorder of adolescents and adults, according to the Harvard Mental Health Letter. They stated that the old belief that the symptoms fade with age now seems to have been an illusion, mainly because hyperactivity tends to subside with age and because adults are rarely observed as closely.[12] How often the symptoms persist is uncertain: Estimates range from 1 percent of the population at age eighteen and 0.3 percent at age twenty-five to figures as high as 2 percent of all adults.

Children with ADHD have a pattern of behavior that sets them up for failure in school and for conflict with their parents. They have difficulty finishing tasks, remembering details, focusing on a book or an assignment, or even remaining seated for more than a few minutes. Some appear to be driven from within as they race wildly from one thing to another. They are often highly bright and creative, yet they are seen as lazy, disruptive, and terribly disorganized.[13]

Researchers have identified a number of core symptoms that are reflected in ADHD children. Many of these characteristics associated with ADHD are ones that teachers need to be aware of because they are often demonstrated in the classroom. All children demonstrate these characteristics from time to time; however, the ADHD child has a consistent overlapping of many of these characteristics. It does not happen one day and the next day disappears but is a repeated behavior over a period of weeks, months, and years.

Inattentiveness. The ADHD child has great difficulty sustaining concentration on tasks and is easily bored unless the task is extremely *interesting* to him or her or the situation is novel, scary, or one-on-one. This child is also easily *distracted* by irrelevant stimuli, such as movement and noise around him, an overly busy classroom, too much daylight, and poor placement in classroom.

Impulsivity. The ADHD child often acts too quickly without thinking ahead and weighing consequences. This type of behavior involves running and fighting, making irritating noise, speaking out of turn, and jumping out of his or her seat without thinking.

Hyperactivity is often seen in children as early as two to three years old. Parents often say that these children never walked. They went from crawling to running. Not only are these children physically active, but they are also verbally active. They are often referred to as chatterboxes.

Not delaying gratification. "It's my turn," "I was here first," or "I've got to have it now!" are phrases one often hears from ADHD children. They tend to go through temper tantrums and fits when things do not go their way. They struggle with the inability to delay gratification.

Noncompliance. Hyperactive children have difficulty following rules. In their minds, rules are for everyone else. Because they tend not to see rules as applicable to them, they are able to accurately state the rules, even in the midst of breaking them. ADHD children can also be aggressively noncompliant, often throwing fits or temper tantrums, yelling, acting defiantly, resisting authority, talking back, or being disrespectful, and they are often referred to as strong willed.

Emotional overarousal. ADHD children have an untimely way of expressing their feelings, either positively or negatively. They often express themselves in the extreme. If they are happy, observers see it through their silly behavior. Negative feelings are expressed through their emotions as tantrum behavior.

Disorganization. ADHD children are often known to lose things. They have messy desks, bookbags, and rooms. They forget important things (times of sport games, where they put their equipment and shoes); lose their homework, pencil, and paper; or forget that they even had homework. They forget rules for both home and school and are poor managers of time, money, and responsibilities.

Social problems. ADHD children have a difficult time playing fairly with other children. They tend to want to be in control, are bossy, have very low frustration levels, and seldom take responsibility for their actions. They tend to blame others for their failures. They are often involved in arguments, fighting, cheating, and lying, and they are the source of other children's frustration. Peers tend to reject them, and younger children often become their targets for playmates.

Self-control. The capacity to inhibit or delay one's initial motor (and perhaps emotional) responses to an event is a critical foundation for the performance of any task.

Teaching Strategies for the Sunday School Teacher

In my experience, classroom management and discipline are the number one concerns of teachers and those who work with children, whether it is in the classroom, church, home, or sports arena. Classroom management is the backbone to effective teaching. Having a clear understanding of the significance of a well-managed classroom will enhance learning in any situation. In my observations of classroom teachers, those who have adequate classroom management skills have the least amount of unwanted behaviors, better interaction and cooperation with students, and are able to be effective in the classroom.

What is classroom management? "It is the dichotomy between the teacher and student as active mediators and constructors of the learning environment, identifying what students need to understand to participate in class lessons, how teachers orchestrate the participation, and how norms, rules, and expectations are signaled and re-signed across time."[14] In other words, the teacher has a very important role in the environment, atmosphere, and order of the classroom. "A student is not above his teacher, but everyone who is fully trained will be like his teacher" (Luke 6:40).

Literature shows students with ADHD and other behavioral problems do best in a structured classroom. This would be a classroom where expectations and rules are clearly communicated and where academic tasks are carefully designed for manageability and clarity.[15]

Sunday school teachers need to have expectations clearly defined for students. Expectations could include attending class on time, obeying classroom rules (listening to one another, respecting each person and their opinion, recognizing that each person is special and a gift from God, etc.), and having necessary materials (Bible, pencil and paper). Seating arrangements and whom the child sits next to are part of controlling students' unwanted behavior. Some classroom management considerations are:

- Have a structured and organized classroom. Does the classroom have rules posted, and are they reinforced on a weekly basis? Structured and organized classrooms have students involved in the learning process from the moment they enter the room until they leave. Students know what the expectations are and what the expected behavior is as well.

- Set limits and boundaries. Do it consistently, predictably, promptly, and plainly. Students need to know, each time they meet, what the limitations are. The rules need to be reinforced for the activity for that day. You need to be sure they know what the consequences are; check for their understanding. Once the students are clear about the boundaries, then proceed with the lesson.

- Don't get into complicated, lawyerlike discussion of fairness. These long discussions are just a diversion. Take charge of your classroom. If a student has a dispute, a disagreement, or an issue, or wants to discuss a matter in lengthy details, let him know that you are available before or after class to discuss personal concerns. When we allow students to use class time for debates, it takes away teachable time from other students, and it discredits us as the leaders.

- Watch for overstimulation. One of the fastest ways of losing control of the classroom is the area of overstimulation. When students become overstimulated, it is difficult to regain control of the classroom. Students start making fun of others, saying negative things, or making unwanted jokes. Closely monitor conversations and students' reactions to the comments made by their peers.

- Carefully consider the child's age and ability before expecting him or her to perform a task. An effective teacher understands the capability of each of her students and what they are able to do. Too high expectations discourage students. They feel that they will never be able to measure up. On the contrast, too low expectations can lead to behavioral problems. Students might feel that the lesson is not challenging enough and thus find other things to entertain them (talking, throwing things around the room, getting out of their seats, drawing while you are talking, etc.).

• Help the student be responsible for his or her actions. The older the student, the greater the responsibility. "He made me do that" or "It was her fault" are not acceptable. If a student breaks a rule, bring it to his or her attention. Help students to see the connection between their behavior and the effect it has on them as well as the class.

• Focus on quality in teaching and not quantity. Teachers have students about one hour a week, and often their goal is to indoctrinate them with as much Bible as time permits. However, students respond better to quality than to quantity. Someone once asked me, "How do you eat a cow?" The answer is one bite at a time. The Bible is not a cow, but the principle is the same.

Classroom management is the foundation for effective instruction for the Sunday school teacher. Without good classroom management, it is next to impossible to motivate students to learn. Good students will eventually lose interest in the lesson even if it is good. Students with ADHD will find it impossible to stay focused. With effective classroom management, good instruction will bring life to the classroom and learning experiences.

Effective instruction is how the lesson is presented to the students. It involves the relationship of the teacher with each student, teachers' ability to motivate each student, how appropriate the lesson is to students' everyday life, and how involved the student is in the learning process.

Teaching the Bible Creatively illustrates that the method can affect the results:

A woman read somewhere that dogs were healthier if fed a tablespoon of cod liver oil each day. So each day she followed the same routine—she chased her dog until she caught it, wrestled it down, and managed to force the fishy remedy down the dog's throat. Until one day when, in the middle of the grueling medical effort, the bottle was kicked over. With a sigh, she loosed her grip on the dog so she could wipe up the mess—only to watch the dog trot to the puddle and begin lapping it up. The dog loved cod liver oil. It was just the owner's method of application the dog objected to.[16]

Almost every child wants to learn more about God and the Bible—but students can be turned off by our methods of application. As a teacher and a teacher of teachers, I have come to realize that students are usually interested in our content (the Bible) but are completely turned off by how it is presented to them. Some suggestions for effective instruction are:

- Begin your lesson with an attention grabber (e.g., question of the day, joke, hands-on learning experience, music).

- Prepare and distribute an outline of the lesson. If you don't have an outline to distribute, write the lesson on the chalkboard. Students benefit from an organized lesson because they like to know what the expectations are. The outline does not have to be extensive. It can include the objective for the day, activities related to the objective, and scheduled time for each activity.

- Pace the lesson to maintain students' attention. Students need time to process. Too much information will contribute to students' lack of motivation.

- Use visual images as much as possible. Use the overhead projector, Power Point, handouts, and chalkboard or dry-erase board.

- Draw the students' attention to important concepts. This will help to assess their comprehension. This will also help the teacher to organize his or her material.

- Frequently use the students' names and interests in examples when presenting.

- Try to include activities that require movement, or occasionally turn the lesson into a game or debate format.

- Use lots of eye contact and proximity control. Students respond more appropriately when teacher is walking around the room and they can interact face to face with the teacher.

- End each class or lesson presentation with a sound closure. Briefly highlight important topics covered; set the stage for the next lesson.

Effective instruction sets the pace for active learning. When ADHD students are actively engaged in the learning process, there is a drastic change in their behavior and attitude toward Sunday school. Children who suffer from ADHD desire to be a part of a group, but often their social skills, inappropriate behavior, and a lack of focus interfere with the learning process.

DISCUSSION STARTER QUESTIONS

1. What experience have you had with children with ADD/ADHD? How does this chapter help you understand them better?
2. What can your church do to teach children with ADHD more effectively? How can it better show them God's love?
3. What principles from this chapter can be translated to a classroom that has no learners with ADHD?

CHAPTER TWENTY

THE ALMOST-UNPARDONABLE SIN:

Is Divorce Treated as a Justice Issue in Your Ministry?

CRAIG KEENER

esus said to His disciples, "Anyone who divorces his wife and marries another woman commits adultery against [his wife]" (Mark 10:11). While I leave aside for the moment other matters of interpretation in this passage, I want to draw attention to the phrase, "against his wife." In Jesus' day some Pharisees (largely in the school of Hillel) allowed husbands to divorce their wives for almost any reason, but the law did not permit wives to divorce their husbands (though under extreme circumstances courts would force the husband to grant his wife a divorce). The wife had no legal recourse to prevent the divorce, and in a society where only men received fair pay for their work, the divorce put the woman at a severe economic disadvantage.

In other words, Jesus treated divorce as a justice issue: It could represent the sin of one person against another person, a betrayal of covenant fidelity. "The Lord has been a witness between you and the wife of your youth, against whom you have dealt treacherously, though she is your companion and your wife by covenant. . . . 'For I hate divorce,' says the Lord, the God of Israel . . . so take heed to your spirit, that you do not deal treacherously" (Malachi 2:14, 16 NASB). We recognize that while some sins, like adultery or fornication, require the consent of both parties, other sins can be a crime committed by one person against another, like murder and rape. We all know that many American divorces today occur by mutual consent or represent the lack of commitment of both spouses, in varying degrees, to make their marriage work. But as in the Bible, many divorces represent one person's betrayal of another person. (I think here especially of divorces involving unrepentant adultery, abandonment, or abuse.)

Yet many evangelicals today refuse to treat divorce as a justice issue, and what is worse, they sometimes abuse the betrayed spouse in the name of opposing divorce. To punish a betrayed spouse in a divorce because we oppose divorce is like punishing a rape victim because we oppose rape. Jesus defended the betrayed party of many divorces of His day and challenged His contemporaries' interpretation, charging that they allowed this betrayal because of the hardness of their hearts. Yet I have witnessed some evangelicals punishing the very people that Jesus was seeking to protect, thereby compounding the offense of the betrayer in oppressing the person betrayed. Is it possible that our abuse of Scripture to oppress others also reflects a hardness of heart?[1]

Learning the Issues Surrounding Divorce

This charge concerning many evangelicals' treatment of divorced people may at first sound too harsh. Unfortunately, however, I could illustrate it abundantly. Since my first book, . . . *And Marries Another,* came out in 1991, many people have written or called to tell me their stories, in addition to those I encounter in the normal course of ministry. One of the more graphic stories was of a man who married a divorced woman; both were later converted to Christianity, and under the teachings of their evangelical church, they could no longer have intercourse. The wife, who accepted the teaching of the church, has not slept with her husband for years. Some churches today continue to teach that all remarriages are adulterous, hence that newly converted members should divorce their current spouses and return to their original ones. (I briefly address the biblical arguments for this position later in this essay.)

But that example is an uncommon one; more commonly I have encountered wives abandoned by husbands who are ministers, where the wives are subsequently abandoned by churches that rally to support popular pastors. In this case the churches fail to take divorce seriously enough. But perhaps even more frequently I have witnessed evangelical churches disciplining and withholding opportunities for ministry from a divorced believer regardless of the grounds for the divorce.

Though it is not the point of this article, I do believe (and argued at length in *And Marries Another*) that even the strictest reading of Scripture should permit the remarriage of the betrayed party; this is the most commonly held evangelical view.[2] Likewise I believe that Scripture when interpreted in its grammatical and historical context does not prohibit biblically remarried persons from engaging in ministry, including that of senior pastor.[3] Many believers who were divorced and remarried before their conversion (or divorced for biblical grounds and then remarried) told me of their hardships in finding an evangelical denomination and local church that would allow them ministry. Many evangelical churches do allow remarried pastors, and even more allow divorced people leadership in various ministries in the church; but many others bar remarried people from various ministries, regardless of the reason for their divorce.

Because this chapter focuses on the issue of discrimination against divorced evangelicals, however, I leave aside those debated issues here and focus on some experiences of one divorced person who has not, at the time of this essay's writing, remarried. Unless one interprets 1 Timothy 3:2 as prohibiting church leadership for all single people, I know of no one who tries to make a biblical case for discriminating against a divorced person who has not remarried. Yet with or without a biblical argument, this discrimination remains a regular occurrence in many evangelical circles.

The story must be told precisely because most evangelicals remain unaware of it. Until I joined the black church and listened to the stories of my brothers and sisters there, I remained comfortably oblivious to the fact that racism was a daily reality many of them experienced. Now I bristle when I hear some white evangelicals pontificating that racism is purely a matter of the past; they speak from their lack of experience and ignore the voices of those who have genuinely experienced racism's reality. Yet I also have observed the same pattern in the treatment of divorced people, and sometimes I think many evangelicals are even less responsive to this issue than to racism. I hear the wounded cry of betrayed Christians when they read Christian periodicals that sometimes lump together all "divorced people," without making distinctions in terms of the reasons they are divorced. I treat here the case of "Stephen," a committed Christian I mentioned in the first chapter of *And Marries Another,* focusing on significant events from the past ten years not included in the book.

The Story of Stephen

Stephen married a woman he believed to be a committed Christian; they met in Bible college and prayed, fasted, studied the Bible, and witnessed together during their courtship. But the pressures of ministry proved difficult, and she grew increasingly uncomfortable as they confronted slander and other forms of hostility against ministers that sometimes occur in churches. She noted that she no longer enjoyed church, and one day she announced her intention to "backslide." Despite Stephen's attempts to prevent it, within two months she had begun an affair with the husband of her closest friend, and within a month or two after that the illicit new couple abandoned their spouses. Although the man had returned to his wife after previous affairs, this time he preferred to remain with Stephen's wife. The unfaithful spouses thus filed for divorces. Persuaded by some evangelical literature on marriage and desperate to save his marriage, Stephen fought the divorce for two years. Eventually, however, she secured the divorce on the grounds of two years' physical separation and, after a few more years of living with her paramour, married him.

During this time Stephen's Christian friends helped hold him together. At the same time, he discovered what most never-divorced Christians do not know: the harshness of some fellow Christians toward divorced persons. One couple far removed from the situation wrote him notifying him that they were breaking off Christian fellowship with him and declaring that his wife's departure must be due to sin in his life. A number of others insisted, like Job's comforters, that God would not have allowed this tragedy if he had loved his wife the way he should have. These same "comforters" would never have endorsed the idea that sickness is due to sin, but divorce so horrified them that they needed an explanation that would protect them from the fear that the same thing could happen to them.

Stephen had never so much as kissed another woman before his marriage, and thirteen years after his wife left him he has not remarried and does not date. He is lonely and does not oppose remarriage, but he also remains afraid. He married a woman who seemed to be a committed Christian, he affirmed his love for her daily and did the best he knew to be a godly husband, and those who knew him best attested as much in letters on his behalf. But if, despite such precautions, his first marriage failed, dare he risk another? He is overcoming the fear now, but part of the fear was generated by the rejection he experienced in some evangelical circles.

Stephen has sacrificed most of his life to serve Christ and promote the evangelical faith. Yet in a number of evangelical institutions over the years he was rejected by search committees solely on the basis of his divorce. The reason he was rejected, of course, is so the institutions may maintain a stand against divorce, but their stand hardly seems consistent: How does it set an example against divorcing one's spouse to keep out people who were divorced against their will? The same institutions would recoil in horror at the idea of rejecting a rape victim as a way of protesting rape. On the strictest reading, Jesus opposed divorce and remarriage as adultery. Yet few of the institutions that reject all divorced candidates (remarried or not) ever inquire as to whether a candidate has committed (literal) adultery or engaged in premarital sex. (One candidate who had engaged in such activities before her conversion five years ago remarked to Stephen her disgust that she was accepted for ministry by one of the same organizations that turned him down.)

In the end, though, it is usually not an institutional policy but personal prejudice that is the primary problem; if several members of a search committee regard Stephen's divorce as an insurmountable obstacle, that is usually sufficient to keep Stephen from being hired. To be sure, Stephen, like the rest of us, often does not know why he is turned down for some positions; obviously there are often a number of qualified candidates for a position. But in at least six instances workers inside the institutions have volunteered to Stephen that he was rejected because he was divorced. In nearly every case, this happened in spite of the fact that Stephen offered full legal documentation for the grounds of his divorce, including his ex-wife's notarized admission concerning the circumstances.

If such discrimination occurred on the basis of race or gender, we would rightly protest it. But although I know some churches that act biblically within their own circles, I do not know of any evangelical organizations that treat divorce as a justice issue enough to take a public stand to defend betrayed persons. More traditional voices might counter that race and gender are different from divorce; divorce, like homosexual behavior, is a sin and should not be protected. This objection recognizes a legitimate truth but sidesteps the essential point of the comparison: We are not talking about defending divorce, but about defending a person sinned against in a divorce, someone who did not choose his or her situation.

Rarely will betrayed believers speak up for themselves, often fearing they will only compound the problem. A few years ago a Christian journalist for a respected Christian magazine called a large number of ministers reportedly betrayed by divorce. The journalist simply sought to learn the trials such ministers faced, but the few who would speak to him did so only on the condition of anonymity, and most of his contacts refused a phone interview altogether. Few people are speaking out; consequently, little is changing.

After a number of years Stephen finally found a peaceful niche and settled into an effective ministry; it seemed like his past would no longer prove an issue. But missions had long been on his heart, and Stephen finally applied to a mainstream evangelical missions organization. Stephen might seem like an ideal missionary in terms of spiritual disciplines: He was praying an hour a day, fasting a day each week, had immersed himself in Scripture, and has led probably more than one hundred people to Christ in personal evangelism. He has been a committed Christian for more than twenty years and has often paid a high price for his commitment. But he shuddered when he discovered the space on the application form asking whether or not he was divorced. As always, Stephen told the truth; he nevertheless hoped that if they took into account any circumstances as they claimed, his documentation would be adequate to attest that he was an innocent party.

A few months later, he received notice indicating that he could not participate in the one-month short-term mission. The stated reason was that he was divorced. In this case the story has a better ending: People within the same organization eventually found even better use for his ministry in other ways. But although Stephen's story has a happy ending, it came only after many years of facing rejection in evangelical circles. I have known others who proved less fortunate than Stephen. Some have left evangelical churches altogether because of the brand they felt they wore.

Getting the Full Story May Be Impossible

In today's increasingly relativist climate, it is easier to dismiss notions of justice surrounding divorce (or other matters) by simply saying, "There is always fault on all sides." To be sure, there is always fault on both sides. Many contribute in some ways to the dysfunction of their marriage, even when the spouse is the one who ultimately breaks up the marriage and remains closed to reconciliation. Further, even where one side shares relatively little fault with regard to the divorce, no spouse (or unmarried person) is sinless. Every husband and wife could use some improvement, and most could use much improvement.

Finally, getting the full, true story is sometimes impossible for anyone but God. But should a divorced person who claims to have been betrayed always bear the burden of proof, especially when there are clear evidences of unrepentant adultery, abandonment, or abuse? Does not God warn us that condemning the innocent is just as sinful as acquitting the guilty (Exodus 23:7)? Are there not many cases where we can speak of a betrayed party and a betrayer, the former no worse a spouse than any given person whose marriage did not break up? For example, I know of wives whose husbands became drug addicts through no fault of the wives and began selling drugs to the children as well as beating their wives. In some cases, the husband then left, but the church continued to hold the wife accountable for years by expecting her to save her marriage!

I am not among those who recommend that we reinstitute the penalties of Old Testament law; nevertheless, I find it instructive that the entire Bible treats adultery very harshly without ever so much as pointing a finger at the betrayed spouse. Both God and the prophet Hosea experienced abandonment, yet few of us would condemn them as guilty for the departure of their spouses. Today, some would condemn as primitive the Bible's notions that some situations involve both guilty and innocent parties. But is that approach really an adequate one for Bible-believing Christians?

What About Guilty Parties?

At least in principle, most evangelicals would agree that we should not discipline those who were sinned against in a divorce. Again at least in principle, most would agree that we do need to exercise discipline where it is clear that one party broke up the marriage through unrepentant adultery, abandonment, or abuse (cf. Matthew 18:15–17). In practice, sometimes it is precisely the difficulty of determining which party (if either) is innocent that leads Christians to lump all divorced people into the same "tolerated but sinful" category. In many divorces, however, one person shares the clear burden of responsibility, and discipline is appropriate.

What About the Repentant Spouse?

But when a person repents after the marriage has already been broken, how should we treat him? To some extent this depends on how broken the marriage is. Genuine repentance always involves restitution; if the innocent party remains single and desires reconciliation, we can work to restore the marriage. This solution cannot work in every case, however. What do we do, for example, if one of the parties has already remarried? When restitution is impossible, should we treat divorce more harshly than other sins?

Toward the beginning of this article I noted that some churches prohibit remarriage so strictly that they would break up second or third marriages to reinstate the first one. Someone might base this practice on David reclaiming Michal after she married another man (2 Samuel 3:14–16). This was clearly an exceptional situation, however. If David and Saul's daughter could bear a child, this would unite the kingdom. More to the point of our discussion, David never divorced Michal; her "marriage" to Paltiel had been invalid under Mosaic Law. Otherwise David could not have "remarried" her (Deuteronomy 24:3–4).

These churches, however, especially appeal to a literal reading of Mark 10:11–12 and Luke 16:18: Remarriage is adultery. Adultery is sleeping with someone while one or both parties are married to someone else, so this statement, if applied literally, would mean that one remains married to the original spouse. In this case, all subsequent marriages are adulterous, and Christians should actually dissolve any marriages after the first. Did Jesus intend us to apply His words so strictly?

For several reasons, I would suggest that He did not. First, we know that Jesus often employed hyperbole, rhetorical overstatement. This was a common Jewish teaching technique in his day, and Jesus used it even in the very context of some of His divorce statements (Matthew 5:29–30; Mark 10:25). Second, the Bible's allowance of exceptions for an innocent party in the cases of adultery or abandonment (Matthew 5:32; 19:9; 1 Corinthians 7:15) suggest that this is hyperbole.[4] If the innocent party is no longer married to the guilty party, the guilty person can hardly remain married to the innocent person! Third, the very context of Mark 10:11–12 suggests that it is hyperbole. Hyperbolically, Jesus said that marriage *could* not be dissolved. More literally, however, He warned that we *must* not dissolve it (Mark 10:9); that is, Jesus was not speaking ontologically (which would require breaking up remarriages) but as a command (forbidding us to break up marriages). Finally, when speaking literally Jesus acknowledged someone as having been married five times and living out of wedlock with one, not having been married once and simply living with the rest (John 4:18).

Thus I would agree that churches should discipline those who commit sexual sin, abuse their spouses, or divorce with inadequate grounds. We should, however, treat the guilty party in a divorce the same way we treat others who commit terrible sins: We should forgive those who demonstrate sincere repentance. Jesus' atonement is the only basis any of us have for salvation.

The issue of church leadership for the guilty party is more debatable. Because church leadership demands proven character (1 Timothy 3:1–13), it is legitimate to withhold such positions from anyone whose previous sins make it difficult for him to be "above reproach" in the community (1 Timothy 3:7). I do not believe this applies to preconversion sins long ago repented of, which would disqualify many more people than divorcés. Nor do I believe that "husband of one wife" (1 Timothy 3:2, 12; Titus 1:6) refers specifically to remarriage (whether after divorce or widowhood). The Greek phrase more naturally suggests marital fidelity, as I have argued elsewhere.[5] Nevertheless, it would seem appropriate to withhold leadership positions until a guilty person has established sufficiently the genuineness of his repentance and commitment. However controversial my comments are regarding the ministry of the guilty party, however, I hope that my readers will at least agree with me concerning the innocent party.

Conclusion

Justice-oriented evangelicals have appropriately tackled many issues of justice in society and some in the church. But one of our most silent areas has been the church's treatment of those whom most of us would agree are betrayed parties in divorces. This silence has sounded especially deafening in view of the fact that the primary sphere of discrimination has been the church—and that church discrimination has included the self-described justice-oriented evangelical segments of the church. To be sure, some may exploit our protests so they can justify sin—as they might twist anything available to rationalize their behavior. But unjust treatment of those who have been wronged is also sin, as is ignoring such unjust treatment. Ignoring oppression, even when it occurs within the church, should not characterize justice-oriented evangelicals.

Returning to our opening Scripture, one might ask if our silence genuinely reflects how Jesus would respond to divorce, or if it seriously distorts it. If Jesus would protect people against being divorced rather than punish those betrayed against their will, we need to begin to do a better job of representing His heart and mind to broken people.

DISCUSSION STARTER QUESTIONS

1. How does your church, denomination, or organization treat divorced people? Do they generally take into account an individual's reasons for being divorced?
2. What does the Bible include as explicit grounds for calling people innocent regarding their divorced state? Are there any other grounds that qualify? Why or why not?

3. When we cannot be certain of the reasons for someone's divorce, or when a person was partly or wholly at fault but has repented, how should we treat him or her? What biblical principles apply here? How can we make our churches or institutions more hospitable or charitable to those who have been divorced? How can we do this without compromising God's standard against divorce?

CHAPTER TWENTY-ONE

SINGLING OUT THE UNMARRIED:

What Do Single People Bring to Ministry?

SHIRLEY WRIGHT MASONGEZI

It has just been recently that I am making a great adjustment of being called by my husband's name. A half-century of singleness still calls for more adjustments. My knowledge of the topic of singles and the church comes from my experiences during the last half of the twentieth century in traditional and evangelical churches in America. Before we can look forward to the twenty-first century, we need to take a look backward. As a baby boomer my experiences may not be very unique, but being a young black single female mathematician before being a Christian gives me a few different dimensions to my observations.

I love being married to my husband. God gave me a great blessing in him so that he could add more depth to my life. But I also enjoyed most of my half century of singleness. Allow me to explain.

Before I was a Christian, life was very humdrum and unfulfilling as I went from one acquisition to the next, as I discovered each previous acquisition did not give me lasting satisfaction. At thirty years of age, I began a quest to find out why God had created me. After attending Bible school I became more and more comfortable with my singleness. In fact, almost a decade after becoming a Christian, I wanted to remain single as I wondered if the gift of celibacy was for me. I was having the time of my life with the One who gave me new life. But the journey to that point in my life took a great deal of serious exploration into God's Word, seeking His will for my life through prayer and godly counsel.

My Relationship with the Church

My first eighteen years of life were spent in a cohesive, middle-class, Midwestern, predominantly African-American church that was dually aligned with the National and American Baptist Conventions. In this context I grew up being encouraged by many aunties and uncles (in the extended family structure of the black culture) to be very active in a variety of spiritual and social activities. My church gave me a global perspective, which caused me to be very aware of several mission fields, in Africa in particular, and developed an attitude and discipline of praise and thanksgiving to the Lord, even though I did not know Him personally.

I enjoyed the challenge of Sunday school, youth choir, and Guild Girls (an American Baptist missions training course for adolescents). During these years the youth group was strongly encouraged to take an active role in the affairs of the local church throughout our collegiate career because the pastor knew the entanglements of this world and the atheistic professors we would encounter.

After college graduation my unanswered questions took me farther away from the local church for almost a decade. In retrospect, I realize my eventual conversion took place because God graciously placed me in a family of prayer warriors. As an aspiring young intellectual, I was totally unaware of the spiritual powerhouses on both sides of my family. My maternal great-grandfather and his youngest son were pastors. Two other paternal uncles were also in full-time ministry. Couple this with the faith of committed Christian parents and grandparents who believed we six children were gifts from God, and each of us had a lofty calling.

When I returned to the church as a Christian single, after receiving Christ through a television ministry, I felt unworthy to hold any significant role; I allowed Satan to put me on a guilt trip for things that had been forgiven and cleansed by Christ's blood. I had not opened a Bible in almost a decade, so I did not know very much about the mercies of God, but only felt the consequences of my sin. As a baby Christian who had the pungent odor of the world, I was not capable of blessing the local body of Christ. But the Lord gave me a call to come and be washed by the Word of God through a home Bible study.

The study had been started by the young professionals in the first church I attended after I made the decision to follow the Lord for the rest of my life. I initially refused to attend despite several invitations from my new friends from the friendly little church, because Friday night continued being my disco night until my first visit to the Bible study. I did not realize I was a new creature and I needed to put to death the deeds of the flesh. It took the sovereignty of God to move me from one apartment to another one that was located next door to where the Bible study was being held on that particular Friday evening. Lovingly and tenaciously my new friends welcomed me into their group even though I was ignorant of the Bible. Their love was very contagious and therefore disarmed my guilt and covered a multitude of my sins. But once I got my theology of salvation straight, I was ready to move ahead, not wanting anything to sidetrack me from what was ahead.

Issues of Singleness

In retrospect I see how incredibly imbalanced my life was before Jesus Christ's transforming work in me. I had a myriad of positive and negative feelings because of my singleness. I had feelings of being "alone" in a married world. During that time I was not equipped to appreciate being alone or being left out in conversations with women friends who were married with kids and thus talked about subjects I could not discuss. I desperately wanted my own children but, when I realized it would not happen unless I adopted, I had a difficult time adjusting emotionally to the reality of the situation. I denied my emotions and feelings for several years by covering the pain with drugs and trying to escape. Rather than learning to appreciate being alone, I hung out with many different people, even though on many occasions they were not very healthy relationships. As a teacher I had a classroom full of children, but I longed to have more personal influence and a lasting relationship with one or two of them that I could truly call my own.

I also felt unfulfilled and unwanted when my first fiancé broke our engagement about a year before we planned to get married. After this emotional catastrophe, I desperately wanted to be accepted by a man, so I called one of my old boyfriends whom I had rejected several years earlier. After a few months of a dead-end relationship, I finally faced up to the fact that God was the one I had my case against. When I finally recognized I was spiritually empty, I accepted it was only possible for Him to fill the void in my life. As I learned who the one true God really is, I began to trust Him with the needs in my personal life, which I had tried to deny for so many previous years. But as I saw eligible bachelors at the church, I wanted to be accepted. I desired to have sex because I had wrongly learned earlier in my life that was how a person received acceptance. For the second time in my life, I was encouraged by the body of believers to pray about those difficult areas that I still wanted to control. At times I felt powerless, but I sensed my need for the Lord to teach me new things, though learning was so uncomfortable.

Each Sunday morning I was being healed from my former life by the warm Christian fellowship, by the preaching of the Word of God, and by the music being sung. My mind was also being renewed by new things I was learning during the Sunday school hour. I soon discovered my insatiable appetite in my newly acquired faith. I was not completely challenged by the sermons each Sunday, so I found myself enjoying Christian television and contemporary gospel music. I was in front of the TV with my open Bible and notebook at least twice a week. We often had devotions in our home while I was growing up, which were concluded by times of prayer. As a result, the influence of prayer on my young life was profound, and I now personally knew the One to whom those prayers were directed. Immediately after my conversion, I discovered my burden for prayer. The first thing I did each day upon entering my apartment after work was to go to my room, close the door, kneel down beside my bed, and pour out my heart in prayer during long periods of precious time.

The year 1980 was a red-letter one, when I led the first person to the Lord. I did not think it would be so easy to invite someone from the intellectual community to attend a Bible study. I was wondering why I never heard evangelism encouraged in the two local churches

I attended during my first few years as a Christian. Could it be that the singles' ministries in those churches were low priority, or were they just missionary dating groups to find Mr. or Miss Right?

God was beginning to develop my burden for people over twenty-five years of age who put their careers as first priority, not wanting to examine the evidence of the reality of God. The gospel was invading my life in a way that I had never imagined. One day when I concluded one of my classroom lectures at the university, I announced that I was a Christian and if anyone wanted to talk about what that means, he or she should feel free to enter into a discussion whenever seeing me on campus. Several students took my statement seriously. In fact, two students were so curious about my definition of a Christian, I had the opportunity to discuss the four spiritual laws with them during my office hours. One of them rose from his chair, knelt beside it, and prayed the sinner's prayer, which was rather shocking for me.

I continued teaching and researching for another year at the university as I sought God for my future. I was led to resign my position and pursue a second career in missions. The transition was a bit complicated, but God gave me grace to go through each step with Him going before me. As I counted the cost, I asked for the blessing of my family before entering the ministry. The elders who blessed me that day are now deceased and among the great cloud of witnesses.

I also received another blessing before I left the university community. My mentor, who was one of the advisors for my Masters degree, begged me not to leave the doctoral program because I would suffer severe personal consequences, perhaps regretting my decision later in life. He suggested if I were patient enough to finish my Ph.D., I would surely be among the upper echelon of women professors in the field of mathematics, who were making an impact on American society as well as the world. He suggested that I could write my own ticket if I persevered just a few more years. His counsel was from a worldly perspective, hoping that I would reconsider my decision to leave a fairly lucrative position that could lead to job security rather than entering the uncertain field of missions where I would be begging people for money in order to subsidize my work on the "dark continent" of Africa.

I was now so comfortable with my single life that I personalized Isaiah 54:5, "For your Maker is your husband," as I told those people who wanted me to find a husband that I had found the most faithful Husband in the entire universe. During these years I looked up stories of singles in the Bible because I considered my singleness as being single-minded for God. For so long I had considered being single a liability, but now I celebrated it as a great asset. I asked God to give me a resolve like the apostle Paul, so that I could one day see a rich harvest of souls in every place that I would travel. I felt as if my life was a cross between the woman at the well and Mary Magdalene. I saw how wrong my thinking had been to feel like I had to have a husband or a man to feel complete. I conversely felt so sinful and inadequate after searching so long for the fallacious "man of my dreams." I had opened my life up to so many ungodly influences during those years of searching.

The Word of God says, "For the Son of Man came to seek and to save what was lost" (Luke 19:10). I knew what I needed, but I thought I was capable of making my own decisions concerning my personal life. When I stopped my search for the good life and allowed God to capture me, I experienced a satisfying peace for the first time, as well as receiving eternal and abundant life.

Other People's Pressures

I felt such a freedom and release from the singleness myths in which I was trapped for several years. Friends and family members would ask why I wasn't interested in getting married. They would say, "You are much too pretty not to have a husband." Many felt sorry for me, and others were condescending, which frankly exhausted my patience. After many years of listening to these types of comments, this was ingrained in my thinking so profoundly that I started believing I couldn't be successful without a man in my life. Several years into my conversion, my father was one of my most empathetic and sensitive allies. In fact, after my conversion I asked his forgiveness for the way I earlier acted like a prodigal daughter. After this our relationship changed completely, until the Lord allowed us to be intimate friends for several years before his death. He jokingly told me not to rush into marriage because he was well aware of the limited choices available. He encouraged me to pursue the ministry in which the Lord had called me and enjoy the relationships of those who were also following the Lord's guidance.

I was captivated by Joseph's life in Egypt, as I tried to extract some biblical principles that I could emulate. I was struggling with purity in my new Christian life, so Joseph's testimony of refusing seduction in Potiphar's house really spoke to me. I asked myself, *How could someone withstand the continual bombardment of sexual temptation and unswervingly remain pure?* I was also touched by his faithfulness, diligence, and availability when doing his job each day. Translating these principles to my life is exactly what I needed because of my former lifestyle. I would do anything to maintain purity. At first I did not think it was possible, but as I submitted my sexual feelings and emotions to the Holy Spirit, I saw victory over this area.

Proper maintenance and a constant reliance on the Spirit of God made my personal relationship with Him more intimate. After I finally cleared the hurdles I stumbled over for several years, I experienced much joy in my single life. All my relationships seemed to improve and take on a depth I had never known. My new identity was that of a Christian who just happened to be single. But even though I was a Christian single, I was first a woman, which I appreciated as a positive force because that is how God created me. I was truly understanding God's plan for singles when I read 1 Corinthians 7:25–40, in which Paul encourages singleness because of the extra time it allows one to offer to the Lord's work. Struggles with temptation continued, but I experienced more victory after starting Bible school. My sexual drive was still alive and well, but it was easier to obey the Spirit year after year as I allowed my mind to be transformed and learned to walk by faith.

The Church's Responsibility

In this new millennium, I see the culture driving the church to a crucial point of decision: Do we retreat as singles become increasingly hostile and more isolated from the church, while we continue to serve those who only enter our doors each Sunday morning, or do we start reinventing how we do church? We have seen too many attempts to make singleness into another youth group. Singles are adults and should be treated as such. There are all sorts of categories of singles: men and women who have never been married and who fit the "traditional" definition of *single;* those who are dating but not engaged; those who are living with someone of the opposite sex or otherwise sexually involved; men and women who are divorced, with or without children; men and women who are widowed. Many are raising their kids, adopted children, or relatives' kids. "Single" is so much more complex than it used to be!

Many churches have been increasingly aware of the needs of single mothers and fathers, who hardly fit any category, yet might perhaps have the greatest needs. Then we have the X and Y generations, who are looking for a different kind of church. This is a real challenge for the church in America, because those under thirty years of age are the ones walking away from the church. Many of them return if and when they have their own children, but if the leadership fails to understand these young people, we could easily lose another generation.

How do we create meaningful connections for all these different categories of singles within the church? Some of our young people today do not receive the same type of encouragement I received when I was growing up. They find it a struggle to make their voices heard within their denominations or their churches, and some are forming informal networks to try to have more impact.

Just as our discipleship ministries are opportunities for spiritual development and growth in an accountability system, our singles ministries should focus on the same biblical principles. Singles can be involved in mentoring, tutorial, or computer training for those who need to be challenged in this area. Some can spend time with the elderly or shop for them, baby-sit the children of single parents, or offer their professional skills to the church for a few hours in time of need. Just as Christian electricians, carpenters, or systems analysts volunteer their services to the local church, there is an untapped population of singles who have the potential to evangelize our communities through their areas of expertise and who often have fewer time commitments or distractions.

Many singles also need sound biblical advice concerning financial investment and household skills. Most married people own their own homes, while most singles rent. How can the church help older singles to establish roots rather than live a "temporary" life forever or until they get married? And how can the church better become "extended family" to singles who are far removed from the love and even the accountability of family?

At certain times, I felt as if I was second best because many singles were overlooked for key positions within the church and our married counterparts were asked to fill those roles, even if the single person was gifted in that area. Christians tend to assume that single people have "failed" to marry, and thus they have no relational skills and can't teach or offer counsel. In most churches, elders, deacons, and other church leaders are almost always married. In the midst of the uncertainty of God being able to use me in the local church, the evangelical church I attended, as well as a parachurch ministry, admonished me to become a student of God's Word, learning how to correctly handle the Word of truth. I am fortunate in the sense that I was not discouraged or frustrated to the point of leaving any local church in which I was a member. I was continually admonished to keep my eyes on the Lord at all times. But many single people continue to feel like "outsiders" in their own churches. When they stop attending for a while, no one seems to notice, and no one calls. And sometimes they leave and never return.

But with a new set of social issues this millennium, how can we fulfill the Great Commission, incorporating more of the single men and women who have merely been entertained on Sunday morning or have been able to attend church anonymously during the last two decades? We will continue to have some churches serve older people. Others will cater to the young, while many aim to embrace all generations and all cultures instead of having separate cultural congregations. Whatever strategy we use to plant churches in this new millennium, let me encourage you to rethink how we can minister to singles who need to know that God loves them and they have a gift from God that they can share in order to change the world.

DISCUSSION STARTER QUESTIONS

1. How are singles involved in your church? Are they, as a rule, treated as adults or adolescents? (If you're not sure, ask a few of them.)
2. Does God keep some people single as punishment or because He doesn't love them enough to give them a mate? If not, what purposes might He have for singleness—both for those who are single and for the church body that includes them? Read Paul's answer in 1 Corinthians 7:8, 32–38.

3. What are some ways singles and marrieds in your church or ministry can get to know each other and better understand each other's needs?

NOTES

Chapter 1: Developing a Biblical Theology of Racial Reconciliation by Dwight Perry

1. Michael O. Emerson and Christian Smith, *Divided by Faith: Evangelical Religion and the Problem of Race in America* (New York: Oxford Univ. Press, 2000), 7. (Emerson is identified in the book as the primary author.) Internal quote is from Eduardo Bonilla-Silva Lewis (unpublished ms.), "'The New Racism': Toward an Analysis of the U.S. Racial Structure, 1960s–1990s," written in 1997.
2. Andrew Hacker, *Two Nations* (New York: Scribner's, 1992), 3.
3. Joseph R. Barndt, *Dismantling Racism* (Minneapolis: Augsburg Fortress, 1991), 28.
4. Emerson and Smith, *Divided by Faith*, 18.
5. Barndt, *Dismantling Racism,* 94.
6. Ibid., 96.
7. Raleigh Washington and Glen Kehrein, *Breaking Down Walls* (Chicago: Moody, 1993), 12.
8. Spencer Perkins and Chris Rice, *More Than Equals* (Downers Grove, Ill.: InterVarsity, 2000), 29.
9. Rodney Cooper, *We Stand Together* (Chicago: Moody, 1995), 17.
10. Lawrence Richards, *Expository Dictionary of Bible Words* (Grand Rapids: Zondervan, 1985), 368.

Chapter 2: Fade to White by Vincent Bacote

1. J. I. Packer, "Is Systematic Theology a Mirage? An Introductory Discussion," in *Doing Theology in Today's World: Essays in Honor of Kenneth S. Kantzer,* ed. John D. Woodbridge and Thomas Edward McComiskey (Grand Rapids: Zondervan, 1991), 23.
2. Ibid.
3. Ibid., 33.
4. Michael O. Emerson and Christian Smith, *Divided by Faith: Evangelical Religion and the Problem of Race in America* (New York: Oxford Univ. Press, 2000), 21–22.
5. For example, see Ibid., 22–49. As Emerson and Smith observe on p. 48, American ideals such as equality and freedom have helped to improve race relations, but not in such a way that racialization has been overcome. There is still significant separation between the races, with differing perceptions of the nature, solution, and urgency of the problem. In terms of the normativity question, readers can ask themselves the following questions: "How do I define what is normal?" "What or who is the norm for a successful American, and what kind of person comes to mind?" If one envisions a white male as the answer to the latter question, then why is that the picture in your mind, and how hard is it to replace that perception with someone non-white? I suggest this exercise because it can reveal the subtle way in which the ideal successful American is perceived as white.
6. Ibid., 75–76.
7. Ibid., 76. Emerson and Smith describe the individualism of white evangelicals as one in which each individual is held responsible for their own actions, and one which gives central importance the individual's personal relationship with Christ. The authors transpose this idea and note that "white evangelicals place strong emphasis on family relationships, friendships, church relationships, and other forms of interpersonal connections. Healthy relationships encourage people to make right choices. For this reason, white evangelicals, as we see, often view social problems as rooted in poor relationships or the negative influence of significant others." Ibid., 77–78. Emerson and Smith define antistructuralism as "the inability to perceive or unwillingness to accept social structural influences" (76).
8. Cheryl Dunlop, general editor at Moody Press, supplied much of the discussion of individualism in the history of the American evangelical white church.
9. "Absent from their [white evangelicals'] accounts is the idea that poor relationships might be shaped by social structures, such as laws, the ways institutions operate, or forms of segregation. Again, understanding evangelicals' cultural tools illuminates why this element is missing. White evangelicals not only interpret race issues by using accountable freewill individualism and relationalism, but they often find structural explanations irrelevant and even wrongheaded." Emerson and Smith, *Divided by Faith,* 78. Emerson and Smith do point out that structural factors are sometimes mentioned by white evangelicals, but in these cases the structures (e.g., government, the media, political leaders) perpetuate racism by the introduction of programs such as affirmative action or by "creating" more of a race problem than actually exists for the sake of maintaining a constituency.
10. Wayne Grudem, *Systematic Theology: An Introduction to Biblical Doctrine* (Grand Rapids: Zondervan, 1994), 21.
11. Ibid.

12. Alister McGrath, "Evangelical Theological Method: The State of the Art," in *Evangelical Futures: A Conversation on Theological Method,* ed. John G. Stackhouse Jr. (Grand Rapids: Baker Books, 2000), 30. McGrath contrasts Grudem's approach with Kevin Vanhoozer's literary genre-sensitive, Riceour-influenced approach as found in *Is There a Meaning in This Text? The Bible, the Reader, and the Morality of Literary Knowledge* (Grand Rapids: Zondervan, 1998).

13. Erickson acknowledges the difficulties in recognizing social sin, including those produced by the social conditioning of one's own group. He articulates social sin through the categories of the world, the powers, and corporate personality, and argues that the solutions to such sins are not only regeneration but also some non-revolutionary attempts to renovate evil structures. See Millard Erickson, *Christian Theology* (Grand Rapids: Baker, 1985), 641–58.

14. Grudem, 490.

15. "Even when respondents assented to the existence of systemic discrimination, they saw it as tangential, even superficial compared to the true problem of negative attitudes and unhealthy relationships. Ann Swidler argues that the cultural tool kit limits possibilities, or, put another way, in providing a set of tools, it withholds others. For those we interviewed, the tools of individualism and personal relationships limited their ability either to recognize institutional problems or to acknowledge them as important." Emerson and Smith, *Divided by Faith,* 79–80.

16. Tony Evans, a reconciliation leader and head of the Urban Alternative in Dallas, said in an interview with *Christianity Today,* "The concerns of black Americans are not of dominant concern, by and large, to white evangelicals." According to Tony Warner, Georgia area director for InterVarsity Christian Fellowship, "White evangelicals are more willing to pursue a white conservative political agenda than to be reconciled with their African-American brothers and sisters. It raises a fundamental question of their belief and commitment to the biblical gospel." Ibid., 66.

17. Docetism is the heresy that argues that Christ only appeared to be human. Theologically, a docetic tendency can be seen when one de-emphasizes the human element in our theological method and results.

18. Willie James Jennings, "Wandering in the Wilderness: Christian Identity & Theology Between Context & Race," in *The Gospel in Black & White: Theological Resources for Racial Reconciliation,* ed. Dennis Okholm (Downers Grove, Ill.: InterVarsity, 1997), 46–47.

19. By "catholic," I have in mind theology pursued as a communal task, where the Christian community, globally understood, participates together in articulating and refining the message of our faith.

20. Kevin J. Vanhoozer, "The Voice and the Actor: A Dramatic Proposal about the Ministry and Minstrelsy of Theology," in *Evangelical Futures,* 104–5.

21. John Stackhouse points out that, demographically speaking, evangelical theology happens to be very white and male, and this is simply the shape of the field. See *Evangelical Futures,* 10.

Chapter 3: The "Right" Way to Praise God by Clarence Shuler

1. C. Eric Lincoln, *The Black Experience in Religion* (Garden City, N.Y.: Anchor Books, 1974), 44.

2. Ibid., 45.

3. Thomas Sowell, *Race and Culture: A World View* (New York: Basic Books, 1994), 1.

4. Harvie M. Conn, *A Clarified Vision for Urban Mission* (Grand Rapids: Zondervan, 1987), 103–4.

Chapter 5: Getting to Know Each Other by Bill McCartney
1. Adapted from "A Call to Unity" by Bill McCartney in *Seven Promises of a Promise Keeper* (Colorado Springs: Focus on the Family, 1994), 157–58.
2. Adapted from *Sold Out* by Bill McCartney (Nashville: Word, 1997), 177–81.

Chapter 7: Understanding Interracial Families by A. Charles Ware
1. Aldore Collier, "Black/White Love Affair Sparks 'Jungle Fever,'" *Jet,* 80, no. 8, 10 June 1991, 56.
2. Tony Pugh, "Interracial Marriages Becoming Commoner," *Indianapolis Star,* 23 March 2001, A9.
3. Peter S. Ruckman, *Segregation or Integration? What Saith the Scripture?* 3d ed. (Pensacola, Fla.: Pensacola Bible Institute, 1962), 5–13.
4. M. R. De Haan, *Dear Doctor: I Have a Problem* (Grand Rapids: Radio Bible Class, 1961), 2, 265–66.
5. A. Charles Ware, *Prejudice and the People of God: Reconciliation Rooted in Redemption and Guided by Revelation,* ed. Eugene Seals (Indianapolis: Baptist Bible College of Indianapolis, 1998), 28.
6. For further discussion of this issue see Dr. Allen P. Ross's article, "Studies in the Book of Genesis, Part 1," in the July–September 1980 issue of *Bibliotheca Sacra.*
7. Don Batten, Ken Ham, and Carl Wieland, *One Blood: The Biblical Answer to Racism,* (Green Forest, Ark.: Master Books, Inc., 1999).
8. John R. Rice, *Negro or White* (Murfreesboro, Tenn.: Sword of the Lord, 1956), 239.
9. Fred and Anita Prinzing, *Mixed Messages: Responding to Interracial Marriages* (Chicago: Moody, 1991), 14.
10. Batten, Ham, and Wieland, *One Blood,* 56–57.

Chapter 9: People Just Like Me by Rod Cooper
1. Bruce W. Fong, *Racial Equality in the Church: A Critique of the Homogeneous Unit Principle in Light of a Practical Theology Perspective* (Lanham, Md.: Univ. Press of America, 1996), xix.
2. Ibid., 176.
3. Ibid., 171.
4. Ibid., 176.

Chapter 10: The Quest for Biblical Community by Henry Lee Allen
1. All societies use some type of technology. See Gerhard Lenski, *Human Societies* (New York: McGraw-Hill, 1970) for evidence. However, massive literacy, a prelude to a scientific or technological culture, is a fairly recent innovation even in Western cultures. See Jacques Barzun, *From Dawn to Decadence: 1500 to the Present* (New York: HarperCollins, 2000).
2. Gerhard Lenski, *Human Societies* (New York: McGraw-Hill, 1970).
3. See interview. *Psychology Today,* American Psychological Association (July 1976), reprinted as Article 9 *Annual Editions in Sociology 1982/83* (Guilford, Conn.: 1983), 52–57.
4. See Hubert M. Blalock and Paul H. Wilken, *Intergroup Processes* (New York: Free Press, 1979).
5. Joel Charon, *Ten Questions,* 4th ed. (Stamford, Conn.: Wadsworth, 2001).
6. JosephR. Feagin, *Racial and Ethnic Relations* (Englewood Cliffs, N.J.: Prentice-Hall, 1984).
7. Clarence Shuler, *Winning the Race to Unity* (Chicago: Moody, 1998).

8. Xenophobia refers to an exaggerated or unhealthy fear of strangers.
9. James F. Downs, *Cultures in Crisis*, 2nd ed. (Beverly Hills: Glencoe, 1975).
10. John Duckitt, *The Social Psychology of Prejudice* (Westport, Conn.: Praeger, 1994).
11. Thom Hopler, *A World of Difference* (Downers Grove, Ill.: InterVarsity, 1981).
12. Daniel Goleman, *Emotional Intelligence* (New York: Bantam, 1995).
13. Gareth Morgan, *Imaginization* (Thousand Oaks, Calif.: Sage, 1997).
14. Jean Lipman-Blumen, *Connective Leadership* (New York: Oxford, 1996).

Chapter 11: The Promise and Peril of Seminary Education by David K. Clark

1. To save repeating myself, all references to *seminaries* and *theological schools* are to evangelical seminaries in English-speaking North America.
2. Richard John Neuhaus, "The Christian University: Eleven Theses," *First Things* 59 (January 1996): 20–22.
3. I will use the term *Anglo* to describe white, English-speaking North Americans, regardless of whether their ancestral heritage is Icelandic, Italian, Polish, or English.
4. Donald Davidson, "On the Very Idea of a Conceptual Scheme," *Proceedings and Addresses of the American Philosophical Association* 47 (1973–74): 5–20.
5. James W. Lewis, "On Wisdom and Strife," *Criterion* 27 (Autumn 1988): 13.
6. Stephen L. Carter, *The Culture of Disbelief: How American Law and Politics Trivialize Religious Devotion* (New York: HarperCollins, Basic Books, 1993), 16.
7. David Gushee quotes Augustine: "Attract Them by Your Way of Life: The Professor's Task in the Christian University," in *The Future of Christian Higher Education*, ed. David S. Dockery and David P. Gushee (Nashville: Broadman & Holman, 1999), 137–53.
8. Gary L. McIntosh and Samuel D. Rima Sr., *Overcoming the Dark Side of Leadership* (Grand Rapids: Baker, 1997).
9. This cross-cultural study categorizes more than one thousand churches from thirty-two countries and five continents into four quadrants: high-quality growing, high-quality declining, low-quality growing, and low-quality declining. Christian A. Schwarz, *Natural Church Development: A Guide to Eight Essential Qualities of Healthy Churches* (Carol Stream, Ill.: ChurchSmart Resources, 1996), 22–23.
10. James M. Kouzes and Barry Z. Posner, *The Leadership Challenge* (San Francisco: Jossey-Bass, 1995), 349.
11. See Robert K. Cooper and Ayman Sawaf, *Executive EQ: Emotional Intelligence in Leadership and Organizations* (New York: Berkley Publishing Group, 1998).
12. E. D. Hirsch Jr., *Validity in Interpretation* (New Haven: Yale Univ. Press, 1967).
13. Craig L. Blomberg, "The Globalization of Hermeneutics," *Journal of the Evangelical Theological Society* 38 (1995): 583.
14. Parker J. Palmer, *Leading from Within: Reflections on Spirituality and Leadership* (Indianapolis: Indiana Office for Campus Ministries, 1990), 5–6.
15. Ibid., 7–8.
16. Reported by C. Douglas Jay, "What Should We Learn from a Sorry Past?" *In Trust* (Spring 2001): 21.
17. See Bethel Seminary's web site, "Global Christian Theology: An Annotated Bibliography with Emphasis on Non-White Theologians" at http://www.bethel.edu/~rakrob/files/global_theology.htm.
18. See Randall Lehmann Sorenson, "Doctoral Students' Integration of Psychology and Christianity: Perspectives via Attachment Theory and Multidimensional Scaling," *Journal for the Scientific Study of Religion* 36 (1997): 530–48.

Chapter 12: Pursuing Faith-Based Opportunities by Glen Kehrein

1. Associated Press Wire: "Prison Population at Record High," John Smith, 25 March 2001.
2. Robert L. Woodson Sr., *The Triumphs of Joseph* (New York: Free Press, 1998), 8.
3. For a historical analysis as to the causes of this shift, see "A Case for Wholistic Ministry: The City, Evangelicals and the Social Gospel," chapter 3 in *A Heart for the City,* John Fuder, ed. (Chicago: Moody, 1999).
4. Nicholas Lehmann, *The Promised Land: The Great Migration and How It Changed America* (New York: Knopf, 1991), 6.
5. Taylor Branch, *Parting the Waters: America in the King Years 1954–63* (New York: Simon and Schuster, 1988), 351–78.
6. Branch, *Parting the Waters,* 470.
7. Michael O. Emerson and Christian Smith, *Divided by Faith: Evangelical Religion and the Problem of Race in America* (New York: Oxford Univ. Press, 2000), 75. Internal quote is from William Martin, *A Prophet with Honor: The Billy Graham Story* (New York: W. Morrow, 1991), 168.
8. Ibid., 109.

Chapter 13: Seeing the Invisible Prejudice by Rosalie de Rosset

1. J. Ellen Foster, "Work for Women," *The Institute Tie* IX, 6 (February 1909): 483.
2. Brent Staples, "Black Men and Public Space," *Harper's* vol. 27 (December 1986): 19.
3. Ibid., 20.
4. Ibid.
5. Dorothy L. Sayers, *Are Women Human?* (Grand Rapids: Eerdmans, 1971), 19.
6. Shirley Chisholm, "I'd Rather Be Black Than Female," *McCall's,* 97:6 (August 1970) 6.
7. Evelyn Christenson, foreword to Lorry Lutz, *Women as Risk-Takers for God* (Carlisle, Cumbria, U.K.: World Evangelical Fellowship, 1997), xi.
8. Sayers, *Are Women Human?* 19.
9. Beth Howard, "Classification: Human," Message Preparation for Women class, Moody Bible Institute, 12 March 1999, 1.
10. Ibid., 2.
11. Lorry Lutz, *Women as Risk-Takers for God,* 242.
12. Foster, "Work for Women," 483.
13. Ibid.
14. Lutz, *Women as Risk-Takers,* 27.
15. Sayers, *Are Women Human?* 47.
16. Ibid.
17. "Prayer from Kenya." *The Oxford Book of Prayer,* ed. George Appleton (Oxford: Oxford Univ. Press, 1985).

Chapter 14: A Plea for Godly Partnership by Ellen Lowrie Black

1. Loren Cunningham and David J. Hamilton, *Why Not Women?* (Seattle, Wash.: YWAM Publishing, 2000), 16.
2. Ibid., 14.

Chapter 15: Moving Past "Women Can't Preach" by Michelle Obleton

1. This is a true story, but all names have been changed.
2. Bruce Bugbee, Don Cousins, and Bill Hybels, *Network: The Right People . . . in the Right Places . . . for the Right Reasons* (Grand Rapids: Zondervan, 1994).

3. Cynthia Perry, "Looking at Women in Ministry," written for the African-American Church Consultation. Arlington Heights, Ill.: Home Missions Baptist General Conference, 1992.

4. Victoria Johnson, *Restoring Broken Vessels: Confronting the Attack on Female Sexuality* (Detroit: Dubar, 1996).

5. George Barna, "Women Are the Backbone of the Christian Congregations in America," *Barna Report,* 6 March 2000.

6. Ibid.

Chapter 16: Retired and Set Aside, an edited interview with Evelyn Christenson

1. Some Scripture quotations in this chapter are paraphrases of the King James Version or the *New American Standard.*

Chapter 17: The Theology of the Wheelchair by Sandy Rios

1. "Sasha's Song" copyright © 1985 Sandy Rios. All rights reserved.

2. Christopher De Vinck, *The Power of the Powerless* (New York: Doubleday, 1988).

Chapter 18: Those We'd Rather Forget by Brad Grammer

1. Marion L. Soards, *Scripture and Homosexuality* (Louisville, Ky.: Westminster John Knox, 1995), 64–65.

2. Joe Dallas, *Desires in Conflict* (Eugene, Ore.: Harvest House, 1991).

3. Mark R. Laaser, *The Secret Sin* (Grand Rapids: Zondervan, 1992), 15.

4. Peter K. Johnson, "Assemblies of God Tackles Problem of Porn Addiction Among Ministers," *Charisma* (January 2001), 24.

5. Dan B. Allender and Tremper Longman III, *The Cry of the Soul* (Colorado Springs: NavPress, 1994), 27.

6. Ibid., 58.

7. Ibid., 62.

8. Kay Arthur, *Lord, I Want to Know You* (Sisters, Oreg.: Multnomah, 1992), 87.

9. George Barna, *The Second Coming of the Church* (Nashville: Word, 1998), 6.

10. Ibid., 6.

Chapter 19: Kids in Constant Motion by Cynthia Perry

1. T. Reid, S. Vasa, J. Maag, and G. Wright, "An Analysis of Teachers—Perceptions of Attention Deficit-Hyperactivity Disorders," *The Journal of Research and Development in Education,* 27 (1994), 195–202.

2. Attention Deficit Hyperactivity Disorder Decade of the Brain. (1997). *Attention deficit hyperactivity disorder* [online]. Accessed at: http://www.nimh.nih.gov

3. E. Hallowell and J. Ratey, *Driven to Distraction: Recognizing and Coping with Attention Deficit Disorder from Childhood Through Adulthood* (Toronto: Pantheon, 1994).

4. H. Taylor and S. Larson, "Teaching Children with ADHD—What Do Elementary and Middle School Social Studies Teachers Need to Know?" *Social Studies,* 89 (July 1998), 161–64.

5. R. A. Barkley, *Taking Charge of ADHD: The Complete Authoritative Guide for Parents* (New York: Guilford Press, 1995).

6. *Attention deficit hyperactivity disorder* [online].

7. Taylor and Larson, "Teaching Children with ADHD," 161–64.

8. Children and Adults with Attention Deficit Disorders Facts Sheets 1–9. CHADD (1995). James Dobson, *Solid Answers: America's Foremost Family Counselor Responds to Tough Questions Facing Today's Families* (Wheaton, Ill: Tyndale, 1997); K. Nadeua, *Attention! Magazine.* 30 (1997), 121–25; S. Raza, "Enhance Your Chances for Success with Students

with Attention-Deficit/Hyperactivity Disorder (ADHD)," *Intervention in School and Clinic* 33 (1997), 56–59.

9. C. Dendy, *Teenagers with ADD: A Parents' Guide* (Bethesda, Md.: Woodbine, 1995); E. Hallowell and J. Ratey, *Driven to Distraction: Recognizing and Coping with Attention Deficit Disorder from Childhood Through Adulthood* (Toronto: Pantheon, 1994); J. Lerner, B. Lowenthal, and S. Lerner, *Attention Deficit Disorders: Assessment and Teaching* (Pacific Grove, Calif: Brooks/Cole Publishing Company, 1995); Cynthia Perry, *ADHD: A Teacher's Guide to Attention Deficit Disorder* [unpublished workbook] (Oak Forest, Ill., 1998).

10. The Harvard Health Letter 1995, 1.

11. http://www.nimh.nih.gov/publicat/learndis.cfm#adhd.

12. Harvard Mental Health Letter (1995).

13. Barkely, *Taking Charge of ADHD:* Dobson, *Solid Answers;* L. Weiss,. *Attention Deficit Disorder in Adults* (Dallas: Taylor, 1992).

14. C. Evertson and C. Randolph, "Classroom Management in the Learning-centered Classroom," in A. Ornstein, ed., *Teaching Theory into Practice* (Boston, Mass.: Allyn & Bacon, 1995), 116–31.

15. "Attention Deficit Disorder: What Teachers Should Know" (CHADD, 1995).

16. Bill McNabb and Steven Mabry, *Teaching the Bible Creatively: How to Awaken Your Kids to Scripture* (Grand Rapids: Zondervan, 1991), 13.

Chapter 20: The Almost-Unpardonable Sin by Craig S. Keener

1. Much of this essay constitutes a revision of my article, "Divorce as a Justice Issue," *Prism* (November 1998): 6–8, 20. I have provided documentation for my biblical arguments more fully in ...*And Marries Another: Divorce and Remarriage in the Teaching of the New Testament* (Peabody, Mass.: Hendrickson, 1991); some are updated and expanded in *A Commentary on the Gospel of Matthew* (Grand Rapids: Eerdmans, 1999), 189–92, 463–69.

2. Luther, Calvin, and most of the Reformers allowed for remarriage if the spouse committed adultery, a view which William Heth and Gordon Wenham (who disagree with it) regard as "the evangelical consensus" in *Jesus and Divorce: The Problem with the Evangelical Consensus* (Nashville: Thomas Nelson, 1984). Many evangelical scholars argue for it today (e.g., Craig Blomberg, "Marriage, Divorce, Remarriage, and Celibacy: An Exegesis of Matthew 19:3–12," *Trinity Journal* 11 [1990]: 161–96; Robert Stein, "Is It Lawful for a Man to Divorce His Wife?" *Journal of the Evangelical Theological Society* 22 [1979]: 115–21; Gary Burge, "You're Divorced—Can You Remarry?" *Christianity Today* [Oct. 4, 1999]: 81–82).

3. I argue against the divorce and remarriage interpretation of 1 Timothy 3:2 in chapter six of *And Marries Another.* My friend William Heth told me that he disagrees with remarriage but would not bar remarried persons from ministry.

4. For documentation for this exception, see again *And Marries Another,* 21–66, especially 28–37, 61–62; *Matthew,* 189–92, 463–69.

5. See note 3 above.

BIBLIOGRAPHY: FOR FURTHER READING

Part One
Unity Between Races in the Church

Barndt, Joseph. *Dismantling Racism.* Minneapolis: Augsburg, 1991.

Cooper, Rodney. *We Stand Together.* Chicago: Moody, 1995.

Emerson, Michael O., and Christian Smith. *Divided by Faith: Evangelical Religion and the Problem of Race in America.* New York: Oxford Univ. Press, 2000.

Hacker, Andrew. *Two Nations.* New York: Scribner's, 1992.

Okholm, Dennis, ed. *The Gospel in Black & White: Theological Resources for Racial Reconciliation.* Downers Grove, Ill.: InterVarsity, 1997.

Perkins, Spencer, and Chris Rice. *More Than Equals.* Downers Grove, Ill.: InterVarsity, 2000.

Perry, Dwight. *Breaking Down Barriers.* Grand Rapids: Baker, 1998.

Walvoord, John F., and Roy B. Zuck. *The Bible Knowledge Commentary: Old Testament.* Wheaton, Ill.: Victor, 1987.

Washington, Raleigh, and Glen Kehrein. *Breaking Down Walls.* Chicago: Moody, 1993.

Winthrop, D. Jordan. *The White Man's Burden: Historical Origins of Racism in the United States.* London: Oxford University Press, 1974.

Part Two
Unity Between Classes in the Church

Blalock, Hubert M., and Paul H. Wilken. *Intergroup Processes.* New York: Free Press, 1979.

Charon, Joel. *Ten Questions,* 4th ed. Stamford, Conn.: Wadsworth, 2001.

Downs, James F. *Cultures in Crisis,* 2nd ed. Beverly Hills: Glencoe, 1975.

Duckitt, John. *The Social Psychology of Prejudice.* Westport, Conn.: Praeger, 1994.

Feagin, Joseph R. *Racial and Ethnic Relations.* Englewood Cliffs, N.J.: Prentice-Hall, 1984.

Goleman, Daniel. *Emotional Intelligence.* New York: Bantam, 1995.

Haley, Alex. *Roots.* New York: Dell, 1976.

Hall, Edward T. "How Cultures Collide," reprinted as Article 9 *Annual Editions in Sociology 1982/83.* Guilford, Conn.: Dushkin, 1983.

Hopler, Thom. *A World of Difference.* Downers Grove, Ill.: InterVarsity, 1981.

Lenski, Gerhard. *Human Societies.* New York: McGraw-Hill, 1970.

Lipman-Blumen, Jean. *Connective Leadership.* New York: Oxford, 1996.

Morgan, Gareth. *Imaginization.* Thousand Oaks, Calif.: Sage, 1997.

Shuler, Clarence. *Winning the Race to Unity.* Chicago: Moody, 1998.

Part Three
Unity Between Genders in the Church

Grentz, Stanley. *Women in the Church: A Theology of Women in Ministry.* Downers Grove, Ill.: InterVarsity, 1995.

Groothuis, Rebecca Merrill. *Good News for Women: A Biblical Picture of Gender Equality.* Grand Rapids: Baker Books, 1997.

Hall, Gretchen Gaebelein. *Equal to Serve.* Grand Rapids: Baker Books, 1987.

Keener, Craig S. *Paul, Women, and Wives.* Peabody, Mass.: Hendrickson Publishers, 1992.

Lutz, Lorry. *Women as Risk-Takers for God.* Carlisle, Cumbria, U.K.: World Evangelical Fellowship, 1997.

Malcom, Kari. *Women at the Crossroads: A Path Beyond Feminism and Traditionalism.* Downers Grove, Ill.: InterVarsity, 1982.

Mickelsen, Alvera, ed. *Women, Authority, and the Bible.* Downers Grove, Ill.: InterVarsity, 1986.

Piper, John, and Wayne A. Grudem, eds. *Recovering Biblical Manhood and Womanhood: A Response to Evangelical Feminism.* Wheaton, Ill., Crossway, 1991.

Rinck, Margaret. *Christian Men Who Hate Women: Healing Hurting Relationships.* Grand Rapids: Zondervan, 1990.

Saucy, Robert L., and Judith K. TenElshof, eds., *Women and Men in Ministry: A Complementary Perspective.* Chicago: Moody, 2001.

Sayers, Dorothy. *Are Women Human?* Grand Rapids: Eerdmans, 1971.

Part Four
Unity Across Other Barriers in the Church

The Elderly and Ministry

Garmatz, Robert. *Never Too Old: How to Involve Older Adults in Your Church.* St. Louis: Concordia, 1992.

Seymour, Robert E. *Aging Without Apology: Living the Senior Years with Integrity and Faith.* Valley Forge, Pa.: Judson, 1995.

Stafford, Tim. *As Our Years Increase: Loving, Caring, Preparing.* Grand Rapids: Pyranee, 1989.

Ministry with the Disabled

Newman, Gene, and Joni Eareckson Tada. *All God's Children: Ministry with Disabled Persons.* Grand Rapids: Zondervan, 1993.

Pierson, Jim. *No Disabled Souls: How to Welcome a Person with a Disability into Your Life and Your Church.* Cincinnati: Standard, 1998.

Tada, Joni Eareckson, and Steve Jensen. *Barrier-Free Friendships: Bridging the Distance Between You and Friends with Disabilities.* Grand Rapids: Zondervan, 1997.

Ministry to Homosexuals and People with AIDS

Dallas, Joe. *Desires in Conflict: Answering the Struggle for Sexual Identity.* Eugene, Oreg.: Harvest House, 1991.

Riley, Mona, and Brad Sargent. *Unwanted Harvest.* Nashville: Broadman & Holman, 1995.

Worthen, Anita, and Bob Davies. *Someone I Love Is Gay: How Family and Friends Can Respond.* Downers Grove, Ill.: InterVarsity, 1996.

Ministry with Children with ADD/ADHD

Barkely, Russell A. *Taking Charge of ADHD: The Complete Authoritative Guide for Parents.* New York: Guilford Press, 1995.

Hallowell, Edward M., and John J. Ratey. *Driven to Distraction: Recognizing and Coping with Attention Deficit Disorder from Childhood Through Adulthood.* Toronto: Pantheon, 1994.

Lerner, Janet W., Barbara Lowenthal, and Sue R. Lerner. *Attention Deficit Disorders: Assessment and Teaching.* Florence, Ky.: Wadsworth, 1994.

Divorced People and Ministry

Braun, Michael A. *Second-Class Christians?* Downers Grove, Ill.: InterVarsity, 1989.

Keener, Craig S. . . . *And Marries Another: Divorce and Remarriage in the Teaching of the New Testament.* Peabody, Ma.: Hendrickson, 1991.

Kysar, Myrna and Robert. *The Asundered: Biblical Teachings on Divorce and Remarriage.* Atlanta: John Knox, 1978.

Single Adults and Ministry

Reed, Bobbie. *Single Adult Ministry for Today.* St. Louis: Concordia, 1996.

Clayton, Valerie and Jerome Clayton. *Victory in Singleness: A Strategy for Emotional Pease.* Chicago: Lift Every Voice, 2002.

Wood, Britton. *Single Adults Want to Be the Church, Too.* Nashville: Broadman, 1977.

TEST
easy

The
ASVAB

by Laura Stradley and Robin Kavanagh
Illustrated by Kara LaFrance

ALPHA

A member of Penguin Random House LLC

Publisher: Mike Sanders
Senior Acquisitions Editor: Janette Lynn
Cover Designer: William Thomas
Book Designer/Layout: Ayanna Lacey
Copy Editor: Laura Caddell
Indexer: Celia McCoy
Proofreader: Monica Stone

This book is dedicated to my children, who are the lights of my life.
—Laura Stradley

To my family, friends, and acquaintances who are serving or have served in the military.
—Robin Kavanagh

Published by Penguin Random House LLC
001-309807-April 2019
Copyright © 2018 by Laura Stradley and Robin Kavanagh

International Standard Book Number: 978-1-46547-352-3
Library of Congress Catalog Card Number: 2018958037

21   20   19   10 9 8 7 6 5 4 3 2 1

Interpretation of the printing code: The rightmost number of the first series of numbers is the year of the book's printing; the rightmost number of the second series of numbers is the number of the book's printing. For example, a printing code of 19-1 shows that the first printing occurred in 2019.

Printed in the United States of America

Reprinted from *The Complete Idiot's Guide to the ASVAB*

Contents

Introduction

Thinking about a career in the military? Congratulations! You're considering one of the most honorable professions in the world. Unlike most other types of jobs you could be exploring right now, you have to go through a long process for the military to determine whether you've got the right stuff to succeed in a specific branch.

You'll be tested on all types of things, such as your physical appearance and health, your psychological health, your character, and even your financial responsibility. But before you get to these assessments, you have to jump one big hurdle: you must pass the Armed Services Vocational Aptitude Battery (ASVAB from here on out).

If you don't know by now, this is a battery of up to 10 tests designed to predict how you will perform once you're in the Army, Navy, Marine Corps, Air Force, or Coast Guard. It will also determine which jobs you're qualified to train for. What you should know right now is that you need to get a minimum score on certain sections of this test to be eligible to enlist.

We offer this book as a general guide to help you prepare for the ASVAB and get your scores to where you want them to be. You may not agree with all of our advice, and some parts may not work for you as an individual—and that's okay. No piece of advice is right for every person. We encourage you to make your test-prep experience your own and pursue whatever works best for you.

When you're using this book, we ask that you keep in mind that we are giving advice based on our extensive research and personal experience with this subject. The information we provide is up-to-date as of the date this book was written, and we have made every effort to ensure the accuracy of the information we provide.

Please be aware that regulations and conditions in the military can change very quickly, which may render some of the information in this book incorrect by the time you read it. It's always best to contact a recruiter for the most up-to-date information about enlistment, the ASVAB, scores, and anything else related to your pursuit of a military career.

How to Use This Book

Studying for a large exam like the ASVAB is a huge undertaking, especially when you consider the amount of math and science you'll be tested on. To help, we've tried to make reading and using this book as easy as possible for you by breaking down all the information you need into five main sections; you can pick and choose what you want to read, and when.

Part 1, A Little Intel Goes a Long Way, gives you lots of information about the different branches of the military, career options, and recruitment. You'll also find out how the test is broken down, what to expect, and the best ways to approach both taking the test and studying for it.

Part 2, Word Up! All about Communication Skills, explains how the ASVAB is divided into two main parts: the Armed Forces Qualifying Tests (AFQT) and the Technical Tests. The AFQT tests you on verbal communication and math abilities. This part takes you through what you'll see on the two AFQT verbal subtests and gives you plenty of room to practice.

Part 3, Math as Easy as Hup-2-3, breaks down the two AFQT math subtests for you and gives you a comprehensive review of the type of math you'll likely encounter on the ASVAB. You'll see a lot of practice questions in the chapters, as well as a separate chapter filled with more chances to practice.

Part 4, Get It Together: Technical Sections, describes all the other subtests, which are considered "technical sections." This is not only because they count toward your job eligibility but also because they test you on general science, physics, electronics, automotive and shop information, and visual logic. Each of the chapters in this part of the book provides review of the subject at hand, plus questions that will help you get some good practice.

Part 5, After-Action Review: Practice Tests, contains three complete practice tests that include both AFQT and job specialty sections. You'll also find an additional test that has only math and verbal sections, so you can get some more practice taking the crucial AFQT (in case you didn't know, this is the part of the test you need to pass to join the military).

We also include three appendixes that give you score breakdowns for each branch of service, locations of testing sites throughout the United States and Puerto Rico, and a listing of resources you can check out to help make the most of your test-prep experience.

Extras

Along the way, be sure to look for these power-packed extras:

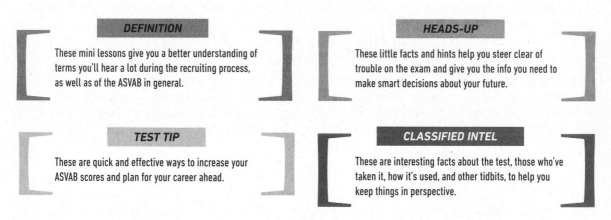

DEFINITION

These mini lessons give you a better understanding of terms you'll hear a lot during the recruiting process, as well as of the ASVAB in general.

HEADS-UP

These little facts and hints help you steer clear of trouble on the exam and give you the info you need to make smart decisions about your future.

TEST TIP

These are quick and effective ways to increase your ASVAB scores and plan for your career ahead.

CLASSIFIED INTEL

These are interesting facts about the test, those who've taken it, how it's used, and other tidbits, to help you keep things in perspective.

Acknowledgments

Laura Stradley:

Special thanks to everyone who helped with the completion of this book, including Rick May for his automotive expertise, and my children for their patience with the process.

Robin Kavanagh:

Special thanks to Keri Cerami, math professor extraordinaire, and Stephen Butkewitsch, our technical editor, who were both invaluable to this project. Also to Tom Kavanagh for his awesome automotive knowledge; Wendy Mamilovich, who helped an old friend; Marilyn Allen, best agent in the world; and all those who have contributed their experiences and tips to this book. And of course, thank you to our team of fabulous editors: Janette Lynn and Laura Caddell.

Special Thanks to the Technical Reviewer

The ASVAB: Test Easy was reviewed by an expert who double-checked the accuracy of what you'll learn here, to help us ensure that this book gives you everything you need to know about preparing for and taking the ASVAB. Special thanks are extended to Stephen Butkewitsch, our technical editor.

Trademarks

All terms mentioned in this book that are known to be or are suspected of being trademarks or service marks have been appropriately capitalized. Alpha Books and Penguin Group (USA) Inc. cannot attest to the accuracy of this information. Use of a term in this book should not be regarded as affecting the validity of any trademark or service mark.

A Little Intel Goes a Long Way

There's an old saying, "Work smart, not hard." It may sound cliché, but there's quite a bit of wisdom in these tried-and-true words. Doing your homework (literally, in the case of test prep) can help make you better informed and ready to strike when the chance arises—which is why gathering intelligence is so important in the military. It's also essential when scoping out your current enemy: the ASVAB.

In this part, we get you up to speed on the different military sectors and careers you may be interested in, what to expect from the recruitment process, and how the ASVAB fits in. Then we get down and dirty about how to take the test and how best to prepare for it, no matter where you are in life.

So You Want to Be in the Military ...

College just isn't for you or isn't affordable right now. A relative you admire served. You feel called to duty as a patriotic American. You're looking to take your life in a new direction. It's a family tradition.

Young people consider joining the military for a lot of reasons and each is deeply personal and unique. Regardless of your motivation for choosing to serve, it's important to learn as much as you can about this life-altering decision and the world you are preparing to step into.

This chapter gives you an overview of the five main branches of the military, what you can expect during recruitment, what recruiters wish candidates knew before signing up, and essential questions to ask along the way.

The Decision of a Lifetime

Enlistment is a decision that will impact your career choices throughout your life. You may find that once you're in the military, it's the place you want to spend the rest of your working years. You could also view your time in the military as a stepping stone toward larger educational and career goals.

Joining the military is a great way to train for different professions while getting paid for gaining hands-on experience in a private-sector industry that interests you. It can also be a place to grow and explore yourself (and the world) while you consider college or your long-term career options.

All of these scenarios make researching the different branches of the military extremely important before you decide which one is right for you. Because the Army, Navy, Air Force, Marines, and Coast Guard offer different opportunities and have different requirements of recruits, now is the time to determine which is the best for helping you reach both short-term and long-term goals.

Air Force

In 1947, the Air Force became an official entity of the U.S. Armed Forces. For the 40 years prior, it had been a part of the Army. After the heavy use of aircraft during World Wars I and II, it was clear that airpower would be a key factor in national defense, especially since the Korean War was well underway only a few years after the end of World War II. President Harry Truman created the Department of the Air Force with the National Security Act of 1947, and the U.S. Air Force has been responsible for guarding the skies ever since.

The Air Force's official mission is to "fly, fight, and win—in air, space and cyberspace." Protecting the United States against missile and airborne attacks, guarding against cyberattacks, and overseeing the national space program are just a few of the branch's charges.

The Air Force is made up of ten major commands in Virginia, Texas, Louisiana, Ohio, Georgia, Colorado, Florida, Illinois, Hawaii, and Germany. Additionally, there are 29 field operating agencies and 3 direct reporting units. The Air Force also offers two reserve units: the Air Force Reserve and the Air National Guard.

In the Air Force, you can explore four main types of occupational specialties that encompass a variety of different jobs. These include the following:

▶ **Mechanical.** These are generally technical specialties, such as Aerospace Maintenance; Air Traffic Controller Operations; Biomedical Equipment; Electrical Power Production; Aircraft Fuel Systems; Heating, Venting, and Air Conditioning (HVAC); Munitions Systems; Missile and Space Systems Electronics Maintenance; Nuclear Weapons; Tactical Aircraft Maintenance; and Vehicle Operations.

▶ **Administrative.** These positions center on the behind-the-scenes work that make everything run smoothly. A sampling of jobs includes Air Transportation, Aviation Resource Management, Information Management, Logistics Plans, Personnel, Materiel Management, Regional Band, and Vehicle Maintenance Control and Analysis.

▶ **General.** Jobs in this category are anything but general. They encompass a wide variety of abilities, interests, and industries—many of which you might not expect. Just a few of the opportunities here include Aerospace Control and Warning Systems, Aerospace Physiology, Airborne Battle Management Systems, Airfield Management, Bioenvironmental Engineering, Cardiopulmonary Laboratory, Communications Signals Intelligence, Contracting, Dental Assistant, Diagnostic Imaging, Graphic Arts, Diet Therapy, Paralegal, Pest Management, Still Photography, and Pararescue.

▶ **Electronics.** These technical specialties deal primarily with electronics systems. Possible jobs include Aerial Gunner, Airborne Mission Systems, Avionics Test Station and

Components, Computer Systems Control, Electrical Systems, Ground Radar Systems, Integrated Avionics Systems, Missile and Space Facilities, Wideband and Telemetry Satellite Systems, and Visual Imagery and Intrusion Detection Systems.

The Air Force will not accept recruits with gauges in their ears. One North Carolina recruiter said that "if you can shine a flashlight through it and see the light on the other side, it is not acceptable." Also, tattoos from the wrist to the tips of the fingers (single wedding band tattoos are the exception) and those from the collar bone to the top of the scalp will also disqualify you from service.

If you're interested in learning more about the Air Force, you can get a lot of good information from its official website, www.af.mil/. The recruitment site is www.airforce.com/.

CLASSIFIED INTEL

Each branch of the military has two websites. One is the official organization site and has a .mil extension on the address. The other is a recruiting site, which has a .com extension. An official site will say *official site* on the home page, and you can assume that the information on the site is accurate and up-to-date. Any other site is produced and maintained by a private company, which means the information may or may not be up-to-date.

Army

When many people talk about the military, they use Army as their go-to reference—and with good reason. It's the oldest and largest branch of America's armed forces. As of May 2018, nearly 500,000 soldiers were serving in the Army on active duty

(as opposed to reserve). The National Guard and the Army Reserves make up about 525,000 additional troops.

The Army's mission is to "fight and win our Nation's wars by providing prompt, sustained land dominance across the full range of military operations and spectrum of conflict in support of combatant commanders."

To achieve this, the Army is broken up into operational and institutional organizations. The operational Army is the units stationed worldwide that are on the ground conducting operations. The institutional Army is the infrastructure that keeps the operational Army ready for action by providing training, administration, and resource-management and logistical functions.

Within these subdivisions, you'll find some 150 different jobs that you can pursue, depending on your interests and qualifications. The Army states that 99 percent of these jobs have civilian applications beyond your time in the service. General areas of occupation include these:

▸ **Administrative Support.** If you're interested in a career in human resources, general administration, law, finance, information services, or even religion, this category is for you. Some of these jobs include Chaplain, Human Resource Specialist, Financial Management Technician, Shower/Laundry and Clothing Repair Specialist, Unit Supply Specialist, and Personnel Systems Manager Officer.

▸ **Intelligence and Combat Support.** In these jobs, you'll work behind the scenes to help collect intelligence and get it to units engaged in combat. Some of these jobs include Interpreter/Translator; Cryptologic Linguist; Chemical, Biological, Radiological, and Nuclear (CBRN)

Specialist; Civil Affairs Specialist; and Small Arms/Artillery Repairer.

▶ **Arts and Media.** Those who work in this category straddle the lines of civilian and military communication. If graphic design, media, music, or journalism is your passion, this is one area you should explore. Some jobs include Public Affairs Specialist, Multimedia Illustrator, Army Bandsperson, and Visual Information Equipment Operator–Maintainer.

▶ **Legal and Law Enforcement.** These jobs are all about keeping the peace and making sure military personnel and property stay safe. Some jobs include Military Police, Firefighter, Attorney, Paralegal, and Criminal Investigations Special Agent.

▶ **Combat.** These soldiers are on the front lines gathering reconnaissance and employing defensive and offensive tactics wherever action is needed. Some jobs include Special Forces Candidate, Cannon Crewmember, Air and Missile Defense Crewmember, Infantryman, and Cavalry Scout.

HEADS-UP

As of 2015, women are eligible for combat jobs in all branches of the service.

▶ **Mechanics.** These jobs help make sure all of the Army's basic and highly advanced equipment stays in good working order. Some jobs include Avionic Communications Equipment Repairer, Artillery Mechanic, Machinist, Biomedical Equipment Specialist, and Multiple Launch Rocket System (MLRS) Repairer.

▶ **Computers and Technology.** All sorts of different jobs fall into this category, including ones dealing with communications, intelligence gathering, graphic arts, mechanics, and explosives. Some include Computer/Detection Systems Repairer, Imagery Analyst, Counterintelligence Agent, Information Technology Specialist, and Avionic and Survivability Equipment Repairer.

▶ **Medical and Emergency.** This is a great way to gain free training and experience in the general medical, veterinary, and dental fields. Some jobs include Animal Care Specialist, Medical Laboratory Specialist, Mental Health Specialist, Optical Lab Specialist, Mortuary Affairs Specialist, and Dental Corps Officer.

▶ **Construction and Engineering.** Interested in carpentry, engineering, plumbing, electrical, or masonry? These are the jobs you should check out. Some include Combat Engineer, Bridge Crewmember, Interior Electrician, Petroleum Supply Specialist, Quarrying Specialist, and Water Treatment Specialist.

▶ **Transportation and Aviation.** These jobs are responsible for the management, coordination, use, and anything else involved in the transport of Army equipment and personnel. Some jobs include Avionic Mechanic, Air Traffic Control (ATC) Operator, Parachute Rigger, Unmanned Aerial Vehicle Operator, and Cargo Specialist.

Policy changes in 2015 decreed that recruits can have tattoos above the wrist bone and below the collar of a t-shirt. Most recruits can expect to spend an average of three to four months in the Delayed Entry Program, which is discussed later in this chapter.

If you're interested in learning more about the Army, go to the official website, www. army.mil/, or the recruiting site, www. goarmy.com.

Coast Guard

The U.S. Coast Guard's domain is the seas and shores that surround the United States and its territories. It is responsible for protecting "the public, the environment, and the United States, economic and security interests in any maritime region in which those interests may be at risk, including international waters and America's coasts, ports, and inland waterways."

This includes enforcing maritime law, providing search-and-rescue operations, and supplying assistance to mariners in U.S. waters. During peacetime, the Coast Guard acts by direction of the Department of Homeland Security. However, during wartime or by direction of the president, the Coast Guard operates under the Navy.

It takes a certain type of personality to be a "Coastie," says Petty Officer Albert Scales, a recruiter in West Orange, New Jersey. He says most members of the service are looking to give of themselves more and that they're more interested in protecting and saving lives. For example, Scales says that when faced with a huge wave (a "big surf," in Coastie-speak) "the average person would say, 'That's a 40-foot wall of water. Why would I want to go into that?' We don't think that way. We just go because someone on the other side needs our help."

The Coast Guard has five main missions: national defense, maritime security, protection of natural resources, maritime mobility, and maritime safety. Compared to the other branches of the service, the Coast Guard has relatively few positions to offer recruits.

> **CLASSIFIED INTEL**
>
> The life of a Coastie is never boring. Every day, on average, the Coast Guard saves 14 lives; conducts 74 search-and-rescue operations; seizes or removes more than 1,000 pounds of illegal drugs at an estimated $12.9 million in value; boards 193 ships and boats; and ensures the safe, secure, and efficient navigation of ships carrying $5.5 billion worth of commerce.

However, if the job you're interested in is unavailable at the time you enlist, you can enter this service as a non-rate, which means that no one job is assigned to you. You will work and be paid as a member of the Coast Guard while you wait for your name to come up for the particular training school. You can also train for many different types of jobs throughout your time in the service.

Generally, enlisted Coast Guard jobs are divided into four main categories:

- **Aviation.** As the name suggests, these jobs involve technical positions that include maintenance of fixed-wing and rotary aircraft. Responsibilities can include inspecting, servicing, and repairing avionics systems; working with airframe systems; repairing aircraft engines, fuselages, wings, rotor blades, and more; filling aircrew positions; and performing search-and-rescue operations.

- **Deck and Ordnance.** These jobs deal with the running and operation of Coast Guard vessels, including law enforcement; small arms and weapons systems; pyrotechnics; tactical command, control, and communications; intelligence gathering; and cryptology.

- **Hull and Engineering.** These jobs deal with the maintenance, running, and operation of Coast Guard vessels. Duties include general and emergency repairs; installation, maintenance, repair, and management of electronics systems and components; maintenance of navigation and communication systems; information management; and mechanical support.

▶ **Administrative and Scientific.** All the other jobs in the Coast Guard fall under this broad category. Duties can include environmental protection, health-care services, restaurant and catering, writing and photography, human resources management and administration, and accounting.

Coast Guard recruits should expect to spend at least a few months in the Delayed Entry Program, which is discussed later in this chapter. Candidates should also know that having tattoos on the hands, chest (visible in a V-neck tee), neck or above, as well as ear gauges, can make you ineligible for enlistment.

For more information about the Coast Guard or recruitment, or to see the Coast Guard in action, go to www.uscg.mil/, www.gocoastguard.com/, or https://www.youtube.com/user/thecoastguardchannel/discussion?disable_polymer=1.

Marine Corps

The United States Marine Corps website says "It's their fighting spirit that sets Marines apart from any other force, but it's also their training and knowledge that gives them the advantage in every battle." If this sounds like fun, you just may have what it takes to become a devil dog, jarhead, or leatherneck—whichever nickname you prefer.

> **HEADS-UP**
>
> The Marine Corps is a very conservative branch of the military, which means standards of appearance are high. If you have tattoos, body art, or piercings, you may not be able to join. Prohibited items include tattoos on the head or neck; sleeve tattoos; and markings that depict gang colors, have sexist or racist messaging, or are related to drugs or illegal activity.

The Corps is an infantry-based command, which means its primary mission is combat and combat support for other branches of the military. Roles include Ground Combat, Aviation Combat, and Combat Support.

At just about 184,000 active-duty personnel as of May 2018, the Marine Corps has the second smallest workforce, after the Coast Guard. This is partly because of the level of skill and dedication needed to succeed in the Corps, but also because of the need for units to be able to deploy task forces anywhere worldwide within 24 hours of receiving orders.

The Marine Corps is a kind of amalgamation of all the other services wrapped into one ultra efficient unit. Marines can execute operations by land, by sea, and by air with efficiency and stealth.

Career opportunities with the Marine Corps are vast. As one recruiter put it, "There's something for everyone" if you qualify physically, academically, and psychologically for the rigors of the more than 500 jobs within about 40 categories that make this branch function. Because of this, we just list a sampling of the job categories, so you can get an idea of whether there's a job that may fit with your interests:

- Air Control/Air Support/Anti-Air Warfare/Air Traffic Control
- Aircraft Maintenance
- Airfield Services
- Ammunition and Explosive Ordnance Disposal
- Artillery
- Aviation Logistics
- Aviation Ordnance
- Avionics
- Chemical, Biological, Radiological, and Nuclear (CBRN) Defense
- Combat Camera (COMCAM)
- Communications
- Data/Communications Maintenance
- Electronics Maintenance
- Financial Management
- Food Service
- Ground Ordnance Maintenance
- Infantry
- Intelligence
- Legal Services
- Meteorological and Oceanographic (METCO)
- Military Police and Corrections
- Music
- Navigation Officer/Enlisted Flight Crews
- Public Affairs
- Supply Administration and Operations
- Training
- Utilities

For more information about the Marine Corps or Marine Corps recruitment, go to www.marines.mil or www.marines.com/.

Navy

The Navy is the branch of the U.S. Armed Forces responsible for defending the country and its interests by sea. The Navy's official mission is to "maintain, train, and equip combat-ready Naval forces capable of winning wars, deterring aggression, and maintaining freedom of the seas."

To carry out this mission, the Navy maintains bases, ships, and other assets worldwide to support offensive and defensive military operations. This means a huge variety of opportunities for those looking for careers that include travel, adventure, and personal challenge—not to mention a ton of variety! Navy jobs are not all about sailing. Navy recruits train in just about any type of job you can think of, from aviation and mechanics, to law enforcement and information technology.

CLASSIFIED INTEL

You can join the Navy even if you don't know how to swim. They will train you until you're a pro. Take it from one recent recruit who had never had a swim lesson in his life before he enlisted. By the time he completed his training, he was certified as a rescue diver.

Because enlisted and officer personnel in the Navy have more than 1,000 different career options, we list only some of the job categories, so you can get an idea of whether there's a job that may fit your interests:

- Arts and Photography
- Aviation
- Business Management
- Computers
- Construction and Building
- Education
- Electronics
- Emergency, Fire, and Rescue
- Energy and Power
- Engineering
- Finance and Accounting
- Food, Restaurant, and Lodging

- ▸ Information Technology
- ▸ Intelligence and Communications
- ▸ Law
- ▸ Law Enforcement and Security
- ▸ Medical and Dental
- ▸ Music
- ▸ News and Media
- ▸ Office and Administrative Support
- ▸ Religion
- ▸ Science
- ▸ Telecommunications
- ▸ Transportation and Logistics
- ▸ World Languages

For more information about the Navy or Navy recruitment, go to www.navy.mil or www.navy.com/.

The Recruitment Experience

Now that you have a general overview of what each branch of the military has to offer, let's talk about recruitment. If you're interested in joining a particular branch, or even just want more information, contacting a recruiter is your best bet.

It's important to understand a recruiter's role before going any further. You may have heard horror stories from friends or on the internet about people having bad experiences with recruiters. Complaints often arise about promises being made and then not fulfilled, high-pressure tactics, and even misleading information.

The truth is that it's a recruiter's job to maintain and increase the numbers of active and reserve personnel in our voluntary armed forces. They have their own goals to

meet and are trained in how to counsel and lead potential recruits through the decision-making process.

However, they also must abide by stringent ethical standards. They are knowledgeable career counselors who are responsible for guiding you through the whole enlistment experience.

CLASSIFIED INTEL

A recruiter or guidance counselor can't promise a specific assignment, location, or job. He or she also can't promise that you will not deploy or force you into signing anything.

The smartest thing for you to do is learn as much as you can about the branch you're interested in, independent of your recruiter. The internet, friends, and family who have had experience with the branch you're thinking about joining are great resources and will help you make the most informed choice. We also give you a taste of what to expect.

From the Door to Contract

When you connect with a recruiter, you'll do a lot of talking. During this time, he or she will discreetly look to see if you and the branch of service you're considering joining are a good fit. Through conversation, the recruiter will try to see if you meet minimum qualifications based on age, physical appearance, prior service record, law violations, educational history, marital status, dependents, and testing. You may even take some sample ASVAB tests to indicate how you would score on the real exam.

From there, your recruiter will decide whether you will likely make it through the enlistment process and fulfill the military's needs. Even if he's not 100 percent sure that you're military material, he'll probably send you to take the ASVAB, as an additional assessment tool.

You'll be sent to either a Military Entrance Processing Station (MEPS) or a Military Entrance Test (MET) site to take the real ASVAB. Larger MEPS sites can provide one-stop shopping for military recruits, so if your recruiter feels you'll do well on the ASVAB, you may complete some of the other entrance requirements:

▸ **Physical and psychological examinations.** Basics like blood pressure, height/weight, vision, and hearing are tested and recorded. Expect blood and drug screenings, and possible strength or stamina tests.

▸ **Moral character assessment tests.** This test also takes place at a MEPS location. These may include extended interviews, credit and criminal background checks, and even a financial history. Requirements for this vary.

Where you go from the ASVAB depends on your scores. If you don't make the grade, you'll have to retake the ASVAB in 30 days. If you do make the grade (see Chapter 2), your next step is to meet with a guidance counselor (if available) or your recruiter to discuss your career options. Now it's up to you to figure out what those options are. Remember that you still have control over where you go from here. After you've gone through all these steps, you'll get an offer from the military stating what your job will be, how much you'll be compensated, and the time of service you'll be responsible for fulfilling (among other things).

Keep in mind that deciding whether to take the deal might involve more than your career goals. According to S. Douglas Smith, Public Affairs Officer with the U.S. Army Recruiting Command, recruits sign on because of incentives that are offered, the location they're offered, and the length of enlistment, in addition to the type of job that's available. Incentives can include signing bonuses of up to $40,000, money for college or help paying back student loans, funds to start business or to buy a house, or even bonuses for prior education and work experience. If you're interested in these incentives, ask about them when discussing your contract.

Once you've reviewed the contract, if you're not happy with the deal they're offering, you're free to walk away without signing. If you decide to sign, make sure that you read the contract carefully and that you understand and agree to all of what's stated before signing.

Also keep in mind the importance of your short-term and long-term goals. A $40,000 signing bonus may seem like a great deal when you're 18, but it could come with an obligation to stay in the military for at least four years. Ask yourself how this affects your career and educational goals before you accept.

After You Sign

Once you sign on the dotted line, you may be raring to pack up and head off to basic training. In reality, most new recruits wait a minimum of three to four months before they have to show up for active duty. If you don't get orders to report for training within a month of enlistment, you'll likely be enrolled in the Delayed Entry Program (DEP). The DEP is designed to control the number of new enlistees who are assigned to training schools by assigning them specific dates when they will begin active duty. Those in the DEP can wait up to a year, although the average wait time is three to four months.

[HEADS-UP

Even after you sign a contract with the military, provisions can help you get out of it if you get a case of buyer's (or, in this case, signer's) remorse.]

If exceptional circumstances arise, you can ask for your active duty date to be pushed back up to an additional year, even if you've been delayed for a full year already. Some high school students can also apply for DEP status so that they can graduate before beginning their service.

Recruiters' Wish List

The fact that you're reading this book means you've probably given some serious thought to joining the service. Probably one of your main concerns is whether military life will be a good fit for you. Believe it or not, your recruiters have wondered the same thing! As ambassadors of the military, they know firsthand the benefits that await you upon enlistment. At the same time, they also know that not everyone is cut out for life in the service.

That's why it's important to look at this equation from their perspective as well. Your recruiter can provide you with the tools and the means to successfully enlist in the military, but they need you to hold up your end of the bargain, too.

Most recruiters wish for a few things, to ensure a smooth process for you and for them:

▶ **A clean record.** In recent decades, very few people have been able to join any branch of service with more than a misdemeanor in their past.

▶ **A reasonable body fat composition.** Each branch of the military differs in what it will allow in terms of height and weight standards. However, each branch has certain minimum qualifications in this department; ask your recruiter for more information if this concerns you.

▶ **Honesty.** When your recruiter asks you questions about your past or your health, or requests information of a personal nature, the best policy is full disclosure. They will most likely find out the truth eventually, and it will save everyone a lot of time if you are honest from day one. Often there are circumstances where disqualifications can be waived.

▶ **The ability to pass the ASVAB.** We saved the best for last! The ASVAB can be challenging for the ill-prepared test-taker. Many recruiters recommend websites like March 2 Success, military.com, and others (see Appendix C) so that you will be familiar with the types of questions on the exam. Other recruiters may require you to take a practice test in their office before they go to the trouble and expense of sending you to a test site. Some recruiting stations even have a portion of their operating budget set aside for ASVAB tutoring.

The point is the ASVAB is not the type of test that people should just assume they can pass without preparation. The more time you spend reviewing the subject matter and answering sample questions, the more likely you will be able to pass the ASVAB on your first try.

Of course, recruiters wish for many other things in addition to this list: punctuality at appointments, returned phone calls, happy moms and dads, cooperative high school officials and guidance counselors, and so forth. That being said, the most important items on their list are the four qualifying areas just mentioned. As you continue to navigate this book, you will most definitely improve your ability to qualify for military service—and check off a box on your recruiter's wish list!

Essential Questions to Ask Your Recruiter

Joining the military is a major decision. Much like the other major decisions you've made in life, you'll want to be sure you have all the facts before you sign on the dotted line. The question is, what facts should you have? When something is new to us, sometimes it's hard to know what questions to even ask. You'll want to know answers to these questions, based on veteran experience:

1. What rank will I be when I enter basic training?

2. If I have college credits, will I be able to enter at an advanced rank? (Most branches of service value college credits and will allow you to enter at an advanced rank—the rate of advancement varies by branch, as does the number of college credits required for this program.)

3. How quickly can I get promoted after basic training?

4. How long is basic training?

5. What is required of me when I arrive at basic training? (Some branches require you to do a certain number of push-ups upon arrival; failure to do so could result in spending extra time at basic training, something no one wants to do!)

6. What happens if I get injured or sick during basic training?

7. What kind of educational benefits will I have when I enter the service? Are any of these benefits available to me before I leave for basic training? (Some branches provide tuition assistance up to $250 per credit hour before you even leave for basic!)

8. Am I eligible for any enlistment bonuses, such as the Army College Fund, college loan repayment, signing bonuses, or station of choice?

9. After I choose the career field I want in the military, is it guaranteed? (Some branches can guarantee better than others.)

10. What is the maximum commitment I will have to the service? (Even if you enlist for four years of service, you are generally obligated to eight years of combined active and inactive service. Inactive simply means that if the military wants you back when your four years are up, they can recall you.)

11. If I don't like the job I enlist for, can I reclass to a different job?

12. If I'm married, will the service pay to move my spouse to my assignment?

13. How soon can my spouse join me—after basic training, after Advanced Individual Training (also known in some branches as on-the-job training), or when I arrive at my first assignment?

14. What kinds of benefits will my spouse be eligible for as a dependent?

15. What is the likelihood that I will get deployed, and what are the average lengths of deployments? (Length of deployment varies by branch.)

16. How much traveling and/or time away from home is required with the job I have selected?

17. Does my career field have a crossover to the Commissioned Officer ranks?

18. What type of pay will I receive besides my base pay? (Generally, you will be eligible for a housing allowance, a food allowance, travel expenses as needed, and a plethora of additional stipends.)

19. What civilian jobs are similar to the military job I have chosen?

20. What type of transition assistance will be provided for me when I'm ready to transfer back to civilian life? (Different branches vary on this—the Army actually contracts this assistance out to the largest outplacement agency in the country, providing a full-service program to soldiers, including resumé writing, job fairs, job preparation workshops, counseling, interviewing skills, and the like, all for free!)

You may want to ask your recruiter dozens of other questions, but hopefully this list has given you a starting point. One last tip: if your recruiter doesn't know the answer, he knows someone who does. Be sure your questions are answered to the extent that you are comfortable with, even if it means a few extra phone calls are made or emails are sent. You won't regret having too much information in the days and months ahead.

> **TEST TIP**
>
> If the information your recruiter or counselor is giving you doesn't match up with your goals, make sure you say so. This is your future and you have to make the decisions that are right for you.

The Least You Need to Know

▶ It's best to learn about the different branches of the military to see if they can offer you the type of training you're interested in.

▶ There are many requirements and steps in the recruitment process that you have to pass in order to enlist.

▶ Recruiters can be a great resource for career counseling, but when considering the information they give you, remember they have quotas to meet.

▶ Think about where you'd like your career to take you and what your long-term goals are before heading to a recruiter.

▶ You're under no obligation to enlist until you sign a contract, and even then, you may still be able to change your mind.

▶ Preparing a list of questions about the issues you're most concerned with in regard to serving in the military can be a big help.

Know Thy Enemy: ASVAB Essentials

By now, you know that being in the Army, Navy, Air Force, Marines, or Coast Guard isn't all about jumping out of airplanes and heading off to combat. For most members of the service, it's a career choice or a training ground to gain the skills they need to work in private-sector industries. Any way you slice it, the military is a world unto itself, and it needs skilled labor just like any other society.

That's where the ASVAB comes in. Just about anyone can walk into a recruiter's office and say they want to enlist. But it's the recruiter's job to figure out whether those who come to them have the right stuff to make it in the military. To do this, recruiters adhere to their branch's code of ethics and entrance standards that every new recruit must meet (some of which we covered in Chapter 1).

The ASVAB is a standardized way to assess the skills of the thousands of strangers who come knocking on recruiters' doors coast to coast. This chapter gives you an overview of what the ASVAB is, how it's divided up, and what you can expect when you take the exam.

ASVAB Breakdown

The ASVAB is a series of short tests aimed at giving the military an idea of your abilities before they hire you. It might be weird to think of the military as an organization that hires people, but that's really all enlistment is about. Each branch of the military wants to fill its ranks with the best and brightest candidates for the myriad jobs that make the organization run.

The ASVAB subtests are designed to reveal a person's natural strengths and abilities, so they can be placed in a job where they will succeed. This is done not only for the benefit of the recruit—after all, a happy serviceperson is one who sticks around—but for the benefit and safety of the organization as a whole. Placing someone who has a low aptitude for mechanical science in the cockpit of an F-15 fighter plane can end up costing lives and millions of dollars in expenses.

> **CLASSIFIED INTEL**
>
> Each of the ASVAB subtests is based on general knowledge that anyone with a high school diploma or GED would know. The majority of the questions contain information that should at least be somewhat familiar to you, even if only vaguely.

With this in mind, the ASVAB is divided into two main parts: the Armed Forces Qualifying Test (AFQT) and the technical tests. One determines basic enlistment eligibility, while the other qualifies you for specific jobs within each of the branches.

Armed Forces Qualifying Test

The AFQT is nothing more than a big math and English exam, very similar to what you'd find on the SAT or ACT. It consists of two math subtests and two verbal subtests, each with specific skill sets being tested.

What can math and English skills tell the military about you? A lot more than you might think.

Take a look at the four subtests that make up the AFQT:

▸ **Word Knowledge (WK).** On the surface, this section tests your vocabulary knowledge. Underneath, it's really measuring your communication skills and ability to use context clues to draw logical conclusions.

▸ **Paragraph Comprehension (PC).** Here you're asked to read short passages and answer questions based on what you read. This is kind of a wolf-in-sheep's-clothing test, since what's really being tested are your analytical skills.

▸ **Arithmetic Reasoning (AR).** This whole test is all about word problems. You're asked to think through these problems, develop the best (and fastest) approach to solving it, and then choose the correct answer out of the four you're given. You're really being tested on your ability to follow directions, think logically, and develop an analytical approach to problem solving.

▸ **Mathematics Knowledge (MK).** On this test, you're asked to demonstrate your elementary math skills, as well as your knowledge of algebra and geometry. This test is straight-up, in that it is designed to measure how good you are at math.

> **HEADS-UP**
>
> When you take the ASVAB, you sit down and take one long test divided into sections. You will not see any section labeled *AFQT* or *technical tests*. It's up to you to prepare for the sections that matter most to you. Since everyone has to pass the AFQT to enlist, math and verbal prep are a must.

Technical Tests

Unlike with the AFQT, how you perform on the technical tests (or technical subtests) does not affect your entrance eligibility. These are a series of subject-specific tests that determine what career path options are open to you:

- **General Science (GS).** This tests you on the basics of physical, earth, and life sciences. Don't worry if you slept through bio; brushing up should be enough to get you through this part of the test.

- **Electronics Information (EI).** If you like tinkering with your DVD player, this test is right up your alley. Here, you'll find all sorts of questions about electrical systems, components, circuitry, terminology, and other technical basics.

- **Automotive and Shop Information (AS).** Strut your stuff (ha, ha!) about all things related to cars, tools, and hardware. Here's where your industrial arts and weekends working on your car pay off.

- **Mechanical Comprehension (MC).** No, you won't find automotive questions in this section. Mechanical comprehension is mostly about physical science, how machines work, and applications of mechanical principles in real life.

- **Assembling Objects (AO).** This section focuses on perception of spatial relationships. Basically, you're given multiple parts of an object, and then you need to answer questions about how they would fit together.

Why You Need to Do Well

We know the prospect of being tested on math, English, science, logic, automotive and shop information, and visual acuity is not the happiest thought in the world. The good news is that you don't have to be an ace in everything to achieve your goals in the military.

What you do need to ace is the AFQT. This is the part of the test that determines whether you can enlist. Each branch of the military has a minimum AFQT score that recruits must achieve to be eligible for enlistment (see Appendix A). These scores vary and can change from month to month. Check with your recruiter for the current minimum score for the branch you're looking to join.

CLASSIFIED INTEL

The Coast Guard has the highest AFQT score requirement of all of the armed forces. Why? Most Coast Guard jobs are heavily based in academics. If you're interested in being a Coastie, be prepared to study hard and take lots of tests during your service.

Technical subtest scores have a much different function in the recruitment process. For some jobs, you need to have only the right math and verbal scores. However, most jobs require recruits to have a certain amount of knowledge and skill (as determined by the ASVAB technical scores) to be able to perform safely and successfully.

For example, it makes sense to have a high aptitude in science, math, and electronics for jobs that concentrate on electrical engineering or weapons programming. These are highly scientific, analytical, and technical specialties that may not suit the strengths of someone who is more naturally inclined toward the arts or humanities. The technical subtests give the military an educated guess about your strengths so that you and your recruiter can make the best decision for your future.

The Two Faces of the ASVAB

The ASVAB actually comes in three versions: the paper and pencil test (PAP), the computer adaptive test (CAT), and the student test. If you were given an aptitude test in high school, you may well have already taken a version of the ASVAB already. The student version is used as a career-counseling tool for high school students.

If your goal is not necessarily to figure out your career path, but to gain entrance into the military, you need to be familiar with both the PAP and CAT tests. Although the information you're tested on is the same, how these tests are administered makes a difference in how well you do. It's not because of the difficulty of the questions or because one test is easier or harder than the other. It's simply a matter of strategy.

Think of it like washing your car. You prepare differently to go to a full-service car wash than you do when washing your car yourself in your driveway. The result— a clean car—is the same, but the method of preparation and execution is different.

Knowing how to approach both tests puts you at an advantage. As mentioned in Chapter 1, you may not have a choice of where you take the ASVAB. Most MEPS facilities offer the CAT, but many MET sites can offer only PAP testing. Conversely, at sites where CAT is available, you may not have the option to take a paper version of the ASVAB. Being prepared no matter what the situation will help you perform better.

Computer Adaptive Test (CAT)

The CAT offers test-takers an alternative to the traditional fill-in-the-bubble paper test. Major standardized tests such as the GMAT, GRE, MAT, and other academic evaluations are administered through a CAT system.

Questions on the CAT ASVAB adapt to how you perform on the test. For example, the first question in every section is at a medium level of difficulty. If you get that one correct, the next question will be a little harder. If you get that first question wrong, the second will be a little easier.

One thing that's important to understand about the ASVAB is that not all questions are counted equally. Two people can take the ASVAB, get the same number of questions correct, and come back with different scores.

All ASVAB questions, regardless of which version you take, are scored as either a 0 or a 1. However, this doesn't mean that each question is worth the same. Scaled ASVAB scores are based on Item Response Theory, which takes into consideration several factors:

▸ Assigned difficulty of questions

▸ How a question discriminates among those at different levels of ability

▸ The likelihood that a guess from a test-taker with a low level of ability will result in a correct answer

So why is this important to know about the CAT ASVAB? Knowing that the difficulty of questions has an impact on your scaled score can help you strategize. Try to get as many questions correct as you can in the beginning of the test. This will ensure that you have harder questions at the beginning, which will increase your scaled score right off the bat. If you start out with a high score, maintaining it is a lot easier than trying to build it up from a lower one.

What to Expect

Like any standardized test, the CAT ASVAB is timed. You'll have a certain amount of time to complete the questions within the section you're working on. The following table shows how the CAT ASVAB is broken up.

Computer Adaptive Test ASVAB Sections and Times

Subject	Number of Questions	Minutes
General Science (GS)	16	8
Arithmetic Reasoning (AR)	16	39
Word Knowledge (WK)	16	8
Paragraph Comprehension (PC)	11	22
Mathematics Knowledge (MK)	16	20
Electronics Information (EI)	16	8
Auto Information (AI)*	11	7
Shop Information (SI)*	11	6
Mechanical Comprehension (MC)	16	20
Assembling Objects (AO)	16	16
Total	145	154

*The Auto Information and Shop Information scores are presented under one label: AS.

The questions will come up one at a time. After you choose your answer, you make your selection electronically. You're then prompted to verify that the selection you made is your final answer.

> **TEST TIP**
>
> Don't just blindly click through the answer verification after you make your selection. Double-check to make sure you didn't make a mistake between the answer you were thinking of and the one you marked. It just might save you from submitting a wrong answer.

Once you verify your answer, you're presented with the next question. This goes on until either the time runs out or you've completed the section. When you're done with one section, you simply move on to the next.

At the end of the test, you get a computer-generated score report that instantly lets you know how you did. Decoding it may take a degree in cryptology, but we walk you through score reports a little later in the chapter.

The CAT ASVAB is also designed so that even the least computer-savvy person can complete the exam. As long as you can move a mouse and click a button, the CAT will be no problem for you. Every testing site gives very detailed and easy-to-follow directions and training on how to take the computerized test. There's also a tutorial that you take before starting the test so that you can try out answering questions without any risk. This gives you good practice and helps familiarize you with what you'll be doing over the coming hours.

Paper and Pencil Test (PAP)

This is the more traditional standardized test most people are used to taking. The PAP ASVAB comes complete with test booklets, answer sheets with rows and rows of tiny bubbles, number 2 pencils, and a *proctor* to make sure everyone is completing the exam according to the rules.

> **DEFINITION**
>
> A **proctor** is someone who is charged with administering an exam. It's this person's responsibility to make sure that all the administrative duties are carried out, all the paperwork is in order, the test is properly timed, and everyone adheres to the rules.

You're most likely to find this test given at MET sites, since they are smaller and often are a part of designated space in a building dedicated to other purposes. The computer and communications equipment needed to administer the CAT requires specific facilities to maintain the integrity of the test. With the PAP, all you need are the test materials, a room, a clock, chairs, and a proctor.

What to Expect

Once you get to the site, you'll be checked in and given instructions on where to go, what to do, and when to do it (good practice for life in basic training). Make sure you bring a picture ID and a few sharpened pencils. Leave the calculator, food, and beverages at home.

When all the administrative stuff is out of the way, the proctor will begin reading instructions, and handing out answer sheets and test booklets. You will be expected to follow these instructions to the letter.

Once administrative duties are taken care of, the test begins. The following table shows how the PAP ASVAB is broken up.

Paper and Pencil ASVAB Sections and Times

Subject	Number of Questions	Minutes
General Science (GS)	25	11
Arithmetic Reasoning (AR)	30	36
Word Knowledge (WK)	35	11
Paragraph Comprehension (PC)	15	13
Mathematics Knowledge (MK)	25	24
Electronics Information (EI)	20	9
Auto and Shop Information (AS)	25	11
Mechanical Comprehension (MC)	25	19
Assembling Objects (AO)	25	15
Total	**225**	**149**

You must wait for the time of each section to run out before you can move on to the next. If you have time left in the section you're working on, you can go back and check answers in that section only. You can't move ahead to the next subtest or leave when the section is complete.

When all is said and done, expect the PAP to take three to four hours. Your scores will be sent to your recruiter within a few days.

CAT and PAP Head-to-Head

As you can see, the CAT and paper ASVAB have major differences, aside from how you record your answers. One of the most important is the difference in time and number of questions. You have slightly more time to complete the CAT than you do the PAP; you also have fewer questions to answer with the CAT, and you don't have to wait for time to run out on a section before moving on to the next. As a result, the average test-taker completes the CAT ASVAB in about 90 minutes.

You may have also noticed that the CAT contains 10 subtests, while the PAP has only 9. The Automotive and Shop Information section of the CAT ASVAB is broken up into two sections. However, the score is reported as a combined scaled total under the AS label.

Because of how the PAP is structured and administered, you can choose to leave questions blank on your answer sheet. You don't have that luxury on the CAT. What's more, you're not penalized for leaving answers blank on the PAP. You do incur a penalty for not completing a section of the CAT. The penalty is in direct proportion to the number of questions left unanswered. This means that not finishing one or two questions will have less of an effect on your score than not finishing 10 questions.

TEST TIP

No matter which version of the test you take, always answer every question. Try to narrow your answer choices and make an educated guess—one based on logic instead of chance.

Scheduling is also a major difference. Test times for the CAT ASVAB are much more flexible than those for the PAP because a proctor is not needed to administer the test. With the PAP, a proctor must be present to handle all the paperwork and maintain a controlled environment. PAP ASVABs are also frequently given at MET sites, where personnel may be sparse. A whole group of recruits may be assembled before a test date is assigned, which makes availability unpredictable.

When considering which test you would prefer, consider the pros and cons of each. Be aware, though, that you may not have a choice in where you're sent to take the ASVAB. Still, knowing which fits better with your skill set and personality can help open a dialogue between you and your recruiter about your options for taking the test.

Computer Adaptive Test

Pros:

▸ The test takes less time and has fewer questions.

▸ The test adjusts to your skill level.

▸ You get your results immediately after you finish the test.

▸ You have more flexible scheduling options.

▸ You can leave when you're done.

▸ Headphones are available to help you tune out the world around you and concentrate on taking the test.

Cons:

▸ The test may not be available at every testing center.

▸ You have to answer every question you're given, in the order they're given. You can't jump around.

▸ You can't change an answer once you finalize it.

▸ If you don't answer a question, you'll receive a score penalty.

Paper and Pencil Test

Pros:

▸ You can jump around within a single section of the test and play to your strengths more easily.

▸ You can go back over questions in a section or change your answers if you have time at the end of a subtest.

▸ The paper test may be more comfortable for those more familiar with this type of format.

▸ You can skip questions and not receive
a score penalty.

Cons:

▸ There's room for error in marking your answers on a form that has bubbles to fill in.

▸ You have to wait for days to get your results.

▸ Scheduling options are not as flexible.

▸ No facilities near you may offer the PAP ASVAB.

▸ You have to wait for the allotted time for each section to run out before you can move on to the next.

Interpreting Your Score Report

The most important part of the ASVAB actually comes after the test. After all, it's the scores you're really interested in, not the test itself.

Seeing a score report for the first time can be intimidating. You'll see all sorts of numbers and abbreviations. Even with a recruiter's help, figuring out what it all means can be tough, so we break it down for you here.

You'll get three main types of scores on your score report:

▸ Standard scores

▸ Composite or line scores

▸ AFQT percentile score

Standard Scores

Standard scores are given for each of the AFQT and technical subtests. They can be anywhere between 0 and 100, based on the number of questions you answered correctly. On the ASVAB, you're not penalized for a wrong answer; you just don't get any points for it. Standard scores look like this:

GS	AR	WK	PC	MK	EI	AS	MC	AO	VE
75	69	58	77	52	46	82	62	55	69

Each of the two-letter designations represents a subtest (see the listing of subtests earlier in the chapter), with the exception of the VE, which indicates your total verbal score.

> **HEADS-UP**
>
> According to the Official ASVAB Enlistment Testing Program, the VE score is a "weighted composite of WK and PC scores and is not computed by simply adding the PC and WK scores."

Composite Scores

Next, you'll see your composite scores, also called *line scores*. These determine your occupational eligibility. They're divided into four branches of the military: Army, Air Force, Navy/Coast Guard, and Marines. The scores are broken down into subcategories specific to the types of jobs offered in each branch. See Appendix A for more detailed information on how these scores are used.

They are also calculated differently, depending on the area of service. For example, the Marines, Army, and Air Force use differently scaled formulas to arrive at their composite scores. The other branches simply add the line scores you got in the required subtests for each of their job categories. You'll see something like this in this section of your score report (explanations of the categories are discussed in Appendix A):

Army:	GT	CL	CO	EL	FA	GM	MM	OF	SC	ST
	123	124	125	126	127	128	129	130	131	132

Air Force:	M	A	G	E
	80	81	82	83

Navy/CG:	GT	EL	BEE	ENG	MEC	MEC2	NUC	OPS	HM	ADM
	120	216	217	121	122	123	218	219	124	125

Marines:	MM	GT	EL	CL
	122	123	124	125

AFQT Percentile Score

The final score on your report is the AFQT percentile. This is the most important score because it determines your overall eligibility. It's determined based on the following formula: $2(VE) + AR + MK$. This means that your VE line score is multiplied by 2 and then added to your AR and MK scores.

Then the score is converted into a percentile that shows how your performance places in relation to others who took the test during a sample period (in 1997, no less!). For example, if your score report places you in the 90th percentile, only about 10 percent of test-takers in a fixed sample scored higher on the overall AFQT than you did.

What If I Don't Make the Grade?

Don't freak out if your scores are not where you need them to be the first time you take the ASVAB. It happens all the time, especially if it's been a long time since you've actively engaged in the subject matter or taken a standardized test.

Every branch of the military has its own policy for retaking the exam. (See Appendix A for more information.) Usually, you have to wait at least 30 days before you can try again.

This is a lot of time to get ready to do your best. The fact that you're reading this test guide in the first place shows that you're already on the path toward success. Also, work with your recruiter to prepare. Your recruiter may be able to give you an in-office test to help you practice, in addition to offering resources to help you study on your own or with a tutor.

However, keep in mind that even if you scored well on all of the necessary tests to qualify for your dream job, there is no guarantee that you will be placed in that position. You may be wait-listed until a spot becomes available in that training school.

ASVAB Scores and Your Military Career

After you enter the service, your ASVAB scores will affect your career only if you want them to. They're not used for general promotions, awards, or other favorable actions. If you want to reclass into another career field or, in some branches of service, be promoted to a more advanced version of the same job, then your scores may come into play. You may

also have the chance to take the test again, except it will be called the Armed Forces Classification Test (AFCT).

The Least You Need to Know

▸ The ASVAB is divided up into 9 to 10 subject-specific subtests, depending on which version you take.

▸ The computer adaptive and paper and pencil versions of the ASVAB are not the same and each has its share of pros and cons.

▸ It's important to find out which version of the test you'll take, and practice strategies specific for each.

▸ You will get a variety of different scores, but it's only your math and verbal scores that determine whether or not you can enlist.

▸ All of your other scores determine job eligibility.

▸ If you don't score high enough to meet the minimum requirements for your branch, you can usually retest in 30 days.

Plan of Attack: General Test-Taking Strategies

At some point, somebody may have told you that you can't study for a standardized test. If that were true, test-preparation companies wouldn't be making millions teaching high school and college students how to pass their college/grad school entrance exams—and there wouldn't be books like this one on library shelves.

The truth is test prep works! But knowing the material you're being tested on is only one piece of the puzzle. Taking the test correctly is as much a part of your score as finding the right answers, and this is what most test-preparation courses focus on. And believe it or not, your scores do go up when you understand how the questions are structured, what to look for, and what to expect at every turn.

This chapter reintroduces you to how to take a standardized test and gives you strategies that help you use the test struc-ture to your advantage.

Rethink Your General Approach

The phrase "standardized test" often evokes sweat and panic among potential test-takers. For some reason, people have been taught to fear these types of exams, a fact that just doesn't make sense to us.

In school, you're given a variety of tests with lots of types of questions. What were the ones you liked best? If you answered multiple choice, you're with just about everyone else. Now think about why you like this type of question instead of, say, fill in the blank or definition. Maybe it's because you can more easily figure out the correct answer because you're given several possibilities.

So why should a whole test full of multiple-choice questions be so daunting? All the answers are already there! The ASVAB is a test based on general knowledge, which someone who has completed high school (or its equivalent) should be familiar with. So with a little brushing up on the subject matter, you should be in good shape for handling the questions.

But that's not the end of the story. It's your job to choose the answer that will get you the points, which can be more complicated than it sounds. Multiple-choice exams are essentially guessing games. How you would phrase the answer isn't necessarily how the answers you have to choose from are presented.

If you adjust the way you approach taking the exam in the first place, you'll be able to get to the correct answers more easily and quickly. These general tips are a good guideline to start with.

Read Carefully

First, always start by making sure that you read the directions and your question very carefully before deciding what a likely answer is. One of the biggest mistakes test-takers make is to assume they know what they're supposed to do on every question. And since you're under tight time constraints, it's very tempting to do this.

However, this is a surefire way to end up missing crucial information in the question itself that leads to the correct answer. Always take your time and make sure you fully understand what the question is asking.

> **TEST TIP**
>
> Pay close attention to questions that have the word *not* in them. They ask you to do the reverse of what you normally would on a question. For example, instead of searching for the one answer choice that the question content supports, you'd be looking at three answer choices that the question backs up and one that doesn't fit. That one is your answer.

Speak for Yourself

After reading the question, your first instinct may be to go right to the answer choices. But doing this may sway your opinion on the correct answer, which you want to avoid.

Instead, take a minute to jot down your own answer to the question. You can use your test booklet if you're taking the PAP or scratch paper if you're taking the CAT. This will help ensure that your answer makes sense to you and that you remember it once you look at the answer choices. Believe it or not, it's very easy to forget your original answer when you start evaluating the answers on the test.

Make the Most of Multiple Choice

Now that you have the answer you think is right, it's time to look at the answer choices you have to work with. Most standardized questions don't ask you to choose the right answer; they ask you to find the best answer out of the four choices you're given.

This is all part of the test design strategy. Those who write these exams want to see that you can not only come up with the correct answer, but also recognize it in varying forms.

Process of elimination is your best friend with the ASVAB—and for multiple-choice exams in general. If you think about it, it makes more sense to look for answers that are wrong simply because there are more of them. Some will be so obviously wrong that you can cross them off quickly. However, others will give you pause. This is where having an answer in mind will help you the most.

Use the answer you came up with on your own to help you narrow down possible "best" answers when there is more than one possibility. Consider each choice and eliminate anything that doesn't fit your original answer. If you can get your odds down from one correct answer out of four to something like one correct answer out of two, your chances of selecting the correct answer go way up.

> **HEADS-UP**
>
> Always choose an answer choice that makes a logical connection to the information—don't just take an instinctual guess.

Always go through all the answer choices before making your selection—even if you're 100 percent sure that your answer is right. Often answer choices are arranged to make you think one is correct at first glance. Using process of elimination will slow you down a little, but you'll be able to think your answer through a little more before making your mark. Remember that wrong answers are not penalized on the ASVAB; you simply don't get any points. The number of questions you complete is not as important as the number you get correct.

It's also important to be flexible when it comes to your answers, because the choices you're given may not match what you were thinking. When this happens, try thinking about the question and your answer from a different perspective, or go over the way you came up with your answer to make sure you didn't miss something.

Putting It Together

Now that you have a new general approach to your test questions, let's try out the steps on an Electronics Information question.

> Which of the following is an example of a conductor?

Read carefully: What is this question asking? Essentially, it's asking you to figure out what a conductor is and be able to identify one.

Speak for yourself: Since this is the Electronics Information section, it's pretty safe to assume that when they say "conductor," they're not talking about a railroad employee. The question has something to do with electricity.

If you know anything about being safe during a lightning storm, you know something about conductors. Conductors transmit electricity and help it move from place to place. Lightning rods are made of metal to attract the electricity away from other objects. It's not safe to swim when there's a thunderstorm. Why? Water's a conductor, too. Both metal and water attract electricity and help it travel from one place to another. While this is far from a definite answer, it's a good place to start. You have a general idea of what you're looking for.

Make the most of multiple choice: Now that we know what a conductor is, let's take a look at the answers and ask, "Is this made of metal or wood?" If the answer is "yes," then you have a possible answer:

(A) garbage bag

(B) plastic storage box

(C) TV antenna

(D) rubber boots

TEST TIP

If one of the answers fits with what you're looking for, don't stop checking the rest of the choices. One of the other answers may be a better fit.

Garbage bags are usually made of plastic or, in some cases, paper, neither of which is metal or water. The same is true of the plastic storage box and the rubber boots. A TV antenna, on the other hand, is usually made of metal. This is the best choice out of the ones you're presented with.

Let's try this question again, this time with a little twist:

> Which of the following is NOT an example of a conductor?

Read carefully: By adding one little word to the question, we've changed your whole purpose in finding an answer. Essentially, the question is asking you to look at a list. Three of the items on the list will be conductors. One will not. You have to choose which one doesn't belong.

Speak for yourself: We said before that metal and water are both conductors. Use this as your starting place again.

Make the most of multiple choice: Now that we know what a conductor is, let's take a look at the answers and ask, "Is this made of metal

or water?" Instead of looking for a "yes," this time look for the one for which the answer is "no":

(A) wire fence

(B) pond

(C) TV antenna

(D) rubber boots

Wire fences are made of metal, so answer A is not a possibility. Ponds are full of water, one of our conductors, and as we said before, TV antennae are usually made of metal. This leaves rubber boots as the best answer.

The Guessing Game

One question most test-takers have is whether they should guess on the test. For some exams, this is a viable strategy because of the way the test is scored. For others, no advantage is gained by guessing.

With the ASVAB, you're not penalized for wrong answers—you simply don't get credit for them. This makes guessing a good idea throughout the test. You have nothing to lose and everything to gain. In fact, on the CAT version of the ASVAB, you'll receive a substantial penalty for any questions that are unanswered.

Does that mean you should just randomly select answers on questions you're having trouble with? No way. This is a wasted opportunity. If you don't know what the answer to the question is, you can still eliminate answer choices that you know are not correct and then make an educated guess based on what's left.

When we say "educated guess," we mean that you choose an answer based on some kind of logic or using information that you have. It's always best to make an educated guess instead of a random one, because it increases your chances of getting the question correct.

Eliminating answers that you know are not right is a great way to start making your educated guess. It automatically increases your chances of getting the question right. Think about it: on any given question ...

> You have a 25 percent chance of choosing the answer that will get you points.

> You increase your chance to 33 percent. if you can eliminate one of those answers.

> You have a 50 percent chance of choosing the right answer. if you eliminate two answers.

Even if you have no idea what the question is asking, you tip the odds in your favor by eliminating at least one of the answers. Here are some specific things to look for in answer choices, usually telltale signs that those choices are not the best answer:

> **Extremes or absolutes.** ASVAB test writers like to keep things neutral. If an answer choice has words that indicate some type of condition that is too far to one side, this is not likely what you're looking for. Watch out for words like *never, always, furious, enraged,* or *overjoyed,* or anything else that hints at an extreme situation.

> **Contradictory information.** Many times, particularly in the verbal sections, answer choices directly contradict the information given in the question, information you're asked to read, and even another answer choice. If it goes against what's in the question or passage, that's a dead giveaway that the choice is most likely wrong. If it goes against another answer choice, this is a signal that at least one of these answers is

wrong—and that one may be right. Spend some time here to figure out which one is your best bet.

> **Similarities.** When you see two answers that are very close in meaning, it's easy to get stuck trying to figure out whether there's a trap there. Generally when this happens, neither answer is correct, and the only thing you gain is more time passed on the clock. If your instincts are telling you that there is something there, see what other answer choices you can eliminate; then come back to these and look for specific reasons you think one might be correct.

Test-Specific Strategies

As we discussed in Chapter 2, the CAT and PAP versions of the ASVAB have some pretty big differences. This means that there are some specific strategies for each type, in addition to the general tips we give you throughout this book.

Here are some tips for taking the CAT:

> **Start off strong.** Since the first question of any CAT section is at a medium level of difficulty, if you get it right, the next question will be harder. Remember that, on the CAT ASVAB, harder questions mean more points. Because it's harder to build up to a high score when you start with a low one, try to get your first five questions correct. This will get your score up at the beginning of the test and make it easier to maintain throughout.

> **Watch where you click.** Choosing a different letter than the choice you mean to mark is a common mistake on the CAT. To avoid this, use your scrap paper to write down the answer

choices and cross off the ones you want to eliminate. Circle the one that you believe is correct, then check and double check that that's the answer you're selecting onscreen. Once you make your selection, you'll be prompted to confirm that this is your choice. Take this opportunity to check again. Better safe than sorry.

▶ **Know before you go.** Get as familiar with the CAT ASVAB as possible before test day. Visit the official ASVAB website for more detailed information: www.official-asvab. com/catasvab_app.htm. When you sit down for the test, spend as much time as you need going through the tutorial so that you're comfortable moving forward.

▶ **When in doubt, click through.** You have only so much time to complete each section, so don't spend too much on any one question. If you're not sure of the answer, make an educated guess and move on. If time is running short, finish the section by randomly choosing answers. You may not get any right, but at least you'll avoid a score penalty by not finishing the section. Be careful not to do this too often, though. Having several wrong answers in a row can significantly affect your CAT score.

Here are some tips for taking the PAP:

▶ **Take notes.** Make use of the test booklet (which you can write on) or scratch paper you're given during the test. Writing down your thoughts, taking notes, and even making lists of A-B-C-D, so that you can check off which answer choices you don't need, can be invaluable ways to work through questions, especially if you learn best by both seeing and doing.

▶ **Watch where you mark.** Filling in the right bubble on the wrong line is common. Use your test booklet or scratch paper to block out all the answer bubbles for the questions following the one you're answering to prevent this mistake. Also, always check and double check that you are filling in the right bubble in the right space. If you make a mistake, make sure you completely erase your mark.

▶ **Skip carefully.** You can move back and forth among questions in a single section. Use this to your advantage by skipping questions that you're having difficulty answering and move on to something else. When you do this, make sure that you continue to mark your answer in the correct spaces on the answer sheet.

▶ **Keep an eye on the clock.** If you know how many questions you have in a section, you can pace yourself accordingly. Be aware of the time as you work on the test. As with the CAT, if it looks like you're running out of time, finish the section you're working on by filling in random answers. You won't be penalized for not completing the section, but you could pick up a few stray points by doing this.

The Least You Need to Know

▶ Rethinking your general approach to taking a
standardized test can help you score better.

▶ You can use the multiple-choice format of the
test to your advantage by eliminating incorrect
answers.

▶ When in doubt, taking an educated guess on a
question you're not sure about can increase the
chances of getting a correct answer.

▶ You can use different strategies to approach
the CAT and PAP versions of the ASVAB, so know
which one you're taking and study accordingly.

Prepare, Prepare, Prepare

Let's face it, studying for what amounts to 10 tests that you have to take in one sitting is a daunting task. You've got to brush up on your algebra and learn a whole bunch of new vocabulary words. Since there are essentially three science sections on the ASVAB, you've got to break out your old textbooks and bone up on biology, chemistry, and physics. On top of all that, you need to get your knowledge of tools, hardware, and automotive systems up to snuff, in addition to having to figure out how to visually put puzzles together!

If you feel like there's just too much to learn and not enough time before you have to take the ASVAB, you're going to psych yourself out before you get anywhere near the test. The best way to get over the anxiety of preparing for what might seem like an insurmountable task is to break it down into smaller, more manageable pieces.

This chapter walks you through some general preparation strategies that will help make your studying more effective, not to mention take some of the pressure off.

Practice Tests and Planning Strategies

It's time to put everything that you've learned about the ASVAB into perspective. Although studying the subject areas you'll find on the test and learning about new strategies for taking this type of exam are extremely helpful tools, practicing is the best way to prepare.

But blindly taking practice test after practice test just to get experience doesn't make much sense. It also takes a lot of time that you could be using more wisely. Your best bet is to think strategically about what you need to accomplish when you take the actual ASVAB and then plan your study approach accordingly.

Using Scores as a Guide

Because the ASVAB gives you scores for general entrance eligibility and job quali-fication, doing well on every section of the test is not absolutely necessary. One way to strategically prepare for the ASVAB is to determine your specific goals and concen-trate on getting the scores you need to make them happen.

HEADS-UP

Remember, even if you score well on all the neces-sary tests to qualify for your dream job, there's no guarantee that you will get that job. Placement depends on the availability of spots in the designated training school and the needs of that branch of the military.

▸ Talk with your recruiter about your interests and aspirations to determine career paths that may interest you.

▸ Find out what technical scores you need to qualify for those jobs.

▸ Assess your skill and comfort level with the subject matter of each sub-test required for that job. The best way to do this is to take practice tests (like those in this book) at home or at your recruiter's office.

▸ When you know what you need the most help with, concentrate most of your study efforts on those subjects.

Your Recruiter, Your Coach

Recruiters are a great resource for what you can realistically expect to encounter as you move forward through recruitment and the ASVAB, in particular. But believe it or not, many people who are preparing for the ASVAB overlook their recruiter as a tool to help them get where they need to be.

At the end of the day, your recruiter is there to help you get through the ASVAB. Your recruiter wants you to succeed, if only to increase his or her enlistment numbers. In many ways, recruiters are like salespeople, and enlistment is a numbers game—but instead of meeting sales goals, they're trying to meet enlistment goals.

That's not to say that they don't genuinely care about your future. They do. People choose recruiting as their profession because they like working with people and want to help them succeed. For all these reasons, many recruiters will do anything they can to help you prepare and get the scores you need. This can include the following types of help:

▸ Recommend a personal tutor, and in some cases, pay for the tutoring via the branch's recruiting budget

▸ In-office timed practice testing

▸ Guidance on what to concentrate on, based on your goals

If you're feeling anxious about taking the test, have questions, or just need a quiet place to study, your recruiter should be your first point of contact. Recruiters don't mind putting in extra time or effort, so don't feel bad about asking for help.

Maximize Your ASVAB Workouts

Chances are if you're reading this book, you're serious about preparing for the ASVAB. Nothing will stop you from getting the scores you want, and you will dedicate yourself to hours upon hours of studying for however many weeks you have between now and the date of your test.

Okay, so that's a little bit extreme, but that's how many people feel when they get ready to study for any type of test in earnest. The point is that over the coming weeks, you plan to invest quite a bit of time and effort into preparing for this exam—in addition to school, work, family, friends, sports, or whatever else you have going on in your life.

That's why it's important that you get the most out of your study time. Let's look at some often overlooked yet highly effective ways to make sure your efforts will make the most impact on test day.

Timing Is Everything

Sure, study and practice will help you increase your ASVAB score. However, all the correct answers in the world won't mean much if you don't have the time to record the answers.

One Marine Corps recruiter in New Jersey said that one of the biggest mistakes potential recruits make when preparing for the ASVAB is not timing themselves on practice tests. If you remember our discussion in Chapter 2 about how the test is broken down, you'll note that for many of the ASVAB subtests, you have more questions than you have minutes to answer.

A certain amount of anxiety accompanies any timed test, let alone one in which you have to answer 20 questions about the

science of electrical components in 9 minutes. If you're a slow reader or have marked test-taking anxiety issues, these can become even more pronounced when taking the ASVAB. The best remedy for this is to practice under the same time constraints you'll face on test day. The more you practice at home, the better idea you'll have about what pace to set, how much time to spend on your questions, and how to keep yourself on target with the clock.

HEADS-UP

Unlike many other standardized exams, the ASVAB does not have provisions for test-takers with learning disabilities or those who may need extra time or a special environment to complete the test.

Timing yourself also goes a long way toward making you more comfortable with working against the clock. The calmer you are when you take the test, the better the experience will be. If you think you might have trouble with this on your own, talk to your recruiter to see if you can come into the office and be timed there.

Study Strategically

It doesn't matter whether you're studying for every section of the ASVAB or only one or two subtests—break down the material you're studying into smaller parts. This will keep you from feeling overwhelmed with information in one sitting. Keeping your mind concentrated in one area will also increase your chances of retention.

Additionally, always make sure you work on a handful of practice questions, no matter what you're studying. Reading and memorizing is great, but you'll benefit from it more if you can apply it right away. For example, if you're studying roots to prepare for the Word Knowledge subtest, answer a few practice questions in the book or online to apply what you learned to actual questions.

Slow and Steady Is the Way

When you sit down to take the ASVAB for real, you'll want to be as comfortable with it as possible. So it's not very realistic to expect to be ready for the test in a week or even two. To effectively study for the ASVAB, you need time.

But nowadays, time is hard to come by, especially when you're trying to learn the structure of a new test, refresh yourself on the subjects and topics you'll be tested on, and test your knowledge by answering practice questions.

Our advice is to schedule a little time every day over a few weeks to work on your ASVAB skills, so it doesn't seem like such a huge task. An hour a day is all you need. This will spread out the work and keep your stress level down. Some tips for doing this include the following:

▸ Give yourself enough time to realistically prepare for the test. There's no rush to enlist. Take the time you need to study now so you can do your best the first time around.

▸ Look at your schedule for the next six to eight weeks and pencil in some study time every day. Then stick to it.

▸ Choose a place where you're comfortable and where you'll be undisturbed, preferably someplace without a phone or computer.

▸ Leave the rest of your hectic life behind. Your study time is yours. Don't let any other worries or concerns about other aspects of your life take precedence.

▸ Have everything you need close at hand. Having to go from one room to another wastes a lot of time.

▸ Don't beat yourself up for missing a study session or two. Life can be unpredictable. Try to adjust your routine if you need to, or sneak in some extra study time later.

Relax, It's Only a Test

After weeks of preparing and thinking about the worlds of possibilities riding on your results, your blood pressure may be sky-high the week you're scheduled to take the test. Putting everything in perspective now is more important than ever.

Taking the ASVAB is not rocket science, nor is it your one-and-only shot at a prosperous future. It's a test, plain and simple. It's made of paper and ink (or, in the case of the CAT ASVAB, software coding). Spill your water on it, and it goes back to being so much man-made material that just sits on a desk.

Now that you've got your head in the game, here are some other things you can do the week leading up to the test, to make sure you're in the best shape possible for taking the ASVAB—and they have nothing to do with studying.

▶ **Take some time off.** A day or so before the test, ease back on the preparation. Better yet, stop altogether. This will give your brain a chance to rest so that it's in top shape on test day. Instead, schedule some leisure time with friends, family, or your favorite video game.

▶ **Get some sleep.** Try to get as much sleep as you can the week of the test. One night's rest is not enough if you want to be as rested and relaxed as possible for the test.

▶ **Eat something.** Have a little something packed with protein the morning of the test. This will help keep your blood sugar up and hunger at bay. The last thing you want is a grumbling stomach while you're trying to concentrate. You also don't want to be overly full, so keep it light. Protein bars are a good idea.

▶ **Pack what you need the night before.** Make sure you have everything you need for the exam with you and ready to go. A photo ID is a must. If you have to borrow or sharpen pencils in the middle of the test, you'll lose precious time. Bring at least five sharp number 2 pencils for the PAP. Find out from your recruiter other specifics you'll need and what you can't bring to the site.

▶ **Arrive early.** Arrive at least 15 minutes before the test begins to take care of any administrative business and ensure you get the seat you want. Traffic and unforeseen events are not excuses for being late for the test, so allow yourself ample time.

▶ **Come up with a plan B.** If you're not feeling well, have a fever, or have recently gone through a stressful or emotional event (good or bad), your test scores may not accurately reflect your abilities. Don't be afraid to reschedule the test. Talk to your recruiter about options if your personal circumstances are not optimal on test day or the days leading up to it.

The Least You Need to Know

▶ You can maximize your study time by developing a strategy based on your goals.

▶ Recruiters are excellent resources if you're looking for help preparing for the ASVAB.

▶ There are a lot of sections to the ASVAB, so concentrate on preparing for only one section at a time and doing a little studying every day.

▶ Getting your answers down in time is crucial on test day, so make sure that when you take your practice tests you time yourself.

▶ Don't spend the week before the test cramming; you'll want to be as relaxed as possible on test day.

Word Up! All about Communication Skills

Words, words, and more words. No matter where you go, you're surrounded by them. And for good reason! We live in the age of information, and effective communication makes the world go round. When you enter the military, however, communication takes on a whole new significance. Your ability to accurately transmit and decode messages in various ways—written and verbal—is crucial when lives are on the line. That's why the ASVAB devotes two whole sections of the Armed Forces Qualifying Test (AFQT) to communication skills.

In this part, you'll learn about the Word Knowledge and Paragraph Comprehension subtests and get some good practice for the types of questions you'll likely face on test day. Plus, you'll get lots of tips for improving your vocabulary, breaking down questions, and translating those pesky paragraphs into real English.

Word Knowledge

Just about every teacher you had in school probably stressed the importance of building your vocabulary skills. Back then, you needed it to pass your tests and write papers that made you sound like the greatest living expert on whatever your topic was. Today you need it to pass the Word Knowledge (WK) section of the ASVAB.

This section of the ASVAB is really nothing more than a big vocabulary test, only better. If you remember back to high school, your vocab tests were probably a list of words you had to define. On the ASVAB, you get four answers to choose from and context clues to help you make the right choice.

This chapter gives you the tools you need to ace this subtest. You'll see what types of questions the Word Knowledge subtest has, review essential strategies for approaching them, and explore ways to build up your vocabulary skills so that you can figure out the correct answer, even when you don't know what the words mean.

Why Do I Have to Take This?

"A picture is worth a thousand words." The truth of this adage has certainly been proven throughout history. But when you're giving orders for executing a mission or putting together a weapon, expressing what you want and need in words is often more effective—not to mention safer.

That's why the ASVAB tests you on your knowledge of vocabulary. This subtest is a way for the military to gauge your communication abilities. When a failure to accurately communicate can result in lives lost, ensuring that new recruits have a minimum-level ability in this area is essential.

New recruits are often shocked at the amount of writing they have to do throughout training and eventually for the job they're placed in. To make it through whatever school you're placed in, perform an administrative task, and even command entire units, you'll be writing in some form pretty much on a daily basis. Your success depends on being able to clearly and efficiently communicate.

What to Expect

The ASVAB tests your understanding of words, how they're used in context, and their general meaning. You'll encounter two types of questions on the Word Knowledge section of the ASVAB—and they both test you on synonyms. This simply means that the correct answer choice means pretty much the same thing as the underlined word in the question.

On the CAT version of the test, you'll have 8 minutes to answer 16 questions, giving you about 30 seconds per question. On the PAP, you'll have to answer 35 questions in 11 minutes. That's less than 20 seconds per question! So both speed and preparation are essential for getting the best score you can on this section.

When faced with a Word Knowledge question, following the multiple-choice general strategies outlined in Chapter 3 should be your first line of defense. But for this to work, you have to know or figure out what all the words in the question mean. We walk you through some ways to do this for both types of questions you'll see on the test.

Simple Definition

The first type of question we look at is the most straightforward: simple definition. You're given a word, and your job is to choose the answer choice that is closest to the meaning of that word:

Joyous most nearly means

(A) happy.
(B) drab.
(C) original.
(D) different.

Seems simple enough, right? Sure, if you know what everything means. If you don't, you still have lots of ways to narrow your answer choices and get some clue to a word's meaning.

Get to the Root of the Problem

Just about every word in the English language is made up of smaller parts. If you've ever wondered why the word *contradict* is used to describe saying something that goes against something else, just look at the word's roots:

▸ The prefix *contra* means "against" or "opposite."

▸ The root *dict* means "speak."

Now put these meanings together, and you can see a clear definition: to speak against or oppose. Many of the words commonly used on standardized tests like the ASVAB use words that have Greek and Latin word roots, prefixes, and suffixes. Don't forget that you're looking for the answer that most nearly matches the word you're given, not the definition that is exactly the same. That's why roots can be a powerful tool for eliminating answer choices.

> **TEST TIP**
>
> When you have a larger, more complex word, look for smaller words within. They can give you a hint at the definition.

You can make this work for you by memorizing a handful of these roots (more on this in "Learn Your Roots," later in this chapter). Then when you see them in a word, you can get a good idea of what the word generally means. Based on this intel, you can then eliminate answer choices that do not match up with this idea.

Try it with the following example:

<u>Enamored</u> most nearly means

(A) angry.
(B) melodious.
(C) infatuated.
(D) angelic.

Look at the root word in the middle, *amor.* Pretty much everyone knows that *amor* means "love," thanks to American pop culture. So the correct answer choice will have something to do with love.

Now look at your answer choices. *Angry* just isn't going to do it. If you don't know what *melodious* means, see if you can pick out a familiar word within the main roots. Look closely, and you'll pick out "melody," which doesn't mean love. Try the same strategy with *angelic,* and you have "angel." Although angels often are associated with love, angels are defined as heavenly beings. Love is not used to define what an angel is. That means this answer choice is likely wrong.

Even if you didn't know that *infatuated* means "possessed of an unreasoning passion or love," you've eliminated all of the other answer choices as being unsuitable for "most nearly" meaning the same as the word in the question.

What's the Connotation?

If you're not sure what the definition of a word is, ask yourself if it has a positive or negative *connotation.*

DEFINITION

Connotation is the implied meaning or the feeling associated with a word. You may choose to say "car accident" instead of "wreck" or "crash" because "accident" doesn't imply as much violence as the other words. Don't confuse connotation with its opposite, *denotation,* which is the literal or dictionary definition.

A correct answer choice will have the same connotation as the word in the question, so depending on what word you're struggling with, you can use this technique to help you eliminate answer choices:

1. If you know that the word in the question is positive, you can eliminate any negative answer choices right away.

2. If you're not sure what one of the answer choices means, see if you can determine whether it is positive or negative. Then compare it to the question word's connotation.

3. If the word you're given in the question is neither positive nor negative, the correct answer must also be neutral. Eliminate any obviously positive or negative answer choices.

To determine the connotation of a word, think about how you've heard it used before and in what context. Say you don't know what the word *malicious* means, but there it is in a practice question. Ask yourself where you've heard that word before and in what situations. What can you connect to it?

Chances are the context in which you've heard this word used have been negative, since *malicious* describes something as being intentionally harmful. This means you can be pretty confident that its connotation is negative, too.

Prefixes and suffixes can also give you a good idea of whether the word you're looking at is positive or negative. Again, memorizing word roots will be a big help here. Here are some to get you started:

- Prefixes that connote positive meanings: *am/ami/amor, ben/bene, gen, grat, pac*

- Prefixes that connote negative meanings: *ant/anti, bel, dys, mal, mis, mor/mort, neg, pug*

Determine Part of Speech

The correct answer choice will be the same part of speech as the word in the question. If you know the word you're given is a noun, you can eliminate any answer choice that is not a noun.

In case you've forgotten your parts of speech, here's a quick review:

- Noun: Words that name a person, place, thing, or idea. "Cat," "home," and "mother" are all nouns.

- Verb: Words that signify action. "Run," "speak," and "smile" are all verbs.

- Adjective: Words that describe or modify a noun. "Willing," "beautiful," and "old" are all adjectives.

- Adverb: Words that describe or modify a verb, adjective, or another adverb; often ending in *ly*. "Happily," "nearly," and "expertly" are all adverbs.

Looking at parts of speech can work both for and against you. It can work against you because some words have multiple definitions and have multiple parts of speech; it can work for you because looking at the part of speech of other words in the question can help you determine which definition of the word is being used in this instance. Look at the following example:

Cow most nearly means

(A) energize.
(B) levitate.
(C) aggravate.
(D) intimidate.

Your first instinct is likely to define cow as a noun, an adult female bovine, whale, elephant, manatee, or other animal. But if you look at the answer choices, you'll see that they're all verbs: to energize, to levitate, to aggravate, to intimidate. This means that the definition of cow you need to concentrate on is the verb form, which means "to frighten or threaten."

Words in Context

The second type of question you'll see on the Word Knowledge subtest of the ASVAB gives you sentences with a single underlined word. Your job is to choose the answer choice that gives the meaning of how the word is used in the sentence:

Thanks to her <u>acute</u> sense of hearing, the woman picked up the kitten's faint cries for help from the sewer below.

(A) dirty
(B) sharp
(C) transparent
(D) luxurious

The sentence isn't there just to make the test question longer. It actually gives you more information that will help lead you to the correct answer. The strategies we discussed earlier for simple definition questions can still be used with these. However, two additional techniques work specifically for these types of questions.

Look for Clues

The sentences in these questions are like gifts from the ASVAB fairy, and you either use them or lose them. Look for context clues within the sentence that hint at the meaning of the word. Some are very obvious, like specific words that modify or apply to the underlined word. Others require a little logic on your part to draw conclusions about what's going on in the sentence and how it relates to the underlined word.

In the example, the word you need to define is *acute*. You know that the word is being used to describe "sense" (a noun), which means it's an adjective. What else does the sentence tell you? Acute hearing helped the woman hear faint cries.

What do you know about faint cries? They're quiet and hard to hear. You would need to have sensitive hearing to pick them up. So, if acute hearing enabled the woman to hear something that wasn't loud, you can infer that the meaning of the word has something to do with being able to be very precise or sensitive.

Now look at the answer choices:

(A) dirty
(B) sharp
(C) transparent
(D) luxurious

You know that *dirty* has nothing to do with being precise or sensitive. *Sharp* is a possibility, since it has multiple definitions, one of which is "sensitive." But you still need to eliminate the other answer choices to be sure. *Transparent* means something is see-through, and *luxurious* is the adjective form of "luxury." Neither of these have meanings close to what you're looking for, which makes B your best answer.

Swap It Out

The second approach is to simply replace the underlined word with the answer choices. This works well when you know the definitions of the answer choices, but are not sure about what the underlined word means. If the answer choice makes sense in the sentence without changing the meaning, chances are that answer is a keeper.

Read the following example:

Mark was such an <u>affable</u> guy, it was no wonder that his many friends voted him the most popular boy in his class.

(A) lackluster
(B) unusual
(C) likable
(D) original

Now replace *affable* with the answer choices, and see what works best:

(A) Mark was such a <u>lackluster</u> guy, it was no wonder that his many friends voted him the most popular boy in his class.

(B) Mark was such an <u>unusual</u> guy, it was no wonder that his many friends voted him the most popular boy in his class.

(C) Mark was such a <u>likable</u> guy, it was no wonder that his many friends voted him the most popular boy in his class.

(D) Mark was such an <u>original</u> guy, it was no wonder that his many friends voted him the most popular boy in his class.

If you don't know what *lackluster* means, you can use one of our previous strategies to get a clue to its meaning: look for smaller words in this complex one that are familiar. The word *luster,* when it stands alone, means "shiny." *Lack* suggests that something is missing—in this case, shine, since that's part of the word. A good guess would be that *lackluster* means "dull" (which it does).

Now that you're familiar with all of the words, what fits? Would a dull or unusual guy have lots of friends and be voted Mr. Popularity? Probably not. How about an original guy? *Original* is a neutral word, suggesting neither positive nor negative connotations. The sentence, however, leans more to the positive than anything else, so "original" is likely not your answer. Would a likable guy have lots of friends and be popular? Of the answers you're given, this makes the most sense.

Build Your Vocab

Probably the best thing that you can do to raise your score on the Word Knowledge section of the ASVAB is to simply increase your vocabulary. The more words you know or are familiar with going into the test, the faster and more efficient you'll be on this subtest.

The key to bulking up your vocab is to do it slowly and steadily. A little work on this each day can pay off big-time in terms of words you know walking into the exam. The following are easy and even entertaining ways to get started.

Word of the Day

You can subscribe to a word-of-the-day website that will email you a new vocabulary word and definition every day. Just click open your message and use that word sometime during the day for maximum retention. You can also have words of the day sent to your phone via text message. A quick online search nets several services that you can subscribe to. We like Merriam-Webster's Word of the Day (see Appendix C).

Hit the Books

Simply reading will help you increase your vocab. It doesn't matter much what you read as just about anything you pick up will likely introduce at least one new word to you. Yes, that romance novel, mystery, issue of *Sports Illustrated,* or even daily newspaper can help you pick up new words. The increased interaction with language will seep into your mindset and familiarize you with more words than you could ever imagine—and it happens automatically.

You can also head to your local library in search of vocabulary guides. Use one of these books to make a list of words you want to learn, and work on learning them a few at a time over a couple weeks.

Memorize in Clusters

So many of the words you'll likely encounter on the ASVAB have similar meanings. For example, *florid, embellish, bombastic, ornate, overblown, flowery,* and *elaborate* all share a single similar meaning: excessively decorated, spoken, or written. Use a good thesaurus and make a list of synonyms for any vocabulary word on your list. This is a great way to get the most out of your study time.

Learn Your Roots

We talked earlier about recognizing prefixes, suffixes, and word roots. This is really an invaluable tool for improving your vocabulary because it gives you the tools for understanding how words are built—which, in turn, clues you into their meaning. The following table compares some common roots, prefixes, and suffixes.

Common Roots, Prefixes, and Suffixes

Root	Meaning	Example
acer/acri	sour, sharp, bitter	acrid
bene	good	benefit
beli/bel/pug	fight, war	pugnacious
circ	around	circuit

Root	Meaning	Example
chron	time	chronological
dic/dict/dit	speak, talk	dictate
loqu/locut/log	speak, talk	dialogue
luc/lum/lun/lus	light	illuminate
mal	bad	malaise
phot/photo	light	photograph
omni	all, ever	omnipresent
path	feel	sympathy
pop	people	population
simil/simul	same	simultaneous
spec/spic	see	conspicuous
sym/syn	together	synchronize
terr/terra	earth	terrain
ver	true	verify
vid/vis	see	visual
viv/vita/vivi	life	vitality

Prefix	Meaning	Example
a/ab/an	away from, without	abdicate
ante	before	antechamber
anti/de	against, opposite	antihero
com/con	with, fully, together	congregation
contra/counter	against, opposite	counteract
inter	between	interoffice
intra	within	intramural
post	after	posthumous
super/supra	above or over	supersede

Suffix	Meaning	Example
able	worth or ability, suggests adjective	capable
acy/cy	state of, suggests noun	accuracy
ant/ent	noun that does something	defendant
ary	relating to, suggests adjective	reactionary
ed	past, suggests verb	walked
ism	belief, suggests noun	feudalism
ist	person, suggests noun	nudist
ful	having/giving, suggests noun/adjective	bountiful
ation/ness	action or condition, suggests noun	intimidation
fy/ify	to cause or form, suggests verb/adjective	justify
ly	in the manner of, suggests adverb	normally
ise/ize	cut off, suggests verb	excise

Let's get in some practice figuring out the meanings of words based on looking at their roots. For each of the following, list as many roots as you can in the first column. Then write what you think the word means in the second column. Look them up in the dictionary to check.

Word	Roots	Meaning
Interoffice	_____	_____
Acerbic	_____	_____
Luminous	_____	_____
Circumvent	_____	_____
Omnipotent	_____	_____
Antebellum	_____	_____
Pugilistic	_____	_____
Malodorous	_____	_____
Anachronistic	_____	_____
Sympathetic	_____	_____

TEST TIP

Prefixsuffix.com (www.prefixsuffix.com) has an extensive list of word roots that you can access for free.

Make Associations

One of the easiest and most lasting ways to learn new words is to associate their meanings with something that makes sense to you. You can do this in a few ways. The first is to come up with a little rhyme or word association that reminds you of the meaning. These are called *mnemonic devices*, and as long as they makes sense to you, they can consist of just about anything. Here are a few to get you started:

▸ Pretentious: Pretends to be all that

▸ Nullify: Make nada or nothing

▸ Miser: Scrooge was a miserable miser

▸ Levity: Levitates or lifts your mood

▸ Concrete: Hard evidence

▸ Intrepid: Bold, gutsy, like the famous aircraft carrier

You can also make associations with words based on where you heard them (a conversation, a book, a movie, a song, and so on), what you were doing when you heard it, the context of what was going on, how you were feeling, and more. A few that work for us include these:

▶ *Curious:* Mr. Olivander, the wand-maker in *Harry Potter and the Sorcerer's Stone,* used *curious* when Harry's wand ended up having the same core as his archenemy's.

▶ *Indubitably:* Burt, in *Mary Poppins,* would say "indubitably" when agreeing with her.

▶ *Vapid:* In the movie *10 Things I Hate About You,* a character used *vapid* to describe the boring and unoriginal student population.

Now it's your turn. Look up and write out the definitions of the following words. Then think of an association for each that means something to you.

Uproar

Definition: _____

Association: _____

Trepidation

Definition: _____

Association: _____

Slovenly

Definition: _____

Association: _____

Acrid

Definition: _____

Association: _____

Jettison

Definition: _____

Association: _____

Vacuous

Definition: _____

Association: _____

Misanthrope

Definition: _____

Association: _____

Torpid

Definition: _____

Association: _____

Enigmatic

Definition: _____

Association: _____

With a little time and practice, you will be in excellent shape to take the ASVAB's Word Knowledge subtest, no matter how much you may have shivered at the thought of studying English in school. And all your hard work will pay off not only on the test, but for the rest of your life as well. A great vocabulary is an asset that can give you an advantage when applying for future jobs and help you make a good impression on new people you meet.

Paragraph Comprehension

You're most likely not going to have to take another test in the military that asks you to read a passage and then answer questions about what you read. You will, however, apply the same skills on a daily basis as you would to pass such a test.

The military needs to know the strength of your communication and analytical skills before they will allow you to enlist. Believe it or not, that's where Paragraph Comprehension (PC) comes in. Answering questions based on complex passages about generalized topics actually shows how you think and understand the world around you.

This chapter introduces you to what you can expect to see on this section of the test, how to approach each type of question, and how to get through this subtest as painlessly as possible. If English has never been a strong subject for you, this chapter will definitely help you.

Why Do I Have to Take This?

The ability to read and understand written materials is something that every branch of the military takes very seriously. Unlike in most civilian jobs, mistakes in communication can end up costing people their lives in the military.

So how does reading boring little paragraphs and answering questions tell anyone how you communicate? It's all about analysis. The ASVAB's Paragraph Comprehension subtest gauges your ability to effectively take in information, to process it, and to make decisions based on what you've read. When you get the correct answer, you show that you can do this effectively.

You need to score well on this section for two reasons:

▸ It's part of the AFQT and in calculating your percentile scores, your verbal raw score is counted *twice*. If you don't make the grade here, you won't be eligible to go further through the enlistment process.

▸ Many jobs require a good PC score to qualify for training. Make sure you know what line scores you need for the jobs you're interested in, so you can study accordingly.

What to Expect

For this section, taking the CAT version of the ASVAB gives you an advantage, especially if you're a slow reader. The PC subtest on the CAT is 11 questions in 22 minutes. On the other hand, you have only 13 minutes to answer 15 questions on the PAP version. That's less than a minute per question!

You can expect to see a short passage (most are just one paragraph, but they can go up to three), with one or more questions that follow. Each question refers to that particular passage.

The good news is that you most likely won't have to read 11–15 paragraphs to complete this section in time. It just doesn't make sense when you've got less than a minute per question. Instead, some simple tweaks to your general approach will save you time and brainpower:

1. **Read the questions first.** You'll find several different types of questions, which we detail later in the chapter. If you know what type of question you're dealing with, you'll know what to look for in the passage. For example, if you get a question that asks you what a word means in a particular sentence, you have to read only enough to figure out how it's used in that one instance. Also make sure you read through the answer choices and understand what they mean.

2. **Attack the passage.** Depending on what type of question you have, deploy the appropriate technique for best finding the information in the passage that gets you the answer you need. Analyze the information and answer the question in your own words.

3. **Eliminate what doesn't fit.** Look for answers that are backed up directly with information from the passage. Get rid of answer choices that are not supported by a specific phrase or sentence in the passage.

TEST TIP

Check reality at the door when you approach a PC question. The only information that matters is what's in the passage. Make your inferences based on your own logic and specific statements from the passage—not what you know to be true in real life.

Now let's take a look at the six main types of questions you'll see on the PC subtest.

Main Idea

Often, you'll be asked to identify the overall point of a passage. Most passages have a predictable format: some kind of topic sentence states or implies the point of the passage, and the rest of the sentences give details or support for that point. Your job is to find that sentence. To make this easier, look for sentences that explain what the passage is about instead of how or why something is what it is. These can appear anywhere in the passage. They often are the first or last sentence, but they can also come in toward the middle.

Plan of attack:

1. Read the passage carefully, making notes when you can.

2. Ask yourself what the passage is about.

3. Eliminate answer choices that don't match your idea.

Purpose

This is a variation on the main idea question. You're not looking for what the passage is about; you're looking for what the speaker hopes to accomplish. Some purposes of a passage can include these:

▸ Inform the reader about something

▸ Show or explain a process

▸ Educate or instruct

▸ Persuade

▸ State an opinion or position

▸ Reason something out

▸ Tell a story

Plan of attack:

1. Figure out what the main idea of the passage is.

2. Ask yourself why the speaker would try to communicate this message. What is he or she hoping to accomplish?

3. Eliminate answer choices that don't match your idea.

Tone

As we discussed in Chapter 5, words can have more to their meaning than what's written in the dictionary. They can also evoke a feeling in the person communicating them and the person receiving the message.

On the ASVAB, you'll be asked to figure out what feelings the *speaker* in a passage is trying to communicate through words. This is called *tone*. When you have a tone question, pay close attention to the language in the passage and the impression you get based on what's said.

Read the following passage:

> The wind gently blows the hair away from my face. My muscles burn with the strain of the motion as my arms and legs work in synchronization with each other. Blood pumps through my veins in time with my steps. The faster I go, the more exhilarated I feel. I love to run.

What kind of vibe do you get from reading this paragraph? Affectionate, energized, and savoring are all good answers. The loving and elaborate description of the everyday action of running tells us that this person doesn't think of it as ordinary, but rather as something reverent.

Plan of attack:

1. Look at the language being used, punctuation, and context clues in the passage.

2. Determine whether the speaker in the passage is excited, somber, apprehensive, happy, and so on.

3. Eliminate answer choices that don't match.

Try it here:

> The tone of this passage can best be described as
>
> (A) reminiscent.
> (B) argumentative.
> (C) mysterious.
> (D) relishing.

Reminiscent means that you're remembering something fondly, which doesn't really apply here, since the speaker is using present tense. *Argumentative* and *mysterious* just don't make sense for this passage. This leaves *relishing,* which means "to take pleasure in." Answer D fits best.

As with main idea questions, you'll have to read the whole passage for tone questions. Vocabulary also plays a key role in this type of question, since many of the answer choices may be more sophisticated than what you'd use every day. Be sure to check out our vocab-building tips in Chapter 5.

Specific Details

Like the name suggests, this type of question asks you to find a specific piece of information in the passage. The beauty of this type of question is that the answers are right in the passage, and often the question will use language similar to what's written in the answer. Knowing this will save you time if you use the general approach outlined earlier in the chapter.

Plan of attack:

1. Read and determine what information the question is asking you to find.

2. Skim the passage to determine where the information you need is located. Read just enough to answer the question in your own words.

3. Eliminate answer choices that don't match your answer.

HEADS-UP

Beware of questions that ask you to determine what's *not* in a passage or can't be inferred from what's written. This runs counter to what you're used to (finding the correct answer), and it's easy to overlook that you're seeking something different.

Give it a try:

A component that can decrease the amount of power in a circuit is a

(A) bulb.
(B) socket.
(C) resistor.
(D) switch.

The question is asking you to look for a word that has something to do with decreasing power. Now skim the passage for those words and see what you find:

Most electrical circuits require a precise balance of components in order to work properly. If too much power travels from the socket into a lamp into which a bulb is plugged, the circuit will overheat and sustain damage. Introducing resistors into the circuit can help decrease the amount of power that reaches the bulb so that it matches exactly what is needed to make the bulb work properly.

The last sentence in the passage talks about resistors being able to decrease power in a circuit. Answer C is correct.

Vocabulary in Context

These questions are probably the easiest on the test, especially since by the time you get to them, you've already had lots of practice with them.

The Word Knowledge (WK) subtest, which comes just before Paragraph Comprehension, has lots of vocabulary-in-context questions—just without an accompanying paragraph. This means you can use Word Knowledge strategies here as well. The Swap-It-Out technique discussed in Chapter 5 also works for this type of question.

Your job is to figure out how the underlined word is being used in a specific sentence. The great thing about this type of question is that you usually have to read only one sentence!

Plan of attack:

1. Go back to the passage and read the sentence that contains the word in the question.

2. Use context clues to determine how the word is being used and what it's intended to mean.

3. Eliminate answer choices that don't match your definition.

TEST TIP

Use your test booklet and/or scratch paper to write down notes about the passage as you read along. This will help keep you on your toes and increase your chances of getting the correct answer.

Inference Questions

Many people consider inference questions to be difficult or tricky because the questions don't give you the answers, as they do in specific detail or vocabulary-in-context questions. It's up to you to draw conclusions (or infer) based on information in the passage.

As with every other question in this section, you'll be presented with a passage of information and a question. Common questions that follow include these:

▸ The author is most likely to agree with which of the following statements?

- Based on the passage, it can be inferred that ....
- According to the passage, it can be assumed that ....

Then you'll get four statements to consider. They might ask you about what happens next, thoughts the author might have, where the story takes place, and other conclusions that could be based on the passage.

Now, you may be asking how you're supposed to know what happens next or what the speaker is thinking. That's where the critical thinking comes in. It's your job to compare the answer choices to information in the passage. Correct answers will always be supported by specific details in the passage.

Plan of attack:

1. Read the question first.
2. Read the passage.
3. Go to each answer choice and ask yourself, "What in the passage tells me this would likely happen or be true?"

Now try this:

According to the passage, it can be assumed that ....

The setup of the question tells us it's a straightforward inference question. Next, read the passage:

> Owning a pet can result in several health benefits. Studies have shown that cat and dog owners tend to suffer fewer cardiovascular ailments such as high blood pressure or cholesterol. Interacting with pets can also result in increased brain activity and have a calming effect on the body.

Now look at the answer choices, and go through them one by one to see what's supported by information in the passage and what's not.

(A) Pet owners live longer.
(B) Cats and dogs are inappropriate pets for children.
(C) The health benefits of owning a dog are greater than those of owning a cat.
(D) A cat would be a good gift for someone who has anxiety issues.

The passage doesn't mention anything about pets affecting length of life or children, so you can eliminate answers A and B. Although the passage does talk about different health benefits from owning dogs and cats, it does not provide a judgment on which is better. This eliminates answer C. Because the passage says that interacting with a pet can have a calming effect on the body, and a cat is a pet, it can be reasonably assumed that answer D is correct.

HEADS-UP

It's really tempting to choose an answer that sounds logical or possible. But remember, it must also be supported by specific information in the passage. If you can't point to a line in the passage as the reason you feel the answer is correct, chances are it's wrong.

The Paragraph Breakdown

Now that you know all about the types of questions you'll see on the test, you can practice getting the information you need out of them. Write down the main idea, purpose, tone, and major details for each of the following passages.

William Henry Harrison had the shortest presidency in American history. He took office on March 4, 1841, and died 32 days later. Harrison was the first president to die in office, and controversy about the title and term of his successor soon developed.

Main idea: _____

_____

Purpose: _____

_____

Tone: _____

Main details: _____

_____

Wine is the result of a fermentation process involving grapes or other fruits whose chemical compositions are conducive to creating alcohol. Wine grapes are first crushed and strained and then the skins discarded. Yeast is added to the mixture. As the yeast consumes the natural sugars in the grape juice, alcohol is produced.

Main idea: _____

_____

Purpose: _____

_____

Tone: _____

Main details: _____

_____

Laws regarding car seats vary from state to state. It is important for parents to know what their local regulations are, not only for the safety of their children, but also to comply with the law. Car dealerships, community groups, and health-care agencies often hold free clinics to check that your car seat is installed properly and to give out car seat information about child age, height, and weight requirements. Every parent can benefit from attending these clinics.

Main idea: _____

_____

Purpose: _____

_____

Tone: _____

Main details: _____

_____

When you fall asleep, your brain literally slows down. The brain waves you create when you're awake take a break and different, slower waves are produced. These theta and delta wave patterns become slower the deeper you sleep. Your body temperature and respiration also decrease, while your brain's need for oxygen increases.

Main idea: _____

_____

Purpose: _____

_____

Tone: _____

Main details: _____

_____

Communication Skills Workout

Practice really does make perfect—and it's the best way to increase your comfort with any section of the ASVAB. Use this section to test out what you learned in Chapters 5 and 6. And remember, you can learn just as much from incorrect answers as you can from those you get right.

Word Knowledge Workout

The following questions test your knowledge of and ability to use vocabulary. Read each question and choose the answer choice that most nearly means the same as the underlined word.

1. Adhere most nearly means

   (A) vent.
   (B) attribute.
   (C) stick.
   (D) sense.

2. Mutation most nearly means

   (A) character.
   (B) lampoon.
   (C) ambassador.
   (D) change.

3. Profuse most nearly means

   (A) beautiful.
   (B) lavish.
   (C) horrid.
   (D) graceful.

4. <u>Strict</u> most nearly means

    (A) lax.

    (B) uncaring.

    (C) rigid.

    (D) parental.

5. He had a <u>voracious</u> appetite after having fasted for three days.

    (A) unquenchable

    (B) healthy

    (C) average

    (D) enviable

6. <u>Respite</u> most nearly means

    (A) surge.

    (B) bastion.

    (C) well.

    (D) break.

7. <u>Zealot</u> most nearly means

    (A) fanatic.

    (B) arbitrator.

    (C) expert.

    (D) leader.

8. <u>Upbraid</u> most nearly means

    (A) reprimand.

    (B) tie.

    (C) fashion.

    (D) lift.

9. The murder was so <u>egregious</u> that the person convicted was given four life sentences.

    (A) questionable

    (B) monstrous

    (C) slight

    (D) average

10. <u>Disdain</u> most nearly means

    (A) contempt.

    (B) comedy.

    (C) disappointment.

    (D) approval.

11. <u>Boon</u> most nearly means

    (A) insight.

    (B) tragedy.

    (C) impediment.

    (D) gain.

12. Because he didn't <u>heed</u> his mother's warning, the boy ran into the poison ivy and got a rash.

    (A) slow

    (B) observe

    (C) initiate

    (D) argue

13. <u>Fervent</u> most nearly means

    (A) excess.

    (B) original.

    (C) mocking.

    (D) heartfelt.

14. <u>Caustic</u> most nearly means

    (A) poisonous.

    (B) scathing.

    (C) believable.

    (D) excessive.

15. <u>Articulate</u> most nearly means

    (A) think.

    (B) arrange.

    (C) create.

    (D) enunciate.

16. The sun's warmth felt so good, all she could do was <u>bask</u> in it.

    (A) heat
    (B) forget
    (C) enjoy
    (D) seek

17. After our first date, Mike and I said good night and went to our <u>respective</u> houses.

    (A) relative
    (B) visual
    (C) individual
    (D) regretful

18. My <u>equivocal</u> response neither confirmed nor denied my involvement.

    (A) definite
    (B) instant
    (C) evasive
    (D) missing

19. <u>Cow</u> most nearly means

    (A) comfort.
    (B) brace.
    (C) repair.
    (D) bully.

20. Our orders are to <u>plaster</u> the downtown area with the 5,000 flyers that were delivered last night.

    (A) blend
    (B) bluster
    (C) cover
    (D) avert

Answers and Explanations

1. **C.** To *adhere* means "to stick," which is why tape is called an *adhesive*— it sticks to things! To *vent* is to "talk out your frustrations." When you *attribute,* you "give credit," and when you *sense,* you "perceive."

2. **D.** If you're an X-Men fan, you know a thing or two about mutation. In the context of the comic or cartoon, mutants are people who have genes that have mutated (changed from the norm) and given them superpowers. So we're looking for a word that implies change. *Character* and *ambassador* refer to people, so those are not possible answers. A *lampoon* is a type of satire (think the National Lampoon movies), which doesn't make sense. That leaves *change.* Since a definition of *mutation* is "the process of changing," that makes this your best bet.

3. **B.** *Profuse* means "extensive," "abundant," "extravagant"—basically, a lot of something! The only answer that applies to quantity is *lavish,* which means "using or giving in great amounts."

4. **C.** Someone who is strict adheres to the rules with little or no deviation. *Lax* is the opposite of this, while *uncaring* implies apathy; people who are *strict* feel strongly about the importance of convention or rules. And while many parents may be strict, *parental* is not a definition of it. This leaves *rigid* as the best answer.

5. **A.** If you had nothing to eat for three days, chances are you would be extremely hungry. The answer you're looking for reflects this type of urgency. *Healthy* and *average* are simply not strong enough to match a starved appetite. *Enviable* has to do with jealousy and nothing to do with hunger. Your answer is *unquenchable,* which means "unable to be satisfied." It's not an exact match, but remember, you're looking for the best choice out of the four you're given.

6. **D.** When you get a respite, you get a rest (this is a good mnemonic). *Surge* is the opposite of resting. A *bastion* is a protective structure, and a *well* is a hole dug that provides water—neither has anything to do with what you're looking for. *Break* is the best choice.

7. **A.** A *zealot* is someone who is extremely devoted to an ideology. While this person may be an *expert, arbitrator,* or *leader,* they don't have to be any of these things in order to be a zealot.

8. **A.** When you see this word, *tie* or *fashion* may look like a good answer choice because you see *braid* in the underlined word. Don't be fooled here. To *upbraid* is to scold or reprimand.

9. **B.** Context clues in the sentence indicate that the answer we're looking for shows an unusually horrible crime. The only answer choice that reflects this is B. If you're not familiar with what *monstrous* means, you can easily associate it with monster, which implies horror that is out of the ordinary.

10. **A.** *Disdain* is a strong negative word. As a noun, it means "a sense of contempt or scorn." That eliminates *comedy* and *approval* as possible answers. *Disappointment* means

"expecting something and then not having that expectation met." Although it's negative, it's not strongly so. *Contempt* is a feeling that something is horrible or vile, both strong negatives.

11. **D.** When you get a boon, you *gain* something that you want, or something that is useful. This makes *boon* a positive. That eliminates *tragedy* as a possible answer. Both *impediment* (something that blocks your way) and *insight* (knowledge) are neutral and have nothing to do with gaining something.

12. **B.** The context clues in this sentence tell us that if the boy had listened to his mother, he would not have suffered the effects of poison ivy. *Observe* is the only answer that makes sense here.

13. **D.** When you do something with fervor, you do it with great emotion and feeling. You put your heart into it. *Fervent* is the adjective form of this word. Although all the answer choices can be done fervently, the only one that defines the word is D, *heartfelt*.

14. **B.** Your first instinct with this question may be to choose *poisonous*. After all, many household cleaners are considered to be caustic. Making the association between the word and "poison" would be natural. However, not all poisons are *caustic*, which refers to "something that is corrosive" or "something that is extremely critical or malicious." *Believable* and *excessive* don't make sense as answers. However, *scathing* refers to something that's bitingly critical or hurtful— which is corrosive to oneself.

15. **D.** This one is a little tricky. *Articulate* can be either an adjective or a verb.

When you are articulate, you have a way with words and can speak clearly and distinctly. When you articulate, you are actively giving a clear description of something. The answer choices tell us that we're dealing with the verb here, since they are all verbs. *Think, arrange,* and *create* have nothing to do with speaking. *Enunciate* means to speak clearly, which makes this the correct answer.

16. **C.** This sentence is talking about how the warm sun makes you feel really good. *Enjoy* is the only answer choice that matches this.

17. **C.** This is a good question to use the Swap-It-Out technique discussed in Chapter 5:

After our first date, Mike and I said good night and went to our <u>relative</u> houses.

After our first date, Mike and I said good night and went to our <u>visual</u> houses.

After our first date, Mike and I said good night and went to our <u>individual</u> houses.

After our first date, Mike and I said good night and went to our <u>regretful</u> houses.

The answer that makes the most sense is C.

18. **C.** In this sentence, the response being discussed doesn't really give any firm information. Is it *definite?* No. *Instant,* maybe, but instant implies time, which has nothing to do with not giving exact information. The response can't be *missing,* since the speaker says that they gave it. So even if you don't know that *evasive* refers to trying to avoid or dodge, it's still the most logical answer.

19. **D.** The obvious answer here may be the big farm animal that makes milk. Unfortunately, that's not one of your answer choices. *Cow* is used here as a verb, which means "to threaten." *Comfort* and *brace* mean the opposite of this, and *repair* has nothing to do with threatening. *Bully* is your best choice.

20. **C.** When you apply plaster to something, you cover it in the substance. So it makes sense that when you distribute a lot of something, like flyers, throughout an area, it's also called *plastering*. In the sentence, the orders are to get as many flyers out in the downtown area as possible. *Cover* is obviously the best choice.

Paragraph Comprehension Workout

Read each passage and answer the questions that follow. Choose the answer choice that best answers the question.

Use the following passage to answer questions 1–2:

While you may think it's the acid in fresh pineapple that causes your tongue to burn if you eat too much, it's actually the work of an enzyme found in the fruit. Bromelain, found in abundance in pineapples, is a natural enzyme that breaks down proteins found in muscles, such as your tongue. This enzyme is also the main substance in commercial meat tenderizer. However, the pain associated with a bromelain burn on the tongue lasts only as long as it takes for the damaged cells to regenerate.

1. Based on the information in the paragraph, it can be inferred that

    (A) adding pineapple juice to a marinade will help tenderize meat.
    (B) burns caused by bromelain cause permanent damage.
    (C) bromelain is what gives pineapple its sweet taste.
    (D) bromelain is a main nutritional component of pineapple.

2. The word <u>abundance</u> in this paragraph most nearly means

    (A) just enough.
    (B) inadequate.
    (C) in great quantities.
    (D) reserved.

Use the following passage to answer question 3:

Babies have 144 more bones than adults. Throughout physical development from birth to adulthood, the 350 bones a person is born with grow and expand, causing many to fuse together. By the time a person stops growing, 206 bones remain.

3. The purpose of this passage is to

    (A) entertain.
    (B) inform.
    (C) postulate a theory.
    (D) dismiss a claim.

Use the following passage to answer questions 4–5:

Increased interest in the ideals of the Enlightenment throughout eighteenth-century Europe was one of the main causes of the French Revolution. As talk of nationalism, individual rights, and democracy spread throughout the starving populace, the inequity between the nobility and the church, and the commoners became more apparent. This led to an extended period of civil unrest and violence as the country struggled to redefine its government.

4. Which of the following would be the best title for this passage?

   (A) The Rise of Napoleon
   (B) The French Revolution's Definitive Cause
   (C) Vive la Révolution
   (D) The Enlightenment's Role in the French Revolution

5. Which was NOT an effect of the Enlightenment ideals on the French populace?

   (A) The masses felt empowered to change their government.
   (B) More people emigrated to other countries in Europe.
   (C) Tolerance for the excesses of the nobility decreased.
   (D) France became increasingly unstable.

Use the following passage to answer questions 6–7:

Rock candy is a sweet treat that is easy to make. Simply create a solution of super-saturated sugar syrup and water. Place the liquid in a container that can sit undisturbed for a number of days. Then put a stick or string in the solution and keep it in a cool, dry place. Within a few days, sugar crystals will have formed on the stick or string.

6. Based on the information in the paragraph, it can be inferred that

   (A) food coloring is needed to make rock candy.
   (B) you have to have a good knowledge of chemistry to make rock candy.
   (C) making rock candy is the simplest task in the world.
   (D) you can't make rock candy in one day.

7. The word solution in this paragraph most nearly means

   (A) a mixture of sugar and water.
   (B) a way to solve a problem.
   (C) a chemical reaction.
   (D) a candy.

Use the following passage to answer questions 8–9:

My favorite band is finally coming to town! I have been a huge fan of their music since the group's first album came out five years ago. Since then, they have only gotten better. I live in such a small town that musicians hardly ever come here to perform. I am the luckiest person, and I can't wait for the concert!

8. Based on the information in the paragraph, it can be inferred that

    (A) the speaker has never attended a concert before.
    (B) the speaker will attend the concert.
    (C) the speaker is a new fan of the band.
    (D) the speaker only casually listens to the band's music.

9. The speaker in this passage is

    (A) angry.
    (B) confused.
    (C) excited.
    (D) ill.

Use the following passage to answer questions 10–11:

Simple, handmade soap is the product of a chemical reaction when fat and lye are combined in precise proportion. Handmade soap is becoming increasingly popular because soap makers often use vegetable oils, such as olive or coconut, as the base for their products. This produces a naturally moisturizing soap that is gentle on the skin, whereas the additives in commercial soaps can irritate and dry out skin.

10. The author would most likely agree with which of the following statements?

    (A) Commercial soap is the best you can buy.
    (B) Selling commercial soap is more profitable than selling handmade soap.
    (C) Handmade soap smells better than commercial soap.
    (D) Handmade soap is better for sensitive skin than commercial soap.

11. According to the passage,

    (A) fat and lye must be combined in precise proportion to make soap.
    (B) animal fat cannot be used to make soap.
    (C) vegetable oils are unpopular ingredients among soap makers.
    (D) lavender is a main ingredient for making soap.

Use the following passage to answer questions 12–13:

Medieval castles served an important function throughout European history. They were tall, strong fortresses that housed military units and protected the surrounding areas. They also acted as homes to ruling nobility and royalty in feudal systems. However, today the roles of castles have been romanticized by their portrayal in children's fairy tales and popular media.

12. According to the passage

    (A) castles are still important in the defense of present-day Europe.

    (B) today, general ideas about medieval castles have been romanticized.

    (C) commoners often lived in medieval castles.

    (D) castles had only one function in medieval history.

13. The main idea of this passage is best described as

    (A) the role of fairytale castles in today's world.

    (B) the architecture of medieval castles.

    (C) how the nobility of medieval England once lived.

    (D) the changing roles of castles in Europe.

Use the following passage to answer questions 14–15:

A vaccine helps protect people and animals from a specific disease by teaching the body how to recognize and destroy the pathogen that causes it. First, a portion of a virus or bacteria, called an *antigen*, is introduced into the body through the vaccine. Then the immune system fights off the antigens. The next time that pathogen makes its way into the body, the body recalls what needs to be done to destroy the invader, thus preventing illness.

14. The word <u>pathogen</u> nearly means

    (A) an immune system response.

    (B) an antidote.

    (C) an invading virus or bacteria.

    (D) a vaccine.

15. This passage illustrates

    (A) a process.

    (B) a decision.

    (C) a memory.

    (D) an incident.

Use the following passage to answer questions 16–17:

I don't understand how I could've lost my keys! They were in my hands when I walked into the room. I went straight to the table and put down my things. Then I went to the kitchen for a snack. When I checked the table for my keys, they weren't there.

16. The speaker of this passage most likely feels

    (A) relaxed.
    (B) confused.
    (C) tired.
    (D) energized.

17. Which of the following is not a reasonable inference based on the passage?

    (A) The keys could have fallen out of sight.
    (B) Other things on the table could be covering the keys.
    (C) She didn't have the keys in her hand when she put her things on the table.
    (D) The keys could have been taken by someone else in the house.

Use the following passage to answer questions 18–20:

Napoleon Bonaparte was forced into exile in 1814 after having tried to dominate Europe through more than a decade of military campaigns. The self-proclaimed emperor was sent to the Italian island of Elba to live out the remainder of his life. However, he soon escaped to retake his throne, though unsuccessfully. Napoleon was finally defeated at the Battle of Waterloo in 1815 and was exiled again, this time to Saint Helena in the Southern Atlantic.

18. The word <u>exile</u> most nearly means

    (A) expulsion.
    (B) repentance.
    (C) subservience.
    (D) terror.

19. According to the passage

    (A) Napoleon won the Battle of Waterloo.
    (B) Napoleon died on Elba.
    (C) Napoleon was not an elected official.
    (D) Napoleon was a hero to the French people.

20. The author of this passage would most likely agree with which of the following statements?

    (A) Napoleon's exile was a just consequence for causing more than a decade of war throughout Europe.
    (B) France never recovered from Napoleon's fall.
    (C) Napoleon is considered a despot by historians.
    (D) Exiling Napoleon so close to Europe was not an effective way to prevent continued aggression from France.

Answers and Explanations

1. **A.** The passage states that bromelain is a main component of commercial meat tenderizer. Since the enzyme is found in abundance in pineapple, it stands to reason that soaking meat in a marinade with pineapple juice would work to tenderize it. The passage does not talk about the nutritional value of bromelain or its effect on taste. The passage also says that cells regenerate from bromelain damage, which contradicts answer B.

2. **C.** Because you can suffer from bromelain burns if you eat pineapple, it's logical to think that there is a lot of it in the fruit. The other answer choices don't make sense.

3. **B.** Because of the factual nature of the content, this passage is clearly intended to inform.

4. **D.** This is a main idea question. Answers A and C are not supported by the information in the passage. Answer B is contradicted by the first sentence, which implies that the French Revolution has more than one cause.

5. **B.** Each of the answer choices except answer B can be proven by specific lines in the passage. The passage does not mention emigration.

6. **D.** Because the passage says that sugar crystals will form in a few days, it's logical to infer that you can't make rock candy in one day. Food coloring isn't mentioned anywhere in the passage, nor is any reference to chemistry made. Answer C is an opinion that the passage does not support. Even if you agree with it, answer D is directly supported by information in the passage, thus making it your best choice.

7. **A.** *Solution* in some contexts could mean a way to solve a problem. In this case, though, it's a sugar/water mixture.

8. **B.** Nothing in the passage suggests that the speaker has never been to a concert. The information in the passage indicates that the speaker is an avid fan and has been so for a long time. The final statement about not being able to wait for the concert suggests that the speaker will attend.

9. **C.** The context of the passage clearly shows that the speaker is excited.

10. **D.** The final sentence in the passage talks about the effects of soap on the skin and how handmade soap is gentler than commercial soap. None of the other answer choices is supported by the passage.

11. **A.** This is a specific detail question. If you look at the passage, the first sentence uses language similar to the first answer choice. Animal fat and lavender are not mentioned in the passage. The popularity of vegetable oil is mentioned, but this contradicts answer C.

12. **B.** This is another specific detail question. Again, the language in the correct answer is similar to where you find it in the passage. All of the answer choices presented except for B are contradicted by information in the passage.

13. **D.** This is an explicit main idea question, but no one sentence states the purpose of the passage. Because the

passage starts talking about the role of castles in medieval Europe and their roles today, answer D is the best choice.

14. **C.** *Pathogen* isn't really defined in the sentence it's presented in; it's defined in the following sentence. Based on this information, you can conclude that a pathogen is an invading virus or bacteria.

15. **A.** This is a different take on the purpose question. The only choice that fits is "a process" because the passage takes you through the steps of how a vaccine works.

16. **B.** The speaker is clearly confused. The facts don't add up to her, and she can't come up with a reason for her keys to be missing.

17. **C.** Watch out for the *not* here. The passage specifically states that the speaker had the keys in her hand when she walked in the room. Because no other information is introduced to suggest that she did anything other than put the keys down on the table, answer C is the best choice.

18. **A.** In this passage, *exile* is used to describe how Napoleon was forced to leave his native country after his fall from power—basically, his expulsion. *Repentance* is to make up for a wrong committed, *subservience* is to be like a servant, and *terror* is extreme fear. The passage doesn't support any of these definitions.

19. **C.** The passage contradicts choices A and B. How the French people viewed Napoleon is not mentioned. However, the passage says Napoleon was a self-appointed emperor, which means he, not the French people, named himself as leader.

20. **D.** The passage does not touch on the justice of Napoleon's exile. The passage also makes no reference to France after Napoleon, historians, or despots, which eliminates answers B and C as possibilities. It is logical to infer that because the passage says that Napoleon escaped from Elba and immediately launched another military campaign, exiling him off the coast of Italy was not effective.

Math as Easy as Hup-2-3

The good news is that to qualify for entrance into the military, you don't have to be a math genius. You just need general skills in arithmetic, algebra, geometry, and logic. The bad news is that you have to show off what you know on two math subtests: Arithmetic Reasoning is all word problems, and Math Knowledge has lots of equations, shapes, and figuring involved.

Never fear, though. This part will refresh your memory and skills in areas of math that you likely haven't thought about since grammar school, such as adding fractions with different denominators. We also take you through more complex types of math that you may not have understood all that well the first time you touched on them in high school—but you sure will this time, with a little practice.

Arithmetic Reasoning

When most people hear the word *arithmetic*, they envision simple math: adding and subtracting, multiplying and dividing, maybe the occasional percent or fraction. No biggie, right? We all learned that in grade school.

Well, that's exactly what the Arithmetic Reasoning (AR) section of the ASVAB tests you on—but it takes everything a step further using word problems. In this section, your understanding and application of basic math skills is put to the test. However, since you're breaking down word problems to get to that basic math, your reading, analytical, and reasoning skills are also being assessed.

This chapter walks you through ways to make these reasoning problems more, well, reasonable. We show you how to break these questions into bite-size pieces (and give you some practice at it), in addition to giving you a review of basic concepts you'll likely encounter on the test.

Why Do I Have to Take This?

Basic math is a skill that everyone in life must have. But as we've said, this section isn't just about the math; it's about how you think. All branches of the military want to make sure their recruits can follow instructions carefully and logically. This is more crucial in the military than in any other type of civilian job, since the security of the nation and the lives of our men and women in the service depend on how well military personnel make decisions. That's why this section is part of the AFQT and is required for military entrance.

What to Expect

The majority of the Arithmetic Reasoning section is made up of word problems that ask you to apply logic and simple arithmetic skills. Your mission here is to pick the mathematical objectives out of a short description of circumstances. To do this, you analyze the word problem and decide what's important to your task and what's not.

Try it with the following word problem that breaks down the difference in the amount of time you have to answer each question on the CAT and PAP versions of this subtest. Then we'll tackle how to break down the question in the next section:

> On the CAT version of the Arithmetic Reasoning subtest, you have 39 minutes to answer 16 questions. On the PAP, you have 36 minutes to answer 30 questions. How much more time per question do you have on the CAT versus the PAP?

Word Problems? No Problem!

Just mentioning the phrase "word problem" is enough to make a lot of people nervous. But with a little strategy and practice, you can build up your confidence to where you're doing better than ever on this section of the ASVAB.

Basic Approach

Since you're taking a test to get into the military, we think you should approach these word problems like you are running a mission. Here are the steps you take:

1. **Gather intel.** In the field, you'd send someone on a reconnaissance mission to get information about a target. On the ASVAB, you simply read the question from beginning to end and try to figure out what it's asking you to do.

2. **Assess the situation.** After you've read the question, translate it into words that make sense to you. This will give you a better understanding of what the question is asking you to do and give you a simpler version to work off of when moving forward.

3. **Devise a plan of attack.** Write out the steps and equations you'll need to solve the problem. Seeing them on your scratch paper will help you keep track of your work as you go along and make sure you're taking a logical approach to solving the problem.

4. **Execute the mission.** Complete all steps needed to formulate the answer. Check and double check your math to make sure that it's accurate and makes sense.

5. **Debrief.** In real life, this is when you would report the results of your mission. On the ASVAB, this is when you eliminate answer choices that don't match the one you've come up with.

Let's try this approach on the word problem from the previous section:

1. **Gather intel.** On the CAT version of the Arithmetic Reasoning subtest, you have 39 minutes to answer 16 questions. On the PAP, you have 36 minutes to answer 30 questions. How much more time per question do you have on the CAT versus the PAP?

2. **Assess the situation.** The question is asking us to find the difference (red flag for subtraction) between two times. But to get those times, we have to figure out how much time there is to answer each question (red flag for division) in each section.

3. **Devise a plan of attack.** We can set up three expressions to help us work through the problem: one to figure out how long you have to work on each question on the CAT, one to do the same for the PAP, and one to calculate the difference. What you write on your scratch paper may look something like this:

Minutes per CAT question = $\frac{39}{16}$

Minutes per PAP question = $\frac{36}{30}$

Minutes per CAT question – minutes per PAP question = final answer

4. **Execute the mission.** Now, let's solve the expressions we've written and find out what answer choice we need to look for:

CAT = $\frac{39}{16}$ = 39 ÷ 16 = 2.4375

(minutes per CAT question)

PAP = $\frac{36}{30}$ = 36 ÷ 30 = 1.2 (minutes

per PAP question)

CAT – PAP = 2.4375 - 1.2 = 1.2375

5. **Debrief.** If this were a question on the ASVAB, you'd now eliminate answer choices that are not in the ballpark of 1.2375 minutes.

Practice Makes Perfect

Not too bad, right? Now let's get some practice in breaking down some more word problems. The point is to get used to the word problem format and to work through the question to the stage where you can start calculating.

For each of the following word problems, read carefully and write in your own words what you think the question is asking you to find out. Next, write out the steps and/or equations you would use to solve the problem.

1. The owner of Arty's Furniture Emporium is planning a holiday sale. A five-piece dining room set is one of the main items he wants to feature. He bought the set wholesale for $1,000 and set the retail price at $2,000. If he wants to make at least a 25% profit when selling the set, what's the lowest amount that he can set the sale price?

What it's asking: _____

_____

How you would solve: _____

_____

_____

2. A car salesman makes a 5% commission on every sale he closes. If the average car sells for $18,500, about how many cars would the salesman have to sell in a month to make enough to pay his $1,500 rent?

What it's asking: _____

_____

How you would solve: _____

_____

_____

3. If a factory can produce 45 widgets in 15 minutes, how many widgets can it produce in an 8-hour work day?

What it's asking: _____

_____

How you would solve: _____

_____

_____

4. A graduating class has 135 students. If $\frac{8}{20}$ of the class's students are women, what number of students are men?

What it's asking: _____

_____

How you would solve: _____

_____

_____

_____

Arithmetic Review

Now that you're feeling more comfortable with word problems, it's time to review some of the math you'll be using on the AR subtest. To start, take a look at some basic terms and symbols. Some may be familiar, while others may be new.

Arithmetic Vocab

Term	Definition
Natural numbers	Counting numbers, like 1, 2, 3, and so on. Natural numbers are always positive, and 0 is not a natural number. When a set of natural numbers includes 0 (0, 1, 2, 3), you're dealing with whole numbers.
Integer	Any whole number and its opposite (the opposite of 3 is –3; the opposite of 5 is –5). –2, –1, 0, 1, and 2 are all integers; –3.1 or 2.5 are not.
Prime number	An integer that can be divided by only 1 and itself. 2, 3, 5, 7, 11, 13, and 17 are prime numbers. 1 is not a prime number because 1 is its only factor.

Term	Definition
Factor	A number that can be evenly divided into a number. Factors of 12 are 1, 2, 3, 4, 6, and 12. They all divide into 12 evenly.
Multiple	The product of two natural numbers: 36 is a multiple of 9 since 9×4 is 36. 14 is a multiple of 7 since $7 \times 2 = 14$.
Product	Answer to a multiplication problem. This and words like *times*, *double*, and *of* in a word problem can indicate the need for multiplication.
Quotient	Answer to a division problem. This and words like *per, out of,* and *into* in a word problem can indicate the need for division.
Sum	Answer to an addition problem. This and words like *total* and *combined* in a word problem can indicate the need for addition.
Difference	Answer to a subtraction problem. This and words like *minus, decrease,* and *fall* in a word problem can indicate the need for subtraction.

Order of Operations

You may remember the "Please Excuse My Dear Aunt Sally," or PE(MD)(AS), rule from grade school. This mnemonic applies to order of operations, or the order in which you perform mathematical processes in an expression with more than one type of the following symbols: +, ×, ÷, and –.

You need to follow a specific order to solve these problems correctly. First, look for any expressions that are separated into parentheses and solve these first, applying any exponents (discussed later in the chapter) that may be present.

Next, move on to multiplication and division, and solve these parts of the expression moving left to right. Finally, perform the addition and subtraction operations, moving left to right. Once the expression in the parentheses has been reduced to a number, repeat the order of operations on the entire expression.

Try this with the following expression: $(3)(4 - 1)^3 + 2 - 4$

1. **Parentheses.** Solve the expression in parentheses: $4 - 1 = 3$.

2. **Exponent.** Apply the exponent to the 3 in the parentheses. This is the same as saying $3 \times 3 \times 3$. The product is 27.

3. **Multiplication.** The new expression is $(3)27 + 2 - 4$. Because the 3 is alone in parentheses, we know we have to multiply it by 27. This gives us 81.

4. **Addition and subtraction.** Now the expression is $81 + 2 - 4$. We solve left to right to finish: $81 + 2 = 83$ and $83 - 4 = 79$.

Always keep order of operations in mind when you have a mixed expression like this. Solving in a different order can lead you to a wrong answer.

Positive and Negative Numbers

If you think of numbers in terms of a line, you'll be able to understand positives and negatives. At the center of the line is 0. All numbers to the right of 0 are positive, and all numbers to the left are negative (0 is a neutral number).

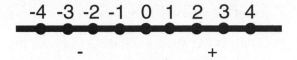

Easy enough, right? The tricky part with positives and negatives come when you start moving up and down that line through addition and subtraction. Remember:

▸ The number on the right of an expression tells you how many units to move and in which direction on the line.

▸ When you see an addition sign (+), you move to the right on the number line.

▸ When you see a subtraction sign (-), you move to the left.

Look at the following expression: $2 - 1$. Your first instinct might be to read this as 2 minus 1, but really, what you're seeing in terms of the number line is $+2 + (-1)$. This expression is telling you to start at the $+2$ position on the number line and move one step to the left, or -1. The result is that you end up at $+1$ on the number line. Try it on the previous number line.

This is the basic idea of how we deal with adding and subtracting positives and negatives in math. Use the previous number line to illustrate the following:

▸ **Positive + Positive =** Move up the number line; for example, $1 + 1 = 2$.

▸ **Positive + Negative =** Move down the number line; for example, $3 + (-4) = -1$.

▸ **Negative + Positive =** Move up the number line; for example, $-2 + 4 = 2$.

- **Negative + Negative =** Move down the number line; for example, $-3 + (-1) = -4$.

- **Negative – Negative =** When you have two negative symbols, they cancel each other out and make a positive. For example, $-2 - (-2)$ is the same as $-2 + 2$, and you would move up the number line when you solve. The answer is 0.

- **Positive – Negative =** With this type of problem, you have two negatives as well: $1 - (-1)$. The negatives become a positive, so you need to move up the number line: $1 - (-1) = 1 + 1 = 2$.

Multiplication and division problems are a little different:

1. Multiply or divide the numbers in the problem like you normally would.

2. Then figure out whether the result is positive or negative. Only the negatives affect the sign of the answer:

   - An odd number of negatives will result in a *negative* answer: $-14 / 7 = -2$ (one negative); $(-2)(-4)(-5) = -40$ (three negatives).

   - An even number of negatives will result in a *positive* answer: $-27/-3 = 9$ (two negatives); $(-4)(-6)(-8)(-10) = 1{,}920$ (four negatives).

Exponents and Roots

When you see a term like x^2, you may automatically think "exponent." However, this is actually a "power." The main number or variable in the term is called the *base*, while the raised number is the exponent. For example, in 4^3, 4 is the base, 3 is the exponent, and all together it's called 4 to the third power (or 4 cubed).

No matter how you say it, though, exponents tell you one thing: how many times to multiply the base times itself. All 4^3 means is $4 \times 4 \times 4$.

Some rules to remember with exponents:

- A base to the first power (x^1) is just the base shown. A base to the zero power (x^0) equals 1.

- When you multiply like variables, you get an exponent: $y \times y = y^2$.

- When multiplying two like variables with exponents, keep the variable the same and add the exponents: $x^2 \times x^4 = x^6$.

- When you apply an exponent to terms in parentheses that have powers, you multiply exponents to simplify the expression: $(x^3)^3 = x^{3 \times 3} = x^9$.

- When you multiply separate powers, you multiply the coefficients and then add the exponents: $3x^2 \times 2x^2 \times 2x^2 = 12x^6$.

- When you divide powers, treat it like a fraction and reduce. Write out the base the number of times indicated in the exponent and cancel out like terms:

$$x^4 \div x^3 = \frac{x^4}{x^3} = \frac{x \times x \times x \times x}{x \times x \times x} = \frac{\cancel{x} \times \cancel{x} \times \cancel{x} \times x}{\cancel{x} \times \cancel{x} \times \cancel{x}} = \frac{x}{1} = x$$

- When you multiply unlike variables with exponents, combine them into one term: $x^2 \times y^2 = x^2 y^2$.

- A negative exponent, such as 4^{-2}, doesn't tell you the number of times to multiply the base by itself. Instead, it tells you how many times to divide the number itself from 1. Take a look at how this works with 4^{-2}:

  1. Calculate the value of 42:
     $4 \times 4 = 16$

2. Write the answer as a fraction: $\frac{16}{1}$

3. Flip the fraction: $\frac{1}{16}$

A number or variable that is raised to the second power is called a *square*. The opposite of a squared base is a square root, the number that when multiplied by itself, equals that power. For example, $10^2 = 10 \times 10 = 100$. If you wanted to find the square root of 100, you would use a radical sign, which would make your expression look like this: $\sqrt{100} = 10$.

For the ASVAB, it's easier to learn some common square roots than to learn how to break them down. Exponents from 1 to 10 are easy: $\sqrt{4} = 2$, $\sqrt{9} = 3$, $\sqrt{16} = 4$. When you're asked to find a square root of a number you're unfamiliar with, knowing the squares of the first 20 natural numbers can help you quickly zero in on the correct square root answer.

Multiples and Factors

When you need to factor a number, what you're doing is figuring out how many pairs of natural numbers can be multiplied to get the number you're factoring. For example, what numbers can you multiply to get 12? 1×12, 2×6, and 3×4. Guess what? You just calculated the factors of 12! 1, 2, 3, 4, and 6 are all factors of 12.

You need to know three things when calculating multiples and factors.

Prime Factorization

This action breaks down a number into the product of its prime factors.

1. Divide out a prime number again and again until you have 1 as an answer.

2. List all the primes you used and multiply.

Let's try this with the number 27:

$$
\begin{array}{r|r}
3 & 27 \\
3 & 9 \\
3 & 3 \\
  & 1
\end{array}
$$

Now list the prime numbers you used on the outside (3, 3, and 3) and then multiply: $3 \times 3 \times 3 = 27$

A good place to start dividing with prime factorization is 2 if you have an even number, 3 if the sum of the digits is a multiple of 3 (for example, 3,654; $3 + 6 + 5 + 4 = 18$, which is a multiple of 3), and 5 for numbers ending in 0 and 5.

Greatest Common Factor (GCF)

The general idea here is to multiply all the common prime factors of two numbers. The product is the highest factor they have in common.

To find the GCF of two numbers:

1. Use prime factorization.

2. Multiply the common factors.

Try it with 32 and 36:

$$
\begin{array}{r|r}
2 & 32 \\
2 & 16 \\
2 & 8 \\
2 & 4 \\
2 & 2 \\
  & 1
\end{array}
\qquad
\begin{array}{r|r}
2 & 36 \\
2 & 18 \\
2 & 9 \\
2 & 3 \\
  & 1
\end{array}
\qquad
\begin{aligned}
32 &= \left[2 \times 2\right] \times 2 \times 2 \times 2 \\
36 &= \left[2 \times 2\right] \times 3 \times 3
\end{aligned}
$$

The only shared factor here is 2×2, or 2^2, which when multiplied, gives you a greatest common factor of 4. If there had been more than one shared factor, you would have multiplied them all, and the product would be your greatest common factor.

Least Common Multiple (LCM)

This is the smallest number that can be divided by two specific numbers.

To find the LCM of two numbers, follow these steps:

1. Use prime factorization.

2. Multiply each factor by the greatest number of times it appears in any one factorization.

Take a look at the following example, where you need to find the LCM of 15 and 25:

$$15 = 3 \times 5$$

$$25 = 5 \times 5$$

$$3 \times 5 \times 5 = 75$$

The factors are 3 and 5. The greatest number of times we see these factors is 5 = twice; 3 = once. Combine each of these occurrences in the expression $3 \times 5 \times 5$, and find that 75 is the smallest number that 15 and 25 can both divide into evenly.

Fractions

Fractions represent a part of a whole, which means that every whole number can be expressed as a fraction: $4 = \frac{4}{1}$. They follow a specific format: $\frac{3}{4}$. The bottom number (denominator) tells us how many pieces make up the whole. The top number (numerator) tells us how many parts of that whole we are dealing with.

> **TEST TIP**
>
> The line between numerator and denominator can also indicate division, which is an essential operation when dealing with fractions. If the sight of a fraction in a problem freaks you out a little, think of it as a division problem instead and treat it that way.

Here are a few things to remember:

▸ When the numerator is less than the denominator, it is a proper fraction: $\frac{2}{3}$.

▸ When the numerator and denominator are the same number, the fraction equals 1: $\frac{2}{2} = 1$.

▸ When the numerator is either equal to or greater than the denominator, you have an improper fraction, which represents something that is either more than or equal to 1: $\frac{10}{4}$.

▸ When you simplify an improper fraction, you break it down into a mixed fraction (a whole number and a fraction together in one term). To do this, divide the bottom number into the top (that result is your whole number) and use the remainder as the numerator of a new fraction, with the denominator remaining the same:

$$\frac{13}{6} = 2\frac{1}{6}.$$

For the most part, you'll be working with proper fractions on the ASVAB. For proper fractions, you need to know how to do the following:

▸ **Simplify.** Reduce a fraction to its simplest form. Always reduce your fractions before attempting any other action with them. Break down both the numerator and denominator into prime factors, and get rid of any factors each side has in common. What's left is the simplified fraction:

$$\frac{9}{36} = \frac{3\times3}{2\times2\times3\times3} = \frac{\cancel{3\times3}}{2\times2\times\cancel{3\times3}} = \frac{1}{4}$$

▶ **Add.** Add only the numerators when the denominators are the same. If your fractions have different denominators, you have to get them to match. Multiply each fraction by the opposite denominator as both numerator and denominator.

For example, if you want to add $\frac{1}{2}+\frac{1}{3}$, you multiply the first fraction by $\frac{3}{3}$, since the denominator opposite the first fraction is 3. You multiply the second fraction by $\frac{2}{2}$, since the denominator opposite the second fraction is 2. The result is $\frac{1}{2}\times\frac{3}{3}=\frac{3}{6}$ and $\frac{1}{3}\times\frac{2}{2}=\frac{2}{6}$. Now add the numerators on the resulting fractions and find that:

$$\frac{3}{6}+\frac{2}{6}=\frac{5}{6}$$

So, what do you do if you have to add mixed fractions? Add the fractions first and then add the whole numbers, including any that result from adding the fractions:

$$2\frac{5}{8}+3\frac{1}{2}$$

Add fractions first:

$$\frac{5}{8}\times\frac{2}{2}=\frac{10}{16}$$
$$\frac{1}{2}\times\frac{8}{8}=\frac{8}{16}$$
$$\frac{10}{16}+\frac{8}{16}=\frac{18}{16}=1\frac{2}{16}=1\frac{1}{8}$$

You had 2 whole numbers to start with: 2 and 3. When adding your fractions, you now have an additional whole number: 1. Add all the whole numbers, including the mixed fraction you've just created: 2 + 3 + 1 = 6.

Your final answer is $6\frac{1}{8}$.

▶ **Subtract.** Apply the same rules you use for addition:

$$\frac{1}{2}-\frac{1}{3}=\frac{3}{6}-\frac{2}{6}=\frac{1}{6}$$

If you have to subtract mixed numbers, turn them into improper fractions before doing anything. To do this, multiply the whole number by the denominator. Then add the product to the numerator. Your denominator stays the same. Try it with $2\frac{3}{8}-1\frac{1}{2}$:

$$2\frac{3}{8}=\frac{8\times2+3}{8}=\frac{19}{8}$$
$$1\frac{1}{2}=\frac{2\times1+1}{2}=\frac{3}{2}$$
$$\frac{19}{8}-\frac{3}{2}$$

Once all your fractions are converted, follow the same steps you would to subtract proper fractions, and simplify your answer back to a mixed fraction:

$$\frac{19}{8}\times\frac{2}{2}=\frac{38}{16}$$
$$\frac{3}{2}\times\frac{8}{8}=\frac{24}{16}$$
$$\frac{38}{16}-\frac{24}{16}=\frac{14}{16}=\frac{7}{8}$$

▶ **Multiply.** Multiply the numerators and denominators straight across. Then simplify the resulting fraction:

$$\frac{1}{3}\times\frac{2}{4}=\frac{2}{12}=\frac{1}{6}$$

If you have to multiply mixed numbers, turn them into improper fractions and follow the same steps as above. When you simplify the answer, turn it back into a mixed number.

- **Divide.** Set up your problem as if you were multiplying. Then flip the numbers of the second fraction, which is called a *reciprocal*, and multiply across:

$$\frac{1}{3} \div \frac{2}{4} = \frac{1}{3} \times \frac{4}{2} = \frac{4}{6} = \frac{2}{3}$$

When dividing mixed numbers, turn them into improper fractions and proceed as you would with any other division problem.

Decimals

Just as every whole number is a fraction, every whole number is a decimal. The decimal place is directly behind the whole number: $4 = 4.0$. Everything after the decimal point is a portion of a whole.

Here are some important things to remember:

- **Add and subtract.** Perform these operations like you would with any other problem. Line up your decimal points before you attempt to solve these problems. This ensures that you keep your numbers in line and that your answer has the decimal in the right place:

$$\begin{array}{r} 12.3 \\ + \ 1.2 \\ \hline 13.5 \end{array}$$

- **Multiply.** Multiply the problem as you normally would. Then count up the *total* number of decimal places in *each* factor of the original expression, and put the decimal point that many places to the left of the last number in your product. Try it with 5.4×2.3:

1. Multiply like normal:

$$\begin{array}{r} 54 \\ \times 23 \\ \hline 162 \\ +1080 \\ \hline 1242 \end{array}$$

2. Since there are two decimal places (one number after the decimal in each of the factors) in the original expression, place the decimal in the answer two places from the right: 12.42

[**CLASSIFIED INTEL**

You can drop any zeroes at the end whenever you deal with decimals.]

- **Divide.** The trick to dividing decimals is working with a whole-number divisor. Turning decimals into whole numbers is as simple as moving the decimal point in the right direction. Here's how you'd approach $215.65 \div 1.729$.

1. Write out the expression like this:

$$1.729\overline{)215.65}$$

2. The outside number is the divisor. Move the decimal point three places to the right so that you have a whole number:

$$1729\overline{)215.65}$$

3. Now move the decimal point of the dividend (the inside number) three places to the right. Since the decimal point is only two places in, add in as many 0s as needed to make up three places:

$$1729\overline{)215650}$$

4. Divide like normal and get 124725. Since the decimal point in the dividend is after the 0, just move it straight up into the quotient to get $1729\overline{)215650.00}$ with quotient 124.73.

▶ **Decimals to fractions.** To convert a decimal to a fraction, make the decimal the numerator and make 1 the denominator. Then move the decimal point to the right until you have a whole number. For each place you move the decimal to the right, add a zero to the denominator. Finally, simplify the fraction:

$$.25 = \frac{.25}{1} = \frac{25}{100} = \frac{1}{4}$$

To turn a fraction into a decimal, simply divide the numerator by the denominator:

$$\frac{1}{2} = 1 \div 2 = .50$$

Percent

Percents represent a part of 100. Whenever you have a question that involves percent, you're dealing with either decimals or fractions (whichever works best for you).

In decimals, 100% is the same as 1. Anything less than 100% is shown to the right of the decimal place: 4% = .04; 50% = .50.

In fractions, 100% is $\frac{100}{100}$. When you want to turn a whole number into a percent expressed as a fraction, simply make the number the numerator and use 100 as the denominator: $4\% = \frac{4}{100}$ Then, if possible, reduce.

In the AR section of the ASVAB, you may be asked to find what percentage one value is of another value. When asked to do this, divide the smaller number by the larger to find the percentage.

Try it here:

> You just got notification that you will receive a $2,160 increase in your salary of $36,000 per year. By what percent did your pay just go up?

This question is asking you to calculate what percent of $36,000 is $2,160. To do this, you divide 36000 ÷ 2160.00 = .06. This means your salary increased by 6 percent.

Ratios

Ratios compare two values and are expressed in three main ways: using fractions, with a colon (:), or using the word *to*. On the ASVAB, they usually express some sort of group relationship. The easiest way to work with ratios is to turn them into fractions and reduce.

> A dance club has 25 men and 45 women. What's the ratio of men to women?

Here you're being asked to write a mathematical statement that shows the relationship of men to women. Write the fraction the way you read it. That means the value for men is the numerator and the value for women is the denominator: $\frac{25}{45} = \frac{5}{9}$

Proportions

When you compare ratios, you use proportions. Like with ratios, it's easiest to treat these as fractions. Two must-knows for the ASVAB:

▸ **Test for equality.** Cross-multiply the fractions. If the products are the same, your proportions are equal.

Test to see if $\frac{2}{4}$ is proportional to $\frac{6}{8}$.

If $2 \times 8 = 4 \times 6$, then it is. In this case, the values on either side of the equals sign are not the same ($2 \times 8 = 16$ and $4 \times 6 = 24$), so these two fractions are not proportional. If the first fraction had been $\frac{3}{4}$, they would have been proportional: $3 \times 8 = 24$ and $4 \times 6 = 24$.

▸ **Solve for an unknown quantity.** Cross multiply the two proportions in fraction format and use a variable (see Chapter 9) for the unknown value. Try it with the following:

$\frac{3}{5} = \frac{x}{10}$ Start by cross multiplying:

$3 \times 10 = 30$ and $5 \times x = 30$. To find the value of x, divide both sides of the second equation by 5:

$$\frac{\cancel{5}}{\cancel{5}} \times x = \frac{30}{5}$$

$$x = 6$$

This gives you a final answer of $x = 6$.

Rates

Rates are special ratios that compare two different measurements. Examples include:

unit price $\left(\frac{\text{Price}}{\text{Number of items}} \right)$, speed $\left(\frac{\text{Distance}}{\text{Time}} \right)$, distance (rate × time), interest

(amount borrowed × interest rate × time of loan), and time $\left(\frac{\text{Distance}}{\text{Rate}} \right)$.

On the AR section of the ASVAB, figure out what the question is asking and plug your values into the appropriate equation. Solve for the missing value.

Averages

Calculating averages is simple math. When asked for an average of something, add up all the terms that are given and then divide by the number of terms. For example, the average of 3, 4, 6, and 7 $= \frac{3+4+6+7}{4} = \frac{20}{4} = 5$.

Scientific Notation

Scientific notation is a way of using exponents to shorten a long number and still have it represent the correct value. To do this:

1. Move the decimal point to the right of the leftmost digit. With 248,500,000, you'd move the decimal eight places to the left, to get 2.48500000.

2. Drop all the 0s at the end of the number: 2.485.

3. Multiply by the power of 10 the number of places you moved the decimal: 2.485×10^8.

Factorials

These look strange but are really easy. Say you get a question that looks like this: 3! All you do is list all the numbers in descending order from 1 to 3 and multiply them together: $3! = 3 \times 2 \times 1 = 6$. Use this same pattern whenever you see a number with an exclamation point after it.

Mathematic Knowledge

If you're anything like we were in high school, the thought of having to sit through an algebra or geometry class was not the most pleasant part of your day. With all the lines, letters (some even in Greek!), shapes, and rules, learning and applying these math skills can be confusing and overwhelming.

The military doesn't expect you to be a math genius, however. The Math Knowledge (MK) section of the ASVAB tests you on only basic math, algebra, and geometry skills that you likely acquired by the time you were a sophomore in high school. The problem is you probably haven't used these skills since then, either.

This chapter goes over what types of questions you'll see on this section of the ASVAB, strategies for working them out, and a thorough review of the main subject areas you'll encounter on the test.

Why Do I Have to Take This?

The purpose of taking algebra in high school isn't as much about learning skills that you'll apply in everyday life as it is to teach you how to think logically. Unless you pursue a technical career that involves math or science, you will likely never have to worry about solving inequalities or manipulating polynomials in real life.

Still, testing you on your ability to work with these types of math problems is a good way to measure your abilities to reason, to follow a multistep process, and to apply logic to a problem. All of these are skills you need to perform just about every job in the military, which could explain why Math Knowledge is part of the AFQT.

The bottom line is that you need to do well on this section to gain entrance to the military as a whole, in addition to qualify for many jobs.

What to Expect

Mathematics Knowledge is a relatively short section. On the CAT, you need to answer 16 questions in 20 minutes (1.25 minutes per question). For the PAP, you've got 25 questions in 24 minutes (just under a minute each).

TEST TIP

If math isn't your strong suit, make sure that you time yourself when you practice for this section. This will help increase your confidence and give you a better idea of what types of questions you can answer quickly and what types require more time.

The questions in this subtest are much more straightforward than those on the Arithmetic Reasoning test. Here you're asked to solve equations, apply algebraic and geometric concepts, and tackle the occasional short word problem. Oh yeah, there are also some basic arithmetic questions.

Keep in mind that many questions will require you to take several steps to come up with the correct answer, so be prepared to look beyond the surface before attacking any of these questions. You'll also have to figure out the answers to all of the math questions on the ASVAB the old-fashioned way. That's right, calculators are not allowed. The only tools you're allowed are pencils and scratch paper, so it's best to get into the habit now.

Plan of Attack

People get flustered on the math sections of standardized tests for many reasons. While this is perfectly normal, we're here to tell you that there really is nothing to fear if you know what to expect and how to approach the questions. Here are a few tricks to take some of the guesswork out of working on this section of the ASVAB:

▸ **Translate the question.** Standardized math tests are notorious for asking you to complete complex questions with many steps. Take some time to really read and understand the question before diving in. Put it in your own words, if you can. You may find that it's asking you to do something other than what you thought at first glance.

▸ **Estimate the answer.** After reading the question, try to estimate the answer. For example, if you need to find a factor of 12, you know you're looking for either 1 or a number less than 12. Eliminate anything that doesn't fit these criteria. This is a quick way to narrow your choices and help you decide whether the answer you've calculated is reasonable. In some cases, it can even lead you to the right answer without having to do much math at all.

▸ **Substitute.** If the question you're dealing with asks you to solve for a variable, try to plug the answer choices into the equation you're working with. This means you don't have to deal with unknowns and you can do simple math with real numbers. The right answer is the one that works in the equation.

▸ **Eliminate.** Again, we can't stress enough how important it is to eliminate answer choices you know are wrong.

Algebra Review

The language of mathematics is very complex. If you're not familiar with the words used to describe numbers, parts of equations, and actions you're supposed to take in a problem, you'll be confused throughout our discussion about the types of math you need to know. So before we dive into the basic concepts of algebra, familiarize yourself with the terms in the following table.

Algebra Vocab

Term	Definition
Expression	Mathematical statement that combines terms and operations, such as $9 + 1$, $5x(9)$ or $4x^2 + 7x - 10$.
Operation	Action you need to take with a value: addition, subtraction, division, or multiplication. See Chapter 8 for more on this.
Equation	A mathematical statement that shows two equal expressions: $7 + 4 = 11$ or $8x = 16$.
Variable	Letter in an equation or an expression that stands in place of an unknown quantity; in $4x = 12$, x is the variable.
Coefficient	Number that multiplies a variable; in $4x = 12$, 4 is the coefficient and means $4 \times x$.
Term	A single number, variable, or combinations thereof. Examples: $8x$, x, xy^2, 15.

Term	Definition
Constant	A number that stands by itself in an expression or equation; in $5x + 2$, 2 is the constant.
Distributive	This just means that whenever you see a number, variable, or expression outside a set of parentheses, you multiply that to each term inside the parentheses. With the expression $x(x + 6)$, you multiply x by every term in the parentheses, which gives you $x^2 + 6x$.

Now let's look at some initial concepts that will help you on a number of ASVAB questions.

Equations

Working with equations is one of the most basic tasks in algebra. If you remember the definition of equation discussed earlier, you're dealing with two amounts that equal each other. It's your job to either solve the equation or solve for one term in the equation. To do this, you'll have to move terms around and make sure what you do to one side of the equation, you do to the other.

Let's say that you're asked to solve for a variable. You do this by isolating the variable to one side of the equation and the numbers to the other. How do you do that? Get rid of the numbers on one side of the equation by canceling it out with a reverse operation (subtraction is the reverse of addition, division is the reverse of multiplication, and so on). Then do the same to the other side.

Check out this example: $14 + x = -4$.

You want to get rid of the 14 so that the x is alone on the left side of the equation. Because the 14 is positive, you add a negative 14 to cancel it out, and then you do the same to the expression on the other side of the equals sign.

$$14 - 14 + x = -4 + (-14)$$

The rest is simple arithmetic. If you remember from Chapter 8, when you add a negative to a negative, you go down the number line, which means your sum is a negative. In this case, $-4 + (-14) = -18$, which leaves you with a final answer of $x = -18$.

Unfortunately, not every problem will have such a nice and neat answer. More often, you're going to have to solve for a variable equaling an expression. Your answers can look more like $x = y + 2$ instead of a simple $x = 2$. If the question you're working on asks you to solve for one variable "in terms of" another, this is what you're going to have to do.

Isolate the variable you're asked to solve for on one side of the equation, the same as you would with a number. The only difference is that you're moving around terms, not just numbers. For example, if you're asked to solve for a in terms of y if $12a - 8y = 9a + 4y + 6$, your goal is to solve until you have a by itself on one side of the equals sign.

Start by adding $8y$ to both sides:

$$12a - 8y + 8y = 9a + 4y + 6 + 8y$$

Now combine *like terms*:

$$12a = 9a + 12y + 6$$

Next, add $-9a$ to both sides:

$$12a + (-9a) = 9a + (-9a) + 12y + 6$$

Now combine like terms again:

$$3a = 12y + 6$$

Finally, divide every term on both sides of the equation by 3:

$$\frac{3a}{3} = \frac{12y+6}{3}$$

$$a = 4y + 2$$

> **DEFINITION**
>
> **Like terms** refers to terms that have the same variables and exponent. For example, with $8 \times 2 + 10x + x - x^2$, the only terms you can add are $10x$ and x to make $11x$ because they share the exact same variable and exponent. (In this case, the exponent is 1, which is implied. See our explanation of exponents in Chapter 8.)

Some equation problems will give you the values of the variables. When you see this, just plug in the numbers and solve according to order of operations.

Inequalities

When you see something that looks like an equation but has a >, <, ≤, ≥, or ≠ sign, you're dealing with an inequality. Here's what these symbols mean:

▸ **Greater than symbol (>).** The value to the left is greater than the value to the right.

▸ **Less than symbol (<).** The value to the left is less than the value to the right.

▸ **Less than or equal to symbol (≤).** The value to the left is less than or equal to the value to the right.

▸ **Greater than or equal to symbol (≥).** The value to the left is greater than or equal to the value to the right.

▸ **Not equal symbol (≠).** The values are unequal.

Without getting too mathematical on you, your job with inequalities is not to find one answer, but to find a range of answers (which you don't have to write out). To do this, work an inequality through like you would any other equation:

$$14 + a < 25$$

$$\cancel{14 + (-14)} + a < 25 - 14$$

$$a < 11$$

Here, your answer is saying that the value of a is some number less than 11.

Simple, right? However, when you multiply or divide an inequality by a negative number, you have to flip the inequality symbol. Take a look:

$$20 > -10a$$

This says 20 is greater than −10. To solve for a in this inequality, you have to divide both sides by −10:

$$\frac{20}{-10} > \frac{-10a}{-10}$$

The 10s on the right cancel each other out, leaving only the a. Divide 20 by −10 and flip the symbol, and you're done: $-2 < a$.

Polynomials

Okay, it's a big word, but all it really means is that you're looking at an expression involving one or more terms that may be separated by an operation. Any expression that has one or more terms is called a *polynomial*. A term with more than three terms is referred to only as a polynomial and does not have a special name. You should be aware of three basic types of polynomials:

▸ **Monomial.** This is a polynomial that has just one term: 5, 10x, and 4xy^2 are all monomials.

▸ **Binomial.** This is an expression with two terms joined by operations: 8xy + 4 and 6 − 2 are binomials.

▸ **Trinomial.** These are expressions with three terms joined by operations, such as $x^2 + 6y + 4$.

On the ASVAB, you're asked to add, subtract, multiply, and divide much more complicated polynomial expressions and equations than the ones you've seen so far. Remember a few rules when you're dealing with polynomials:

▸ **Simplify before you solve.** Combine like terms. To do this, simply add the coefficients.

▸ **Multiply or divide.** Where you can, apply multiplication and/or division operations. To do this, multiply or divide coefficients like you normally would. Then do the same to the variables and exponents. For multiplication, you can multiply and combine unlike bases: $(8x)(2xy^3) = 8 \times 2$ and $x \times x \times y \times y \times y = 16x^2y^3$.

With division, treat the operation like a fraction. For example, with $\frac{24a^2}{4a^6}$, you would reduce the coefficients like you would any fraction: $\frac{6a^2}{a^6}$. Next, reduce the exponents. An easy way to do that is to write out the base the number of times indicated in the exponent: $\frac{a \times a}{a \times a \times a \times a \times a \times a}$.

In this example, the top two a's cancel out two of the a's on the bottom: $\frac{\cancel{a \times a}}{\cancel{a \times a} \times a \times a \times a \times a}$, leaving four behind in the denominator. Your final answer to this problem would be $\frac{6}{a^4}$.

▶ **Use FOIL when multiplying or dividing binomials.** FOIL stands for "first, outer, inner, and last," or the order in which you would multiply or divide terms (most often multiplication). Take a look:

$(3x + 1)(2x - 4)$, you multiply *first* terms $3x \times 2x$, *outer* terms $3x \times -4$, *inner* terms $1 \times 2x$, and *last* terms 1×-4. The resulting equation looks like this:

$(3x + 1)(2x - 4) = (3x \times 2x) + (3x \times -4) + (1 \times 2x) + (1 \times -4)$

Now solve what's in parentheses:

$(3x + 1)(2x - 4) = (6x^2) + (-12x) + (2x) + (-4)$

Finally, simplify the expression by combining like terms:

$(3x + 1)(2x - 4) = 6x^2 + (-10x) + (-4)$

TEST TIP

The final expression you have in this example is a quadratic expression. We explain more about this later in this chapter. For now, memorize this format so you can recognize it easily.

Simple Polynomial Factoring

Factoring polynomials is a common algebraic task that challenges you to find out what smaller expressions make up a larger expression. Unfortunately, this means you have to work backward to figure out what was multiplied to get the expression or equation you're given. It's not as bad as it sounds. We break it down for you piece by piece.

Let's start with simple factoring. The first thing you need to do is figure out the GCF (see Chapter 8), or the largest factor that two

or more terms share (variables included). If variables are also involved, you need to look for the variable term with the lowest common exponent. For example, if you're looking for the GCF for $27x^2 + 15x$, your GCF would actually be $3x$, because 3 is the greatest factor 27 and 15 have in common and x^1 is shared by both terms.

After you've determined the GCF, divide each term by the GCF. Place the simplified terms separated by their operations in parentheses and place the GCF outside.

Let's try it. Factor the previous expression: $27x^2 + 15x$. We know the GCF is $3x$, so we start by breaking down each term into prime factors:

$27x^2 = 3 \times 3 \times 3 \times x \times x$

$15x = 3 \times 5 \times x$

What do both of these have in common? One $3 \times x$. Simplify each of these by crossing out one $3 \times x$ in each expression:

$27x^2 = 3 \times 3 \times \cancel{3 \times x} \times x$

$15x = \cancel{3 \times} 5 \times \cancel{x}$

Now combine like terms and place the new expression in parentheses with $3x$ outside: $27x^2 + 15x = 3x(9x + 5)$. To check to see if you're right, multiply each term in parentheses by $3x$: $3x \times 9x = 27x^2$ and $3x \times 5 = 15x$.

Factoring Quadratic Expressions

Now that you have a good idea of how to work simple factoring, let's move on to something a little more complicated: factoring quadratic expressions.

If you're presented with an expression that has the following structure or if the expression you're left with after factoring out the GCF has this structure, think quadratic expression: $ax^2 + bx + c$. Here, the x's can be any variable, a and b are coefficients, and c is a constant. All of the following are quadratic expressions:

$y^2 + 13y + 30; x^2 + 10x + 25; a^2 + 7a + 12.$

When you factor quadratic expressions, you're actually working FOIL backward to find the two binomials that when multiplied, make up the quadratic. You do this in a few simple steps, which we show you using $x^2 + 9x + 14$.

First, create two sets of binomials, with the expression's variable as the first term: $(x \quad)(x \quad)$.

To figure out the second terms in each of the parentheses, list out the factors of the last term. Now find two that when added together equal the coefficient of the middle term. With the previous example, we would break down 14 into factors: 1×14 and 2×7. (It's a good idea to do this with negatives as well.)

When you add 2 and 7, you have 9, which is the coefficient of the middle term. Plug these numbers into the parentheses: $(x + 2)(x + 7)$. Finally, figure out whether you need positive or negative signs and where. Because both 2 and 7 are positive, use an addition sign in both sets of parentheses (shown previously). If the 2, 7, or both had negatives, you would use a subtraction sign in the parentheses.

To check your work, FOIL the binomials you've made. The answer should be the original equation:

$(x + 2)(x + 7) = (x \times x) + (x \times 7) + (2 \times x) + (2 \times 7)$

$(x + 2)(x + 7) = (x^2) + (7x) + (2x) + 14$

$(x + 2)(x + 7) = x^2 + 9x + 14$

TEST TIP

If you want to save a lot of time and brain power, when you're asked to factor a quadratic expression, FOIL the answer choices. The one that equals the expression in the question is your answer.

Geometry Review

Many people find geometry to be much easier to handle than algebra. This could be because there are more steadfast rules in geometry and fewer exceptions. Like algebra, geometry is meant to teach you logic. Unlike algebra, geometry has many more practical applications, such as figuring out how much flooring you need for a room based on its dimensions.

The type of geometry that's on the ASVAB concentrates mostly on a handful of concepts that you need to brush up on to get you through. Familiarize yourself with the terminology in the following table.

Geometry Vocab

Term	Definition
Polygon	A closed two-dimensional shape made up of at least three sides. Examples are a triangle, a hexagon, and a quadrilateral.
Area	The space an object occupies. Usually measured in square units.
Perimeter	The distance around an object.
Vertex	The point where the two lines that make up an angle intersect.

(continues)

Term	Definition
Line	A 180° angle that stretches infinitely in two directions.
Ray	Part of a line that has one finite endpoint but goes on infinitely in one direction.

Lines

Lines form the basis of geometry, and you'll see them in many forms. For the purpose of an ASVAB question, the most important things to know about lines are that they're infinite (they stretch in either direction without end) and can be segmented. Some specific line types you should know include the following:

▶ **Line segment.** This is a part of a line with two endpoints. It's often broken up into several smaller segments that are labeled with letters. The midpoint is the marking directly in the center of the line.

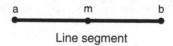

Line segment

You may be asked to identify certain parts of a line segment, such as its midpoint; calculate the length of a line segment based on information given; or apply properties of certain types of lines to figure out lengths or angle values.

▶ **Parallel lines.** These are special types of lines that run next to each other but never meet.

Parallel lines

▶ **Perpendicular lines.** Two lines are perpendicular if they intersect at a point and the resulting angles are all 90°. See the following diagram for an example.

Perpendicular lines

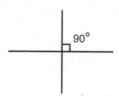

Angles

Angles are simply formed when two lines, rays, or line segments intersect at a common point; they are measured in degrees. Angles you should know include these:

▶ **Right.** Angle that looks like an *L*. It measures 90°; the lines are perpendicular.

▶ **Acute.** Any angle that is less than 90°.

▶ **Obtuse.** Any angle that is more than 90°.

▶ **Straight.** A straight line is actually a 180° angle. This is an important number to remember because it can help you calculate the degrees of other angles in a geometry question.

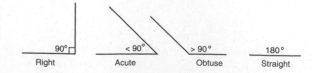

Now that you know the basics, memorize these special types of angles and their properties. Not only can you be asked to identify these types of angles on the test, but knowing the rules associated with them will enable you to figure out missing values of angles in ASVAB questions.

- **Adjacent.** Two angles that share a common side. Adjacent angles look like one large angle that's split at the vertex. The sum of the two angles is equal to the larger angle.

- **Supplementary.** Two angles that together make a straight line. The sum of the angles equals 180°.

- **Complementary.** Two angles that together make a right angle, so the sum of the angles equals 90°.

- **Corresponding.** You'll often see these as a set of parallel lines with another line, called a *transversal*, running through both. This creates a set of angles with specific properties and relationships. Memorize the relationships outlined on the following diagram.

questions involving triangles ask you to determine missing values before you get to the main part of the problem, which may be calculating area or some other task.

Memorize these basic rules about angle relationships in triangles. They'll help you quickly calculate missing values:

- Triangles have three internal angles. They also have external angles. Each internal angle is adjacent to an exterior angle (see the following diagram).

- The three internal angles of a triangle always add up to 180°.

- The sum of an internal angle and its adjacent external angle always is 180°.

- You can calculate the value of an internal angle if you know the value of the adjacent external angle. Simply subtract the value of the external angle from 180. In the following diagram, the external angle is 45°. 180 − 45 = 135, which means the adjacent internal angle is 135°.

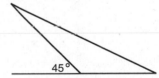

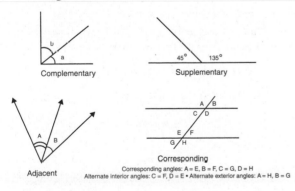

Complementary

Supplementary

Corresponding

Adjacent

Corresponding angles: A = E, B = F, C = G, D = H
Alternate interior angles: C = F, D = E • Alternate exterior angles: A = H, B = G

- You can figure out the value of an external angle by adding the two internal angles that do not touch the external angle. In the following diagram, you would add 88 + 42 to find the value of angle *x* (130°).

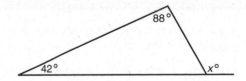

Triangles

Triangles are an ASVAB favorite. Learning the types of triangles there are and the rules associated with them will help you through many types of questions. A lot of times,

You should also be familiar with several special triangles:

▸ **Similar triangles.** These are two triangles that have internal angles that are equal to each other and, therefore, have proportional sides. In the following diagram, the degrees of angles g, d, and f are the same in each triangle. This means that side a is proportional to side x, side c is proportional to side y, and side b is proportional to side z (with the same proportion).

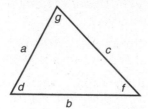 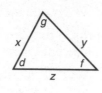

▸ **Congruent triangles.** Two triangles whose corresponding side lengths and angles are the same values.

Congruent

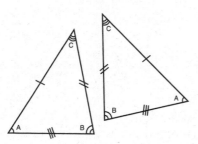

To test if two triangles are congruent, ask the following questions. If the answer to any of these is yes, you have congruent triangles:

▸ Are all three corresponding side values equal?

▸ Are two corresponding sides and the angle they make equal?

▸ Are two corresponding angles and the side they share equal?

▸ Are two corresponding angles and a side they don't share equal?

Common triangles include the following:

▸ **Isosceles.** A triangle with two sides of equal length and, therefore, two angles that are equal.

▸ **Equilateral.** A triangle with all side lengths and angles equal. Angles are always 60°.

▸ **Right.** A triangle with one angle equal to 90°.

Isosceles   Equilateral   Right

Now that you're familiar with common triangles and their properties, let's talk about what you'll be asked to do with this information on the test. Most often you'll need to find the perimeter (value of the length around), area (value of the space within), or a missing value. Here's what you do:

▸ **Perimeter.** Add the lengths of all three sides.

▸ **Area.** Determine the length of the base of a triangle, divide by half, and then multiply by the height using the equation $A = \frac{1}{2}bh$. Take a look at the following diagram.

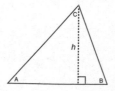 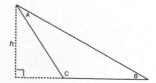

The base of a triangle is the length of the bottom line, and the height is the distance between the triangle's highest point and the base. Often, you'll see this indicated as a dotted line running from the base to the top angle. A triangle's area is represented in square units (cm², ft²) when units of measure are given in the problem.

- **Missing value of an angle(s).** Determine what type of triangle you're looking at, and label the diagram with the values you're given in the problem. Then use the rules discussed earlier in this section to calculate the values you need. For instance, if you're given a right triangle and told that one angle is 30°, you know the other is 60°.

- **Missing side of a right triangle.** When you know the value of any two sides of a right triangle, you use the Pythagorean theorem to calculate the other: $a^2 + b^2 = c^2$. Memorize this formula and the following diagram. Substitute the two sides for the corresponding letters in the equation. Then solve for the missing side.

Pythagorean Theorem

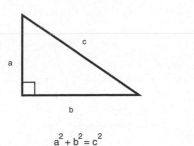

$$a^2 + b^2 = c^2$$

HEADS-UP

When you solve for a missing side of a right triangle, you have to figure out the square root to get the actual length of the side, because in the equation, each of the sides are squared.

Quadrilaterals

Quadrilaterals are polygons that have four sides and corners. You need to know these quadrilaterals:

- **Parallelograms.** These are quadrilaterals that have opposite sides that are parallel and equal in length. This makes the opposite angles also equal. Rectangles, rhombi, and squares are all parallelograms.

- **Rectangles.** These are parallelograms with four right angles. The sides that run parallel to each other are equal.

- **Squares.** All four sides are congruent and angles are right angles. A square is a special type of rectangle.

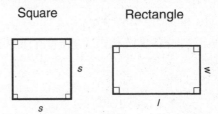

Like with triangles, you should know how to calculate area and perimeter for each of these. With perimeter, you add the values of all the sides. With area, you multiply the value of the length times the value of the width. In the previous rectangle, if length = 4 in. and width = 2 in., you'd multiply 4 × 2 and find that the area is 8 in². For a parallelogram, you'd multiply the base times the height. The height is found in the same way as for a triangle.

You should know two special types of quadrilaterals:

- **Rhombus.** This is a parallelogram that has four sides of equal length and diagonals that intersect at right angles (a square is one type of rhombus). Take a look at the following diagram.

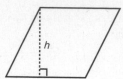

To calculate the area of a rhombus, you multiply the base by the height. For example, if the height line in the previous diagram is 10 in. and the base (which can be any side) is 8 in., the area would be 80 in².

▶ **Trapezoid.** This is a quadrilateral with at least two sides that run parallel to each other. To calculate the area of a trapezoid, you use the following formula: $A = \frac{1}{2} \times h \times (b_1 + b_2)$. In this case, b_1 and b_2 are the values of the bases (top and bottom lines of the following figure).

Trapezoid

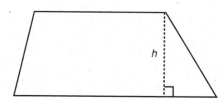

If in the previous diagram b_1 = 12 in, b_2= 18 in, and h – 6 in, this is how you would work the equation:

$$A = \frac{1}{2} \times 6 \times (12 + 18)$$

$$A = \frac{1}{2} \times 6 \times 30$$

$$A = \frac{1}{2} \times \frac{6}{1} \times 30$$

$$A = \frac{6}{2} \times 30$$

$$A = 3 \times 30$$

$$A = 90 \ \text{in}^2$$

Circles

Circles are a lot easier to work with than you might think. Memorize a few essential bits of information, and you'll do fine:

▶ **Radius (r).** This is a segment that's drawn from the center of a circle to the edge. A circle can have an infinite number of radii.

▶ **Diameter (d).** This is a segment whose endpoints are on the circle and that goes through the center of the circle. Double the value of any radius, and you get the diameter.

▶ **Circumference (c).** This is the distance around a circle.

▶ **Chord.** This is a segment in a circle that touches any two points of the edge. A diameter is a type of chord.

▶ **pi (π).** This is a mathematical constant that appears in many formulas involving circles. All you need to know is that it equals about 3.14 or $\frac{22}{7}$, which is enough to get you through your ASVAB calculations.

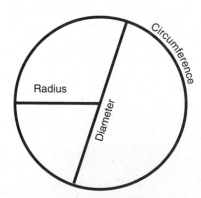

These gems of wisdom about circles and the following formulas should help you tackle just about any circle question on the ASVAB:

▶ Circumference: $C = 2\pi r$

▶ Area: $A = \pi r^2$

Solid Figures and Volume

If you see a solid figure on the ASVAB, it will likely be either rectangular or cylindrical. You're most often asked to figure out volume or surface with rectangular solids (think cubes).

Cube

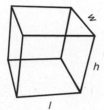

The two main tasks you'll be asked to complete with solids are volume and total surface area:

▶ **Rectangular solids.** Use the following formula to figure out volume: $V = l \times w \times h$. Plug in the values for length, width, and height, or solve for a missing value based on the information given in the question. These values will always be notated with l, w, and h. To calculate surface area, use the following formula: $2lw + 2wh + 2lh$.

▶ **Cylindrical solids.** For cylindrical solids, the formula is $V = \pi r^2 h$. Plug in the values of the radius, pi, and height to get your answer or solve for a missing value based on the information given in the question. To calculate total surface area, use the formula $TSA = 2\pi r(r + h)$.

Math Skills Workout

Arithmetic Reasoning

Carefully read the following word problems and choose the best answer for each.

1. A concert hall can hold 1,253 people. If tonight's show sold only 82% of the hall, about how many tickets were sold?

   (A) 226
   (B) 568
   (C) 1,027
   (D) 1,171

2. Erin bought half as many bolts at the hardware store as Jason and double the number that Brooke bought. If Brooke bought 18 bolts, how many did Jason buy?

   (A) 28
   (B) 36
   (C) 56
   (D) 72

3. Which of the following is the same as 4,683,000,000?

   (A) 4.683×10^9
   (B) 4.6830×10^{10}
   (C) 4.6830×10^{11}
   (D) 4.683×10^{12}

4. A flight leaves New York City traveling at 520 miles per hour. After three hours in the air, how far will that plane have traveled?

    (A) 1,040 miles

    (B) 1,560 miles

    (C) 1,875 miles

    (D) 2,056 miles

5. Your test grades for the semester are 82, 73, 94, 87, and 78. What is your test average?

    (A) 82.8

    (B) 85.3

    (C) 87.65

    (D) 96.4

6. The cost of tuition at the local college is increasing by $255 per credit. Last year, you paid $9,900 for 12 credits worth of classes. How much will you pay this year for the same number of credits?

    (A) $825

    (B) $1,081

    (C) $9,990

    (D) $12,960

7. A carnival grab bag game has 36 prizes. Of the prizes available, 14 are for boys, 14 are for girls, and 8 are unisex. If you closed your eyes and picked, what is the probability of drawing a girl or unisex prize?

    (A) $\frac{1}{2}$

    (B) $\frac{1}{3}$

    (C) $\frac{11}{18}$

    (D) $\frac{13}{18}$

8. It takes Bob $1\frac{1}{2}$ hours to mow one lawn.

There are 15 lawns on his block, and $\frac{1}{3}$ of the homeowners want Bob to mow their lawn today. If Bob starts the first lawn at 10:00 A.M., when will he finish the last one?

    (A) 7:30 A.M.

    (B) 4:00 P.M.

    (C) 5:30 P.M.

    (D) 6:00 P.M.

9. Mrs. Menkin's class is going to the zoo. There are 24 students in the class, plus Mrs. Menkin and two class parents. If each car can seat four people, how many cars are needed to drive everyone to the zoo?

    (A) 6

    (B) 7

    (C) 8

    (D) 9

10. Marge can carry up to 22 pounds in her backpack. She needs to move 10 five-pound bags of sugar from her car to her house. What is the fewest number of trips she would have to make in order to move all of the sugar from the car to the house?

    (A) 1

    (B) 2

    (C) 3

    (D) 4

11. You buy a new car for $12,465. At the dealership, you write a check for $3,000 as your down payment, and then sign a five-year loan for the remainder of the purchase price at an interest rate of 6%. By the end of the loan, how much will you have paid for the car in total?

    (A) $2,839.50
    (B) $9,465.00
    (C) $13,032.90
    (D) $15,304.50

12. A class of 789 students declare their majors. About 14% will study biology, 23% will study English, 46% will study business, and the rest will study liberal arts. About how many students total will study business and liberal arts?

    (A) 363
    (B) 497
    (C) 542
    (D) 694

13. Tom begins walking to Journal Square at a rate of 4 miles per hour. At the same time, Adrienne begins walking toward the same destination at 2 miles per hour. If Tom lives 8 miles away and Adrienne lives 3 miles away, how long could Adrienne stop for coffee in order to get to Journal Square at the same time as Tom?

    (A) $\frac{1}{2}$ hour
    (B) $\frac{3}{4}$ hour
    (C) 1 hour
    (D) 2 hours

14. 5!

    (A) 15
    (B) 56
    (C) 120
    (D) 132

15. On the whale-watching trip, $\frac{3}{4}$ of the 216 participants registered online. What is the ratio of people who did not register online to those who did?

    (A) 1:2
    (B) 1:3
    (C) 2:3
    (D) 3:4

16. You need to buy bread, eggs, milk, and orange juice at the store. The bread is $2.33, the eggs are $3.69, the milk is $2.65, and the juice is $3.45. The cashier rings you up and adds 6% sales tax. If you give her $20 to pay for your groceries, what will your change be?

    (A) $4.45
    (B) $5.67
    (C) $6.28
    (D) $7.15

17. Your new office is 365 ft². The office manager estimates one cubicle will take up 12 ft² of space. If you wanted $\frac{1}{5}$ of the office to house cubicles, how many cubicles would you need to purchase to fill this space?

    (A) 5
    (B) 6
    (C) 7
    (D) 9

18. You just found a library book that is a year and a half overdue. If the library you took it from charges 10¢ per day in fines, how much money will you owe when you return it?

    (A) $5.42
    (B) $36.50
    (C) $54.75
    (D) $541.50

19. A gallon of gas is $2.68, and your car has a 15-gallon tank. You start a 650-mile road trip with an empty tank and fill up every 325 miles. Assuming you do not use any gas while at your destination and you fill up your tank once home, how much money will you spend on gas round-trip?

    (A) $80.40
    (B) $120.60
    (C) $160.80
    (D) $201

20. Music lessons for your child will cost $1,265 per year. If you get a part-time job that pays $6.05 per hour, how many hours will you have to work in a year to pay for the music lessons?

    (A) 209.09
    (B) 290.90
    (C) 2,090.90
    (D) 2,909.90

Answers and Explanations

1. **C.** This question is all about percents. Calculate 82 percent of 1,253: $.82 \times 1,253 = 1,027$.

2. **D.** The wording here is tricky, so ask yourself what the question is really looking for. You need to find out how many bolts Jason bought. You know that Brooke bought 18 bolts and that Erin bought twice as many as Brooke did. Multiply 18×2, and you'll find that she bought 36 bolts. You also know that Erin bought half as many bolts as Jason, which is another way of saying he bought twice as many as she did. Multiply 36×2, and you have your answer: 72.

3. **A.** Notice the answer choices. This involves scientific notation. Discard answers B and C, since they retain a 0 at the end of the number, which is not done with scientific notation. If you count the total number of places in the original number, you'll see that there are only 10 of them, so the correct answer can't be D. This leaves A, which follows the correct format for scientific notation.

4. **B.** This is a simple rate problem. Use the Distance = Rate × Time formula to solve for the distance: $D = 520 \times 3$.

5. **A.** You need to figure out the average here, so add all the numbers together and divide by the number of terms you added. Your equation will look like this: $\frac{(82+73+94+87+78)}{5} = 82.8$.

6. **D.** You need to take several steps to solve this problem. First, you have to figure out how much each credit cost last year. To do this, divide $9,900 by 12, which results in $825 per credit.

Next, calculate how much the tuition increase raised the price per credit: $825 + $255 = $1,080. Finally, multiply the new price per credit by the number of credits from last year: $1,080 \times 12 = $12,960.

7. **C.** This is a probability problem. There are 36 total possible outcomes. Because you're being asked the chances of drawing two types of prizes, you need to add the number of possible positive outcomes, which would be 14 girl's prizes and 8 unisex prizes. Use these numbers to make your fraction and reduce:

$$P = \frac{\text{Number of positive outcomes}}{\text{Number of total possible outcomes}}$$

$$P = \frac{14+8}{36}$$

$$P = \frac{22}{36} = \frac{11}{18}$$

8. **C.** Start by calculating the number of lawns Bob has to mow: $\frac{15}{1} \times \frac{1}{3} = \frac{15}{3} = 5$. Then multiply the answer by how long it takes Bob to mow one lawn:

$$\begin{array}{r} 1.5 \\ \times\ 5 \\ \hline 7.5 \end{array}$$

. Finally, count 7.5 hours past 10:00 A.M., and you'll see Bob will be done by 5:30 P.M.

9. **B.** There are 27 people who need to get to the zoo. Divide this number by 4 (the number of people who can fit in one car) and you'll get 6.75. Since there's no such thing as .75 of a car, round up to the next whole number. They will need seven cars total.

10. **C.** Since each bag of sugar weighs 5 pounds, the backpack can hold only 4 at a time (5 × 4 = 20). Two trips will take eight bags into the house, leaving two bags left. This means it will take three trips to transport all the bags into the house.

11. **D.** You need to do many things to find the answer to this problem. First, subtract the down payment from the price of the car: 12,465 − 3,000 = $9,465. This is the amount that will be financed through the loan. Next, use the rate formula for calculating interest discussed in Chapter 8: amount borrowed × interest rate × time of loan. Plug in the values you have: 9,465 × .06 × 5 = 2,839.50. Because the question asks how much you've paid for the car in total, add this value to the total price of the car, which gives you $15,304.50.

12. **B.** Add the total percentages you're given in the problem and subtract that from 100. This gives you 17, which is the percent of students who declared liberal arts as their major. Add this value to 46, the percent of business majors, to find that the total percent you're working with is 63. Turn 63 into a decimal and multiply by the total number of students: .63 × 789 = 497.

13. **A.** You need to figure out how long it will take Tom and Adrienne to reach Journal Square based on their individual paces. Apply the formula Distance = Rate × Time for each of them:

Adrienne: $3 = 2t$

$\frac{3}{2} = t$

$1\frac{1}{2} = t$

Tom: $8 = 4t$

$\frac{8}{4} = t$

$2 = t$

Now subtract Adrienne's time from Tom's to find that she will arrive at Journal Square a half hour before Tom.

14. **C.** This is a factorial: 5 × 4 × 3 × 2 × 1 = 120.

15. **B.** If $\frac{3}{4}$ of the participants registered online, then $\frac{1}{4}$ did not. Figure out how many people this is by multiplying (or .25) by 216 (the total number of participants): .25 × 216 = 54. Subtract this value from 216 to find the number of people who did register online: 216 − 54 = 162. Now set up a ratio (54:162) and reduce it to lowest terms using 54 as the greatest common factor. The final ratio is 1:3. More simply, we can note that the total number 216 is irrelevant, as

$\frac{1}{4} : \frac{3}{4} = 1 : 3$.

Alternatively, you could find that $\frac{1}{4}$ of participants did not register online, leaving ¾ who did. The ratio then would be $\frac{1}{4} : \frac{3}{4}$, which reduces down to 1:3.

16. **D.** Add all the prices together: $12.12. Next, multiply the total by .06 (the sales tax): .73. Then add those two amounts together and subtract from the total amount of money you give to the cashier: ($20):

$$\begin{array}{r} 20.00 \\ -12.85 \\ \hline \$7.15 \end{array}$$

17. **B.** To figure out how many feet can be dedicated to cubicles, you need to calculate how much $\frac{1}{5}$ of 365 is. In mathematical terms, this translates to $\frac{1}{5} \times \frac{365}{1} = 73$. Now that you know that only 73 ft² can be used, divide that amount by 12, the area one cubicle will take up. You'll get 6.08, which rounded to the nearest whole number is 6.

18. **C.** One year is 365 days. Divide that by 2 to find that half a year is 182.5 days. Add the two numbers together (365 + 182.5 = 547.5) and multiply by 10¢ (which is the same as saying .10):

$$
\begin{array}{r}
547.50 \\
\times \quad .10 \\
\hline
00000 \\
+ \ 547500 \\
\hline
54.7500
\end{array}
$$

The amount of the fine is $54.75.

19. **D.** Start by figuring out how much a full tank of gas would cost at the price indicated: $2.68 × 15 = $40.20. Now figure out how many times you'll gas up based on the information in the question. Since 325 is half of 650, you'll fill up five times: once before leaving, once at the 325-mile mark, once when you get to or leave your destination, once 325 miles into your return trip, and once when you get home. Multiply the price per tank by 5, and your answer is $210.

20. **A.** Divide the amount of money needed by the hourly rate to get the number of hours that you will have to work:

$$6.05\overline{)1265.00}$$

$$
\begin{array}{r}
209.09 \\
605\overline{)126500.00} \\
- \ 1210 \\
\hline
550 \\
- \ \ 000 \\
\hline
5500 \\
- \ 5445 \\
\hline
550 \\
- \ \ 000 \\
\hline
5500 \\
- \ 5445 \\
\hline
55
\end{array}
$$

Mathematics Knowledge

For each question, choose the best answer.

1. Reduce the following expression into lowest terms: $\frac{4x+2}{6x+4}$

    (A) x + 1

    (B) 2x + 1

    (C) $\frac{x}{2x+1}$

    (D) $\frac{2x+1}{3x+2}$

2. Solve for x: $x^2 + 12 = 48$.

    (A) 2

    (B) 4

    (C) 5

    (D) 6

3. A letter in an equation or expression that stands in place of an unknown quantity is a

    (A) ray.

    (B) variable.

    (C) constant.

    (D) coefficient.

4. Solve for y: $4y = 128$.

    (A) 32

    (B) 36

    (C) 38

    (D) 42

5. $\frac{6a}{3a^4} \times \frac{4b^3}{a^3} =$

    (A) $\frac{8ab^3}{a^7}$

    (B) $\frac{8ab^3}{3a^7}$

    (C) $\frac{8b^3}{a^6}$

    (D) $\frac{24ab^3}{a^6}$

6. Factor $y^2 + 8y + 15$.

    (A) (y + 4)(y + 3)

    (B) (y + 2)(y + 6)

    (C) (y + 5)(y + 2)

    (D) (y + 5)(y + 3)

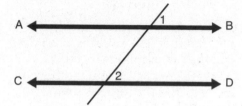

7. In the figure, $\overrightarrow{AB}$ and $\overrightarrow{CD}$ are parallel. If angle 1 is 53º, then angle 2 is

    (A) 43°

    (B) 53°

    (C) 68°

    (D) 127°

8. If two triangles have three corresponding sides of equal value, they are

    (A) congruent.

    (B) similar.

    (C) right.

    (D) acute.

9. A circle's radius is 8 in. What is its circumference?

    (A) 22.58 in.

    (B) 25.32 in.

    (C) 50.24 in.

    (D) 201.06 in.

10. $\sqrt{81} =$

   (A) 8

   (B) 9

   (C) 10

   (D) 11

11. Solve for b: $ab \mid c = d^2$.

   (A) b = d2 + c – a

   (B) b = d2 – c – a

   (C) $b = \frac{d^2+c}{a}$

   (D) $b = \frac{d^2-c}{a}$

12. $\frac{14a}{10b} \div \frac{7b^2}{5a} =$

   (A) $\frac{a^2}{b^3}$

   (B) $\frac{a^{-2}}{b^{-3}}$

   (C) $\frac{98ab^2}{50ab}$

   (D) $\frac{50ab^2}{98ab}$

13. $\frac{9}{11} \times 2\frac{4}{6} =$

   (A) $1\frac{9}{10}$

   (B) $1\frac{4}{5}$

   (C) $2\frac{2}{11}$

   (D) $2\frac{1}{12}$

14. $24.45\overline{)794.3}$

   (A) 25.854

   (B) 28.936

   (C) 32.487

   (D) 46.289

15. A trapezoid has a base of 9 in., a second base of 7 in., and a height of 5 in. What's the area?

   (A) 16 in²

   (B) 28 in²

   (C) 35 in²

   (D) 40 in²

16. $(3y \times 4z)(7y \times 3z)$

   (A) 252yz

   (B) 322yz

   (C) 252y²z²

   (D) 322y²z²

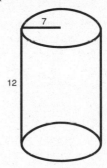

17. The volume of the cylinder above is about

   (A) 1,846 in³

   (B) 1,923 in³

   (C) 2,421 in³

   (D) 3,556 in³

18. If one angle in a right triangle is 42°, the remaining angle will be

   (A) 20°.

   (B) 36°.

   (C) 48°.

   (D) 90°.

19. If $14a + 2 > 100$, $a >$

    (A) 2

    (B) 4

    (C) 5

    (D) 7

20. If the *a* side of a right triangle is 4 ft and the *b* side is 6 ft, the area of the triangle is

    (A) 10 ft².

    (B) 12 ft².

    (C) 16 ft².

    (D) 36 ft².

Answers and Explanations

1. **D.** Factor each of the expressions on either side of the fraction bar. You can factor 2 out of both:

    $\frac{4x+2}{6x+4} = \frac{2(2x+1)}{2(3x+2)}$.

2. **D.** Isolate the x by adding –12 to each side of the equation. This leaves you with $x^2 = 36$. Now figure out the square root of 36, which is 6.

3. **B.** A ray is a part of a line with one endpoint and another side that stretches to infinity. A constant is a number that stands by itself in an expression or equation. A coefficient is a number that multiplies a variable. A variable is a letter that stands in place of an unknown quantity.

4. **A.** This is a simple equation. Isolate the y by dividing each side by 4. This gives you 32 as your answer.

5. **C.** Treat this like any other problem multiplying fractions. Multiply the terms straight across: $\frac{6a}{3a^4} \times \frac{4b^3}{a^3} = \frac{24ab^3}{3a^7}$. Then reduce. $3a$ can go into $24ab^3$ once, which leaves you with $\frac{8b^3}{a^6}$.

6. **D.** This is a quadratic equation. Sure, you could do the math to break everything down, but this problem can actually be solved very easily. Take a quick look at the answers to see which numbers, when added, equal 8. That leaves you with B and D. Next ask if the numbers, when multiplied, equal 15. The only one you're left with is D, which is correct.

7. **B.** These two angles are corresponding, which makes their value the same.

8. **A.** This is one of the tests you can apply to see if two triangles are congruent. Right and acute triangles have specific types of angles, and *similar* refers to two triangles that have internal angles that are equal to each other and have proportional sides.

9. **C.** Apply the $C = 2\pi r$ formula here: $2 \times 3.14 \times 8 = 50.24$.

10. **B.** The square root of 81 is 9, since $9 \times 9 = 81$.

11. **D.** The only difference between this type of equation and one with numbers is that you're not solving for a specific quantity. You approach it the exact same way. Since we're solving for b, we need to isolate it to one side. Start with c and subtract that quantity from both sides. Then divide both sides by a. This gives you your final answer:

    $$ab + c = d^2$$
    $$ab + c - c = d^2 - c$$
    $$\frac{ab}{a} = \frac{d^2-c}{a}$$
    $$b = \frac{d^2-c}{a}$$

12. **A.** Approach this like you would any other division-of-fractions problem. Turn it into a multiplication expression and flip the second fraction. Multiply straight across and reduce: $\frac{14a}{10b} \times \frac{5a}{7b^2} = \frac{70a^2}{70b^3} = \frac{a^2}{b^3}$.

13. **C.** The easiest way to approach this is to turn the mixed fraction into an improper fraction and multiply straight across: $\frac{9}{11} \times 2\frac{4}{6} = \frac{9}{11} \times \frac{16}{6} = \frac{144}{66}$.

Then divide the denominator into the numerator and write out the remainder as a fraction. Reduce where you can: $\frac{144}{66} = 2\frac{12}{66} = 2\frac{2}{11}$.

14. **C.** This is simple division of decimals. Move the decimal point in the divisor two places to the right. Then do the same with the dividend and add a 0 after the 3. Divide down and move the decimal point straight up into the quotient to get 32.4867.

15. **D.** Apply the $A = \frac{1}{2} \times h \times (b_1 + b_2)$ equation here:

$A = \frac{1}{2} \times h \times (b_1 + b_2)$

$A = \frac{1}{2} \times 5 \times (9 + 7)$

$A = \frac{1}{2} \times 5 \times 16$

$A = \frac{1}{2} \times 80$

$A = \frac{1}{2} \times \frac{80}{1} = \frac{80}{2} = 40$

16. **C.** Order of operations applies here. Solve what's in parentheses first. Start with the coefficients and then move on to the variables:

$(3y \times 4z)(7y \times 3z)$

$3 \times 4 = 12$

$y \times z = yz$

$7 \times 3 = 21$

$y \times z - yz$

Combine each to get $12yz \times 21yz$. Repeat with the remaining expression:

$12 \times 21 = 252$

$y \times y \times z \times z = y^2z^2$

Your final answer is $252y^2z^2$.

17. **A.** Use the formula for finding the volume of a cylinder for this question: $V = \pi r^2 h$.

When you plug in the numbers from the question, you find:

$V = 3.14 \times 7^2 \times 12$

$V = 3.14 \times 49 \times 12$

$V = 153.86 \times 12$

$V = 1,846.32$

18. **C.** We know that right triangles are named so because they have one 90° angle. If another angle is 42°, all you have to do is subtract the measure of these two angles from 180 to figure out the value of the third angle: $180 - (90 + 42) = 48$.

19. **D.** Approach this like you would a regular equation and solve for the value of a. Start to isolate a by adding −2 to each side of the inequality: $14a + 2 + (-2) > 100 + (-2)$. The new inequality is $14a > 98$. Next, divide both sides by 14: $\frac{14a}{14} > \frac{98}{14}$. The final inequality is $a = 7$.

20. **B.** In a right triangle, the b side is the base and the a side is the height. Plug in the values given into the formula for calculating the area of a triangle:

$A = \frac{1}{2}bh$

$A = \frac{1}{2} \times 6 \times 4$

$A = \frac{1}{2} \times \frac{24}{1}$

$A = \frac{24}{2} \times 12$

PART

4

A B C D
A B C D
A B C D
A B C D
A B C D
A B C D
A B C D
A B C D
A B C D
A B C D
A B C D
A B C D
A B C D
A B C D
A B C D
A B C D

Get It Together: Technical Sections

So far, we've helped you bone up on the skills you need to pass the math and verbal sections of the ASVAB, on which you need to get minimum scores to even qualify for entrance. Now it's time to start thinking about what job you might want to pursue and what tests you'll need to pass to get you there.

In this part, we go over each of the Military Occupational Specialty qualifying subtests and their accompanying subject areas: General Science, Electronics Information, Auto Information and Shop Information, Mechanical Comprehension, and Assembling Objects.

General Science

"The whole of science is nothing more than a refinement of everyday thinking."

—Albert Einstein

Often referred to as the father of modern physics, Albert Einstein is arguably one of the most famous scientists in the history of the world. He published over 450 works during his lifetime, developed legendary scientific theories, and possessed extreme intelligence. For that reason, this quote seemed like the perfect introduction to this chapter. After all, if *Einstein* thinks science is based on everyday thoughts, it must be so!

Throughout this chapter, we discuss terms and concepts commonly found on the General Science (GS) section of the ASVAB, as well as in everyday life. Your ability to apply textbook theories to the world around you will greatly enhance your understanding of science, as well as your ability to score well on the science subtest of the ASVAB.

Why Do I Have to Take This?

The technical subtests on the ASVAB are a good indicator of skill and aptitude. In the chapters that follow, we tell you about each of these tests and what types of jobs require you to do well on them. That's right, all the technical subtests count toward your Military Occupational Specialty (MOS) score requirements, and how well you do on them directly influences your career options.

Although training costs vary by branch and job, most estimates suggest that the cost of training for *each* service member is between $50,000 and $100,000. Clearly, the military wants to get selection right on the first try!

Here's where knowing what you want to do with your career can help you on the ASVAB. Look up the job you're interested in pursuing in your area of service and see what line scores you need for it. You'll likely find General Science (GS) listed in those dealing with general maintenance, technical applications, electronics, and medicine. If your future career lies along these lines, acing the GS subtest is critical.

What to Expect

The General Science section of the ASVAB covers a wide variety of concepts, primarily from the life, physical, and earth sciences. As we begin to "dissect" these disciplines, you may start having flashbacks to your junior high and high school science classes. The good news is that you don't have to sit through years of those classes again!

Even better, you've probably already learned most of the information on the ASVAB tests. And despite the fact that the GS section covers a wide range of topics, there are actually only 25 questions on the PAP and 16 questions on the CAT that you'll have to answer.

Most of the strategies outlined in earlier chapters of this book lend themselves nicely to the science subtest as well. The other advantage you have is that science is all around us. Although you may not remember all the terminology from your teenage school years, you now have the ability to apply these terms to actual life experiences.

Using your experiences in life to help understand and remember scientific terms is one of the biggest advantages you have on this section of the test. Now let's turn our attention to some of the main subjects you may see on the test.

Life Science Review

Life science is a broad field of study that deals with living organisms, their life processes, and their relationship with the environment. It actually encompasses several other branches of science, including the many derivatives of biology, such as cellular biology (which includes genetics), health, and nutrition. Let's examine each of these in greater detail.

Biology Basics

Biology is the study of life and living organisms. Due to the magnitude of this subject, scientists have broken biology down into smaller, more manageable subcategories, including zoology (the study of animals), botany (the study of plants), ecology (the study of the environment), and so forth.

HEADS-UP

The Greek root *ology* means "study of." If you see a word with this suffix and are not sure what the word means, you already know that it means the study of something. Look to the other parts of the word to see if you can figure out the meaning. For example, the root *bio* means "life," so *biology* translates into "the study of life."

We get into some of these subcategories momentarily. First, however, let's discuss the four unifying principles of biology:

▸ **Cell theory.** All living organisms are made of cells, which are the basic units of life. From bacteria, to fungi, to plants and animals, cells make up the structure of every life form on Earth.

▸ **Gene theory.** Traits such as intelligence, physical characteristics, and the like get passed on from generation to generation through genes. Genes are located on chromosomes, which are threadlike strands of DNA found in cells.

▸ **Evolution theory.** Genetic changes in a population are inherited over several generations, no matter how large or small. For example, after being introduced into a foreign environment in Australia, toxic toads grew longer legs that helped them escape to other sections of the country in order to survive.

▸ **Homeostasis theory.** This principle addresses an organism's ability to maintain a constant internal environment, regardless of external changes. Think of the human body. It has to be at the right temperature at all times for the internal environment to be able to sustain all vital functions. This is why you sweat when you exercise or sit too long in the sun; it's also the reason you shiver in the cold. The body is trying to balance the internal and external environments.

These four principles demonstrate how easily we can relate to the science of biology. Let's look now at some sample concepts from the specific biological subcategories just listed.

Zoology

As you can guess from the name, zoology is the study of animals. One of the most important things for you to know about zoology for the ASVAB is a concept called *taxonomy*, also known as biological classification. This is a method by which scientists classify living things. Living organisms can be divided into the following classifications (listed from largest to smallest):

▸ **Domain.** Only three: Eukaryota (living things with cells that have a nucleus), Bacteria (single-cell prokaryotes with no nucleus and cell membrane is made of unbranched fatty acid chains), and Archaea (single-cell prokaryote, similar to both eukaryotes and bacteria with different rRNA, cell wall, and membrane chemistry).

▸ **Kingdom.** Broken up into five groups: Animalia (animals, vertebrates, invertebrates), Plantae (plants, mosses), Fungi (mushrooms, molds), Protista (slime molds, some algae), and Monera (bacteria, some pathogens).

▸ **Phylum.** Based on one of two things: either the physical characteristics of an organism (such as having a spine or a shell) or the degree of its evolutionary relation to others of its population.

▸ **Class.** Defined by history and a general consensus among the scientific community, which are generally described as a major group of organisms.

▸ **Order.** Groups of organisms based on more specific characteristics than class.

▸ **Family.** More specific classification of organisms within an order.

- **Genus.** First of the final two classifications of an organism. Genus and species work together to make a specific identification of an organism.

- **Species.** The most specific classification. Members of a species look similar and reproduce with each other, but not with other species.

TEST TIP

If the Domain classification is new to you, well, it's new to the scientific field, too. As more research takes place, scientists are changing what they know about the world. Domain has only been added to biology courses in the past decade and may not be on the ASVAB.

A good way to remember the order of classifications is to use a mnemonic device. In this case, you take the first letter of each word and turn it into a silly sentence, such as "Dear Keen People Can Often Find Good Sales."

Any living organism on the planet can be classified using the previous ranks, as well as their specific subclassifications. Take a look at the following table to understand how a human being is classified:

Rank	Classification	Explanation
Domain	Eukaryota	Living things with cells that have nuclei.
Kingdom	Animalia	Animals: Multicellular, heterotrophic, eukaryotic organisms.
Phylum	Chordata	Chordates: Animals with skulls.

Rank	Classification	Explanation
Class	Mammalia	Mammals: Animals that have hair and give milk to their young.
Order	Primata	Primates: Includes monkeys and apes; adapted for climbing trees, rely on vision, and have large brains.
Family	Hominidae	Fist-walking and knuckle-walking hominids, or great apes.
Genus	*Homo*	Humans possessing specific and specialized development of memory, learning, and teaching.
Species	*Homo sapiens*	Literal translation: "Wise man." Highly developed, with specialized ability to learn; able to actively transform environment; can acclimatize, control, and farm; can create urban establishments, infrastructures, and advanced technology.

Botany

Botany is the study of plants. An important concept to know in this branch of biology is photosynthesis. This is a process that green plants use to turn sunlight, water, and carbon dioxide into energy, in the form of oxygen and sugar.

The process of photosynthesis takes place in the chloroplasts, which are located in the leaves of the plants. The chloroplasts, which are so tiny they must be viewed through a microscope, use an element called *chlorophyll* to facilitate the photosynthetic process. Chlorophyll absorbs red and blue light, making it impossible to see these colors with our eyes. Green light, on the other hand, is not absorbed and, therefore, causes plants to appear green.

The energy from the absorbed red and blue light interacts with the water within the plant. This action results in the creation of molecules that the plant uses to turn its water and carbon dioxide into sugars. When photosynthesis occurs, a chemical reaction takes place:

$$6CO_2 + 6H_2O \text{ (+ light energy)} \rightarrow C_6H_{12}O_6 + 6O_2$$

In plain English, this equation says that carbon dioxide (the air we exhale) plus water and sunlight get converted into sugar and oxygen (which we inhale).

The actual process of photosynthesis takes place in two parts:

▶ **Light-dependent reactions.** When light reaches a plant cell, molecules in the chlorophyll absorb wavelengths of red and blue light (among others, but these are the most effective for photosynthesis). This influx of energy starts a reaction with the electrons and protons of the molecules, which then kick-starts the production of adenosine triphosphate (ATP), nicotinamide adenine dinucleotide phosphate (NADPH), and oxygen.

▶ **Light-independent reactions.** Sometimes called *dark reactions*, these processes do not actually take place in the dark; they just don't need photons to take place. During this stage of photosynthesis, the energy and products of the light-dependent reactions (ATP, NADPH, and oxygen) are used to convert carbon dioxide and water into carbohydrates and oxygen that nourish the plant and heterotrophs that eat the plant.

Ecology

Ecology is the study of the environment and how organisms live and interact within different habitats. All life on Earth depends on keeping a careful balance within and among these habitats, which is why climate change is such a concern. Even slight changes in abiotic (nonliving, like a rise in temperature) and biotic (living, like increased populations of predators) conditions can have devastating consequences for a habitat and all those who interact with it.

Within any ecosystem you will find:

▶ **Producers.** Organisms that produce their own food. Remember photosynthesis? That is how plants produce their own food, which makes them producers.

▶ **Consumers.** Organisms that eat other organisms for food. Carnivores eat only meat. Herbivores eat only plants. Omnivores eat both. They can be broken down into primary (herbivores), secondary (carnivores and omnivores), and tertiary levels (omnivores or carnivores that will eat secondary consumers).

▶ **Decomposers.** Organisms that break down wastes and dead organisms.

Producers, consumers, and decomposers are very important links in the food chain. Producers provide nutrition for consumers, and decomposers break down the organic wastes producers and consumers leave behind. An example of this is an ear of corn (producer) being eaten by Farmer Jim (consumer). Farmer Jim throws the outer leaves of the corn into his compost pile, then eats the kernels off the cob and throws the cob in the pile as well. Decomposers in the compost break down all of that waste and turn it into rich soil. Farmer Jim later takes that soil and uses it to fertilize his corn field so he can grow more corn.

In reality, though, this cycle of survival is more complex than that. After all, Farmer Jim isn't the only one who eats his corn; so do birds, rodents, pigs, bacteria, and other organisms. That's where the concept of the food web comes in. A food web takes into consideration all of the different food chains within an ecosystem or environment and looks at how they all affect each other.

Relationships among organisms within any given ecosystem are symbiotic: what affects one affects the others in some way and there is some benefit to the populations as a result of these interconnected relationships. Types of symbiotic relationships within an ecosystem can be:

▸ **Mutual.** All organisms in the relationship benefit.

▸ **Parasitic.** One or a group of organisms benefits while another is harmed.

▸ **Commensal.** One or a group of organisms benefits while another is not affected at all.

Cellular Biology

Cellular biology examines what cells do, what they're made of, and what their purpose is. There are billions (if not trillions) of cells in the adult human body.

Although cells are microscopically small, they are actually comprised of several

important components called *organelles*. Check out these simple illustrations of the two main types of cells.

> **DEFINITION**
>
> **Organelles** are structures within a cell that perform specific functions. Think of them as the organs of a cell that make it work the way it's supposed to.

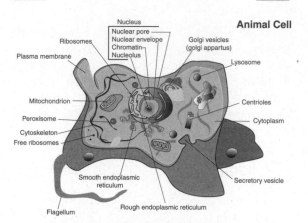

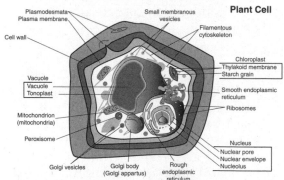

As you prepare for the ASVAB, you should become familiar with some of the terms noted in each illustration:

▸ **Nucleus.** This is the central part of the cell, which contains the DNA and RNA for growth and reproduction, as well as controlling how the genetic code is expressed by the cell.

- **Plasma cell membrane.** This is a semi porous enclosure that surrounds the cell. It acts as a boundary, holding all the contents inside the cell and preventing foreign substances from entering the cell.

- **Cytoplasm.** This term refers to the whole of a cell's internal components that are suspended within cytosol, a fluid that makes up the majority of a cell. Cytosol is made up of electrolytes, proteins, carbohydrates, and organelles.

- **Endoplasmic reticulum.** This transports cellular materials. It's also involved with synthesis and modification of those materials.

- **Ribosome.** These units use RNA (a molecule similar to DNA, discussed later in this section) to build proteins.

- **Golgi.** This is the location in the cell where newly made proteins can mature and become functional.

- **Mitochondria.** This is the unit in which nutrients are converted into energy. Mitochondria have a membrane enclosure around them.

- **Lysosome.** This organelle contains the necessary digestive enzymes for the cell.

Cells have a variety of processes that they undergo on a regular basis, one of the most important being cell division. There are two main types of cell division:

- **Mitosis.** This is the process of dividing one cell into two cells, each with its own complete nucleus and the exact genetic coding of the original cell. All cells (except those involved with sexual reproduction) undergo mitosis. Your body undergoes mitosis every time you get a cut and new skin grows back. Weightlifters also experience mitosis when they grow bigger muscles from working out.

- **Meiosis.** This method of cell division is used in sexual reproduction. In animals, the number of chromosomes per cell is halved, which results in a gamete cell. For example, in humans, male and female gametes have 23 unpaired chromosomes, while all other cells in the human body have 46. When two gamete cells combine, the outcome is a new cell with a combination of information from each gamete. In other organisms, meiosis may result in a spore. A spore is a reproductive structure often found in bacteria, plants, algae, fungi, and some protozoa.

Genetics

Within discussions of cell reproduction, you often hear about genetics, which is a branch of science that examines heredity and variation in living organisms. When cells divide, they either create an exact copy of themselves or create a cell with half its genetic material that waits to join with another similar cell.

Some key terms to understand in this subject area include:

- **Gene.** This is the basic unit of heredity and contains the information needed to build, maintain, and reproduce cells.

- **DNA.** Thanks to popular television shows like *Law & Order* and *CSI*, most people are familiar with the term *DNA*, which is short for deoxyribonucleic acid. DNA contains the genetic instructions used in the development and functioning of all known living organisms and some viruses.

- **Chromosome.** This is a specific type of DNA that is joined with protein and contains genetic information, as well as nucleotide sequences and regulatory elements specific to the organism.

- **RNA.** Short for ribonucleic acid, RNA is similar to DNA. The two differ slightly structurally; RNA is single-stranded, compared to the double-stranded composition of DNA. RNA is needed to synthesize proteins.

- **Nucleotides.** These are molecules that, when joined, comprise the structural units of RNA and DNA. They play an important role in metabolism.

- **Metabolism.** This is the set of chemical reactions that allows organisms to grow, reproduce, maintain structure, and respond to the environment. Metabolism also breaks down organic matter to harvest energy, and it influences how much food an organism requires.

- **Amino acids.** These molecules are critical to life. They also play a key role in metabolism. Amino acids form linear chains of proteins, which catalyze the chemical reactions of metabolism. Amino acids are used in the food industry as flavor enhancers, as well as in biodegradable plastics and drugs.

- **Proteins.** These linear chains of amino acids are also known as *polypeptides*. Proteins are organic compounds that are essential to cellular processes. They are a necessary component of animals' diets as well. Through the process of digestion, proteins are broken down into free amino acids, which are then used in metabolism.

Health

Our bodies are incredibly complex machines. They truly "embody" the concept of teamwork, from the organs working together within each system to the microscopic units working together in each cell. In this section, we examine some of the major systems that operate within the human body.

Circulatory System

- **The team.** This system controls the flow of blood in the body using vessels, muscles, arteries, veins, capillaries, and the heart to accomplish the mission.

- **The process.** Blood leaves the heart through the left ventricle, picking up oxygen in the aorta on its way out. (The aorta is the largest artery in the body.) The oxygen-rich blood enables cells in the rest of the body to do their work. After circulating throughout the body, the blood heads back to the heart through veins. As it filters through the lungs, the blood deposits the carbon dioxide (which we exhale) and replaces it with oxygen (which we inhale).

Respiratory System

▶ **The team.** The respiratory system works hand in hand with the circulatory system. This is the team that actually supplies the blood with oxygen. The "team" is comprised of the mouth, nose, trachea, lungs, and diaphragm.

▶ **The process.** Oxygen enters the body through the mouth and nose, passing through the trachea into the chest cavity. To get to the lungs, the oxygen then travels through a little maze of pipes known as the *bronchi* and *bronchial tubes*. Upon arrival in the lungs, it settles in small sacs called *alveoli* to await the diaphragm pumping out carbon dioxide. Finally, the diaphragm pulls the oxygen all the way through the lungs and completes the process.

Digestive System

▶ **The team.** Main players in this system that convert food to energy are the mouth, throat, esophagus (food tube), stomach, liver, gall bladder, intestines, rectum, and anus.

▶ **The process.** Food enters the mouth and begins to be broken down when you chew, mixing the food with saliva. When you swallow, you move the food into the esophagus, which brings it down into the stomach. Here, acid and other chemicals your body makes break down the food even more. Juices from the pancreas and liver (by way of the gall bladder) combine with the contents of the stomach in the small intestine to perform most of the digestive work. Nutrients are broken down and routed to the right systems, while solid wastes are passed on to the large intestine through the rectum and out the anus.

Excretory System

▶ **The team.** This system regulates the chemical composition of the body by removing waste, retaining the right amount of water, and balancing all of this with salt and nutrients. The kidneys, liver, lungs, and skin are all involved with the excretory system.

▶ **The process.** The kidneys' job is to filter waste from the blood and excrete it with water through urine. The liver also serves as a filter, removing unnecessary amino acids. The skin, often referred to as the largest organ in the body, is another excretory agent that generally filters out salt and water in the form of perspiration.

CLASSIFIED INTEL

You've probably heard of people who've died of dehydration, meaning they did not have enough water in their body. But people have also died of overhydration because the salt amounts weren't balanced with water levels, something controlled by the excretory system.

Reproductive System

▶ **The team.** This system was designed to ensure survival of the species. Female reproductive organs are located within the pelvis and are designed to produce eggs, transport and sustain these cells, nurture and develop offspring, and produce hormones. The male reproductive organs have essentially the same function (using sperm instead of eggs), with their location being both inside and outside the pelvis.

▶ **The process.** Remember back to your sex ed classes for this one. A woman's ovaries hold eggs, each of which can be fertilized by a single sperm to create a baby. Every month, an egg is released from an ovary and travels into the fallopian tube, where it stays until fertilized. If it is fertilized, it embeds in the lining of the uterus and begins to grow and form a placenta. If it isn't fertilized, it is shed along with the lining of the uterus through menstruation.

Nutrition

As you prepare for the military, you are most likely training intellectually for the ASVAB (using this book) and physically for the fitness demands of the service. In fact, nutrition and fitness will actually be intertwined with one another, your career, and your success in the military.

Most branches of the armed forces have rigorous standards for cardiovascular and muscular fitness, as well as height, weight, and body fat composition. Your ability to excel in these areas will have a direct impact on your level of success in the military. Your knowledge of this information will also positively affect your score on the General Science section of the ASVAB, so learning about nutrition is a win-win situation! Let's take a few minutes to cover some of the basics.

Every physical activity requires energy, which we gain through our body stores and the food we eat. This energy is measured in calories. Caloric intake is not the only important factor in the creation of energy, though. Nutrient balance is critical for both energy and health. Many of us probably remember the old food pyramid that taught us about balanced nutrition when we were kids.

Some of the specific nutrients that you should be familiar with include the following:

- **Proteins.** We discussed these earlier; in terms of nutrition, they are essential to growth and repair of muscle and other body tissues. They can be found most commonly in meats, eggs, dairy, seeds, and nuts.

- **Fats.** This is one source of energy that we need, but we should try to consume it in moderation. Good fats are found in olive oil, salmon, almonds, and avocados.

- **Carbohydrates.** Our main source of energy, these are found in foods like whole grains, fruits, chocolate, and honey.

- **Minerals.** These are inorganic elements that are critical to our normal functions and are found in many foods. Some examples of minerals include iron, zinc, copper, calcium, and magnesium.

- **Vitamins.** These are essential to many chemical processes in the body and are also found in a variety of foods. Some examples include vitamin A, found in fish oil, eggs, milk, and dark leafy vegetables; vitamin D, found in cheese, eggs, and breakfast cereals; vitamin K, found in spinach, parsley, and broccoli; and vitamin C, found in citrus fruits, melons, peppers, and tomatoes.

- **Water.** This is essential to normal body function. It serves as a vehicle for carrying other nutrients; furthermore, more than 60 percent of the human body consists of water.

- **Fiber.** This is the fibrous indigestible portion of our diet, essential to the health of the digestive system. It includes oatmeal, soybeans, whole grains, and artichokes.

Earth Science Review

Much like its name suggests, earth science deals with the origin, structure, and phenomena associated with planet Earth. But believe it or not, this includes topics that are not strictly terrestrial. It also includes studies about the atmosphere, weather, and space. This section explores all these areas.

Geology

We start our discussion with geology, which examines Earth's physical structure. An easy way to remember this is to remember that *geo* means "Earth." Therefore, geologists are scientists who study the Earth—or, more specifically, the lithosphere (the outer portion of Earth).

Just like an onion, the Earth is made up of several layers:

- **Lithosphere.** You probably know this as the crust. It encompasses the solid rocky top layer of the planet (the one on which we live) and part of the upper mantle. On the surface, you have the Continental crust (the land that makes up the continents) and the Oceanic crust (the land under the oceans). The entire lithosphere is only about 125 miles deep, and the crust only about 45 miles of that!

- The entire lithosphere is divided into tectonic plates, which pretty much float on top of the asthenosphere, which is made up of semi liquid rock. Because of this, tectonic plates shift, which result in earthquakes, volcanic eruptions, and the occasional sinking/creation of an island. The grooves where tectonic plates meet are called *fault lines*.

- **Mantle.** This is the next layer down. It's about 1,800 miles thick and makes up about 85 percent of Earth's total volume. The mantle is divided into several layers: the upper mantle (which is made up of the lithosphere and asthenosphere); transition region; lower mantle; and D'', or D double-prime, layer.

- The rock in the mantle is made up mostly of ferro magnesium silicates and the layer changes in texture from very rigid for a few miles, to soft and hot for several more miles and then back to rigid again.

- Pressure and temperature in this layer are both very high. In fact, the majority of the Earth's heat comes from this layer and the movement of convection currents (heat) through the mantle is believed to be responsible for the movement of tectonic plates.

- **Outer core.** The outer core is about 1,400 miles thick and is made entirely of molten rock. Though you may associate molten rock with lava, when it's underground, it's called *magma*. The two main elements found in the outer core are iron and nickel.

- **Inner core.** This is the final layer of the Earth. It's about 800 miles thick and made of solid iron and nickel. Temperatures and pressure in the inner core are higher than anywhere else on the planet, yet the metals that make it up remain solid.

Rocks

▸ More than 3,700 known mineral rocks are present in the Earth's crust. These rocks are divided into three main categories:

▸ **Igneous rock.** All rocks on Earth are originally created as this type of rock; it is the result of molten lava that has cooled and hardened. These rocks are further categorized depending on where the liquid rock cooled and hardened. If the igneous rock was formed underground, it is referred to as an intrusive rock. Remember this by thinking, "*in*side the Earth, *in*trusive rock." If the lava cooled on the surface of the Earth, it is called *extrusive rock*.

▸ **Sedimentary rock.** As igneous rocks weather the elements of wind and water, they get worn down. After thousands of years, they form particles not much larger than dirt. Often, they come to rest on the bottom of lakes, streams, and oceans. As these layers of rock interact with other minerals, they get heavier and more closely bonded. Eventually, they form solid layers of sedimentary rock. *Fossils* are usually found in these layers.

> **DEFINITION**
>
> **Fossils** are skeletons of living organisms that have been preserved over time by rock. Soft sedimentary rock, such as shale, often houses fossils.

▸ **Metamorphic rock.** Deeply entrenched in the folds of the Earth, this rock forms from igneous and sedimentary rock. The heat from Earth's interior layers basically "cooks" metamorphic rock, causing the finished product to look very different than its original version. Marble is a beautiful example of this.

▸ Rocks are often classified based on their hardness. This is determined by testing a rock's resistance to scratching and comparing the results to the Mohs, scale of mineral hardness, which gives a 1 to 10 rating (1 being the softest and 10 the hardest). Soft rock, like talc or graphite, scores a 1. Minerals such as feldspar, quartz, and topaz are toward the middle (scoring 6, 7, and 8, respectively). Diamonds top the scale at 10, as they're the hardest known mineral on Earth.

Meteorology

Meteorology is arguably the category of earth science that affects our daily lives the most. This science studies atmospheric conditions, particularly as they relate to weather. Let's examine this intriguing science that has the power to make or break weekend plans!

Atmosphere

This is a collection of layers containing various gases that sustain life on Earth. Gases include ozone, oxygen, nitrogen, carbon dioxide, and argon. You should familiarize yourself with several layers of atmosphere:

▸ **Troposphere.** This is the layer closest to Earth and extends up into the sky where clouds form; the upper part/transition layer of the troposphere is called the *tropopause*. The entire layer extends up to 12 miles high, is the only layer of our atmosphere that can support life, and is also known as the *lower atmosphere*.

▸ **Stratosphere.** This is the layer above the troposphere and is about 12 miles high as well. Ozone and about 19 percent of the atmosphere's total gases are present in this layer. The higher up in the stratosphere you get, the higher the temperature rises. This results in the formation of ozone, which helps deflect solar radiation from reaching the lower atmosphere.

▸ **Mesosphere.** This layer extends about 53 miles above the planet. The mesosphere has the opposite effect of the stratosphere in that the higher you go, the colder it gets. It's in this layer that smaller meteorites and other space debris that make it through the top layer of the atmosphere burn up.

▸ **Thermosphere.** This layer extends about 430 miles above the planet and is also known as the *upper atmosphere*. It is also the hottest layer, reaching up to 3,600°F. This is caused by the heavy absorption of solar radiation by the molecules in the very thin air.

▸ **Exosphere.** This is the final layer of the atmosphere, and extends to about 6,200 miles above the surface of the planet. It marks the barrier between the Earth's atmosphere and space, and is where satellites orbit.

Barometric Pressure

You've probably heard your meteorologist talk a lot about barometric pressure. This is simply a measure of the weight of the air as it pushes down on an area of Earth. Important things to know include:

▸ High pressure generally indicates good or improving weather. Beautiful sunny days are the result of high barometric pressure.

▸ Low or falling pressure suggests poor weather is looming. Barometric pressure falls sharply just before a tornado and remains low throughout a hurricane.

Front

This is what happens when two different types of air masses meet. Because their density is not the same they won't mix, but rather they form a wall or boundary. A cold front forms when a mass of cold air moves toward and meets a mass of warm air. Rain and thunderstorms often result, as well as lower temperatures.

A warm front occurs at the boundary where cold air meets warm air. The resulting weather is usually more stable and widespread, with some precipitation possible and in extreme cases ice storms in winter.

Clouds

Clouds are formations of gaseous water. In English, this means that when water evaporates from the Earth, it changes states from liquid to gas (see our physical science discussion). As the water reverts to a liquid state and settles in the atmosphere, clouds begin to form. Once the clouds begin to take shape, meteorologists can identify the type of cloud based on how high it is in the sky and how it looks. That's why most clouds have two parts to their name: the first part deals with their height, the second with their appearance.

High-level clouds get the prefix *cirro*, while midlevel clouds get the prefix *alto*. Low-level clouds don't have any prefix attached to their names. The following list of identifiers typically applies to the second half of a cloud's name:

▸ **Cumulus.** Puffy like cotton balls; often appear in groups.

- **Cirrus.** Wispy, like shreds of cotton; made of ice crystals.

- **Cumulonimbus.** Tall and thick; sometimes called *thunderheads* because they often bring thunderstorms.

- **Stratus.** Look like a thick, flat blanket; all one color but can look pink or orange during sunrise or sunset.

CLASSIFIED INTEL

Air has to be just a bit dirty for clouds to form. The water vapor needs something on which to condense, such as dirt or dust particles.

Astronomy

Astronomy is the study of matter in outer space, including celestial bodies and the universe as a whole. Because Earth is a part of this, it's considered an area of focus in earth science.

Since there's a whole universe of information we could share with you about astronomy, we focus on only a few key concepts and terms, to provide a general understanding of the subject. Let's start with some general vocabulary.

Astronomy Vocab

Term	Definition
Star	An object that shines because of nuclear reactions that release energy from its core.
Sun	A star around which planets and other celestial objects move.

Term	Definition
Planet	A celestial body larger than an asteroid that moves around and receives light from a star.
Solar system	The system of planets and other objects orbiting a star, such as the sun.
Galaxy	A group of stars, gas, and dust held together by gravity. Our galaxy is known as the Milky Way.
Asteroid	A rock or minor planet orbiting the sun. There is a whole belt of asteroids between Mars and Jupiter, and another beyond Pluto.
Meteor	Also known as a *shooting star*. This occurs when a particle of dust enters Earth's atmosphere.
Meteorite	An object from outer space, such as a rock, that falls into the Earth and lands on its surface.
Comet	A small, frozen mass of dust and gas revolving around the sun.
Constellation	Groupings of stars named by astronomers. For example, the Big Dipper is part of the Great Bear, one of the most famous constellations.
Light year	The distance a ray of light would travel in one year—about six trillion miles.
Phases	The perceived change in the shape of the moon, Mercury, and Venus, depending on how much of the sunlit side is facing the Earth. Some examples of moon phases include new, half, crescent, and full.

Term	Definition
Black hole	The area around a tiny (yet massive) object that appears black. In actuality, light cannot escape this region because of an incredibly strong gravitational field.
Binary star	Two stars orbiting each other that look like one star.
Equinox	Around March 21 and September 22. On these days, day and night are the same length of time all over the world.

Now that you're familiar with some of the terms you may see on the ASVAB relating to astronomy, let's talk about some specific concepts you should be familiar with.

Planets

You may have learned in school that our solar system is made up of nine planets, but that assessment has changed several times over the years as scientists learn more about space.

In 2006, Pluto was designated as a dwarf planet and no longer qualified for full planetary status. Therefore, the eight planets in our solar system are (in order from proximity to the sun): Mercury, Venus, Earth, Mars (all considered inner planets), Jupiter, Saturn, Uranus, and Neptune.

TEST TIP

You probably learned some kind of mnemonic device for remembering the planets in school. It needs a little tweaking, due to Pluto's untimely demise as a planet. Try: My Very Earnest Mother Just Served Us Noodles; My Very Easy Method Just Speeds Up Naming; and My Very Educated Mother Just Showed Us Nebulas.

Kepler's Laws of Planetary Motion

Johannes Kepler, a famous astronomer, created a set of laws that have proven applicable to all planets. They include:

1. The sun is the center of the galaxy, and all of the planets move around the sun in elliptical orbits.

2. Like the axis upon which the Earth rotates, the planets revolve around the sun attached to imaginary lines that extend out from the center of the sun. This means that the planets never move any closer or farther from the sun than the path of the ellipse they follow when rotating the sun.

3. The amount of time it takes a planet to make one full trip around the sun depends on how far away the planet is from the sun. Based on this law, the time it takes Mercury to travel around the sun a single time is less than the time it takes Earth to make a single trip around the sun.

In addition to Kepler's laws, you should know that planets can have satellites (moons), which revolve around the planet, not the sun. Some planets, like Jupiter and Saturn, have multiple moons. Earth only has one.

Eclipses

These occur when our view of one object in the sky is blocked by either another object or the Earth's shadow. Eclipses come in two types:

▶ **Solar.** The moon appears between Earth and the sun, temporarily casting Earth in shadow. During a total eclipse, all you can see is a beautiful ring of light surrounding a blackened moon. It is dangerous to look directly at a solar eclipse, even with sun glasses. Solar eclipses are best viewed through a pinhole projector.

Solar Eclipse

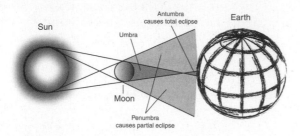

Not to scale

▶ **Lunar.** During this magnificent scientific event, the moon passes behind Earth, which blocks sunlight from the moon and casts it in shadow (called an umbra). Lunar eclipses can last as long as an hour and a half, and actually cause the moon to appear red. For all of you stargazers, it's perfectly safe to view, since the moon does not create its own light.

Lunar Eclipse

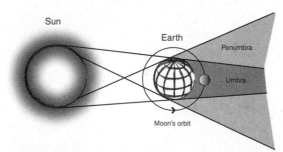

Not to scale

Physical Science Review

Physical science examines the nonliving systems found in natural science. Two examples of this include chemistry and physics. Let's discuss a few of the basics from each of these disciplines.

Chem Lab

Chemistry is the study of matter, which is anything that has mass and volume. Most often, chemists study substances that are considered microscopic, such as atoms, the states of matter, and chemical reactions. Consider a few basic facts regarding each of these chemistry subtopics.

Atoms

This is the basic unit of matter. Atoms have three primary components:

▶ **Protons.** These are the positively charged particles in an atom. They actually comprise the nucleus; different atoms have different numbers of protons, which make up the atomic number or charge of the atom.

▶ **Electrons.** These are the negatively charged particles surrounding the nucleus of an atom, forming "clouds" called *orbitals*. They are the smallest part of the atom, and their purpose is to balance the positively charged protons.

▶ **Neutrons.** Much like the root indicates in the word *neutron*, neutrons are the particles that have no charge in the atom—they are neutral. However, neutrons have a major effect on the mass and radioactivity of an atom. All atoms have neutrons (with the exception of hydrogen).

Two additional terms you should know related to atoms are ion and isotope. An ion is an atom that has an electrical charge due to the addition or subtraction of electrons. An isotope is two or more forms of the same element that contain different numbers of neutrons.

Element

This word describes a chemical substance that can't be separated into simpler parts by chemical means. Elements you might be familiar with include oxygen (O), hydrogen (H), copper (Cu), and aluminum (Al). All of the known elements are listed on The periodic table of elements and are classified according to atomic number and atomic weight. It's a good idea to memorize the symbols for common elements when you prep for the ASVAB. A great interactive tool for exploring elements is the Elements Database (www.elementsdatabase.com/).

Compound

When two or more elements chemically bond together in a fixed ratio, a compound is formed. Unlike with elements, compounds can be broken down into simpler atoms through chemical means.

Compounds are described by *molecular* formulas, which show the atoms that are present in the compound, in what concentrations, and sometimes in what forms.

> **DEFINITION**
>
> A **molecule** is a combination of two or more atoms that are chemically bonded.

For example, if you combine one atom of carbon (C) and two atoms of oxygen (O), you create the compound carbon dioxide (CO_2). The number of atoms is represented in the smaller number of the compound symbol.

Matter

As we said earlier, matter is anything that has mass and volume. Therefore, it is all around us. Despite this all-encompassing definition, matter can be categorized into the following states:

▶ **Solid.** Atoms in this state are very close together (dense), so much so that the substance has a definite shape and volume. A major force is needed to change the shape of a solid.

▶ **Liquid.** Atoms in this state are not as closely bonded and tend to move so that a liquid takes the shape of whatever is containing it. However, it does have a measurable volume. Heat has the greatest effect on the change of a liquid.

▶ **Gas.** Atoms in this state are very loosely bonded and will fill the entirety of any container that holds it (think of helium inside a balloon). Gases do not take on any form of their own, nor do they have any measurable volume.

Chemical Reactions

These occur when two or more molecules interact, and some kind of chemical change happens as a result of that interaction. Though this action may cause change (the reaction), the molecules involved remain the same. The creation of compounds is a chemical reaction. Perhaps you've heard what happens when you combine hydrogen and oxygen: with the right number of molecules, you get a substance called water!

Physics Lab

Physics, which is the study of force and motion, also operates by a variety of laws. This section should be a comfortable fit for you, then, scientifically speaking! Many key concepts in physical science (including Newton's laws) are further detailed in Chapter 15, but some additional ones you should familiarize yourself with include the following:

▶ **Velocity.** The rate of motion in a specific direction. Velocity is measured in distance (such as kilometers) per time frame (such as seconds or hours) in a given direction. For example, a car might travel 35 kilometers per hour in a northern direction (35 km/h north).

▶ **Acceleration.** The rate of change in velocity of an object. If an object changes its velocity by the same amount each second, this is known as constant acceleration. When the rate of acceleration is variable, it is known as nonconstant acceleration. Constant acceleration would take place if a car increased directional speed by 5 miles per hour every second. The acceleration would be constant at 5 mph/s.

On the other hand, if the car gradually increased speed, allowing for slow drivers and lane changes, the acceleration might vary from second to second. It would be nonconstant, with 5 mph/s the first second, 2 mph/s in the next second, 6 mph/s after that, and so forth.

▶ **Friction.** Two objects rubbing against one another, sometimes resulting in a force that holds back movement of a sliding object. For example, sandpaper on wood creates friction as it smooths the surface of the wood. The brakes on a car apply friction to the wheels, slowing them down.

▶ **Momentum.** This describes the mass of an object multiplied by its velocity. For example, a fire engine might have a mass of 11,000 kilograms and a velocity of 20 meters per second heading west on the interstate. The momentum of the fire truck would be 220,000 kg-m/sec.

▶ **Gravity.** A force of attraction between mass and the universe. The strong force of gravity on Earth pulls everything toward the center of the planet. For this reason, no one falls off the round world as it spins and rotates.

▶ **Force.** Any influence that can cause a change in the velocity of an object. Have you ever heard someone say, "Boy, the force of the wind out there was really strong today"? Wind can be a force against a variety of things, such as a sailboat or a vehicle. Wind can cause a sailboat to change directions, slow down, or speed up. Forces are measured in newtons using the following formula: Force = Mass × Acceleration.

▶ **Work.** A force that is applied to one object and results in either the movement of that object or a transfer of energy to an object. We perform work when we lift an object, type on the keyboard, wash vegetables for dinner, and so forth. To calculate work, use the following formula: Work = Force × Distance. Work is measured in joules, a basic unit of energy.

Let's say you use your strong muscles and apply a force against the leg press machine of 100 newtons. In fact, you are so strong that you push the weights 2 whole meters! Plug these numbers into the previous formula to find that your leg press results in 200 joules of work.

We know better than anyone that all this information is a lot to take in. Heck, we wrote it! But the best way to assimilate this into your brain is to attack actual questions. Flip ahead to Chapter 17 to practice answering General Science questions.

Electronics Skills

As we progress through the age of information technology, it has become almost essential for the average person to be computer literate, capable of telecommunication, and cyber-connected from all over the world. Modern jobs depend on these skills in both the civilian sector and the military community. Even the ASVAB exam you're prepping for is graded electronically—including the paper and pencil version!

Our world has become so dependent on electronics that we probably can't imagine a day without using something electronic, even if it's just a lightbulb. Electronic technology has enhanced the quality of our lives in many ways.

Electronics are a fundamental component in the modern military; your score on the electronics subtest will indicate whether a career in electronics might be a good fit for you. This chapter reviews the terms and theories often seen on the Electronics Information (EI) subtest, which will help you prepare for a variety of questions.

Why Do I Have to Take This?

Often soldiers are portrayed as camouflage-clad warriors who crawl around in the dirt, run through jungles, and scale rough terrain in search of the enemy. Well, this depiction is certainly true—but it is only one piece of the modern soldier's composition.

These days, the military is equipped with some of the most technologically advanced equipment in the world. Infantry have night-vision goggles and global positioning systems, pilots have heat sensors and lasers to guide missiles, musicians have professional sound and recording equipment, and so on. There is even such a thing as an unmanned vehicle that can detect sniper location and mortar fire, and then fire back accordingly.

True enough, all this information is interesting—but what's the point? Well, here's the deal: military technology can only help accomplish the mission when the service members know how to use, maintain, and repair it. This is where people with electrical aptitudes and knowledge come in.

As with most jobs in the military, you don't have to be a civilian electrician to become one in the service. You simply have to demonstrate an initial propensity for that type of work by scoring well on the electronics subtest of the ASVAB.

Much like the correlation between civilian auto mechanics and military mechanics, electricians have skills that carry over from one sector to the other, too. This makes a military career in electrical work that much more desirable, because your marketability after service is fantastic. Plus, you'll receive training and gain experience on Uncle Sam's nickel, so to speak!

CLASSIFIED INTEL

Dozens of jobs in the electronics field require knowledge similar to that of an electrician: heating and air-conditioning technicians, refrigeration mechanics and installers, line installers and repairers, electrical and electronics installers and repairers, electronic home entertainment equipment installers and repairers, and elevator installers and repairers.

Civilian electricians perform a variety of tasks, including drilling holes; setting anchors; measuring, fabricating, and attaching conduits; creating and drawing diagrams for entire electrical systems, and

more. In the military, electronics knowledge and skills are extremely valuable and offer you the opportunity to work in areas that simply aren't accessible to civilians.

Consider the following:

▸ With the Navy's state-of-the-art ships, highly technical submarines, advanced aircraft, and cutting-edge weapons systems, electronics are an integral part of nearly everything the Navy does.

▸ The Air Force uses incredibly technical equipment, performing nuclear treaty monitoring, nuclear event detection, and avionics that preserve our nation's security.

▸ The Army has always been a forerunner in the field of simulation-based training, offering some of the most advanced flight simulators in the world.

▸ The Coast Guard has used technology in their own right to save lives, enhance law enforcement techniques, and modernize telecommunications at sea.

▸ The Marines have advanced combat operations through the development of software-based systems that target information sharing and increase the speed of network communications.

If you decide to pursue a degree when your service is over, the coursework you completed can transfer into college credits within a network of more than 1,800 colleges nationwide. You'll also receive extensive on-the-job training with communications systems and highly sophisticated computerized equipment.

In short, scoring well on the electronics section of the ASVAB is your key to an exciting career that's loaded with military excitement and civilian job growth later.

What to Expect

The EI subtest gives you about 30 seconds to answer each question. The CAT consists of 16 questions that must be completed in 8 minutes, and the PAP gives you 9 minutes to answer 20 questions.

But here's the good news: these questions are designed much like the questions on the science subtest—either you know the answers or you don't. There's one clearly defined right answer—nothing abstract, and no need for extensive logic or reasoning.

You'll be asked to apply your knowledge of electronic terms and concepts to questions regarding basic electricity, wiring, and electrical systems. More specifically, you should be familiar with circuits, voltage, and grounding. You'll also see questions on amplitude and frequency, sound waves, inductors, and AM radio signals.

Your best bet for excelling on this subtest is to implement one of the military's favorite phrases: attention to detail. The Army used to employ this terrific little expression as a training tool to help soldiers learn from their mistakes in basic training.

In fact, just to be sure the soldiers remembered this key piece of advice, it was drilled into them as they executed dozens of push-ups! The drill sergeant would yell, "Down!" As the soldier completed the downward motion of the push-up, he (or she) yelled, "Attention to detail!" On the up command, the punishment—er, *learning*—continued as soldiers yelled, "Teamwork is the key!"

So use this fun (but true) anecdote to your advantage. Find a buddy and study the information presented in this chapter. Pay close attention to details, remember the terminology, and look for root words on the test that you're already familiar with. Adhering to these steps will go a long way toward helping you earn the score you want on the EI subtest.

Supercharged Electricity Review

When it comes to the language of electronics, the following table defines a few terms you should know before you go any further.

Must-Know Terms

Term	Definition
Electricity	Flow of electrons through a conductor, such as copper or aluminum wire
Conductor	A material through which electricity can flow easily
Current (I)	Flow of electricity through a conductor
Ampere (A)	Measure of current
Insulator	A material through which electricity flows poorly or not at all
Voltage	Strength with which current flows through a conductor
Volt (V)	Measure of voltage
Resistance	Hindrance to electric flow
Ohm (Ω)	Measure of resistance
Power (P)	Amount of energy transferred during a specified time
Watt (W)	Measure of electric power

In the sections that follow, we break down electricity into four simple topics: current, voltage, circuits, and Ohm's law.

Electricity 101

To explain electricity, we should really start with square one: matter, atoms, and electrons (okay, squares one, two, *and* three!). Do those terms sound familiar? They should, if you've read this book in chapter order. If not, flip back to Chapter 11 and take a minute to brush up on these concepts. They provide the foundation for basic electricity principles.

Electrons carry a negative charge with them wherever they go—you might say they never leave home without it. If a bunch of them all head out in the same direction, *bang!* You've got electricity.

[
CLASSIFIED INTEL

If you lined up a million electrons "shoulder to shoulder" (so to speak), they would barely stretch across the top of a pin!
]

Here are some interesting facts that demonstrate just how amazing electricity is:

▸ Electricity travels 186,000 miles per second. That's eight times around the world in a single second!

▸ Water is a good conductor of electricity. The human body is made up of 60 percent water, so if you touch electricity, expect a very unpleasant reaction. At a minimum, you will probably experience a simple shock; at worst, death.

▸ Electricity always takes the shortest path to the ground. As a conductor of electricity, you should take care not to touch anything connected to electricity. Touching a tree with a fallen power line resting on it could be fatal.

A Current Affair

As electrons move together, they create something known as an electric current. To make electricity useful for human purposes, we capture the flow of negative electrons using a conductor.

[
HEADS-UP

Conductors include almost any metal, such as iron, gold, silver, copper, or mercury. Most household wiring uses copper and is covered with an insulator, such as rubber, to make handling such wires possible.
]

To understand the concept of flow, picture two funnels. The first funnel has a very wide spout, allowing a great amount of water to pass through at one time. The second funnel has a very narrow spout, enabling only a sliver of water to pass through. If you placed the two funnels side by side and poured water into them, you would see far more water per second passing through the larger-spouted funnel than the smaller-spouted one.

Using the same concept, some household appliances require more current than other appliances. For example, hair dryers and microwaves need more current than nightlights and alarm clocks. Current is measured in amperes (or amps, for short).

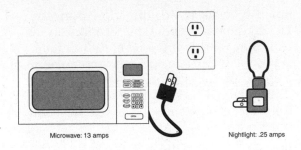

Microwave: 13 amps   Nightlight: .25 amps

Crank Up the Voltage

If you want to know how much electrical force a power source applies, you're looking for the voltage. Think of this as the amount of force pushing the current through a conductor. If you pushed the water through the smaller funnel spout discussed earlier instead of just letting it flow naturally, you would increase the speed and force at which it exits the funnel.

Currents flowing from a power source, such as the electric company, a gas-powered generator, or a battery, operate much like the water in the funnel spout. Each produces and sends out a certain amount of voltage, which pushes current along a conductor at a certain rate.

Voltage in the United States is fairly standard for most homes. Household fixtures (such as lamps, televisions, and vacuum cleaners) typically run on 120 volts; some larger appliances, such as ranges and air conditioners, need 240 volts.

Testing All Circuits

As electrons flow through wires or other types of conductors, the path they take is called a *circuit*.

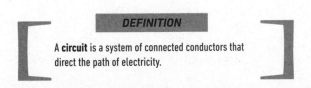

DEFINITION

A **circuit** is a system of connected conductors that direct the path of electricity.

The circuit is functional only if a source of electricity is present to push the electrons along their path. That's why a hair dryer cord (or any other cord) is completely harmless—and useless—when it's not plugged in. Some of the most common electricity sources include batteries, wall outlets, and solar panels.

As long as electrons are able to move along their desired paths, the circuit is complete. A complete circuit may also be referred to as closed. An easy way to remember this is that *complete* and *closed* both start with the letter *c*. As soon as you turn off that hair dryer, light, or other electrical appliance, though, you have stopped the circuit. When the electrons stop moving, the circuit is called open.

Simple Circuit

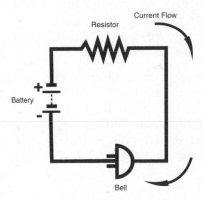

A basic circuit, such as the one shown, starts with a power source that generates a negative electric current, which then flows through a conductor until it meets a positive charge that closes the circuit. Along the way, it can meet resistors, loads, or other components that can change the path and properties of the energy. These can include the following:

▸ **Diode.** Allows current to flow in only one direction. (We discuss diodes in detail later in the chapter.)

- ▸ **Capacitor.** Stores charge in a circuit, often temporarily for rapid release.

- ▸ **Fuse.** Prevents a circuit from overloading due to too much current.

- ▸ **Wire.** Medium through which current travels in a circuit.

- ▸ **Switch.** Opens or closes the circuit.

- ▸ **Battery.** Type of power source in the circuit.

- ▸ **Transformer.** Transfers electricity from one source to another.

- ▸ **Resistor.** Provides resistance to the current flowing through a circuit.

- ▸ **Aerial.** Produces or receives electromagnetic waves. Can also be called an *antenna*.

- ▸ **Amplifier.** Increases current or voltage.

- ▸ **Lamp.** Turns electrical energy into light energy.

- ▸ **Motor.** Turns electrical energy into kinetic energy.

When you see movement from positive to negative on a circuit diagram, you're seeing the flow of current. Electrons, which carry electrical energy, move from negative to positive in a circuit. In other words, current and electrons actually flow in opposite directions.

But not all currents flow the same way. Alternating current (AC) describes the two types of currents that flow from sources of power. AC flows in both directions, reversing itself multiple times per second. It is commonly used by the power company for industrial and domestic customers alike. "DC (direct current) travels" travels in only one direction: from power source to destination. Batteries are a common example of DC.

Since we're discussing direction of current, let's talk about diodes for a second. You can compare this component to the arrow signs that indicate a one-way street. Traffic responds to the sign by flowing in only one direction on a one-way street, which helps limit excess movement of cars, trucks, and other vehicles.

Likewise, a diode allows electrical current to flow in one direction but blocks it from traveling in the opposite direction. Most diodes are made of silicon and have a variety of functions. For one thing, they can be used as light sensors and emitters called *light emitting diodes* (LEDs).

Diodes can also convert AC to DC in a process known as *rectification*. The alternator in your car (which uses the energy produced from your engine to charge your battery) is a good example of a diode that converts AC to DC.

Now that we know *how* electric current flows through a circuit, you may be wondering *what* uses all this electricity. If you've spent any time with an electrician or if you've done electrical work yourself, you may have heard the term *load*. A load is anything that uses the electricity from a circuit. Have you ever had to replace the heating element in your oven or, better yet, changed a lightbulb? Heating elements, lightbulbs, and motors are all examples of *loads*.

> **DEFINITION**
>
> A **load** is part of a circuit that converts one type of energy to another (for example, electric to kinetic energy). See Chapter 15 for more information about energy.

When planning a circuit or learning how one works, schematics are usually involved. This is a technical way of mapping out all the parts in a circuit using commonly accepted symbols. The following diagram illustrates common symbols used in circuit schematics.

Circuit Symbols

For the purposes of passing the EI section of the ASVAB, you should know about these two main types of circuits, which are diagramed here using some of the symbols we just showed you:

▶ **Series.** A circuit that provides a single-flow path. Think about strings of lights in which, if one bulb goes out, the whole string does.

Series Circuit

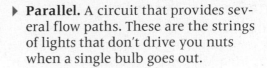

▶ **Parallel.** A circuit that provides several flow paths. These are the strings of lights that don't drive you nuts when a single bulb goes out.

Parallel Circuit

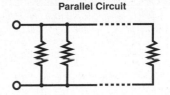

Before we wrap up our discussion on circuits, we need to discuss resistance. As the name implies, resistance is anything that impedes the flow of a current.

When current moves freely, it is said to have low resistance. The amount of resistance in a wire depends on its *gauge,* length, and composition.

DEFINITION

Wire thickness is called **gauge**. Gauge is expressed in reverse of what you might expect: a large wire has a small gauge, and a small wire has a large gauge. The larger the gauge, the higher the resistance.

Good conductors of electricity offer low resistance. One example is copper, which most modern homes are wired with. Resistance causes friction, which causes heat. The higher the resistance, the hotter a wire can get.

Have you ever touched the plug on your hair dryer or portable heater after it's been in use? It's so hot that it can actually burn your skin—so we don't recommend trying this little experiment at home! Resistance is measured in ohms, which leads us to our next topic: Ohm's law.

The Zen of Ohm's Law

With a basic understanding of voltage and current, you can understand how all of this is applied. Ohm's law is a good place to start because it defines the proportional relationship among currents, voltage, and resistance within a circuit.

Ohm's law states that electric current is directly proportional to voltage—the higher the voltage, the greater the current. It also states that electric current is inversely proportional to resistance—the higher the resistance, the lower the current. To find out how much current you have, you divide the voltage by the resistance.

You can express Ohm's law in a number of different ways. Understanding this concept will likely get you through several ASVAB questions on this subtest. Memorize these simple equations and use them to calculate any of the following.

Related Ohm's Law Equations

Value Sought	Equation	Translation
Ampere (A)	$A = \frac{V}{\Omega}$	amps $= \frac{\text{volts}}{\text{ohms}}$
Watts (W)	$W = V \times A$	watts = volts $\times$ amps
Voltage (V)	$V = A \times \Omega$	volts = amps $\times$ ohms
Ohms (Ω)	$\Omega = \frac{V}{A}$	ohms $= \frac{\text{volts}}{\text{amps}}$

Since formulas can feel a bit abstract, let's practice some ways you might apply these equations on the test, so you get a more concrete idea of what to expect.

1. You're building a circuit that has a voltage of 240. You add a resistor of 60 ohms. What is your amperage?

    (A) 4A

    (B) 6A

    (C) 8A

    (D) 10A

This question is asking you to calculate amperage. Using Ohm's law, you divide your voltage (240) by your resistance (60) and come up with answer A (4A).

2. What would your power be if you have 2 amps and 120 volts?

    (A) 40W

    (B) 120W

    (C) 240W

    (D) 360W

This question is asking you to find the wattage, which is a measure of power. If you know that your voltage is 120V and your current is 2A, you can determine that your power usage is 240W, answer C. (P = 120 × 2)

3. How many volts would you need to complete a circuit with 50 amps of current and 10 ohms of resistance?

    (A) 300V

    (B) 600V

    (C) 500V

    (D) 1,200V

Since you're being asked to find voltage, use the voltage equation here and multiply your amps by your ohms, giving you 500 volts, answer C.

Now that you understand the difference in ohms, volts, and watts, you should familiarize yourself with the following related terms. EI subtest questions asking for these definitions have been known to pop up:

- **Ohmmeter.** Measures resistance
- **Voltmeter.** Measures differences in voltage
- **Wattmeter.** Measures power
- **Ammeter.** Measures current

Ups and Downs of Frequency and Waves

In addition to the basic concepts regarding power and electricity, the ASVAB asks questions pertaining to frequency, waves, and principles thereof. The following sections will get you up to speed in each of these areas in no time.

Frequency Explained

Frequency is an important electronic concept that can be applied in a variety of situations. Remember our discussion a few pages back about alternating current? Well, frequency applies to electric power, because AC has a specific number of cycles per second, known as *frequency*.

> **DEFINITION**
>
> **Frequency** is a measure of any periodic event expressed as the number of complete cycles per second. This measurement applies to AC power, waves (sound, light, electromagnetic, and the like), computer clock speed, and so forth.

Frequency is measured in hertz (Hz), after the German physicist Heinrich Hertz. He was the first scientist to prove the existence of electromagnetic waves. In the United

States, our AC has a frequency of 60Hz. When there are fewer cycles per second, the frequency is said to be lower. Other developed countries run AC power on either 50Hz or 60Hz.

To envision frequency, it may help to picture a wave that looks like the letter *S*, rotated 90 degrees. If you measure the full shape of the *S* from beginning to end, you have calculated one oscillation. This is known as 1Hz of frequency.

Another way to measure frequency is to divide the number of times an event occurs by the amount of time given. Your frequency is then $\frac{\text{Times Event Takes Place}}{\text{Amount of Time Elapsed}}$.

To understand frequency better, imagine the Marine Corps physical fitness test. During the abdominal crunch event, each soldier must complete as many crunches as possible (using proper form) in 2 minutes. Let's say that Private Johnny completes 100 crunches in 2 minutes, earning the maximum score possible for this event. His frequency would be 0.83Hz per second.

Ride the Waves

A wave is a disturbance that is transmitted through space and time. It usually includes a transfer of energy as well. There are water waves in the ocean, light waves from the sun, sound waves from noise, and so forth.

Waves come in a variety of shapes and forms. The three most common types of waves include transverse, longitudinal, and surface waves:

- **Transverse waves** cause particles in the medium where the wave is located to travel in a perpendicular direction to the wave itself. Examples of transverse waves include radio, heat, and light waves.

- **Longitudinal waves** cause particles in the medium to move parallel to the wave direction. A sound wave is a good illustration of this. For example, the medium may be a room, a concert hall, an outdoor venue, or even a car in which a sound is located. The particles that vibrate in the room are air particles, and they move alongside the sound wave.

- **Surface waves** cause particles in the medium to move in a circular direction. Ocean waves exemplify this principle, as do certain types of seismic waves (which can cause earthquakes).

Several characteristics can be universally applied to all waves:

- **Reflection.** This is a change in wave direction after it strikes a reflective surface. A mirror is a good reflective surface for light waves. A reflective surface in acoustics might be a wall or a rock, which then causes echoes.

- **Refraction.** This is a change in wave direction because of a change in the wave's speed from entering a new medium. A good example of refraction is when you place a straw in a glass of water. Under the water, the straw appears to be broken. The water is considered the new medium, which caused the light wave speed to change once the straw entered the water.

- **Diffraction.** This is the bending of waves as they interact with obstacles in their path. A good example of this occurs with sound waves. If you and your friend are having a conversation outdoors and, for some reason, you step behind a tree while she is talking, you can still hear her voice.

The sound waves bend around the tree, such that if you keep backing up behind the tree, eventually the sound of her voice will be no different than if the tree wasn't even there. This is because the wavelengths begin to even out again as they get farther away from the obstacle. Diffraction also tends to be more pronounced with longer wavelengths, making it easier to hear low frequencies (such as the booming bass from a car driving by) than high frequencies (such as the guitar or vocalist in that car).

- **Interference.** This is when two waves come into contact with each other and collide. Have you ever tried to use a walkie-talkie or handheld radio, and you could actually hear someone else's conversation? Or maybe you had a baby monitor for a sleeping child, and you heard a lot of static coming through the speaker. These are both examples of interference in sound waves, which tends to occur when two things have the same frequency.

- **Dispersion.** This occurs when a wave splits up by frequency. A rainbow is a great example of dispersion of light waves. The white light is scattered into different wavelengths of various colors.

- **Rectilinear propagation.** This is the movement of waves in a straight line. Even if you throw a rock into a pond and bend the front of a wave, though, the wave is still moving in a generally straight line.

As we mentioned in our discussion of frequency, waves are often depicted in a never-ending letter *S* shape, rotated 90°. Three types of measurements are important to know for the ASVAB:

- ▸ **Wavelength.** Measures the distance from one peak or crest of a wave to the next corresponding peak or crest.

- ▸ **Wave speed.** Multiply the wavelength measure by the frequency.

- ▸ **Amplitude.** This measures the height of a wave. It's calculated by slicing a line down the middle of the *S*. You then measure from the midline to the top of a crest to determine amplitude.

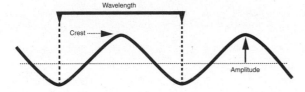

Finishing Touches

As we wrap up our discussion on electronics, here are a few last tips for the ASVAB. Some of the questions may ask you to define acronyms that you are familiar with, even if you don't actually know what each letter stands for. After you get rid of any answer choice that does not start with the same letters as the acronym, eliminate any others that don't make sense for the subject you're working with.

TEST TIP

Remember your root word and prefix breakdowns from Chapter 5. They still apply, even to electronics.

Also, if you're not sure about the meaning of a word or term, look to the roots of the words to get a clue about their meaning. For example, if you are asked a question about bipolar junction transistors, take the first word apart and look for prefixes or root words that you are familiar with. *Bi* means

"two," as in *bicycle* (two wheels) and *biannual* (twice per year). *Polar* means "opposite," as in the north and south poles. In the case of electronics, it refers to positive and negative charges or flows of electricity.

You also know that the word *junction* refers to a place where two roads meet. In electronics, it is a place where two wires meet or where two devices with different electrical properties meet. Thus, if all you knew was that bi means two, polar means opposite, and junction is a meeting place, you could figure out this electrical definition.

You could also pick it out graphically using the same basis of knowledge. Just look for a picture that has two lines that meet and look like a sideways *T*; this represents the junction. Then look for two lines coming out of the sideways "t," one of which probably has an arrow on it. The two lines coming from the junction will be going in different directions, representing the "bi" and "polar" aspects of the question. And there you have it!

Using the knowledge you gained through this chapter, as well as the rest of the book, should position you to do well on this portion of the ASVAB. Now flip ahead to Chapter 17 and test your knowledge on some practice questions.

Auto Information

"It takes 8,460 bolts to assemble an automobile and one nut to scatter it all over the road."

—Author unknown

Cars are such amazing machines; they're built from hundreds of parts, all beautifully crafted and designed to work in perfect harmony with one another—until one poor decision is made by the driver, that is. That beautiful piece of machinery can suddenly become a 4,000-pound battering ram.

This is a risk the military can't afford to take, which is why the ASVAB has a section that tests aptitude for Auto Information (AI). Throughout this chapter, we discuss the function of several key systems in the modern automobile, as well as the importance of proper maintenance and repair.

Why Do I Have to Take This?

People join the military for all kinds of reasons. One of the biggest advantages to joining the service, however, is the ability to gain training and experience in the career of your choice, at no cost to you.

If you enjoy doing physical work more than sitting at a desk, the automotive field might be a good choice for you. This field has excellent transferability to similar civilian professions when your tour of duty is over, such as automotive and heavy equipment mechanics, auto and construction equipment dealers, and so forth. With automotive skills, you might also work for farm equipment companies or for state highway agencies.

Auto mechanics and heavy equipment repair technicians are a critical cog in the wheel of the military. They transport the troops safely in and out of battle, ensure the replenishment of necessary supplies, and keep military operations mobile.

> **CLASSIFIED INTEL**
>
> Gen. George Washington once said, "There is nothing so likely to produce peace as to be well prepared to meet an enemy." In the modern military, this means maintaining mechanized equipment so that it functions properly on a moment's notice.

What to Expect

This particular subtest is designed a bit differently than the other sections of the ASVAB. First of all, it is much shorter than most of the other tests. The CAT has only 11 questions, and you'll have 7 minutes to answer them.

Secondly, the PAP combines Auto Information with the Shop Information subtest, asking you to answer a total of 25 questions on both subjects—in just 11 minutes. Regardless of which test version you take, your auto and shop skills are combined for scoring purposes under the AS category.

As in the other technical sections on the ASVAB, you'll be able to put your life experiences to the test here. Most of the questions address basic maintenance and terminology associated with cars, which means that even someone without a formal automotive education might have some basic knowledge as an owner/operator.

The other thing to keep in mind before you take the ASVAB is that some questions may not even require specific automotive knowledge. You may encounter a question or two that asks you to use a multistep process to figure out what happens next. The idea is to use logic and an understanding of the steps to arrive at a conclusion.

You will probably also find a lot more questions that use diagrams, asking you to identify parts of the illustration. Regardless of how the question is structured, though, the next few pages will help you prepare for anything that comes your way on the automotive subtest!

Things That Make You Go Vroom

Automakers have radically simplified the driver's role in the maintenance, upkeep, and running of our cars. In most cases, we turn a key, fill up the tank, change the oil and tires ... and that's it. That's all the labor and responsibility involved in using and enjoying our favorite 2-ton toy.

Considering how quick and painless maintaining a car nowadays is, it's quite amazing when we consider what goes on under the hood. Here's a look at the main systems that make your car go.

Engine Basics

The engine is the heart of your car and the most important component for making it go. In fact, most of the other major systems all work in conjunction to make sure the engine can do its job: providing the energy to propel the car forward.

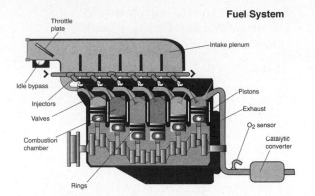

Fuel System

Throttle plate

Intake plenum

Idle bypass

Injectors

Valves

Pistons

Exhaust

O₂ sensor

Catalytic converter

Combustion chamber

Rings

Most engines operate using a four-stroke combustion cycle broken down into the following:

▸ **Intake stroke.** The *pistons* are at the top of the cylinders in the engine. The crankshaft and camshaft move to open the fuel intake valves and lower the pistons (with precision timing). The downward motion of the pistons draw in an exact ratio of fuel and air until the combustion chamber of each cylinder is full.

DEFINITION

Pistons are cylinders in an engine that fit tightly into larger cylinders and move under pressure created by the explosions in the combustion chamber.

▸ **Compression stroke.** The crankshaft moves the pistons back up to the top of the cylinders, which greatly compresses the fuel-air mixture.

▸ **Power stroke.** When the piston reaches the top, the spark plugs fire at exactly the right time to ignite the fuel. This causes an explosion in the combustion chamber that drives the piston back down.

▸ **Exhaust stroke.** As the pistons rise once more, the camshaft opens the

exhaust valves, which enables the waste gases caused by combustion to collect in the exhaust manifold and be routed to the exhaust system.

Ignition and Starting Systems

The purpose of the ignition system is to create a spark that will ignite the fuel–air mixture in the cylinder of an engine. The spark must occur at exactly the right instant and must reoccur several thousand times per minute for each cylinder in the engine to run properly.

A simple version of an ignition system may look something like this:

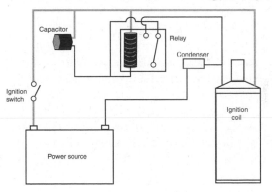

Ignition System

Capacitor

Relay

Condenser

Ignition switch

Ignition coil

Power source

The ignition and starting systems work together to start your car. Starting old and new cars alike involves the following steps:

1. Turning the key to the first position activates the ignition.

2. Power transfers from the 12.6-volt battery through the ignition switch to the ignition coil, which exponentially multiplies that power and sends it to the distributor (if present) and spark plugs.

3. When you turn the key to the next position, you engage the solenoid, a relay that powers the starter motor and turns electrical energy into mechanical energy.

4. Once engaged, the starter motor causes the fly wheel on the engine to turn, which also moves the engine's crankshaft and camshaft.

5. Rods connected to the crankshaft move the pistons inside the engine up and down.

6. The piston movement draws in air and fuel (the ratio of which is regulated by the fuel system).

7. The ignition system ignites the air–fuel mixture on the engine's combustion stroke, which we described already in the "Engine Basics" section.

Keep in mind that this overview is a very simplified version of what occurs during the ignition process. There are several other key components involved that you should be aware of, including spark plugs, the battery, the ignition coil, and the distributor (or coil pack). Depending on which ignition system your car has, these parts will vary in composition.

Traditional Ignition Systems

In older cars that use mechanical or electronic ignition systems, key components include the following:

▸ **Spark plugs.** Spark plugs receive the battery's voltage through an ignition coil. As the battery power travels through the coil, it intensifies exponentially to ignite the air–fuel mixture. In a split second, the 12 volts from the car's battery are converted to up to 20,000 volts for the spark plugs!

▸ **Battery.** The battery stores electrical energy and supplies a car with the initial source of energy.

▸ **Ignition coil.** The ignition coil is essentially an electrical transformer that uses electromagnetic induction to increase voltage. Energy is then directed to the spark plugs through the distributor.

▸ **Distributor.** The distributor, which has a replaceable cap and rotor, takes the current from the ignition coil and sends it to the spark plugs within each cylinder of the engine via a spark plug wire. Precise timing is needed to ensure the sparks light at the correct times.

[**CLASSIFIED INTEL**

We know that spark plugs ignite little explosions inside an engine. But did you know that it's at a rate of over 4,000 explosions per minute for a four-cylinder car traveling 50 miles per hour?]

Distributorless Ignition Systems

Most cars nowadays have a distributorless system, which was designed to eliminate the distributor and fire the spark plugs directly from the ignition coils, at a ratio of one coil for every two spark plugs. Notable components include:

▸ **Spark plugs.** They can receive far more volts (closer to 50,000) than earlier plugs, resulting in a hotter spark and more efficient burning of the fuel-air mixture.

▸ **Coil pack.** In place of the distributor, there are multiple coils; each coil serves one or two spark plugs. A typical six-cylinder engine has three coils that are mounted together in a coil "pack." Each individual coil has a spark plug wire coming out either side, connecting the coil to the appropriate spark plugs. The coil fires both spark plugs at the same time.

The Ignition Switch Connection

Almost everything in your car that uses electricity to run is connected to the ignition switch. In most cars, this small device acts as an intermediary between the battery and the rest of the car's electrical components (which we tell you all about in the next section).

Once the car is started, the alternator takes over and uses the energy generated by your engine to recharge the battery. When the alternator stops working properly, the battery doesn't get charged, and what you may have suspected to be a dead battery is actually a bigger problem—bad news for your checkbook!

Electrical System

A car's electrical system consists of a battery, starter, solenoid, alternator or generator, voltage regulator, and fuse panel (box). The purpose of this system is to provide the initial source of power to the ignition system and to provide continuous power to all your car's accessories, such as the radio, air conditioning, headlights, defroster, windshield wipers, and the like.

Let's examine this system in more detail. Check out our diagram of a basic electrical system, and then read about its main components next.

Electrical System

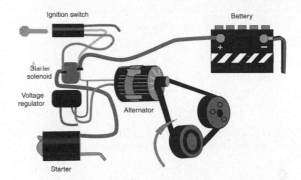

▶ **Battery.** The primary purpose of the battery is to start the engine (see our earlier discussion on starting and ignition systems). The battery also provides about 12 volts of DC to the electrical accessories of the car when the engine isn't running or when it's idling. Auto batteries have six cells that are stacked with positive and negative lead plates that sit in a solution of sulfuric acid and water; these plates store the energy needed to accomplish all the battery's tasks.

▶ **Starter.** This small electric motor consumes the greatest amount of power in the whole electrical system. Its main job is to start the combustion process in the engine by turning the crankshaft.

▶ **Solenoid.** A key component in the ignition system, the solenoid is sometimes referred to as a starter relay. The reason for this nickname is that the solenoid operates much like a relay runner, whose job is to pass the baton to the next runner in the race. The solenoid receives a sizable electric current from the battery and a small electric current from the ignition switch. Upon receipt of the current from the ignition switch, the solenoid knows to pass the battery's current on to the starter.

▸ **Alternator.** The main role of the alternator is to charge the battery. The alternator is connected to the engine by a belt, which is where it receives the necessary power to charge the battery. In so doing, it helps to power all the electrical devices in the car.

▸ **Voltage regulator.** This part does exactly what its name implies: it maintains the proper voltage level for the electrical system. It helps eliminate power surges, spikes, and brownouts, which can harm the car's electronic devices. Many newer cars house these regulators inside the alternators, although some American models and older cars have an exterior design.

▸ **Fuse panel.** Much like the circuit breaker or fuse box in your home, the fuse box in a car helps control the function of things like headlights, dashboard lights, radios, clocks, and so forth. Fuse boxes are usually located near the bottom of the dashboard or under the hood.

Fuel System

This is undoubtedly the system that the average driver deals with the most often. Every time we fill up the gas tank, we are working with a key component in the fuel system: gas. The main purpose of this system is to store and supply fuel to the combustion chamber in the engine, where it combines with air, vaporizes, and then burns to give the engine energy.

A few key components you should become familiar with include fuel, fuel pumps, fuel filters, and fuel injectors (or carburetors in older cars).

Fuel

Cars are typically equipped with one of two engine types: a diesel engine, which uses diesel fuel; or a gasoline engine, which uses gasoline.

▸ **Gasoline.** A complex blend of hydrogen and carbon, with additives mixed in to improve performance. It burns more cleanly than diesel fuel, but gas engines are typically less efficient than diesel engines.

▸ **Diesel fuel.** This is also a combination of carbon and hydrogen compounds that requires additives for performance. However, diesel fuel vaporizes at a much higher temperature than gasoline, gets better gas mileage, and is denser than gasoline.

Fuel is stored in a tank, where it stays until the fuel pump siphons it out and brings it to where it's needed.

Fuel Pump

Older engines were often built without this key component, relying on gravity to carry the fuel to the engine via a hose. However, in designs that don't utilize gravity, fuel pumps are essential.

These pumps feed fuel to the engine from the fuel tank. In older cars that used carburetors, the fuel pump had a mechanical design and was usually mounted outside the fuel tank. In newer cars with higher-pressure fuel injection systems, the fuel pumps tend to be electric and are mounted inside the fuel tank.

Fuel Filter

These devices filter out dirt and rust particles in the fuel before they reach the engine. They are usually made of cartridges with filter paper inside, similar to the paper used in coffee filters. Fuel filters are found in most modern vehicles; they improve engine performance by allowing it to burn cleaner fuel.

> **TEST TIP**
>
> Most modern vehicles use an electronic fuel injection system controlled by a computer to regulate the air-fuel ratio going to the engine. Older ones relied on a carburetor, which relied on a low-pressure system to mix fuel and air.

Fuel Injector

This part consists of a nozzle and a valve; it mixes fuel with air inside the internal combustion engine. Unlike carburetors, fuel injectors forcibly pump fuel through a small space under high pressure directly into the engine's cylinders. Fuel injectors began replacing carburetors in the late 1980s.

Drivetrain System

We have discussed all the components needed to get your engine up and running. Now let's look at how all of that makes a car go. This is what the drivetrain system is for—taking the energy from the engine and using it to make the vehicle move. The transmission and chassis are the main parts of this system.

Transmission

Transmissions are either manual or automatic. Their purpose is to match the speed of the engine to enable the car to travel at the speed the driver wants. This is accomplished through a set of gears, each of which allows a specific amount of *torque* from the engine to move parts in the chassis that enable the car to move.

> **DEFINITION**
>
> **Torque** refers to the amount of force that enables a rotating motion. When you use a screwdriver, you apply torque to make your screw twist into place.

Each gear has limitations as to how much torque can be passed on. Once that limit is reached, the next gear must be selected. In a manual transmission vehicle, the driver would engage the clutch, which disengages the transmission from the engine, and use the gear shift to engage the next gear.

This is done by computer automation with an automatic transmission, though there is no clutch. Automatic transmissions use a torque converter, which is a hydraulic component that brings the energy from the engine to the transmission.

Chassis

When we talk about the chassis, we are speaking mostly about the system that controls the wheels. This includes the steering wheel, steering column, and drive system.

Modern vehicles have front-wheel, rear-wheel, or four-wheel drive systems. Because the ASVAB is unlikely to ask about the latter, we are going to discuss the first two systems used to propel a vehicle:

▶ **Front-wheel drive.** The two front wheels turn to move the vehicle. The transmission sends power to the front *differential*, which then moves the universal joints in the front axle to cause the wheels to move. The rear wheels move in response to the forward motion from the front wheels.

▶ **Rear-wheel drive.** In this configuration, the two rear wheels receive the power from the transmission through a drive shaft. This is a rotating metal rod that runs from the transmission to the rear axle. It connects with universal joints and a differential to enable the rear wheels to propel the vehicle forward.

We will get into the brake and suspension systems later in this chapter.

Exhaust System

The purpose of the exhaust system is to direct exhaust gas away from the controlled combustion inside the engine. It is also designed to reduce the noise of the engine, maintain performance, and reduce or eliminate harmful emissions.

Whew! That's quite a job description! The exhaust team has a few key players, which vary depending on the size and style of the vehicle. A basic exhaust system may look something like this:

Exhaust System

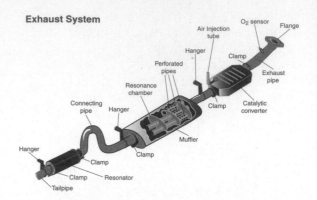

Some of the most common parts include the exhaust manifold, an assortment of pipes, the catalytic converter, and muffler.

Exhaust Manifold

This is a very heavy component that connects to the engine at multiple points, so that it can collect the excess gases from the cylinder head or heads (depending on the design of the engine) during the exhaust stroke. When the exhaust valve opens, the gases are pushed into the manifold, where they collect before moving to the exhaust pipe.

Pipes

Many pipes carry out exhaust functions. Some of these include the following:

▶ **Exhaust pipe.** The exhaust pipe transports the gases and vapor away from the engine farther down the exhaust system. It connects to the catalytic converter.

▶ **Intermediate pipe.** This connects the catalytic converter to the muffler. Not all cars have this pipe.

▶ **Tailpipe.** This is the last step in the exhaust process, guiding gases out and away from the vehicle. It's usually at least a foot long (if not longer), to help prevent gases from reentering the inside of the car.

Catalytic Converter

This is a simple device created in the 1970s to control the emissions of a car. Cars mostly emit nitrogen gas, carbon dioxide, and water vapor. Most modern cars are built with three-way catalytic converters to help control emissions of all three of these gases.

Muffler

The main job of the muffler is to silence exhaust gas noises. Essentially, it absorbs and dissipates noises while continuing to move the exhaust gases on their way out the tailpipe. Mufflers are typically located near the rear of the vehicle and tend to be round, oval, or even custom shaped.

Cooling System

Although many of the systems in our cars have changed over the years (particularly through the age of technology), the cooling system has evolved very little from the original design used in Ford's Model T.

Almost 100 years later, most cooling systems still circulate liquid coolant through the engine and back out to the radiator, where it is cooled by the air blowing through the front grill of the vehicle.

There are actually two types of cooling systems used in cars: liquid cooled and air cooled. The latter of these is less common and is occasionally found in older vehicles. For the purpose of this exam, we discuss the liquid-cooled systems.

> **CLASSIFIED INTEL**
>
> The inside of an engine's combustion chamber can reach temperatures that exceed 4,500° Fahrenheit. No wonder engines need a cooling system to keep things from overheating!

Several key components allow the cooling system to do its job, including a water pump, the engine passages through which the liquid travels (water jackets), a radiator, a radiator cap, and a thermostat. These components help maintain homeostasis in the engine, regardless of the outside air temperatures. (Remember the term *homeostasis* from Chapter 11?)

- **Water pump.** The water pump provides the pressure needed to circulate coolant through the cavities of the engine.

- **Water jackets.** Liquid coolant travels through the engine block and heads, picking up heat from the engine. As it exits the hot engine, the coolant travels through a rubber hose connected to the radiator.

- **Radiator.** The radiator reduces the temperature of the coolant after it exits the engine. It consists of a parallel network of small tubes through which the hot fluid flows. This fluid faces the front grill and a fan system that forces cool air through the radiator, helping to cool the fluid.

- **Radiator cap or pressure cap.** As the coolant picks up heat from a 4,500°F engine, it becomes very hot and expands. If the coolant gets too hot, it runs the risk of boiling; the radiator cap is therefore needed to maintain pressure in the cooling system, which raises the boiling point of the water. The excessively hot liquid takes up more space than the system can hold, so it is released into a reserve tank until it is cool enough to return to the engine. This mechanism helps keep the pressure within the system at the right level, prevents hoses and other parts from bursting, and is known as a closed cooling system.

▶ **Thermostat.** Much like your home has a thermostat to control the air temperature, a vehicle has a thermostat to help control the temperature of the engine. It is located between the engine and the radiator, and it functions by opening and closing a valve to regulate the flow of coolant to the engine. Ideally, the thermostat doesn't allow too much coolant through, so the engine can heat up sufficiently for the vehicle to function properly; at the same time, it pushes enough coolant through so that the engine doesn't overheat.

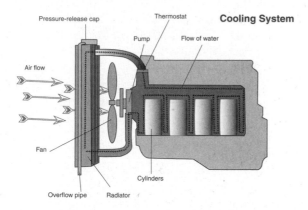

Cooling System

Now that we've taken you through each of the main systems that support your car's vital functions, it's time to move on to the systems that keep everything together.

Brake System

Braking is pretty simple, and it all starts with the brake pedal. When you push the brake, you signal the master cylinder in the engine to send pressurized fluid through the brake lines to the assemblies attached to the front and/or rear wheels. The pressurized fluid moves the pistons in the assemblies, which move the parts of the brake that provide the friction to slow the wheel.

Generally, modern cars are designed with front-wheel disc brakes and rear-wheel drum brakes, so it's important to know how both work.

Disc Brakes

This type of brake relies on friction and heat to slow a vehicle. Although the same principle applies to drum brakes, disc brakes are considered superior in design and operation. They have a reduced chance of overheating, tend to be more responsive than drum brakes when applied hard, and offer better performance in wet weather. These advantages come at a cost, though.

Disc brakes are more expensive than drums. Let's take a moment to examine their components: brake pads, rotors, and calipers.

▶ **Brake pads.** These are metallic blocks that apply friction to both sides of the rotors. Newer-style pads can also be made from ceramic and other materials. Brake pads have a little metal clip that scrapes against the rotor when the pads are getting worn and need to be replaced. The sound of metal scraping on metal is an easy indication that it's time to perform maintenance on the brake system.

▶ **Rotors.** These are made of machined steel and are mounted to the spindle assembly, which allows the car to turn and the wheels to spin.

▶ **Calipers.** This is the part that houses the brake pads; they are mounted so that they straddle the rotor. The caliper contains at least one piston. When you press the brake pedal, hydraulic pressure (fluid power) is exerted on the piston, which then forces the pad against the rotor. Friction between the pads and the rotors (which are sometimes referred to as discs) causes the car to slow down.

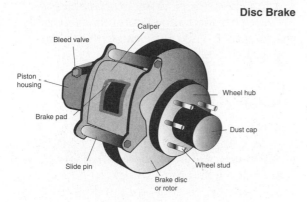

Disc Brake

Bleed valve
Caliper
Piston housing
Brake pad
Slide pin
Wheel hub
Dust cap
Wheel stud
Brake disc or rotor

Drum Brakes

These brakes function similarly to disc brakes, even though they tend to be slightly less effective. The parts of a drum brake include a backing plate, brake shoes, a brake drum, and a wheel cylinder.

▶ **Backing plate (or mounting plate).** This is where each of the drum elements is attached.

▶ **Brake shoes.** These can be functionally compared to the brake pads from the disc system. The main difference is that, whereas the brake pads are flat, the shoes are curved and push out instead of in. Like disc brakes, drum brakes have a small metal clip to alert the driver that the shoes are getting worn and should be replaced.

▶ **Brake drum.** This is a hollow metal cylinder that's attached to the wheel. It fits snugly around the brake shoes so that when the shoes press against it, the resulting friction slows the vehicle.

▶ **Wheel cylinder.** This is located at the top of the backing plate. It houses two pistons, one on either side. When you step on the brake, hydraulic fluid forces each piston out of the cylinder.

The pistons are slotted at the end so that the shoe fits into their groove. When you take your foot off the brake, they are then retracted by a set of springs into the cylinder so that they're ready to perform the whole process all over again.

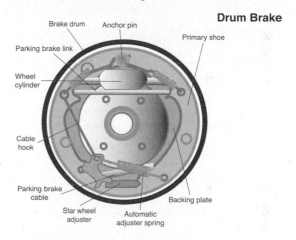

Drum Brake

Brake drum
Anchor pin
Primary shoe
Parking brake link
Wheel cylinder
Cable hook
Parking brake cable
Star wheel adjuster
Automatic adjuster spring
Backing plate

The Emergency Brake

The emergency brake (or parking brake) controls the rear brakes through a series of steel cables that the driver operates via a hand lever or foot pedal. Emergency brakes are considered secondary braking devices in terms of design and safety. That is, if the *hydraulic system* of the front and rear wheels fails, a mechanical emergency brake can bypass the failed system to stop the vehicle.

Visit science.howstuffworks.com/hydraulic. htm for an animated explanation of hydraulic systems.

Drum emergency brakes have two main components:

▸ **Braking cable.** This circumvents the wheel cylinder and controls the brakes directly by pushing the rear shoe against the drum.

▸ **Rear shoe.** This is quite a bit larger than the front shoe in the drum brake. It engages the drum and eliminates its ability to turn.

Cars with disc brakes on the rear wheels have additional components in an emergency brake and are designed in one of two ways:

▸ Using an existing rear-wheel caliper, a lever is added to a mechanical corkscrew device inside the caliper piston. When the driver engages the parking brake, the brake cable pulls on the lever. The corkscrew device then pushes the piston against the pads, thereby stopping the vehicle mechanically.

▸ The other emergency brake system for rear-wheel disc brakes uses a mechanical drum brake unit that is mounted inside the rear rotor. Here the brake shoes are connected to a lever that is pulled by the parking brake cable. Once again, the vehicle is able to stop mechanically rather than hydraulically as the lever pushes the shoes against the drum unit.

Often drivers choose not to use parking brakes on vehicles with automatic transmissions. The problem with this is that lack of use can cause the parking brake cables to become corroded and eventually inoperable. Occasional use helps the cables stay clean and functional.

Suspension

The suspension system includes the various components that connect a vehicle to its wheels. A lot of people talk about suspension when they talk about how well a car rides. A good system does the following:

▸ Makes for a smooth ride by minimizing road noise, bumps, and vibrations

▸ Contributes to the car's handling and braking

▸ Protects the car from damage and wear and tear

To accomplish all these goals, automakers have to strike just the right balance within the various components of the system. One of the ways they accomplish this is by maximizing the friction between the tires and the road surface. When your car hits a bump, the wheel that hit the bump experiences vertical acceleration as it moves up and down.

Without suspension, the wheel can lose contact with the road completely, only to slam back down moments later because of gravity. Suspension helps absorb the energy of the vertically accelerated wheel, maximizing tire friction on the road and minimizing passenger discomfort.

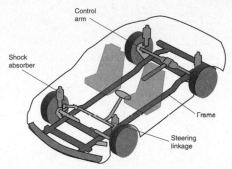
Car Suspension

Control arm

Shock absorber

Frame

Steering linkage

Let's take a moment to discuss some of the main components found in a suspension system:

▸ **Shock absorber or damper.** As the name implies, the shock absorber helps smooth the jolt of a bump and absorbs the energy created by that bump.

▸ **Control arm.** Triangular in shape, the control arm pivots in two places, to manage the motion of the wheels.

▸ **Frame.** This supports the car's engine and body and is a key structural element of the car.

▸ **Steering linkage.** This is a series of arms, rods, and ball sockets that allow the wheels to swivel when the driver turns the steering wheel. As a result, the car is able to turn.

▸ **Springs.** There are several different types of springs in the suspension system, including coil springs, leaf springs, torsion bars, and air springs. Generally, their purpose is to absorb the motion of the wheels.

▸ **Antisway or stabilizer bars.** These help prevent a car from rolling during a sharp turn.

Types of Suspension Systems

There are two main types of suspension systems: front wheel and rear wheel. Each of these can be further categorized as dependent or independent.

▸ **Front-wheel dependent.** In this design, the front wheels are connected by an inflexible axle, forcing them to move in unison. Although these are still commonly found in trucks, they haven't been used on cars in decades.

▸ **Front-wheel independent.** This design was developed in 1947 and allows the wheels to move *independently* of one another—hence the name. This is the most common front-wheel suspension system for cars.

▸ **Rear-wheel dependent.** Similar to the dependent front-wheel suspension system, a solid axle connects the rear wheels in this design.

▸ **Rear-wheel independent.** This construction is similar to that of the front-wheel independent system, but it is a simplified version. In rear-wheel independent systems, there is no steering rack. (The steering rack enables the wheels to turn from side to side and is unnecessary in the back.)

Some cars have specialty suspension systems, such as Formula One racers, hot rods (built between the 1940s and 1960s), Volkswagen Baja Bugs, and so forth.

Cars are incredibly complex, intricate machines that you could spend months—even years—studying. Hopefully, however, our condensed review has simplified a few of the major systems every car has. For more information, see *The Complete Idiot's Guide to Auto Repair* (see Appendix C), and don't forget to check out the practice questions in Chapter 17.

Shop Information

Have you ever toyed with the idea of woodworking or carpentry? What about some minor home repairs or decorating projects? If any of these ideas have ever struck your fancy, here are a few fun facts about carpentry that you might get a kick out of:

▶ The word *carpenter* originates from the Latin word *carpentrius*, which means "maker of a carriage."

▶ Carpenter frogs were so named because of the hammerlike sound of their call.

▶ British and Australian carpenters are sometimes referred to as "chippies."

All fun aside, this chapter is designed to cover some wood and metal shop basics, so that you'll be well prepared for the ASVAB. Take a few minutes to familiarize yourself with the terms in this chapter, and you'll be on your way to an excellent technical score for this subtest!

Why Do I Have to Take This?

No matter how tight the job market is at any given time, you can usually be sure that employers will want a few years of training and experience. If that's not enough, the qualifications keep expanding, the requirements for each job are loaded, and there is little job security.

But here's the good news: there is one employer with locations all over the world who wants to hire people with *no* experience, pay a reasonable salary, offer incredible benefits, and train employees to do the kind of work they enjoy! This is no joke—we're talking about the U.S. Armed Forces, of course.

While it's certainly true that there are sacrifices and great commitments required of military service members, the opportunities are vast. The military is looking for people who have an interest in carpentry, not necessarily an acquired skill.

That's why it's important to brush up on the technical skill sections of the ASVAB. Scoring well on the technical subtests is the first step in securing the job of your choice in the military.

More specifically, a good score on the Shop Information subtest is critical if your dream job involves any type of hands-on building or repair work.

What to Expect

The Shop Information subtest won't take up too much of your time on the CAT version of the ASVAB. You'll be asked only 11 questions, and you'll have 6 minutes to choose your answers. The score you receive from this section is called Shop Information, or SI.

Once you've completed the entire ASVAB, your SI score is combined with your Auto Information (AI) score. On your score report, your line score will be labeled AS, which indicates your combined Auto and Shop scores.

On the PAP, the Shop and Auto subtests are already combined in one section, giving you the combination AS score right off the bat. Because the two subtests are already joined on the PAP, you will have a total of 11 minutes in which to answer 25 questions about both subjects.

The great part about this subtest is that you can rely heavily on practical knowledge rather than book knowledge alone. You will also find that diagrams are sometimes used to communicate test material, which is particularly helpful if you are a visual learner. You will see similar diagrams throughout this chapter.

Basic Hand Tools Review

Hand tools have been around since the dawn of civilization. If time is a testament to quality, it's safe to say that hand tools have proven their worth over the millennia.

Here's a brief list of some popular categories of tools that have made their way to some ASVAB exams.

Shaping Tools

These tools are used to contour objects, usually wood or metal. They are designed to make curves, incisions, scores, and other intricate forms.

▸ **Planes.** Plane tools are used to flatten, smooth, and narrow the width of wood. Two specific types of planes are jack and block planes. A jack plane is typically used for smoothing the edge of wood or reducing its size. When the jack plane is used on the edge of wood, it tends to have a curved blade. A straight-bladed jack plane is generally selected for smoothing wood joints.

A block plane is an ideal general-purpose type of plane. It is small, can fit into tight spaces, and is used to trim wood edges and joints as well. The versatility of this tool makes it useful for home improvement projects and carpenter work alike.

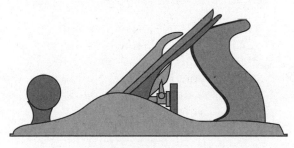

Jack plane

▶ **Chisels.** These tools are highly versatile. They are essential in joint making, boat building, timber framing, and dozens of other applications. Wood chisels are the most common, though cold chisels, which are used on metal, may also come up on your test.

Wood chisels range in size from ⅛ inch to 2 inches wide and are used to chip away or completely cut wood. Though they come in many shapes and widths, depending on the use, the basic design has a handle made of wood or metal and a flat, sometimes U-shaped blade with a sharp cutting tip. To use a chisel, grasp the handle and use the strength of your own hand or a mallet of some kind to push the chisel into the wood. With each pound, the blade of the chisel makes a cut.

▶ **File.** A file functions similar to a nail file, even if the design is a bit different. Files can be used on wood, metal, or plastic to shape, trim, and smooth surfaces. Basically, a file is a hand-held steel bar that is covered with tiny ridgelike grooves—sometimes crisscrossed. It is used after a saw to smooth out rough edges, but before sandpaper or another abrasive that is finer.

▶ **Rasp.** A rasp is similar to a file, but is designed strictly for wood. Rasps are generally larger than files, too, with more pointed ridges. These ridges are often referred to as "teeth" because of their size and sharpness. Rasps, too, should be used in between the saw and the sandpaper steps, though before filing.

Saws

These are thin pieces of metal with jagged edges used to cut through wood or metal. They usually have a wood or metal handle and can be operated using a back-and-forth motion. While many people prefer power tools these days, hand saws still have a lot of value for woodworkers and carpenters. Some examples of common hand saws include the following:

▶ **Hack saw.** This tool is most commonly used for cutting metal or bone. It is designed with a fine-toothed blade that is held in place using tension and an arched metal frame. The handle is usually shaped like the grip of a pistol, and the blade is able to cut on both push and pull strokes.

▶ **Crosscut saw.** This type of saw is best used for cutting wood against (perpendicular) the grain, and is comprised of a blade and a handle. The teeth work like a knife cutting across the wood and can have various patterns, depending on the use.

- **Rip saw.** The opposite of the crosscut saw, the rip saw is for cutting with the grain. Its blade mimics the end of a chisel, which creates a smoother cut through the wood. The teeth are usually larger than those of a crosscut saw, but the two look very similar.

- **Coping saw.** This is a thin-blade saw used for detail work and cutting out interior spaces on wood. The blade stretches between the ends of a large, open metal arch, close to a C shape. The blade is removable, so the saw can be positioned for interior cuts.

- **Miter saw.** Although there are some exceptional powered miter saws, this hand tool still brings a lot to the table. Also known as a *miter box*, this saw is ideal for making angled cuts, such as those on a picture frame. It consists of a small hack saw that is guided and steadied by a framework that helps the user make a perfect cut at the desired angle.

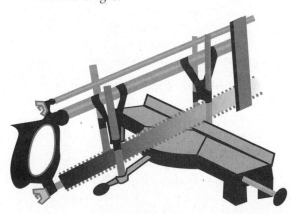

Miter saw

Hammers

The hammer may be the most basic household necessity in terms of tools and is extremely versatile. What you may not have realized, however, is the vast number of hammer variations. Consider some of the most common hammer types:

- **Rubber mallet.** The beauty of this tool is that it is able to withstand the effects of both water and oil, giving the user more freedom of application. The rubber mallet features a nonmarring rubber head, making it ideal in situations when a steel head could damage the material being hammered. It may be used on sheet metal, upholstery, plasterboard, and even toys!

- **Curved claw hammer.** When you think of a hammer, this is likely what you picture. It consists of a rounded metal head on one side and a curved claw on the other that can be used for pounding *and* pulling nails in or out of wood or even concrete.

- **Ball-peen hammer.** This hammer looks similar to the curved claw hammer, minus the claw. In its place is a ball-shaped sphere of steel. It is most commonly used in construction projects, woodworking, and auto repairs. The spherical peen end of the hammer is sometimes used in conjunction with chisels or metal shaping.

Ball-peen hammer

- **Sledgehammer.** This is a large hammer, usually requiring two hands to swing it. The head is heavy and flat on the ends, which enables it to deliver a great amount of force to a wide area and perform tasks that would be unwieldy for smaller hammers. Sledgehammers are often used in demolition to break up rock or concrete.

Screwdrivers

These common shop tools come in many different shapes, sizes, and styles. A screwdriver is used to manually twist a screw into a piece of wood, plastic, or metal. Generally, the purpose is to fasten two materials to one another. There are two types:

- **Phillips-head screwdriver.** This tool is a staple in most homes and in most industrial workshops. Why? Its pointy, tapered end with an X shape at the bottom makes it easier to connect the tip of the screwdriver with the head of the screw, particularly at awkward angles. The X shape provides more stability to the connection between screw and screwdriver, and makes turning the screw much easier.

- **Flathead screwdriver.** This type of screwdriver has a single, flat end that fits into a slotted screw. On top of a flathead screw is a single groove into which the screwdriver tip fits. However, this configuration can make the screwdriver slip easily.

Flathead   Phillips head

Screwdrivers

CLASSIFIED INTEL

There are two more types of screwdrivers you may see on the ASVAB. The only difference is the shape of the head. The Robertson has a square tip, and the Torx has a six-point star.

Wrenches

A wrench is designed to provide torque to tighten or loosen things like screws, nuts, and bolts. Wrenches come in a variety of types:

- **Open-end wrench.** This wrench is one that is most often depicted to symbolize tools of all kinds. It has an open end that is nonadjustable and fits around the right-sized nuts and bolts. This wrench design is quite versatile, though it sometimes causes slippage if the tool isn't exactly the right size for the job.

- **Box-end wrench.** The ends of this wrench are grooved circles designed to wrap around the head of a bolt. These are great for getting a good grip and reducing slippage, especially when you need to use a lot of force.

- **Combination-end wrench.** This wrench has an open design at one end with a box design at the other end.

- **Adjustable-end wrench.** Much like the name implies, the adjustable wrench is designed with a set of clamps at one end that can expand and contract with a simple screw adjustment. It is the most versatile wrench for most household and shop projects.

CLASSIFIED INTEL

Adjustable wrenches are also sometimes referred to as Crescent or spanner wrenches.

- **Pipe wrench.** This is actually considered a form of the adjustable wrench, but it is more specific in terms of its abilities and applications. This is a popular tool for mechanics, plumbers, and handymen, with adjustable claws on one end that allow it to grip differently sized objects.

- **Allen wrench.** This is an L-shaped bar with a hexagonal head. It is used to turn Allen screws, which are commonly found in ready-to-finish or -assemble furniture.

- **Socket wrench.** Also known as a *ratchet*, this wrench uses separate, removable sockets to tighten different sizes of nuts and bolts. These wrenches are used in automotive repairs, as well as other household projects.

Adjustable wrench   Pipe wrench   Socket wrench   Allen wrench

Wrenches

Nuts, Bolts, Screws, and Nails

Speaking of hammers, screwdrivers, and wrenches, let's take a look at some of things they are used to turn.

- **Nails.** These are thin fasteners that have flat, nonscored heads, smooth shanks, and pointed tips. They come in many sizes and are designed for many purposes, such as fastening wood, masonry, drywall, trim, roofing, etc.

- **Bolts.** Bolts are fastener that works with a nut to create stability. Unlike with a screw, a bolt does not have a pointed tip and cannot work alone. Its external threads must wind into the internal ones of a nut in order to fasten. Bolt heads are turned by wrenches and are usually either hexagonal or square. They can be used with both wood and metal and have varying numbers of threads.

- **Wing nut.** This is a nut that can be tightened on a bolt with just fingers. It has two metal pieces that look like wings, which are used by fingers to turn the nut.

- **Lock nut.** This is a nut that has built-in features that make it more difficult for the nut to come loose. Features may include a crownlike or plastic/nylon ring on one side of the nut.

- **Wood screws.** These screws have a smooth shank below a flat head, pushing the start of the threads to the bottom of the shank. The tip is sharp, and the threads bore into the wood. The screw is designed with a shank to allow two pieces of wood to pull against each other when fastened. It also reduces heat in the wood caused by friction during rotation, which can result in a weakened fastener.

- **Machine screws.** Similar to bolts in shape and function (may use a nut), these screws are turned by a screwdriver, not a wrench. They are usually much smaller than bolts and are used to fasten metal.

Clamps and Vises

These are very useful tools that are used to hold an item in place or hold two objects together to prevent movement. There are several different types:

- **Hand screw.** Quite simply, this type of clamp tightens around an object using two long screws. The screws are rotated by hand, causing the jaws of the clamp to apply inward pressure to the object being held. The jaws are usually made of wood blocks.

- **C-clamp.** These are relatively small clamps that consist of a metal curve that looks like a C. A screw with a foot can be turned at the bottom of the C to extend as far as you need to clamp it around an object.

- **Pipe clamp.** This clamp holds a pipe in place so that the pipe may be cut, threaded, lifted, or suspended. The clamp itself is a metallic strap or band, and it is also used to stop leaks.

- **Bar clamp.** This clamp has adjustable jaws that are attached to a long bar. A screw mechanism tightens the large jaws, which are often used for wide-width projects.

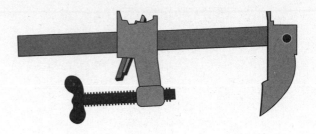

Bar clamp

- **Vise.** Vises are like clamps, except that they are usually stationary and screwed into a wall or table. They are generally heavy and hold items in place. Some common ones are bench and pipe vises.

Pliers

These tools are designed to allow the user to grip an object so that it can be held, bent, compressed, or turned. Common types include:

- **Needle-nose.** These have two long-pointed jaws that can fit into small spaces. Good for working with wires or other thin objects, tasks where precision or intricacy are important, or when there is limited work space. May have a wire cutter built in.

- **Linesman.** The jaws of these pliers are a little shorter and chunkier than those of the needle-nose. Shallow ridges near the tip are good for gripping, while side cutters are often found behind the jaws. Used mostly in metal work, they are also handy for electricians working with thick or multiple wires.

- ▶ **Slip-joint.** The joint that controls the open and close action of the jaws has an adjustable pivot point, which allows you to grip a variable range of widths.

- ▶ **Locking.** A type of adjustable plier that can be used as a clamp or vise. A screw or lever opens the large, often serrated jaws, and closing the handle closes the jaws and locks them into place.

Combination Slip Joint Pliers

Drills and Drill Bits

A drill is a tool with a rotating bit that is used for boring holes into certain materials. Although the power drill has largely replaced the hand drill, some woodworkers prefer to use a hand drill. Hand drills require very little maintenance but offer the operator total control.

Hand Drill

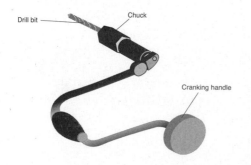

Drill bit

Chuck

Cranking handle

The three main parts of a hand drill include the chuck, the cranking handle, and the drill bit. The chuck is a clamping device that holds the drill bit in place; if it is too loose, the bit could slide out of the drill. The cranking handle turns the main shaft of the hand drill, to which the chuck and drill bit are attached. When the cranking handle is operated, the drill bit rotates and bores into the material that needs a hole.

The drill bit is a removable component that slides into the chuck and actually does the cutting. It comes in a variety of different sizes, depending on the size of the hole that's needed.

There are several different types of drill bits:

- ▶ **Auger bit.** This bit is specifically made for drilling large deep holes in wood. Furthermore, it's best used in conjunction with a hand drill. The center point of the bit has small threads that help pull the bit into the wood. The rest of the bit has a spiral shape with chisel-like edges that cut the wood as the bit rotates.

- ▶ **Spade bit.** Typically, you use this bit when you need to make a larger hole than a twist bit will allow. The shape resembles a flat shovel with a point at the end. These bits may also be known as *flat wood bits* and, as evidenced by their pseudonym, are mostly used on wood.

- ▶ **Carbide-tipped masonry bit.** This type of bit is designed for use with brick, stone, quarry tile, or concrete. Because of the hardness of the surface that's being drilled, the masonry bit is rarely used in hand drills anymore. However, the tip of the bit is prone to overheating, so the slow rotational speed of a hand drill is sometimes more suitable for this type of bit.

- **Twist bit.** This is undoubtedly the most common type of drill bit for the average handyman or do-it-yourselfer. Twist bits are great for use on wood, metal, and plastics, and are generally made of high-speed steel or carbon steel. They can also be found less often in titanium nitride. Twist bits cut using the front edges of the bit and withdraw waste via the spirals.

- **Countersink.** This is used to create a hole in which the top part of the hole is enlarged. The purpose is to allow the head of a screw or bolt to lie flush with (or slightly below) the surface of the wood or metal.

Measuring Tools

We will skip the basics of rulers and measuring tapes here, and instead talk about three essentials for anyone's toolbox.

- **Square.** More than a ruler, a square provides a straight edge to draw lines and measure right angles. A square comes in various sizes and shapes, with some including a level for increased accuracy.

- **Calipers.** While pliers have jaws, calipers have legs that are used to measure either the internal or external width of a three-dimensional object.

- **Level.** This tool helps you measure the evenness of a horizontal surface. Modern levels have a small glass tube filled with liquid and a bubble, which becomes centered when the surface being measured is even.

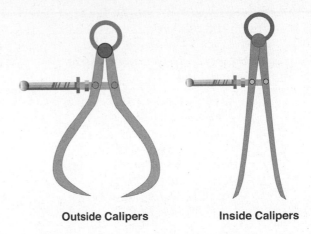

Outside Calipers   Inside Calipers

Power Tools Review

The military is a big proponent of the saying "Work smart, not hard." In many instances, power tools have fit the bill with this old adage. Power tools are powered by an electric motor, a compressed-air motor, or, in rare cases, a gasoline engine.

Many of the tools we've discussed, such as wrenches and hammers, can only be found in the hand-tool section of your hardware store. However, some shaping tools and saws have power counterparts:

- **Router.** This power tool cuts the surface of metal or wood and is usually used in the finishing stages of a project. It can smooth rough edges, buff surfaces, and sand wood.

- **Lathe.** Like a router, a lathe is a shaping power tool that can be used with either metal or wood. The item being cut rotates on the axis of the lathe, while the edge that needs shaping is pressed against a fixed cutting or abrading tool (often a chisel or sandpaper).

▶ **Power saws.** All kinds of power saws are on the market today, depending on the type of cut needed. Two examples of popular power saws include these:

   ✳ **Circular saw.** This is one of the most common saws in use today. Depending on the blade it's equipped with, it can cut wood, steel, masonry, or ceramic tile. Its primary function is to make straight, continuous cuts.

   ✳ **Jigsaw.** This type of saw does just the opposite of the circular saw. It is designed to make cuts in different directions and shapes. It has a narrow blade that moves vertically in a reciprocating motion and can make intricate cuts and curves.

▶ **Power drills.** Like hand drills, power drills cut holes but with far less effort than their nonelectric counterparts. Power drills also use removable bits in a variety of widths, depending on the size needed for the hole. Different kinds of drills include these:

   ✳ **Pistol grip.** Probably the most common, the pistol grip can be found in both corded and cordless varieties. It's typically used for standard projects, such as drilling holes in drywall to hang pictures, drilling through wood, and so on.

   ✳ **Hammer drill.** This drill uses an action similar to its namesake and is used most frequently in drilling masonry. A jackhammer is an example of a hammer drill.

   ✳ **Drill press.** This is a fixed tool that is typically either mounted to a workbench or bolted to the floor. Its main advantages are that it takes less human effort to operate, and the project can be more securely held in place during the drilling process.

Hundreds of tools out there can really make or break even the smallest project. Tools have not only simplified our lives, but they have also created the products we use every day. Understanding some basic hand and power tools will help you succeed not only on the ASVAB but also at home. To test your knowledge of shop tools, turn to Chapter 17 for practice questions, answers, and explanations.

Mechanical Comprehension

If you like solving problems, enjoy tinkering with broken appliances, or have ever had an inkling to become an engineer, you'll really find your stride with the Mechanical Comprehension (MC) section of the ASVAB. If not, hang in there anyway! Remember, military jobs are made up of a combination of ASVAB scores. You want to score as high as possible on every technical subtest so that you have the largest pool of jobs available to you. In this chapter, we help you review basic mechanical principles, theories, and applications that will help you get the score you're looking for.

Why Do I Have to Take This?

As you are no doubt aware, the military has become increasingly reliant on electronic systems as the primary mode of doing business—even on the battlefield. As we discussed in Chapter 12, each branch of service needs skilled technicians to operate, maintain, and repair these systems.

Since the military is willing to train individuals to do a job, it's in their best interest to select the right personnel. In this case, that includes individuals who have the ability to learn the technical pieces of the job, as well as an ability to see the bigger picture in the absence of textbook methods or clearly assigned directives. This is where the MC section of the ASVAB comes in.

What to Expect

One of the main reasons the ASVAB wants to test your mechanical comprehension knowledge is to determine whether you're capable of locating and repairing faults in electronic control systems. This is accomplished via fault-diagnosis questions, which tend to be abstract in nature. They require logic and an awareness of principles rather than straight mathematical calculations.

This skill is needed because electronic systems often provide very little physical evidence of the reason they are malfunctioning. In such a case, the process of elimination combined with logic is the best way to go.

The other tool that will help you ace this section of the test is basic terminology knowledge. All the mechanical intuition in the world won't help you if you don't know the language. We provide many of the fundamentals for you in this chapter.

The important point is not to feel intimidated or overwhelmed by the prospect of learning (or relearning) a few vocabulary words. You'll be required to learn a whole new language when you join the military anyway, so consider this practice for the real thing!

And keep in mind that if you're taking the CAT, you'll have to answer 16 questions in 20 minutes. On the PAP, you'll have 19 minutes to answer 25 questions. Let's get started with some of those mechanical terms now.

Mechanical Basics

Like the military (and many of the subject areas you've already read about in this book), mechanical science has a language all its own. Some of these terms are quite simple, and even someone with no scientific background would be able to identify them: *pounds, motion, speed, acceleration, force, energy, work, pressure,* and so on.

Familiarize yourself with the following terms:

Must-Know Terms

Term	Definition
Mass	The amount of matter an object has. Can be measured in kilograms.
Matter	Anything that occupies space and has mass.
Motion	Rate at which an object changes position.
Speed	How fast an object is moving.
Velocity	Speed and direction of an object in motion.
Acceleration	The rate of change in velocity; can be positive or negative.
Work	Transfer of energy through force over a distance.
Force	Something that does work on an object, often changing its motion.
Energy	The amount of work a force can produce.
Potential energy	Stored energy, with the potential for doing work on an object.
Kinetic energy	Energy of motion.

Now that you have a general idea of the topics we'll be discussing, let's dive into specifics.

Energy Review

Energy has numerous forms, including kinetic, potential, gravitational, electromagnetic, chemical, elastic, thermal, sound, and light.

Whew! That's a long list, and it doesn't stop there! But don't panic: you only need to know the basics for the ASVAB. Besides, a few of the energy forms should sound familiar from our electronics discussion in Chapter 12. Let's take a look at two types of energy often seen on the ASVAB: potential and kinetic.

Potential Energy

If you know what the word *potential* means, you're already halfway there when it comes to understanding this concept. *Potential* means having a latent possibility, a capacity to develop, or the ability to become something. Therefore, if an object has *potential energy*, it has the possibility and capability of becoming another kind of force, usually motion energy.

> ### DEFINITION
> **Potential energy** is energy that is stored in an object. When released it is converted into a different type of energy, often kinetic.

The simplest example of potential energy occurs when you stretch a rubber band. If you hold the rubber band in the stretched position, it has potential energy or the ability to do work. (We get to this later in this chapter.) When you release the rubber band, it goes flying across the room using kinetic (or motion) energy.

A rubber band is also said to have elastic energy. Elastic energy is found in objects that can rearrange themselves and then restore their shape later. A spring is another example of elastic energy.

Another way of describing potential energy is as follows: it exists in any object with mass that's located in a force field. One example of a force field is a gravitational field.

Gravity is the force that makes objects fall to the ground. For example, the Earth exerts a natural force of attraction between it and objects near its surface, drawing them toward the ground like a magnet. With this in mind, you're now prepared to measure potential energy.

One way to determine the gravitational potential energy of an object is to multiply its mass (m) by the gravitational force (g) exerted on it and its height (h) above the Earth's surface: PE = mgh.

Keep in mind that gravitational force is always represented as 9.8 meters per second squared, or $9.8 \frac{m}{s^2}$. Now consider this example:

If you have an object with a mass of 10 kilograms located 15 meters above the Earth, what is the object's potential energy?

Plug the numbers into the formula as follows:

$$PE = 10 \times 9.8 \times 15$$

$$PE = 1,470 \text{ joules}$$

You just calculated gravitational potential energy!

Kinetic Energy

As we mentioned earlier, kinetic energy is also known as *motion energy*. Whenever an object is in motion, it is said to have kinetic energy.

Everything that we see moving has kinetic energy, as a matter of fact. A good example of kinetic energy involves hypothetically positioning a large rock at the top of a hill and giving it a shove. As soon as the rock started rolling downhill, it would begin converting its potential energy into kinetic energy. If the rock ran over some flowers, it would be "doing work" on the flowers by flattening them.

Kinetic energy, potential energy, and work are all measured in units called *joules*. To measure kinetic energy, you multiply the object's mass (in kilograms) by the square of its velocity (v), and then multiply that value by $\frac{1}{2}$:

$$KE = \frac{1}{2}mv^2$$

We discuss velocity in greater detail when we review motion. For the purposes of this equation, though, you should know that velocity is a measure of the speed and direction in which an object is moving.

Let's practice measuring kinetic energy using the following example:

Suppose you have a vehicle that weighs 2,000 kilograms. If the vehicle is traveling at a speed of 10 meters per second, how much kinetic energy does it possess?

The answer to this question can be computed as follows:

$KE = \frac{1}{2} \times 2{,}000 \text{ kg} \times (10 \text{ m/s})^2$

$KE = \frac{1}{2} \times 2{,}000 \text{ kg} \times 100 \text{ m}^2/\text{s}^2$

$KE = \frac{1}{2} \times 200{,}000 \text{ m}^2/\text{s}^2$

$KE = 100{,}000 \text{ kg m}^2/\text{s}^2$ or 100,000 joules

Now consider this:

If you have another vehicle that weighs 3,000 kilograms moving at a speed of 6 meters per second, which vehicle has more kinetic energy? Use the same formula to determine the second vehicle's kinetic energy using the figures supplied in the example.

$KE = \frac{1}{2} \times 3{,}000 \text{ kg} \times (6 \text{ m/s})^2$

$KE = \frac{1}{2} \times 3{,}000 \text{ kg} \times 36 \text{ m}^2/\text{s}^2$

$KE = \frac{1}{2} \times 108{,}000 \text{ m}^2/\text{s}^2$

$KE = 54{,}000 \text{ kg m}^2/\text{s}^2$ or 54,000 joules

Subtract the totals and you'll see that the first vehicle has more kinetic energy than the second.

Work Review

Work and energy are inextricably intertwined. It should come as no shock, then, to hear that work is actually defined as a transfer of energy. More specifically, work is the amount of energy that is transferred through force over a distance.

To visualize the transfer of energy through force and distance, picture a tennis game. If you've ever played tennis, you know this is a good example of hard work!

The tennis player does work on the racket by swinging it. The energy is transferred from the athlete to the racket. Next, the racket does work on the ball and transfers energy to it. If the tennis player did enough work to start with, the ball will go flying over the net with enough force that the opponent will miss it!

If you want to measure work, you need to multiply force by distance: $W = fd$.

Let's use a simple example we're all familiar with to calculate this formula. Suppose you have to push a box across a 15-meter room. If you use 20 newtons of force to accomplish this, you would generate 300 joules of work:

$W = f \times d$

$W = 20 \times 15$

$W = 300 \ joules$

Now, this works if you are pushing an object from one place to another. What happens if you lift an object? In this case, you have to also account for the impact of gravity with this equation: $W = mass \ x \ gravity \ x \ height$. Why? Because when you lift an object, you must overcome the force of gravity, which is quantified through downward-acting gravitational acceleration.

Let's try that out. Suppose you have a 2kg bag of groceries on the floor and you need to move it to a place 2 meters above where it is. Here is how you would apply the formula:

$W = m \times g \times h$

$W = 2 \times 9.8 \times 2$

$W = 39.2 \ joules$

Remember from our discussion of potential energy, gravitational force is represented by the gravitational acceleration constant of 9.8 meters per second squared—and this is how we got the value of g in the equation above.

Motion Review

Motion is simply movement of any kind. It could be something as large as a jet soaring through the sky or as small as a vibration generated by a single voice. To fully grasp the concept of motion, you need some knowledge of the law—Newton's law, that is!

Sir Isaac Newton is known to many as the greatest scientist in the history of the world—even greater than Albert Einstein! Born in the mid-1600s, Newton is also credited with completely initiating classical mechanics, optics, and even mathematics. But he's most well known for his laws of motion.

Newton's First Law

Newton's first law is also known as the *law of inertia*. It states that objects tend to resist changes in motion. An object in motion tends to stay in motion, and an object at rest tends to stay at rest, unless a force is exerted upon it.

It's important to understand the difference between mass and weight. Weight, although similar to mass, measures the amount of gravitational force exerted on an object. If that force is altered—say, by going to the moon—weight changes. The mass of an object, however, is the same anywhere in the universe, regardless of gravitational pull.

To figure out the mass of an object, you multiply its volume (*v*) by its density (*d*): Mass = *dv*. To calculate weight, you multiply the mass (*m*) of the object by the *gravitational acceleration* (*g*) exerted on the object: Weight = *mg*.

> **DEFINITION**
>
> **Gravitational acceleration** is the scientific name for what we think of as the force or pull of gravity. On Earth, it is always equal to $9.8 \frac{m}{s^2}$ or $32.2 \frac{ft}{s^2}$.

Mass is expressed in metric units, usually kilograms or variations thereof. Though in the United States we tend to use our own system of measurement (the Standard or Customary system), most of the world uses metric. This is why most units of measure in math and science are metric.

In the United States, weight is usually expressed in pounds. The metric system expresses weight in newtons. Most people in other areas of the world measure an object's mass, not its weight. That's why you hear the term *kilograms* more often than *newtons*.

Newton's Second Law

This law of motion states that the acceleration of an object is directly proportional to the net force acting on the object. It also states that an object accelerates in the direction of the net force acting on it.

Basically, this law is all about how a force influences the speed of an object. To calculate force, you multiply the mass (*m*) of the object by its acceleration (*a*): F = *ma*.

Consider this example:

> If you are trying to close an over-stuffed suitcase and you push the lid down, in what direction will the lid move?

No, this is not a trick question. You're right—the lid moves in a downward motion as you easily guessed. That's because an object moves in the direction of the force acting upon it. Now for part two of the question:

> As you try to close the suitcase with one hand, you realize that you're getting nowhere, so you switch to two hands. By exerting twice as much pressure, the lid accelerates downward:
>
> (A) Slightly
> (B) Not at all
> (C) Twice as much
> (D) Three times as much

Again, the answer is probably fairly obvious—it's letter C. Twice the force causes an object to accelerate twice as fast. Here's the last part of the question:

> You finally get the frustrating lid closed on the overstuffed suitcase, but by now you are so aggravated that you decide to give it a good shove. In fact, you're so steamed that you also shove the suitcase next to it (even though it closed without a problem). The overstuffed suitcase is five times as large as the other piece you pushed. How quickly does the bursting luggage accelerate, compared to the lighter piece next to it?

The correct answer is one fifth as fast. When an object has five times the mass of another object, it will accelerate one fifth as fast. Acceleration, therefore, is directly proportionate to force and inversely proportionate to mass.

Newton's Third Law

The law of reciprocal action is pretty straightforward and very famous: "For every action, there is an equal and opposite reaction." Chances are, you heard about this as a kid. It means that every motion results in the creation of another motion that runs in the opposite direction. For example, when you do a 5-mile march, your feet push against the ground with every step you take. What you don't feel is that the ground is simultaneously pushing against you (which is partially the reason why your feet ache when you're done).

Now if you strap on "full battle rattle" (as soldiers sometimes call it) and head underwater for training exercises, the force you exert is countered by the force of the water all around you—not just what's under your feet. Though your weight is much lighter in this environment, you feel the force everywhere.

Speed

Now that we've discussed the basics of motion, let's look at some of the tools used to measure it. We'll start with speed, the rate at which an object moves. If you've ever driven a car, you are familiar with the formula for calculating speed:

$$\text{Speed} = \frac{\text{Distance}}{\text{Time}}$$

This means that if you drive 20 miles per hour, your speed will take your car 1 mile every 3 minutes.

Consider another example. Let's say Private Snuffy fails to make his bed one morning, and you want to measure the speed of Drill Sergeant Joe's wrath. As Drill Sergeant Joe comes running out of the barracks, he covers about 50 meters in 5 seconds, headed in a straight line for Private Snuffy. What is Drill Sergeant Joe's speed?

Using the formula for speed, you can determine that this swift (and angry) drill sergeant will cover about 10 meters every second.

Velocity

Velocity is a measure of both the speed and direction an object moves. If Drill Sergeant Joe ran at the same rate of speed and in a straight line to Private Snuffy, we would say he maintained constant velocity. Speed and direction have to be unchanging for constant velocity to occur.

However, if Drill Sergeant Joe had to run around some obstacles to get to Private Snuffy, his direction would no longer be constant. So even if his speed never wavered, the velocity would not be considered constant anymore.

Acceleration

Speaking of change, what happens when an object speeds up (increases velocity)? In general, this change is known as acceleration (a) and is calculated by subtracting the initial rate of velocity (vi) from the final rate of velocity (*vf*), and dividing that value by the length of time (*t*) in which the change occurs: $Acceleration = \frac{vf\text{-}vi}{t}$.

Imagine how it feels when an airplane prepares for takeoff. Usually, the pilot positions the plane at the beginning of the runway, pauses for a few seconds, and then hits the gas (so to speak). Your body presses into the seat as the plane accelerates rapidly down the runway.

Now, if the plane goes from 4 miles per second to 10 miles per second in 2 seconds, you would say the plane is accelerating 3 miles per second per second ($3\frac{mi}{s^2}$).

Gravitational Acceleration

When an object is allowed to fall with only the force of gravity acting on it (we call this *freefalling*), the ratio of weight to mass is constant. This means that, in theory, a car and a paper clip dropped in an environment with no air friction would both hit the ground at the same time; the ratio of weight to mass is the same for both the heavy object and the light object.

Now apply this knowledge to the following question. Will a car and a paper clip fall at the same speed when dropped from a tall building? The answer is not quite. Though the car may have more than 500 times the mass of a paper clip, it also has 500 times the force against it, which would theoretically cause them to fall at the same speed. However, air friction and wind resistance can make for some deviation from this rule.

Although it's often safe to ignore air friction in calculating equations on paper, it can make quite a difference in reality, as any paratrooper will tell you.

Pressure

You can't discuss force without addressing pressure. Simply put, pressure is a measure of continuous force that is applied to an object. Pressure is calculated using the formula: $P = \frac{Force}{Area}$.

For this calculation, you want your measure of force to be in pounds and area to be in square inches. The reason? Pressure is generally expressed in pounds per square inch or psi.

Let's try this out. How much pressure would Private Snuffy need to set a heat press to for it to apply 15 pounds of force to a metal sheet that is 5 in²?

Plug in your numbers: $P = \frac{15}{5} = 3$. This means that Snuffy would only have to set the heat press to 3 psi to achieve the desired result.

Centripetal Acceleration

Another term you should familiarize yourself with is *centripetal force,* which occurs when an object gets pulled into a circular path. Basically, the circular motion also results in an inward force on that object.

Have you ever gone to a carnival and ridden on the swings? The swings are attached to long chains that are likewise attached to arms connected to a base that turns. This construction causes the swings to travel in a circular motion (once the ride begins) because of centripetal force. Simultaneously, the swings move outward from the center, due to centrifugal force resulting from the centripetal acceleration, or rotating motion.

Gear Review

Because gears are used in so many mechanical devices, they are an essential concept for you to review. Gears are small wheels with teeth that mesh with other toothed wheels to do one of the following: (1) change the speed of a mechanism, (2) change the motion of a device, or (3) change the direction of the machinery.

When gears reduce the speed of machinery, this is known as gear reduction. The motor or mechanism slows down so that it can produce a more forceful output. In other words, more work gets done, even though it takes longer to do it.

The reason gears are used to reduce the speed of a mechanism is to achieve something called mechanical advantage, which enables people to accomplish a task with less effort by allowing simple machinery to do work for them. We discuss this in more detail in the following section.

A driving gear is one that is motorized by some force. When its teeth interlock with another gear, the motion from the driving gear turns the second gear in the opposite direction. Take a look at the following figure:

If the small gear in the middle is the driving gear, it causes the other gears to move based on the force of its motion. Because it turns to the left, the other gears it propels turns to the right.

Before we wrap up our discussion on gears, let's take a moment to cover one more concept that you'll likely see on the ASVAB: gear ratio. To understand the idea behind gear ratio, picture a 10-speed bike. When the bike is in its lowest gear, you have a 1:1 ratio, meaning every full turn of your bike pedals results in one full turn of the bike wheels.

If you're going uphill, it takes a lot of effort to pedal using the 1:1 ratio. As you begin shifting gears to get the bike uphill with less effort, you are lowering the gear ratio. Eventually, you may settle on a gear that allows you to turn the pedals three full rotations for one full wheel rotation, or 3:1. The advantage here is that the gears are taking on more of the work so you can expend less energy pedaling.

One easy way to determine the ratio of two gears is to count their teeth. Look at the following figure:

In the figure, the gear on the left has 12 teeth, while the gear on the right has 6 teeth. This makes the gear ratio 12:6, or 2:1.

As described in the bike example, gear ratio directly influences the rate at which the two gears turn. Therefore, if we have a gear ratio of 2:1, we know that for every one turn the larger gear makes, the smaller gear turns twice. See Chapter 8 for more information on ratios and reducing fractions.

Pulley Review

Pulleys are simple machines that make heavy work a lot easier. A pulley is made up of a grooved wheel attached to an axle that allows the wheel to turn. If you run a rope through the groove and attach the rope to an object, lifting that object becomes easier. This is mechanical advantage again. Here's how it works:

1. In a simple one-wheeled pulley system, the only real advantage is changing the direction of force you use to lift the weight. If you have to lift a 100-pound object a distance of 4 meters, a pulley does not change that. However, instead of having to push the weight straight up in the air, the pulley allows you to use a downward pulling motion, which may feel easier.

2. In a basic two-wheeled pulley system, there is a force-distance trade-off, causing a distinct mechanical advantage. By inserting a second pulley into the system, you now have the ability to disperse the weight of the object between the two pulleys.

   A 100-pound object now feels like 50 pounds when you pull the rope. However, to move the object 4 meters, you must now pull the rope twice as far, or 8 meters in this example. You have to pull the rope a longer distance, but you have a lesser force to deal with.

3. If you add two more pulleys, for a total of four pulleys, you have made your task even easier. The same concept applies with the force and distance ratio—you have half the force to move, but twice the distance to pull the rope. Your object now feels like a mere 25 pounds because of the number of pulleys you can use to distribute the weight. However, you have

to pull the rope 16 meters now just to raise the object the original 4 meters! This process continues with the addition of pulleys.

There are three main types of pulleys:

▸ **Fixed.** The axle is connected to a stationary object, such as a hook or wall. A clothesline is a good example of a fixed pulley. This simple machine changes the direction of force, though, which makes it *feel* easier to move an object; in fact, you actually have to apply *more* effort than the load just to move it.

▸ **Compound.** This pulley system blends several fixed or movable pulleys to maximize mechanical advantage. A block and tackle is a common type of compound pulley, often used in the shipping industry. Mechanical advantage increases with the number of additional pulleys added to the system.

▸ **Movable.** The axle here is not attached to anything except the pulley wheel, meaning that the pulley actually moves with the load. These are commonly found in weightlifting machines. With this system, you have a mechanical advantage of 2; this means you can apply half the force of the object to move it. You do, however, have to pull or push the pulley up and down.

Fixed pulley

Compound pulley

Movable pulley

Lever Review

Much like pulleys, *levers* also make life easier in terms of lifting heavy objects.

The object on which a lever pivots is called a *fulcrum*. To better envision a lever-and-fulcrum combination, picture a seesaw (or teeter-totter) from your childhood days. You sat on one end, and the force of your weight pushed that end of the seesaw down to the ground. Then your friend had to try to climb onto the opposite end. (This was always difficult because that end was sticking up high in the air, due to your weight at the other end!)

If your friend weighed more than you, you shot up into the air. If your friend weighed less than you, you remained on the ground and had to push up with your leg muscles to get the seesaw moving. If your friend weighed about the same as you, this was ideal, because you could take turns going up and down with little effort.

The fulcrum was the object in the middle of the seesaw that anchored it to the ground. On a classic seesaw, the fulcrum was positioned exactly at the midpoint of the lever. However, this is not necessarily the case with all levers. Take note of the variance in fulcrum location with each class of lever:

▸ **1st-class lever.** The fulcrum is located between the load and the effort. Good examples include a seesaw, scissors, a claw hammer, and a wheel and axle.

▸ **2nd-class lever.** The load is between the effort and the fulcrum. Good examples include a nutcracker, a

wheelbarrow, a wrench, and a springboard diving board.

▸ **3rd-class lever.** The effort is between the fulcrum and the load. For this type of lever to work properly, the fulcrum is usually attached to the lever. Good examples include tongs, tweezers, and a stapler.

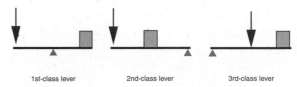

1st-class lever   2nd-class lever   3rd-class lever

Once you understand how levers and fulcrums work, you can begin applying numbers and weights to these diagrams. Let's examine a few basic equations now.

In a 1st-class lever situation, such as a seesaw, you have the following variables: the distance from the fulcrum (d_1) to weight number 1 (w_1), and the distance on the other side of the fulcrum (d_2) to weight number 2 (w_2).

The lever just shown is balanced as follows:

$$w_1 \times d_1 = w_2 \times d_2$$

To better understand how to apply this equation to a word problem you may see on the ASVAB, consider this scenario.

> Little Isabella weighs 45 pounds. She wants to play on the seesaw with her friend Sarah. Sarah also weighs 45 pounds. They both sit equidistant from the pivot point (or fulcrum) on the seesaw, which is 2 meters. Is the lever balanced?

The answer is yes, the lever is balanced, because $45 \times 2 = 45 \times 2$. If Sarah weighed less than Isabella (or vice versa), the lever would not be balanced.

Here's another situation you may encounter with a lever:

> Thomas weighs 55 pounds, but his twin sister Sarah weighs only 45 pounds. If they are sitting 20 feet away from each other on a very large seesaw, how far away should the fulcrum be placed from each child?

First of all, let's put Thomas on the left side of the seesaw and call the distance between him and the fulcrum x. On the right side of the seesaw, we will place Sarah. The distance between her and the fulcrum will be known as $20 - x$. (Remember, 20 is the full distance between the two children, which is where that number came from in this word problem.)

Now we multiply Thomas's weight by x. This is equated to Sarah's weight multiplied by $20 - x$. See the following equation with the numbers plugged in:

$55x = 45 (20 - x)$

Now solve for x:

$55x = 900 - 45x$

$55x + 45x = 900 - 45x + 45x$

$100x = 900$

$x = 9$

Now that we know x equals 9, we know that Thomas should be placed 9 feet from the fulcrum on the seesaw. As for Sarah, we said she should sit $20 - x$ feet away from the fulcrum. In this case, that means she needs to be 11 feet away from the fulcrum. Her lesser body weight is now properly offset by Thomas's greater body weight because of the variance in distances to the fulcrum.

For more help with lever word problems, check out www.psychometric-success.com/faq/faq-mechanical-comprehension-tests. The main thing to remember for this section of the ASVAB is to think outside the box. This section is testing your ability to solve problems more than just reiterate a bunch of memorized facts. Be sure to practice some of these word problems in Chapter 17, too.

Assembling Objects

Did you know that you use your visual intelligence every day? This skill comes in handy whenever you read a map, pack your groceries in your car, or even play games like Tetris or Snoodoku (a version of the popular puzzle game Sudoku that uses faces instead of numbers). By using your sense of sight and analytical skills, you gain information about the world around you and figure out the relationship between objects and their surroundings.

These skills are very important in the military, which is why the Assembling Objects (AO) test was added to the ASVAB several years ago. This chapter introduces you to this one-of-a-kind subtest and walks you through how to approach the questions.

Why Do I Have to Take This?

Believe it or not, figuring out how objects are connected measures your *spatial intelligence* and problem-solving abilities.

By gauging your spatial intelligence, the military gets an idea of how you might perform a multitude of tasks, including these:

▶ Estimating distance

▶ Strategizing an attack

▶ Repairing machinery

▶ Navigating military transports

▶ Executing missions

▶ Conducting accurate reconnaissance

Many jobs in each branch of the Armed Forces require good visualization and spatial perception. Yet as of this writing, the Navy is the only service that requires scores from the AO subtest for job eligibility.

Even if you're not planning to enlist in the Navy, your chosen service may look at your AO score anyway, to gain some more insight into your potential. Any way you slice it, doing well on this section is a good idea.

What to Expect

Regardless of which version of the ASVAB you take, you'll have the AO subtest as your last hurdle to jump before completion. On the CAT, expect to see 16 questions for which you'll have 16 minutes to record your answers. On the PAP, you'll get 9 more questions to answer and 1 less minute in which to answer, for a grand total of 25 questions in 15 minutes on this version of the test.

So, what exactly will you have to do in this section? In a nutshell, the AO subtest is all about solving puzzles—literally. Each question will have a sample drawing that depicts one of two scenarios: two shapes with connection points or a series of shapes that fit together in a certain way.

Following the sample are four answer choices, which will be some iteration of what's in the sample. Depending on the question, you will be required to either (1) choose the answer choice that accurately

shows how the two shapes will be joined if a straight line connected the two points in the example, or (2) determine how the pieces in the example would fit together to make a whole.

The best approach to all these questions is the process of elimination, which means discarding prospective answer choices that clearly don't work. We get into specifics of what to look for in the next two sections, which detail how to approach the two types of AO puzzles you'll see on the ASVAB.

The Right Connections

Connector questions are very straightforward and look something like this:

> In the following diagram, which figure best shows how the objects in the first box would touch if points A and B were connected?

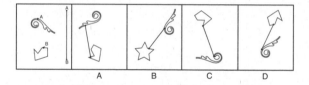

The first box is the sample. It shows a curvy, flourished shape and one that has sharp angles. Point A is marked as a dot where the curled end meets the straight part of the flourish. Point B is right next to the left side of the flat portion at the top of the jagged shape.

The shapes are repeated in various positions in boxes A through D. You're looking for the answer choice that has the two points connecting at the exact same place as shown in the sample. Look at the points in each choice and determine if they match up with the example.

    (A) The points are at different places on both shapes.

    (B) A star replaces the jagged shape, so obviously it doesn't match.

    (C) Again, the points are at different places on both shapes.

    (D) The points do match in the same places shown in the sample.

Using process of elimination, the correct answer is clearly D.

Feeling good about connectors? You should. They're pretty easy to figure out once you get used to them and know what you're looking for in a correct answer. Some of the most common reasons you'll find to eliminate a choice on an AO question include these:

▸ The points don't match up with those shown in the sample.

▸ One or more shapes have been changed from those shown in the sample.

▸ One or more shapes have been "mirrored," or changed into a mirror image of themselves. Mirror images may look exactly the same, but they're not.

▸ The connecting line is not coming into the point at the correct angle.

Let's try another question and see what we can eliminate based on these reasons.

    In the following diagram, which figure best shows how the objects in the first box would touch if points A and B were connected?

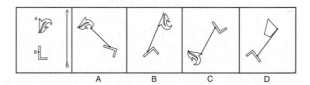

In this question, we have a leaflike flourish and what looks like an *L*. Point A is shown at the tip of one of the leaf's points, and point B is shown toward the middle of the vertical line in the *L*. Now let's look at the answer choices:

    (A) Two issues here. First, the placement of point A is different from the sample. Second, the *L* is mirrored.

    (B) Although the points appear to be in the same spots on both shapes, the shapes themselves are mirrored.

    (C) Although both shapes are rotated, the points connect at the correct places on both shapes. If answer D doesn't have any obvious flaws, this is most likely the answer that will get you the points.

    (D) A quadrilateral is shown in this choice instead of the leaf, making it an incorrect answer.

The best answer is C.

Even if this type of visualization is difficult initially (or just plain weird), a little practice will get you in ship shape in no time. In addition to working with the more than 100 AO problems in this book, you can help build the skills you need to ace connector questions by reading maps or doing some simple sketching. This type of work has proven useful in enhancing a person's visual-spatial skill set.

Making the Pieces Fit

If you're good at figuring out how to best organize your kitchen cupboards or you like to curl up on rainy Sundays and do jigsaw puzzles, you'll love this type of AO question.

As with connector questions, puzzle questions give you a sample box with several shapes. Your task this time is to figure out how they fit together. Some answer choices will form a complete shape. Others will simply show the shapes touching in some way.

Either way, you should approach these questions the same way you would a connector question. Furthermore, you should use the same common reasons to eliminate answer choices—looking for connection points being the obvious exception.

Let's take a look at an AO puzzle question:

Which answer choice best shows how the objects in the first box would appear if they were fitted together?

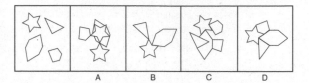

The sample has four shapes: a star, a triangle, a six-sided figure, and a five-sided figure. Now go through the answer choices and look for reasons to eliminate some:

(A) Two of the shapes are layered, which may make it difficult to discern what shape is in the back. However, there is a more obvious error here; there are two stars instead of one. This is not a match.

(B) We're looking for a puzzle with four shapes. This one has only three.

(C) This answer has too many shapes! Although all the sample shapes are there and in the correct proportion, a quadrilateral has been added, which eliminates this answer.

(D) This answer shows all the shapes in the right size and number.

The correct choice is D.

Let's try another one:

Which answer choice best shows how the objects in the first box would appear if they were fitted together?

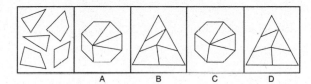

This question gives us five shapes, but this time they make up a whole object. Since all of them are angular and look similar, we need to look carefully at how each of the answer choices is constructed. All we need is one piece that doesn't match the sample to eliminate the answer choice:

(A) The diamond shape in the sample is less proportionate than the one in this answer, which also affects the sizes of the other shapes in the choice.

(B) None of the shapes in this answer choice match up in size or shape with those in the sample.

(C) The diamond shape in this choice matches the one in the sample, as do the rest of the shapes within. So far, this is the best choice.

(D) The same issues in answer B apply here. The shapes are way off.

The best choice is answer C.

Even if you weren't sure that the shapes in answer C matched the sample perfectly, there were enough more noticeable reasons to eliminate the other answer choices. Using this approach can help you turn a tough AO puzzle into something more manageable.

To help sharpen your skills at putting shapes together, try computer games like Tetris, in which you fit shapes together to make whole lines. If you prefer to work offline, try any of the following:

▸ Putting together classic jigsaw puzzles

▸ Searching for hidden pictures, such as those found in *Highlights* magazine

▸ Scrutinizing the *I Spy* or *Where's Waldo?* books to locate a specific object

Technical Skills Workout

General Science

1. Biology is the study of

    (A) life and living organisms.
    (B) origin, structure, and phenomena associated with planet Earth.
    (C) nonliving systems found in natural science.
    (D) matter.

2. Genes are located on

    (A) dominant alleles.
    (B) recessive alleles.
    (C) chromosomes.
    (D) proteins.

3. Which biological classification can be found between phylum and order?

    (A) family
    (B) class
    (C) genus
    (D) species

4. Mushrooms and molds are part of the kingdom

    (A) Protista.
    (B) Animalia.
    (C) Plantae.
    (D) Fungi.

Ⓐ Ⓑ Ⓒ Ⓓ

Ⓐ Ⓑ Ⓒ Ⓓ

Ⓐ Ⓑ Ⓒ Ⓓ

Ⓐ Ⓑ Ⓒ Ⓓ

Ⓐ Ⓑ Ⓒ Ⓓ

Ⓐ Ⓑ Ⓒ Ⓓ

5. Where are chloroplasts located?

    (A) gametes

    (B) chromosomes

    (C) plant leaves

    (D) carbon dioxide

6. A habitat is

    (A) an environment in which
    an organism or a group of
    organisms normally live.

    (B) a region in the Northern
    Hemisphere that has cone-
    bearing trees.

    (C) the study of the environment.

    (D) a home for multiple biomes.

7. Light-independent reactions

    (A) take place in the dark.

    (B) are part of photosynthesis.

    (C) need photons.

    (D) create ATP, NADPH, and oxygen.

8. A family of cells that live closely
   together is defined as a(n)

    (A) organ.

    (B) tissue.

    (C) system.

    (D) body.

9. Newly formed proteins mature in the

    (A) mitochondria.

    (B) nucleus.

    (C) golgi.

    (D) lysosome.

10. Which cells do NOT undergo mitosis?

    (A) skin cells

    (B) hair cells

    (C) fingernail cells

    (D) sex cells

11. In meiosis, the number of chromo-
    somes in gamete cells is

    (A) doubled.

    (B) the same as in all other cells.

    (C) halved.

    (D) dependent on DNA composition.

12. Spores are created by

    (A) bacteria, plants, and algae.

    (B) animals and humans.

    (C) genes and chromosomes.

    (D) the excretory system.

13. The system that oxygenates blood is
    the

    (A) circulatory system.

    (B) respiratory system.

    (C) digestive system.

    (D) excretory system.

14. Overhydration is a problem because

    (A) the body doesn't have enough
    water.

    (B) sugar levels become unbalanced
    with water levels.

    (C) water intake is too fast for the
    respiratory system.

    (D) salt levels become unbalanced
    with water levels.

15. What percent of the body is comprised of water?

    (A) less than 30 percent
    (B) more than 80 percent
    (C) less than 50 percent
    (D) more than 60 percent

16. Vitamin D can be found in which foods?

    (A) spinach and parsley
    (B) fish oil and leafy veggies
    (C) cheese and eggs
    (D) citrus fruits and tomatoes

17. Earth's crust is approximately how many miles deep?

    (A) 10
    (B) 180
    (C) 1,800
    (D) 3,000

18. Clouds that are puffy and often found in groups are called

    (A) cirrus.
    (B) cumulus.
    (C) stratus.
    (D) cumulonimbus.

19. The smallest part of an element is

    (A) a compound.
    (B) matter.
    (C) a proton.
    (D) a molecule.

20. The outermost level of Earth's atmosphere is the

    (A) mesosphere.
    (B) exosphere.
    (C) troposphere.
    (D) thermosphere.

Answers and Explanations

1. **A.** Answer B is the definition of earth science, answer C is the definition of physical science, and answer D is the definition of chemistry.

2. **C.** Choices A and B refer to specific types of traits, such as those used in determining eye color, hair color, and the like. Choice D is wrong because proteins are organic compounds found in cells that are designed to assist in the digestive process.

3. **B.** Remember taxonomy order using the mnemonic device "Dear Keen People Can Often Find Good Sales."

4. **D.** The Protista kingdom includes slime molds and some algae. The Animalia kingdom includes animals, vertebrates, and invertebrates. The Plantae kingdom includes plants and mosses.

5. **C.** Gametes are sexual reproductive cells. Chromosomes are threadlike strands of DNA located in the nucleus of cells. Carbon dioxide is one of the elements in photosynthesis that gets converted to sugar and oxygen.

6. **A.** Choice B describes a coniferous forest. Choice C is the definition of ecology. Choice D is wrong because biomes are major regional biological communities, such as a forest or desert. Habitats are located within a single biome, rather than multiple biomes living within a habitat.

7. **B.** Sometimes called "dark reactions," this process does not actually take place in the dark; it needs more than photons to take place. During this stage of photosynthesis, the energy and products of the light-dependent reactions (ATP, NADPH, and oxygen) are used to convert carbon dioxide and water into carbohydrates and oxygen that nourish the plant and the heterotrophs that eat the plant.

8. **B.** An organ is a group of tissues working together. A system is a group of organs working together. A body is multiple systems working together.

9. **C.** Mitochondria convert nutrients to energy. The nucleus is the "command center" of the cell. Lysosomes contain the necessary digestive enzymes for the cell.

10. **D.** Sex cells are the only ones listed that do not undergo mitosis.

11. **C.** Refer to our discussion on meiosis for additional information about sexual reproduction in animal cells.

12. **A.** Spores are the reproductive structure produced by bacteria, plants, algae, fungi, and some protozoa.

13. **B.** Choice A is wrong because the circulatory system controls the flow of blood, but it doesn't supply it. Choice C is wrong because the digestive system converts food to energy. Choice D is wrong because the excretory system regulates the chemical composition of the body.

14. **D.** Choice A describes *de*hydration, not *over*hydration. The other selections have nothing to do with overhydration.

15. **B.** Up to 80 percent of the human body can be made of water, depending on size.

16. **C.** Choice A describes vitamin K. Choice B describes vitamin A. Choice D describes vitamin C.

17. **A.** Choice B is simply wrong, while choices C and D describe the depth of the mantle and the outer core, respectively.

18. **B.** Cirrus clouds are wispy and made of ice crystals. Stratus clouds are uniform in color and density. Cumulonimbus clouds are tall and thick.

19. **D.** Choice A is wrong because a compound is created when two or more elements combine. Choice B is wrong because matter is anything with mass and volume. Choice C is wrong because a proton is a positively charged particle inside an atom.

20. **B.** The atmospheric layers listed from closest to Earth to the farthest are: troposphere, stratosphere, mesosphere, thermosphere, and exosphere.

Electronics Skills

1. <u>Current</u> is defined as

    (A) the flow of air through a conductor.

    (B) the flow of electricity through a conductor.

    (C) the strength with which current flows through a conductor.

    (D) the amount of energy transferred during a specified time.

2. Ohms measure

    (A) voltage.

    (B) current.

    (C) electrical power.

    (D) resistance.

3. Household wiring is most commonly made of

    (A) copper.

    (B) iron.

    (C) mercury.

    (D) silver.

4. Which of the following is NOT an example of a power source?

    (A) electric company

    (B) wall outlet

    (C) gas-powered generator

    (D) battery

5. A circuit is

    (A) a system of connected conductors that direct the path of electricity.

    (B) a material through which electricity passes.

    (C) something through which electricity cannot pass.

    (D) a measurement of electrical pressure.

6. A circuit is complete when it is

    (A) closed.

    (B) open.

    (C) full.

    (D) hot.

7. Alternating current (AC) travels

    (A) to the source of power only.

    (B) from the source of power only.

    (C) to and from the source of power.

    (D) to and from the diodes.

8. A bulb in your strand of Christmas lights goes out, which causes them all to go out. What type of circuit do these lights operate on?

    (A) parallel

    (B) LED

    (C) switch

    (D) series

9. The thickness of a 12-gauge wire is _____ than a 3-gauge wire.

    (A) more thick

    (B) less thick

    (C) the same

    (D) not enough information to tell

10. You have a 100-watt lightbulb and 20 volts of electrical pressure. How many amps of current do you have?

    (A) 5
    (B) 2,000
    (C) 200
    (D) 6

11. If you have 6 ohms of resistance and 2 amps of current, how many volts do you have?

    (A) 3
    (B) 12
    (C) 18
    (D) 2

12. Suppose you have 15 volts of pressure and 5 ohms of resistance. How many amps do you have?

    (A) 75
    (B) .33
    (C) 3
    (D) 750

13. Frequency is measured in

    (A) ammeters.
    (B) hertz.
    (C) AM.
    (D) FM.

14. The number of complete cycles per second in any given periodic event is called

    (A) wave.
    (B) refraction.
    (C) frequency.
    (D) dispersion.

15. Suppose you are trying to earn the world record for bouncing a Ping-Pong ball on the paddle without dropping it. If you bounce it 2,500 times over the course of 300 minutes, what is your frequency?

    (A) .14 hertz
    (B) 750,000 hertz
    (C) .12 hertz
    (D) 50 hertz

16. Particles in a medium move parallel to the wave direction in a

    (A) transverse wave.
    (B) longitudinal wave.
    (C) surface wave.
    (D) seismic wave.

17. The bending of waves as they interact with obstacles in their path is

    (A) dispersion.
    (B) rectilinear propagation.
    (C) diffraction.
    (D) reflection.

18. Amplitude measures the

    (A) height of a wave.
    (B) speed of a wave.
    (C) distance from one wave peak to another.
    (D) intensity of a wave.

19. Which device is used to measure power?

    (A) ohmmeter
    (B) voltmeter
    (C) wattmeter
    (D) ammeter

20. Radio, heat, and light waves are

    (A) longitudinal.

    (B) surface.

    (C) parallel.

    (D) transverse.

Answers and Explanations

1. **B.** Choice A is wrong because air has nothing to do with current. Choice C is wrong because it describes voltage. Choice D is wrong because it describes power.

2. **D.** Choice A is wrong because voltage is measured by volts. Choice B is wrong because current is measured by amperes. Choice C is wrong because electric power is measured by watts.

3. **A.** The other choices depict other common conductors of electricity, but they are not found in household wiring.

4. **B.** Power is not generated from the wall outlet, although it's often part of an electric circuit.

5. **A.** Choice B is wrong because it describes a conductor, choice C describes an insulator, and choice D describes voltage.

6. **A.** An open circuit is not complete because the electrons have stopped moving, so choice B is wrong. Choices C and D are also wrong.

7. **C.** Choice A is not only wrong, but it is impossible. Current has to come from a power source of some kind. Choice B is wrong because it describes direct current (DC). Choice D is wrong because current doesn't come from a diode; a diode directs the flow of current in some situations.

8. **D.** Choice A is wrong because on a parallel circuit there are enough paths for the current to flow so one malfunctioning light won't cause the whole strand to go out. Choice B is wrong because LED stands for light emitting diodes and is not a type of circuit. Choice C is wrong because a switch is not a type of circuit, either.

9. **B.** Thick wire has a small gauge; thin wire has a larger gauge.

10. **A.** To determine amps when you know volts and watts, use the following formula: $W = V \times A$.

11. **B.** To determine volts, multiply amps by ohms.

12. **C.** To determine amps, divide volts by ohms.

13. **B.** Choice A is wrong because an ammeter is a device used to measure current. Choice C is wrong because AM stands for amplitude modulated and is a carrier signal for radio waves. Choice D is wrong for the same reason, although it stands for frequency modulated.

14. **C.** Choice A is wrong because a wave is a disturbance that is transmitted through space and time. Choice B is wrong because refraction is a change in wave direction because of a change in wave speed as it enters a new medium. Choice D is wrong because dispersion occurs when a wave is split up by frequency.

15. **A.** To determine frequency, divide the number of occurrences by the total time.

16. **B.** Choice A is wrong because transverse waves cause particles to move in a perpendicular direction to the wave. Choice C is wrong because surface waves cause particles to move in a circular direction to the wave. Choice D is wrong because seismic waves are a type of surface wave.

17. **C.** Choice A is wrong because dispersion occurs when a wave is split up by frequency. Choice B is wrong because rectilinear propagation is the movement of waves in a straight line. Choice D is wrong because reflection is the change in wave direction after it strikes a reflective surface.

18. **A.** Choice B is wrong because it describes wave speed. Choice C describes wavelength, and choice D is simply wrong because, depending on what type of wave you are trying to measure, there are different methods of calculating intensity.

19. **C.** Choice A is wrong because it measures resistance, choice B is wrong because it measures the difference in voltage, and choice D is wrong because it measures current.

20. **D.** Choice A is wrong because longitudinal waves include sound waves, for example. Choice B is wrong because surface waves include ocean waves, for example. Choice C is wrong because parallel is a direction of particle movement within a wave medium, not a type of wave.

Automotive Skills

1. The purpose of a transmission is to
   - (A) route electricity from the battery to the spark plugs.
   - (B) keep gas and air moving throughout the engine.
   - (C) match the speed of the engine to the speed the driver sets.
   - (D) keep the engine cool.

2. Pistons are
   - (A) solid cylinders or discs in an engine that move up and down.
   - (B) suppliers of the initial source of energy for the car.
   - (C) electrical transformers.
   - (D) devices that take current from the ignition coil and send it to the spark plugs.

3. Water jackets can be found in which automotive system?
   - (A) drivetrain
   - (B) chassis
   - (C) cooling
   - (D) suspension

4. Which components comprise a car's electrical system?
   - (A) spark plugs, battery, ignition coils, coil pack
   - (B) pipes, muffler, catalytic converter
   - (C) water pump, radiator, pressure cap, thermostat
   - (D) battery, starter, solenoid, alternator

5. About how many volts of power does the battery provide to electrical accessories in the car?
   - (A) 6
   - (B) 12
   - (C) 120
   - (D) 6,000

6. What component does a coil pack replace in modern vehicles?
   - (A) distributor
   - (B) ignition coil
   - (C) starter
   - (D) generator

7. The voltage regulator
   - (A) converts battery voltage.
   - (B) helps eliminate power surges.
   - (C) regulates voltage in the cooling system.
   - (D) times spikes so they will coincide with brownouts, to cancel each other out.

8. A type of engine that uses gasoline may be called a(n)
   - (A) diesel engine.
   - (B) external combustion engine.
   - (C) internal combustion engine.
   - (D) hydrogen engine.

9. What did older engines rely on to carry fuel to the engine?
   - (A) gravity
   - (B) fuel pump
   - (C) fuel injectors
   - (D) electric filters

10. Which of the following is NOT a function of the exhaust system?

 (A) reduces the noise of an engine
 (B) filters out dirt and rust particles in the fuel
 (C) maintains performance
 (D) reduces or eliminates harmful emissions

11. The pipe that connects the exhaust pipe to the muffler is the

 (A) tailpipe.
 (B) resonator pipe.
 (C) intermediate pipe.
 (D) X-pipe.

12. Three-way catalytic converters most commonly control emissions of

 (A) nitrogen, carbon dioxide, and water vapor.
 (B) nitrogen, carbon monoxide, and hydrogen.
 (C) hydrogen, water vapor, and helium.
 (D) carbon monoxide, hydrogen, and sulfur.

13. The thermostat

 (A) prevents coolant from boiling.
 (B) picks up heat from the engine.
 (C) provides pressure needed to circulate coolant through the engine cavities.
 (D) controls the temperature of the engine.

14. What do disc brakes rely on to slow a vehicle?

 (A) backing plate
 (B) brake shoes
 (C) heat and friction
 (D) liquid coolant

15. Brake shoes can be compared to which disc brake component?

 (A) brake pads
 (B) rotors
 (C) calipers
 (D) wheel cylinder

16. Emergency brakes are considered a

 (A) primary braking device.
 (B) secondary braking device.
 (C) hydraulic braking device.
 (D) fluid braking device.

17. The suspension system connects the

 (A) fuel system to the exhaust system.
 (B) shock absorber to the steering linkage.
 (C) vehicle to its wheels.
 (D) dependent to the independent wheel systems.

18. Which wheel design hasn't been used on cars in decades?

 (A) front-wheel independent
 (B) front-wheel dependent
 (C) rear-wheel independent
 (D) rear-wheel dependent

19. A wheel system that uses a solid axle to connect rear wheels is called

    (A) front-wheel independent.
    (B) front-wheel dependent.
    (C) rear-wheel independent.
    (D) rear-wheel dependent.

20. Which element of the electrical system uses the most power?

    (A) solenoid
    (B) starter
    (C) alternator
    (D) voltage regulator

Answers and Explanations

1. **B.** The purpose of a transmission is to match the speed of the engine to enable the car to travel at the speed the driver wants. This is accomplished through a set of gears, each of which allows a specific amount of torque from the engine to move parts in the chassis that enable the car to move.

2. **A.** Choice B describes a battery. Choice C describes an ignition coil. Choice D describes the distributor.

3. **C.** Water jackets enable liquid coolant to travel through the engine block and heads, picking up heat from the engine.

4. **D.** Choice A is wrong because it describes a distributorless ignition system. Choice B is wrong because it describes the exhaust system. Choice C is wrong because it describes the coolant system.

5. **B.** The battery provides about 12 volts of DC current to the electrical accessories of the car when the engine isn't running or when it's idling.

6. **A.** Choices B and C are still found in modern cars. A generator (as in choice D) has been replaced by an alternator in modern cars.

7. **B.** Choice A is wrong because the ignition coil converts voltage. Choice C is wrong because voltage is regulated by the electrical system, not the cooling system. Choice D is wrong because voltage regulators try to eliminate spikes and brownouts, not time them to occur simultaneously.

8. **C.** Diesel engines use diesel fuel. There is no such thing as an external combustion engine. Hydrogen engines do not use gasoline.

9. **A.** Choice B is wrong because fuel pumps are used in newer cars to carry fuel to the engine, not older cars. Choice C is wrong because a fuel injector forcibly pumps fuel under high pressure in newer cars. Choice D is wrong because there is no such thing as an electric filter in cars.

10. **B.** Choice B is a function of the fuel filter in the fuel system. All other choices relate to the exhaust system.

11. **C.** Choice A is wrong because the tailpipe is the last piece of tubing in the exhaust process. Choice B is wrong because a resonator is not a pipe. It is a secondary silencing mechanism that may be used when standard mufflers don't adequately control noise. Choice D is wrong because an X-pipe describes a specially shaped piping system used to equal the pressure in a dual exhaust system.

12. **A.** None of the other answers have the correct combination of gases controlled by catalytic converters.

13. **D.** Choice A refers to a radiator cap or a pressure cap. Choice B refers to the passages in the engine through which liquid coolant travels, and choice C refers to a water pump.

14. **C.** Choices A and B describe components of drum brakes. Choice D uses a term from the cooling system, not the elements disc brakes use for stopping.

15. **A.** Choices B and C refer to other elements of disc brakes. Neither of these functions similarly to the brake shoes of drum brakes. Choice D is wrong because it describes another component of the drum brake system.

16. **B.** Choice A is wrong because disc and drum brakes are the primary system used for braking. Choice C is wrong because emergency brakes rely on a mechanical system, whereas the primary brakes use hydraulics. Choice D is just wrong.

17. **C.** Choice A doesn't make sense and has nothing to do with the suspension system. Choice B refers to components of the suspension system, and choice D refers to two separate types of suspension systems.

18. **B.** All of the other designs are still in use.

19. **D.** Choices A and B refer to the front wheels, so they are wrong. Choice C uses a flexible system to connect rear wheels.

20. **B.** Each choice represents an element of the electrical system, but only the starter uses an exorbitant amount of power in that system.

Shop Information

1. Which of the following is NOT a function of shaping tools?

   (A) contour objects
   (B) make curves
   (C) make incisions
   (D) cut large sections of wood or metal

2. A cold chisel is used for

   (A) creating pockets for door hinges.
   (B) cutting cold wood.
   (C) cutting cold metal.
   (D) wooden boat building.

3. Rasps are generally used on

   (A) wood.
   (B) metal.
   (C) plastic.
   (D) all of the above.

4. A hand saw used for cutting metal or bone is a

   (A) crosscut saw.
   (B) hack saw.
   (C) miter saw.
   (D) circular saw.

5. A Tuttle saw works best on

   (A) soft wood.
   (B) any wood.
   (C) hard wood.
   (D) old wood.

6. What types of projects usually require the use of a ball-peen hammer?

   (A) anything with upholstery
   (B) something with toys or plaster board
   (C) one that requires the removal of nails
   (D) some auto repairs and woodworking tasks

7. Which type of hammer is often referred to as a baby sledge?

   (A) tinner
   (B) engineer
   (C) ball peen
   (D) curved claw

8. The end of a Phillips head screwdriver looks like a(n)

   (A) x.
   (B) narrow slot.
   (C) star.
   (D) hexagon.

9. Which of the following is NOT one of the three main parts of a hand drill?

   (A) chuck
   (B) cranking handle
   (C) crankshaft
   (D) drill bit

10. An auger bit is used to

    (A) drill large, deep holes in wood.
    (B) make a larger hole than a twist bit will create.
    (C) make a hole where the top part of the hole is enlarged.
    (D) make holes in stone or quarry.

11. Which tool should you use to loosen nuts and bolts?

    (A) plane tool

    (B) wrench

    (C) screwdriver

    (D) clamp

12. This type of clamp typically has wood jaws.

    (A) hand screw

    (B) C-clamp

    (C) pipe clamp

    (D) bar clamp

13. Crescent, spanner, and pipe wrenches are all forms of

    (A) socket wrenches.

    (B) open-end wrenches.

    (C) adjustable-end wrenches.

    (D) Allen wrenches.

14. What type of clamp uses two long screws to force the clamp jaws toward one another, thereby holding an object in place?

    (A) hand screw

    (B) pivot screw

    (C) jack screw

    (D) vise screw

15. Which type of clamp is similar to a version of locking pliers?

    (A) pipe clamp

    (B) bar grip

    (C) vise grip

    (D) power clamp

16. Which of the following is NOT a function of a router?

    (A) contour plastic

    (B) smooth rough edges

    (C) buff surfaces

    (D) sand wood

17. A fixed cutting tool often used in conjunction with a powered lathe is a

    (A) circular saw.

    (B) jigsaw.

    (C) chisel.

    (D) rasp.

18. The most common type of power drill is the

    (A) hammer drill.

    (B) pistol grip.

    (C) drill press.

    (D) crank drill.

19. A saw with a narrow blade that moves in a vertical and reciprocating motion is a

    (A) circular saw.

    (B) miter saw.

    (C) table saw.

    (D) jigsaw.

20. What type of general-purpose plane tool can fit into tight spaces and is used to trim wood edges and joints?

    (A) chisel

    (B) jack plane

    (C) router

    (D) block plane

Answers and Explanations

1. **D.** Cutting large sections of an object is the job of a saw, not a shaping tool. All the other choices are functions of shaping tools.

2. **C.** Choice A describes a wood chisel. Choices B and D are wrong because cold chisels are used specifically to cut cold metals, not wood.

3. **A.** The other surfaces can be used with a file but not a rasp.

4. **B.** Choice A is wrong because a cross-cut saw is used for cutting wood against the grain. Choice C is wrong because a miter saw is used for making angled cuts, often for picture frames. Choice D is wrong because it is not a hand saw.

5. **C.** Tuttle saws work best on hard woods.

6. **D.** Choices A and B describe a rubber mallet hammer. Choice C describes a curved claw hammer.

7. **B.** An engineer's hammer is called a baby sledge because it looks similar to the sledge but smaller. It generally weighs between 1 and 5 pounds.

8. **A.** Choice B describes a flathead. Choice C, describes a seldom-used tool called a Torx screwdriver, which is sometimes used in some seatbelt systems. Choice D describes an Allen wrench.

9. **C.** Crankshafts are found in automobiles, not a hand drill.

10. **A.** Choice B is wrong because it describes a spade bit. Choice C is wrong because it describes a countersink. Choice D is wrong because it describes a carbide-tipped masonry bit.

11. **B.** Plane tools are used to flatten, smooth, and narrow the width of wood. Screwdrivers are used in conjunction with screws, not nuts and bolts. Clamps are used to fasten an item in place.

12. **A.** This type of clamp tightens around an object using two long screws and wooden blocks. The screws are rotated by hand, causing the jaws of the clamp to apply inward pressure to the object being held.

13. **C.** Crescent, spanner, and pipe wrenches all have specific functions as adjustable wrenches.

14. **A.** When the screws of a hand screw are rotated, they cause the jaws of the clamp to apply inward pressure, holding an object in place.

15. **C.** Choice A is wrong because a pipe clamp is used to hold a pipe in place for cutting, threading, lifting, or suspending. Choice B is wrong because a bar clamp uses a screw mechanism to tighten its large jaws. Choice D is wrong because a power clamp does not resemble locking pliers. It may be used in welding projects and is often made of cast aluminum.

16. **A.** Routers are used with metal and wood, not plastic.

17. **C.** Lathes are used to shape metal or wood by rotating the item on the axis of the lathe. The edge of the item needing to be cut is pressed against a fixed cutting object, like a chisel or sandpaper.

18. **B.** Choice A is usually used for drilling masonry—a jackhammer is a good example of this type of drill. Choice C is wrong because a drill press is a fixed tool mounted to a workbench or the floor. Choice D is wrong because a crank drill is what people sometimes call a hand drill. None of these are as popular as the pistol-grip power drill.

19. **D.** Choices A and C are wrong because they both have circular blades. Choice B is wrong because miter saws have straight horizontal or circular blades, too.

20. **D.** Choices A and C are wrong because they are not plane tools. Choice B is wrong because it cannot easily fit into tight spaces and isn't considered general purpose like the block plane.

Mechanical Comprehension

1. Transferring energy through force over a distance is called

    (A) potential energy.

    (B) kinetic energy.

    (C) work.

    (D) motion.

2. When an object can rearrange itself and then restore its original shape later, it has

    (A) elastic energy.

    (B) spring energy.

    (C) gravitational energy.

    (D) chemical energy.

3. The formula for gravitational potential energy is

    (A) $PE = \frac{mg}{h}$

    (B) $PE = mgh$

    (C) $PE = \frac{m}{gh}$

    (D) $PE = \frac{mh}{g}$

4. If a sailor who weighs 64 kilograms is running at a rate of 8 meters per second, what is his kinetic energy?

    (A) 4,096 joules

    (B) 131,072 joules

    (C) 256 joules

    (D) 2,048 joules

5. Work is

    (A) force times distance.

    (B) force times distance multiplied by one half.

    (C) force divided by distance squared.

    (D) force divided by distance.

6. What unit is used to measure work?

    (A) newtons

    (B) joules

    (C) meters

    (D) kilograms

7. Gravitational pull on Earth is

    (A) $9.8 \frac{m}{s^2}$

    (B) $32.2 \frac{m}{s^2}$

    (C) $9.8 \frac{m^2}{s}$

    (D) $98 \frac{m}{s}$

8. Newton's second law of motion states that

    (A) an object in motion tends to stay in motion.

    (B) an object at rest tends to stay at rest.

    (C) the acceleration of an object is directly proportionate to the net force acting on it.

    (D) for every action, there is an equal and opposite reaction.

9. If you run 6.2 miles in 31 minutes, what is your speed?

    (A) 1 mile every 4 minutes

    (B) $\frac{2}{10}$ of a mile every minute

    (C) 2 miles every 6 minutes

    (D) $\frac{6}{10}$ of a mile every 2 minutes

10. When you are driving due north at 60 miles per hour, what type of motion do you use?

    (A) constant acceleration
    (B) gravitational acceleration
    (C) constant negative speed
    (D) constant velocity

11. If an elephant and a chipmunk both jump off a ledge that exists in a vacuum, who will hit the ground first?

    (A) the elephant
    (B) the chipmunk
    (C) both will hit at the same time
    (D) there's no way to tell

12. When an object gets pulled into a circular path, this is known as what?

    (A) centripetal acceleration
    (B) centrifugal force
    (C) circular force
    (D) constant force

13. The most common type of gear is the

    (A) helical gear.
    (B) bevel gear.
    (C) worm gear.
    (D) spur gear.

14. When a driving gear engages with another gear, in which direction does the second gear turn?

    (A) the same as the driving gear
    (B) the opposite of the driving gear
    (C) depends on what type of driving gear you have
    (D) depends on the size of the driving gear

15. This simple machine is made of a grooved wheel attached to an axel. Often a rope is run through the wheel to make lifting heavy things easier. What type of machine is this?

    (A) gear
    (B) lever
    (C) pulley
    (D) fulcrum

16. A clothesline is an example of a

    (A) fixed pulley.
    (B) moveable pulley.
    (C) compound pulley.
    (D) level pulley.

17. A seesaw is an example of a

    (A) gear.
    (B) pulley.
    (C) lever.
    (D) mechanical advantage.

18. In a 3rd-class lever, the effort is between the _____ and the _____.

    (A) fulcrum, load
    (B) load, lever
    (C) fulcrum, gear
    (D) middle, end of the lever

19. If you have a 1st-class lever with a load 2 meters to the right of the fulcrum and 3 meters to the left of the fulcrum, is the lever balanced?

    (A) yes
    (B) no
    (C) not enough information
    (D) yes, as long as the load on the left side is wider than the load on the right side

20. The force that makes objects fall to the ground is

   (A) centripetal.
   (B) gravity.
   (C) joules.
   (D) kinetic.

Answers and Explanations

1. **C.** Choice A is wrong because potential energy is defined as stored energy or an object with the potential to do work. Choice B is wrong because kinetic energy is the energy of motion. Choice D is wrong because motion is defined as when an object changes position over a period of time.

2. **A.** Choice B is wrong because a spring is an example of elastic energy. Choice C is wrong because gravitational energy is energy associated with a gravitational field. Choice D is wrong because chemical energy is a form of potential energy related to the molecular structure of atoms.

3. **B.** Potential energy is measured by multiplying mass (m) by gravitational force (g) by height above Earth's surface (h).

4. **D.** The formula for kinetic energy is:
$$KE = \tfrac{1}{2}mv^2$$

5. **A.** None of the other formulas represent work.

6. **B.** Joules are used to calculate work and energy.

7. **A.** Gravitational acceleration, also known as *gravitational pull*, is always represented by the same mathematical figure (on Earth).

8. **C.** Choices A and B are wrong because they express Newton's first law of motion. Choice D is wrong because it expresses Newton's third law of motion.

9. **B.** Speed is calculated using the following formula: $Speed = \frac{Distance}{Time}$

10. **D.** Constant velocity means that speed and direction are both unchanging.

11. **C.** If two objects fall at the same time, the ratio of weight to mass is the same for both heavy and light objects. In a vacuum that has no wind resistance or air friction, both would hit the ground at the same time because of this concept.

12. **A.** Choice B is wrong because centrifugal force occurs when outward force is placed on a body that is traveling in a circular direction. Choices C and D are not names for types of force.

13. **D.** Spur gears are found in such common appliances as washing machines, clothes dryers, electric screwdrivers, and the like.

14. **B.** The motion from the driving gear, which is motorized by some force, causes the second gear to turn in the opposite direction.

15. **C.** Choice A is wrong because a gear is a small wheel with teeth that meshes with other toothed wheels. Choice B is wrong because a lever is a rigid bar that pivots on a fixed point. Choice D is wrong because a fulcrum is the pivot on which a lever turns.

16. **A.** Choice B is wrong because a moveable pulley is not attached to anything except the pulley wheel, which would make hanging clothes rather difficult! Choice C is wrong because a compound pulley is far more involved than a simple clothesline system. Choice D is wrong because a level is not a type of pulley.

17. **C.** A seesaw uses a lever and a ful-
    crum. Choices A and B are wrong
    because no gears or pulleys are
    involved with a seesaw. Choice D is
    wrong because mechanical advan-
    tage is the reason simple machines
    are used; it is not a specific type of
    machine.

18. **A.** Examples of 3rd-class levers
    include tongs, tweezers, and staplers.

19. **C.** 1st-class levers are balanced only
    when the products of the load weight
    and distance from that load to the ful-
    crum are equal for each side of the
    lever. However, this problem does not
    give you the weight of the loads, and
    therefore, there is not enough infor-
    mation to answer the question.

20. **B.** Choice A is wrong because centrip-
    etal force occurs when an object gets
    pulled in a circular path. Choice C is
    wrong because a joule is the unit used
    to measure work and energy. Choice
    D is wrong because kinetic is the
    energy of motion.

Assembling Objects

1. Which answer choice best shows how the objects in the first box would appear if they were fitted together?

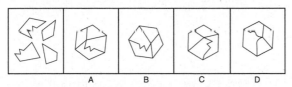

2. Which answer choice best shows how the objects in the first box would appear if they were fitted together?

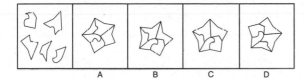

3. In the following diagram, which figure best shows how the objects in the first box would touch if points A and B were connected?

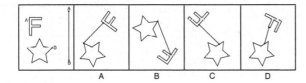

4. Which answer choice best shows how the objects in the first box would appear if they were fitted together?

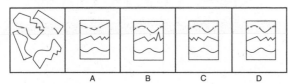

5. In the following diagram, which figure best shows how the objects in the first box would touch if points A and B were connected?

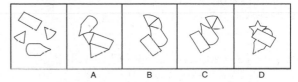

6. Which answer choice best shows how the objects in the first box would appear if they were fitted together?

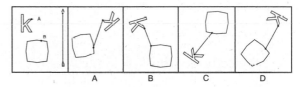

7. In the following diagram, which figure best shows how the objects in the first box would touch if points A and B were connected?

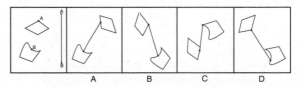

8. Which answer choice best shows how the objects in the first box would appear if they were fitted together?

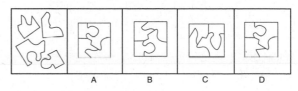

9. Which answer choice best shows how the objects in the first box would appear if they were fitted together?

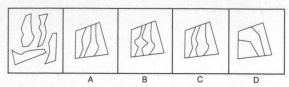

10. In the following diagram, which figure best shows how the objects in the first box would touch if points A and B were connected?

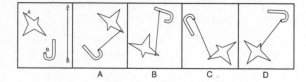

11. In the following diagram, which figure best shows how the objects in the first box would touch if points A and B were connected?

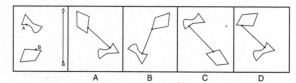

12. Which answer choice best shows how the objects in the first box would appear if they were fitted together?

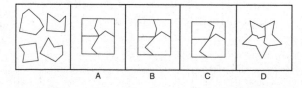

13. In the following diagram, which figure best shows how the objects in the first box would touch if points A and B were connected?

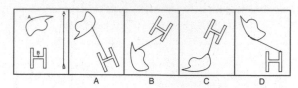

14. Which answer choice best shows how the objects in the first box would appear if they were fitted together?

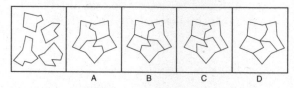

15. In the following diagram, which figure best shows how the objects in the first box would touch if points A and B were connected?

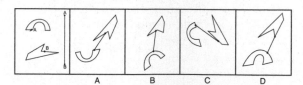

16. Which answer choice best shows how the objects in the first box would appear if they were fitted together?

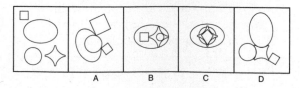

17. In the following diagram, which figure best shows how the objects in the first box would touch if points A and B were connected?

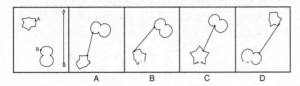

18. Which answer choice best shows how the objects in the first box would appear if they were fitted together?

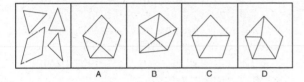

19. In the following diagram, which figure best shows how the objects in the first box would touch if points A and B were connected?

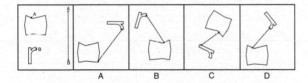

20. Which answer choice best shows how the objects in the first box would appear if they were fitted together?

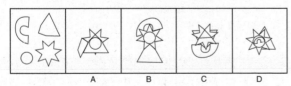

Answers and Explanations

1. **B.** One of the pieces in answer A is mirrored. Two of the shapes in answer C have been changed from the sample. In answer D, only one shape has not been changed.

2. **C.** The shapes in answer A are elongated. Some of the shapes in answer B have been altered. Answer D is completely mirrored.

3. **A.** Answer B has the A connection on the wrong part of the *F*. Both connection points are in the wrong places in answers C and D.

4. **D.** The several shapes in answers A and B don't match the sample. Answer C has mirrored shapes.

5. **B.** Answers A and C have the A connection in the wrong place on the diamond shape. Answer D has the B connection in the wrong place.

6. **C.** In answer A, one of the pie pieces is now a larger triangle. The large piece with the curved angle tip in answer B has one side that is not curved anymore. Answer D doesn't have the two pie pieces.

7. **D.** The angle at which the line connects to the A point on the *k* in answer A doesn't match the diagram. The point on the four-sided figure in answer B is on the corner instead of toward the middle, and the connection point on the *k* in answer C doesn't match the sample.

8. **A.** The pieces in answer B are mirrored. Some of the shapes in answers C and D don't match the sample.

9. **C.** The shapes in answers A and B are different from those in the sample. Answer D has only three shapes, whereas the sample has four.

10. **C.** The *J* in answer A is mirrored. The connection point on the *J* in answer B is in the wrong place, while the connection point on the star in answer D is in the wrong place.

11. **A.** The connection points on the four-sided figure in answers B and C don't match the sample. In answer D, the connection on the four-sided figure is in the right place, but the angle it connects from is wrong.

12. **A.** Some of the shapes in answers B and C are different from those in the sample. Answer D has only three shapes, whereas the sample has four.

13. **A.** The connection points on the rounded figures in answer B and C are in the wrong places. The connection point on the *H* in answer D is also in the wrong place.

14. **B.** Answer A is completely mirrored. The angles in the shapes in answers C and D don't match the sample.

15. **A.** The connection points on the rainbow shape in answers B and D don't match the sample. The connection point on the angled figure in answer C doesn't match the sample.

16. **D.** The star shape in answer A is now a square. The circle in answer B is much smaller than in the sample. The small square in answer C has been turned into a diamond.

17. **B.** The A connections in answers A and D are off. The eight-sided figure in answer C has been replaced with a star.

18. **D.** The overall shape of answer A is right, but the pieces that make it up are off. Answer B has an extra piece. Answer C has only three pieces, whereas the sample has four.

19. **D.** The connection point on the four-sided figure in answer A doesn't match the sample. The four-sided figure in answers B and D has been mirrored.

20. **B.** There is no rainbow shape in answer A, and there is now a four-sided shape in its place. The circle in answer C has been replaced with a triangle. In answer D, the size of the rainbow shape has been reduced.

PART

5

After-Action Review: Practice Tests

Now that you've learned everything you've ever wanted to know about vocabulary, reading, reasoning, math, science, and visual intelligence—and much, much more—it's time to prep for the real thing.

This part offers you three complete practice ASVAB tests, along with an additional AFQT practice test to help you test your knowledge, speed, and accuracy. Attempting practice questions under the same conditions as the real ASVAB is a crucial part of preparing for the exam. Trial and error, plus answers and detailed explanations for every question, can be even more of an effective learning tool than straight studying.

Practice Test 1

General Science

Time: 11 Minutes

Questions: 25

Directions: This section tests your general knowledge in the area of science. Carefully read each question and choose the best answer.

1. If a car is traveling at "constant velocity," what is the car doing?

    (A) maintaining constant speed with no change in direction
    (B) maintaining constant speed on a circular track
    (C) maintaining constant direction at varying speeds
    (D) driving too fast on a circular track

2. Which planet is farthest from the sun?

    (A) Mercury
    (B) Earth
    (C) Neptune
    (D) Uranus

3. Which of the following are the three states of matter?

    (A) liter, milliliter, gram
    (B) proton, electron, neutron
    (C) solid, liquid, gas
    (D) hydrogen, oxygen, carbon

4. Rock that is heated melts to become

    (A) oxide.

    (B) carbonate.

    (C) magma.

    (D) granite.

5. The majority of elements on the periodic table are

    (A) metals.

    (B) nonmetals.

    (C) metalloids.

    (D) alkali metals.

6. The process that allows the skin to grow back after you get a cut is called

    (A) homeostasis.

    (B) mitosis.

    (C) stem cell reproduction.

    (D) collagen.

7. Human DNA has how many chromosomes?

    (A) 23

    (B) 36

    (C) 46

    (D) 43

8. The hardest material on Earth is

    (A) topaz.

    (B) quartz.

    (C) diamond.

    (D) calcite.

9. The system that regulates growth, hormones, and metabolism is the

    (A) musculoskeletal system.

    (B) nervous system.

    (C) digestive system.

    (D) endocrine system.

10. The moon shines because

    (A) it reflects the light of the sun.

    (B) it is a giant ball of fire.

    (C) there is no gravity on the moon.

    (D) it is reflecting the light of the Earth.

11. A substance made up of one type of atom is called a(n)

    (A) nucleus.

    (B) microscopic.

    (C) compound.

    (D) element.

12. Olfaction refers to the sense of

    (A) sight.

    (B) smell.

    (C) hearing.

    (D) touch.

13. The mineral needed to make bone is

    (A) calcium.

    (B) iron.

    (C) iodide.

    (D) fluoride.

14. Which of the following words does NOT describe a form of water condensation near the surface of the Earth?

    (A) dew

    (B) frost

    (C) fog

    (D) rain

15. Dense connective tissue, usually found in joints is

    (A) cartilage.

    (B) muscle.

    (C) tendon.

    (D) ligament.

16. Most metal in the Earth's crust is

    (A) aluminum.
    (B) oxygen.
    (C) iron.
    (D) calcium.

17. The most extensive part of digestion occurs in the

    (A) stomach.
    (B) small intestine.
    (C) large intestine.
    (D) pancreas.

18. Clouds that are low, appear uniformly gray, and often cover the whole sky are called

    (A) stratus.
    (B) cirrus.
    (C) cumulus.
    (D) cirrocumulus.

19. Mass is measured in

    (A) newtons.
    (B) centigrade.
    (C) Celsius.
    (D) kilograms.

20. Eukaryota is

    (A) a kingdom.
    (B) a phylum.
    (C) an order.
    (D) a domain.

21. Unreactive gases on the periodic table of elements, called *noble gases*, tend to do which of the following?

    (A) react mostly with transition metals
    (B) combine with most other gases
    (C) not react to other elements
    (D) explode

22. A key source of energy for the human body is

    (A) insulin.
    (B) enzymes.
    (C) carbohydrates.
    (D) cholesterol.

23. When rock weathers, it breaks down and produces

    (A) sediment.
    (B) glaciers.
    (C) coral reefs.
    (D) fossils.

24. How long does it take the Earth to orbit the sun?

    (A) 1 day
    (B) 365 days
    (C) 7 days
    (D) 88 days

25. What type of storm causes clouds to become electrically charged?

    (A) tornadoes
    (B) thunderstorms
    (C) tsunamis
    (D) snowstorms

Arithmetic Reasoning

Time: 36 Minutes

Questions: 30

Directions: This section tests your ability to reason through mathematical problems using basic arithmetic. Carefully read each question and choose the answer choice that best answers the question.

1. A real estate agent completes the sale of a $2.2 million home. She will get a 6% commission. Of that amount, she has to give 40% to the firm she works for. About how much money will she actually take home from the sale?

   (A) $50,000
   (B) $80,000
   (C) $95,000
   (D) $135,000

2. On Election Day, 5,500 people voted for two candidates. If Candidate A received 3,080 votes, by what percentage did Candidate B lose the election?

   (A) 7%
   (B) 10%
   (C) 12%
   (D) 44%

3. 5!

   (A) 55
   (B) 100
   (C) 120
   (D) 123

4. The senior center has 145 members. If 29 are men and the rest are women, what is the ratio of men to women?

   (A) $\frac{2}{5}$
   (B) $\frac{5}{10}$
   (C) $\frac{5}{8}$
   (D) $\frac{1}{4}$

5. If you travel from point A at 60 miles per hour to point B 120 miles away, how long will you be on the road?

   (A) 1.5 hours
   (B) 2 hours
   (C) 2.25 hours
   (D) 3 hours

6. If you make a 15% down payment on a $23,462 car, how much money do you have left to pay?

   (A) $19,942.70
   (B) $22,733.21
   (C) $43,000.00
   (D) $86,000.00

7. Kelly purchased a book for $3.45 at an online store. She did not have to pay tax, but she did have to pay $7.32 in shipping charges. How much was her total purchase cost?

   (A) $9.22
   (B) $10.47
   (C) $10.77
   (D) $11.82

8. Farmer Joe harvested enough hay over the last four years to make 22, 30, 35, and 32 bales of hay, respectively. If Joe sold each bale for $25, what's the average amount of money he took in over the last four years?

   (A) $650.22
   (B) $743.75
   (C) $1,572.64
   (D) $2,975.75

9. If the value of a bond increases by $0.25 per week, how much will a $25 bond be worth after seven years?

   (A) $13
   (B) $43
   (C) $91
   (D) $116

10. $\sqrt{81} =$

   (A) 9
   (B) 10
   (C) 11
   (D) 12

11. You have to buy pencils, markers, erasers, and paper to get ready for the upcoming school year. The local stationery store sells packages of pencils for $1.25, markers for $1.75, erasers for 50¢, and paper for $2.50. If you buy one package of each for each of your three children, how much will all your school supplies cost?

   (A) $17
   (B) $18
   (C) $19
   (D) $20

12. When school lets out for the summer, 75% of the students in Miss George's class said they would start camp within the week. The rest were going on vacation. If Miss George had 28 students in her class, what is the ratio of students who were going to camp versus those going on vacation?

   (A) 1:3
   (B) 3:1
   (C) 4:5
   (D) 5:4

13. Your test scores are 89, 63, 75, 80, 85, and 92. What is your average test grade?

   (A) 68.9
   (B) 73.7
   (C) 78.2
   (D) 80.6

14. A class of 126 students fills out surveys about their future plans. Every student responds: 36 women and 90 men. If $\frac{3}{4}$ of the women and $\frac{5}{6}$ of the male respondents said they were going to college, about how many total students said they are pursuing other options?

    (A) 15
    (B) 22
    (C) 24
    (D) 102

15. A cookie jar has four chocolate chip cookies, two oatmeal cookies, five sugar cookies, and three gingerbread cookies. If you close your eyes and pick a cookie at random, what are the chances that you'll take out any other cookie besides oatmeal?

    (A) 6/7
    (B) 2/14
    (C) 1/7
    (D) 5/14

16. Sabrina is three years older than Draydon, who is $\frac{1}{3}$ Scott's age. If Scott just turned 18, how old is Sabrina?

    (A) 7
    (B) 8
    (C) 9
    (D) 10

17. Addie is planning a road trip to Las Vegas. If she lives 426 miles away, about how fast would she have to drive if she wanted to make it there in six hours?

    (A) 70 mph
    (B) 71 mph
    (C) 75 mph
    (D) 80 mph

18. If your boss gives you $67 from a sale that you rang up as $342.50, what percentage of commission did you get?

    (A) 19.6
    (B) 20.9
    (C) 22.8
    (D) 25.4

19. You want to tile your kitchen floor, which is 6.5 ft by 12.5 ft. How many whole 2 × 2—ft tiles will you need to buy to cover the entire floor?

    (A) 18
    (B) 19
    (C) 20
    (D) 21

20. What is three-fifths of 185?

    (A) 101
    (B) 105
    (C) 111
    (D) 220

21. The widget factory can make 45 widgets in two hours. If it ran six hours a day, how many widgets could it make in half of a seven-day week?

   (A) 427.5
   (B) 472.5
   (C) 574.2
   (D) 752.4

22. If a car costs $3,985, how much money would you owe if you made a down payment of $\frac{2}{3}$ the price?
   (A) $1,328.33
   (B) $1,458.60
   (C) $1,574.80
   (D) $1,628.90

23. It takes Jim 45 minutes to walk 2.5 miles. If he has to meet Casey at a park seven miles away at 12:30 P.M., what time would he have to start walking to make it there on time?

   (A) 10:14 p.m.
   (B) 10:14 a.m.
   (C) 10:24 p.m.
   (D) 10:24 a.m.

24. You make 30 bracelets and bring them to school. One-third of the class wants one bracelet each. If you have 24 bracelets left at the end of the day, how many students did you give bracelets to?

   (A) 3
   (B) 6
   (C) 9
   (D) 12

25. Say you need to earn an extra $3,689 this year to afford a cruise to Aruba this summer. You get a part-time job that pays $8.49 per hour. How many hours will you have to work to earn enough money to pay for the trip?

   (A) 226.89
   (B) 368.20
   (C) 434.51
   (D) 552.28

26. If you draw a chalk circle on your driveway with a diameter of 22 feet, what is its radius?

   (A) 11 feet
   (B) 22 feet
   (C) 44 feet
   (D) 66 feet

27. A bag holds four red beads, three blue beads, and eight black beads. If you reach into the bag, what is the probability you will draw a blue bead?

   (A) $\frac{1}{5}$

   (B) $\frac{3}{16}$

   (C) $\frac{4}{15}$

   (D) $\frac{8}{15}$

28. If 17 of the 132 English faculty on a community college campus has a doctorate degree, about what percentage of the total faculty does NOT?

   (A) 24%
   (B) 56%
   (C) 82%
   (D) 87%

29. Your favorite band is playing at the stadium near your house. When you call to get tickets, you find out that only 38% of the seats have been sold. If the stadium has 1,500 seats, how many are still available?

    (A) 390
    (B) 570
    (C) 930
    (D) 1,280

30. Nora plays racquetball twice a week with Jan and three times a week with Blaine. If she has to pay $3.75 for each player, including herself, how much money does she spend on racquetball games per week?

    (A) $7.50
    (B) $11.25
    (C) $18.75
    (D) $37.50

Word Knowledge

Time: 11 Minutes

Questions: 35

Directions: This section tests your knowledge of and ability to use vocabulary. Read each question and choose the answer choice that most nearly means the same as the underlined word.

1. The police needed <u>concrete</u> evidence that showed the woman committed the crime before they could make an arrest.

    (A) inconsistent
    (B) tangible
    (C) merited
    (D) difficult

2. <u>Expectant</u> most nearly means

    (A) anticipant.
    (B) incorrect.
    (C) beloved.
    (D) normal.

3. Her <u>inventive</u> ideas were what won the team high marks for creativity in the competition.

    (A) frigid
    (B) optimal
    (C) clever
    (D) dispassionate

4. <u>Opulent</u> most nearly means

    (A) simple.
    (B) advanced.
    (C) meager.
    (D) luxuriant.

5. <u>Omnipotent</u> most nearly means

    (A) encompassing.
    (B) supreme.
    (C) panoramic.
    (D) interesting.

6. <u>Germane</u> most nearly means

    (A) suited.
    (B) foreign.
    (C) harsh.
    (D) benign.

7. <u>Meander</u> most nearly means

    (A) navigate.
    (B) attack.
    (C) zigzag.
    (D) forgive.

8. <u>Atrocious</u> most nearly means

    (A) horrible.
    (B) unmoving.
    (C) excited.
    (D) lonely.

9. The intrepid warrior stood vigil over the sleeping campers throughout the night, never taking his eyes away from the path where enemies could approach.

   (A) outgoing
   (B) meek
   (C) gutsy
   (D) arrogant

10. Succinct most nearly means

    (A) amuse.
    (B) match.
    (C) heavy.
    (D) blunt.

11. Vociferous most nearly means

    (A) loud.
    (B) singular.
    (C) decision.
    (D) selective.

12. Frugal most nearly means

    (A) open.
    (B) cheap.
    (C) fortunate.
    (D) easy.

13. Judicious most nearly means

    (A) intuitive.
    (B) instructive.
    (C) judgmental.
    (D) prudent.

14. Even though Mary said she was happy, her mother's astute senses alerted her that there was something her daughter was worried about.

    (A) dull
    (B) buried
    (C) sharp
    (D) clouded

15. Her tendency to say what she thought whenever she liked made most people view her as abrasive.

    (A) incredulous
    (B) tactless
    (C) available
    (D) instinctive

16. Incorrigible most nearly means

    (A) calm.
    (B) sincere.
    (C) respectful.
    (D) unruly.

17. Stringent most nearly means

    (A) mainstream.
    (B) severe.
    (C) offensive.
    (D) wicked.

18. After an immense search effort that encompassed hundreds of miles, the man was not able to locate a source of water for the village.

    (A) heroic
    (B) fortuitous
    (C) intimate
    (D) tremendous

19. Potent most nearly means

    (A) eligible.
    (B) strong.
    (C) makeshift.
    (D) irritating.

20. Bigotry most nearly means

    (A) antagonism.
    (B) admiration.
    (C) chauvinism.
    (D) transcendence.

21. I didn't mean to belittle the club's generous financial contribution to the charity by suggesting we aim for a higher goal next year.

    (A) demean
    (B) praise
    (C) insist
    (D) exclaim

22. Opponent most nearly means

    (A) acquaintance.
    (B) friend.
    (C) catalyst.
    (D) antagonist.

23. Eloquent most nearly means

    (A) elegant.
    (B) articulate.
    (C) mumbled.
    (D) relatable.

24. Florid most nearly means

    (A) short.
    (B) ornate.
    (C) simple.
    (D) exponential.

25. Dialogue most nearly means

    (A) insist.
    (B) argue.
    (C) chat.
    (D) accuse.

26. One of Anne's favorite weekend activities was going to the bookstore to peruse the new titles released that week.

    (A) examine
    (B) interact
    (C) eliminate
    (D) sanctify

27. The car that tapped my rear bumper caused only superficial damage.

    (A) significant
    (B) internal
    (C) external
    (D) permanent

28. Mischievous most nearly means

    (A) playful.
    (B) obedient.
    (C) forgiven.
    (D) uninitiated.

29. It took nearly two years of physical therapy, but Liam was able to recuperate from having both legs broken in a car accident.

    (A) respond
    (B) reconstitute
    (C) relive
    (D) recover

30. <u>Reticence</u> most nearly means

    (A) openness.

    (B) intelligence.

    (C) historic.

    (D) reserve.

31. Having already been through a bad divorce, Ted was <u>averse</u> to the idea of getting married again.

    (A) affectionate

    (B) resistant

    (C) perplexed

    (D) efficient

32. <u>Predecessor</u> most nearly means

    (A) instigator.

    (B) infiltrator.

    (C) ancestor.

    (D) substitute.

33. <u>Procrastinate</u> most nearly means

    (A) delay.

    (B) force.

    (C) retaliate.

    (D) pursue.

34. Mary chose a fast-paced, inspiring story to <u>uplift</u> the mood of her early morning class.

    (A) moisten

    (B) entrance

    (C) forego

    (D) elevate

35. <u>Militant</u> most nearly means

    (A) instinctive.

    (B) revolutionary.

    (C) proper.

    (D) reserved.

Paragraph Comprehension

Time: 13 Minutes

Questions: 15

Directions: This section tests your ability to read and understand written information, as well as come to logical conclusions based on a text. Read each passage and answer the questions that follow. Choose the answer choice that best answers the question.

(1) Organic foods and other natural products should be more accessible to the general consumer. (2) Too often they are only found online, which requires shipping, or in specialty shops in remote areas. (3) Being able to purchase a variety of organic foods at your local grocery store would make it easier for consumers to live healthy lifestyles. (4) It would also stimulate sales for this growing industry.

1. The main idea of this passage is stated in which sentence?

(A) 1
(B) 2
(C) 3
(D) 4

Use the following passage to answer questions 2–3:

The Louisiana Purchase was a strategic political move for President Thomas Jefferson. Since 1762, this 828,800-square-mile expanse of land between the East and West Coasts had been controlled by the Spanish and French. By purchasing the Louisiana Territory from Napoleon in 1803, Jefferson was able to secure trade access to the port of New Orleans and greatly increase the United States' standing as a formidable country.

2. The Louisiana Purchase was

(A) a significant part of American history.
(B) a strategic move for Spain.
(C) a way to antagonize Canada.
(D) insignificant in comparison to the wars going on in Europe at the time.

3. The main idea of the passage is that

(A) no forethought went into the consequences of the Louisiana Purchase.
(B) without the Louisiana Purchase, Jefferson would not have been reelected.
(C) the Louisiana Purchase was not supported by American allies.
(D) the Louisiana Purchase was a strategic move to improve America's economic and political standing in the world.

Use the following passage to answer questions 4–6:

Deforestation is a serious issue that more people should take an active part in preventing. Not only does the decline of vegetation and trees in certain sections of Earth contribute to global warming, but habitats for myriad species are also being destroyed. As a result, these species are facing certain extinction.

If too many types of plants and animals no longer exist on Earth, serious ecological consequences may occur. These include increased populations of insects and pests, interruptions in the food chain that can lead to famine and pestilence worldwide, the breakdown of entire ecosystems, and an increase in the speed of global warming. It is every citizen's responsibility to educate themselves about the dangers of deforestation and how they can do their part in slowing down its progress.

4. The author would most likely support

   (A) legislation approving the building of housing developments on nature preserves.
   (B) a community education program that teaches people how they can contribute to reforestation efforts.
   (C) increased imports from South American farms that have recently expanded into the rainforest.
   (D) efforts to support a boost in the timber industry.

5. In the passage, <u>myriad</u> most nearly means

   (A) a finite amount.
   (B) a disproportionate amount.
   (C) many types of.
   (D) interesting.

6. The tone of this passage can best be described as

   (A) contemplative.
   (B) persuasive.
   (C) dispassionate.
   (D) lazy.

Use the following passage to answer questions 7–8:

Coffee beans are not actually beans but rather roasted seeds of coffee berries. After the seeds are separated from the berries, they're fermented, cleaned, and air-dried. Now called *green coffee beans*, they must be roasted before they are consumed. The internal temperature must be raised to at least 205° Celsius to produce caffeol oil, which produces the flavor commonly associated with coffee.

7. What is produced when the internal temperature of a coffee bean reaches at least 205° Celsius?

   (A) caffeine
   (B) caffeol oil
   (C) dark coloring
   (D) extra flavor

8. According to the paragraph,

   (A) coffee beans can be eaten directly from the plant.
   (B) coffee beans taste like berries.
   (C) coffee beans must be cleaned before they are fermented.
   (D) coffee beans are seeds.

Use the following passage to answer questions 9–10:

The U.S. Constitution mandates that the federal government take a national census every 10 years. The data is used to calculate how many congressional seats are appointed per state, to determine the number of electoral votes each state gets, and to set state and municipal funding. Census data also gives comprehensive demographic information about the population.

9. In this paragraph, the word <u>mandates</u> most nearly means

   (A) enlists.
   (B) believes.
   (C) requires.
   (D) restricts.

10. The purpose of this passage is to

   (A) inform.
   (B) persuade.
   (C) incite.
   (D) evaluate.

Use the following passage to answer questions 11–12:

Vitamin C is an essential nutrient for maintaining good health. It helps boost the immune system, acts as a natural antihistamine, and can help wounds heal faster. While citrus fruits, such as oranges and lemons, are the foods most often associated with vitamin C, many other fruits and vegetables are rich in this nutrient. Red peppers, cantaloupe, strawberries, kiwi, and mangoes are all good choices for someone looking to increase the amount of vitamin C in their diet.

11. According to the passage, vitamin C would be something a person should add to their diet if they

   (A) were preparing for a test.
   (B) were looking to run faster.
   (C) had a paper cut.
   (D) needed to sleep better.

12. A good title for this passage would be

   (A) How to Live a Healthy Life
   (B) Simple Homeopathic Remedies
   (C) Nutrients and Your Health
   (D) The Health Benefits of Vitamin C

Use the following passage to answer questions 13–15:

Everyone should take an interest in their local government. Not enough people attend their local town council meetings and are not informed about the decisions their leaders are making about laws that can affect their lives. It's our responsibility as American citizens to monitor the actions of our elected officials and hold them accountable. If we don't, then who will?

13. According to the passage, the average citizen

    (A) is not informed about the actions of their local government.
    (B) attends town council meetings regularly.
    (C) has a good understanding of how local government works.
    (D) pays attention to their surroundings.

14. In the passage, <u>accountable</u> most nearly means

    (A) is interested in an outcome.
    (B) has assets at stake.
    (C) is responsible for one's actions.
    (D) is informed about circumstances.

15. The author of this passage would most likely agree with which of the following statements?

    (A) Too many people come to council meetings.
    (B) Elected officials must answer to the public.
    (C) Council meetings are the best place to air a grievance about the community.
    (D) Town councils should recognize citizens more often.

Mathematics Knowledge

Time: 24 Minutes

Questions: 25

Directions: This section tests your knowledge of basic mathematics, algebra, and geometry. Carefully read each question and choose the answer choice that reflects the best answer.

1. $(a + 5)(a + 8)$

    (A) a2 + 3a + 40

    (B) a2 + 13a + 40

    (C) a3 + 3a + 40

    (D) a3 + 13a + 40

2. If $b = 4$, then $5 \times b^3 + \frac{3b}{2} =$

    (A) 326

    (B) 345

    (C) 425

    (D) 623

3. $y^2 \times y^3 \times y^4 \times y^5 =$

    (A) y1

    (B) y–10

    (C) y14

    (D) y120

4. A *vertex* is

    (A) the space an object occupies.

    (B) a single number or variable, or combinations of them.

    (C) an action you need to take with a value.

    (D) the point where the two lines that make up an angle intersect.

5. Solve for x: $4x - 3 < 5 + 2y$

    (A) x < 2 + 2y

    (B) x < $\frac{8+2y}{4}$

    (C) x > 2 – 2y

    (D) x > $\frac{8-2y}{4}$

6. $32.6\overline{)4} =$

    (A) .122

    (B) .123

    (C) .124

    (D) .125

7. Solve for y: $x + 2y - 4x + 6 = 2$

    (A) $y = -2 + \frac{3x}{2}$

    (B) $y = -2 + 3x$

    (C) $y = 4 - \frac{3x}{2}$

    (D) $y = 2 + \frac{3x}{2}$

8. If a rectangular solid has a length of 3 meters, a height of 5 meters, and a width of 10 meters, what is its total surface area?

    (A) 30 m2

    (B) 60 m2

    (C) 150 m2

    (D) 190 m2

9. $12.475 \times 20.2 =$

    (A) 25.19950

    (B) 251.9950

    (C) 2519.950

    (D) 25199.50

10. $6\frac{1}{4} \div \frac{5}{8} =$

    (A) $5\frac{5}{24}$

    (B) 8

    (C) 10

    (D) $5\frac{6}{24}$

11. Solve for x: $3x + 5^2 \neq 7 - 12$

    (A) 7

    (B) -10

    (C) 11

    (D) -16

12. Factor: $b^2 - 14b + 24$

    (A) $(b + 2)(b + 12)$

    (B) $(b - 2)(b + 12)$

    (C) $(b + 2)(b - 12)$

    (D) $(b - 2)(b - 12)$

13. A quadrilateral with two sets of parallel sides is called a

    (A) parallelogram.

    (B) polygon.

    (C) trapezoid.

    (D) rhombus.

14. If side a in a right triangle equals 6 and the hypotenuse equals 7.8, the value of side b equals

    (A) 24.84

    (B) 60.84

    (C) $\sqrt{24.84}$

    (D) $\sqrt{60.84}$

15. $[(6 + 4)^2 + (14 - 8)] - \frac{2}{3} \times \frac{9}{2} =$

    (A) 52

    (B) 54

    (C) 103

    (D) 106

16. Solve for a: $\frac{3}{6} = \frac{a}{12}$

    (A) 6

    (B) 8

    (C) 12

    (D) 15

17. In the following diagram, the value of side b is proportional to the value of side

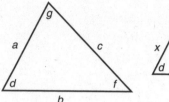

    (A) x.

    (B) y.

    (C) z.

    (D) d.

18. What is 16,597,000,000 equal to in scientific notation?

    (A) 1.6597×109

    (B) 1.6597×1010

    (C) 1.6597×1011

    (D) 1.6597×1012

19. $2\frac{4}{5} - \frac{7}{8} =$

    (A) $\frac{40}{37}$

    (B) $\frac{37}{40}$

    (C) $1\frac{23}{40}$

    (D) $1\frac{37}{40}$

20. In an isosceles right triangle, two sides are

    (A) divisible.
    (B) equal.
    (C) unequal.
    (D) complimentary.

21. The following shape is a

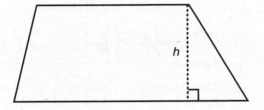

    (A) rhombus.
    (B) hexagon.
    (C) trapezoid.
    (D) chord.

22. 8! =

    (A) −20
    (B) 36
    (C) 22,961
    (D) 40,320

23. Factor: $c^2 - 121$

    (A) (c + 11) (c − 11)
    (B) (c − 11) (c + 11)
    (C) (c + 11) (c + 12)
    (D) (c + 11) (c − 12)

24. Two angles that share a common side are

    (A) adjacent.
    (B) congruent.
    (C) similar.
    (D) straight.

25. One side of a square is 15.2 ft. What is the area of the square?

    (A) 30.4 ft^2
    (B) 60.8 ft^2
    (C) 121.6 ft^2
    (D) 231.04 ft^2

Electronics Information

Time: 9 Minutes

Questions: 20

Directions: This section tests your knowledge of basic electronics principles and applications. Carefully read each question and choose the answer choice that reflects the best answer.

1. In what direction does current flow on a circuit diagram?

   (A) positive to negative
   (B) positive to neutral
   (C) negative to positive
   (D) negative to neutral

2. Insulators are often made from

   (A) copper.
   (B) plastic.
   (C) rubber.
   (D) iron.

3. The following is the symbol for a

   (A) fuse.
   (B) wire.
   (C) capacitor.
   (D) diode.

4. If you have 15 volts and 180 watts of power, how many amps do you have?

   (A) 10
   (B) 12
   (C) 270
   (D) 280

5. What type of power source is represented in the following diagram?

   (A) gas-powered generator
   (B) circuit
   (C) diode
   (D) battery

6. What pushes electrons along their path in a circuit?

   (A) protons
   (B) electricity
   (C) ohms
   (D) amps

7. Heating elements, lightbulbs, and motors are all examples of

   (A) conductors.
   (B) switches.
   (C) loads.
   (D) circuits.

8. If you have a wave whose speed is 20m/s and length is 2 meters, its frequency is

   (A) 40Hz.
   (B) 22Hz.
   (C) 18Hz.
   (D) 10Hz.

9. The following is the symbol for a(n)

(A) transformer.
(B) resistor.
(C) battery.
(D) aerial.

10. If you have 50 volts and 10 ohms, how many amps do you have?

(A) 5
(B) 500
(C) .20
(D) 25

11. Resistance causes

(A) friction.
(B) power surges.
(C) circuit malfunction.
(D) electric shock.

12. The type of frequency easiest to hear is

(A) low.
(B) high.
(C) midrange.
(D) none of the above—they are all equal.

13. If you have 15 volts and 5 amps, how many ohms do you have?

(A) 75
(B) 10
(C) 20
(D) 3

14. This device is used to measure power:

(A) ohmmeter.
(B) voltmeter.
(C) wattmeter.
(D) ammeter.

15. What is used to measure alternating current?

(A) frequency
(B) direct current
(C) electromagnetic
(D) amplitude modulated

16. What is the purpose of the following diagram?

(A) to convert AC to DC power
(B) to smooth and increase DC voltage
(C) to supply AC power to electronic circuits
(D) to convert main AC supply to low-voltage AC

17. When two things have the same frequency, the result is

(A) scattered wavelengths.
(B) interference.
(C) rectilinear propagation.
(D) waves bending.

18. If you have 15 volts and 1 ohm of resistance, how many amps do you have?

(A) 16
(B) 14
(C) 15
(D) 1

19. If you have a wave whose wavelength
    is 4 meters and a frequency of 3Hz,
    what is the wave speed?

    (A) 7 meters per second

    (B) .75 meters per second

    (C) 12 meters per second

    (D) 1 meter per second

20. Good conductors of electricity offer
    _____ resistance:

    (A) high

    (B) 5 ohms of

    (C) 10-gauge

    (D) low

Automotive and Shop Information

Time: 11 Minutes

Questions: 25

Directions: This section tests your knowledge of automotive components and principles, as well as general shop tools and applications. Carefully read each question and choose the answer choice that reflects the best answer.

Refer to the following diagram to answer questions 1–3:

Ignition System

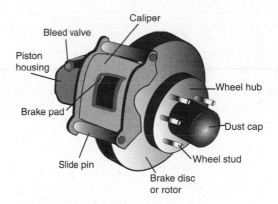

1. The battery transfers power through the _____ to the _____ after you turn the key.

   (A) ignition switch, ignition coil
   (B) capacitor, relay
   (C) condenser, ignition coil
   (D) relay, power source

2. The *solenoid* is another word for which part pictured in the diagram?

   (A) capacitor
   (B) relay
   (C) condenser
   (D) ignition coil

3. In what position is the ignition switch as illustrated in the diagram? Is power being passed through the circuit?

   (A) open; yes, power is being passed through the circuit
   (B) closed; yes, power is being passed through the circuit
   (C) open; no, power is not being passed through the circuit
   (D) closed; no, power is not being passed through the circuit

Use the previous diagram to answer questions 4–6.

4. Which type of brake is pictured?

   (A) drum brake
   (B) disc brake
   (C) emergency brake
   (D) secondary brake

5. Which of the parts pictured in the diagram houses the brake pads?

   (A) slide pin
   (B) wheel hub
   (C) rotor
   (D) caliper

6. After pressing on the brake pedal, hydraulic pressure is exerted on what?

   (A) bleed valve
   (B) brake pad
   (C) piston
   (D) dust cap

7. What function does a differential perform?

   (A) It enables the wheels to turn on the axels.
   (B) It reduces the noise of the engine.
   (C) It allows wheels to rotate at different speeds.
   (D) It houses the brake lines.

8. Which part is used to control the emissions of the car?

   (A) tailpipe
   (B) catalytic converter
   (C) exhaust pipe
   (D) muffler

9. Which part of the exhaust system is the last to guide gases out and away from the vehicle?

   (A) exhaust pipe
   (B) catalytic converter
   (C) exhaust manifold
   (D) tailpipe

10. What is the second stroke in the four-stroke process?

   (A) power stroke
   (B) intake stroke
   (C) compression stroke
   (D) exhaust stroke

11. A piston is in which position in a cylinder at the beginning of the four-stroke process?

   (A) up
   (B) down
   (C) open
   (D) closed

12. What is the purpose of the ignition system?

   (A) to stop the car
   (B) to provide the initial source of power to the suspension system
   (C) to keep the engine cool
   (D) to create a spark that will ignite the fuel–air mixture in the cylinder of the engine

13. Carburetors have been replaced by what component of the fuel system in modern cars?

    (A) fuel injector

    (B) fuel filter

    (C) fuel pump

    (D) alternator

14. The radiator consists of a network of _____ that cools hot fluid from the engine.

    (A) pumps

    (B) calipers

    (C) pistons

    (D) tubes

15. A brake drum is

    (A) solid.

    (B) hollow.

    (C) full of brake fluid.

    (D) attached to the calipers.

Use the previous diagram to answer questions 16–17.

16. What type of hammer is pictured?

    (A) rubber mallet

    (B) ball-peen

    (C) engineer's hammer

    (D) tinner's hammer

17. What type of work is the hammer NOT suited for?

    (A) metal shaping

    (B) construction projects

    (C) auto repairs

    (D) driving rivets into sheet metal

Use the previous diagram to answer questions 18–19.

18. What type of tool is pictured?

    (A) hand drill

    (B) Allen wrench

    (C) auger bit

    (D) bar clamp

19. Why would a woodworker prefer the pictured tool over its powered counterpart?

    (A) It is easier to use.

    (B) It can bore larger holes.

    (C) It is faster to use.

    (D) It offers total control.

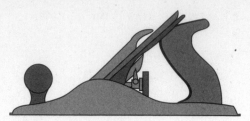

Use the previous diagram to answer questions 20–22.

20. What type of tool is pictured?

    (A) pipe clamp
    (B) hand screw
    (C) jack plane
    (D) block plane

21. What is the purpose of the pictured tool?

    (A) to smooth out wood joints
    (B) to trim wood edges in tight spaces
    (C) to apply inward pressure to an object
    (D) to hold a pipe in place for cutting or threading

22. Which category does the tool pictured fit into?

    (A) cutting tools
    (B) shaping tools
    (C) clamping tools
    (D) power tools

23. Which of the following is NOT a common type of saw?

    (A) hack
    (B) miter
    (C) chisel
    (D) crosscut

24. Which type of power drill is generally bolted to a workbench or the floor?

    (A) pistol grip
    (B) hammer drill
    (C) drill press
    (D) jigsaw drill

25. What type of tool has tiny, ridgelike grooves used to smooth out rough edges of wood, metal, or plastic?

    (A) file
    (B) rasp
    (C) chisel
    (D) crosscut saw

Mechanical Comprehension

Time: 19 Minutes

Questions: 25

Directions: This section tests your knowledge and application of basic mechanical principles. Carefully read each question and choose the answer choice that reflects the best answer.

1. Suppose your son is playing tee ball, and he strikes the ball with the bat. The ball rolls along the ground all the way down the first baseline. Which of the following is NOT an example of work being done in this scenario?

    (A) Your son does work on the bat.

    (B) The bat does work on the ball.

    (C) The ball does work on the bat.

    (D) The ball does work on the ground.

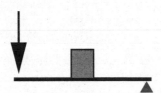

2. Which type of lever is pictured above?

    (A) 1st class

    (B) 2nd class

    (C) 3rd class

    (D) 4th class

3. Suppose you are trying to balance stacks of books on a 1st-class lever. One stack weighs 25 pounds, and the other stack weighs 50 pounds. If the books are placed 15 meters from one another on the lever, how far should each stack be from the fulcrum?

    (A) The 50-pound stack should be 5 meters from the fulcrum, while the 25-pound stack should be 10 meters from the fulcrum.

    (B) The 50-pound stack should be 10 meters from the fulcrum, while the 25-pound stack should be 5 meters from the fulcrum.

    (C) The 50-pound stack should be 15 meters from the fulcrum, while the 25-pound stack should be 15 meters from the fulcrum.

    (D) The 50-pound stack should be 25 meters from the fulcrum, while the 25-pound stack should be 50 meters from the fulcrum.

4. A nutcracker, wheelbarrow, and wrench are all examples of which type of lever?

    (A) 2nd class

    (B) 3rd class

    (C) 1st class

    (D) 4th class

5. Mechanical advantage _____ with each additional pulley.

    (A) decreases

    (B) remains the same

    (C) changes, depending on what size the pulleys are,

    (D) increases

6. What is the formula that is used to demonstrate a balanced load on a 1st-class lever?

    (A) $w_1 \div d_1 = w_2 \times d_2$

    (B) $w_1 \times d_2 = w_2 \div d_2$

    (C) $w_1 \times d_1 = w_1 \div d_2$

    (D) $w_1 \times d_1 = w_2 \times d_2$

7. If you have a 40-pound object that is being lifted 8 meters on a fixed pulley, what is your mechanical advantage?

    (A) 1

    (B) 2

    (C) 3

    (D) 4

8. Suppose you have two gears. For each circle the larger gear makes, the smaller gear makes four circles. What is the gear ratio?

    (A) 1:1

    (B) 4:1

    (C) 1:4

    (D) 4:4

9. Suppose you have two gears. One has 200 teeth, and the other has 40 teeth. What is the gear ratio?

    (A) 1:1

    (B) 200:1

    (C) 5:1

    (D) 40:1

10. Which of the following is NOT a purpose for gears?

    (A) change the speed of a mechanism

    (B) change the weight of an object

    (C) change the motion of a device

    (D) change the direction of machinery

11. When an object falls with only the force of gravity acting on it, we call this

    (A) friction.

    (B) acceleration.

    (C) speed.

    (D) freefalling.

12. If you are traveling at a rate of 60 kilometers per hour and you decrease your speed to 45 kilometers per hour over the course of 5 seconds, what is your negative acceleration?

    (A) 3 kilometers per hour per second

    (B) 15 kilometers per second per second

    (C) 5 seconds per mile per second

    (D) 15 miles per second per mile

13. What does velocity measure?

    (A) the change in speed during a given time

    (B) the speed and direction of an object

    (C) the direction and friction of an object

    (D) the gravitational pull on an object

14. The law of reciprocal action states what?

    (A) For every action, there is an identical reaction.

    (B) For every motion, there is an unequal and similar reaction.

    (C) For every action, there is an equal and opposite reaction.

    (D) For every acceleration, there is an identical velocity.

15. Which type of lever is pictured above?

    (A) 1st class

    (B) 2nd class

    (C) 3rd class

    (D) 4th class

16. Newton's second law states that an object accelerates in the direction of what?

    (A) the net force acting on it

    (B) the electromagnetic pressure around it

    (C) the gravitational pull exerted on it

    (D) none of the above

17. What is the formula for force?

    (A) Force = Mass × Velocity

    (B) Force = Mass × Acceleration

    (C) Force = Acceleration × Velocity

    (D) Force = Acceleration × Density

18. Suppose that you kick a box that weighs 1 pound and then you kick another box that weighs 10 pounds. Assume that you kick both with the same amount of effort. How far will the lightweight box move compared to the heavy one?

    (A) the same distance

    (B) 10 times as far

    (C) one-tenth as far

    (D) twice as far

19. How is weight expressed in the metric system?

    (A) pounds

    (B) kilograms

    (C) joules

    (D) newtons

20. How do you determine the mass of an object?

    (A) Volume × Density

    (B) Weight × Height

    (C) Speed × Velocity

    (D) Width × Acceleration

21. Movement of any kind is called what?

    (A) mass

    (B) speed

    (C) acceleration

    (D) motion

22. Suppose you apply 20 newtons of force against an object for 10 meters. How much work have you done?

    (A) 10 joules

    (B) 20 joules

    (C) 30 joules

    (D) 200 joules

23. Suppose an object with a mass of 50 kilograms travels at a rate of 5 meters per second. What is the object's kinetic energy?

    (A) 55 joules
    (B) 250 joules
    (C) 625 joules
    (D) 1,250 joules

24. Adding additional pulleys to a single-wheel pulley system

    (A) reduces the force needed to move an object.
    (B) increases the distance of rope you have to pull.
    (C) makes the weight you are moving feel lighter.
    (D) all of the above.

25. Suppose you have two balanced objects on a 1st-class lever, but you know the mass of only one of them. Object #1 weighs 18 kilograms. It is clearly heavier than object #2. If you set the objects 30 feet apart on the lever, with object #1 sitting 10 feet from the fulcrum, how heavy is object #2?

    (A) 9 kilograms
    (B) 10 kilograms
    (C) 11 kilograms
    (D) 12 kilograms

Assembling Objects

Time: 15 Minutes

Questions: 25

Directions: This section tests your ability to visualize how objects fit together. Carefully read each question and choose the answer choice that reflects the best answer.

1. In the following diagram, which figure best shows how the objects in the first box would touch if points A and B were connected?

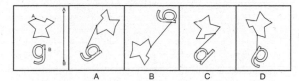

2. Which answer choice best shows how the objects in the first box would appear if they were fitted together?

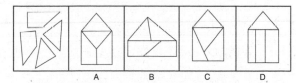

3. In the following diagram, which figure best shows how the objects in the first box would touch if points A and B were connected?

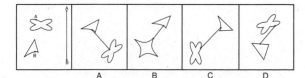

4. Which answer choice best shows how the objects in the first box would appear if they were fitted together?

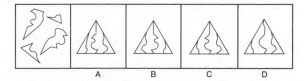

5. In the following diagram, which figure best shows how the objects in the first box would touch if points A and B were connected?

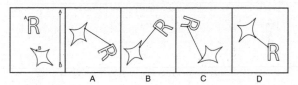

6. Which answer choice best shows how the objects in the first box would appear if they were fitted together?

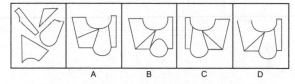

7. In the following diagram, which figure best shows how the objects in the first box would touch if points A and B were connected?

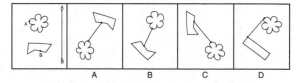

8. Which answer choice best shows how the objects in the first box would appear if they were fitted together?

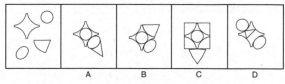

9. Which answer choice best shows how the objects in the first box would appear if they were fitted together?

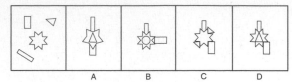

A   B   C   D

14. Which answer choice best shows how the objects in the first box would appear if they were fitted together?

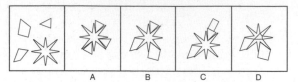

A   B   C   D

10. In the following diagram, which figure best shows how the objects in the first box would touch if points A and B were connected?

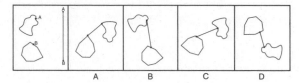

A   B   C   D

15. In the following diagram, which figure best shows how the objects in the first box would touch if points A and B were connected?

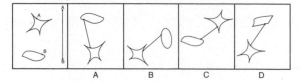

A   B   C   D

11. In the following diagram, which figure best shows how the objects in the first box would touch if points A and B were connected?

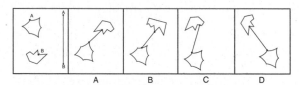

A   B   C   D

16. Which answer choice best shows how the objects in the first box would appear if they were fitted together?

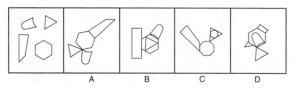

A   B   C   D

12. Which answer choice best shows how the objects in the first box would appear if they were fitted together?

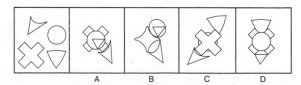

A   B   C   D

17. In the following diagram, which figure best shows how the objects in the first box would touch if points A and B were connected?

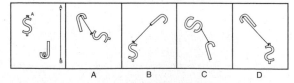

A   B   C   D

13. In the following diagram, which figure best shows how the objects in the first box would touch if points A and B were connected?

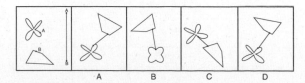

A   B   C   D

18. Which answer choice best shows how the objects in the first box would appear if they were fitted together?

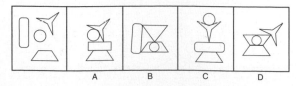

A   B   C   D

19. In the following diagram, which figure best shows how the objects in the first box would touch if points A and B were connected?

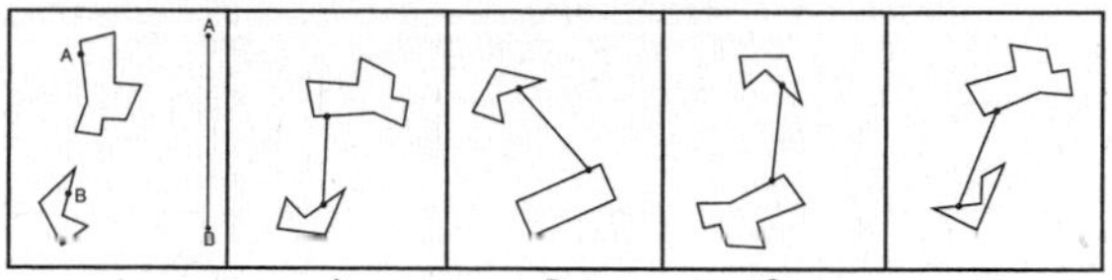

A B C D

20. Which answer choice best shows how the objects in the first box would appear if they were fitted together?

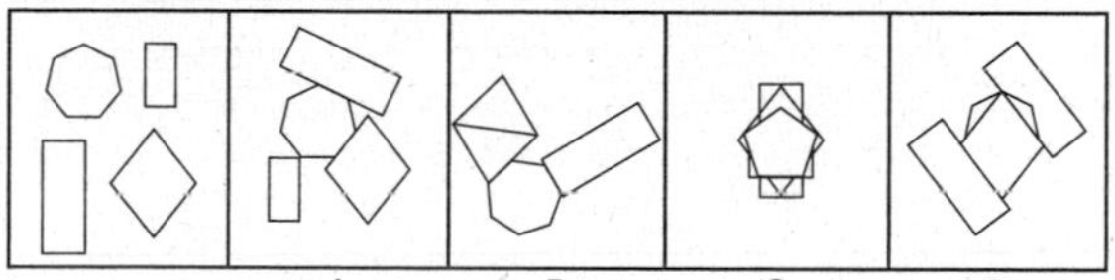

A B C D

21. In the following diagram, which figure best shows how the objects in the first box would touch if points A and B were connected?

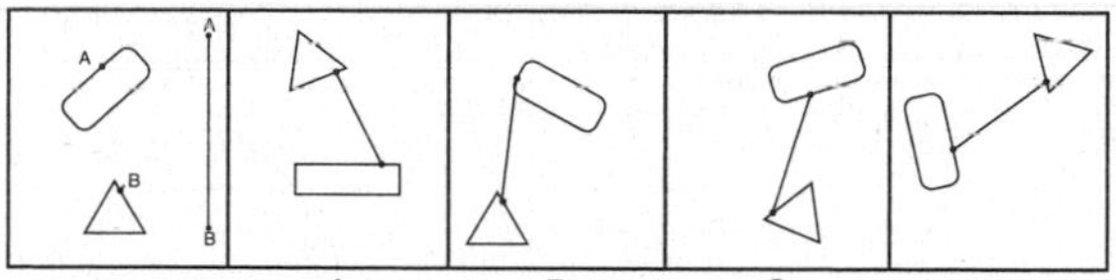

A B C D

22. Which answer choice best shows how the objects in the first box would appear if they were fitted together?

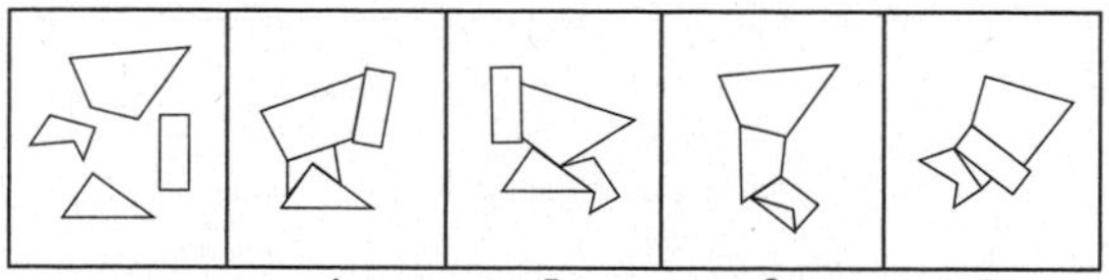

A B C D

23. In the following diagram, which figure best shows how the objects in the first box would touch if points A and B were connected?

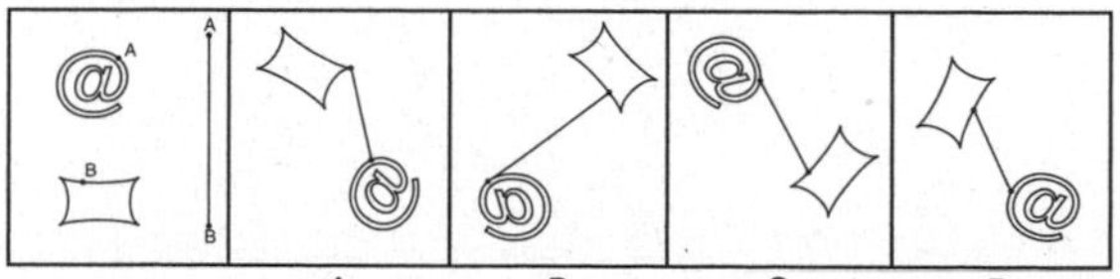

A B C D

24. Which answer choice best shows how the objects in the first box would appear if they were fitted together?

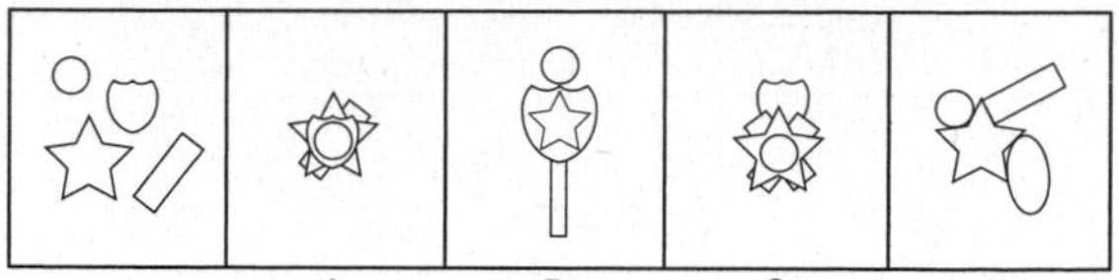

A D C D

25. In the following diagram, which figure best shows how the objects in the first box would touch if points A and B were connected?

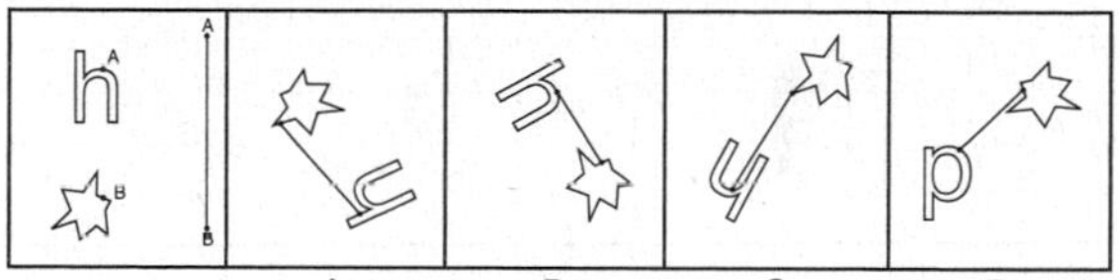

A B C D

Practice Test 1: Answers and Explanations

General Science

1. **A.** Eliminating answer choices here is a good idea. Because we're dealing with *constant* velocity, we can assume that any answer choice that suggests variation is wrong. That gets rid of C. There is no suggestion of circular tracks in the name. You can infer that you're looking for an answer choice that's all about speed and direction remaining the same, or "constant."

2. **C.** The planets in order from the sun are Mercury, Venus, Earth, Mars, Jupiter, Saturn, Uranus, and Neptune.

3. **C.** Hydrogen, oxygen, and carbon are elements. Protons, electrons, and neutrons are parts of an atom. Liter, milliliter, and gram are metric measurements that you have probably seen on soda bottles and other food products.

4. **C.** Magma, by definition, is melted rock. Carbonate and oxide are not types of rock, and granite is a solid rock.

5. **A.** Ninety-two out of 117 elements are metals. There are only 12 nonmetals and 5 metalloids. Alkali metals are not a separate category on the periodic table; they fall under the metals category.

6. **B.** Mitosis is the process of dividing one cell nucleus into two nuclei. Answer A is wrong because homeostasis refers to the body maintaining equilibrium or a stable state internally, despite external conditions. Answer C is wrong because stem cell reproduction uses mitosis to create stem cells, not skin cells. Answer D is wrong because collagen is a protein found in connective tissue.

7. **C.** Human DNA has 23 *pairs* of chromosomes for a total of 46. Each chromosome contains a strand of DNA and many of our genes, which is the basic way we inherit traits from our ancestors.

8. **C.** Diamond rates a 10 on the Mohs, scale of mineral hardness and is considered the hardest substance on Earth. Quartz is 7, topaz is 8, and calcite is only 9. So even if you weren't sure that diamonds were the hardest substance on the planet, it's surely the hardest of your answer choices.

9. **D.** The endocrine system involves all the organs and glands that regulate hormones, which, in turn, affect growth and metabolism. The musculoskeletal system deals with muscles and bones. The nervous system involves nerves and the process of sensing electrical messages throughout the body. The digestive system turns food into energy and takes the nutrients needed to sustain the body.

10. **A.** The moon shines by reflecting sunlight. Like Earth, half of the moon is always lit by the sun's direct rays, and the other half is in shadow.

11. **D.** By definition, an element is a chemical substance made up of a single type of atom. A nucleus is part of an atom. Microscopic refers to the size of something—namely, that it's so small that it can be viewed only with a microscope. A compound is a combination of two or more elements.

12. **B.** Choice A is wrong because the sense of sight is vision. Choice C is wrong because the sense of hearing is audition. Choice D is wrong because the sense of touch is somatic sensation.

13. **A.** Choice B is wrong because iron is needed to make hemoglobin, the protein used to carry oxygen throughout the body. Choice C is wrong because iodide is a component of radioactive waste. Choice D is wrong because fluoride helps prevent tooth decay.

14. **D.** Rain is water condensation that accumulates in clouds. All the other choices refer to different forms of condensation near the ground: dew is liquid, frost is frozen, and fog is vapor.

15. **A.** Even if you didn't know that cartilage acts as a cushion in joints, you could get this right through process of elimination. Choice B is wrong because muscles are tissues that cause motion and are used to move joints. Choice C is wrong because tendons connect muscles to bones. Choice D is wrong because ligaments connect bones to other bones at joints.

16. **A.** You can eliminate answers B and D right away because they are not metals: oxygen is a gas and calcium is a mineral. Aluminum is the most abundant metal in Earth's crust, with iron coming in second.

17. **B.** The stomach helps break down food so that it can be absorbed into the system. The large intestine deals with the waste products of food after all the nutrition is taken out by the small intestine (which is the most complex part of the digestion process). The pancreas produces secretions and hormones to aid in digestion.

18. **A.** Stratus clouds are the ones that look like there's a blanket in the sky. Cirrus clouds are thin and wispy, and found high in the sky. Cumulus clouds look billowy, like cotton balls. Cirrocumulus clouds are high in the sky but are patchy, like a blend the of the thinness of cirrus clouds and the puffiness of cumulus.

19. **D.** Newtons measure force. Both centigrade and Celsius measure temperature. Kilograms measure mass.

20. **D.** Eukaryota is one of three domains: Eukaryota (living things with cells that have a nucleus), Bacteria (single-celled prokaryotes with no nucleus and cell membrane is made of unbranched fatty acid chains) and Archaea (single-cell prokaryote, similar to both eukaryotes and bacteria with different rRNA, cell wall, and membrane chemistry).

21. **C.** As the name suggests, unreactive gases do not react to other elements or nearly anything. This includes combining and exploding.

22. **C.** Carbohydrates are quickly and easily converted into sugar, the body's main source of energy. Insulin and enzymes are created by the body to aid in digestion and the absorption and metabolism of food. Cholesterol is a fatlike substance the body produces to help with the production of cells and hormones.

23. **A.** Glaciers are made of ice, not rock. Coral reefs are produced by living creatures, not the weathering of rock. Fossils are remains of a living organism preserved in rock. Sediment is what's left of rock after it has been worn down by time and erosion and transported by wind or water.

24. **B.** The 365-day calendar year marks one entire revolution of Earth around the sun.

25. **B.** A tornado may be accompanied by lightning or electrical activity in the atmosphere, but it is not defined by these characteristics. Snowstorms deliver frozen crystals of water, not electricity. Tsunamis are not even storms but tidal waves. This leaves thunderstorms, which are defined by the electrical activity they create.

Arithmetic Reasoning

1. **B.** First calculate how much 6% of $2.2 million is: $2,200,000 × .06 = $132,000. Next, figure out what 40% of $132,000 is: $132,000 × .40 = $52,800. Finally, subtract the second total from the first: $132,000 − $52,800 = $79,200.

2. **C.** First figure out the difference between the election totals: 5,500 − 3,080 = 2,420. Then calculate what percentage 2,420 votes is of the 5,500 total: 2,420 ÷ 5,500 = .44 or 44%. Next, subtract 100 − 44 to find out the percentage of votes the winning candidate got: 56. Last, find the difference between the percentages: 56% − 44% = 12%. Candidate B lost by 12%.

3. **C.** This is a factorial. Calculate: 5! = 5 × 4 × 3 × 2 × 1 = 120.

4. **D.** The number of men = 29. The number of women = 116. Make these the numerator and denominator of a fraction, and then reduce: $\frac{29}{116} = \frac{1}{4}$.

5. **B.** This is a rate question. Your job is to figure out the time based on the distance and rate. Plug your values into this equation and solve:

   Time = $\frac{\text{Distance}}{\text{Rate}}$

   Time = $\frac{120}{60}$ = 2

6. **A.** Calculate how much 15% of $23,462 is ($3,519.30). Then subtract that number from $23,462. The answer is $19,942.70.

7. **C.** This is straight-up adding decimals:

   ```
    3.45
   +7.32
   10.77
   ```

8. **B.** This is a multistep process using simple math. First add each of the values of hay and multiply the sum by 25: (22 + 30 + 35 + 32) × 25 = 119 × 25 = $2,975. Now divide this amount by 4, the number of years in the question, to find the average: $743.75.

9. **D.** Multiply .25 × 52 to find out how much the value of the bond increases in a year: $13. Now multiply 13 × 7 to calculate how much the bond's value will increase in 7 years: $91. Now add that to the base amount of the bond: 25 + 91 = $116.

10. **A.** 9 × 9 = 81

11. **B.** Start by adding the cost of each of the types of supplies you need to buy:
    Pencils: $1.25
    Markers: $1.75
    Erasers: $.50
    Paper: $2.50
    1.25 + 1.75 + .50 + 2.50 = 6
    Now multiply that amount by the number of children who need supplies to get the total cost: $6 × 3 = $18.

12. **B.** Figure out how many students make up 75% of the class by multiplying 28 × .75 = 21. This means that 21 students are going to camp and 7 are not. Since the question asks for the ratio of students who are going to camp versus those going on vacation, your ratio should read 21:7. Now reduce to 3:1.

13. **D.** Add the scores and divide by 6: $89 + 63 + 75 + 80 + 85 + 92 = 484$; $\frac{484}{6} = 80.6$.

14. **C.** Calculate how many college-bound women make up $\frac{3}{4}$ of female respondents: $.75 \times 36 = 27$. Now calculate how many college-bound men make up $\frac{5}{6}$ (or .83) of the male respondents: $.83 \times 90 = 74.7$. You can round this up to 75. Since you know that $27 + 75 = 102$ people are pursuing college, subtract this amount from the total number of respondents: $126 - 102 = 24$.

15. **A.** Your total number of cookies is 14. If you were looking to find your chances of picking an oatmeal cookie at random, the probability would be $\frac{2}{14}$, or $\frac{1}{7}$ when you reduce, since there are only two oatmeal cookies in the jar. However, the question asks about your chances of picking any of the *other* cookies. Since there are 12 cookies that are not oatmeal your probability is $\frac{12}{14}$, which reduces to $\frac{6}{7}$.

16. **C.** Use what you know about Scott to figure out Draydon's age (she is $\frac{1}{3}$ of Scott's age): $\frac{1}{3} \times \frac{18}{1} = \frac{18}{3} = 6$.
Now add 3 to that (the number of years Sabrina is older than Draydon), and you have 9 as Sabrina's age.

17. **B.** We can use the Distance = Rate × Time formula here. We know that the distance is 426 miles and the time is 6 hours. Plug these numbers into the formula and solve:

$426 = r \times 6$

$\frac{426}{6} = r$

$71 = r$

18. **A.** Divide the amount of the commission by the amount of the sale to find the rate of commission to get .19562. Round up to get the answer that fits best: 19.6%.

19. **D.** First, figure out the area of the floor by multiplying length times width: $6.5 \times 12.5 = 81.25$. Now calculate the area of each tile: $2 \times 2 = 4$. Last, divide 81.25 by 4: 20.31. Since we're talking about whole tiles in this question and your decimal shows that more than 20 tiles will be needed, you have to round to the nearest full tile. Your answer is 21.

20. **C.** $\frac{3}{5} \times 185 = \frac{3}{5} \times \frac{185}{1} = \frac{555}{5} = 111$

21. **B.** First figure out how many widgets are produced in an hour: $\frac{45}{2} = 22.5$. Now figure out how many hours it would run during half of a seven-day workweek. Since the factory works only six hours per day, multiply that by 7: $6 \times 7 = 42$. Next divide that amount by 2, since you want to find out how many hours the factory produces widgets in half of a workweek: $\frac{45}{2} = 21$. Now multiply that amount by 22.5: $21 \times 22.5 = 472.5$.

22. **A.** Calculate the amount of money you made for the down payment: $\$3,985 \div 3 = \$1,328.33$. This is the value of one-third of the car's price, or what is owed after your down payment.

23. **D.** Calculate how long it would take Jim to walk 7 miles. You can use a proportion for this: $\frac{45}{2.5} = \frac{t}{7}$. Cross multiply to figure out the missing value:

$45 \times 7 = t \times 2.5$

$315 = t \times 2.5$

$\frac{315}{2.5} = t$

$126 = t$

It will take Jim 126 minutes to walk to the park. Subtract this from 12:30, and you'll find he has to leave his house at 10:24 A.M.

24. **B.** Though this may look like a complicated question, it's really simple subtraction. Since those whom you gave the bracelets to got only one each, subtract 24 from 30 to get your answer of 6.

25. **C.** Division will do the trick here. Divide 3,689 by 8.49 to find that you need to work 434.51 hours to earn the money for the trip.

26. **A.** The value of a radius is half the diameter:

$\frac{22}{2} = 11$

27. **A.** There are 15 beads total. Three are blue. Write out a ratio of $\frac{3}{15}$ and reduce to $\frac{1}{5}$.

28. **D.** Figure out how many members of the faculty do not have doctorates: $132 - 17 = 115$. From this number, you can eliminate answers A and B, since you can estimate that 115 is well over 56% of 132. Now divide that number by the number of total faculty to get the percentage: $\frac{115}{132} = .87$.

29. **C.** Multiply the number of total seats by the percentage sold already: $.38 \times 1,500 = 570$. Now subtract this total from 1,500: $1,500 - 570 = 930$.

30. **D.** Calculate the cost for each person by multiplying the cost of a game by the number of times per week they go:

Nora: $5 \times 3.75 = 18.75$

Jan: $2 \times 3.75 = 7.50$

Blaine: $3 \times 3.75 = 11.25$

Now add the sums to get $37.50.

Word Knowledge

1. **B.** If you do a quick swap of the underlined word for the answer choices, you can eliminate answers C and D right away; they just don't make sense. If you had *inconsistent* evidence, the police would likely not be able to make an arrest, since such evidence would be unreliable. The best choice here is answer B, which means something that can be touched or is actual.

2. **A.** Break this word down into its base word: *expect*. When you expect something, you anticipate it. Answer A has the base word of "anticipate." All the other answer choices don't fit.

3. **C.** The sentence tells us that the woman's ideas were creative, so the correct answer will have something to do with creativity. *Frigid* is cold, *optimal* is favorable, and *dispassionate* is without passion or enthusiasm. This leaves *clever*, which involves showing mental skill and creativity.

4. **D.** *Opulent* means "luxurious" or "finely appointed." Answers A and C are the opposite of this meaning, and answer B has nothing to do with luxury. Answer D is most likely, especially since *luxury* is the base word in this choice.

5. **B.** This is a good word to break down by roots. *Omni* means "all-encompassing" and *potent* means "power." The correct answer will mean "all-powerful." Answers A and C have that encompassing aspect of the prefix but say nothing about power. Answer D just doesn't fit with what we're looking for; whereas answer B is a decent fit, since *supremacy* implies encompassing power.

6. **A.** *Germane* means "appropriate" and has a neutral connotation. Answers C and D have negative and positive connotations, respectively, and answer B is the opposite of "appropriate." If something is suited to something else, it is appropriate, making A the best choice.

7. **C.** When you think of *meander*, think of a winding river that snakes its way down a mountain making lots of twists and turns. Many water parks also have a "meandering river" ride where you float lazily on an inner tube around a long, twisty circle. A river can't *navigate, attack,* or *forgive,* but it sure can *zigzag,* which makes C your best choice.

8. **A.** A great way to remember the definition of *atrocious* is to remember your Mary Poppins: "Supercalifragilisticexpialidocious. Even though the sound of it is something quite atrocious!" A very long word like that certainly does sound "awful," which is what it means.

9. **C.** One of the most revered aircraft carriers in the United States is the USS Intrepid, which is now in a museum in New York City. The military would never name an enormous ship in its fleet designed to be used in times of war with a word that means *meek* (shy) or *arrogant* (full of oneself). Such a vessel needs to project strength and valor—guts, if you will.

10. **D.** *Succinct* describes something that's short, sweet, and to the point. *Amuse, math,* and *heavy* don't make sense. However, when you're *blunt,* you get to the point fast and with few words.

11. **A.** The root *voc* tells you that this word has something to do with speaking, and the suffix *ous* tells you that this word is an adjective. Even if you know nothing else about this word, you can get this answer correct. *Decision* is a noun, so it's out. A voice might be singular, but it can't be selective. Given the choice between *singular* and *loud*, the latter is the best choice, since volume is a more logical attribute for a voice than how many there are. By the way, *vociferous* means "crying out loudly."

12. **B.** *Frugal* means "to be cautious with money." Any way you slice it, "cheap" is the best answer.

13. **D.** *Judicious* refers to someone who is practical and expedient in their decisions. *Intuitive* (using one's feelings) and *instructive* (giving direction) just don't fit. Someone who is *judicious* may be judgmental, but that is not a characteristic needed to define the word. *Prudent* is the best choice.

14. **C.** To be *astute* is to be very aware or intuitive. Answers A and D are the opposite of this. Answer B has nothing to do with this definition.

15. **B.** Something that is *abrasive* is harsh or causes friction. Within the context of the sentence, *abrasive* refers to harsh speech. Answers A, C, and D have nothing to do with being harsh, as *incredulous* means "unbelievable," *available* means "open," and *instinctive* means "going with a feeling." Answer B is correct because *tactless* means "speaking without concern for others' feelings or reactions," which is usually harsh.

16. **D.** A good little mnemonic for *incorrigible* is "you don't want to encourage incorrigible behavior," which gives you a clue that such behavior is negative. Answers A, B, and C describe behavior that is not generally negative, making answer D your best choice.

17. **B.** You can make an association here, as *stringent* means the same as "strict," "severe," and "stern." Answer A has nothing to do with these things. While you may be tempted to go with either answers C or D, remember that you're looking for a word that defines the underlined word. Someone can sometimes be offensive or wicked while being stringent, but they are always severe, which is why answer B is the best answer.

18. **D.** A search that encompasses hundreds of miles is very large. This means the answer you want has something to do with size. Answer D is the only one that addresses size, as *heroic* describes bravery, *fortuitous* describes a chance happening, and *intimate* describes a degree of personal interaction.

19. **B.** As we said earlier, the root in *potent* means "power." Your correct answer here will have some connection to this idea. The only one that fits the bill is answer B.

20. **C.** Even if you didn't know the exact definition of bigotry, you've likely heard the word used in conjunction with negative sentiments, which gives it a negative meaning. Answer B is positive, and answer D is neutral, as *transcendence* means "to go beyond." Both answers A and C are negatives, but *antagonism* means "aggression," while *chauvinism* means "prejudice," which is what bigotry is.

21. **A.** To *belittle* is to reduce the importance of something. Answer A is the only answer choice that reflects this meaning. Answer B is the opposite, and the other answers have nothing to do with this definition.

22. **D.** The base word here is *oppose*, which means "to go against." The first three answers run counter to this definition, as they all indicate relationships that go with or help. Even if you didn't know the meaning of *antagonist*, the prefix *ant* in answer D is a good sign that this word goes against something.

23. **B.** *Eloquent* is an adjective that describes beautiful or well-spoken speech. Such speech may be elegant or relatable, but it does not need to be in order to be considered eloquent. If speech is mumbled, it is the opposite of elegant. This leaves answer B, *articulate*, as the best choice.

24. **B.** *Florid* describes something that is greatly embellished. Answers A and C do not match this definition. Answer D applies to growth, not embellishment, whereas answer B refers specifically to decorating or embellishing a great deal.

25. **C.** The prefix *di* means "two" and the root *logue* means "speak." This word refers to two speakers engaging in communication. Though each answer choice involves some kind of communication, only answer C, *chat*, involves two participants, by definition.

26. **A.** When you go to a bookstore, chances are, you're going to look at books. You can't *interact* with them, since they are not alive. You likely wouldn't *eliminate* them, especially if going to a bookstore is a favorite activity. *Sanctify* means "to make something holy," which doesn't really make sense, either. Answer A, *examine*, is the logical choice.

27. **C.** A tap on the bumper of a car isn't likely to cause much damage to either vehicle. Therefore, you can eliminate answers A and D. Likewise, such an accident probably would not damage the inside of the car, which eliminates answer B from the running as well.

28. **A.** *Mischief* is the base word here and implies causing trouble without intent to harm. *Obedient* refers to doing what you're told. *Forgiven* means "to be pardoned." *Uninitiated* means "lacking experience." Answer A, *playful*, is the best choice, since it's the only one even remotely related to the underlined word.

29. **D.** Physical therapy for broken bones usually results in some kind of recovery. Swap out answer choices here to find that D is the only one that makes sense in the sentence.

30. **D.** *Reticence* means "quiet" or "reserved in nature." Answer A is the opposite. Answer B has nothing to do with this meaning. Answer C, in addition to having no connection with *reticence*, is also the wrong part of speech.

31. **B.** Someone who has been through a bad divorce is likely to be wary of getting married again. Answer A runs opposite to this idea. Answer C refers to confusion, which doesn't fit, either. Answer D has nothing to do with being wary.

32. **C.** A *predecessor* is someone who comes before another. An *instigator* causes something to happen. An *infiltrator* is a spy. A *substitute* stands in for someone. An *ancestor* is someone who lives before another in a family line, making it the best choice.

33. **A.** When you *procrastinate,* you push off what you can do today until tomorrow. In other words, you delay having to do something. Answer B means "to go through with strength." Answer C means "to get revenge." Answer D means "to go after."

34. **D.** Students in an early morning class are likely to still be feeling the effects of sleep. The teacher in the sentence is using inspirational material to bring their spirits up (*uplift*). Clearly, D is your best bet.

35. **B.** To be *militant* is to be extremely aggressive, which means answers C and D are not a good fit. Though militants can run on instinct (answer A), they are not defined by it. Answer B, *revolutionary*, suggests aggression to an extreme.

Paragraph Comprehension

1. **A.** The main idea of this passage is stated in the first sentence.

2. **A.** Use process of elimination here. No mention of strategy on Spain's part was made in the passage, nor did the passage mention Canada or European wars. The best choice is answer A because by making the purchase "Jefferson was able to secure trade access to the port of New Orleans and greatly increase the United States' standing as a formidable country."

3. **D.** The passage does not support any answer choice other than D.

4. **B.** The speaker is clearly arguing for people to become involved in the fight against deforestation. Every choice other than answer B goes against that stance.

5. **C.** If you swap out *myriad* for the answer choices, you'll find that answer C makes the most sense. There's no indication of a specific amount, its proportions, or level of interest.

6. **B.** As we said before, the speaker is clearly urging action against deforestation. She's not thinking it over or lacking in enthusiasm, which eliminates the other answers as possibilities.

7. **B.** This is a specific detail question, and the answer is found in the last sentence: "The internal temperature must be raised to at least 205° Celsius to produce caffeol oil." Caffeine and coloring aren't mentioned in the passage. Flavor is, but it says that caffeol oil produces the flavor we associate with coffee. It does not mention extra flavor anywhere.

8. **D.** This is an inference question. You need to use information in the passage to prove each answer true or false. The passage says that green coffee beans must be roasted before they can be consumed. This eliminates answer A. The passage says that coffee beans come from berries, but it says nothing about them tasting like berries. It also says that coffee beans must be fermented before they're cleaned. These two details eliminate answers B and C. The first sentence clearly states that coffee beans are "roasted seeds of coffee berries," which makes answer D the best choice.

9. **C.** *Mandate* means "to require." If you use the swapping technique with this question, you'll see that answer C is the only choice that fits the sentence.

10. **A.** The passage talks about the census, why it's conducted, and how it's used. No opinion or conclusion is stated, so *persuade* and *evaluate* aren't possible answers. The information is very neutral and does not ask the reader to take any action, which eliminates *incite* as an answer. More than anything, the passage informs the reader about the census, making answer A the best answer.

11. **C.** This is another inference question. There's no information in the passage about vitamin C being helpful for test preparation, running speed, or better sleep. It does say that it can help wounds heal faster. Because a paper cut is a wound, it's logical to think that adding vitamin C to your diet can be beneficial.

12. **D.** This is a main idea question. In the passage, the main idea is the first sentence: "Vitamin C is an essential nutrient for maintaining good health." The best choice is answer D because it includes these key ideas.

13. **A.** This is an inference question. The information in the passage contradicts answer B, and there is no information to support answers C and D. Answer A is directly supported by the second sentence in the passage.

14. **C.** "Monitor the actions of our elected officials" tells us that the speaker is urging people to keep an eye on politicians. This sets up the rest of the sentence, which talks about holding them responsible for their actions. The only choice that fits this idea is answer C.

15. **B.** This is another inference question. The best approach is to go to each answer choice and ask why the author would agree with it:

(A) "Too many people come to council meetings": The author wouldn't agree because the passage says, "Not enough people attend their local town council meetings."

(B) "Elected officials must answer to the public": This is a good choice because the author says, "It's our responsibility as American citizens to monitor the actions of our elected officials and hold them accountable."

(C) "Council meetings are the best place to air a grievance about the community": There's no mention of grievances or public speaking in the passage.

(D) "Town councils should recognize citizens more often": There's no reference to citizens being recognized in the passage.

Mathematics Knowledge

1. **B.** Use FOIL for this:

   First: $a \times a = a^2$

   Outer: $8 \times a = 8a$

   Inner: $5 \times a = 5a$

   Last: $5 \times 8 = 40$

   Your new expression is: $a^2 + 8a + 5a + 40$

   Combine like terms: $a^2 + 13a + 40$

2. **A.** Plug in 4 wherever you see *b:*

   $5 \times b^3$

   $5 \times 4 \times 4 \times 4$

   Now solve according to order of operations:

   Multiply: $(5 \times 4 \times 4 \times 4 = 320) +$

   $\left(\frac{3 \times 4}{2} = \frac{12}{2}\right)$

   Divide: $320 + \left(\frac{12}{2} = 6\right)$

   Add: $320 + 6 = 326$

3. **C.** When multiplying two like variables with exponents, keep the variable the same and add the exponents: $y^2 \times y^3 \times y^4 \times y^5 = y^{2+3+4+5} = y^{14}$.

4. **D.** A vertex is the point where the two lines that make up an angle intersect. Area is the space an object occupies. An operation is an action you need to take with a value. A term is a single number or variable, or combinations of them.

5. **B.** Solve this like any other equation:

   $4x - 3 < 5 + 2y$

   $4x -3+3 < 5 + 3 + 2y$

   $4x < 8 + 2y$

   $x \ \frac{8+2y}{4}$

6. **B.** Move your decimal points in this equation and add zeroes after the 4 in the dividend to find your answer. Take the division as far as you have to in order to get to one of the answer choices: $32.6 \div 4 = .1226$. Remember to round if you have the option. In this case, since you came up with .1226, you would round up to .123.

7. **A.** Start by combining like terms:

   $x + 2y - 4x + 6 = 2$

   $2y + x - 4x + 6 = 2$

   $2y - 3x + 6 = 2$

   Now subtract 6 from both sides:

   $2y - 3x +6-6 = 2 - 6$

   $2y - 3x = -4$

   Next, add $-3x$ to both sides:

   $2y -3x+3x = -4 + 3x$

   $2y = -4 + 3x$

   Finally, divide both sides by 2:

   $\frac{2y}{2} = \frac{-4+3x}{2}$

   $y = -2 + \frac{3x}{2}$

8. **D.** Use the total surface area formula for rectangular solids here: $2lw + 2wh + 2lh$. The question has $l = 3$, $w = 10$, and $h = 5$:

   $(2 \times 3 \times 10) + (2 \times 10 \times 5) + (2 \times 3 \times 5)$

   $60 + 100 + 30 = 190$ m^2

9. **B.** Take out the decimal points and multiply these two numbers as usual. Now count the number of decimal places in the original question. 12.475 has three places, while 20.2 has one. The decimal point in your final answer will be four places from the right: 251.995.

10. **C.** Turn your mixed number into an improper fraction by multiplying 6×4 and then adding 1 (from the numerator): $6\frac{1}{4} = \frac{25}{4}$. Now multiply the mixed fraction by the reciprocal of $\frac{5}{8}$: $\frac{25}{4} \times \frac{8}{5} = \frac{200}{20} = 10$.

11. **B.** Attack this like any other equation and solve for x:

    $3x + 5 \times 5 \ne 7 - 12$

    $3x + 25 \ne -5$

    $3x + \cancel{25 - 25} \ne -5 - 25$

    $3x \ne -30$

    $x \ne \frac{-30}{3} = -10$

12. **D.** This is a quadratic expression. You can either FOIL the answer choices or factor the expression: $b^2 - 14b + 24$.

    Set up your binomials: $(b\ )(b\ )$

    Now list factors of 24:

    1×24

    2×12

    3×8

    4×6

    If you add 2 and 12, you get 14, which is the middle term; if you multiply them, you get the final term, which is 24. Add these terms to your binomial shells. Now we figure out the signs. Since one of our original terms is negative, both signs in the final binomials will be negative. The final answer is $(b - 2)(b - 12)$.

13. **A.** A parallelogram is a quadrilateral with opposite sides that are parallel and equal in length. Trapezoids and rhombi are types of parallelograms with their own distinct properties that distinguish them from simply having the definition of a parallelogram. A polygon is an enclosed figure with three or more sides.

14. **C.** Use the Pythagorean theorem here to solve for the missing value: $a^2 + b^2 = c^2$.

    $(6 \times 6) + b^2 = (7.8 \times 7.8)$

    $36 + b^2 = 60.84$

    $b^2 = 60.84 - 36 = 24.84$

    $b = \sqrt{24.84}$

    Since your answer choices don't ask for an exact answer, $\sqrt{24.84}$ is enough to get you through this question.

15. **C.** This one is all about order of operations. Start with the brackets, since they tell you that what's inside must be solved before moving on to anything else:

    Parentheses: $(6 + 4 = 10)$; $(14 - 8 = 6)$

    New expression: $[(10)^2 + (6)]$

    Exponents: $(10 \times 10 = 100)$

    New expression: $[100 + (6)]$

    Addition: $100 + (6) = 106$

    Now that the expressions in the brackets have been solved, take a look at the new expression: $106 - \frac{2}{3} \times \frac{9}{2}$.

    Go back to the beginning of order of operations and start again. Since there are no parentheses or exponents, start with multiplication:

    Multiply: $\frac{2}{3} \times \frac{9}{2} = \frac{18}{6} = 3$

    New expression: $106 - 3$

    Subtraction: $106 - 3 = 103$

16. **A.** This is another proportion. Cross multiply and solve for the missing value:

$\frac{3}{6} = \frac{a}{12}$

$3 \times 12 = 6a$

$36 = 6a$

$\frac{36}{6} = a$

$6 = a$

17. **C.** These are similar triangles, since they have internal angles that are equal to each other and, therefore, have proportional sides. The degrees of angles g, d, and f are the same in each triangle. This means that side a is proportional to side x, side c is proportional to side y, and side b is proportional to side z.

18. **B.** With scientific notation, you move the decimal point to the right of the leftmost digit. With 16597000000, you'd move the decimal 10 places to the left to get 1.6597000000. Now drop all of the 0s after the 7 to get 1.6597. Finally, multiply this number by 10 to the 10th power (the number of decimal spaces you moved): 1.6597×10^{10}.

19. **D.** Turn the mixed number into an improper fraction and set up a new expression:

$2\frac{4}{5} - \frac{7}{8} = \frac{14}{5} - \frac{7}{8}$

Now make the denominators the same by multiplying each fraction by its opposite denominator:

$\frac{14}{5} \times \frac{8}{8} = \frac{112}{40}$

$\frac{7}{8} \times \frac{5}{5} = \frac{35}{40}$

Finally, subtract the two new fractions and reduce:

$\frac{112}{40} - \frac{35}{40} = \frac{77}{40} = 1\frac{37}{40}$

20. **B.** Isosceles right triangles have two equal sides.

21. **C.** This is a trapezoid because it's a quadrilateral with just parallel sides. A rhombus has two sets of sides that run parallel. A hexagon is a six-sided polygon. A chord is a segment in a circle that touches any two points of the edge.

22. **D.** This is factorial, so calculate: $8 \times 7 \times 6 \times 5 \times 4 \times 3 \times 2 \times 1 = 40{,}320$.

23. **A.** Both terms here are perfect squares. Calculate the square roots of both terms and place in a set of binomial expressions: $\sqrt{c^2} = c$; $\sqrt{121} = 11 : (c\ 11)(c\ 11)$. We need a positive and negative sign here to make these work when FOIL is applied, so our answer is $(c + 11)(c - 11)$.

24. **A.** Adjacent angles share a common side. *Congruent* and *similar* are terms used to describe triangles. A straight angle is one that's 180°.

25. **D.** All sides of a square are equal. Multiply $15.2 \times 15.2 = 231.04$ to find the area.

Electronics Information

1. **A.** Choices B and D are wrong because there are no neutral charges in current flow. Choice C is wrong because it describes the flow of electrons instead of current.

2. **C.** Choices A and D are wrong because they describe conductor material rather than insulator. Choice B is wrong because it is not a material typically associated with wiring.

3. **D.** The diode looks like an arrow pointing in the direction that current flows.

4. **B.** The formula for this problem is Watts = Volts × Amps. Insert the values you have and solve for the missing amount.

5. **D.** Choice A is wrong because a gas-powered generator uses a different symbol. Choices B and C are wrong because they are not power sources.

6. **B.** Choice A is wrong because protons aren't involved in electric currents. Choice C is wrong because ohms measure the resistance in a current. Choice D is wrong because amps measure current; they don't push it along.

7. **C.** Choice A is wrong because conductors are the materials through which electricity can pass. Choice B is wrong because a switch is an electrical control element. Choice D is wrong because a circuit is a system of connected conductors that direct the path of electricity.

8. **D.** To calculate frequency, divide wave speed by wavelength.

9. **B.** The resistor diagram looks like a never-ending letter *W*.

10. **A.** To determine amps, you must divide volts by resistance.

11. **A.** The other choices are all incorrect because they have nothing to do with resistance.

12. **A.** Low-range frequencies have the longest wavelengths, making them easier to hear.

13. **D.** To answer this question, use the following formula: $\Omega = \frac{volts}{amps}$

14. **C.** Choice A is wrong because an ohmmeter is used to measure resistance. Choice B is wrong because a voltmeter is used to measure the difference in voltage. Choice D is wrong because it is used to measure current.

15. **A.** Choices B, C, and D are wrong because they are all types of current, and therefore cannot measure another type of current.

16. **B.** The diagram illustrates a DC voltage capacitor, which increases and smooths DC voltage.

17. **B.** Choice A is wrong because scattered wavelengths occur during dispersion. Choice C is wrong because rectilinear propagation is the movement of waves in a straight line. Choice D is wrong because the bending of waves occurs during diffraction.

18. **C.** To solve for the missing value, you use the following formula:

    $amps = \frac{volts}{ohms}$

19. **C.** Wave speed is calculated by multiplying wavelength and frequency.

20. **D.** Good conductors of electricity offer low resistance, such as copper. Choice A is wrong because it is the opposite of the right answer. Choice B is wrong because there is no exact resistance number used to determine "a good conductor." Choice C is wrong because gauge refers to wire thickness, not resistance.

Automotive and Shop Information

1. **A.** Refer back to the seven steps we listed in the beginning of the chapter that are involved in starting a car. After turning the key, the next set of activities are as follows: power transfers from the battery (power source) through the ignition switch to the ignition coil, which sends power to the distributor (if present) and spark plugs.

2. **B.** The solenoid is also called a *relay* because it receives current from the battery and passes it on to the starter. This function is similar to that of a relay runner in a race.

3. **C.** When switches are in the open position, power cannot be passed through the circuit. When the circuit is closed, it is complete.

4. **B.** A disc brake is distinguishable by brake pads, calipers, and rotors. Choice D is wrong because a secondary brake is another way of referring to an emergency brake.

5. **D.** Choice A is wrong because the slide pin is used to hold the calipers together. Choice B is wrong because the wheel hub holds the rotors and allows the car to turn. Choice C is wrong because the rotors don't house the brake pads, but they provide a rubbing surface for friction material and help disperse heat during braking.

6. **C.** Choice A is wrong because the brake lines hold brake fluid and sometimes get air bubbles in them. The bleed valve is opened to empty the brake lines of fluid and air. Choice B is wrong because the brake pad is designed to apply friction to both sides of the disc brake. Choice D is wrong because the dust cap is used to keep contaminants, such as dust and dirt, out of the hub bearing.

7. **C.** A differential allows wheels to rotate at different speeds. This is needed when turning, as each wheel travels a different distance.

8. **B.** Catalytic converters were designed in the 1970s to control harmful exhaust pollutants like nitrogen gas, carbon dioxide, and water vapor.

9. **D.** Choice A is wrong because the exhaust pipe is the first step in the process of transporting gases and vapors through the exhaust system. Choice B is wrong because catalytic converters control harmful emissions. Choice C is the first stop for exhaust once it leaves the engine.

10. **C.** The four-stroke process is as follows: intake, compression, power, exhaust.

11. **A.** The piston starts the four-stroke process in the up position. During the intake stroke, the crankshaft and camshaft move to open the fuel intake valves and lower the pistons (with precision timing). During the compression stroke, the piston moves back up to compress the fuel-air mixture. When the piston reaches the top, the spark plugs fire at exactly the right time to ignite the fuel. This causes an explosion in the combustion chamber that drives the piston back down. Finally, the exhaust stroke makes the pistons rise once more, the camshaft opens the exhaust valves, which enables the waste gases caused by combustion to collect in

the exhaust manifold and be routed to the exhaust system.

12. **D.** Choice A is wrong because it describes the brake system. Choice B is wrong because the electrical system is responsible for providing the initial source of power to the ignition system. Choice C is incorrect because it describes the cooling system.

13. **A.** Choice B is wrong because the fuel filter keeps rust and dirt particles out of the fuel before they reach the engine. Choice C is wrong because the fuel pump feeds fuel to the engine from the fuel tank. Choice D is wrong because the alternator is not even part of the fuel system.

14. **D.** Hot fluid flows through a series of radiator tubes to be cooled by a fan system and air coming through the front grill.

15. **B.** Choice A is wrong because it is the inverse of the correct choice. Choice C is wrong because brake fluid is located in the brake lines, not the cylinder. Choice D is wrong because calipers are not part of a drum brake system; brake drums are attached to the wheel.

16. **B.** The peen of the hammer is depicted by the ball-shaped sphere of steel directly across from the hammer head.

17. **D.** The hammer best suited for driving rivets into sheet metal is a tinner's hammer.

18. **A.** Hand drills are characterized by a cranking handle, a chuck, and a drill bit, as depicted in the diagram.

19. **D.** The other three choices are all reasons to use a power drill, not a hand drill.

20. **C.** None of the other choices resemble this type of tool.

21. **A.** Choice B is wrong because it describes the role of a block plane. Choice C is wrong because it describes the role of a hand screw. Choice D is wrong because it describes the role of a pipe clamp.

22. **B.** A jack plane is a type of plane tool, which falls under the category of shaping.

23. **C.** A chisel is a type of shaping tool, not a saw.

24. **C.** Choices A and B are wrong because a pistol grip drill is handheld, as is a hammer drill. Choice D is wrong because a jigsaw is a type of saw, not drill.

25. **A.** Choice B is wrong because rasps are used for wood surfaces only. Choices C and D are wrong because they don't have tiny ridgelike grooves used for smoothing surfaces.

Mechanical Comprehension

1. **C.** The ball cannot do work on the bat if the bat struck it; however, the bat can do work on the ball in this situation.

2. **B.** A 2nd-class lever positions the load between the fulcrum and the effort.

3. **A.** To calculate this equation, you should perform the following procedure:

   Multiply the larger weight by x. That is the left side of the equation.

   Multiple the smaller weight by (the distance between the two weights minus x). That is the right side of the equation.

   Solve for x.

   $50x = 25(15 - x)$

   $50x = 375 - 25x$

   $75x = 375$

   $x = 5$

   You now know that the larger weight should be 5 feet from the fulcrum. Since the two weights were 15 feet apart to begin with, you can deduce that the second weight must be 10 feet from the fulcrum.

4. **A.** Choice B is wrong because a 3rd-class lever is exemplified by tongs, tweezers, and staplers. Choice C is wrong because a 1st-class lever is exemplified by a seesaw, scissors, or a hammer claw. Choice D is wrong because a 4th-class lever doesn't exist.

5. **D.** Each time a pulley is introduced to a pulley system, the mechanical advantage increases.

6. **D.** Balancing the weights on a 1st-class lever requires that the products of each weight and its distance from the fulcrum are equal.

7. **A.** The easiest way to calculate mechanical advantage (without regard to friction and other unknown factors) is to count the number of rope lengths you have in the pulley system. In this case, there is one pulley with one rope section. Therefore, you have a mechanical advantage of 1.

8. **B.** Gear ratio is used to determine the rate at which two gears turn.

9. **C.** To determine gear ratio by number of teeth, divide the larger number of teeth by the smaller number. In this case, $\frac{200}{40} = 5$. Therefore, you have a 5:1 ratio.

10. **B.** Gears perform each of the other tasks listed. Although gears may cause an object to *feel* lighter, they don't actually change the weight of the object.

11. **D.** Choice A is wrong because friction occurs when two objects rub against one another. Choice B is wrong because acceleration occurs when there is a rate of increase of velocity. Choice C is wrong because speed is defined as distance traveled over a unit of time.

12. **A.** Negative acceleration is calculated in the same manner as acceleration. The change in velocity per hour is divided by the time interval.

13. **B.** Velocity is the speed and direction of an object.

14. **C.** The law of reciprocal action is considered Newton's third law.

15. **A.** A 1st-class lever is characterized by a fulcrum located in between the load and the effort.

16. **A.** Newton's second law states that the acceleration of an object is directly proportional to the net force acting on the object; furthermore, the object accelerates in the direction of the net force acting on it.

17. **B.** None of the other formulas represent force.

18. **B.** Newton's second law applies to this question.

19. **D.** Most countries use mass to measure an object, which is why you may be more familiar with the term *kilogram* than *newton*. However, a newton is the metric expression of weight.

20. **A.** None of the other choices offers the appropriate formula for mass.

21. **D.** Choice A is wrong because mass is defined by the volume and density of an object. Choice B is wrong because speed is distance traveled per unit of time. Choice C is wrong because acceleration is the rate of increase of velocity.

22. **D.** Work is calculated by multiplying force times distance.

23. **C.** Kinetic energy is calculated using the following formula: $KE = \frac{1}{2}mv^2$
$KE = mv^2$.

24. **D.** All of these answers are correct. The more pulleys you add to a pulley system, you have half the force to move, but twice the distance to pull the rope. The object you move now feels lighter because of the number of pulleys you can use to distribute the weight.

25. **A.** Plug the numbers into the formula as follows:

$18(10) = x(30 - 10)$

$180 = 30x - 10x$

$180 = 20x$

$9 = x$

Practice Test 1: Answers and Explanations   273

Assembling Objects

1. **B.** This is a pretty simple one. Answer A has the B connection in the wrong place on the *g*. Answer C has a *p* instead of a *g*, and answer D is mirrored.

2. **A.** The shapes in answer B are changed from the sample and one is mirrored, which eliminates it as a possibility. Choices C and D both have shapes different from the sample. Answer A is your best bet.

3. **C.** Both shapes in answer C have been rotated so that points A and B are connected in the right place. The A connection in answer A is wrong. There's a star shape instead of an *X* shape in answer B, and the triangle in answer D has been changed.

4. **C.** The shapes in answers A and D are not the same shape or size as those of the sample. Answer B contains mirrored images, which means it can't be correct.

5. **A.** Notice the little flag on the dot indicating point B in the sample. This tells you the angle the connecting line has to come in at. The line in answer B comes into point B at a different angle than that in the sample. The A connection in answer C is in the wrong place, and the B connection in answer D is also wrong.

6. **D.** Some of the shapes in answers A and B do not match those in the sample. Answer C contains all mirrored pieces. Everything in answer D is the same as the sample.

7. **C.** The five-sided figure in answer A is mirrored. The flower shape in answer B has five petals instead of six, and the five-sided figure in answer D has been replaced by a rectangle.

8. **B.** All the answer choices except answer B contain at least one shape that doesn't match the sample.

9. **D.** The star in answer A is different from the sample. The triangle in answer B is smaller and a different shape. There's an extra piece in answer C. This makes answer D the best choice.

10. **D.** Choices A and C have one connector placed on the wrong section of one of the objects. The top object in choice B is rotated too much and at an angle to make the connection to point A exactly the same as it is in the example.

11. **D.** The A connection in answer A and the B connection in answer C are in the wrong place. The top shape in answer B is not the same as in the example.

12. **C.** There are extra pieces and changed shapes in answer A. The cross in answer B is markedly different from the sample, and the second triangle is missing. In answer D, at least one of the triangles is the wrong shape. Even though the circle is behind the cross in answer C, it's still your best choice.

13. **D.** The top shape in answer A and the bottom shape in answer B are different from the sample. Both the A and B connections in answer C are in the wrong place.

14. **B.** There are no quadrilaterals in answer A, which eliminates it as a possibility. One of the quadrilaterals in answer C is not the same as the sample, and the triangle in D doesn't have a flat bottom like the one in the sample.

15. **C.** The B connection in answer A is in the wrong place and the rounded object doesn't match the sample. Answers B and D have incorrect shapes included in the connection. This leaves only C as a possible choice.

16. **A.** There's a rectangle in answer B that should not be there. The hexagon in answer C was changed to an octagon, and there is a piece missing. Answer D has five pieces instead of four.

17. **A.** Answer B has the B connection in the wrong place. Instead of a dollar sign in answer C, there is an *S*, and the B connection is in the wrong place. Finally, the figures are mirrored in answer D.

18. **C.** The rounded rectangle from the sample now has squared edges in answer A. In answer B, the star was replaced by a triangle. The rectangle in answer D has been replaced with another trapezoid.

19. **C.** The bottom shape is mirrored in answer A. The bottom shapes in answers B and D do not match the sample.

20. **A.** The diamond in answer B has been split into two shapes. The seven-sided figure in answer C was replaced with a pentagon. There are five shapes in answer D, and the smaller rectangle is now the same size as the larger one.

21. **D.** The rounded rectangle in answer A has been replaced by a regular one. The A connection and the B connection in answer B is in the wrong place. In answer C, the angle of the B connection doesn't match the sample.

22. **B.** The angles in two of the shapes are skewed in answer A. Two pieces in both answers C and D have also been changed in shape and size.

23. **C.** The B connection in answer A is in the wrong place. The @ in answer B is mirrored. Both the A and B connections are in the wrong place in answer D.

24. **A.** The proportions of all the shapes in answer B are off. There are two rectangles in answer C instead of just one. In answer D, the shield has been replaced with an oval.

25. **B.** The A and B connections in answers A and C are in the wrong place. There's a *p* in answer D instead of an *h*.

Practice Test 2

General Science

Time: 11 Minutes

Questions: 25

Directions: This section tests your general knowledge in the area of science. Carefully read each question below and choose the answer choice that best answers the question.

1. The study of plants is called
    (A) botany.
    (B) ecology.
    (C) zoology.
    (D) chemistry.

2. If a species' body composition changes in response to survival needs, the theory of _____ applies.
    (A) cell regeneration
    (B) gene therapy
    (C) evolution
    (D) homeostasis

3. All of the following are aspects of thermodynamics theory except:
    (A) Energy never disappears.
    (B) Energy transfer cannot be completed in single-cell organisms.
    (C) Energy gets converted to other forms.
    (D) Energy transfer is not completely efficient.

4. Archaea is a

    (A) domain.
    (B) phylum.
    (C) class.
    (D) order.

5. Plants appear green because

    (A) photosynthesis produces green energy.
    (B) chlorophyll absorbs all red and blue light, causing plants to appear green.
    (C) the chloroplasts absorb green light.
    (D) they grow from seeds.

6. Which chemical reaction represents the process of photosynthesis?

    (A) $6CO_2 + 6H_2O$ (+ light energy) $C_6H_{12}O_6 + 6O_2$
    (B) $8CO + 6H_2O$ (+ light energy) $C_6H_{12}O_6 + 8O_2$
    (C) $6CO_4 + 12H_2O$ (+ light energy) $C_6H_{12}O_6 + 6O_4$
    (D) $6CO + 6H_2O$ (+ light energy) $C_6H_{12}O_2 + O_2$

7. An important element essential to human life that plants produce is

    (A) light.
    (B) carbon dioxide.
    (C) oxygen.
    (D) water.

8. The dark shadow cast when the moon passes behind the Earth, fully blocking sunlight from the moon, is called a(n)

    (A) penumbra.
    (B) corona.
    (C) eclipse.
    (D) umbra.

9. Any influence that can cause a change in the velocity of an object is

    (A) energy.
    (B) work.
    (C) force.
    (D) friction.

10. Which cell organelle contains digestive enzymes?

    (A) ribosome
    (B) golgi
    (C) mitochondria
    (D) lysosome

11. The two main types of cell division are

    (A) DNA and RNA.
    (B) mitosis and meiosis.
    (C) endoplasmic and cell plasma.
    (D) nucleus and nucleotide.

12. Weightlifters' muscles get larger due to

    (A) protein growth.
    (B) chromosome change.
    (C) mitosis cell division.
    (D) metabolism conversion.

13. Which biological term is used to describe the basic unit of heredity?

    (A) nucleotide

    (B) gene

    (C) metabolism

    (D) amino acid

14. A group of stars, gas, and dust held together by gravity is a

    (A) sun.

    (B) binary star.

    (C) galaxy.

    (D) constellation.

15. Muscles, veins, arteries, and capillaries are all part of the

    (A) respiratory system.

    (B) digestive system.

    (C) circulatory system.

    (D) excretory system.

16. The kidneys

    (A) pass solid waste out of the body.

    (B) pull oxygen all the way through the lungs.

    (C) allow blood to deposit carbon dioxide and pick up oxygen.

    (D) filter waste from the blood.

17. The body's main source of energy comes from

    (A) fats.

    (B) carbohydrates.

    (C) minerals.

    (D) vitamins.

18. Which of the following serves as a vehicle for carrying nutrients needed by the body?

    (A) proteins

    (B) fats

    (C) fiber

    (D) water

19. Which portion of our diet includes fibrous, indigestible foods?

    (A) fats

    (B) vitamins

    (C) fiber

    (D) proteins

20. From surface to center, the layers of Earth are

    (A) crust, mantle, outer core, inner core.

    (B) mantle, inner core, outer core, crust.

    (C) crust, inner core, outer core, mantle.

    (D) mantle, crust, inner core, outer core.

21. When liquid molten rock flows beneath Earth's surface, it is called

    (A) magma.

    (B) lava.

    (C) volcano.

    (D) nickel.

22. The outer core of Earth is made up primarily of

    (A) iron and copper.

    (B) iron and nickel.

    (C) nickel and magnesium.

    (D) nickel and copper.

23. The air pressing down on Earth is measured in terms of

   (A) warm front.
   (B) barometric pressure.
   (C) temperature.
   (D) cumulonimbus.

24. NaCl is the chemical symbol for salt. Which two elements make up this compound?

   (A) hydrogen and mercury
   (B) sodium and chlorine
   (C) sodium and aluminum
   (D) chlorine and copper

25. Abiotic conditions

   (A) are nonliving things that affect an ecosystem.
   (B) are living things that affect an ecosystem.
   (C) describe an ecosystem.
   (D) have no effect on ecosystems.

Arithmetic Reasoning

Time: 36 Minutes

Questions: 30

Directions: This section tests your ability to reason through mathematical problems using basic arithmetic. Carefully read each question and choose the answer choice that best answers the question.

1. John wants to give his two employees a raise. Employee 1 earns $245 per week, and Employee 2 earns $396 per week. If he increased their weekly pay by 6%, how much more would he have to allocate to pay his employees per 4-week pay period?

   (A) $34.76
   (B) $38.46
   (C) $134.23
   (D) $153.84

2. Mr. X has four dates per week. At this rate, how many dates will he have over the course of a year?

   (A) 208
   (B) 215
   (C) 287
   (D) 306

3. Jon makes $32,890 per year. Amy makes $545.50 per week. How much more per week does Jon make?

   (A) $32.50
   (B) $56.20
   (C) $87.00
   (D) $632.50

4. Out of the 750 books in the local library, 150 are romance novels, 200 are mysteries, and the rest are non-fiction books. What percentage of the total collection are romance novels?

   (A) 20%
   (B) 25%
   (C) 50%
   (D) 55%

5. If you made $15,625.35 during the first half of the year and 7% more for the second half of the year, what's the total amount of money you made over the entire year?

   (A) $30,050.67
   (B) $32,344.47
   (C) $42,433.74
   (D) $82,779.23

6. The produce section of a grocery store held a sale on peaches. Over the course of the sale, 125 peaches were sold. During the same time, 85 regular-priced apples were also sold. What is the ratio of peaches to apples sold during this sale period?

   (A) 85:210
   (B) 125:210
   (C) 17:25
   (D) 25:17

7. Thirty-two is what percentage of 128?

    (A) 15%
    (B) 20%
    (C) 25%
    (D) 55%

8. Bailey brings three kids to the movies with her. The price for adults is $5.25 and for children is $3.75. In the lobby, she meets her friend and invites her to come see the movie with her and the kids. Assuming that Bailey and her friend are adults, how much will it cost for all five people to see the movie?

    (A) $9.52
    (B) $10.50
    (C) $11.25
    (D) $21.75

9. If you travel at a consistent rate of 13 miles per hour, about how long will it take you to travel 87 miles?

    (A) $6\frac{9}{13}$ hours

    (B) $6\frac{2}{13}$ hours

    (C) $7\frac{2}{4}$ hours

    (D) $9\frac{3}{6}$ hours

10. If you add –12 to –13, you get

    (A) 25
    (B) –25
    (C) –1
    (D) 1

11. April's mother is 67 and is 32% older than April. About how old is April?

    (A) 42
    (B) 43
    (C) 45
    (D) 46

12. $5 \times 4 \times 3 \times 2 \times 1$ is also known as a(n)

    (A) constant.
    (B) inequality.
    (C) factorial.
    (D) variable.

13. Jack makes $0.35 on every copy of his new CD that is sold. If each costs $14.95, what portion of sales goes to Jack?

    (A) 2.34%
    (B) 6.23%
    (C) 6.75%
    (D) 7.54%

14. Your garden is 4-feet wide by 6-feet long. You want to build another garden for your friend that is bigger but still proportionate. If you make your friend's garden 9-feet wide, how long would it have to be to still be in proportion to yours?

    (A) 8 feet
    (B) 9 feet
    (C) 10.8 feet
    (D) 13.5 feet

15. For every $2 that you spend at a particular restaurant, 75¢ is given to charity. If you spend $138 there over the course of the month, how much of your money will have been donated?

    (A) $28.55

    (B) $51.75

    (C) $103.50

    (D) $151.75

16. What part of the following expression would you evaluate first according to order of operations: $[2 \times 4 + (3^2 - 3)^4] + (-6) - 9$.

    (A) $(32 - 3)$

    (B) 2×4

    (C) $(32 - 3)4$

    (D) $[2 \times 4 + (32 - 3)4]$

17. Jordan makes $622 per week as a waitress. If she has to pay 12% of that to her landlord for rent, how much does she have left over for other expenses each month?

    (A) $298.56

    (B) $345.65

    (C) $2,189.44

    (D) $2,488

18. Emma and Tim both collect baseball cards. If Emma has 32 cards and hers outnumber Tim's cards by a ratio of 4:1, how many cards does Tim have?

    (A) 6

    (B) 8

    (C) 24

    (D) 32

19. If you could wash four loads of laundry at the laundromat for $10.75, how many full loads could you wash for $23.63?

    (A) 6

    (B) 7

    (C) 8

    (D) 9

20. Your latest scores on a particular video game are 10,965; 15,637; and 16,222. What is your average score based on these numbers?

    (A) 14,274.67

    (B) 15,274.67

    (C) 23,724.67

    (D) 42,824

21. Four-sixths plus $\frac{2}{8}$ equals:

    (A) $\frac{12}{11}$

    (B) $\frac{11}{12}$

    (C) $1\frac{2}{5}$

    (D) $1\frac{5}{8}$

22. Barry is organizing a trip to the botanical gardens for himself and 14 friends. Among them, they have five cars. Two hold four passengers, two hold five passengers, and one holds only three passengers. How many more people would they have to invite to fill up all the cars?

    (Λ) 3

    (B) 4

    (C) 5

    (D) 6

23. You have to move 27 one-pound bags of sand from the garage to your car. You can carry two bags at a time. How many trips will you have to make to move all the bags?

    (A) 11
    (B) 13
    (C) 14
    (D) 16

24. Private Snuffy can complete 50 push-ups in three minutes, which is 15 more than his closest competitor in his training class. By what percentage would his competitor need to increase to reach Snuffy's performance?

    (A) 28%
    (B) 30%
    (C) 38%
    (D) 43%

25. At what percentage would a savings account have to accrue annual interest to increase a deposit of $235 to about $263 in a year?

    (A) 2%
    (B) 6%
    (C) 12%
    (D) 21%

26. $2 \times 2 \times 2 \times 2 \times 2$ is another way of writing

    (A) 22
    (B) 23
    (C) 24
    (D) 25

27. The square root of 169 is:

    (A) 11
    (B) 12
    (C) 13
    (D) 14

28. The odds on a horse in a race are paid 9:1. If you placed a $75 bet on the horse and it won, how much money would you win?

    (A) $525
    (B) $675
    (C) $775
    (D) $955

29. One lap on a track is equal to one quarter of a mile. If you ran 29 laps, about how many miles have you traveled?

    (A) 6
    (B) 7
    (C) 8
    (D) 9

30. In the following expression, which number is a base?

    $7^6 + 14 - 12 + (-3)$

    (A) 7
    (B) 14
    (C) –12
    (D) –3

Word Knowledge

Time: 11 Minutes

Questions: 35

Directions: This section tests your knowledge of and ability to use vocabulary. Read each question and choose the answer choice that most nearly means the same as the underlined word.

1. <u>Conceited</u> most nearly means

    (A) humble.
    (B) noble.
    (C) proud.
    (D) loud.

2. <u>Insurmountable</u> most nearly means

    (A) conquered.
    (B) undefeatable.
    (C) friendly.
    (D) surrounded.

3. <u>Extraordinary</u> most nearly means

    (A) unexpected.
    (B) reliable.
    (C) morose.
    (D) melancholy.

4. <u>Open</u> most nearly means

    (A) simple.
    (B) advanced.
    (C) meager.
    (D) accepting.

5. <u>Intricate</u> most nearly means

    (A) frigid.
    (B) optimal.
    (C) complex.
    (D) dispassionate.

6. <u>Antediluvian</u> most nearly means

    (A) outdated.
    (B) incorrect.
    (C) beloved.
    (D) normal.

7. <u>Profuse</u> most nearly means

    (A) hard.
    (B) generous.
    (C) merited.
    (D) difficult.

8. After my mother's funeral, I thanked her friends for being so <u>solicitous</u> in their kind offer to help with the preparations.

    (A) grateful
    (B) false
    (C) active
    (D) concerned

9. The calm attorney was known for her <u>forbearance</u> when facing particularly aggressive opponents in court.

    (A) temper
    (B) vitality
    (C) patience
    (D) abrasiveness

10. Regal most nearly means

   (A) majestic.
   (B) ruddy.
   (C) uninterested.
   (D) ruined.

11. Insipid most nearly means

   (A) brave.
   (B) darkened.
   (C) dull.
   (D) trite.

12. Foresight most nearly means

   (A) affluence.
   (B) intuition.
   (C) contagion.
   (D) influence.

13. Frequent most nearly means

   (A) obstructive.
   (B) censorious.
   (C) recurrent.
   (D) blatant.

14. Even though the newspapers were all predicting a landslide win for the other candidate, the mayor was resolute in his belief that he would win the election.

   (A) steadfast
   (B) depressed
   (C) anxious
   (D) appreciative

15. The increasing length of the war quickly depleted the country's finances and manpower.

   (A) infused
   (B) drained
   (C) sustained
   (D) marginalized

16. Ubiquitous most nearly means

   (A) somniferous.
   (B) omnipotent.
   (C) omniscient.
   (D) omnipresent.

17. The duplicitous thief betrayed his comrade by giving him less than an equal cut of their latest heist.

   (A) demented
   (B) honorable
   (C) dishonest
   (D) disavowed

18. Capitulate most nearly means

   (A) surrender.
   (B) delay.
   (C) waver.
   (D) intrude.

19. It took a while for the exchange student to assimilate into her new family's culture, but soon she was speaking French and darting about the village like a native.

   (A) construct
   (B) reject
   (C) blend
   (D) grieve

20. Benevolent most nearly means

    (A) inferior.
    (B) egotistic.
    (C) blinded.
    (D) giving.

21. Lanky most nearly means

    (A) stout.
    (B) gangly.
    (C) broad.
    (D) small.

22. Metamorphosis most nearly means

    (A) transformation.
    (B) incantation.
    (C) inclination.
    (D) excitation.

23. Obligate most nearly means

    (A) exist.
    (B) deceive.
    (C) appreciate.
    (D) compel.

24. Enrich most nearly means

    (A) treat.
    (B) stir.
    (C) augment.
    (D) react.

25. Indoctrinate most nearly means

    (A) force.
    (B) train.
    (C) incite.
    (D) believe.

26. Her sanguine smile and optimistic words of encouragement in even the toughest circumstances helped make Jane the ideal candidate for team leader.

    (A) darkening
    (B) threatening
    (C) confident
    (D) unconscious

27. Mystify most nearly means

    (A) perplex.
    (B) clarify.
    (C) deify.
    (D) stupefy.

28. Because of my dyslexia, I often transpose *p* and *b* when I write the word *plumber*; it ends up looking like *blumper*.

    (A) impress
    (B) switch
    (C) ruin
    (D) berate

29. Bait most nearly means

    (A) mislead.
    (B) carry on.
    (C) bleed.
    (D) harass.

30. The anesthetic from my dental work earlier in the day was still in effect, thus making me garble my words in the meeting.

    (A) jumble
    (B) squeak
    (C) plait
    (D) berate

31. Belie most nearly means

   (A) predict.
   (B) confirm.
   (C) contradict.
   (D) forage.

32. Heady most nearly means

   (A) upset.
   (B) thrilling.
   (C) delusory.
   (D) exhausting.

33. Knowing that everyone else in the house was sick, I thought I'd take some extra vitamin C to try to fortify my immune system so I would not get sick, too.

   (A) strengthen
   (B) enlighten
   (C) enliven
   (D) invigorate

34. Dictate most nearly means

   (A) passive.
   (B) aggressive.
   (C) utter.
   (D) behave.

35. Gracious most nearly means

   (A) tangible.
   (B) raucous.
   (C) tactless.
   (D) congenial.

Paragraph Comprehension

Time: 13 Minutes

Questions: 15

Directions: This section tests your ability to read and understand written information, as well as come to logical conclusions based on a text. Read each passage, and answer the questions that follow. Choose the answer choice that best answers the question.

Use the following passage to answer questions 1–2:

(1) The Nile River is an important source of water in Africa. (2) Authorities have argued over the years about its exact length, as no definite consensus on its source has been reached. (3) As of 2018, it is estimated to be about 4,123 miles long, flowing south to north through Burundi, Democratic Republic of Congo, Egypt, Eritrea, Ethiopia, Kenya, Rwanda, South Sudan, Sudan, Tanzania, and Uganda.

(4) Settlements and farms tend to center around the river. (5) Its use as a source of water for agricultural purposes has resulted in the production of many different types of foods upon which these countries rely for sustenance and income. (6) The Nile also serves as a source of hydroelectric power that helps support many communities in the countries through which it flows.

1. How many countries does the Nile run through?

    (A) 8
    (B) 9
    (C) 10
    (D) 11

2. Which sentence best conveys the main point of the passage?

    (A) 1
    (B) 2
    (C) 3
    (D) 4

Use the following passage to answer questions 3–5:

(1) Antarctica is the only continent that acts as a living laboratory for scientific research. (2) Though the benefits of having such a vast land that has not had much interference from human inhabitants are great, the extreme climate makes long-term study a challenge. (3) Maintaining temporary settlements that can support the manpower and equipment necessary to conduct experiments in temperatures that average –56°F throughout the year and can drop below –150°F in the winter is a constant issue.

(4) Furthermore, because of Antarctica's position over the southern pole of the Earth, it is lit by the sun for only six months throughout the year. (5) This presents issues for generating and maintaining sources of power during the months when the sun does not shine on the continent, especially since there are no sources of energy that can be drawn from towns or villages.

3. A research team planning to conduct a study in Antarctica might face issues with

    (A) providing heat that would protect their team members and equipment.

    (B) providing food and shelter for their team members and equipment.

    (C) providing light and electricity to conduct experiments and use computer equipment.

    (D) all of the above.

4. Which sentence best conveys the main point of the passage?

    (A) 1

    (B) 2

    (C) 4

    (D) 5

5. The tone of this passage can be described as

    (A) impassioned.

    (B) accusatory.

    (C) matter of fact.

    (D) sour.

Use the following passage to answer questions 6–7:

Animals are often classified by the type of food they eat. Most people are familiar with the two main types of this classification system: carnivores and herbivores. Carnivores are animals that eat only the flesh of other animals. Herbivores are plant eaters or vegetarians. They do not consume meat at all. What many people are not aware of is the third class, named omnivores. The name comes from the roots *omni*, which means "all" or "all-encompassing," and *vore*, which means "to devour." In short, omnivores eat both meat and plants to provide for their bodies.

6. According to the passage, humans can generally be classified as ·

   (A) carnivores.
   (B) herbivores.
   (C) omnivores.
   (D) semivores.

7. The root *herb* most likely means

   (A) having to do with plants.
   (B) having to do with meat.
   (C) having to do with men.
   (D) having to do with speaking.

Use the following passage to answer questions 8–10:

My class is so excited to be going to their first Broadway show. Even though we all live within comfortable proximity to New York City, many of us are too encumbered by our daily responsibilities to take the time to add cultural enrichment into our lives. It's easier and less of a drain on your time and money to consume television and internet media versus having to purchase tickets to art exhibits, concerts, or plays.

Also, the amount of time you have to schedule is considerable when you take into account covering the distance between your house and the venue, any transportation delays that may happen along the way, and the time you will actually spend enjoying the experience once you get to your destination. Even though these obstacles may prevent some from taking advantage of the wealth of cultural experience New York City has to offer, making the time to do so is always rewarding.

8. According to the passage, one of the reasons more people in the New York City area don't seek out cultural enrichment more is

   (A) lack of transportation.
   (B) demands on time and money.
   (C) lack of interest in the arts.
   (D) increases in interesting television programming.

9. The author would most likely agree with

   (A) a union strike that causes plays in New York City to have to be cancelled.
   (B) increases in ticket prices to Broadway shows.
   (C) a board of education proposal to set aside funding for an annual trip to the Museum of Modern Art for high school juniors.
   (D) a class about how to read and navigate a trip using maps.

10. The author's purpose is to

  (A) examine obstacles people experience in accessing cultural experience and encourage them to overcome those obstacles.
  (B) dissuade moviegoers from seeing the latest action film.
  (C) encourage students to conduct research about cultural activities.
  (D) admonish those who do not include cultural experiences in their lives.

Use the following passage to answer questions 11–13:

We decided to take our trip to Florida rather suddenly. The opportunity to take the family to visit the theme parks in the Orlando area for so little money was one we could not pass up. We have only a week to make all of our preparations. This includes: notifying our jobs that we need a few days off; telling the girls' schools that they will not be in class and arranging for their assignments in advance; hiring a house sitter that can make sure the mail is taken in and the cats have food and water; and arranging for transportation to and from the airport. We also need to get identification for the girls, as they are too young to have driver's licenses and we didn't have enough time to apply for passports. Their birth certificates will have to do, though I'm not sure where they are right now.

11. The trip the author is talking about is

  (A) unexpected.
  (B) unwelcome.
  (C) inconvenient.
  (D) unfavorable.

12. What type of identification will the author use for her children?

  (A) student IDs
  (B) driver's licenses
  (C) passports
  (D) birth certificates

13. The author's tone is

  (A) upset.
  (B) relaxed.
  (C) hurried.
  (D) defiant.

Use the following passage to answer questions 14–15:

Listening is a skill that needs to be developed and is not simply innate to human beings. There is a big difference between physically hearing what is going on around you and understanding and processing that information. Internal and external forces, such as preoccupied thoughts and background noises, can command more of our attention than we realize. The result is that we do not actively listen to the messages around us, and much of the information presented to us does not add to our consciousness or intellect.

14. Based on information from the passage, one way to listen better would be to

    (A) conduct conversations in loud areas.
    (B) decrease the amount of background noise when conversing with someone.
    (C) concentrate on past experiences instead of on what's being said.
    (D) think about upcoming events.

15. In the passage, the word <u>innate</u> most nearly means

    (A) inborn.
    (B) acquired.
    (C) blessed.
    (D) opportune.

Mathematics Knowledge

Time: 24 Minutes

Questions: 25

Directions: This section tests your knowledge of basic mathematics, algebra, and geometry. Carefully read each question and choose the answer choice that reflects the best answer.

1. If $x = 8$ and $y = 2$, then $y^3 + 2x - (x^2 + 11) =$

   (A) 60
   (B) 23
   (C) −51
   (D) 51

2. $\sqrt{144} =$

   (A) 11
   (B) 12
   (C) 14
   (D) 20

3. $(6x + 2)(2x - 4) =$

   (A) 12x2 + (−20x) + (−8)
   (B) 12x2 + (−28x) + (−8)
   (C) 12x2 + (−28x) + 8
   (D) 12x2 + (−28x) + (−8)

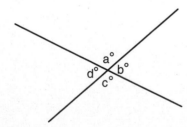

4. If angle $a = 102°$, then angle $d =$

   (A) 32°
   (B) 65°
   (C) 78°
   (D) 102°

5. If $7x - 12 \geq 3x + 8$, then x

   (A) ≥ 5
   (B) ≤ 5
   (C) ≥ 20
   (D) ≤ 20

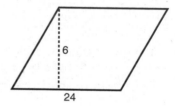

6. The area of this rhombus is:

   (A) 36
   (B) 72
   (C) 144
   (D) 150

7. On line segment AC, point B is located 4 away from points A and C. Point B is the

   (A) midpoint.
   (B) vertex.
   (C) radius.
   (D) ray.

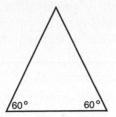

8. What is the value of the third angle in this triangle?

   (A) 36°
   (B) 45°
   (C) 60°
   (D) 90°

9. Factor: $y^2 - 13y + 30$

   (A) $(y - 3)(y - 10)$
   (B) $(y - 6)(y - 12)$
   (C) $(y + 3)(y + 10)$
   (D) $(y + 3)(y - 10)$

10. You're laying carpet in a room that is 12 feet long by 30 feet wide. You have only half the amount of carpet needed to complete the job. How many more square feet of carpet do you need to get?

    (A) 50 ft²
    (B) 80 ft²
    (C) 95 ft²
    (D) 180 ft²

11. If in a right triangle, $a = 5$ and $b = 7$; c equals about

    (A) 8.60
    (B) 12
    (C) 17.2
    (D) 74

12. 22% =

    (A) $\frac{1}{22}$
    (B) $\frac{1}{4}$
    (C) .22
    (D) 2.2

13. A number that stands by itself in an expression or equation is called a(n)

    (A) operation.
    (B) variable.
    (C) coefficient.
    (D) constant.

14. $\frac{9}{11} \div \frac{3}{7} =$

    (A) $\frac{27}{77}$
    (B) $1\frac{10}{11}$
    (C) $\frac{77}{27}$
    (D) $2\frac{23}{27}$

15. In scientific notation, 6,538,900,000 is:

    (A) 6.5389 × 109
    (B) 65.389 × 108
    (C) 653.89 × 107
    (D) 6538.9 × 106

16. $\frac{7}{10}$ is the same as:

    (A) 7 × 10
    (B) 7 ÷ 10
    (C) 7 − 10
    (D) 7 + 10

17. Your office is holding a pool to predict when your boss's baby will be born. There are 20 spots total, and employees can pick only 1 spot. If there are only five spots left and you choose one of them, what is the probability of you winning the pool?

(A) $\frac{1}{2}$

(B) $\frac{1}{5}$

(C) $\frac{1}{20}$

(D) $\frac{2}{20}$

18. 16% of 642 =

(A) 10.272

(B) 102.72

(C) 1027.2

(D) 10,272

19. $\frac{8}{9} + \frac{4}{7} =$

(A) $\frac{2}{3}$

(B) $\frac{3}{8}$

(C) $\frac{12}{16}$

(D) $1\frac{29}{63}$

20. Factor: $y^2 - 9$

(A) $(y - 3)(y - 3)$

(B) $(y + 3)(y + 3)$

(C) $(y - 3)(y + 3)$

(D) $(y - 6)(y + 3)$

21. When multiplying or dividing positive and negative numbers, an even number of negatives will result in

(A) a negative answer.

(B) a positive answer.

(C) a neutral answer.

(D) an unequal answer.

22. Adding the values of all three sides of a triangle will give you its

(A) perimeter.

(B) area.

(C) absolute value.

(D) hypotenuse.

23. A proportion

(A) compares products.

(B) compares two values.

(C) compares sums.

(D) compares ratios.

24. What is the greatest common factor of 42 and 68?

(A) 2

(B) 4

(C) 8

(D) 12

25. If $p = 4$, solve for x: $2x + p^2 - 14 = 0$.

(A) 0

(B) 1

(C) −1

(D) 2

Electronics Information

Time: 9 Minutes

Questions: 20

Directions: This section tests your knowledge of basic electronics principles and applications. Carefully read each question and choose the answer choice that reflects the best answer.

1. What does the letter *I* represent in terms of electricity?

   (A) power
   (B) current
   (C) ampere
   (D) resistance

2. What type of particle is required in the production of electricity?

   (A) proton
   (B) neutron
   (C) electron
   (D) diode

3. Electricity always takes the _____ path to the ground.

   (A) least resistant
   (B) longest
   (C) lowest
   (D) most circuitous

4. Why do household wires require insulators?

   (A) because cold electrons move too slowly
   (B) because exposed wires release dangerous gases into the air
   (C) because insulators allow people to handle wires without getting shocked
   (D) all of the above

5. Which of the following appliances would require the most current?

   (A) nightlight
   (B) 100-watt lightbulb
   (C) hair dryer
   (D) none of the above—current is the same for every appliance

Use this diagram for questions 6–7.

6. What does the previous symbol represent?

   (A) diode
   (B) capacitor
   (C) transformer
   (D) a sequence of resistors in a circuit

7. More specifically, the diagram depicts what kind of circuit?

   (A) series
   (B) parallel
   (C) standard
   (D) open

8. This electronic device is used to prevent a circuit from suffering damage due to too much current:

   (A) resistor
   (B) transformer
   (C) switch
   (D) fuse

9. This symbol can be compared to a road sign that is used to direct traffic down one-way streets.

   (A)

   (B)

   (C)

   (D)

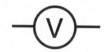

Use the diagram to answer questions 10–11.

10. What does the previous diagram illustrate?

    (A) voltage
    (B) voltmeter
    (C) amperes
    (D) vertical current

11. What is the purpose of the electronic element depicted in the diagram?

    (A) to demonstrate the amount of force an electrical source applies
    (B) to measure voltage
    (C) to determine how much current is flowing through the circuit
    (D) to determine the direction of current flow

12. The acronym *LED* stands for

    (A) lamp-ending diagram.
    (B) light-energy direction.
    (C) light-emitting diode.
    (D) load-electricity diagram.

13. What material typically is used to make a diode?

    (A) silicon
    (B) copper
    (C) rubber
    (D) machined steel

14. Which of the following symbols represents a component that turns electrical energy into kinetic energy?

    (A) —(M)—

    (B) —⊗—

    (C) ▽

    (D) ⌇

15. Which of the following is an example of a load?

    (A) electrons
    (B) copper
    (C) lightbulb
    (D) current

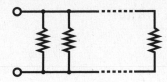

16. The previous diagram illustrates which of the following?

    (A) resistors in a parallel circuit
    (B) series circuit
    (C) diode
    (D) transformer

17. Ohm's law states that electric current is directly proportional to _____.

    (A) resistance
    (B) voltage
    (C) amperes
    (D) watts

18. Which of the following is NOT a factor pertaining to the amount of resistance in a wire?

    (A) gauge
    (B) length
    (C) composition
    (D) color

19. If you have 20 volts and 5 amps, how much resistance do you have?

    (A) 100 ohms
    (B) 4 ohms
    (C) 25 ohms
    (D) not enough information

20. If you have 10 ohms of resistance and 2 amps of current, how much voltage do you have?

    (A) 5 volts
    (B) 8 volts
    (C) 6 volts
    (D) 20 volts

Automotive and Shop Information

Time: 11 Minutes

Questions: 25

Directions: This section tests your knowledge of automotive components and principles, as well as general shop tools and applications. Carefully read each question and choose the answer choice that reflects the best answer.

1. Which system makes the light and power systems work?

    (A) exhaust system
    (B) electrical system
    (C) fuel system
    (D) suspension system

2. Which system deals with the movement of the wheels and the manner in which cars react to terrain?

    (A) exhaust system
    (B) electrical system
    (C) fuel system
    (D) suspension system

3. When the engine receives a full cylinder of gas and air, this is known as which stroke in the four-stroke cycle?

    (A) intake
    (B) compression
    (C) power
    (D) exhaust

4. Brake pistons move under what type of pressure?

    (A) air
    (B) hydraulic
    (C) heat
    (D) mechanical

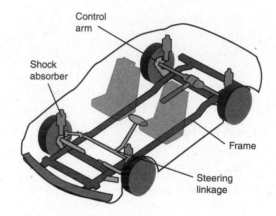

Use this diagram to answer questions 5–7.

5. Which part of the diagram helps smooth the jolting of a bumpy road?

    (A) control arm
    (B) frame
    (C) shock absorber
    (D) steering linkage

6. Which part shown in the diagram can pivot in two places to handle wheel activity?

    (A) control arm
    (B) frame
    (C) shock absorber
    (D) steering linkage

7. Which part shown in the diagram has a series of arms, rods, and ball sockets that allow the wheels to swivel as needed?

   (A) control arm
   (B) frame
   (C) shock absorber
   (D) steering linkage

8. The amount of force that enables a rotating motion is called

   (A) resistance.
   (B) torque.
   (C) shifting.
   (D) combustion.

9. How many coils are found in a typical coil pack for a six-cylinder engine with a distributorless ignition system?

   (A) 3
   (B) 4
   (C) 5
   (D) 6

10. Once your car is running, how does the battery get recharged?

    (A) Energy from the spark plugs is transferred to the battery.
    (B) The solenoid sends electric current to the battery.
    (C) The alternator recharges it.
    (D) The voltage regulator monitors and recharges the battery.

11. Which part of the car's battery stores energy?

    (A) positive post
    (B) negative post
    (C) lead plates
    (D) battery cables

12. Where are fuse boxes generally located in a car?

    (A) near the bottom of the dashboard or under the hood
    (B) near the top of the dashboard or under the driver's seat
    (C) in the trunk or in the driver's door panel
    (D) none of the above

13. Which of the following is NOT true of diesel fuel?

    (A) It vaporizes at a higher temperature than gasoline.
    (B) It gets better gas mileage than gasoline.
    (C) It is denser than gasoline.
    (D) It burns less efficiently than gasoline.

14. In newer cars, fuel pumps tend to be mounted where?

    (A) alongside the fuel filter
    (B) on top of the fuel injector
    (C) inside the fuel tank
    (D) wherever there is space

15. Which of the following is NOT a key function of the exhaust system?

    (A) reduce engine noise
    (B) maintain performance
    (C) reduce or eliminate harmful emissions
    (D) absorb road bumps

16. Which tool is often used in creating pockets for door hinges?

    (A) cold chisel
    (B) file
    (C) wood chisel
    (D) rasp

17. Which type of saw generally has alternating cutting edges on the blade and cuts wood against the grain?

    (A) hack saw
    (B) crosscut saw
    (C) miter saw
    (D) circular saw

18. Which type of hammer is best used when a steel-headed tool could damage the material being hammered into?

    (A) curved claw
    (B) rubber mallet
    (C) ball-peen
    (D) sledge hammer

19. Which part of a hand drill turns the main shaft?

    (A) cranking handle
    (B) cranking chuck
    (C) cranking bit
    (D) cranking miter

20. If you want a screw to lie flush with a piece of wood, which type of drill bit should you use for your project?

    (A) carbide-tipped masonry bit
    (B) spade bit
    (C) countersink
    (D) auger

21. A pipe wrench is actually a form of what other kind of wrench?

    (A) open end
    (B) combination end
    (C) adjustable end
    (D) all of the above

22. An Allen wrench is

    (A) V-shaped.
    (B) L-shaped.
    (C) T-shaped.
    (D) I-shaped.

23. This tool is also known as a ratchet and is used to tighten different-sized nuts and bolts:

    (A) hand screw
    (B) Phillips head screwdriver
    (C) monkey wrench
    (D) socket wrench

24. Which tool is used to stop leaks and features a metallic strap or band?

    (A) bar clamp
    (B) pipe clamp
    (C) vise grip
    (D) band clamp

25. A jackhammer can be categorized as what type of drill?

    (A) drill press
    (B) hammer drill
    (C) claw drill
    (D) circular drill

Mechanical Comprehension

Time: 19 Minutes

Questions: 25

Directions: This section tests your knowledge and application of basic mechanical principles. Carefully read each question and choose the answer choice that reflects the best answer.

1. Which of the following types of energy is NOT found in a rubber band?

   (A) potential energy
   (B) kinetic energy
   (C) elastic energy
   (D) electromagnetic energy

2. Suppose you have an object whose mass is 20 kilograms and is located 2 meters above Earth. What is the object's gravitational potential energy?

   (A) 40 joules
   (B) 98 joules
   (C) 200 joules
   (D) 392 joules

3. *Matter* is

   (A) energy of motion.
   (B) how fast an object is moving.
   (C) speed, plus the direction of motion.
   (D) anything that occupies space and has mass.

4. You have an object whose gravitational potential energy equals 6,272 joules, and the mass equals 64 kilograms. What is the height above Earth's surface?

   (A) 9.8 meters
   (B) 10 meters
   (C) 98 meters
   (D) 1,000 meters

5. How can you determine the ratio of the gears?

   (A) measure the width of each gear
   (B) measure the circumference of each gear
   (C) count the teeth and multiply them together
   (D) count the teeth and divide the larger number by the smaller number

6. When Sergeant Bob does push-ups, the force of his hands against the ground results in equal pressure from the ground against his hands. This is known as what law?

   (A) the law of reciprocal action
   (B) the law of reaction
   (C) the law of reverse inertia
   (D) the law of resistance

7. Suppose it takes you 800 joules of work to move a distance of 50 meters against a force. If you cut your distance in half, what happens to your workload?

   (A) It stays the same.
   (B) It doubles.
   (C) It gets halved.
   (D) No way to tell.

8. If instead you double the force you are acting against, what happens to your workload?

   (A) It stays the same.
   (B) It doubles.
   (C) It gets halved.
   (D) No way to tell.

9. If instead you double the force you are carrying *and* cut the distance in half, what happens to your workload?

   (A) It stays the same.
   (B) It doubles.
   (C) It gets halved.
   (D) No way to tell.

10. When you lean against the countertop in your kitchen, the countertop also pushes against you. Which one of Newton's laws does this concept apply to?

    (A) first
    (B) second
    (C) third
    (D) all three

11. If the gear in the middle of the previous diagram causes the other gears to turn in opposite directions, it is a

    (A) compound gear.
    (B) fixed gear.
    (C) moveable gear.
    (D) driving gear.

12. An object is in mechanical equilibrium

    (A) when it simplifies the workload.
    (B) when it undergoes Newton's third law.
    (C) when its acceleration and velocity are equal.
    (D) when there is no acceleration.

13. Suppose you have a 70-kilogram object that needs to be lifted 15 meters. In a basic two-wheeled pulley system, how much weight does it feel like you're lifting?

    (A) 35 kilograms
    (B) 55 kilograms
    (C) 70 kilograms
    (D) 140 kilograms

14. Suppose you have a 20-kilogram object that needs to be lifted 40 meters. In a basic four-wheeled pulley system, how far do you have to pull the rope?

(A) 20 meters
(B) 60 meters
(C) 80 meters
(D) 160 meters

15. What is a force-distance trade-off?

(A) the definition of simple machines
(B) the concept behind building simple machines
(C) when an object feels lighter, but you are forced to pull the rope farther to raise it the original distance
(D) when an object becomes lighter through the addition of pulleys but the pulleys are placed farther away from the object

16. How much force is needed to exert 15 pounds per square inch of pressure on a 25 in² metal panel?

(A) 225 pounds
(B) 350 pounds
(C) 375 pounds
(D) 400 pounds

17. When gears reduce the speed of machinery, this is known as

(A) simple mechanics.
(B) gear reduction.
(C) gear advantage.
(D) speed reduction.

18. When two objects with different masses freefall, why might they theoretically fall at the same speed?

(A) The object with the smaller mass also has proportionately more force acting on it.
(B) Gravitational pull causes everything to fall at the same speed when there is no air resistance.
(C) The law of acceleration causes all objects to accelerate at the same rate.
(D) Wind resistance and air friction would have an equalizing effect on the two objects.

19. Suppose you are in a car race. When the race begins, you increase your speed from 0 kilometers per hour to 120 kilometers per hour over the course of 10 seconds. What is your rate of acceleration?

(A) 3 m/s2
(B) 4 m/s2
(C) 5 m/s2
(D) 10 m/s2

20. If you are traveling at a speed of 30 miles per hour, what is the distance you cover in one minute?

(A) 2 miles
(B) 30 miles
(C) $\frac{1}{2}$ mile
(D) 1 mile

21. Consider the following figures. An object has a mass of 50 kilograms, acceleration of 8 kilometers per second², and a speed of 20 kilometers per hour. Using the relevant figures, calculate the amount of force needed to set this object in motion.

   (A) 400
   (B) 160
   (C) 800
   (D) 20

22. What does mass measure?

   (A) the gravitational force exerted on an object
   (B) the amount of material in an object
   (C) the density of cells in an object
   (D) the volume of an object

23. What kind of movement constitutes motion?

   (A) movement of mass
   (B) movement measured by Newtons
   (C) kinetic energy
   (D) any kind

24. Kinetic energy is energy that has been converted from another kind of energy. Which of the following does NOT convert to kinetic energy?

   (A) chemical
   (B) potential
   (C) negative acceleration
   (D) all of the above

25. Potential energy exists in

   (A) any object that exists in a force field.
   (B) any object that has kinetic energy.
   (C) any object that can retain its original shape, even after being rearranged.
   (D) any object.

Assembling Objects

Time: 15 Minutes

Questions: 25

Directions: This section tests your ability to visualize how objects fit together. Carefully read each question and choose the answer choice that reflects the best answer.

1. In the following diagram, which figure best shows how the objects in the first box would touch if points A and B were connected?

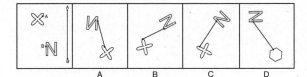

2. Which answer choice best shows how the objects in the first box would appear if they were fitted together?

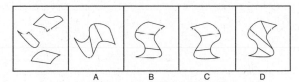

3. In the following diagram, which figure best shows how the objects in the first box would touch if points A and B were connected?

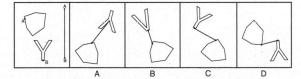

4. Which answer choice best shows how the objects in the first box would appear if they were fitted together?

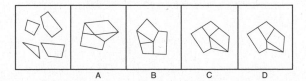

5. In the following diagram, which figure best shows how the objects in the first box would touch if points A and B were connected?

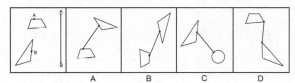

6. Which answer choice best shows how the objects in the first box would appear if they were fitted together?

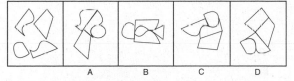

7. In the following diagram, which figure best shows how the objects in the first box would touch if points A and B were connected?

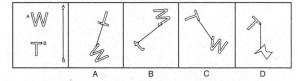

8. Which answer choice best shows how the objects in the first box would appear if they were fitted together?

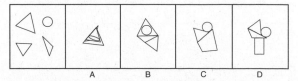

9. In the following diagram, which figure best shows how the objects in the first box would touch if points A and B were connected?

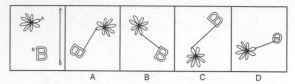

10. Which answer choice best shows how the objects in the first box would appear if they were fitted together?

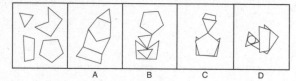

11. In the following diagram, which figure best shows how the objects in the first box would touch if points A and B were connected?

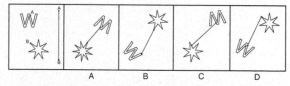

12. Which answer choice best shows how the objects in the first box would appear if they were fitted together?

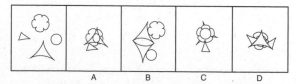

13. In the following diagram, which figure best shows how the objects in the first box would touch if points A and B were connected?

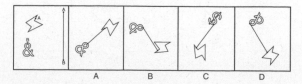

14. Which answer choice best shows how the objects in the first box would appear if they were fitted together?

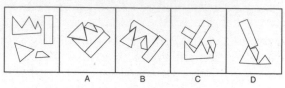

15. In the following diagram, which figure best shows how the objects in the first box would touch if points A and B were connected?

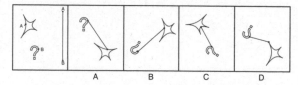

16. Which answer choice best shows how the objects in the first box would appear if they were fitted together?

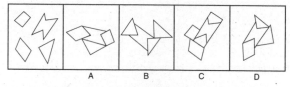

17. In the following diagram, which figure best shows how the objects in the first box would touch if points A and B were connected?

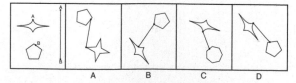

18. Which answer choice best shows how the objects in the first box would appear if they were fitted together?

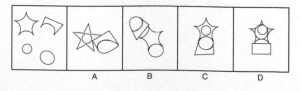

19. In the following diagram, which figure best shows how the objects in the first box would touch if points A and B were connected?

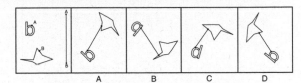

20. Which answer choice best shows how the objects in the first box would appear if they were fitted together?

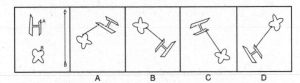

21. In the following diagram, which figure best shows how the objects in the first box would touch if points A and B were connected?

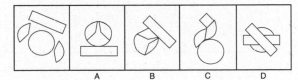

22. Which answer choice best shows how the objects in the first box would appear if they were fitted together?

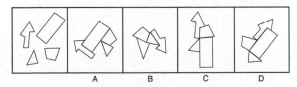

23. In the following diagram, which figure best shows how the objects in the first box would touch if points A and B were connected?

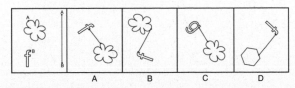

24. Which answer choice best shows how the objects in the first box would appear if they were fitted together?

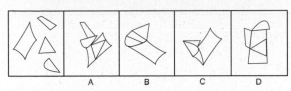

25. In the following diagram, which figure best shows how the objects in the first box would touch if points A and B were connected?

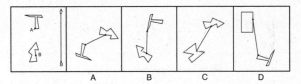

Practice Test 2: Answers and Explanations

General Science

1. **A.** Choice B is wrong because ecology is the study of the environment. Choice C is wrong because zoology is the study of animals. Choice D is wrong because chemistry is the study of matter.

2. **C.** Choice A is wrong because cell theory states that all living organisms are made up of cells. Choice B is wrong because gene theory states that traits get passed on from generation to generation through genes. Choice D is wrong because homeostasis theory addresses an animal's ability to maintain a constant internal temperature.

3. **B.** All the other choices are correct statements regarding thermodynamics theory.

4. **A.** Archaea is a domain, along with Eukarya and Bacteria.

5. **B.** All the other choices were false statements.

6. **A.** None of the other choices have the correct photosynthesis formula.

7. **C.** During photosynthesis, plants convert carbon dioxide, water, and sunlight to sugar and oxygen.

8. **D.** An umbra is the main shadow that is seen during an eclipse that completely covers the sun or moon. A penumbra is a much lighter, outer shadow that only covers part of the sun or moon. A corona is the upper atmosphere of the sun that is visible during a solar eclipse, as the moon blocks all but the outer edges of the sun during a total solar eclipse.

9. **C.** Force is any influence that can cause a change in the velocity of an object. Energy is the amount of work a force can produce. Work is the transfer of energy through force over a distance. Friction is two objects rubbing against one another, sometimes resulting in a force that holds back movement of a sliding object.

10. **D.** Choice A is wrong because ribosomes contain RNA units to build proteins. Choice B is wrong because golgi allow newly made proteins to mature and become functional. Choice C is wrong because mitochondria convert nutrients into energy.

11. **B.** Mitosis is the process of cell division in which each cell completely divides and has its own nucleus. Meiosis is the process of cell division used in sexual reproduction.

12. **C.** All cells undergo mitosis except those involved with sexual reproduction. Hair, muscle, nail, and skin cells all undergo mitosis as they grow and replace old cells.

13. **B.** Choice A is wrong because nucleotides play an important role in metabolism. Choice C is wrong because metabolism is a set of chemical reactions that allows organisms to grow, reproduce, maintain structure, and respond to the environment. Choice D is wrong because amino acids also play a role in metabolism.

14. **C.** A sun is a star around which planets and other celestial objects move. A binary star is two stars orbiting each other that look like one star. A constellation is a grouping of stars named by astronomers.

15. **C.** Choice A is wrong because the respiratory system includes the mouth, nose, trachea, lungs, and diaphragm. Choice B is wrong because the digestive system includes the mouth, throat, esophagus, stomach, liver, gall bladder, and the like. Choice D is wrong because the excretory system includes the kidneys, liver, lungs, and skin.

16. **D.** Choice A is wrong because it describes the large intestine. Choice B is wrong because it describes the diaphragm. Choice C is wrong because it describes the lungs.

17. **B.** Choice A is wrong because while fats do provide us with energy, most dietary energy comes from carbohydrates. Choice C is wrong because the main job of minerals is to assist in normal bodily functions. Choice D is wrong because vitamins play a key role in many chemical processes.

18. **D.** Choice A is wrong because the main function of protein is to assist in growth and muscle repair. Choice B is also wrong—see the explanation about fats in the preceding answer. Choice C is wrong because fiber is the fibrous indigestible portion of our diet, essential to the health of the digestive system.

19. **C.** See previous answer explanations for additional information on choices A, B, and D.

20. **A.** The crust is closest to the surface of Earth, running about 10 miles deep. The mantle comes next and extends inward approximately 1,800 miles toward the center of Earth. Following the mantle is the outer core, which is nearly 3,000 miles deep. Lastly, the inner core is thought to be approximately 900 miles deep.

21. **A.** Choice B describes liquid molten rock that flows above Earth's surface. Choices C and D do not describe any form of liquid rock.

22. **B.** None of the other choices depict the main elements found in Earth's outer core.

23. **B.** Choice A is wrong because a warm front occurs when an advancing mass of *warm* air rises over a mass of cold air. Choice C is wrong because temperature is a degree of hotness or coldness in the environment. Choice D is wrong because cumulonimbus is a type of cloud.

24. **B.** Na is the chemical symbol for sodium. Cl is the chemical symbol for chlorine.

25. **A.** The word root *bio* means "life," and the prefix *a* means "against" or "opposite." Abiotic conditions include temperature and weather changes, sink holes, volcanic movement, and other nonliving changes that can affect an ecosystem.

Arithmetic Reasoning

1. **D.** John currently pays $245 + $396 = $641 to his employees each week. If he increases this by 6% (641 × .06 = 38.46), he will have to allocate $38.46 more per week to pay his employees. Multiply this by 4 and you will find how much more he has to pay per period: $38.46 × 4 = $153.84.

2. **A.** Since there are 52 weeks in a year, multiply 52 × 4 to find that Mr. X will have been on 208 dates over the course of a year.

3. **C.** Divide 32,890 by 52 to figure out Jon's weekly salary: $632.50. Now subtract to get 87.

4. **A.** According to the question, 150 out of 750 books are romances. This is a ratio of $\frac{150}{750}$, which reduces to $\frac{1}{5}$, which is also the fraction form of 20%.

5. **B.** Multiply 15,625.35 by .07 to figure out how much more you made the second half of the year: 15,625.35 × .07 = 1,093.77. Now multiply 15,625.35 × 2 to find your regular annual earnings: $31,250.7. Finally, add 1,093.77 to this amount to find you've made $32,344.47 for the year.

6. **D.** Your ratio of peaches to apples is 125:85, which reduces to 25:17.

7. **C.** Divide 32 by 128. The answer is 25%.

8. **D.** Figure out how much Bailey will have to pay for both the children and the adults:

   Adults: 5.25 × 2 = 10.50

   Children: 3.75 × 3 = 11.25

   Now add the products. Admission for all five people will cost $21.75.

9. **A.** Use the Distance = Rate × Time formula here:

   $87 = 13 \times t$

   $\frac{87}{13} = t$

   $6\frac{9}{13} = t$

10. **B.** Translate this into an expression: $-12 + -13$. When you add two negatives, you go down the number line, so add the two numbers and place a negative in front of your answer: $12 + 13 = -25$.

11. **D.** Calculate 32% of 67: .32 × 67 = 21.44.

    Now subtract this amount from 67: 67 − 21.44 = 45.56

    Round up because your tenths decimal is 5 or higher. April is about 46 years old.

12. **C.** When you have a list of sequential numbers multiplied in order from greatest to least, you have a factorial.

13. **A.** Divide .35 by 14.95 and then multiply by 100 to get 2.34%.

14. **D.** Set up a proportion here based on your garden's dimensions and those of your neighbor's. Use a variable to stand in for the unknown quantity: $\frac{4}{6} = \frac{9}{x}$. Now cross multiply to solve

for x:

$6 \times 9 = 4x$

$54 = 4x$

$\frac{54}{4} = x$

$13.5 = x$

15. **B.** Calculate the percentage of every dollar that goes to charity by dividing 0.75 by 2. This leaves you with 0.375. Now multiply that amount by $138: $138 \times .375 - \$51.75$.

16. **A.** Since parentheses come first in order of operations, you should look for those. The only expression in parentheses is inside the brackets. Brackets are a step up from parentheses, so you would look there first anyway. So it's logical that among the expressions within the brackets, you would solve ($3^2 - 3$) first. Exponents are second, so ($3^2 - 3$)^4 is not correct. Answer D, [$2 \times 4 + (3^2 - 3)^4$], is also not correct because you would not solve the whole expression first, but one smaller part.

17. **C.** Multiply 622×4 to find out how much she makes per month ($2,488). Next, multiply this amount by .12: $2,488 \times .12 = \$298.56$. Now subtract this amount from $2,488: $2,488 - \$298.56 - \$2,189.44$. This is how much Jordan has to spend on other expenses.

18. **B.** Start your calculation with a proportion: $\frac{4}{1} = \frac{32}{x}$. Now cross multiply and solve for x:

$32 \times 1 = 4x$

$\frac{32}{4} = x$

$8 = x$

This tells us that Tim has eight cards.

19. **C.** Divide 10.75 by 4 to find out that one load costs $2.6875.

Now divide $23.63 by this amount to get 8.79. Since this number is not nine full loads, you have to round down to eight, because you need to find the number of entire loads the amount will pay for. You'll have change left over, but eight loads in the wash.

20. **A.** Add all the numbers to get 42,824.

Now divide that number by 3 to get this: $42,824 \div 3 = 14,274.67$

21. **B.** Translate this into two fractions:

$\frac{4}{6} + \frac{2}{8}$

Multiply each fraction by the opposite denominator to get a common denominator:

$\frac{4}{6} \times \frac{8}{8} = \frac{32}{48}$

$\frac{2}{8} \times \frac{6}{6} = \frac{12}{48}$

Finally, add these two new fractions together and reduce: $\frac{32}{48} + \frac{12}{48} = \frac{44}{48} = \frac{11}{12}$

22. **D.** Including Barry, 15 people are scheduled to go on the trip. The total number of seats available are $4 + 4 + 5 + 5 + 3 = 21$. Subtract $21 - 15 = 6$. He needs six more people to fill all the cars.

23. **C.** If you take two bags at a time, you can move 26 bags in 13 trips. You will have to make one more to get the remaining bag, so your total is 14 trips.

24. **D.** Divide 15 by 35 (the number of push-ups the competitor can complete) to find that Snuffy's competitor would need to increase his numbers by 42.8% to catch up to Snuffy. Round this up to 43 and you have your answer.

25. **C.** Subtract 263 – 235 = 28. Now multiply each of the answer choices by 235. The one that equals 28 is the correct answer:

    $235 \times .02 = 4.7$

    $235 \times .06 = 14.1$

    $235 \times .12 = 28.2$

    $235 \times .21 = 49.35$

    Answer C is the best choice.

26. **D.** This is an extended way of writing 2^5.

27. **C.** $13 \times 13 = 169$

28. **B.** Start with a proportion to show the ratio of the odds and how much money is bet:

    $\frac{9}{1} = \frac{x}{75}$.

    Now cross multiply and solve for *x:*

    $9 \times 75 = x$

    $675 = x$

29. **B.** Divide 29 by 4 to get 7.25. Round this down, since it's below half. The best answer is B.

30. **A.** The main number or variable in a term is called the *base*, while the raised number is the exponent. In this question, the only place this is applicable is with the term 7^6. Clearly, 7 is the base and 6 is the exponent.

Word Knowledge

1. **C.** *Conceited* means "to be full of one-self." Answer A is the opposite of this. Answer B describes honorable moral character. Answer D describes something that makes a lot of sound.

2. **B.** *Surmount* means "to overcome." Add the prefix *in,* and the meaning changes to "unable to overcome." Answer A is the opposite of this meaning. The other two answer choices don't make sense.

3. **A.** *Extraordinary* is something that's special or unexpected. Answer B is the opposite of this meaning. *Morose* and *melancholy* are similar in that they both refer to something that's gloomy, sad, or depressing.

4. **D.** *Open* has several definitions. From the answer choices, it's clear that you're looking for the adjective form, which means "accepting."

5. **C.** Something that is *intricate* artfully combines many things to make a whole. *Frigid* means "cold." *Optimal* means "the best." *Dispassionate* means "without strong emotion." *Complex* is the best choice.

6. **A.** The prefix *ante,* which means "before," tells you that there is some kind of time connection. The only answer choice that has any connection to time is A, which is the main definition of the word.

7. **B.** *Profuse* means "generous" or "wide-spread." None of the other answers make sense with this definition.

8. **D.** You can infer from the sentence that the "kind offer" was most likely out of concern for the aggrieved daughter. The other answer choices don't make sense in this context.

9. **C.** *Forbearance* describes restraint or grace under pressure, which the lawyer in the sentence is known for having, according to the context clues. Even if you didn't know this, if you swapped out the underlined word with any of the other answer choices, they wouldn't have made sense in this context.

10. **A.** A good association here is "His regal, royal majesty." Each of these words means the same thing: noble, ceremonial, imperial, and so on.

11. **C.** *Insipid* means "dull" or "uninteresting." *Trite* means "overused" or "clichéd." The other answer choices have nothing to do with either, which makes answer C the best choice.

12. **B.** Break down this word into smaller parts. *Sight* obviously means "to see." The prefix *fore* means "coming before." With this as a working definition, answer B makes the most sense, since it talks about instinct and knowledge.
Affluence is a state of wealth and power. A *contagion* is something that spreads disease (think contagious). *Influence* is having the ability to affect something.

13. **C.** How is *frequent* being used here? Is it an adjective or a verb? The fact that the answer choices are all adjectives tells us we're dealing with the definition of frequent that means doing something "often." *Obstructive* is "getting in the way." *Censorious* is "critical." Blatant is "obvious."

14. **A.** The sentence talks about someone who believes against the odds. The mayor is determined to keep hope alive. *Steadfast* means to stay firm in a belief. Answer B and D don't make sense with the context clues in the sentence, which tell us the underlined word would mean the opposite of what the beginning of the sentence implies. Answer D just doesn't make sense.

15. **B.** Logic (and history) tells us that a lengthy war drains resources. It would not *infuse* (increase), *sustain* (keep steady), or *marginalize* (keep out of the center of attention) money or manpower.

16. **D.** *Ubiquitous* means "all around." *Somniferous* is something that causes sleep (the root *som* means "sleep"). *Omnipotent* means "all powerful." *Omniscient* means "all knowing." *Omnipresent* means "all encompassing."

17. **C.** The context clues tell us the thief is being deceitful or dishonest. *Demented* means "irrational," which could apply in this context. However, there is no indication about the thief's intent other than to cheat his partner. *Disavowed* is to deny association or knowledge of something, which clearly doesn't fit in this case.

18. **A.** *Capitulate* means "to agree" or "to surrender." To *waver* is to go back and forth, and to *intrude* is to interrupt, neither of which makes sense.

19. **C.** The context clue, "like a native," tells us that the student's situation has changed and that though she felt foreign at the beginning of the sentence, by the end she fits in much better. *Blend* is the only answer choice that works with this meaning.

20. **D.** The root *bene* means "good," so the correct answer will have something to do with being good or having attributes considered to be good. *Inferior* means "less than." *Egotistic* means "concerned with the self." *Blinded* means "unable to see." *Giving* is the best choice, since this is generally considered a "good" attribute.

21. **B.** *Long, lanky,* and *gangly* are often used interchangeably when describing someone who is very tall and thin. They all have negative connotations to them. All of the other words describe sizes that oppose long and thin.

22. **A.** If you read Franz Kafka's *Metamorphosis* (about a man who turns into a bug) or remember grade school science class lessons about caterpillars turning into butterflies, you know answer A is the best choice. *Incantation* is a spell. *Inclination* is a desire. *Excitation* is something that creates excitement.

23. **D.** When you're *obligated* to do something, you're responsible for seeing it done. This *compels* (drives) you to do it. *Exists* means "to be." *Deceive* means "to trick." *Appreciate* means "to value."

24. **C.** *Enrich* means "to enhance." Even if you didn't know that *augment* means "to change or enhance," you could eliminate every other answer choice.

25. **B.** To *indoctrinate* is to teach someone about a belief or ideology. *Force* and *believe* don't fit here. To *incite* means to start something. Any way you look at it, answer B is the only choice that has anything to do with teaching, and it is your best choice.

26. **C.** Leaders need to be strong, and the sentence describes Jane as being inspirational and optimistic. The correct answer will have something to do with this. The only answer that comes close is C. (*Sanguine* has several definitions, and "confident" is one of them.)

27. **A.** Mysteries are mystifying because they cause confusion and puzzle people's minds. *Perplex* means "to confuse." *Clarify* means "to make clear." To *deify* is to make something a god or godlike. To *stupefy* is to astonish or amaze, not necessarily to confuse.

28. **B.** In the sentence, we see that the *p* and *b* in the sentence have been switched, or *transposed*.

29. **D.** Bait has many definitions. In this case, *bait* means "to tease or harass," since none of the other words are related to any other definition of bait (a lure, to lure, an attack by a dog, and so on).

30. **A.** Anyone who has had their mouth numbed in the dentist's chair knows that the anesthetic impairs one's ability to speak. Using context clues, you can figure out that to *garble* is to make something unintelligible or all messed up. *Jumble* means "to mix up." *Plait* means "to braid." *Berate* means "to scold."

31. **C.** To *belie* is to give a false impression or contradict the truth.

32. **B.** A good mnemonic to make here is "Intoxication goes right to your head." *Heady* means "intoxicating" or "exhilarating." The only word you might have trouble with in this question is *delusory*, which means "deceptive." It's a form of *delusion* and does not fit.

33. **A.** The sentence is clearly telling us that *fortify* means "to strengthen," since the speaker's goal is not to get sick. The other choices don't make sense in the sentence.

34. **C.** The root *dict* means "to speak," so the correct answer will have to do with speaking. *Utter* is another word for "speak." Answers A and B are adjectives, which means they can't be right, since *dictate* is a verb. Answer D has nothing to do with speaking.

35. **D.** The base word here is *grace,* which means the correct answer will have something to do with elegance or politeness. *Tangible* means "able to be touched." *Raucous* means "loud." To be *tactless* is to be unconcerned with how one's actions impacts others. *Congenial* means "friendly" or "pleasant." Out of all of these choices, D is your best bet.

Paragraph Comprehension

1. **D.** Sentence 2 lists Burundi, Democratic Republic of Congo, Egypt, Eritrea, Ethiopia, Kenya, Rwanda, South Sudan, Sudan, Tanzania, and Uganda as the countries the Nile runs through.

2. **A.** The main point of the passage is best described in sentence 1: "The Nile River is an important source of water in Africa." The rest of the passage backs up this statement with specific examples and details.

3. **D.** From the information in the passage about the inhospitable living conditions, lack of power, and lack of sunlight, all the answer choices would be issues a research team planning to study in Antarctica would face.

4. **B.** Sentence 2 says, "Though the benefits of having such a vast land that has not had much interference from human inhabitants are great, the extreme climate makes long-term study a challenge." The majority of the passage supports this statement, making it the main idea.

5. **C.** The speaker's tone really doesn't convey any emotion, which makes C the best choice.

6. **C.** Even if they choose to be vegetarians or vegans, humans are omnivores, categorically, since we eat both meat and plants in our diets.

7. **A.** You can infer from the passage that *herb* has to do with plants, since it's part of the word defined as "plant-eater."

8. **B.** The passage states that "many of us are too encumbered by our daily responsibilities to take the time to add cultural enrichment into our lives." Specifically, it discusses demands on time and money as barriers to cultural enrichment. The other answer choices aren't supported by information from the passage.

9. **C.** From the author's tone, you can infer that he or she would support any effort that would enable people to enjoy culture more easily or frequently. Answer C is the only one that would accomplish this.

10. **A.** Answer A is directly supported by the final sentence in the passage: "Even though these obstacles may prevent some from taking advantage of the wealth of cultural experience New York City has to offer, making the time to do so is always rewarding."

11. **A.** The only indication we get from the passage that applies to the answer choices is that the trip was last-minute and unexpected.

12. **D.** The last sentence says she will use birth certificates. The passage says she doesn't have passports and the kids are too young for driver's licenses. Student IDs are never mentioned.

13. **C.** Since time is the main issue throughout this paragraph, the author's tone is most likely hurried rather than upset. She is definitely neither relaxed or defiant.

14. **B.** The passage states, "Internal and external forces, such as preoccupied thoughts and background noise, can command more of our attention than we realize." Based on this information, it stands to reason that if you decrease the amount of background noise, you will be able to listen better. All the other answer choices are contradicted by information from the passage.

15. **A.** *Innate* means "at birth." Answer B is contradicted by the context of the sentence in which *innate* is used. Answers C and D just don't make sense.

Mathematics Knowledge

1. **C.** When you plug in the numbers given in the question, you have $2^3 + 2 \times 8 - (8^2 + 11)$. Follow order of operations to solve.

2. **B.** The square root of 144 is 12 because $12 \times 12 = 144$.

3. **A.** Use FOIL here.

   $(6x + 2)(2x - 4) = 12x^2 + (-24x) + 4x + (-8)$

   Now combine like terms.

   $(6x + 2)(2x - 4) = 12x^2 + (-20x) + (-8)$

4. **C.** Looking at the diagram, you can see that the angle is acute, so any answers over 90° are out. This eliminates answer D. Angles a and d are supplementary, which means that the total of their degrees is 180. To solve, subtract 102 from 180, and you'll see that the value of angle d is 78.

5. **A.** Solve this inequality like an equation. Start by moving $3x$ to the left of the ≥ symbol, and −12 to the right.

   $7x - 3x \geq 8 + 12$

   Combine like terms:

   $4x \geq 20$

   Now divide both sides by 4: $\frac{4x}{4} \geq \frac{20}{4}$.

   Because we did not multiply or divide the inequality by a negative number, the symbol stays the same. The final answer is $x \geq 5$.

6. **C.** To calculate the area of a rhombus, we multiply the base times the height. Here it's 24×6, which equals 144.

7. **A.** Because point B is equidistant from the two endpoints, it marks the midpoint.

8. **C.** The two sides on the bottom are 60°, which means the other angle has to be 60° as well. This makes the triangle equilateral.

9. **A.** This is a quadratic expression. You can either FOIL the answer choices or factor the expression: $y^2 - 13y + 30$.

   $(y\ )(y\ )$

   List factors of 30:

   1×30

   2×15

   3×10

   If you add −3 and −10, you get −13, which is the middle term. Multiply them to get the positive 30 term. The final answer is $(y - 3)(y - 10)$.

10. **D.** Calculate the area of the room. Since we know it's a rectangle, multiply the length times the width to get 360 ft². Then divide by half to find the missing amount: 180 ft².

11. **A.** Use the Pythagorean theorem here to solve for the missing value: $a^2 + b^2 = c^2$.

    $(5 \times 5) + (7 \times 7) = c^2$

    $25 + 49 = c^2$

    $74 = c^2$

    $\sqrt{74} = c$

    $8.6 = c$

12. **C.** Another way of writing 22% is .22.

13. **D.** A constant is a number that stands by itself in an expression or equation.

14. **B.** Remember, when you divide fractions, you're really multiplying them. The first fraction stays the same, but you flip the numbers of the second fraction (which is called a *reciprocal*), multiply across, and reduce:

$$\frac{9}{11} \div \frac{3}{7} = \frac{9}{11} \times \frac{7}{3} = \frac{63}{33} = 1\frac{10}{11}$$

15. **A.** With scientific notation, you move the decimal point to the right of the leftmost nonzero digit. With 6538900000, you'd move the decimal 9 places to the left to get 6.538900000. Now drop all the 0s after the 9 to get 6.5389. Finally, multiply this number by 10 to the ninth power (the number of decimal spaces you moved): you then get 6.5389×10^9.

16. **B.** Using a fraction bar to separate terms means division.

17. **C.** This is less complicated than it looks. You are choosing 1 spot out of 20, which makes your chances of winning $\frac{1}{20}$. Whoever else has chosen does not make a difference in your calculations.

18. **B.** Multiply the two terms without regard to the decimal points. In the product, add the two decimal places back in to get 102.72.

19. **D.** Make the denominators the same by multiplying each fraction by its opposite denominator:

$$\frac{8}{9} \times \frac{7}{7} = \frac{56}{63}$$

$$\frac{4}{7} \times \frac{9}{9} = \frac{36}{63}$$

Now add the two new fractions and reduce:

$$\frac{56}{63} + \frac{36}{63} = \frac{92}{63} = 1\frac{29}{63}$$

20. **C.** Both terms here are perfect squares. Calculate the square roots of both terms and place in a set of binomial expressions: $\sqrt{y^2} = y$; $\sqrt{9} = 3$: (y 3) (y 3). Since the sign in the original expression is negative, one sign in your binomials will be negative and the other positive: (y − 3) (y + 3).

21. **B.** An even number of negatives results in a positive answer: $\frac{-27}{-3} = 9$ (two negatives); (−4) (−6)(−8)(−10) = 1,920 (four negatives).

22. **A.** Perimeter is the distance around an object, no matter what type of object it is.

23. **D.** The definition of a proportion is a comparison of ratios.

24. **A.** Let's start with prime factorization of both 42 and 68:

2⌊42	2⌊68
3⌊21	3⌊34
7⌊7	7⌊17
1	1

Now multiply common factors:

$$42 = 2 \times 3 \times 7$$

$$68 = 2 \times 2 \times 17$$

The only shared factor here is 2, which makes it your highest common factor.

25. **C.** Plug in your value for *p* and solve using order of operations.

Electronics Information

1. **B.** Choice A is wrong because power is represented by the letter *P*. Choice C is wrong because amperes are represented by the letter *A*. Choice D is wrong because resistance is measured by the ohm symbol, Ω.

2. **C.** Electricity is comprised of electrons, all of which carry a negative charge. Choice A is wrong because protons have a positive charge. Choice B is wrong because neutrons do not carry any charge. Choice D is wrong because a diode is not a type of atom.

3. **A.** Because electricity always takes the least resistant path to the ground, people have to be very careful what they touch; a fallen tree on a power line could give someone a very serious shock.

4. **C.** None of the other choices offer truthful statements.

5. **C.** While voltage seldom varies, current frequently varies based on the needs of each object using it.

6. **D.** The other choices are incorrect.

7. **A.** This diagram shows a series circuit, as it is a single-flow path.

8. **D.** Choice A is wrong because a resistor is used to provide resistance to the current flowing through a circuit. Choice B is wrong because a transformer is used to transfer electricity from one source to another. Choice C is wrong because a switch is used to open or close a circuit.

9. **C.** Choice A is wrong because it represents a capacitor. Choice B is wrong because it represents a wire. Choice D is wrong because it represents a switch. Choice C represents a diode, which allows current to flow in only one direction.

10. **B.** None of the other terms apply to this diagram.

11. **B.** Choice A is wrong because it describes voltage. Choice C is wrong because it describes amperes. Choice D is wrong because it touches on principles of magnetism, polarity, and so forth.

12. **C.** None of the other choices correctly describe the acronym.

13. **A.** Choice B is wrong because copper is used in conductors. Choice C is wrong because rubber is used for insulators. Choice D is wrong because it is not a material commonly used for diodes.

14. **A.** Choices B, C, and D are wrong because they represent lamps, aerials, and fuses, respectively. A motor is the only answer choice that can convert electrical energy into kinetic energy.

15. **C.** Choice A is wrong because electrons create electricity when they are grouped together and traveling in the same direction. Choice B is wrong because copper is an example of a conductor. Choice D is wrong because current is the flow of electricity.

16. **A.** The other choices are incorrect.

17. **B.** Choice A is wrong because current is *inversely* proportional to resistance. Choice C is wrong because ampere is a unit of measure for current. Choice D is wrong because watts measure power.

18. **D.** All other choices reflect factors pertaining to resistance in a wire.

19. **B.** To calculate this question, use the following formula and plug in the numbers you have: $\text{amps} = \frac{\text{volts}}{\text{ohms}}$

20. **D.** To calculate this question, use the following formula and plug in the numbers you have: volts = amps × ohms.

Automotive and Shop Information

1. **B.** Choice A is wrong because the exhaust system converts excess gases from the engine and releases them to the air. Choice C is wrong because the fuel system stores and supplies fuel to the combustion chamber of the engine, where it combines with air, vaporizes, and burns to give the engine energy. Choice D is wrong because the suspension system deals with the movement of the wheels and the manner in which the car reacts to terrain.

2. **D.** Choice B is wrong because the electrical system makes the lights and power systems work. See additional explanations in the previous answer.

3. **A.** Choice B is wrong because, during the compression stroke, the piston is moving upward, compressing the fuel–air mixture. Choice C is wrong because the power stroke occurs when the spark plug emits a spark to ignite the gasoline mixture. Choice D is wrong because the exhaust stroke causes the exhaust valve to open, and exhaust exits via the tailpipe.

4. **B.** Brake pistons move under hydraulic pressure, also known as fluid pressure.

5. **C.** Choice A is wrong because the control arm manages the motion of the wheels. Choice B is wrong because the frame supports the car's engine and body. Choice D is wrong because the steering linkage allows the wheels to turn as a result of the motion of the steering wheel.

6. **A.** See explanations in the previous answer for additional guidance.

7. **D.** See explanations in the previous answer for additional guidance.

8. **B.** This is the definition of torque.

9. **A.** Distributorless ignition systems are designed to fire the spark plugs directly from the ignition coils at a ratio of one coil for every two spark plugs. A typical six-cylinder engine has three coils that are mounted together in a coil "pack." Each individual coil has a spark plug wire coming out either side, connecting the coil to the appropriate spark plugs. The coil fires both spark plugs at the same time.

10. **C.** Each of the other choices contain false statements and parts that have nothing to do with battery recharge.

11. **C.** Auto batteries have six cells that are stacked with positive and negative lead plates that sit in a solution of sulfuric acid and water; these plates store the energy needed to accomplish all the battery's tasks.

12. **A.** Fuse panels, or fuse boxes, help control the function of many things, such as the headlights, dashboard lights, radios, and clocks.

13. **D.** Diesel burns more efficiently than gasoline.

14. **C.** In older cars, fuel pumps either didn't exist or were mounted outside the fuel tank.

15. **D.** Absorbing road bumps is a function of the suspension system.

16. **C.** Choice A is wrong because a cold chisel is used when cutting cold metals to remove waste metal. Choices B and D are wrong because files and rasps are used to smooth rough edges.

17. **B.** Choice A is wrong because a hack saw does not have alternating cutting edges. Choice C is wrong because a miter saw cuts using both sides of the blade. Choice D is wrong because a circular saw can cut with *or* against the grain, not necessarily just one way.

18. **B.** Choices A, C, and D are all wrong because they all have steel heads.

19. **A.** Choices B and C both list other hand drill parts, although they are not supposed to be prefaced with the word *cranking*. In addition, their job is not to turn the main shaft of the drill. Choice D is not a component of a hand drill.

20. **C.** A countersink is used to create a hole in which the top part of the hole is enlarged. That way, the screw head will go all the way down into the wood so that the surface of the wood is smooth.

21. **C.** A pipe wrench is a more specific version of an adjustable-end wrench. The adjustable clamps on one end are designed especially to grip a variety of objects used by mechanics, plumbers, and handymen.

22. **B.** None of the other choices offer the right answer.

23. **D.** Socket wrenches are frequently used for automotive repairs and other household projects. They come equipped with removable and varying-sized sockets.

24. **B.** A pipe clamp is used to hold a pipe in place so that it can be cut, threaded, lifted, or suspended. It is designed as described in the question.

25. **B.** Choice A is wrong because a drill press is usually bolted to the floor or to a workbench; as a result, it cannot possibly perform the kind of demolition work that a jackhammer does. Choices C and D are the names of a hammer and a saw, respectively.

Mechanical Comprehension

1. **D.** When you stretch a rubber band, it has potential energy—the possibility of doing work. When you release it, it has kinetic energy—motion energy. The fact that the rubber band can be stretched and retain its original shape suggests that it has elastic energy.

2. **D.** The formula for gravitational potential energy is $PE = mgh$, or mass × gravity × height above Earth:

   $PE = 2 \times 9.8 \times 20$

   $PE = 392$ joules

3. **D.** Choice A is the definition of kinetic energy. Choice B is the definition of speed. Choice C is the definition of velocity.

4. **B.** Use the same formula from question 2 and solve for the missing value.

5. **D.** Gear ratio can be calculated by counting the number of rotations each gear makes. The other option is to count the teeth on each gear. Divide the number of teeth on the larger gear by the number of teeth on the smaller gear.

6. **A.** Newton's third law is known as the law of reciprocal action, which states that for every action there is an equal and opposite reaction.

7. **C.** Work is directly proportionate to distance traveled.

8. **B.** Work is directly proportionate to force.

9. **A.** See the explanations for the previous two answers.

10. **C.** Newton's third law of reciprocal action states that for every action there is an equal and opposite reaction.

11. **D.** Choices A, B, and C all describe types of pulleys instead of gears.

12. **D.** None of the other choices offer accurate statements.

13. **A.** A two-wheeled pulley system offers mechanical advantage that causes an object to feel half as heavy.

14. **D.** In a four-wheeled pulley system, the object gains enough mechanical advantage to make it feel four times easier to lift. However, it also forces you to pull the rope four times farther to raise the object to the intended height.

15. **C.** None of the other choices offer factual statements.

16. **C.** Pressure is calculated by the following formula: Pressure = Force ÷ Area. Pressure is measured in psi (pounds per square inch), force in pounds, and area in square units. Plug in the numbers from the question and solve for force:

    $P = F \div A$

    $15 = F \div 25$

    $25 \times 15 = F \div \cancel{25 \times 25}$

    $375 = F$

17. **B.** Choices A, C, and D are not the correct terms for the description that was given.

18. **A.** None of the other choices offer factual statements.

19. **A.** Acceleration is calculated using the following formula: (Final rate of velocity – initial rate of velocity) ÷ Time. Before you can plug in your numbers, you must take your kilometers per hour and convert them into meters per second. The first is easy: 0 km/h = 0 m/s. Since there are 3,600 seconds in an hour, divide 120 by 3,600 to get .03 km/s. Now, this has to be turned into meters per second by multiplying .033 by 1,000. This gives you 33.33. Subtract 0 from 33.33 and divide by 10. This gives you 3.33 m/s². Since your tenths and hundredth digits are below 5, round down to 3 m/s².

20. **C.** Speed is calculated by dividing distance by time.

21. **A.** Force = Mass × Acceleration.

22. **B.** Choice A is wrong because it defines weight. Choices C and D don't describe mass or weight.

23. **D.** Any kind of movement is considered motion.

24. **C.** Choices A and B both convert to kinetic energy. Choice C, however, is not a form of energy.

25. **A.** Choice B is wrong because objects have potential energy before they ever get kinetic energy. Choice C is wrong because it describes elastic energy. Choice D is wrong because not every object has potential energy (although, most do).

Assembling Objects

1. **C.** The *N* in answer A is mirrored. The connection points are in the wrong place on both shapes in answer B. Answer D replaces the *X* shape with a hexagon.

2. **B.** The center shape in answer A is different from the sample. Answer C is mirrored. The shapes in answer D are different from the sample and an extra shape has been added.

3. **C.** The connection points in answers A and D are in the wrong places. Answer B replaces the *Y* shape with a *V* shape.

4. **C.** Answers A and D have different shapes than those in the sample. The triangle in answer B is not the same as the one in the sample.

5. **B.** The triangle in answer A is not the same as in the sample. The circle in answer C replaces the trapezoid shape from the sample. The connection points in answer D are in the wrong places.

6. **C.** The rounded shape from the sample has been turned into a complete circle in answer A, and the quadrilateral from the sample is a triangle in answer B. One of the curved shapes from the sample is a quadrilateral in answer D.

7. **C.** One of the shapes in answers B and D have been changed. The connection point on the *T* is in the wrong place.

8. **B.** The circle from the sample is replaced with an oval in answer A. Two of the triangles from the sample have been replaced with one quadrilateral in answer C, and now there are three pieces to this puzzle instead of four. The third triangle from the sample has been replaced by a rectangle in answer D.

9. **A.** The flower in answer B is shaped differently than the one in the sample. The *B* in answer C is mirrored and the one in answer D has been replaced by an *e*.

10. **A.** There are two triangles instead of one in answer B. The quadrilateral in answer C is smaller than the one in the sample. The pentagon is missing in answer D.

11. **D.** The star in answer A has nine points, not seven, as in the sample. The connection point on the *W* in answer B and on the star in answer C is in the wrong place.

12. **C.** In answer A, the circle is now an oval. The small triangle in answer B has been replaced with a large, curvy one. In answer D, there are five shapes instead of the four shown in the sample.

13. **B.** The angled shape in answer A has been mirrored. The ampersand in answer C has been replaced with a dollar sign. In answer D, the connection on the angled shape is in the wrong place.

14. **A.** The triangle in answer B doesn't match the one from the sample. There is an extra rectangle in answer C and no triangle. The large jagged piece is missing in answer D.

15. **A.** The connection point on the question mark in answer A is in the wrong place. The connection point on the starlike shape in answer C is in the wrong place. The question mark in answer D is mirrored.

16. **A.** In answers B and D, one of the four-sided shapes now has three sides. Answer C has five pieces instead of the four shown in the sample.

17. **D.** The star shape in answer A is not the same as in the sample. In answer B, both connection points are off. In answer C, the five-sided shape now has seven sides.

18. **C.** The star in answer A is different from the one in the sample. Answer B has two ovals instead of an oval and a circle. The shape with the flat bottom and curved top has been replaced with a rectangle in answer D.

19. **D.** The connection to the angled shape in answer A comes in at the wrong angle. Both connection points in answer B are in the wrong places. The *b* in answer C has been mirrored.

20. **A.** Three of the shapes in answer B don't match the sample. The rectangle in answer C is now a square. In answer D, the shapes have changed and there are now only three instead of four.

21. **D.** The connection point to the *H* shape in answer A is wrong. The *H* shape in answer B has been mirrored. The *X*-like shape in answer C has been rounded out.

22. **D.** The shape of the arrow is changed in answer A. There is no large rectangle in answer B. Two shapes in answer C are mirrored.

23. **B.** Both connection points in answer A are in the wrong places. The *f* in answer C has been changed into a *g*. The flower shape in answer D has been replaced with a hexagram.

24. **B.** The shape of the triangle is changed in answer A. Only two of the shapes in answer C match the sample. The largest shape from the sample is missing from answer D.

25. **A.** The connection point to the *T* shape in answer B is wrong. Both shapes in answer C are different from those in the sample, while only one is different in answer D.

Practice Test 3

General Science

Time: 11 Minutes

Questions: 25

Directions: This section tests your general knowledge in the area of science. Carefully read each question and choose the answer choice that best answers the question.

1. A producer

    (A) eats other organisms for food.
    (B) survives in extreme cold.
    (C) creates its own food.
    (D) eats only plants.

2. Genetic information is found in

    (A) endoplastic reticulum.
    (B) lysosome.
    (C) golgi.
    (D) chromosomes.

3. Digestion begins when

    (A) food enters the mouth and is broken down.
    (B) food enters the stomach.
    (C) stomach contents enter the small intestine.
    (D) contents of the stomach move from the small intestine to the large intestine.

4. The rate of change of velocity of an object is

    (A) work.
    (B) physics.
    (C) acceleration.
    (D) friction.

5. If a car increases its speed by 2 miles per hour every second, this is known as

    (A) constant acceleration.
    (B) constant velocity.
    (C) negative velocity.
    (D) nonconstant acceleration.

6. On the Periodic Table, Cu stands for

    (A) curium.
    (B) carbon.
    (C) copper.
    (D) chromium.

7. Hard, closely packed molecules that can hold their own shape fall under which state of matter?

    (A) liquid
    (B) plasma
    (C) solid
    (D) gas

8. When you combine 1 atom of carbon with 2 atoms of oxygen, what type of chemical structure do you have?

    (A) a compound
    (B) an electron
    (C) an atom
    (D) an element

9. The subscript number of a compound symbol represents the number of

    (A) chemical bonds.
    (B) atoms.
    (C) neutrons and electrons.
    (D) negative elements.

10. Neutrons affect the _____ and _____ of an atom.

    (A) mass, charge
    (B) charge, magnetism
    (C) bond strength, density
    (D) mass, radioactivity

11. Which type of eclipse is dangerous to look at?

    (A) lunar
    (B) planetary
    (C) solar
    (D) binary

12. Which of the following is NOT one of Kepler's laws of planetary motion?

    (A) The planets move in elliptical orbits.
    (B) An imaginary line joins the center of a planet to the center of the sun and sweeps the same amount of space all the time.
    (C) The time it takes a planet to orbit the sun is based on how far away from the sun it is.
    (D) The distance from Earth to the sun is measured in astronomical units.

13. Twice a year, day and night are the same length all over the world. This is known as what?

    (A) Lunar New Year
    (B) solstice
    (C) equinox
    (D) astronomical equivalency

14. A celestial body larger than an asteroid that moves around and receives light from a star is known as a(n)

    (A) galaxy.
    (B) asteroid.
    (C) meteorite.
    (D) planet.

15. The prefix *cirro* describes clouds that are

    (A) high in the sky.
    (B) midlevel in the sky.
    (C) low in the sky.
    (D) transparent.

16. When two different types of air masses meet, what is formed?

    (A) clouds
    (B) barometric pressure
    (C) front
    (D) tornado

17. Clouds form in the

    (A) troposphere.
    (B) stratosphere.
    (C) mesosphere.
    (D) thermosphere.

18. Because the atomic molecules are so spread out in the thermosphere, this causes it to be very

    (A) hot.
    (B) cold.
    (C) wet.
    (D) thick.

19. Which gas is NOT commonly found in the atmosphere?

    (A) oxygen
    (B) argon
    (C) nitrogen
    (D) xenon

20. Which of the following is the scale used to determine rock hardness?

    (A) Ohm's
    (B) Kepler's
    (C) Hertz'
    (D) Mohs'

21. Skeletons of living organisms found in rock are called

    (A) shale.
    (B) fossils.
    (C) graphite.
    (D) archaeology.

22. Igneous rock that was formed and remains underground is known as

    (A) lava.
    (B) intrusive rock.
    (C) extrusive rock.
    (D) sediment.

23. Another word for *polypeptide* is

    (A) chromatid.
    (B) nucleotide.
    (C) riboflavin.
    (D) protein.

24. Which of the following is an example of tissue?

    (A) circulatory system
    (B) femur
    (C) muscle
    (D) cell

25. The lithosphere is made up of

    (A) the Earth's crust and part of the upper mantle.
    (B) the Earth's mantle and outer core.
    (C) the Earth's inner and outer core.
    (D) none of the above.

Arithmetic Reasoning

Time: 36 Minutes

Questions: 30

Directions: This section tests your ability to reason through mathematical problems using basic arithmetic. Carefully read each question and choose the answer choice that best answers the question.

1. Amy bought three pairs of shoes at $17.95, $22.95, and $26.95 each. She added a pair of socks for $5.65 and a necklace for $18.50 to her purchase. Assuming there is no sales tax, what was her total at the register?

   (A) $68
   (B) $75
   (C) $92
   (D) $560

2. If you have three quarters, two pennies, six dimes, and a nickel in your pocket, what's the probability you'll pull out a penny the next time you pick out a coin?

   (A) $\frac{1}{4}$

   (B) $\frac{1}{6}$

   (C) $\frac{1}{2}$

   (D) $\frac{1}{12}$

3. Miriam is three times as old as Kenny. If Kenny is half of Adriana's age, and she is 42, how old is Miriam?

   (A) 18
   (B) 21
   (C) 45
   (D) 63

4. Barry needs to make 15% more money this year than his annual salary pays. Instead of getting a raise, Barry is offered extra hours at work at a rate of $11.50 per hour. If his annual salary is $32,425, about how many extra hours would he have to work to make the money that he needs?

   (A) 423
   (B) 444
   (C) 482
   (D) 499

5. You read six books in a month. At this rate, how many do you read in a week?

   (A) 1.5
   (B) 2.2
   (C) 2.8
   (D) 2.9

6. Your college tuition is $326 per credit. An increase of 7% is announced for the following semester. What will the new cost of tuition per three-credit class be?

   (A) $22.82
   (B) $348.82
   (C) $1,046.46
   (D) $3,046.46

7. In a group discussion, $\frac{3}{5}$ of the participants favor the proposed change to the rules. If there are 30 people in the group, how many will likely vote to approve the measure?

   (A) 6
   (B) 18
   (C) 29
   (D) 30

8. A sandbox is 3 feet wide, 3 feet long, and 3 feet tall. How much sand can it hold?

   (A) 9 ft²
   (B) 9 ft³
   (C) 27 ft²
   (D) 27 ft³

9. A man visits his wife's grave six times per year since her passing. If he has been there 27 times, how long has it been since he lost his wife?

   (A) 4.5 years
   (B) 5 years
   (C) 5.5 years
   (D) 6 years

10. Recording studio time costs $235 per hour. If it takes four sessions of eight hours at a time to record an album, how much would it cost to record albums for five new artists?

    (A) $1,175
    (B) $37,600
    (C) $67,300
    (D) $73,600

11. A salesperson makes a 16% commission on everything she sells. If she sold $6,283 worth of merchandise this month and put 12% of her earnings into a savings account, how much did she add to the account this month?

    (A) $10.28
    (B) $95.65
    (C) $120.63
    (D) $1,005.28

12. Which of the following numbers is not an integer:

    (A) 1
    (B) –1
    (C) 2
    (D) 2.3

13. A dance club starts letting people in at 10:00 P.M. In the first hour, 10 men and 15 women are admitted, and none leave. In the second hour, 25 men and 20 women are admitted. Again, none leave. In the third hour, 11 women and 7 men leave and no more people are admitted into the club. What is the ratio of men to women in the club by 1 A.M.?

    (A) 7:6
    (B) 5:8
    (C) 8:3
    (D) 11:1

14. Your lunches at the local diner this week cost you $4.65, $5.32, and $7.27. Assuming you left a 15% tip for each meal, what's the average amount of money you spent on lunch?

    (A) $2.58
    (B) $6.61
    (C) $9.35
    (D) $17.24

15. If you can type 36 words per minute, about how long would it take you to type a 453-word essay?

    (A) 4

    (B) 6

    (C) 13

    (D) 25

16. Which of the following is a prime number?

    (A) 1

    (B) 4

    (C) 9

    (D) 11

17. Marc bought three times as many carrots as Dave. Dave bought half as many as Jen. If Jen bought 10 carrots, how many did Marc buy?

    (A) 10

    (B) 15

    (C) 25

    (D) 40

18. Using order of operations, which term would you address first in the following expression? $-6 + -3 - 4^3 + 6$

    (A) $-6 + -3$

    (B) $(-3) - 43$

    (C) $43 + 6$

    (D) 43

19. In a gymnastics competition, Mary received a 5.4, 3.9, 4.8, 4.9, and 5.1 for her floor routine. What is her average score?

    (A) 4.28

    (B) 4.82

    (C) 15.7

    (D) 24.5

20. Negative six minus negative six equals

    (A) 0.

    (B) 6.

    (C) –12.

    (D) 18.

21. A room measures 16.2 feet long by 8.5 feet wide. What is its area?

    (A) 24.7 ft²

    (B) 137.7 ft²

    (C) 321.84 ft²

    (D) 898.23 ft²

22. Erin needs to buy five apples to make her famous pie. She needs three Golden Delicious, one Granny Smith, and one Red Delicious. At the store, she finds Golden Delicious apples marked down 10% from their usual price of 89¢ apiece. The Granny Smith and Red Delicious apples are marked at 75¢ and 65¢ apiece, respectively. If she doesn't have to pay tax on her purchase, how much money will she need to buy all the apples she needs?

    (A) 80¢

    (B) $1.80

    (C) $2.80

    (D) $3.80

23. The answer to an addition problem is a

    (A) product.

    (B) quotient.

    (C) sum.

    (D) difference.

24. When the numerator is less than the denominator, you have a(n)

    (A) proper fraction.
    (B) improper fraction.
    (C) mixed number.
    (D) simplified fraction.

25. In three years, Jed will be four times as old as Terry. If Terry will be 12 next year, how old is Jed now?

    (A) 14
    (B) 23
    (C) 53
    (D) 85

26. A MEPS site has 68 potential recruits come in on Saturday to take the ASVAB. Of those who come in, 72% will pass the AFQT. About how many recruits will have to retake the ASVAB to get into the military?

    (A) 10
    (B) 19
    (C) 49
    (D) 80

27. On opening day at the amusement park, there were 26 ice cream vendors and 42 hot dog vendors providing food for the park's patrons. What's the ratio of ice cream vendors to hot dog vendors?

    (A) 6:7
    (B) 13:21
    (C) 14:23
    (D) 9:26

28. What is 345.876 divided by 23.1?

    (A) 8.64
    (B) 11.78
    (C) 12.85
    (D) 14.97

29. A CD collection has 25 titles. Of these, 10 are classic rock, 3 are hard rock, and the rest are adult contemporary. What is the probability that you could choose a classic rock CD the first time you reached for a random title and a hard rock CD the second time (assuming you kept the first CD with you and did not return it to the collection)?

    (A) $\frac{1}{20}$
    (B) $\frac{3}{40}$
    (C) $\frac{5}{20}$
    (D) $\frac{5}{40}$

30. How many minutes are in a day?

    (A) 60
    (B) 240
    (C) 1,440
    (D) 86,400

Word Knowledge

Time: 11 Minutes

Questions: 35

Directions: This section tests your knowledge of and ability to use vocabulary. Read each question and choose the answer choice that most nearly means the same as the underlined word.

1. <u>Nuisance</u> most nearly means

   (A) annoyance.
   (B) forbearance.
   (C) clarity.
   (D) argument.

2. <u>Authoritative</u> most nearly means

   (A) loud.
   (B) irritating.
   (C) commanding.
   (D) conceited.

3. <u>Perverse</u> most nearly means

   (A) able.
   (B) wicked.
   (C) appreciative.
   (D) wired.

4. <u>Sonorous</u> most nearly means

   (A) religious.
   (B) grave.
   (C) jubilant.
   (D) echoing.

5. I went back to the classroom so I could <u>retrieve</u> the pencil case I left in my desk.

   (A) recover
   (B) collect
   (C) embrace
   (D) forget

6. Believing everything everyone tells you is not an <u>astute</u> way to collect information.

   (A) forgivable
   (B) efficient
   (C) discerning
   (D) pardonable

7. <u>Efface</u> most nearly means

   (A) implement.
   (B) thicken.
   (C) break.
   (D) erode.

8. <u>Palatable</u> most nearly means

   (A) edible.
   (B) cross.
   (C) insipid.
   (D) brave.

9. When her money ran out for the third time that month, the girl <u>entreated</u> her parents to send some more for her basic expenses.

   (A) annoyed
   (B) begged
   (C) smiled
   (D) soothed

10. <u>Variance</u> most nearly means

    (A) quickness.

    (B) ability.

    (C) likeability.

    (D) difference.

11. Jade's friends loved how friendly and <u>gregarious</u> she got when they went out on Friday nights.

    (A) reticent

    (B) reserved

    (C) sociable

    (D) suspicious

12. The <u>spare</u> room had only a cot and a pillow in it.

    (A) small

    (B) unadorned

    (C) ornate

    (D) spacious

13. <u>Superfluous</u> most nearly means

    (A) unnecessary.

    (B) essential.

    (C) immortal.

    (D) gracious.

14. <u>Affix</u> most nearly means

    (A) argue.

    (B) berate.

    (C) stick.

    (D) savor.

15. <u>Hasten</u> most nearly means

    (A) accelerate.

    (B) pause.

    (C) cry.

    (D) drop.

16. Seattle's <u>temperate</u> climate makes it ideal for those who are not overly fond of extremely cold or hot weather.

    (A) lacking

    (B) excessive

    (C) seasonal

    (D) moderate

17. <u>Viral</u> most nearly means

    (A) spreadable.

    (B) secret.

    (C) submissive.

    (D) surreptitious.

18. The heartfelt tribute video <u>evoked</u> tears from the late musician's most devoted fans.

    (A) extinguished

    (B) stirred

    (C) belied

    (D) criticized

19. <u>Increment</u> most nearly means

    (A) blaze.

    (B) gel.

    (C) increase.

    (D) concern.

20. <u>Raze</u> most nearly means

    (A) demolish.

    (B) uplift.

    (C) create.

    (D) fasten.

21. <u>Vituperative</u> most nearly means

    (A) creative.

    (B) impassioned.

    (C) blasé.

    (D) offensive.

22. With the help of the increased winds and dry weather, the smoking leaves where the cigarette had been dropped had quickly turned into a <u>conflagration</u> that endangered whole neighborhoods.

    (A) inference
    (B) blaze
    (C) creation
    (D) beast

23. <u>Auspicious</u> most nearly means

    (A) egotistic.
    (B) unfortunate.
    (C) favorable.
    (D) interrogative.

24. <u>Baleful</u> most nearly means

    (A) sinister.
    (B) loose.
    (C) flammable.
    (D) sticky.

25. Blake did not want to serve on a jury, so he did not register to vote in hopes that he could <u>circumvent</u> being added to the list of county residents that makes up the jury pool.

    (A) volunteer
    (B) facilitate
    (C) celebrate
    (D) avoid

26. <u>Lather</u> most nearly means

    (A) censure.
    (B) foam.
    (C) rubber.
    (D) hide.

27. <u>Vapid</u> most nearly means

    (A) clever.
    (B) uninspiring.
    (C) mean-spirited.
    (D) energizing.

28. <u>Clarity</u> most nearly means

    (A) transparency.
    (B) reason.
    (C) tranquility.
    (D) abrasiveness.

29. <u>Invigorate</u> most nearly means

    (A) appreciate.
    (B) value.
    (C) refresh.
    (D) concentrate.

30. Though she smiled when she said she was delighted to be part of the committee, her resentful tone proved her words to be <u>spurious</u>.

    (A) serious
    (B) believable
    (C) angry
    (D) disingenuous

31. <u>Blockade</u> most nearly means

    (A) brink.
    (B) passage.
    (C) cordon.
    (D) crater.

32. <u>Vocation</u> most nearly means

    (A) occupation.
    (B) interest.
    (C) belief.
    (D) relief.

33. Grill most nearly means

    (A) undermine.
    (B) interrogate.
    (C) appreciate.
    (D) blast.

34. Malady most nearly means

    (A) prize.
    (B) windfall.
    (C) function.
    (D) woe.

35. Emblazon most nearly means

    (A) display.
    (B) forget.
    (C) explode.
    (D) speak.

Paragraph Comprehension

Time: 13 Minutes

Questions: 15

Directions: This section tests your ability to read and understand written information, as well as come to logical conclusions based on a text. Read each passage and answer the questions that follow. Choose the answer choice that best answers the question.

Use the following passage to answer questions 1–3:

Vinegar is an extremely versatile substance that can be used all around the house. First, its highly acidic properties make it an excellent natural food preservative. Mixing vinegar with garlic, dill, and other spices produces a brine that can be used to pickle vegetables or marinate meats.

Vinegar is also an effective nonchemical cleaner that can be used on all sorts of surfaces, including metal, wood, glass, fabrics, and linoleum. Though its odor is very pungent and distinct in itself, vinegar solutions can be used to clean and deodorize coffee makers, microwaves, sinks, and bathrooms. It can also be used to treat areas of the house that have been soiled by pets. It even works as a natural way to prevent infestations of fleas and ticks on animals.

1. In the passage, the word <u>versatile</u> most nearly means
   (A) having many uses.
   (B) malodorous.
   (C) gentle.
   (D) pleasing.

2. Vinegar might be a good substance to help treat a(n)
   (A) fever.
   (B) coffee stain on the rug.
   (C) heartburn.
   (D) abrasion.

3. One reason you might choose to bathe your pet in a vinegar solution is that
   (A) you want to make their coat shine.
   (B) you want them to stop wetting the rug.
   (C) you want to clean paint off of their fur.
   (D) you want to get rid of fleas.

Use the following passage to answer questions 4–5:

Most people think of communication in terms of a one-way process where a sender encodes a message that is transmitted to a receiver. However, advancing research in communication studies indicates that most communication is systemic, meaning that conception and transmission of a message is only one part of the equation. Listener-centric models of communication are taking center stage today. These assert that communication takes place simultaneously through verbal and nonverbal signals from sender to receiver and back. Furthermore, internal communication, such as thoughts and perception of external stimuli, are also taking place and influencing how both the sender and receiver interpret messages and form their responses.

4. A good title for this passage might be:

   (A) Listen Up: Things Are Not What They Seem
   (B) Sender-Focused Communication Is the Future
   (C) Communication as an Interactive Process
   (D) Listener-centric Communication Models Gain Acceptance

5. According to the passage, thoughts and perceptions are forms of

   (A) external communication.
   (B) internal communication.
   (C) external stimuli.
   (D) external foci.

Use the following passage to answer questions 6–7:

Pablo Neruda was a Chilean poet best known for his contributions to the surrealist movement in the 1970s. He was born Neftalí Ricardo Reyes Basoalto, but he wrote under the pseudonym Pablo Neruda as a teenager because his father did not approve of his taking an interest in writing. Neruda's work features a variety of voices that swing from highly romantic and excited to deeply troubled and depressed. This is of little surprise, since surrealism is characterized by building dreamlike situations through which the unreal becomes real and is examined through artistic interpretation. The spectrum of emotions and thoughts brought to life through surrealistic writing and art stands out among other styles and genres for its tendency to flaunt unreality while exploring very real ideas.

6. Surrealism is

   (A) a type of poem.
   (B) no longer seen in the artistic community.
   (C) a genre of artistic expression.
   (D) grounded in reality.

7. In the passage, the word pseudonym most nearly means

   (A) false name.
   (B) deception.
   (C) recitation.
   (D) belief.

Use the following passage to answer questions 8–10:

(1) Competition for consumer attention has gotten drastically out of hand over the past few decades. (2) When media first started to become an established part of our lives, we were restricted to advertisements that could be printed in magazines or newspapers, or broadcast on television or the radio. (3) With the increasing pervasiveness of the internet; the advent of cell phones and video messaging; and the appearance of programmed media in venues like hotel lobbies, elevators, and even bathrooms and the DMV, consumers are inundated with communication of all sorts.

(4) It's getting to the point where you can't go anywhere without being constantly pressed for your attention to some product, service, or other item essential to your existence. (5) Is there nothing we can do to lessen the amount of communicational baggage we are forced to carry around with us all the time?

8. The speaker comes across as

   (A) calm.
   (B) understanding.
   (C) complacent.
   (D) frustrated.

9. The speaker would most likely NOT support

   (A) the removal of news tickers from the bottoms of television screens.
   (B) digital billboards attached to sides of buses.
   (C) reduced dependence on cell phones.
   (D) more time playing board games with her family.

10. Which sentence best expresses the main idea of the passage?

   (A) 1
   (B) 2
   (C) 4
   (D) 5

Use the following passage to answer questions 11–13:

Is capital punishment a just punishment for murder? This is one of the most debated topics in American society and exemplifies the type of argument that asks one of the essential questions of our existence: what is justice? Because laws are created by people, one could say that justice is what is deemed to be moral and right by the majority of people. But what of those who do not agree with these ideas? Are their impressions of justice any more or less valid within the scope of the universe?

Is there any such thing as a universal right or wrong? Certainly, most cultures find killing to be wrong, yet every culture kills, whether it is deemed to be right or wrong. Does this mean that killing is a universal right, even though large numbers of people believe it to be wrong? Questions such as these will likely never be answered because for every definitive opinion given, there will also be a counter opinion that is just as persuasive. Therefore, arguing for or against capital punishment is a futile task.

11. The speaker in this passage is

   (A) addressing a text.
   (B) arguing with someone else.
   (C) debating with himself.
   (D) responding to a comment.

12. This passage consists of

   (A) a series of questions, answers, and speculation.
   (B) incontrovertible facts.
   (C) academic research.
   (D) biased opinion.

13. In the end, the speaker decides that

   (A) debating the topic is essential.
   (B) every academic should debate this topic.
   (C) there will be only one answer to this debate.
   (D) debating the topic is useless.

Use the following passage to answer questions 14–15:

Guido " Guy" Fawkes is remembered as a key player in the failed attempt to assassinate England's King James I in 1605. As a member of a secret group of dissenters who wanted to overthrow the Protestant government that persecuted Puritans and Catholics, Fawkes was charged with making sure the Gunpowder Plot of 1605 went off without a hitch.

The plan was to ignite a cache of explosives underneath Parliament while King James and most of the aristocracy were present. One of the members of Fawkes's group, however, betrayed the plan to a member of Parliament. Authorities were sent to intercept Fawkes as he was about to light the explosives, and instead of dying in the fire as he intended to, Fawkes was arrested for treason.

Though the plot did not come to fruition, Fawkes is remembered throughout Great Britain today through an annual Bonfire Night commemorating the event that was supposed take place, as well as references in literature, movies, television, and more.

14. It can be inferred that Guy Fawkes was

    (A) politically disinterested.

    (B) a revolutionary.

    (C) loyal to King James I.

    (D) looking forward to traveling to Spain.

15. In the passage, the phrase <u>come to fruition</u> most nearly means

    (A) have much impact.

    (B) last very long.

    (C) come to happen.

    (D) mean anything in the scope of history.

Mathematics Knowledge

Time: 24 Minutes

Questions: 25

Directions: This section tests your knowledge of basic mathematics, algebra, and geometry. Carefully read each question and choose the answer choice that reflects the best answer.

1. If $b = 6$, $b + 12 - 3b \times 2b =$
   - (A) 12
   - (B) –12
   - (C) 198
   - (D) –198

2. $\frac{5}{9} \div \frac{3}{9} =$
   - (A) $\frac{5}{27}$
   - (B) $1\frac{2}{3}$
   - (C) $\frac{3}{5}$
   - (D) $2\frac{3}{5}$

3. $3^{-4} =$
   - (A) $\frac{12}{1}$
   - (B) $\frac{1}{12}$
   - (C) $\frac{1}{81}$
   - (D) $\frac{81}{1}$

4. You have a cylindrical barrel that is 5 feet tall and 6 feet wide. What is its volume?
   - (A) 30 ft³
   - (B) 47.1 ft³
   - (C) 52.3 ft³
   - (D) 141.3 ft³

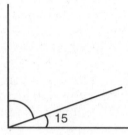

5. If the previous angles are complementary, the value of the missing angle is
   - (A) 75.
   - (B) 90.
   - (C) 130.
   - (D) 180.

6. In $c^2 + 3x + 12$, c^2 is a
   - (A) coefficient.
   - (B) constant.
   - (C) equation.
   - (D) term.

7. Factor $a^2 - 13a + 22$
   - (A) $(a - 12)(a - 1)$
   - (B) $(a - 2)(a - 11)$
   - (C) $(a + 2)(a - 11)$
   - (D) $(a + 1)(a - 12)$

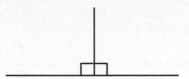

8. These angles are

    (A) supplementary.
    (B) complementary.
    (C) adjacent.
    (D) parallel.

9. If $12x + 6 > 7x - 4$, then $x >$

    (A) –2
    (B) 2
    (C) –5
    (D) 5

10. $b^2 \div b^4 =$

    (A) b–1
    (B) b
    (C) b2
    (D) b3

11. All four sides are congruent and angles are right angles in a

    (A) pentagon.
    (B) hexagon.
    (C) triangle.
    (D) square.

12. When you know the value of any two sides of a right triangle, you use _____ to calculate the other side.

    (A) $A = \frac{1}{2}bh$

    (B) the Pythagorean theorem

    (C) $A = \frac{1}{2}h(b_1 + b_2)$

    (D) $A = \pi r^2$

13. If in a right triangle $a = 6$ and $b = 9$, $c =$

    (A) 10.816
    (B) 11.618
    (C) 12.562
    (D) 17.853

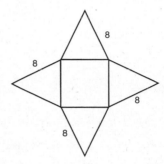

14. If the triangles in the figure are equilateral, the area of the square is

    (A) 10.
    (B) 16.
    (C) 24.
    (D) 64.

15. The greatest common factor of 24 and 36 is

    (A) 8.
    (B) 9.
    (C) 12.
    (D) 16.

16. The area of a circle with a diameter of 11 inches is

    (A) 52.425 in.²
    (B) 94.985 in.²
    (C) 268.598 in.²
    (D) 379.94 in.²

17. What action breaks down a number
    into the product of its prime factors?

    (A) simplification
    (B) factorial
    (C) scientific notation
    (D) prime factorization

18. Solve for a: $\frac{9}{13.5} = \frac{a}{6}$

    (A) 4
    (B) 8
    (C) 12
    (D) 16

19. The total surface area of a cylindrical
    solid that has a radius of 5 feet and a
    height of 12 feet is:

    (A) 60 ft.^{2}
    (B) 112 ft.^{2}
    (C) 533.8 ft.^{2}
    (D) 635.6 ft.^{2}

20. The least common multiple of 12 and
    8 is

    (A) 16.
    (B) 24.
    (C) 32.
    (D) 36.

21. The value of the external angle is:

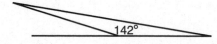

142°

    (A) 38°
    (B) 46°
    (C) 86°
    (D) 125°

22. The area of a trapezoid with a height
    of 9, a top base value of 6, and a
    bottom base value of 14 is

    (A) 20.
    (B) 50.
    (C) 90.
    (D) 10.

23. All of the following are tests to deter-
    mine whether two triangles are
    congruent EXCEPT

    (A) Are all three corresponding side
        values equal?
    (B) Are two corresponding angles
        and the side they share equal?
    (C) Are two sides perpendicular?
    (D) Are two corresponding angles
        and a side they don't share
        equal?

24. Factor: $42x^2 + 28x$.

    (A) 2x(21x + 14)
    (B) 14x(3x + 2)
    (C) 14x(3x − 2)
    (D) 21x(2x + 7)

25. Simplify: $\frac{18y+27}{9}$.

    (A) $\frac{9}{18y+27}$
    (B) $\frac{6y+9}{3}$
    (C) 2y − 3
    (D) 2y + 3

Electronics Information

Time: 9 Minutes

Questions: 20

Directions: This section tests your knowledge of basic electronics principles and applications. Carefully read each question and choose the answer choice that reflects the best answer.

1. The previous symbol represents

   (A) fuse.

   (B) capacitor.

   (C) diode.

   (D) DC voltage capacitor.

2. As you drive down the road unbuckled, your car gives you a gentle reminder in the form of a bell sound. The sound occurs every three seconds. You choose to ignore it for five minutes. What is the frequency of the seatbelt alarm?

   (A) 20 times per minute

   (B) 60 times per minute

   (C) 3 times per minute

   (D) 5 times per minute

3. What is the formula to calculate resistance?

   (A) Ohms = Amps × Watts

   (B) Ohms = Watts ÷ Amps

   (C) Ohms = Volts × Amps

   (D) Ohms = Volts ÷ Amps

4. The previous symbol represents

   (A) fuse.

   (B) motor.

   (C) voltmeter.

   (D) amplifier.

5. If you have 10 amps and 100 watts, how many volts do you have?

   (A) 10

   (B) 1,000

   (C) 90

   (D) 100

6. The formula for amperes is:

   (A) Amps = Volts ÷ Resistance

   (B) Amps = Volts ÷ Watts

   (C) Amps = Volts × Resistance

   (D) Amps = Volts × Watts

7. The idea that waves generally move in a straight line is called what?

   (A) interference

   (B) refraction

   (C) rectilinear propagation

   (D) longitudinal

8. The previous symbol represents

    (A) aerial.

    (B) resistor.

    (C) transformer.

    (D) lamp.

9. What do electrons flow through most readily?

    (A) insulators

    (B) conductors

    (C) loads

    (D) ammeters

10. How much electrical force is required for most household appliances?

    (A) 100 watts

    (B) 100 volts

    (C) 120 watts

    (D) 120 volts

11. The previous symbol represents

    (A) AC voltage capacitor.

    (B) wire.

    (C) battery.

    (D) switch.

12. What does a basic circuit start with?

    (A) resistor

    (B) load

    (C) power source

    (D) diode

13. What is the formula for voltage?

    (A) Volts = Amps × Watts

    (B) Volts = Watts ÷ Amps

    (C) Volts = Ohms × Amps

    (D) Volts = Amps ÷ Ohms

14. Which type of current is commonly used by the power company for industrial and residential customers alike?

    (A) alternating

    (B) direct

    (C) amplified

    (D) frequency modulated

15. Computer clock speed is measured using which type of unit?

    (A) newton

    (B) hertz

    (C) joule

    (D) kilogram

16. If you have a wave that measures 6 meters between peaks, an amplitude of 8 meters, and a frequency of 24 hertz, what is the wave speed?

    (A) 48

    (B) 4

    (C) 3

    (D) 192

17. Which of the following is true of high frequencies?

    (A) They have low pitches and long wavelengths.

    (B) They have low pitches and short wavelengths.

    (C) They have high pitches and short wavelengths.

    (D) They have high pitches and long wavelengths.

18. The previous symbol represents

    (A) battery.

    (B) capacitor.

    (C) diode.

    (D) DC voltage capacitor.

19. When sound waves bend around an object, this is known as what?

    (A) dispersion

    (B) diffraction

    (C) deflection

    (D) distancing

20. What is the formula for wattage?

    (A) Watts = Amps × Ohms

    (B) Watts = Volts ÷ Amps

    (C) Watts = Volts × Amps

    (D) Watts = Volts ÷ Ohms

Automotive and Shop Information

Time: 11 Minutes

Questions: 25

Directions: This section tests your knowledge of automotive components and principles, as well as general shop tools and applications. Carefully read each question and choose the answer choice that reflects the best answer.

1. What drives the piston downward into the exhaust stroke of the four-stroke combustion cycle?

    (A) ignition of gasoline
    (B) hydraulics
    (C) compression
    (D) the weight of the cylinder

2. A camshaft

    (A) ignites fuel and air in a combustion engine.
    (B) injects fuel into a combustion engine.
    (C) moves pistons in a combustion engine.
    (D) opens valves in a combustion engine.

3. A clutch

    (A) changes gears in a transmission.
    (B) disengages the transmission from the engine.
    (C) is attached to the drive shaft.
    (D) activates the solenoid.

4. Which of the following is NOT a type of ignition system in use by cars today:

    (A) mechanical ignition
    (B) hydraulic ignition
    (C) electronic ignition
    (D) distributorless ignition

5. Of the systems listed in question 4, which one is the most modern?

    (A) mechanical ignition
    (B) hydraulic ignition
    (C) electronic ignition
    (D) distributorless ignition

6. What type of joints does a differential move in front- and rear-wheel drive vehicles?

    (A) hinge joints
    (B) ball joints
    (C) universal joints
    (D) axel joints

7. What device in a car helps control the amount of harmful gases emitted by the engine through the exhaust system?

    (A) muffler
    (B) catalytic converter
    (C) exhaust manifold
    (D) intermediate pipe

8. The ignition switch holds battery power back until what?

    (A) the spark plugs ignite
    (B) you activate the ignition with your key
    (C) the solenoid relays the current
    (D) the alternator stops working

9. Almost everything in your car that uses electricity is connected to what?

   (A) brake lines
   (B) coil pack
   (C) voltage regulator
   (D) ignition switch

10. What can happen to a parking brake that goes unused for lengthy periods of time?

    (A) It can get corroded.
    (B) The brake cable can snap.
    (C) The brake cable can become loose.
    (D) The hydraulics stop functioning.

11. What device is used to alert drivers that brake pads are worn and should be replaced?

    (A) small metal clip
    (B) slide pin
    (C) ceramic blocks
    (D) steel drums

12. Another term for *backing plate* is

    (A) wheel.
    (B) hub plate.
    (C) mounting plate.
    (D) wheel well.

13. What causes brake pads to press against the rotors?

    (A) calipers
    (B) hydraulic pressure
    (C) friction
    (D) brake shoes

14. On which system do emergency brakes operate?

    (A) electronic system
    (B) mechanical system
    (C) hydraulic system
    (D) none of the above

15. Which element of the suspension system helps prevent the car from rolling during a sharp turn?

    (A) steering linkage
    (B) stabilizer bars
    (C) control arm
    (D) damper

16. During which phase of a woodworking project should a rasp be used?

    (A) before sawing
    (B) after sanding
    (C) after sawing, before sanding
    (D) before and after sawing

17. Which type of saw should you use to cut the corners of a picture frame?

    (A) hack
    (B) jigsaw
    (C) miter
    (D) table

18. If you had to break up a slab of concrete, which hammer would be the best choice to use?

    (A) curved claw hammer
    (B) tinner hammer
    (C) ball-peen hammer
    (D) sledgehammer

19. Which type of screwdriver has a square tip?

    (A) Torx
    (B) Robertson
    (C) Phillips
    (D) flathead

20. Which type of screwdriver provides more stability for the connection of the screw and screwdriver?

    (A) flathead
    (B) cabinet
    (C) Phillips
    (D) none of the above

21. What tool would you use to measure the internal width of a hole that needs a bolt and nut?

    (A) calipers
    (B) level
    (C) square
    (D) none of the above

22. Twist bits are most commonly used with

    (A) wood.
    (B) metal.
    (C) plastic.
    (D) all of the above.

23. The combination-end wrench has an open end at one end and a _____ design at the other end.

    (A) clamp
    (B) socket
    (C) box
    (D) screw

24. Which tool is often used when assembling ready-to-finish furniture?

    (A) Allen wrench
    (B) hand screw
    (C) bar clamp
    (D) socket wrench

25. A jigsaw has what type of blade?

    (A) circular, jagged
    (B) narrow, reciprocating
    (C) wide, reciprocating
    (D) circular, with short teeth

Mechanical Comprehension

Time: 19 Minutes

Questions: 25

Directions: This section tests your knowledge and application of basic mechanical principles. Carefully read each question and choose the answer choice that reflects the best answer.

1. Suppose you have an object whose mass is 50 kilograms, and it is located 4 meters above Earth. What is the object's gravitational potential energy?

    (A) 200 joules
    (B) 490 joules
    (C) 540 joules
    (D) 1,960 joules

2. What is the definition of negative acceleration?

    (A) slowing down
    (B) Acceleration – x
    (C) Acceleration ÷ Speed
    (D) 0 – Acceleration

3. Work is

    (A) something that changes an object at rest into an object in motion.
    (B) transferring energy through force over a distance.
    (C) any object that changes distance over a period of time.
    (D) energy of motion.

4. When potential energy is released, it is converted to what type of energy?

    (A) work
    (B) chemical
    (C) motion
    (D) gravitational

5. A spring has three main types of energy. What are they?

    (A) potential, light, and sound
    (B) kinetic, potential, and thermal
    (C) elastic, kinetic, and potential
    (D) electromagnetic, potential, and elastic

6. 9.8 m/sec/sec is the constant for

    (A) energy.
    (B) force.
    (C) gravity.
    (D) velocity.

7. What is the kinetic energy of a tricycle moving at 2 kilometers per hour if it weighs 10 kilograms?

    (A) 20 joules
    (B) 10 joules
    (C) 40 joules
    (D) 12 joules

8. Which of the following objects has greater kinetic energy? Object 1 is a paper airplane with a mass of 2 kilograms and a velocity of 15 kilometers per hour; object 2 is a rolling ball with a mass of 4 kilograms and a velocity of 10 kilometers per hour.

(A) Object 1 has greater kinetic energy.

(B) Object 2 has greater kinetic energy.

(C) Object 1 has the same kinetic energy as object 2.

(D) Not enough information.

9. If you have two variables, force times distance, what are you trying to calculate?

(A) mass

(B) matter

(C) work

(D) motion

10. According to Newton's first law, an object tends to resist changes in motion unless

(A) it undergoes negative acceleration.

(B) it has an equal and opposite reaction to the motion.

(C) a force is exerted upon it.

(D) gravitational pull forces the change.

11. This is an example of a

(A) 1st-class pulley.

(B) fixed pulley.

(C) moveable pulley.

(D) compound pulley.

12. Velocity is a measure of both the _____ and _____ in which an object moves.

(A) speed, acceleration

(B) speed, distance

(C) speed, direction

(D) speed, force

13. During freefall, how quickly do objects accelerate downward?

(A) 9.8 m/s²

(B) 8.9 m/s²

(C) 3.14 m/s²

(D) 6.2 m/s²

14. What is an inward force that causes an object to turn?

(A) gravitational pull

(B) centrifugal force

(C) centripetal force

(D) metric force

15. When a gear causes a motor or mechanism to slow down, what is the result?

    (A) increased speed
    (B) increased motion
    (C) more forceful output
    (D) more forceful input

16. This type of gear is designed such that the teeth are angled inward. The result is that contact spreads slowly across each tooth. What type of gear is this?

    (A) helical
    (B) spur
    (C) bevel
    (D) worm

17. Suppose you have a bicycle wheel that turns one time for every six full pedal rotations. What is the gear ratio?

    (A) 1:6
    (B) 6:1
    (C) 2:1
    (D) 1:2

18. If you are a cyclist going uphill, which gear ratio would offer the easiest pedaling for you?

    (A) 1:4
    (B) 2:1
    (C) 9:3
    (D) 4:1

19. When an axle is connected to a stationary object, such as a hook or a wall, this is known as what type of pulley?

    (A) fixed
    (B) stationary
    (C) immobile
    (D) compound

20. The definition of fulcrum is

    (A) the weight of a lever.
    (B) the load that is placed on either side of a lever.
    (C) the mechanical advantage associated with a lever.
    (D) the object on which a lever pivots.

21. Which of the following is NOT an example of a 2nd-class lever?

    (A) wheelbarrow
    (B) nutcracker
    (C) scissors
    (D) wrench

22. If you place two weights on a 1st-class lever and one weight is heavier than the other, which one should sit closer to the fulcrum for the lever to balance?

    (A) the lighter weight
    (B) the heavier weight
    (C) neither; they should sit equidistant
    (D) not enough information to tell

23. When the products of weight and distance from the fulcrum for each side of a 1st-class lever are equal, the lever is considered

   (A) complete.
   (B) incomplete.
   (C) balanced.
   (D) rearranged.

24. Suppose you have a 20-kilogram weight on one side of a 1st-class lever, and it is placed 6 meters from the fulcrum. Suppose you have another 12-kilogram weight to place on the other side. How far apart should the objects be from one another to achieve balance?

   (A) 16 meters
   (B) 6 meters
   (C) 12 meters
   (D) 20 meters

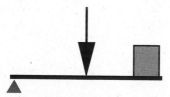

25. Which type of lever is pictured?

   (A) 1st class
   (B) 2nd class
   (C) 3rd class
   (D) 4th class

Assembling Objects

Time: 15 Minutes

Questions: 25

Directions: This section tests your ability to visualize how objects fit together. Carefully read each question and choose the answer choice that reflects the best answer.

1. In the following diagram, which figure best shows how the objects in the first box would touch if points A and B were connected?

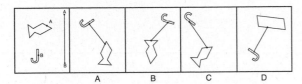

2. Which answer choice best shows how the objects in the first box would appear if they were fitted together?

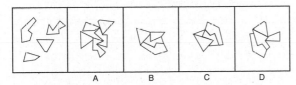

3. In the following diagram, which figure best shows how the objects in the first box would touch if points A and B were connected?

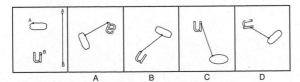

4. Which answer choice best shows how the objects in the first box would appear if they were fitted together?

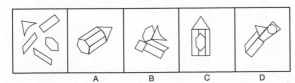

5. In the following diagram, which figure best shows how the objects in the first box would touch if points A and B were connected?

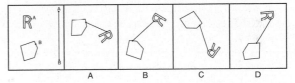

6. Which answer choice best shows how the objects in the first box would appear if they were fitted together?

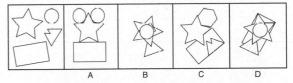

7. In the following diagram, which figure best shows how the objects in the first box would touch if points A and B were connected?

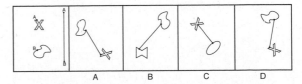

8. Which answer choice best shows how the objects in the first box would appear if they were fitted together?

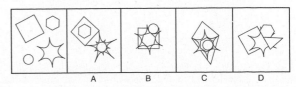

9. Which answer choice best shows how the objects in the first box would appear if they were fitted together?

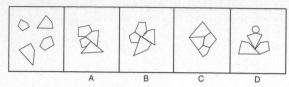

10. In the following diagram, which figure best shows how the objects in the first box would touch if points A and B were connected?

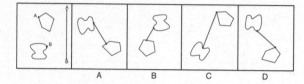

11. In the following diagram, which figure best shows how the objects in the first box would touch if points A and B were connected?

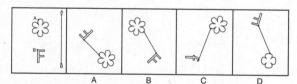

12. Which answer choice best shows how the objects in the first box would appear if they were fitted together?

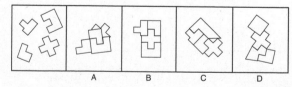

13. In the following diagram, which figure best shows how the objects in the first box would touch if points A and B were connected?

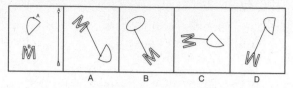

14. Which answer choice best shows how the objects in the first box would appear if they were fitted together?

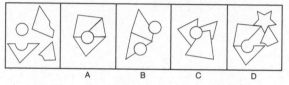

15. In the following diagram, which figure best shows how the objects in the first box would touch if points A and B were connected?

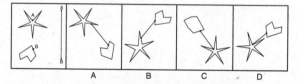

16. Which answer choice best shows how the objects in the first box would appear if they were fitted together?

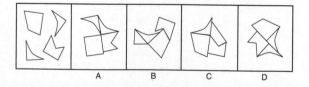

17. In the following diagram, which figure best shows how the objects in the first box would touch if points A and B were connected?

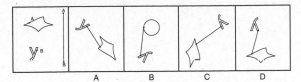

18. Which answer choice best shows how the objects in the first box would appear if they were fitted together?

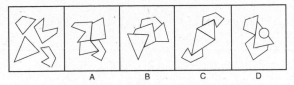

19. In the following diagram, which figure best shows how the objects in the first box would touch if points A and B were connected?

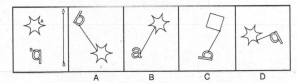

20. Which answer choice best shows how the objects in the first box would appear if they were fitted together?

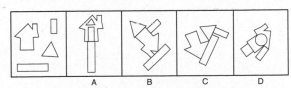

21. In the following diagram, which figure best shows how the objects in the first box would touch if points A and B were connected?

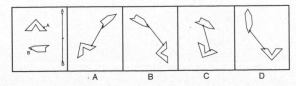

22. Which answer choice best shows how the objects in the first box would appear if they were fitted together?

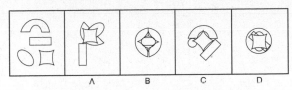

23. In the following diagram, which figure best shows how the objects in the first box would touch if points A and B were connected?

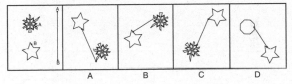

24. Which answer choice best shows how the objects in the first box would appear if they were fitted together?

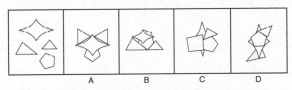

25. In the following diagram, which figure best shows how the objects in the first box would touch if points A and B were connected?

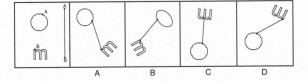

Practice Test 3: Answers and Explanations

General Science

1. **C.** Producers are organisms that produce their own food. They may be able to survive in extreme cold, but they are not defined by this. Answers A and D do not apply.

2. **D.** Chromosomes are a specific type of DNA that is joined with protein and contains genetic information, as well as nucleotide sequences and regulatory elements specific to the organism. All the other answer choices are organelles found within a cell.

3. **A.** All of the other parts of the digestive process happen after breaking down food by chewing.

4. **C.** The rate of change of the velocity of an object is defined as acceleration.

5. **A.** Constant acceleration means an object increases speed by the same amount every second.

6. **C.** Curium is Cm. Carbon is C. Chromium is Cr.

7. **C.** Liquids cannot hold their own shape. Plasmas and gases have atoms that are quite spread out.

8. **A.** A compound is created when two or more elements are combined or bonded.

9. **B.** Choices A, C, and D are false statements.

10. **D.** Neutrons have no charge, and therefore cannot affect the charge of an atom. They have no effect on magnetism, bond strength, or density. They can affect the mass of an atom, and adding neutrons to an atom can cause it to become radioactive.

11. **C.** Choice A is wrong because in a lunar eclipse, the moon passes behind Earth, blocking sunlight from the moon. Since the moon doesn't create its own light, it is safe to view. Choices B and D are not types of eclipses.

12. **D.** All the other choices are Kepler's laws; choice D is a true statement, but is not one of Kepler's laws.

13. **C.** Choice A is wrong because Lunar New Year is a holiday that occurs in January every year and is celebrated in Asian countries; it is also called Chinese New Year. Choice B is wrong because solstice occurs twice each year when the days begin getting either longer or shorter, depending on whether it is summer or winter solstice. Choice D has nothing to do with the length of days and nights.

14. **D.** A galaxy is a group of stars, gas, and dust held together by gravity. An asteroid is a rock or minor planet orbiting the sun. A meteorite is an object from outer space, such as a rock that falls into Earth.

15. **A.** Choice B is wrong because mid-level clouds are identified with the prefix *alto*. Choice C is wrong because low-level clouds do not have a prefix. Choice D is wrong because it has nothing to do with cloud prefix identification.

16. **C.** Choice A is wrong because clouds are formations of gaseous water. Choice B is wrong because barometric pressure is the weight of air as it pushes down on a portion of Earth. Choice D is wrong because a tornado results from barometric pressure that has plummeted.

17. **A.** Choice B is wrong because this is where the ozone exists. Choice C is wrong because the mesosphere is the coldest region in the atmosphere. Choice D is wrong because this is the atmospheric layer closest to space.

18. **B.** Even though the atoms in the thermosphere have very high energy, there is very little heat. Heat is felt when energy is transferred from one atom to another. When atoms are very spread out, they cannot easily transfer energy.

19. **D.** The atmosphere is made up of 78 percent nitrogen, 21 percent oxygen, and .93 percent argon. In addition, you may find ozone and carbon dioxide in the atmosphere, as well as some other trace amounts of neon, helium, methane, krypton, and hydrogen.

20. **D.** Choice A is wrong because ohms are used to measure resistance in electric circuits. Choice B is wrong because Kepler is famous for his planetary laws. Choice C is wrong because Hertz is the name of the scientist who first proved the existence of electromagnetic waves.

21. **B.** Choice A is wrong because shale is a soft, sedimentary rock that often houses fossils. Choice C is wrong because graphite is a type of rock. Choice D is wrong because archaeology is the study of past human life.

22. **B.** Choice A is wrong because lava is liquid molten rock that flows above Earth's surface. Choice C is wrong because extrusive rock is igneous rock that has cooled on the surface of Earth. Choice D is wrong because sediment is worn-down particles of igneous rock that settles in the beds of lakes, streams, and oceans.

23. **D.** Chromatids are what make up a chromosome. Nucleotides are joined molecules that comprise the structural units of DNA and RNA. Riboflavin is a vitamin.

24. **C.** Choice A is wrong because it describes a system. Choice B is wrong because it describes a bone. Choice D is wrong because a bunch of cells together comprise tissue, but a single cell does not.

25. **A.** The lithosphere encompasses the solid, rocky top layer of the planet (the one on which we live) and part of the upper mantle.

Arithmetic Reasoning

1. **C.** Use simple addition.

2. **B.** This is a probability question, so start by counting the total number of coins in your pocket: $3 + 2 + 6 + 1 = 12$. Since the question asks about the chances you'll pull out a penny, use this value as the top number of your fraction to figure out the probability. The total number of coins will be the bottom number.

   Finally, reduce: $\frac{2}{12} = \frac{1}{6}$.

3. **D.** Start by calculating Kenny's age: $.5 \times 42 = 21$. Now multiply that value by 3 to get Miriam's age, which is 63.

4. **A.** Calculate 15% of 32,425: $32,425 \times .15 = 4,863.75$. Now divide this amount by 11.50 to get 422.934. Round this up and you'll have 423 as your answer.

5. **A.** Divide 6 by 4 (number of weeks in a month) to get the answer: 1.5.

6. **C.** First calculate how much a 7% increase in your per-credit tuition will be: $.07 \times \$326 = \$22.82$. Now add this amount to the current per-credit price: $\$326 + \$22.82 = \$348.82$. Finally, multiply this total by 3: $\$348.82 \times 3 = \$1,046.46$.

7. **B.** Calculate: $\frac{3}{5} \times \frac{30}{1} = \frac{90}{5} = 18$

8. **D.** This is a volume question. Since we're dealing with a rectangular solid, plug in the numbers from the question into the following formula:

   $V = l \times w \times h$

9. **A.** Divide 27 by 6 to get 4.5.

10. **B.** Start by multiplying the number of hours by sessions for one album: $4 \times 8 = 32$. Now multiply this number by the number of artists to see how many total hours will be needed to record all the music: $32 \times 5 = 160$. Finally, multiply that by \$235 to get the total cost: $160 \times \$235 = \$37,600$.

11. **C.** First, figure out how much the salesperson made by multiplying $.16 \times \$6,283 = \$1,005.28$. Now figure out how much she puts in her savings account: $.12 \times \$1,005.28 = \$120.63$.

12. **D.** An integer is any whole number and its opposite. Answer D is a decimal, not a whole number.

13. **A.** Start by figuring out how many men and women come and go by 1 A.M.:

    Men: $10 + 25 + (-7) = 28$

    Women: $15 + 20 (-11) = 24$

    Now set up your ratio like it's said in the question (men to women) and reduce: $28:24 = 7:6$.

14. **B.** Add the cost of all your lunches, and then multiply that sum by .15 to calculate that you've paid \$2.586 in tips. Now add $\$17.24 + \$2.586 = \$19.826$ to get the total amount spent throughout the month. Finally, divide this total by 3 to get an average of \$6.6086, which rounds up to \$6.61.

15. **C.** Divide 453 by 36 to find it would take 12.58 minutes to type the essay. Round this up to 13 to get your answer.

16. **D.** A prime number is an integer that can be divided only by 1 and itself. One is not a prime number because 1 is its only factor.

17. **B.** Jen bought 10 carrots. This means Dave bought 5 carrots. Since Marc bought three times the number of carrots as Dave, he bought 15 carrots.

18. **D.** Since there are no parentheses, you address the exponent first, which is answer D.

19. **B.** This is a simple average question. Add up all of the scores and divide by 5: 5.4 + 3.9 + 4.8 + 4.9 + 5.1 = 24.1. Then divide 24.1 by 5 to get 4.82.

20. **A.** This translates to −6 − −6. The two negative signs cancel each other out and make a positive. Therefore, you are really dealing with −6 + 6, which equals 0.

21. **B.** Multiply length times width to get the area of a rectangle: 16.2 × 8.5 = 137.7 ft².

22. **D.** Calculate the cost of each apple:

    Golden Delicious: $.89 − (.89 × .10) = .89 − .089 = $.80

    Granny Smith: $.75

    Red Delicious: $.65

    Now multiply by the number you need of each and add the products:

    Golden Delicious: $.80 × 3 = $2.40

    Granny Smith: $.75 × 1 = $.75

    Red Delicious: $.65 × 1 = $.65

    $2.40 + $.75 + $.65 = $3.80

23. **C.** A product is the answer to a multiplication problem. A quotient is the answer to a division problem. A difference is the answer to a subtraction problem.

24. **A.** When the numerator is either equal to or greater than the denominator, you have an improper fraction. When you simplify an improper fraction, you break it down into a mixed fraction (a whole number and a fraction together in one term). A simplified fraction is one that is in its smallest form.

25. **C.** According to the question, Terry is 11 right now. That means in 3 years, he'll be 14. In 3 years, Jed will be four times this number: 4 × 14 = 56. So today Jed is 53, since 56 − 3 = 53.

26. **B.** Since you have to retake the ASVAB if you don't pass it, you need to figure out how many recruits passed the test and subtract that from the total number who took the test:

    Pass: .72 × 68 = 48.96 (round up to 49)

    Fail: 68 − 49 = 19

27. **B.** Set up the ratio just like it's said in the question, and reduce: 26:42 = 13:21.

28. **D.** Move your decimal points and divide to get 14.97.

29. **A.** Find the probability of both of these events and then multiply to get your answer:

    Classic rock: $\frac{10}{25}$

    Hard rock: $\frac{3}{24}$

    Notice that the denominator in the hard rock fraction is 24, not 25. This is because, according to the question, you did not return the classic rock CD, so you thus reduced the total number of CDs you could have chosen from.

    Now multiply the fractions and reduce: $\frac{10}{25} \times \frac{3}{24} = \frac{30}{600} = \frac{3}{60} = \frac{1}{20}$

30. **C.** There are 60 minutes in an hour and 24 hours in a day: 60 × 24 = 1,440.

Word Knowledge

1. **A.** Something that is a *nuisance* is annoying. *Forbearance* means "calm" or "patience." *Clarity* means "clearness." *Argument* means "a position" or "a disagreement."

2. **C.** Though those who are *authoritative* may be loud, irritating, or conceited, what defines them is their power to command.

3. **B.** *Perverse* can mean "stubborn" or "wicked." None of the other answer choices make sense with this definition.

4. **D.** The root *son* means "sound," so your answer will have something to do with sound. That eliminates choices A and B. You may like option C as an answer, but you can be *jubilant* (excited, happy) without emitting sound. You cannot *echo* without sound, though.

5. **A.** The sentence tells us that the pencil case belongs to the speaker and implies that she was previously in the classroom. This means she needs to get it again. If she were to collect it, this would imply it's the first time she's getting the pencil case in her possession, which goes against the context clues in the sentence.

6. **C.** When you take all information to be fact, you're simply collecting it, not evaluating it at all. The context clues tell us that the underlined word is the opposite of what the sentence is talking about (see the *not* before *astute*). Therefore, *discerning* (evaluative) is the correct answer.

7. **D.** *Efface* means "to rub or wear away," so this answer makes the most sense.

8. **A.** Connect the base word in *palatable* to your mouth, and you'll get a good clue to the meaning of the word. Something that's palatable tastes good and can be eaten. *Cross* means "angry." *Insipid* means "uninteresting." *Brave* talks about nerve.

9. **B.** Swap out your answer choices here, and *begged* will be the only one that makes sense.

10. **D.** An association you can make here is in the base word, *vary*, which means "to change." *Variance*, therefore will have something to do with change. Answer D is the only choice that implies this.

11. **C.** Using the context clues, you can tell Jade is friendly and active with her friends. Answers A and B mean "quiet" and "keeping to oneself." Answer D means "doubtful." Answer C makes the most sense.

12. **B.** Don't be fooled here into thinking "spare room" means "extra room." If you look at the context clues in the sentence, you'll see that it's talking about how it's decorated. There is very little in the room and no indication of its size. Answer B is the best choice.

13. **A.** *Superfluous* means "extra," and answer A is the only one that makes sense with this definition.

14. **C.** *Affix* means "to fasten" something. A good mnemonic: "affix a sticker." *Berate* means "to scold." *Savor* means "to enjoy."

15. **A.** The base word here is *haste,* which means "speed" or "hurry." The correct answer will have to do with hurrying, which is what you do when you accelerate.

16. **D.** The context clues of "ideal for those who are not overly fond of extremely cold or hot weather" tell us that *temperate* relates to conditions somewhere in the middle.

17. **A.** Think about how viruses spread—really easily—and you'll be able to remember the definition of *viral*. *Submissive* means "passive." *Surreptitious* means "secretive."

18. **B.** *Evoke* means "to cause." You can infer from the sentence that the fans were emotionally moved by the tribute, which makes all the other answer choices not fit.

19. **C.** *Increment* is an increase in something. None of the other answer choices make sense.

20. **A.** A good connection to make is "raze one building to make room for another," as this is often the context in which you hear *raze* being used. However, it does not mean to build them; it means to destroy or demolish them.

21. **D.** *Vituperative* describes speech that intends to harm and offend. It may be impassioned or creative, but it is not defined by this. *Blasé* means uncaring, so that doesn't fit.

22. **B.** The sentence talks about a small flame that grows large. The only answer that makes sense is answer B.

23. **C.** *Auspicious* means "positive" or "lucky." To be *egotistic* is to be concerned with oneself. *Unfortunate* is the opposite of *auspicious*. *Interrogative* refers to questioning.

24. **A.** *Baleful* is a negative word that means "menacing" or "threatening." Answer A is the only one that makes sense.

25. **D.** It's obvious from the context of the sentence that Blake is trying to avoid jury duty.

26. **B.** Think of when you shampoo your hair. The foam that forms is called *lather*.

27. **B.** *Vapid* means "dull" or "uncreative." Answers A and D don't fit with this, nor does answer C.

28. **A.** We talked earlier about *clarity*, meaning "being clear" or "transparent." *Tranquility* refers to peace, and *abrasiveness* means "grainy."

29. **C.** *Invigorate* means "to add life to" or "to refresh." None of the other answer choices come anywhere close to this definition.

30. **D.** The sentence tells us that the woman is being false with her words. *Disingenuous* means "insincere."

31. **C.** Look to the base word here, which is *block*. A blockade prevents transportation. *Brink* means "edge." *Passage* is the opposite. A *crater* is a sunken hole. A *cordon* is a barrier.

32. **A.** *Vocation* is another word for a job.

33. **B.** *Grill* is being used as a verb here. When you grill someone, you question them thoroughly.

34. **D.** The prefix *mal* tells you the word is a negative. Answers A through C are either positive or neutral.

35. **A.** To *emblazon* is to splash or make something very noticeable. Answer A makes the most sense.

Paragraph Comprehension

1. **A.** In the sentence, *versatile* describes many uses.

2. **B.** The passage says vinegar is a good cleaner and deodorizer for coffee makers and fabric.

3. **D.** The passage states that a vinegar solution is good for treating a flea infestation. None of the other choices is supported.

4. **D.** This is the best choice because it talks about listener-centric communication and its increased recognition, which is the main idea of the passage.

5. **B.** The passage talks about thoughts and perceptions as internal communication.

6. **C.** The final sentence in the passage directly supports answer C.

7. **A.** The sentence this word is used in talks about how Neruda used a name that wasn't his real one.

8. **D.** Throughout the passage, the speaker uses language that indicates she is upset with the situation, an emotion that runs counter to answers A through C.

9. **B.** All the other answer choices advocate activities that take you away from media interaction.

10. **A.** The passages focuses on the information presented in the first sentence: "Competition for consumer attention has become drastically out of hand over the past few decades."

11. **C.** Since no other source of information is being presented to us, it can be assumed that all the debate is coming from the speaker.

12. **A.** Answer B is too extreme and inaccurate. Answer C is unfounded by the information in the passage. There is no indication of bias one way or another in the speaker's words, which eliminates answer D.

13. **D.** The final sentence reads, "Therefore, arguing for or against capital punishment is a futile task."

14. **B.** The passage talks about Fawkes being part of a plan to overthrow the government, which defines being a revolutionary. This goes against answers A and C. Answer D has no relevance to the passage.

15. **C.** If you swap out the answer choices with the word in the passage, this answer makes the most sense.

Mathematics Knowledge

1. **D.** Substitute 6 for b and solve:

    $b + 12 - 3b \times 2b =$

    $6 + 12 - (3 \times 6) \times (2 \times 6)$

    $6 + 12 - 18 \times 12$

    $6 + 12 - 216$

    $18 - 216$

    -198

2. **B.** Since we're dividing fractions, flip the second fraction and multiply across to get your answer. Then reduce:

    $\frac{5}{9} \div \frac{3}{9} = \frac{5}{9} \times \frac{9}{3} = \frac{45}{27} = 1\frac{18}{27} = 1\frac{2}{3}$

3. **C.** A negative exponent, such as 3^{-4} doesn't tell you the number of times to multiply the base by itself. Instead it tells you how many times to divide the number by 1. Start by calculating the value of 3^4: $3 \times 3 \times 3 \times 3 = 81$. Now write the answer as a fraction and flip it: $\frac{81}{1} \rightarrow \frac{1}{81}$.

4. **D.** Volume for a cylindrical solid uses the formula $V = \pi r^2 h$ If you plug in your values from the question, you get the following:

    $V = 3.14 \times 3^2 \times 5$

    $V = 3.14 \times 9 \times 5$

    $V = 141.3 \text{ ft}^3$

    Note that 3 stands in for the value of the radius. That's because this value is half the diameter, which is represented by the width value in the question.

5. **A.** Complimentary angles are two angles that share a common side and whose combined value equals 90°.

6. **D.** A term is a single number, variable, or combinations thereof. A coefficient is a number that multiplies a variable. A constant is a number that stands by itself in an expression or equation. An equation is a mathematical statement that shows two equal expressions.

7. **B.** This is a quadratic expression. You can either FOIL the answer choices or factor the expression: $a^2 + 13a - 22$.

    $(a\ )(a\ )$

    List factors of 22:

    1×22

    2×11

    If you add 2 and 11, you get 13, which is the middle term. Since one of our original terms is negative, both signs in the final binomials will be negative. The final answer is $(a - 2)(a - 11)$.

8. **A.** Supplementary angles together make a straight line. The sum of the angles equals 180°.

9. **A.** Solve like any other equation, keeping track of the direction of the inequality.

    $12x + 6 - 6 > 7x - 4 - 6$

    $12x + 6 - 6 - 7x > \overline{7x} - \overline{7x} - 4 - 6$

    $5x > -10$

    $x > -2$

10. **B.** When you divide powers, treat them like a fraction and reduce. Write out the base the number of times indicated in the exponent and cancel out like terms:

    $b^5 \div b^4 = \frac{b^5}{b^4} = \frac{b \times b \times b \times b \times b}{b \times b \times b \times b} = \frac{\overline{b \times b \times b \times b} \times b}{\overline{b \times b \times b \times b}} = \frac{b}{1} = b$

11. **D.** Pentagons have five sides. Hexagons have six sides. Triangles have three sides.

12. **B.** Answer A is the formula for finding the area of a triangle, not the missing side of a right triangle. Answer C is used to find the area of a trapezoid. Answer D is used to find the area of a circle.

13. **A.** Use the Pythagorean theorem here to solve for the missing value: $a^2 + b^2 = c^2$.

$$(6 \times 6) + (9 \times 9) = c^2$$

$$36 + 81 = c^2$$

$$117 = c^2$$

$$\sqrt{117} = c$$

$$10.816 = c$$

14. **D.** All sides of an equilateral triangle are equal. Therefore, each of the sides of the square equals 8. To calculate the area of a square, you multiply the value of 2 sides: $8 \times 8 = 64$.

15. **C.** Calculate prime factorization on both 24 and 36:

2⌐24	2⌐36
2⌐12	2⌐18
2⌐6	3⌐9
2⌐3	3⌐3
1	1

Now multiply common factors:

$$24 = 2 \times [2 \times 2 \times 3]$$

$$36 = [2 \times 2 \times 3] \times 3$$

The shared factors here are $2 \times 2 \times 3$, which, when multiplied, gives you a highest common factor of 12.

16. **B.** To calculate the area of a circle, use the following formula: $A = \pi r^2$. Since you know the diameter is 11, divide that by 2 and use that value for the radius. Your math should look like this:

$$A = 3.14 \times 5.5 \times 5.5$$

$$A = 94.985 \text{ in}^2$$

17. **D.** This is the definition of prime factorization.

18. **A.** To solve for the missing value, cross multiply and complete the equation:

$$13.5a = 9 \times 6$$

$$13.5a = 54$$

$$a = \frac{54}{13.5}$$

$$a = 4$$

19. **C.** To calculate total surface area, use the formula: $TSA = 2\pi r(r + h)$. Plug in your values and solve.

20. **B.** To find the LCM of two numbers, calculate prime factorization on both 8 and 12:

2⌐8	2⌐12
2⌐4	2⌐6
2⌐2	3⌐3
1	1

Our common factors are 2 and 3. Next, multiply each factor by the greatest number of times it appears in any one factorization. Since 2 appears three times and 3 appears once, your expression will be $2 \times 2 \times 2 \times 3 = 24$.

21. **A.** You can calculate the value of this external angle because you know the value of the adjacent internal angle and, together, the angles equal 180°. Subtract the value of the internal angle from 180 to get 38 as your answer.

22. **D.** Use the following formula to calculate the area of a trapezoid:

$$A = \tfrac{1}{2} \times h \times (b_1 + b_2)$$

$$A = \tfrac{1}{2} \times h \times (b_1 + b_2)$$
$$A = \tfrac{1}{2} \times 9 \times (6 + 14)$$
$$A = \tfrac{1}{2} \times 9 \times 20$$
$$A = \tfrac{1}{2} \times 180$$
$$A = 90$$

23. **C.** The four tests to determine if two triangles are congruent are as follows:

Are all three corresponding side values equal?

Are two corresponding sides and the angle they make equal?

Are two corresponding angles and the side they share equal?

Are two corresponding angles and a side they don't share equal?

24. **B.** Start by breaking down each term into prime factors:

$42x^2 = 2 \times 3 \times 7 \times x \times x$

$28x = 2 \times 2 \times 7 \times x$

What do both of these have in common? $2 \times 7 \times x$ (which equals $14x$). Next, simplify each of these by crossing out one 2, 7, and x in each expression:

$42x^2 = \cancel{2} \times 3 \times \cancel{7} \times x \times \cancel{x}$

$28x = 2 \times \cancel{2} \times \cancel{7} \times \cancel{x}$

Now combine like terms and place the new expression in parentheses with $14x$ outside: $42x^2 + 28x = 14x\,(3x + 2)$.

25. **D.** Simply divide the upper part of the fraction by 9 to get $2y + 3$.

Electronics Information

1. **A.** See the symbol chart in Chapter 12, page 129, for additional guidance.

2. **A.** Over the course of 60 seconds, your seatbelt alarm will sound 20 times. You allow this to continue for 5 minutes, resulting in a total of 100 alarms. To calculate frequency, you divide the total number of times an event takes place by the total length of time that has elapsed. In this case, $100 \div 5 = 20$.

3. **D.** None of the other choices offer the correct formula.

4. **D.** See the symbol chart in Chapter 12, page 129, for additional guidance.

5. **A.** To calculate volts, use the following formula: Watts = Volts × Amps.

6. **A.** None of the other choices offer the correct formula.

7. **C.** Choice A is wrong because interference occurs when two waves come into contact with one another. Choice B is wrong because refraction occurs when a wave changes direction after encountering a medium of different composition. Choice D is wrong because longitudinal is a type of wave, not a principle of wave movement.

8. **C.** See the symbol chart in Chapter 12, page 129, for additional guidance.

9. **B.** Choice A is wrong because insulators surround the conductors through which electrons flow. Choice C is wrong because loads are circuit parts that convert one type of energy to another. Choice D is wrong because ammeters are used to measure current.

10. **D.** Electrical force refers to voltage, so choices A and C are wrong. Choice B is also wrong because most household appliances in the United States either run on 120 volts or occasionally 240 volts. In other countries, most appliances run on 220 volts.

11. **B.** See the symbol chart in Chapter 12, page 129, for additional guidance.

12. **C.** A power source is required to get electrons moving along their path. This is why a hair dryer cord that isn't plugged in is basically useless.

13. **C.** None of the other choices offer the correct formula.

14. **A.** Choice B is wrong because it is commonly used by batteries. Choices C and D are wrong because they are actually radio waves.

15. **B.** CPU clock speed, AC power, and waves are all measured in hertz (Hz).

16. **D.** Wave speed is calculated by multiplying wavelength and frequency.

17. **C.** Low frequencies have long wavelengths and low pitches, and B and D are simply incorrect statements.

18. **A.** See the symbol chart in Chapter 12, page 129, for additional guidance.

19. **B.** Choice A is wrong because dispersion occurs when a wave is split up by frequency. Choices C and D are wrong because they are not terms commonly associated with waves bending around obstacles.

20. **C.** None of the other choices offer the correct formula.

Automotive and Shop Information

1. **A.** In the four-stroke combustion cycle, the pistons start in the up position. When the intake valve opens, the crankshaft drives the pistons down to receive a full cylinder of fuel and air. This is known as the *intake step*. As the pistons slide back up, they compress the mixture, which is why the next step is called *compression*. When the pistons reach the top position once again, the spark plugs emit a spark to ignite the mixture. This is known as the *power stroke*. The ignition of gasoline drives the pistons back down so that they can release exhaust gases through the exhaust system.

2. **D.** Spark plugs ignite the fuel-air mixture in an engine. The fuel injector pumps fuel into an engine. The crankshaft moves the pistons.

3. **B.** A gear shift is used to change gears in a transmission. The whole transmission, not the clutch, is attached to the driveshaft in rear-wheel drive vehicles. The solenoid is used in the ignition process.

4. **B.** Although hydraulics are used in cars today, they are not considered a type of ignition system.

5. **D.** Ignition systems made prior to 1975 were called mechanical ignitions. During the 1970s and 1980s, the electronic ignition system became popular. In the mid-1980s, the distributorless system was invented, and it is still in use today.

6. **C.** Differentials move universal joints.

7. **B.** Catalytic converters control the amount of harmful gas emissions from cars. They focus mostly on nitrogen, carbon dioxide, and water vapor.

8. **B.** Choices A, C, and D are all fictitious statements.

9. **D.** The ignition switch acts as an intermediary between the battery and the rest of the car's electronic components with a few exceptions, such as your interior lights.

10. **A.** When parking brakes go unused, they can become corroded and eventually inoperable.

11. **A.** As brake pads get worn, a small metal clip scrapes against the rotor. The sound of scraping metal alerts the driver that the pads need to be replaced.

12. **C.** The other terms are not interchangeable with *backing plate*.

13. **B.** Choice A is wrong because calipers are designed to house the brake pads. Choice C is wrong because friction is the result of the pads squeezing either side of a disc brake. Choice D is wrong because brake shoes are a component of drum brakes, whereas brake pads are part of the disc brake system.

14. **B.** Emergency brakes are considered secondary braking devices because they operate using a mechanical system. They are designed this way so that if the hydraulic system used by the primary disc or drum brakes fails, the emergency brake can still slow the car.

15. **B.** Choice A is wrong because the steering linkage is designed to allow cars to swivel and turn. Choice C is wrong because the control arm is designed to manage the motion of the wheels. Choice D is wrong because *damper* is another term for the shock absorber. The shock absorber is built to smooth the jolt of a bump in the road.

16. **C.** The sharp teeth of a rasp help smooth rough edges from a saw. However, the teeth are too rough to smooth the wood as well as sandpaper.

17. **C.** Miter saws come in both the hand tool and the powered tool varieties. Either one is ideal for making picture frames because of the angle on which the saw cuts.

18. **D.** None of the other answer choices have the weight needed to break up concrete. A sledgehammer is the proper tool for this type of job.

19. **B.** A Torx screwdriver has a six-sided star head; a Phillips has an X; and a flathead a single slit.

20. **C.** Because of the *X* shape on the end of a Phillips head screwdriver and the matching shape on the screw, the tool fits snugly inside the head of the screw. This causes less slippage than a flathead.

21. **A.** Calipers have legs that are used to measure either the internal or external width of a three-dimensional object.

22. **D.** Twist bits are the most common type of drill bit because it can be used on a variety of materials.

23. **C.** Combination-end wrenches use a box design to slip vertically over fasteners, which means you can't accidentally use the wrong size; it just won't fit.

24. **A.** None of the other tools are commonly used on this type of project.

25. **B.** A jigsaw's blade is designed to allow it to make intricate cuts and curves in a variety of different directions.

Mechanical Comprehension

1. **D.** The formula for gravitational potential energy is $PE = mgh$, or mass × gravity × height above Earth:

   $PE = 4 \times 9.8 \times 50$

   $PE = 1{,}960$ joules

2. **A.** None of the other answers represent negative acceleration.

3. **B.** Choice A is the definition of force. Choice C is the definition of motion. Choice D is the definition of kinetic energy.

4. **C.** Motion energy is another term for kinetic energy, which is what potential energy is converted to.

5. **C.** When a spring is tightly coiled, it has potential energy. When it is released, the ensuing movement demonstrates kinetic energy. The ability to restore its original structure demonstrates elastic energy.

6. **C.** On Earth, acceleration due to gravity is approximately 9.8 meters per second per second.

7. **A.** Kinetic energy is determined by taking half the value of (mass times velocity squared).

8. **A.** Object 1 has a kinetic energy of 225 joules:

   $KE = .5 \times 2 \text{ kg} \times 15^2$

   $KE = .5 \times 2 \times 225$

   $KE = 1 \times 225$

   $KE = 225$

Object 2 has a kinetic energy of 200 joules:

$KE = .5 \times 4 \text{ kg} \times 10^2$

$KE = .5 \times 4 \times 100$

$KE = 2 \times 225$

$KE = 200$

9. **C.** Work = Force × Distance

10. **C.** Choices A and D are wrong because they are not involved with any of Newton's laws of motion. Choice B is wrong because it refers to Newton's third law.

11. **D.** This pulley system blends several fixed or movable pulleys to maximize mechanical advantage.

12. **C.** None of the other choices offer the combination of factors that defines velocity.

13. **A.** Objects that are free falling are under the influence of gravity only, which means that they accelerate at a rate of 9.8 m/s^2.

14. **C.** Choice A is wrong because gravitational pull is the force that causes an object to fall toward Earth. Choice B is wrong because centrifugal force is an outward force that causes an object to turn. Choice D is wrong because it is not specifically related to circular motion.

15. **C.** Gears offer the mechanical advantage of slowing the work process but increasing the force of output.

16. **A.** Choice B is wrong because a spur gear does not have teeth that are angled inward. Choice C is wrong because bevel gears are mounted on perpendicular shafts with a variety of teeth styles. Choice D is wrong because a worm gear has teeth that mesh with a partially threaded shaft instead of another gear.

17. **B.** Ratios are determined by counting the number of rotations for each gear and dividing the larger number by the smaller number.

18. **D.** With a 4:1 ratio, the force is easier, even if the process takes longer. This is called gear reduction.

19. **A.** A fixed pulley is mounted to a stationary object. Although there is only a mechanical advantage of 1 with this type of pulley, it still has the advantage of making the work *seem* easier.

20. **D.** Choice A is wrong because the weight of the lever actually has nothing to do with a fulcrum. Choice B is wrong because the load on either side of the lever is completely separate from the pivot point. Choice C is wrong because the mechanical advantage of a lever has nothing to do with a fulcrum.

21. **C.** A pair of scissors operates under the principle of a 1st-class lever.

22. **B.** This answer can be determined using the following formula: Heavy weight × X = Lower weight (distance between the two objects – X). Although we didn't use any numbers in this question, if you plugged in a set of numbers, you would be able to see the answer.

23. **C.** A 1st- and a 3rd-class lever are depicted as such due to the placement of force, fulcrum, and effort, not because of balancing purposes.

24. **A.** This answer was derived from the formula described previously in the answer to question 22:

$$20 (6) = 12 (x - 6)$$

$$120 = 12x - 72$$

$$192 = 12x$$

$$16 = x$$

In this case, x is the distance between the two weights on the lever.

25. **C.** A 3rd-class lever positions the effort between the fulcrum and the load.

Assembling Objects

1. **C.** The larger shape in answer A is mirrored and the A connection is too far toward the top. Answer B has the A connection in the wrong place. Answer D has the sharp-angled object changed.

2. **B.** There are five shapes instead of four in answer A. Several shapes were changed in answers C and D.

3. **D.** The *u* in answer A has been changed to an *a*. Connection point A in answer B is in the wrong spot. The connector line reaching point B in answer C comes in at the wrong angle.

4. **A.** One of the four-sided figures in answer B is smaller than in the sample. The rectangular shapes in answer C have been changed. Only the slanted rectangular shape and the full rectangle are the same as in the sample in answer D.

5. **C.** The A connection point in answer A is in the wrong place. The *R* in answer B is mirrored. The D connection point in answer D is in the wrong place.

6. **D.** The mountain shape has been replaced with two circles in answer A. The rectangle in answer B is much smaller than it should be. The circle is now a hexagon in answer C.

7. **D.** The B connection is in the wrong place in answer A. One of the objects in both answers B and C has been completely replaced.

8. **B.** The star shape in answer A is different from the sample. The large square has been replaced with a diamond in answer C. The circle has been replaced with a triangle in answer D.

9. **C.** The four-sided shape is three-sided in answer A. The irregular five-sided figure is a proportional pentagon in answer B. One of the angular shapes has been replaced with a circle in answer D.

10. **D.** The connection points in answers A and C are in the wrong places. The five-sided figure in answer B is now a perfect pentagon.

11. **D.** Answer B has the A connection at the top middle of the flower petal, whereas the sample has it on the side of the petal. Answers C and D have shapes that don't match the sample.

12. **B.** The *L* shape is duplicated in answer A, and one of the other shapes is missing. The largest shape has been changed from the sample in answer C. There are two new shapes in answer D.

13. **C.** The B connection in answer A is in the wrong place. The rounded object in answer B has been replaced with an oval. Both connection points in answer D are wrong.

14. **A.** There is an extra circle in answer B. The largest piece in answer C is longer than in the sample. In answer D, the circle has been replaced with a star.

15. **D.** Both connection points in answer A are wrong. The star is misshapen in answer B. The A connection point in answer C is wrong and the angular shape has been changed.

16. **D.** The disproportional four-sided figure has been replaced with a rectangle in answer A. The curved triangle has been replaced with a flat one in answer B and a four-sided shape in answer C.

17. **C.** The A connection point in answer A is in the wrong place. The angled shape in answer B has been replaced with a circle. The B connection point in answer D is in the wrong place.

18. **B.** The triangle is now a four-sided figure in answer A. One of the pieces of the sample has been duplicated and replaces another piece in answer C. There is also an extra triangle. One of the original shapes has been replaced with a circle in answer D.

19. **A.** The *q* in answer B has been changed to *a*. The star in answer C is now a square. The B connection point in answer D is in the wrong place.

20. **B.** The triangle in answer A is much smaller than it should be and also has different angles. The house has been replaced with an arrow shape in answer C. The triangle is now a circle in answer D.

21. **B.** The B connection point in answer A is in the wrong place. Both connection points in answer C are in the wrong place. The angled shape in answer D has been replaced.

22. **A.** There are two rainbow shapes in answer B now instead of one. The oval in answer C has been turned into a circle. The rainbow in answer D is now a circle.

23. **B.** The A connection point in answer A is in the wrong place. Both connection points in answer C are in the wrong place. The snowflake shape in answer D has been replaced with an octagon.

24. **D.** One of the triangles has been changed to match the other in answer A. The pentagon in answer D has changed, as has the size of the star shape. The larger triangle in answer C has been replaced with a four-sided figure.

25. **D.** The A connection point in answer A is in the wrong place. The circular shape in answer B has been replaced with an oval. The B connection point in answer C is in the wrong place.

AFQT Practice Test

Arithmetic Reasoning

Time: 36 Minutes

Questions: 30

Directions: This section tests your ability to reason through mathematical problems using basic arithmetic. Carefully read each question and choose the answer choice that best answers the question.

1. If you made $726.35 per week for the first half of the month and 10% more per week for the second half of the month, how much money did you make over the entire month?

   (A) $1,452.70
   (B) $1,597.97
   (C) $2,905.40
   (D) $3,050.67

2. The average time a song on a particular album plays is 2 minutes and 35 seconds. Assuming all of the songs on the album are about the average length, how many complete songs could you play during a 10-minute car ride to the store?

   (A) 3
   (B) 4
   (C) 5
   (D) 6

3. A cylindrical pool is 6 feet tall and 10 feet wide at its diameter. How much water can it hold?

    (A) 147 ft²

    (B) 471 ft²

    (C) 147 ft³

    (D) 471 ft³

4. Aaron wants to dedicate at least 20% of his free time after work three days per week to working out in the gym. If he has 7 hours of free time after work on an average day, how many hours will he have to spend at the gym in a week to meet this goal?

    (A) 1.4

    (B) 4.2

    (C) 4.3

    (D) 5.2

5. Two runners leave the same starting point at the same time. Runner A moves at a pace of 4.2 miles per hour. Runner B moves at a pace of 3.6 miles per hour. After 2.25 hours, how much farther has Runner A gone?

    (A) 1.35 miles

    (B) 1.82 miles

    (C) 2.45 miles

    (D) 8.12 miles

6. You want to cash in part of your 401(k) early to put a down payment on a house. Currently, you have $15,689 in your account. You're allowed to take up to 50% of this amount to put toward the purchase of a new home and will have to pay a 12% penalty. How much money will you have after the penalty is paid, if you take the full amount allowed?

    (A) $6,903.16

    (B) $7,844.50

    (C) $8,362.78

    (D) $9,956.22

7. Sarah will be 6 on her birthday next week. If Max takes her out for ice cream today and he is 6 times her age, how old is he?

    (A) 15

    (B) 25

    (C) 30

    (D) 36

8. Emily has to write a 12-page paper for her history class. After working all night, she has completed 7 pages. What percent of the total paper does she have left to complete?

    (A) 35%

    (B) 42%

    (C) 58%

    (D) 100%

9. A child's toy wish list has a train, airplane, doll, video game, and soccer ball on it. What's the probability she will get a toy that's a vehicle?

(A) $\frac{1}{5}$

(B) $\frac{2}{5}$

(C) $\frac{3}{5}$

(D) $\frac{4}{5}$

10. Fourteen is what fraction of twenty-one?

(A) $\frac{2}{3}$

(B) $\frac{7}{8}$

(C) $\frac{2}{21}$

(D) $\frac{14}{3}$

11. The members of your team are 25, 18, 21, 23, 28, and 26. What's the average age?

(A) 20.5

(B) 23.5

(C) 26.3

(D) 141

12. Murray decided to buy a sofa for $1,937. When he had the sales clerk ring up his purchase, he found that he had to pay 7% sales tax and that the sofa was 15% off. How much did Murray end up paying for the sofa in all?

(A) $1,478.04

(B) $1,528.40

(C) $1,646.48

(D) $1,761.73

13. Your friend is an avid collector of sci-fi memorabilia and acquires 6 new pieces per quarter year to add to her collection. If she's been collecting at this rate for 15 years, how many pieces of memorabilia does your friend's collection contain?

(A) 24

(B) 180

(C) 275

(D) 360

14. Ray mowed three lawns, cleaned two gutters, and raked three yards. If he charges $22 for each job he performs on the ground and $28 for any job he needs to climb a ladder for, how much money did he make doing these jobs?

(A) $56

(B) $132

(C) $188

(D) $210

15. If it takes 4 cups of sugar to make one batch of brownies that yields 24 pieces, how many cups of sugar would you need to make 132 brownies?

(A) 22

(B) 23

(C) 25

(D) 28

16. It has been 16 years since Jane has seen a Broadway play. For Max, it has been only $\frac{1}{3}$ as long. How many years has it been since he's seen a Broadway play?

    (A) $4\frac{1}{3}$ years

    (B) $5\frac{1}{3}$ years

    (C) $5\frac{2}{3}$ years

    (D) $5\frac{7}{25}$ years

17. Your son leaves for sleep-away camp on Monday, June 26. He promises to write you every day until he gets home on August 4, and twice every Sunday. If he does not write home on the day he arrives, how many letters can you expect to get by the time he comes home?

    (A) 23

    (B) 39

    (C) 44

    (D) 48

18. Private Joe can bench press 125 pounds on a 15-pound bar. Private Jane can bench press 135 pounds on a 10-pound bar. How much more weight can Private Jane press?

    (A) 5 pounds

    (B) 8 pounds

    (C) 10 pounds

    (D) 12 pounds

19. You're used to getting up at 8 A.M. In boot camp, you have to get up at 4:30 A.M. Assuming you go to bed at the same time every night, how much less sleep will you get over the course of one full week?

    (A) About $\frac{1}{4}$ of a day

    (B) About $\frac{1}{2}$ of a day

    (C) About $\frac{2}{4}$ of a day

    (D) About 1 day

20. You buy a new phone for $185 and receive a 35% rebate check in the mail. How much is the check for?

    (A) $46.75

    (B) $64.75

    (C) $67.54

    (D) $76.45

21. A lecture hall has 266 people attending a speech about biology. Of these people, 60 are history majors, 144 are biology majors, and the rest are undeclared. What is the ratio of history majors to biology majors?

    (A) 5:12

    (B) 30:31

    (C) 12:5

    (D) 31:30

22. Of your neighbors, $\frac{5}{8}$ are in favor of a block party and $\frac{1}{6}$ are in favor of a block-long garage sale. None are in favor of any other kind of activity. How many are in favor of having some kind of neighborhood activity?

    (A) $\frac{6}{8}$

    (B) $\frac{3}{8}$

    (C) $\frac{19}{24}$

    (D) $\frac{21}{19}$

23. What is negative four plus positive eight?

    (A) –4

    (B) 4

    (C) –12

    (D) 12

24. If for every time a bicycle wheel turns once, you have to pedal three times, what's the ratio of wheel turns to times you have to pedal?

    (A) 3:1

    (B) 1:3

    (C) 2:3

    (D) 2:4

25. Your monthly rent is $875. If it increases by $200 for the last three months of the year, how much will you pay in rent over the course of the entire year?

    (A) $1,075

    (B) $3,225

    (C) $7,875

    (D) $11,100

26. In 724.9654, the 6 is in the

    (A) ones place

    (B) tens place

    (C) tenths place

    (D) hundredths place

27. A dance club has 125 women whose hair is either blond, brown, red, or black. Twenty percent are blonde, 20% are brunette, and 20% are redheaded. What is the ratio of women with black hair to those who are brunette?

    (A) $\frac{2}{1}$

    (B) $\frac{1}{2}$

    (C) $\frac{50}{2}$

    (D) $\frac{25}{4}$

28. On Tuesday, Bill bought $89.75 worth of items from the grocery store. On Wednesday, he returned the $1.29 spaghetti, the $2.47 box of dog treats, and the $5.63 value package of floor cleaner to the store. After having returned the items, how much money did he end up spending at the store between the two days?

    (A) $9.40

    (B) $18.80

    (C) $80.36

    (D) $99.20

29. If Assembly Line A can produce 14 boxes of chocolate per half hour and Assembly Line B can produce twice as much as that, how many boxes can they produce together over 12 hours?

    (A) 168

    (B) 336

    (C) 672

    (D) 1,008

30. If you rounded $25.36 to the nearest dime, you would have

    (A) $25.30

    (B) $25.37

    (C) $25.40

    (D) $30.00

Word Knowledge

Time: 11 Minutes

Questions: 35

Directions: This section tests your knowledge of and ability to use vocabulary. Read each question and choose the answer choice that most nearly means the same as the underlined word.

1. Desecrate most nearly means

    (A) cater.
    (B) violate.
    (C) package.
    (D) surround.

2. Grueling most nearly means

    (A) difficult.
    (B) empty.
    (C) nourishing.
    (D) arresting.

3. Listless most nearly means

    (A) disorganized.
    (B) bored.
    (C) confused.
    (D) impotent.

4. Excel most nearly means

    (A) master.
    (B) recognize.
    (C) interest.
    (D) complete.

5. Stride most nearly means

    (A) progress.
    (B) originate.
    (C) break.
    (D) listen.

6. Provoke most nearly means

    (A) speak.
    (B) release.
    (C) call.
    (D) incite.

7. Vogue most nearly means

    (A) search.
    (B) fad.
    (C) model.
    (D) belief.

8. Haughty most nearly means

    (A) tight.
    (B) severe.
    (C) smug.
    (D) giving.

9. Liberal most nearly means

    (A) progressive.
    (B) conservative.
    (C) fastidious.
    (D) outspoken.

10. Garner most nearly means

    (A) placate.
    (B) generate.
    (C) invest.
    (D) blanket.

11. <u>Conviction</u> most nearly means

    (A) mask.
    (B) felony.
    (C) certainty.
    (D) bluster.

12. <u>Accomplice</u> most nearly means

    (A) bereavement.
    (B) relation.
    (C) cohort.
    (D) caregiver.

13. <u>Optimistic</u> most nearly means

    (A) oppressive.
    (B) secretive.
    (C) positive.
    (D) owed.

14. Although the teacher had told her student that if he did not improve his homework grades he would not pass the course, he still took a <u>blasé</u> attitude to her comments and completing his assignments.

    (A) studious
    (B) unconcerned
    (C) slight
    (D) average

15. <u>Translucent</u> most nearly means

    (A) crystalline.
    (B) motionless.
    (C) vague.
    (D) beautiful.

16. <u>Lackluster</u> most nearly means

    (A) muddy.
    (B) vengeful.
    (C) optimistic.
    (D) shiny.

17. <u>Compensate</u> most nearly means

    (A) annihilate.
    (B) move.
    (C) provide.
    (D) repay.

18. Our <u>ruse</u> would have worked if our little brother hadn't told mother that we were only pretending to be sick.

    (A) regret.
    (B) trick.
    (C) incite.
    (D) flower.

19. <u>Languid</u> most nearly means

    (A) belonging.
    (B) fortunate.
    (C) drooping.
    (D) trusted.

20. The damage the illness did to my immune system leaves me <u>vulnerable</u> to all sorts of common infections.

    (A) exposed
    (B) over the top
    (C) brilliant
    (D) aged

21. <u>Prosaic</u> most nearly means

    (A) appreciative.
    (B) supporting.
    (C) dull.
    (D) artistic.

22. When Paige received an expensive new sports car for her 16th birthday, her brother was <u>indignant</u>, because he'd only gotten a new game system for his.

    (A) angry
    (B) healthy
    (C) average
    (D) pacified

23. <u>Calling</u> most nearly means

    (A) arrangement.
    (B) fortune.
    (C) officiant.
    (D) vocation.

24. <u>Misrepresent</u> most nearly means

    (A) stutter.
    (B) deceive.
    (C) orate.
    (D) gripe.

25. <u>Astronomical</u> most nearly means

    (A) valid.
    (B) stellar.
    (C) negligent.
    (D) huge.

26. <u>Infer</u> most nearly means

    (A) ramble.
    (B) diverge.
    (C) conclude.
    (D) reluctant.

27. <u>Fastidious</u> most nearly means

    (A) painstaking.
    (B) generous.
    (C) arousing.
    (D) eager.

28. Although Jimmy was <u>apprehensive</u> about being away from home for the first time, it helped that he had his best friend with him as he took the bus to camp.

    (A) anxious
    (B) fantastical
    (C) courteous
    (D) reluctant

29. When the man thought about the negative consequences, he knew he would <u>rue</u> lying to get more money from his insurance company.

    (A) listen
    (B) anticipate
    (C) regret
    (D) welcome

30. <u>Perimeter</u> most nearly means

    (A) measurement.
    (B) boundary.
    (C) charity.
    (D) consent.

31. <u>Conservative</u> most nearly means

    (A) calculating.
    (B) accepting.
    (C) innovative.
    (D) traditional.

32. <u>Frantic</u> most nearly means

    (A) beleaguered.
    (B) overworked.
    (C) wild.
    (D) produced.

33. <u>Sacred</u> most nearly means

    (A) revered.
    (B) exceptional.
    (C) belated.
    (D) perfect.

34. <u>Gravity</u> most nearly means

    (A) ineptitude.
    (B) mirth.
    (C) seriousness.
    (D) pull.

35. <u>Malicious</u> most nearly means

    (A) official.
    (B) inappropriate.
    (C) designed.
    (D) harmful.

Paragraph Comprehension

Time: 13 Minutes

Questions: 15

Directions: This section tests your ability to read and understand written information, as well as come to logical conclusions based on a text. Read each passage and answer the questions that follow. Choose the answer choice that best answers the question.

A website is series of pages that are interconnected through hyperlinks. The structure of a website consists of a central page, called a *home page*, which contains the main information a visitor needs to know about the site. There is also a navigation bar that gives a listing of the other main information sections. After clicking the mouse on a specific link on the navigation bar, the corresponding page will come up on the screen.

1. According to the passage, what would you use to click on a specific link when visiting a website?

    (A) navigation bar

    (B) hyperlink

    (C) mouse

    (D) blog

Use the following passage to answer questions 2–3:

Drinking coffee can help treat a headache. Caffeine works to block certain chemicals in the brain that make you sleepy and in the process, causes blood vessels to tighten up. Closing off or restricting the flow of blood vessels that are feeding a headache can help bring relief.

2. Caffeine affects the

    (A) brain.

    (B) cardiovascular system.

    (C) only A.

    (D) both A and B.

3. The author would most likely support

    (A) drinking coffee as a sleep aid.

    (B) drinking coffee as a natural headache remedy.

    (C) using coffee as a treatment for areas of the brain that need more blood.

    (D) all of the above.

Use the following passage to answer questions 4–6:

Colombia is the northwestern-most country in South America. Its northern border with Panama is the only direct land connection between Central and South America. Grassy plains, expansive mountain ranges, marshland, and coastal lowlands dominate the country's topography. Colombia's main products include coffee, cattle, sugar cane, chemicals, coal, and petroleum.

4. In this paragraph, the word topography most nearly means

   (A) exports.

   (B) landforms.

   (C) imports.

   (D) elevation of mountains.

6. What country separates Central and South America?

   (A) Panama

   (B) Guatemala

   (C) Colombia

   (D) Uruguay

5. The tone of this passage is

   (A) positive.

   (B) urgent.

   (C) negative.

   (D) neutral.

Use the following passage to answer questions 7–8:

We have to get the new deck built before the end of the month. I've called three contractors already and can't find one that can complete the task for the right price. I'm thinking of asking a coworker about the contractor he hired to build the new addition onto his house. He seemed to be happy with the man's work.

7. The next step the speaker will likely take is to

   (A) do the work himself.

   (B) hire one of the contractors that did not come in at price.

   (C) contact his coworker about his contractor.

   (D) look for other contractors in the phone book.

8. According to the paragraph, the speaker is concerned about

   (A) time.

   (B) cost.

   (C) reliability.

   (D) all of the above.

Use the following passage to answer questions 9–11:

Wind farms are one of the leading sources of sustainable energy in the United States. Such farms contain one or more turbines with giant blades that are turned by the wind. This action converts the kinetic energy of the wind into mechanical energy through the rotation of the blades. The mechanical energy is then routed to a generator within the turbine, which converts that energy into yet another form, electricity.

9. A good title for this passage would be

   (A) Wind Farms Produce the Most Electricity in the Nation
   (B) Sustainable Energy Now!
   (C) Wind Farms: A Sustainable Energy Source Based on Science
   (D) The U.S. Switches its Power Supply to Wind Energy

10. According to the passage, wind has

   (A) kinetic energy.
   (B) potential energy.
   (C) mechanical energy.
   (D) rotational energy.

11. The purpose of this passage is to

   (A) incite action.
   (B) inform.
   (C) publicize.
   (D) editorialize.

Use the following passage to answer questions 12–15:

The introduction of electronic devices that keep us constantly connected to work, friends, and family, coupled with the increasingly long workweek, is resulting in chronic exhaustion among U.S. adults. This increases levels of stress the body experiences and thus leads to increased levels of adrenaline. This means that chemically our bodies are constantly on edge, which costs a lot of physical and mental energy.

Most adults aren't even aware of the amount of stress they are under during a normal workday because they have become desensitized to the effects in order to get through the tasks they have on their plate. The physical costs of this desensitization, however, are greater than one might imagine.

12. In this passage, the word <u>desensitized</u> most nearly means

    (A) more able to physically handle something.

    (B) becoming more aware of one's surroundings.

    (C) losing the ability to feel or notice something.

    (D) more able to remember.

13. According to the passage, a cause of exhaustion is

    (A) lack of time away from work.

    (B) constant interaction with electronic communication devices.

    (C) chemical imbalances caused by external stressors.

    (D) all of the above.

14. The tone of this passage is

    (A) flippant.

    (B) concerned.

    (C) glib.

    (D) bored.

15. The speaker would most likely support

    (A) a stress-awareness campaign being distributed to employees at Fortune 500 companies.

    (B) an increase in the number of hours in the standard workweek.

    (C) the introduction of computer software that would forward calls to a built-in hands-free phone in your car.

    (D) a political candidate whose agenda includes increasing the country's gross national product.

Mathematics Knowledge

Time: 24 Minutes

Questions: 25

Directions: This section tests your knowledge of basic mathematics, algebra, and geometry. Carefully read each question and choose the answer choice that reflects the best answer.

1. Reduce the following to lowest terms:
   $$\frac{3x + 9}{2x+6}$$
   (A) $1\frac{1}{2}$
   (B) $\frac{3(x+3)}{2(x+3)}$
   (C) $\frac{3}{2}$
   (D) $\frac{2(2x+3)}{2(x+3)}$

2. The following diagram is an example of a

   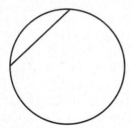

   (A) circumference.
   (B) chord.
   (C) radius.
   (D) diameter.

3. $k^2 - 2k + 6$ is a
   (A) coefficient.
   (B) constant.
   (C) quadratic expression.
   (D) variable.

4. $(b - 7)(b + 4) =$
   (A) b2 – 3b + 28
   (B) b2 – 3b – 28
   (C) b2 – 11b – 28
   (D) b2 – 11b + 28

5. $2\frac{5}{6} \div \frac{2}{7} =$
   (A) $9\frac{11}{12}$
   (B) $12\frac{9}{12}$
   (C) $\frac{12}{119}$
   (D) $6\frac{11}{12}$

6. $4 + a^2 < 2a - 3$ means
   (A) 4 + a² is less than 2a – 3
   (B) 4 + a² is greater than 2a – 3
   (C) 4 + a² is equal to 2a – 3
   (D) 4 + a² is greater than or equal to 2a – 3

7. A mathematical constant that appears in many formulas involving circles is
   (A) ≠
   (B) Ω
   (C) ≤
   (D) π

8. Factor: $b^2 - 10b - 24$

    (A) (b + 3) (b – 8)

    (B) (b + 3) (b + 8)

    (C) (b + 2) (b – 12)

    (D) (b – 4) (b + 12)

9. $7! =$

    (A) –14

    (B) 28

    (C) 4,005

    (D) 5,040

10. $\frac{a^2 d}{cd} \times \frac{4y}{2ay} =$

    (A) $\frac{2c}{a}$

    (B) $\frac{2a}{c}$

    (C) $\frac{4a}{c}$

    (D) $\frac{4c}{a}$

11. $x^0 =$

    (A) 0

    (B) 1

    (C) 2

    (D) 3

12. The square root of 196 is

    (A) 14

    (B) 15

    (C) 16

    (D) 17

13. $3 + 2 [1 + 2(1 + 2)]^2$

    (A) 36

    (B) 49

    (C) 98

    (D) 101

14. In the following diagram, what is the value of angle 3?

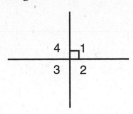

    (A) 30°

    (B) 45°

    (C) 90°

    (D) 180°

15. $(x^3)^3$

    (A) x–4

    (B) x6

    (C) x9

    (D) x–9

16. The three internal angles of a triangle always add up to

    (A) 90°

    (B) 90 ft²

    (C) 180°

    (D) 180 ft²

17. Factor: $a^2 - 49$

    (A) (a – 7)(a – 7)

    (B) (a + 7)(a + 7)

    (C) (a + 7)(a – 7)

    (D) none of the above

18. Solve for a: $\frac{3}{a} = \frac{9}{12}$

    (A) 4

    (B) 5

    (C) 6

    (D) 7

19. If $a = 2$, $a - 6 + 3a - 4a =$

    (A) 3
    (B) –3
    (C) 6
    (D) –6

20. $\frac{4}{8} \times \frac{10}{5} =$

    (A) $\frac{1}{4}$

    (B) $\frac{1}{2}$

    (C) 1

    (D) 2

21. Simplify: $(2x^2)(14x) + x - xy =$

    (A) 28x3 + x – xy
    (B) x(28x2 + 1 – y)
    (C) 28x3 + x2y
    (D) 28x5y

22. Factor: $10y + 15xy + 50y^2$

    (A) y(10 + 15x + 50y)
    (B) 5(2y + 3xy + 10y)
    (C) 5x(2 + 3y + 10y2)
    (D) 5y(2 + 3x + 10y)

23. What is the area of a pool table that is 8.2 feet long by 5.6 feet wide?

    (A) 45.9 ft²
    (B) 45.9 ft³
    (C) 52.9 ft²
    (D) 54.9 ft³

24. You have a box that is 4 feet tall, 4 feet wide, and 3 feet long. What is its volume?

    (A) 48 ft²
    (B) 48 ft³
    (C) 88 ft²
    (D) 88 ft³

25. A monomial is

    (A) any expression that has more than three terms.
    (B) an expression with three terms joined by operations.
    (C) a polynomial that has just one term.
    (D) an expression with two terms joined by operations.

AFQT Practice Test: Answers and Explanations

Arithmetic Reasoning

1. **D.** Multiply your weekly pay by .10 (10%) to find out how much more you made in the last two weeks of the month: 72.64. Now add this to your weekly rate: 798.99. Multiply the original rate of pay by 2 and your new rate by 2, then add the products: $(726.35 \times 2) + (798.99 \times 2) = 1452.7 + 1597.97 = \$3,050.67$.

2. **A.** Convert your time into seconds. Ten minutes equals 600 seconds; 2 minutes and 35 seconds equals 155 seconds. Now divide 600 by 155 to get 3.87. Since the question asks how many *complete* songs you could play during the ride, you have to round down to 3 instead of rounding up to 4, since you know three can definitely play in this time.

3. **D.** This is a volume question. Think back to geometry for this one and calculate the volume of a cylinder using the following formula: $V = \pi r^2 h$. Plug in the numbers from the question to get the following (remember, radius is half the value of diameter, and pi is about 3.14):

   $V = 3.14 \times 5^2 \times 6$

   $V = 3.14 \times 25 \times 6$

   $V = 78.5 \times 6$

   $V = 471$

   Volume is always expressed in cubes, so your answer is 471 ft³.

4. **B.** Calculate 20% of 7 to get the amount of time he wants to spend at the gym per day: 1.4 hours. Now multiply by the number of days he will go, and you have 4.2 hours in the gym per week total.

5. **A.** Calculate the distance per rate each runner goes using the Distance = Rate × Time formula:

   Runner A: $D = 4.2 \times 2.25 = 9.45$

   Runner B: $D = 3.6 \times 2.25 = 8.1$

   Now subtract Runner A's distance from Runner B's to get 1.35 miles.

6. **A.** Fifty percent of 15,689 is 7,844.5. Multiply this amount by the penalty percentage: $7,844.5 \times .12 = 941.34$. Subtract this amount from 7,844.5 to find you'll have $6,903.16 to put toward your house.

7. **C.** Max is 30 because Sarah is 5 today and he is 6 times older.

8. **B.** A simple equation will help you with this one: $7 = y \times 12$. Isolate the y by dividing both sides by 12:

   $$\frac{7}{12} = \frac{y \times \cancel{12}}{\cancel{12}}$$

   $$\frac{7}{12} = y$$

   $$.583 = y$$

   This shows that she has completed about 58% of her paper. Now subtract this amount from the total (100%), and you'll find she has 42% left to complete.

9. **B.** Two out of the total items on the list are vehicles. Since there are five items total, the probability is $\frac{2}{5}$.

10. **A.** Use the same equation here that we did in question 8. But instead of calculating the percentage, we're looking for the fraction:

    $$14 = y \times 21$$

    $$\frac{14}{21} = \frac{y \times \cancel{21}}{\cancel{21}}$$

    $$\frac{14}{21} = y$$

    $$\frac{2}{3} = y$$

11. **B.** Add all the numbers together to get 141. Divide this sum by the number of terms you added to get it—in this case: 6.

12. **D.** Start by figuring out what the discounted price of the sofa is: $1,937 \times .15 = 290.55$; $1,937 - 290.55 = 1,646.48$. Now multiply that amount by the sales tax: $1,646.48 \times .07 = 115.2515$. Finally, add that amount to 1,646.48 to get your final answer of $1,761.73.

13. **D.** First, find out how many new pieces your friend acquires per year by multiplying 6×4. This gives you 24 pieces. Now multiply that by 15 to find that she has 360 pieces of sci-fi memorabilia.

14. **C.** Ray does six ground jobs and two ladder jobs. He earns $132 and $56, respectively. Add them together to find that he earned $188 that day.

15. **A.** A quick way to solve this is to turn it into a proportion: $\frac{4 \text{ cups}}{24 \text{ brownies}} = \frac{x \text{ cups}}{132 \text{ brownies}}$. To solve for x, multiply 4×132 to get 528. Now divide 528 by 24 to get the value of x:

    $$\frac{132}{24} = 22$$

16. **B.** Multiply your two amounts to find the answer: $\frac{16}{1} \times \frac{1}{3} = \frac{16}{1} = 5\frac{1}{3}$

17. **C.** First count the number of days between June 26 and August 4 (remember he did not write on the day he arrived at camp):

    June = 4 days

    July = 31 days

    August = 4 days

    Add them together: 4 + 31 + 4 = 39. Now calculate how many Sundays occur during this time. If June 26 is a Monday, then July 2, 9, 16, 23, and 30 are Sundays your son will be at camp. Add 5 to 39 to find that you'll expect 44 letters.

18. **A.** Add the total weight each can lift and subtract Private Joe's number from Private Jane's:

    Private Joe: 125 + 15 = 140

    Private Jane: 135 + 10 = 145

    The difference is 5 pounds.

19. **D.** You lose 3.5 hours of sleep per day. Multiply this over a seven-day week, and you end up losing 24.5 hours total. This equals about a whole day.

20. **B.** Multiply 185 by .35 to get $64.75.

21. **A.** The ratio is 60:144. Both of these numbers have 12 as a common factor. If you divide both by 12, you have 5:12, which is your final answer.

22. **C.** Find a common denominator and add the fractions.

23. **B.** Write this as an expression: −4 + 8. You start on the negative side of the number line and move eight steps to the right. When you stop, you're at +4.

24. **B.** Write this like you would say it: 1 wheel turn equals 3 times you have to pedal, or 1:3.

25. **D.** Out of 12 months, you pay $875 for nine months ($875 × 9 = $7,875). For three months, you pay $1,075 ($1,075 × 3 = $3,225). For the whole year, you pay $11,100 (that is, $7,875 + $3,225 = $11,100).

26. **D.** The second place to the right of the decimal point is the hundredths place. The first place to the right is the tenths. The other two places in the answers are to the left of the decimal.

27. **A.** Twenty-five women in the club are brunette, since 20% of 125 is 25. Those with hair colors other than brown, blond, and red make up 40% of the women, which equals about 50. Written the way the question reads, the ratio of women with other colors of hair to those who are

    brunette is $\frac{50}{25} = \frac{2}{1}$.

28. **C.** Add up the total of the items Bill returned: 1.29 + 2.47 + 5.63 − 9.39. Now subtract this amount from the total of his bill on Tuesday: 89.75 − 9.39 = $80.36.

29. **D.** First calculate how much Assembly Line A can produce in an hour: 14 × 2 = 28. Now multiply that number by 12 to see how much it can produce in 12 hours: 28 × 12 = 336. Now multiply that number by 2 to determine how much Assembly Line B can produce in that amount of time: 336 × 2 = 672. Add 336 + 672 to get the total they both make in 12 hours.

30. **C.** The nearest dime in this case would be $.40, since 36 would round up to 40, not down to 30.

Word Knowledge

1. **B.** Chances are, you've heard the word *desecrate* used in negative ways, such as to desecrate a grave or something holy. The word means "to soil or violate." All the other answer choices are neutral, but answer B is definitely negative.

2. **A.** If something is *grueling*, it is difficult or challenging. Answers B and C don't fit this description. Answer D, *arresting*, means "visually stunning," which also doesn't fit. An interesting association you might make with the word *grueling* is "Gruel is difficult to swallow."

3. **B.** *Listless* means "without energy or interest." Answers A and C don't fit with this definition. Answer D, *impotent*, means "powerless."

4. **A.** To *excel* means to do something extremely well. Answers B through D don't agree with this definition, but you may feel reluctant to choose A as your answer. Remember that master can be used as both a noun and a verb, and its verb form means "to become very skilled."

5. **A.** If you're familiar with the Stride Rite brand of shoes, making the connection between *stride* and its definition of "moving forward," "walking," or "progressing" will be a natural one.

6. **D.** Don't confuse *insight*, which means "perceptiveness," with *incite*, which means "to provoke" or "to start something." Although *calling* and *speaking* (answers C and A, respectively) may be involved with inciting, they are not necessary to define the word. The same is true of answer B, *release*. This makes D the best choice.

7. **B.** An easy association with the word *vogue* is to think about the fashion magazine with the same name. Fashion is all about what's the best now, and those perceptions are fleeting, just like fads are. Answers A and D have nothing to do with this, and though you might be tempted to choose answer C because of the link between *fashion* and *model*, *fad* is the choice that most nearly means "vogue."

8. **C.** *Haughty* means someone is arrogant or smug. The word speaks directly to someone's high opinion of himself. None of the other answer choices do this.

9. **A.** Liberal politicians are most associated with progressive beliefs. Answer B is the opposite of this, as *conservative* means to act with restraint or to be traditional. Answer C means "to pay close attention to detail." And though if you are liberal you may be outspoken (answer D), *liberal* is not defined by such a quality.

10. **B.** *Garner* means the same as "generate." A cool association for *garner*: Jennifer Garner generates interest wherever she goes. *Placate* means "to soothe," *invest* means "to have a stake in something," and *blanket* means "to cover."

11. **C.** *Conviction* can have many meanings. The one we're most familiar with is likely being found guilty of a crime. However, none of the answer choices reflect this definition (answer B, *felony*, describes the crime itself, not being found guilty). Another definition of conviction is a strong belief. Answer A means "to cover or conceal," and answer D means "to speak without real belief," which is the opposite of what we're looking for. Answer C is your best bet.

12. **C.** A good way to remember what *accomplice* means is to associate it with the word *accompany*, which means to "go with." An accomplice is someone who aids in a crime. Answer A means "mourning," answer B means "to have a connection to," and answer D means "someone who aids someone else in their care." Though answers B and D may seem like possible choices, if you carefully consider their meanings, you'll see that they don't connect like answer C does. A *cohort* is a "partner in crime."

13. **C.** *Optimistic* refers to being positive or having a positive outlook. Answers A and B have negative connotations/meanings to them. *Oppressive* refers to something that holds something else back, and to be *secretive* is to hold information back. Answer D really has nothing to do with what we're looking for.

14. **B.** Context clues in the sentence indicate that the answer we're looking for shows that the student did not change his attitude and/or did not think the teacher's advice was important. The only answer choice that reflects this is B. *Studious* means "interested in or engaging in study." The other answer choices don't really make any sense.

15. **A.** Two roots that can help you in this question. *Trans* means "through," and *luc* means "light." From this, you can deduce that *translucent* has to do with light being able to pass through something. The only answer that fits is *crystalline,* which describes something very clear.

16. **A.** Break this word into smaller words, and you'll get a good clue to its definition. To *lack* is to not have, and *luster* means "shine." Answer D is the opposite of this. Answers B and C don't really have anything to do with lacking shine. However, if something is *muddy* (answer A), it will definitely not shine.

17. **D.** *Compensate* means to pay someone for something, so the answer you're looking for has something to do with payment. Answer A means "to destroy." Answer B means "to change something's position." Answer C means "to give." While you may be thinking C is a good choice, when you see that answer D means "to pay someone back," you'll find that it's the stronger choice.

18. **B.** The sentence tells us that the children were pretending to be sick, which means *ruse* has something to do with pretending or tricking. Answers A and D don't make sense with what we're looking for. Answer C not only doesn't make sense, but it's also the wrong part of speech (a verb when we need a noun).

19. **C.** The Latin root *lang* means "to be weakened." The correct answer choice will have something to do with inability to support something. The only one that makes sense is answer C, *drooping,* which implies a lack of strength to hold oneself upright.

20. **A.** If you use Swap It Out for this question, you'll find that answers B and C don't fit. This leaves A and D for you to consider. The sentence talks about how an illness damaged the immune system, which implies that some harm has made it exposed. Age is not necessary to define this, so answer A is the best choice.

21. **C.** *Prosaic* means something is straightforward or lacking in imagination. This eliminates answer D. Answers A and B don't really fit the meaning we're working with, whereas answer C fits it exactly.

22. **A.** The sentence implies that the brother is upset at the unfairness of the situation. *Healthy* and *average* are simply not strong enough to match a starved appetite. *Pacified* has to do with calming, which is the opposite of what we need. Your answer is *angry*. It's not an exact match, but remember, you're looking for the best choice out of the four you're given.

23. **D.** *Calling* can be either a noun or a verb. A quick look at the answer choices tells you that you're dealing with the noun form of the word (all the answers are nouns). In this case, *calling* means some kind of job or profession. Answers A and B don't fit. Answer C means someone who acts in an official capacity of some kind. While this can be a job, it doesn't have to be and doesn't define *job* or *profession*. Answer D, *vocation*, does.

24. **B.** The answer we're looking for has something to do with standing in for someone in a bad way. Answer A means "to not be able to speak fluidly." Answer C means "to speak publicly." Answer D means "to complain." None of these are a great fit. Answer B, *deceive*, means "to knowingly present an impression that is not the truth." While this isn't the best match in definition, the idea is the same: representing an image with bad or ill intent.

25. **D.** A good association to make with *astronomical* is to think of it in terms of space. Space, the universe, and everything associated with them are so large that you can't even conceive of it all. Answer A means "correct." Answer B refers to the average or every day. Answer C means "careless." This makes answer D the best choice.

26. **C.** When you *infer*, you use all the information you are given to come to your own conclusion about what's going on. Answer A means "to talk on and on." Answer B means "to split apart from something." Answer D means that you don't really want to do something. Answer C is the best choice, as it means "to come to a conclusion."

27. **A.** As we said earlier, *fastidious* means "to pay close attention to detail." The only answer choice that makes sense here is A, *painstaking*, which means "to pay very close attention to detail."

28. **A.** If you swap out the answer choices with the underlined word, you'll find that *anxious* is the only one that makes sense in this context.

29. **C.** In the sentence, the man is considering negative consequences for actions he has already committed. When this happens, he likely regrets those actions. Our answer has to do with regret. Answers B and D run counter to this, and answer A has nothing to do with it.

30. **B.** If you think back to our discussions on geometry, you'll remember that a *perimeter* is the distance around something, or its boundary. You can make the same connection here. You can cross off answers C and D right away. Answer A has a vague connection to the math side of this word, but we're looking for answer B, which speaks to its actual meaning.

31. **D.** We had *liberal* earlier, and now we have *conservative,* its opposite. So, we're looking for an answer that's the opposite of *progressive* (looking to change). That eliminates answers B and C right away. Answer A means "to scheme," which doesn't define the opposite of *progressive.* Answer D, *traditional,* does represent ideas that support how things have always been.

32. **C.** One of Harrison Ford's movies is entitled *Frantic.* Why? The character he plays has his wife mysteriously disappear while the couple is in Paris. He has to find her against huge odds before anything bad happens to her, which makes him frantic to save her. Answers B and D don't make sense with this association. Answer A, *beleaguered,* means "to be annoyed or harassed," which isn't the case here. Answer C is the best choice.

33. **A.** Something that is revered is holy or sacred. *Exceptional* means "special," but not necessarily "holy." *Belated* means "late," which doesn't make sense. *Perfect* means "without flaws," which also doesn't necessarily mean "holy."

34. **C.** *Gravity* is another one of those words that has multiple definitions. If you look at the answer choices, you'll see that there really isn't any one that describes a pull toward Earth. This means you have to think of another definition. Your original thought can help you here. The pull of gravity helps you experience weight, so you can associate it with being heavy. Gravity, when used in respect to a situation, refers to being very serious—or heavy, as opposed to light. *Ineptitude* is not being skilled at something. *Mirth* is amusement, and *surface* is simply the outer portion of an object.

35. **D.** If you remember back to Chapter 5, we discussed *malice* as an intent to harm. *Malicious* is the adjective form of this word, which makes answer D the only choice that fits.

1. **C.** The last sentence talks about using a mouse to click on links.

2. **D.** The passage talks about caffeine affecting both the brain and blood vessels. Since blood vessels are part of the cardiovascular system, both answers A and B are correct.

3. **B.** The passage contradicts answers A and C, which makes answer D wrong as well.

4. **B.** The sentence uses the word *topography* to describe a variety of geographic landforms.

5. **D.** This is an informative passage that has no sense of emotion coming from the speaker. This makes "neutral" the most logical choice.

6. **A.** The second sentence in the passage says that Panama "is the only direct land connection between Central and South America."

7. **C.** The passage doesn't give us any indication that the speaker wants to or even can perform the work himself. Because he's posing the possibility of seeking a recommendation from his coworker, it's unlikely that his next step will be to hire someone he's gotten a quote from already or to look for someone he knows nothing about. Contacting his coworker is the next logical step, based on the information in the passage.

8. **D.** The speaker says, "We have to get the new deck built before the end of the month," "I've called three contractors already and can't find one that can complete the task for the right price," and "I'm thinking of asking a coworker about the contractor he hired ... he seemed to be happy with the man's work." All this implies that he is concerned about time, cost, and reliability.

9. **C.** This makes the most sense, since the passage describes the scientific process of how wind turbines make electricity. There is no emotion present, which rules out answer B. And although the passage says that wind farms are a "leading" source of sustainable energy, there's no indication that all of the U.S. power supply comes from this energy source or that this source produces the most energy in the country.

10. **A.** The sentence "This action converts the kinetic energy of the wind into mechanical energy through the rotation of the blades" tells us that the wind has kinetic energy.

11. **B.** Since this passage describes a process without emotion or any call to action, it is clearly intended to inform.

12. **C.** The sentence talks about being unaware of physical effects. It doesn't talk about any increased physical ability or memory, which eliminates answers A and D. Answer B runs contrary to how the word is used in the sentence.

13. **D.** Each of the answer choices is mentioned in the passage. This makes answer D the best choice.

14. **B.** *Flippant* and *glib* imply speaking in an uncaring way. The speaker obviously cares about this subject; she appears to be concerned with the negative consequences of this life-style. This makes answer B the best choice.

15. **A.** The author states that "most adults aren't even aware of the amount of stress they are under during a normal workday because they have become desensitized to the effects in order to get through the tasks they have on their plate." This supports answer A.

Mathematics Knowledge

1. **A.** Factor out what you can from each side of the division bar. Then get rid of terms that cancel each other out:

$$\frac{3x+9}{2x+6} = \frac{3(x+3)}{2(x+3)} = \frac{3}{2} = 1\frac{1}{2}$$

2. **B.** A chord is a segment in a circle that touches any two points of the edge. A diameter is a type of chord, but its endpoints have to go directly through the center of the circle. The line in this diagram does not.

3. **C.** This is an example of a quadratic expression: $ax^2 + bx + c$.

4. **B.** Use FOIL here: $(b - 7)(b + 4)$

   First: $b \times b = b^2$

   Outer: $b \times 4 = 4b$

   Inner: $-7 \times b = -7b$

   Last: $-7 \times 4 = -28$

   Your new expression is: $b^2 + 4b - 7b - 28$

   Combine like terms: $b^2 - 3b - 28$

5. **B.** Turn $2\frac{5}{6}$ into an improper fraction: $2 \times 6 + 5 = 17$. So, your new fraction is $\frac{17}{6}$. Since you're dividing fractions, multiply by the reciprocal of $\frac{2}{7}$: $\frac{17}{6} \times \frac{7}{2} = \frac{119}{12}$. Now turn your product back into a mixed number by dividing 12 into 119. You get $9\frac{11}{12}$.

6. **A.** The < symbol shows that the value to the left is less than the value to the right.

7. **D.** A mathematical constant that appears in many formulas involving circles is known as pi (π).

8. **C.** FOIL the answer choices to find that only C produces the original expression.

9. **D.** This is a factorial, so you need to calculate $7 \times 6 \times 5 \times 4 \times 3 \times 2 \times 1 = 5,040$.

10. **B.** Multiply straight across and then take out lowest terms:

$$\frac{a^2d}{cd} \times \frac{4y}{2ay} = \frac{4 \times a^2 \times d \times y}{2 \times acdy} = \frac{2a}{c}$$

11. **B.** Any base to the 0 power equals 1.

12. **A.** $14 \times 14 = 196$

13. **D.** Start with the inner expression in parentheses (not the brackets, which indicate that all processes within must be addressed first), and find 3 to be the answer. The parentheses around the 3 indicate that we must multiply. Within the brackets, we multiply 2×3 first, then add $1 + 6$. Next, apply the exponent to the 7 to get 49. Next, multiply 2×49 to get 98; finally, add the 3.

14. **C.** These angles are perpendicular, which makes them all 90°.

15. **C.** When you apply an exponent to terms in parentheses that have powers, you multiply exponents to simplify the expression: $(x^3)^3 = x^{3 \times 3} = x^9$.

16. **C.** The three internal angles of a triangle always add up to 180°.

17. **C.** This involves simple factoring, since you have a binomial made up of squares. Break it into two binomial expressions that have the roots of the squares. In this case, $\sqrt{a^2} = a$ and $\sqrt{49} = 7$. Since our original expression has a negative, at least one of our signs is going to be a negative as well. If we FOIL the binomials, the two middle terms will have to cancel each other out in order to give us our original expression. This means one sign will be negative and the other positive. In this case, it doesn't matter which. The correct answer is $(a + 7)(a - 7)$.

18. **A.** Cross multiply to solve for the missing value. If $3 \times 12 = 36$, then $a \times 9 = 36$. Divide both sides by 9 and find that $a = 4$.

19. **D.** Plug in the value of a into the expression, and then follow order of operations:

    $a - 6 + 3a - 4a$

    $2 - 6 + (3)(2) - (4)(2)$

    Multiply first: $2 - 6 + 6 - 8$

    Solve left to right: $2 - 6 = -4$; $-4 + 6 = 2$; $2 - 8 = -6$

20. **C.** Multiply straight across and simplify:

    $\frac{4}{8} \times \frac{10}{5} = \frac{40}{40} = 1$

21. **B.** Combine as many like terms as possible here, and then see what you can factor out:

    $(2x^2)(14x) + x - xy$

    $28x^3 + x - xy$

    $x(28x^2 + 1 - y)$

22. **D.** Common factors are 5 and y, which, when multiplied, equal $5y$. Now break down each term into prime factors:

    $10y = 2 \times 5 \times y$

    $15xy = 5 \times 3 \times x \times y$

    $50y^2 - 5 \times 5 \times 2 \times y \times y$

    Simplify each of these by crossing out one $5 \times y$ in each expression:

    $10y = 2 \times \cancel{5 \times y}$

    $15xy = 3 \times \cancel{5} \times x \times \cancel{y}$

    $50y^2 = 2 \times y \times \cancel{5} \times 5 \times \cancel{y}$

    Simplify each term and place the new expression in parentheses with $5y$ outside: $10y + 15xy + 50y^2 = 5y (2 + 3x + 10y)$.

23. **A.** This is a simple area problem. Multiply length times width and express in square feet: $8.2 \times 5.6 = 45.9$ ft².

24. **B.** This is a volume problem. Multiply your height by width by depth, and express in cubic feet: $4 \times 4 \times 3 = 48$ ft³.

25. **C.** Know about the root *mon*, which means "one," to help you remember that a monomial is a polynomial that has just one term.

ASVAB Scores by Military Job

Combinations of scores from the ASVAB subtests, called composite scores or line scores, determine qualification for a military job. Each branch of service has different formulas for each job category, which we outline below. Note that these computations are subject to change and were confirmed with The Official ASVAB Testing Program as of July 2018. It's best to check with a recruiter or www.official-asvab.com/military_app.htm for the most up-to-date information.

Air Force

The Air Force currently requires a minimum AFQT score of 31 for those with a high school diploma. If you have a GED or alternative diploma, plan on achieving at least a 50.

The Air Force has its own listing of composite scores. Listed here are the combination of subtests per composite:

- Mechanical (M): AR + 2(VE)+ MC + AS
- Administrative (A): VE + MK
- General (G): VE + AR
- Electronic (E): AR + MK + EI + GS

If you don't make the grade the first time, you can retest within 30 days. If your second test doesn't go as planned, you can take a third test 30 days later. After that, you will have to wait 6 months before you can try again.

The Air Force calls its enlisted jobs Air Force Specialty Codes (AFSCs). According to one North Carolina recruiter, you should aim for a minimum of the following scores to open up the largest number of job possibilities:

- Mechanical: 47
- Administrative: 65
- General: 54
- Electronic: 70

For a complete list of Air Force Career Fields and their corresponding jobs, check out www.airforce.com/careers/browse-careers/.

Army

We begin the list of composite scores with the Army, the oldest and largest branch of service. While the Army requires at least a 31 on the AFQT for admission if you have a high school diploma or college degree, the minimum score if you have a GED or alternative diploma is 50. The Army is limited to the number of recruits it can accept with a GED or alternative diploma, so it's best to consult a recruiter about your qualifications.

The Army determines job qualification using 10 separate composite scores from various subtests of the ASVAB. If you're not sure what the acronyms stand for, check the list on the inside front cover of the book for explanations.

- Clerical (CL): WK + PC + AR + MK
- Combat (CO): WK + PC + AS + MC
- Electronics (EL): GS + AR + MK + EI
- Field Artillery (FA): AR + MK + MC
- General Maintenance (GM): GS + AS + MK + EI
- General Technical (GT): WK + PC + AR

- Mechanical Maintenance (MM): AS + MC + EI
- Operators and Food (OF): WK + PC + AS + MC
- Surveillance and Communications (SC): WK + PC + AR + AS + MC
- Skilled Technical (ST): WK + PC + GS + MC + MK

If you don't make the grade the first time, you can retest within 30 days. If your second test doesn't go as planned, you can take a third test 30 days later. After that, you will have to wait 6 months before you can try again.

The Army calls all of its enlisted jobs a Military Occupational Specialty, or MOS. The Army has grouped these occupations according to industry, or job field (in Army language). For an updated list of Army MOSs with their corresponding composite scores, check out www.goarmy.com/careers-and-jobs.html. This enables you to browse MOS according to job category, as well as get additional career advice information.

Marine Corps

The minimum AFQT score to enter the Marine Corps is 31, and the Corps is extremely limited on the number of recruits they can accept with a GED or alternate diploma. The minimum score for those cases varies from recruiter to recruiter.

The Marine Corps uses four composite scores to determine job qualification:

- Clerical (CL): VE + MK
- Electronical (EL): AR + MK + EI + GS
- Mechanical (MM): AR + EI + MC + AS
- General Technical (GT): VE + AR + MK

If you don't make the grade your first time, you can retest in 30 days and then again 30 days after. If you've still not scored high enough, a recruiter will make the decision about whether or not you can retest again.

As in the Army, the Marines call their jobs Military Occupational Specialties (MOSes). Each MOS is further categorized according to occupational fields. Check out www.todaysmilitary.com/working/career-fields-and-profiles for more information about jobs in the Marine Corps.

Navy and Coast Guard

The next-oldest branch of service is the Navy. For those with a high school diploma or college degree/credits, the Navy requires a minimum AFQT score of 31. For those with a GED or alternative diploma, the requirement is at least 50. The Navy is limited to the number of recruits it can accept with a GED or alternative diploma, so it's best to consult a recruiter about your qualifications.

For the Coast Guard—the smallest branch of the military—you need to score a minimum of a 36 on the AFQT. It's rare for the Coast Guard to accept members with a GED or alternative degree, and a waiver is needed. These are granted on a case-by-case basis and a minimum AFQT score of 54 is necessary.

Both the Navy and Coast Guard use 10 composite scores to determine job qualifications. The Coast Guard does not use the Assembling Objects scores in their requirements. The 10 composite scores are as follows:

- General Technical (GT): VE + AR
- Electronics (EL): AR + EI + GS + MK
- Basic Electricity and Electronics (BEE): R + GS + 2MK

- Engineering (ENG): AS + MK
- Mechanical Maintenance (MEC): AR + AS + MC
- Mechanical Maintenance 2 (MEC2): AO + AR + MC
- Nuclear Field (NUC): AR + MC + MK + VE
- Operations Specialist (OPS): VE + AR + MK + AO
- Health (HM): GS + MK + VE
- Administrative (ADM): MK + VE

If you do not get the minimum AFQT score for entrance into the Navy, you can retest 30 days later. If you still have not gotten the score you need, you can take the test again after another 30 days and then a period of 60 days later, which can be repeated as needed thereafter.

For the Coast Guard, you can retest after 30 days. If you need to retest again, you must wait 6 months.

Unlike the Army, the Navy refers to its jobs as Ratings instead of MOSs. The Navy has fewer jobs than the Army, so they are listed individually instead of by field. To view the full inventory of Navy enlisted jobs, go to www.navy.com/index.php/careers or www.navycs.com/asvab-test.html.

You can learn more about Coast Guard jobs in Chapter 1 and at www.gocoastguard.com.

MEPS Locations

As you go through the enlistment process, you will make at least one trip to the nearest Military Entrance Processing Station (MEPS). This is a major part of the enlistment procedure, as MEPS is the place where you will complete your military physical exam and all of the final contractual paperwork. Furthermore, you will be sworn in at MEPS, and you will very likely take your ASVAB exam there as well. In this appendix, we've provided a comprehensive listing of MEPS locations nationwide. Not every state has a MEPS station, but for those that do, we list each location with the appropriate mailing address and the nearest major city.

Alabama

Montgomery
Maxwell Air Force Base—Gunter Annex
705 McDonald Street
Building 1512
Montgomery, AL 36114-3110
Phone: 334-416-7863
Fax: 334-416-5034

Website: www.mepcom.army.mil/Units/
Eastern-Sector/8th-Battalion/Montgomery/

Alaska

Anchorage
1717 C Street
Anchorage, AK 99501
Phone: 907-274-9142
Fax: 907-274-7268

Website: www.mepcom.army.mil/Units/
Western-Sector/5th-Battalion/Anchorage/

Arizona

Phoenix
2800 N. Central Avenue
Suite 300
Phoenix, AZ 85004-1007
Phone: 602-258-1703
Fax: 602-258-8206

Website: www.mepcom.army.mil/Units/
Western-Sector/7th-Battalion/Phoenix/

Arkansas

Little Rock
1520 Riverfront Drive
Little Rock, AR 72202-1724
Phone: 501-666-6377
Fax: 501-663-5863

Website: www.mepcom.army.mil/Units/
Western-Sector/11th-Battalion/Little-Rock/

California

Los Angeles
1776 Grand Avenue
El Segundo, CA 90245
Phone: 310-640-6050
Fax: 310-640-9754

Website: www.mepcom.army.mil/Units/
Western-Sector/7th-Battalion/Los-Angeles/

Sacramento
1651 Alhambra Blvd.
Suite 100
Sacramento, CA 95816
Phone: 916-455-9000
Fax: 916-455-9012

Website: www.mepcom.army.mil/Units/
Western-Sector/7th-Battalion/Sacramento/

San Diego
4181 Ruffin Road
Suite B
San Diego, CA 92123
Phone: 858-874-2400, ext. 241
Fax: 858-874-0415

Website: www.mepcom.army.mil/Units/
Western-Sector/7th-Battalion/San-Diego/

San Jose
546 Vernon Avenue
Mountain View, CA 94043
Phone: 650-603-8201
Fax: 650-603-8225

Website: www.mepcom.army.mil/Units/
Western-Sector/7th-Battalion/San-Jose/

Colorado

Denver
721 19th Street
Suite 275
Denver, CO 80202
Phone: 303-623-1020, ext. 234
Fax: 303-623-2210

Website: www.mepcom.army.mil/Units/
Western-Sector/3rd-Battalion/Denver/

Florida

Jacksonville
7178 Baymeadows Way
Jacksonville, FL 32256
Phone: 904-737-5220
Fax: 904-737-5339

Website: www.mepcom.army.mil/Units/
Eastern-Sector/10th-Battalion/Jacksonville/

Miami
7789 NW 48th Street
Suite 150
Miami, FL 33166
Phone: 305-463-0891, ext. 248
Fax: 305-629-8923

Website: www.mepcom.army.mil/Units/
Eastern-Sector/10th-Battalion/Miami/

Tampa
3520 West Waters Avenue
Tampa, FL 33614-2716
Phone: 813-932-0079, ext. 1105
Fax: 813-932-8763

Website: www.mepcom.army.mil/Units/
Eastern-Sector/10th-Battalion/Tampa/

Georgia

Atlanta
1500 Hood Avenue
Building 720
Fort Gillem, GA 30297-5000
Phone: 404-469-3090
Fax: 404-469-5367

Website: www.mepcom.army.mil/Units/
Eastern-Sector/10th-Battalion/Atlanta/

Hawaii

Honolulu
490 Central Avenue
Pearl Harbor, HI 96860
Phone: 808-471-8725
Fax: 808-471-2888

Website: www.mepcom.army.mil/Units/
Western-Sector/5th-Battalion/Honolulu/

Idaho

Boise
550 West Fort Street
MSC 044
Boise, ID 83724-0101
Phone: 208-334-1450, ext. 202
Fax: 208-334-1580

Website: www.mepcom.army.mil/Units/
Western-Sector/3rd-Battalion/Boise/

Illinois

Chicago
8700 W. Bryn Mawr Avenue
Suite 200
Chicago, IL 60631
Phone: 773-714-3008
Fax: 773-714-8150

Website: www.mepcom.army.mil/Units/
Eastern-Sector/6th-Battalion/Chicago/

Indiana

Indianapolis
5541 Herbert Lord Drive
Indianapolis, IN 46216
Phone: 317-554-0531
Fax: 317-554-0541

Website: www.mepcom.army.mil/Units/
Eastern-Sector/6th-Battalion/Indianapolis/

Iowa

Des Moines
7105 NW 70th Avenue
Building S-71
Johnston, IA 50131
Phone: 515-224-0125, ext. 312
Fax: 515-224-4906

Website: www.mepcom.army.mil/Units/
Western-Sector/1st-Battalion/Des-Moines/

Kentucky

Louisville
600 Dr. Martin Luther King, Jr., Place
Room 477
Louisville, KY 40202
Phone: 502-540-8350
Fax: 502-582-6566

Website: www.mepcom.army.mil/Units/
Eastern-Sector/8th-Battalion/Louisville/

Louisiana

New Orleans
400 Russell Avenue
Belle Chasse Naval Air Station
Bldg. 556
Belle Chasse, LA 70143
Phone: 504-678-3535
Fax: 504-678-8925

Website: www.mepcom.army.mil/
Units/Western-Sector/11th-Battalion/
New-Orleans/

Shreveport
2715 Alkay Drive
Shreveport, LA 71118-2509
Phone: 318-216-4915
Fax: 318-671-6097

Website: www.mepcom.army.mil/Units/
Western-Sector/11th-Battalion/Shreveport/

Maine

Portland
510 Congress Street
3rd Floor
Portland, ME 04101-3403
Phone: 207-775-0910
Fax: 207-775-2947

Website: www.mepcom.army.mil/Units/
Eastern-Sector/2nd-Battalion/Portland-ME/

Maryland

Baltimore
850 Chisholm Avenue
Fort Meade, MD 20755
Phone: 301-677-0010
Fax: 301-677-0440

Website: www.mepcom.army.mil/Units/
Eastern-Sector/12th-Battalion/Baltimore/

Massachusetts

Boston
Barnes Building
495 Summer Street
5th Floor
Boston, MA 02210
Phone: 617-753-3100
Fax: 617-753-3997

Website: www.mepcom.army.mil/Units/
Eastern-Sector/2nd-Battalion/Boston/

Springfield
551 Airlift Drive
Westover ARB
Chicopee, MA 01022
Phone: 413-593-9543, ext. 200
Fax: 413-593-9485

Website: www.mepcom.army.mil/Units/
Eastern-Sector/2nd-Battalion/Springfield/

Michigan

Detroit
1172 Kirts Boulevard
Troy, MI 48084-4846
Phone: 248-244-8534
Fax: 248-244-9352

Website: www.mepcom.army.mil/Units/
Eastern-Sector/6th-Battalion/Detroit/

Lansing
120 East Jolly Road
Lansing, MI 48910
Phone: 517-887-1714
Fax: 517-877-9160

Website: www.mepcom.army.mil/Units/
Eastern-Sector/6th-Battalion/Lansing/

Minnesota

1 Federal Drive
Suite 3201
Fort Snelling, MN 55111
Phone: 612-725-1757
Fax: 612-725-1749

Website: www.mepcom.army.mil/Units/
Western-Sector/1st-Battalion/Minneapolis/

Mississippi

Jackson
Dr. A. H. McCoy Federal Bldg.
100 W Capitol St.
Jackson, MS 39269
Phone: 601-355-3835, ext. 203
Fax: 601-352-5708

Website: www.mepcom.army.mil/Units/
Eastern-Sector/8th-Battalion/Jackson/

Missouri

Kansas City
10316 NW Prairie View Road
Kansas City, MO 64153-1350
Phone: 816-891-9490
Fax: 816-891-8258

Website: www.mepcom.army.mil/Units/
Western-Sector/11th-Battalion/Kansas-City/

St. Louis
Robert A. Young Federal Building
1222 Spruce Street
St. Louis, MO 63103-2816
Phone: 314-331-4040
Fax: 314-331-5699

Website: www.mepcom.army.mil/Units/
Western-Sector/11th-Battalion/St-Louis/

Montana

Butte
22 W. Park Street
Butte, MT 59701
Phone: 406-723-8883, ext. 222
Fax: 406-782-7797

Website: www.mepcom.army.mil/Units/
Western-Sector/3rd-Battalion/Butte/

Nebraska

Omaha
4245 S. 121st Plaza
Omaha, NE 68137
Phone: 402-733-7474
Fax: 402-733-7660

Website: www.mepcom.army.mil/Units/
Western-Sector/1st-Battalion/Omaha/

New Jersey

Fort Dix
Building 5645 Texas Avenue
Fort Dix, NJ 08640
Phone: 609-562-6050, ext. 2306
Fax: 609-562-5207

Website: www.mepcom.army.mil/Units/
Eastern-Sector/2nd-Battalion/Fort-Dix/

New Mexico

Albuquerque
10500 Copper Ave NE
Suite J
Albuquerque, NM 87123
Phone: 505-246-8020
Fax: 505-246-8861

Website: www.mepcom.army.mil/Units/
Western-Sector/3rd-Battalion/Albuquerque/

New York

Albany
Leo W. O'Brien Federal Building
North Pearl Street & Clinton Avenue
Albany, NY 12207
Phone: 518-649-9888
Fax: 518-320-9869

Website: www.mepcom.army.mil/Units/
Eastern-Sector/4th-Battalion/Albany/

Buffalo
2024 Entrance Avenue
Building 799
Niagara Falls ARS, NY 14304-5000
Phone: 716-501-9012
Fax: 716-501-9027

Website: www.mepcom.army.mil/Units/
Eastern-Sector/4th-Battalion/Buffalo/

New York City
Fort Hamilton Military Community
116 White Avenue
Brooklyn, NY 11252-4705
Phone: 718-630-4646
Fax: 718-765-7338

Website: www.mepcom.army.mil/Units/
Eastern-Sector/2nd-Battalion/New-York/

Syracuse
6001 East Molloy Road
Building 710
Syracuse, NY 13211-2100
Phone: 315-455-3012
Fax: 315-455-7807

Website: www.mepcom.army.mil/Units/
Eastern-Sector/4th-Battalion/Syracuse/

North Carolina

Charlotte
3545 Whitehall Park
Suite 200
Charlotte, NC 28273
Phone: 704-504-2498
Fax: 704-504-1335

Website: www.mepcom.army.mil/Units/
Eastern-Sector/12th-Battalion/Charlotte/

Raleigh
2625 Appliance Court
Raleigh, NC 27604
Phone: 919-834-7787
Fax: 919-755-1303

Website: www.mepcom.army.mil/Units/
Eastern-Sector/12th-Battalion/Raleigh/

North Dakota

Fargo
657 2nd Avenue North
Suite 210
Fargo, ND 58102
Phone: 701-234-0473
Fax: 701-234-0597

Website: www.mepcom.army.mil/Units/
Western-Sector/1st-Battalion/Fargo/

Ohio

Cleveland
20637 Emerald Parkway Drive
Cleveland, OH 44135-6023
Phone: 216-267-1286, ext. 201
Fax: 216-522-9860

Website: www.mepcom.army.mil/Units/
Eastern-Sector/4th-Battalion/Cleveland/

Columbus
775 Taylor Road
Gahanna, OH 43230
Phone: 614-868-8430, ext. 220
Fax: 614-856-9065

Website: www.mepcom.army.mil/Units/
Eastern-Sector/6th-Battalion/Columbus/

Oklahoma

Oklahoma City
301 Northwest 6th Street
Suite 150
Oklahoma City, OK 73102
Phone: 405-609-8700
Fax: 405-609-8639

Website: www.mepcom.army.mil/
Units/Western-Sector/11th-Battalion/
Oklahoma-City/

Oregon

Portland
7545 NE Ambassador Place
Portland, OR 97220-1367
Phone: 503-528-1630
Fax: 503-528-1640

Website: www.mepcom.army.mil/Units/
Western-Sector/5th-Battalion/Portland-OR/

Pennsylvania

Harrisburg
4641 Westport Drive
Mechanicsburg, PA 17055
Phone: 717-691-6180
Fax: 717-691-8039

Website: www.mepcom.army.mil/Units/
Eastern-Sector/4th-Battalion/Harrisburg/

Pittsburgh
William S. Moorhead Federal Building
1000 Liberty Avenue
Suite 1917
Pittsburgh, PA 15222-4101
Phone: 412-395-5873
Fax: 412-395-5454

Website: www.mepcom.army.mil/Units/
Eastern-Sector/4th-Battalion/Pittsburgh/

Puerto Rico

San Juan
15 Calle 2
Suite 310
Guaynabo, PR 00968-1741
Phone: 787-277-7500
Fax: 787-277-7507

Website: www.mepcom.army.mil/Units/
Eastern-Sector/10th-Battalion/San-Juan/

South Carolina

Fort Jackson
2435 Marion Avenue
Fort Jackson, SC 29207
Phone: 803-751-6522
Fax: 803-751-5744

Website: www.mepcom.army.mil/Units/
Eastern-Sector/12th-Battalion/Fort-Jackson/

South Dakota

Sioux Falls
2801 South Kiwanis Avenue
Suite 200
Sioux Falls, SD 57105
Phone: 605-334-0280
Fax: 605-332-8412

Website: www.mepcom.army.mil/Units/
Western-Sector/1st-Battalion/Sioux-Falls/

Tennessee

Knoxville
710 Locust Street, Room 600
Knoxville, TN 37902
Phone: 865-291-9400
Fax: 865-531-8741

Website: www.mepcom.army.mil/Units/
Eastern-Sector/8th-Battalion/Knoxville/

Memphis
1980 Nonconnah Blvd
3rd Floor
Memphis, TN 38132
Phone: 901-344-0028
Fax: 901-396-8124

Website: www.mepcom.army.mil/Units/
Eastern-Sector/8th-Battalion/Memphis/

Nashville
20 Bridgestone Park
Nashville, TN 37214-2428
Phone: 615-928-4994
Fax: 615-833-2570

Website: www.mepcom.army.mil/Units/
Eastern-Sector/8th-Battalion/Nashville/

Texas

Amarillo
1100 South Fillmore
Suite 100
Amarillo, TX 79101
Phone: 806-379-9037
Fax: 806-374-9332

Website: www.mepcom.army.mil/Units/
Western-Sector/9th-Battalion/Amarillo/

Dallas
Federal Building
207 South Houston Street
Suite 400
Dallas, TX 75202
Phone: 214-655-3200
Fax: 214-655-3213

Website: www.mepcom.army.mil/Units/
Western-Sector/9th-Battalion/Dallas/

El Paso
6380 Morgan Avenue
Suite E
El Paso, TX 79906-4611
Phone: 915-568-3505
Fax: 915-568-4477

Website: www.mepcom.army.mil/Units/
Western-Sector/9th-Battalion/El-Paso/

Houston
701 San Jacinto Street
PO Box #52309
Houston, TX 77052-2309
Phone: 713-718-4229
Fax: 713-718-4228

Website: www.mepcom.army.mil/Units/
Western-Sector/9th-Battalion/Houston/

San Antonio
2850 Stanley Road
Suite 103
Ft. Sam Houston, TX 78234-2712
Phone: 210-295-9045
Fax: 210-295-9151

Website: www.mepcom.army.mil/Units/
Western-Sector/9th-Battalion/San-Antonio/

Utah

Salt Lake City
5416 West Amelia Earhart Drive
Suite 130
Salt Lake City, UT 84116
Phone: 801-975-3701
Fax: 801-975-3715

Website: www.mepcom.army.mil/
Units/Western-Sector/3rd-Battalion/
Salt-Lake-City/

Virginia

Fort Lee
2011 Mahone Avenue
Fort Lee, VA 23801-1707
Phone: 804-765-4000
Fax: 804-765-4190

Website: www.mepcom.army.mil/Units/
Eastern-Sector/12th-Battalion/Fort-Lee/

Washington

Seattle
4735 East Marginal Way South
Seattle, WA 98134-2388
Phone: 206-766-6400, ext. 7525
Fax: 206-766-6430

Website: www.mepcom.army.mil/Units/
Western-Sector/5th-Battalion/Seattle/

Spokane
8510 W. Highway 2
Spokane, WA 99224
Phone: 509-456-4641
Fax: 509-747-1988

Website: www.mepcom.army.mil/Units/
Western-Sector/5th-Battalion/Spokane/

West Virginia

Beckley
409 Wood Mountain Road
Glen Jean, WV 25846
Phone: 304-465-0208
Fax: 304-465-3194

Website: www.mepcom.army.mil/Units/
Eastern-Sector/12th-Battalion/Beckley/

Wisconsin

Milwaukee
11050 West Liberty Drive
Milwaukee, WI 53224
Phone: 414-359-1315
Fax: 414-359-1390

Website: www.mepcom.army.mil/Units/
Eastern-Sector/6th-Battalion/Milwaukee/

Resources

You can find tons of great resources out there to help you prepare for the ASVAB overall, bone up on specific subject areas, and gain extra practice. You can also find out a lot about your career options, enlistment requirements, and other information to help you make the best decision possible for your future. We recommend checking out the following books and websites.

Books

Bhatt, Sonal, and Rebecca Dayton. *The Complete Idiot's Guide to Geometry.* Alpha Books, 2014.

DePree, Christopher, and Alan Axelrod Ph.D. *The Complete Idiot's Guide to Astronomy, 4th Edition.* Alpha Books, 2008.

Fotiyeva, Izolda. *The Complete Idiot's Guide to Algebra Word Problems.* Alpha Books, 2010.

Guch, Ian, and Kjirsten Wayman Ph.D. *The Complete Idiot's Guide to Organic Chemistry.* Alpha Books, 2008.

Guch, Ian. *The Complete Idiot's Guide to Chemistry.* Alpha Books, 2011.

Handwerker, Mark J. *Science Essentials, High School Level: Lessons and Activities for Test Preparation.* Jossey-Bass, 2004.

Hewitt, Paul G., and John A. Suchocki. *Conceptual Physical Science, 6th Edition.* Addison Wesley, 2016.

Kavanagh, Robin A. *Vocabulous You! An Interactive Guide to Building Vocabulary for Standardized Tests, College, On the Job and Everyday Life*. Kindle Edition, 2011.

Miller, Mark Richard, and Rex Miller. *Audel Machine Shop Tools and Operations, 5th Edition*. Audel, 2004.

Moulton, Glen E. *The Complete Idiot's Guide to Biology*. Alpha Books, 2004.

Pancella, Paul V., and Marc Humphrey. *The Complete Idiot's Guide to Physics*. Alpha Books, 2015.

Seifert, Mark F. *The Complete Idiot's Guide to Anatomy, Illustrated*. Alpha Books, 2008.

Stribling, Dave. *The Complete Idiot's Guide to Auto Repair and Maintenance*. Alpha Books, 2015.

Thompson, Frances McBroom. *Math Essentials, High School Level: Lessons and Activities for Test Preparation*. Jossey-Bass, 2005.

Wheater, Carolyn. *The Complete Idiot's Guide to Algebra I*. Alpha Books, 2015.

Websites

Algebra Help.com: www.wyzant.com/resources/lessons/math/algebra

ASVAB Career Exploration Program (for high school students): www.asvabprogram.com

Careers in the Military.com: www.careersinthemilitary.com/

How Stuff Works.com: www.howstuffworks.com/

Khan Academy—Math: www.khanacademy.org/math

Khan Academy—Science: www.khanacademy.org/science

March 2 Success.com: www.march2success.com/

Merriam-Webster's Word of the Day: www.merriam-webster.com/word-of-the-day/

Military.com website: www.military.com/

Military Entrance Processing Command website: www.mepcom.army.mil/

Navy Armed Forces Qualification Test Requirements: www.navycs.com/asvab-test.html

Official Air Force website: www.airforce.com

Official Army website: www.goarmy.com

Official Coast Guard website: www.gocoastguard.com/

Official Marine Corps website: www.marines.com

Official Navy website: www.navy.com

Official Site of the ASVAB Testing Program: www.official-asvab.com/

Prefixsuffix.com: www.prefixsuffix.com

Purplemath.com: www.purplemath.com/index.htm

Today's Military.com: www.todaysmilitary.com/

Index